A STUDY OF WAR

THE UNIVERSITY OF CHICAGO PRESS · CHICAGO
THE BAKER & TAYLOR COMPANY, NEW YORK; THE CAMBRIDGE UNIVERSITY
PRESS, LONDON; THE MARUZEN-KABUSHIKI-KAISHA, TOKYO, OSAKA,
KYOTO, FUKUOKA, SENDAI; THE COMMERCIAL PRESS, LIMITED, SHANGHAI

A STUDY OF WAR

VOLUME I

by

QUINCY WRIGHT

Professor of International Law
The University of Chicago

The University of Chicago Press

Chicago · Illinois

TO COLLEAGUES
ASSOCIATES AND ASSISTANTS
WHO COLLABORATED
IN THIS
STUDY OF WAR

FOREWORD

THIS study of war was initiated at the University of Chicago in 1926. It has involved consultations with numerous members of the University of Chicago faculty and others and the preparation of over fifty studies by research assistants and members of the faculty. Sixteen of these have been published in books or as journal articles. A more extensive account of the investigation and the titles of the special studies are contained in Appendix I of this volume. A number of other co-operative investigations of war, which contributed ideas and inspiration for this study, are mentioned in Appendix II.

The study was proposed with the object of stimulating research in the field, but, in addition, it was hoped that the results might eventually be summarized and, if possible, co-ordinated with one another and with the vast literature of the field. The present writer, who has had general supervision of the study, attempted such a summary in a series of ten lectures at the University of Chicago in the spring of 1933, in part repeated in five lectures at the Graduate Institute of International Studies at Geneva in the autumn of 1934 and published by that Institute.

While the present writer has had the advantage of collaboration and discussion with his colleagues and with the large number of assistants who have worked on the project, he assumes responsibility for the present work. He wishes particularly to thank Professor Warder Clyde Allee, Professor Sewall Wright, and Mr. Louis T. Olom for reading the appendix on animal war; Professor William Lloyd Warner for reading the chapter on primitive war; Professor Eugene Staley for reading the chapter on the utilization of resources; and Professors William Fielding Ogburn, Louis Wirth, and Charles Edward Merriam for reading the entire manuscript. Professor Louis Gottschalk and Dr Hymen Ezra Cohen read and criticized the earlier publication of lectures. Many of their suggestions have been incorporated to the great improvement of the work. Messrs. James C.

vii

King, James T. Russell, Carl J. Nelson, William T. R. Fox, John A. Bekker, Sidney Hyman, Frank L. Klingberg, and Carl Christol gave valuable assistance in collecting and analyzing statistical data. Without the continuous encouragement and constructive criticism of his wife, Louise Leonard Wright, the author might never have completed the manuscript, and certainly the reader's troubles would have been greater.

The writer wishes also to thank the *American Journal of International Law*, the *American Political Science Review*, the *Public Opinion Quarterly*, the *Political Quarterly*, *Politica*, the *American Sociological Review*, the *Annals of the American Academy of Political and Social Science*, the *Scientific Monthly*, the Graduate Institute of International Studies, and Longmans, Green and Company for permission to reprint extracts from articles and books of his which they had previously published.

This investigation, begun in the hopeful atmosphere of Locarno and completed in the midst of general war, has convinced the writer that the problem of preventing war is one of increasing importance in our civilization and that the problem is essentially one of maintaining adaptive stability within the world-community, only possible if larger sections of the public persistently view that community as a whole.

Very little happens in the world that does not have a bearing upon the problem of war. Developments in any region of the world and in any field of thought or action may unleash conflicts in remote areas. War in Ethiopia induced a radical change in American neutrality legislation. The writings of Karl Marx and the experiments of the Wright brothers at Kitty Hawk were as important for war today as the policies of Hitler or Chamberlain.

So rapid has been the shrinking of the world as a result of inventions in the means of travel, transport, and communication, so rapid has been the acceleration in the rate of social change as a result of the conscious organization of technical and political invention itself, that the problems of functional synchronization and international adjustment have become increasingly difficult. Conflicts are more frequent, more difficult to resolve, more likely to spread.

To trace with any precision the influence upon world-stability of any incident, invention, discovery, personality, institution, or movement in the immediate or more distant future lies beyond our present power. Suggestions of probabilities and of methods for reducing their margins of error is the most that this study hopes to do. Continuous thought and study, closely integrated with practical effort by our own and successive generations, is the price that must be paid for a less violent world. But neither thought nor action can be effective without a clear and widespread vision of the world as a whole, of the interactions of its past and its present, of the interrelations of its regions, and of the interdependence of its peoples.

QUINCY WRIGHT

UNIVERSITY OF CHICAGO
November 11, 1941

TABLE OF CONTENTS

VOLUME I

VOLUME II

xi

ANALYTICAL TABLE OF CONTENTS
OF VOLUME I

xiii

APPENDIXES

LIST OF ILLUSTRATIONS

LIST OF TABLES

PART I

INTRODUCTION

CHAPTER I

OBJECTIVES OF THE STUDY

TO DIFFERENT people war may have very different meanings. To some it is a plague which ought to be eliminated; to some, a mistake which should be avoided; to others, a crime which ought to be punished; and, to still others, it is an anachronism which no longer serves any purpose. On the other hand, there are some who take a more receptive attitude toward war and regard it as an adventure which may be interesting, an instrument which may be useful, a procedure which may be legitimate and appropriate, or a condition of existence for which one must be prepared.[1]

To people of the latter type war is not a problem. They take it for granted, whether with eagerness, complacency, or concern. Its details may prove unexpected or disagreeable, but they are not interpreted as presenting a problem of war-in-general. They can be satisfactorily handled by the professional historian, diplomat, international lawyer, or strategist.

To the first group, however, war-in-general is a problem, and it is to that group that this study is especially addressed. It is believed that this group has increased during the past century, and especially in the last twenty-five years, until it constitutes a majority of the human race, although in some countries and regions it may be in the minority.

I. THE PROBLEM OF WAR

This growth of the opinion that war is a problem may be attributed to four types of change: (*a*) the shrinking of the world, (*b*) the acceleration of history, (*c*) the progress of military invention, and (*d*) the rise of democracy.

a) *The shrinking world.*—Modern technology has made the world of today smaller in travel and transport time than was Europe or the United States in 1790 and smaller in communication time than was or is the House of Commons or Independence Hall. The result has

[1] See Appen. III.

3

been that people in every section of the world have become interdependent in their economy, culture, and politics. They have become more aware of, and more affected by, all wars, even distant
ones. Formerly wars were unknown to the average man unless near
at hand. Now any war interferes with almost everyone's normal way
of life.

b) *The acceleration of history.*—The progress of science and invention and the rapid intercommunication of ideas and techniques have
conspired to accelerate the speed of social change. While formerly a
man might expect the technical and economic skills, the social and
moral code, and the scheme of values which he received from his
father to last through life, today each of these may change several
times in a single life. Education must emphasize the processes of
learning and living rather than traditional techniques and dogmas.
But even with modern education the rapid and radical changes required are difficult for both individuals and institutions. Tempos
differ between regions, classes, and groups with the result of greater
tensions and more conflicts and wars than in more leisurely centuries.

c) *The progress of military invention.*—The introduction into the
modern world since the eighteenth century of universal military
service, efficient national propaganda, and centralized totalitarian
government; the industrialization of military transport and equipment; and the inventions of the submarine, aircraft, poison gas, and
high explosives, rendering national commerce, industry, and population generally vulnerable to attack, have given war a totalitarian
character unprecedented in history. As a result of this change in the
character of war and of the increased economic interdependence of
peoples, war has tended to spread more rapidly, to destroy larger
proportions of life and property, and to disorganize the economy of
states more than ever before. Either the preparation for, the waging of, or the recovery from war has tended to dominate the political,
economic, and social life of peoples.

d) *The rise of democracy.*—The growth of communication and
literacy and the general rise in the standard of living have tended to
create a national consciousness among the various peoples. This has
meant that a favorable public opinion has become a necessary condi-

tion of successful foreign policy and that increased participation of people in government has been widely insisted upon. Foreign policies and wars have ceased to be mysteries but have become human acts which people can influence if not control. While the responsibility for war may be difficult to locate, war is commonly looked upon as human rather than as a visitation of either God or the devil. Democracy has stimulated the will of people to eliminate war, although it has not yet enlightened their intelligence as to the means.

Because the world is getting smaller, because changes occur more rapidly, because wars are more destructive, and because peoples are more impressed by the human responsibility for war, the recurrence of war has become a problem for a larger number of people.

2. THE RELATIVITY OF WAR

This study attempts to clarify the problem of war by exhibiting the relativity of war (*a*) to history, (*b*) to the point of view, and (*c*) to social and political controls.

a) *To history.*—The first part of the study attempts to show the great diversity in the forms and conditions of international violence at different times and places. War is not a constant factor, or a periodic recurrence, but one which varies in character and incidence according to conditions. Particular emphasis has been given to the variations in the nature of hostilities in four great stages of organic history. Primitive human warfare differs radically from warfare among animals. Warfare in the historic civilizations differs from both. And warfare in the period of modern history has been a different thing from warfare at any other time or place.

In the face of this tremendous variability, it is meaningless to say that war is inevitable because of the pugnacity of man as an animal. While man has original drives that make war possible, that possibility has only been realized in appropriate social and political conditions.

b) *To the point of view.*—The second part of the study attempts to show the great diversity in the attitudes toward and the concepts of war when viewed from different points of view. War has objective and subjective, universal and particular, aspects which may be differently stressed. One aspect emphasizes its violence, another the conflict out of which it arises, another the attitudes it engenders, and another the conditions which define and regulate it. From each point of view war is a different thing. Attention has been directed especially to the technical, sociological, psychological, and legal points of view, each of which has a vast literature. If the problem of war is to be dealt with, that problem must be clearly defined. If we are going to eliminate war, we must know exactly what we are going to eliminate. It may not be possible to eliminate all violence, or all conflict, or all hatreds, or all abnormal conditions, but it may be possible to eliminate war if properly defined, although the costs must always be counted.

c) To social and political controls.—The third part of the study attempts to suggest political, economic, and social changes which might reduce the frequency of war or eliminate it altogether. Political groups have increased in size from the clan, village, and tribe to the kingdom, nation, and federation; and peace has been striven for within these enlarging areas with varying degrees of success. The devices of successful political construction have been many, and, though the diversion of internal conflict to external enemies and the maintenance of fear of invasion have usually been important, new methods of educating for citizenship, of serving the public, of compromising conflicting interests, of propagandizing group symbols, and of stimulating general participation in common tasks have gained a measure of success.

The problem of organizing a world for peace is novel in human history. It could not even be thought of until all sections of the human family had come into contact with one another after the discoveries of the Renaissance period, and it was not in the realm of practical politics until the modern era of rapid world-communication by electrical means. While the organization of consent has in past times superseded the organization of violence in many lesser areas, it is only in the last centuries that the organization of consent could even be conceived of in the world as a whole.

Possible procedures for dealing with the aggressive state, the international feud, the oscillations of political tension, and the incipient war are dealt with so as to indicate the influence which intelligent social construction might have on the incidence and character of war. The relativity of ideas to the practical progress of action in the field is emphasized. Planning for peace cannot take place in the armchair. It can take place only in practical action to meet international problems. Such activity, however, will not contribute to peace in the long run unless its direction, whatever temporary divergencies may be necessary, is guided by a distant star and its details, however insignificant, are assimilated in growing world-institutions, thus solidifying the gains which have been made.

CHAPTER II

SCOPE AND ORGANIZATION OF THE STUDY

I. DEFINITION OF WAR

IN THE broadest sense war is a *violent contact* of *distinct* but *similar* entities. In this sense a collision of stars, a fight between a lion and a tiger, a battle between two primitive tribes, and hostilities between two modern nations would all be war. This broad conception is used in the historical section of this study, though reference is made in the appropriate chapters to the progressive narrowing to which the meaning of the word "war" is normally subjected, as investigation proceeds from animal through primitive to civilized and modern war.

In the analytic section dealing with contemporary war, a narrower definition is needed. For this purpose war will be considered the *legal condition* which *equally* permits two or more *hostile groups* to carry on a *conflict* by *armed* force.[1]

These two definitions are not unrelated. The terms of the second, however, instead of being external descriptions, equally applicable to physical, biological, and social phenomena, have subjective implications, applicable only to human social phenomena. Instead of "violence," implying any event accompanied by rapid destruction of structures, there is reference to "armed force," implying a very specific type of violence—modern military technique—and its conscious employment to achieve an end. Instead of "contact," applicable whenever there is no separation of time and space in the relations of

---

[1] The writer has elsewhere defined war in the legal sense as *"a condition or period of time in which special rules permitting and regulating violence between governments prevail,* or a procedure of regulated violence by which disputes between governments are settled," and war in the material sense as *"an act or a series of acts of violence by one government against another,* or a dispute between governments carried on by violence" ("Changes in the Conception of War," *American Journal of International Law,* XVIII [October, 1926], 762). Many of these characteristics are implied by the briefer definition: "War . . . . [is] the *condition* which prevails while *groups* are *contending* by *arms*" (*American Sociological Review,* III [August, 1938], 461). See also Vol. II, chap. xvii, of this work.

entities, the word "conflict" is used, with the implication that war is a definite and mutually understood pattern of behavior, distinguishable not only from other patterns of behavior in general but from other forms of conflict. Instead of "distinct" entities, implying any entities separable by external observations, the expression "hostile groups" is used, thus confining the entities, which may be at "war," to that small class known as social groups and implying that these groups feel conscious of their distinctiveness by maintaining attitudes of hostility toward one another. Instead of "similar" entities, implying resemblance in such observable qualities as size, structure, and appearance, the warring entities are said to have equality under law. This suggests that in spite of their hostility they are members of a higher group which originates this law.

This conception of war is also related to the specialized definitions which have been elaborated for professional purposes by lawyers, diplomats, and soldiers and for scientific discussion by sociologists and psychologists.

International lawyers and diplomats have usually followed Grotius' conception of war as "the condition of those contending by force as such,"[2] though they have often excluded from the conception duels between individuals and insurrections, aggressions, or other conditions of violent contention between juridical unequals. Furthermore, they have insisted that "force" refers to military and naval activities, that is, to "armed force," thus excluding from the definition contentions involving only moral, legal, or economic force. With these refinements, the legal concept of war becomes equivalent to that adopted here. The word "conflict" is substituted for the

---

[2] *De jure belli ac pacis* i. i. 2, citing Cicero *On Duties* i. xi. 34. Lieber's Code (U.S. War Department, Gen. Ord. 100 [1863], art. 20; *Rules of War* [1917], art. 10, note) defines war as "a state of armed hostility between sovereign nations or governments." For various definitions of war see Wright, "Changes in the Conception of War," *op. cit.*, pp. 761 ff. Some of these definitions include the idea of "proper methods" or "just objects," but it is only in a very limited sense that failure to conform to such standards renders the situation any the less war in the legal sense. Professional military men have often sought to emphasize such factors, recognized in Gentili's conception of war antedating that of Grotius—"a properly conducted contest of armed public forces" (*De jure belli* [1588] i. 2; G. G. Wilson and G. F. Tucker, *International Law* [9th ed.; Boston, 1935], p. 245).

broader term "contention," which might include competition as well as conflict.[3]

Grotius criticized Cicero's definition of war as simply "a contending by force" because, he said, war was "not a contest but a condition." Modern dictionaries, however, have followed Cicero, and sociologists have accepted the same popular conception with the qualification that violent contention cannot be called war unless it involves actual conflict and constitutes a socially recognized form or custom within the society where it occurs. From the sociological point of view war is, therefore, a socially recognized form of intergroup conflict involving violence.[4]

Legal and sociological definitions suggest that "states of war" are separated by exact points of time from "states of peace" which pre-

[3] Robert E. Park and E. W. Burgess (*An Introduction to the Science of Sociology* [Chicago, 1921], pp. 506, 574) define "conflict" as interaction with, and "competition" as interaction without, contact.

[4] George Simmel, "The Sociology of Conflict," *American Journal of Sociology*, IX (January, 1904), 490 ff.; A. M. Carr-Saunders, *The Population Problem* (London, 1922), p. 305. Professor Louis Wirth, on examining this manuscript, suggested that "war is organized conflict carried out in accordance with institutionalized rules for regulating the violence it involves." Horace Kallen ("Of War and Peace," *Social Research*, September, 1939, p. 373) writes: "Peace and war as facts differ formally rather than materially, and are distinguishable by their locus and implements rather than by their intrinsic qualities as human behavior. There are endless varieties of violent conflicts between individuals, groups and nations. War is the name we give to one such variety. Peace is the name for all the others. Peace, it would appear, is the aggregation of chronic, diffuse, unorganized domestic conflicts; war is conflict acute, organized, unified and concentrated at the peripheries of a society's habitat. And because the distinction between war and peace amounts to no more, the suppression if not the complete elimination of war as an instrument of policy is not hopeless." While accepting this conception of war, others have not considered peace as the mere absence of war but as a positive condition of justice and co-operation: Augustine *De civitate Dei* xix. 13; Robert Regout, *La Doctrine de la guerre juste* (Paris, 1935), p. 40; Q. Wright, "The Munich Settlement and International Law," *American Journal of International Law*, XXXIII (January, 1939), 14; Lewis F. Richardson, "Generalized Foreign Politics," *British Journal of Psychology* (Suppl. Monograph XXIII [Cambridge, 1939]), p. 7. Diderot defined war as "a convulsive and violent disease of the body politic" (*Encyclopédie*); Georg Cohn described it as "a social 'superindividual' psychical state of pathological or hypnotic character" (*Neo-neutrality* [New York, 1939], p. 262), and J. M. Kenworthy called it "a stupid, useless and indefensible crime" (*Peace or War* [New York, 1927], p. 309); but such qualifications seem to be applicable only in restricted times and places (see Scott Nearing, *War, Organized Destruction and Mass Murder by Civilized Nations* [New York, 1931], pp. 125 ff.).

cede and follow them. International lawyers have attempted to elaborate precise criteria for determining the moment at which a war begins and ends,[5] but they have not been entirely successful, and, furthermore, they have been obliged to acknowledge the occurrence of interventions, aggressions, reprisals, defensive expeditions, sanctions, armed neutralities, insurrections, rebellions, mob violence, piracy, and banditry lying somewhere between war and peace as those terms are popularly understood.[6] The recognition of such situations casts doubt upon the reality of a sharp distinction between war and peace and suggests the utility of searching for a variable of which war and peace are extreme conditions. Such a variable might be found in the external forms or the internal substance of international relations.

Philosophically minded military writers have sought the first, emphasizing the degree in which military methods are employed. Thus, Clausewitz defined war as "an act of violence intended to compel our opponents to fulfill our will," and elsewhere he emphasized the continuity of violence with other political methods. "War," he wrote, "is nothing but a continuation of political intercourse, with a mixture of other means."[7]

Psychologists, ignoring the form, have found the substance of war in the degree of hostile attitude in the relation of states. Thus, Hobbes compared the oscillations of war and peace to the weather: "As the nature of foul weather lieth not in a shower or two of rain, but in an inclination thereto of many days together; so the nature of war consisteth not in actual fighting, but in the known disposition thereto during all the time there is no assurance to the contrary."[8] As the weather may manifest many degrees of fairness or foulness, so the relations of any pair of states may be cordial, friendly, correct, strained, ruptured, hostile, or any shade between.

We may thus conceive of the relations of every pair of states as

[5] Q. Wright, "When Does War Exist?" *American Journal of International Law*, XXVI (1932), 362 ff.; H. W. Briggs, *The Law of Nations* (New York, 1938), pp. 718 ff.

[6] T. E. Holland, *Studies in International Law* (Oxford, 1898), pp. 130 ff.; *Letters on War and Neutrality* (London, 1916), pp. 8 ff.; A. E. Hindmarsh, *Force in Peace* (Cambridge, 1933); H. Kallen, above, n. 4.

[7] *On War* (London, 1911), I, 2; III, 121.   [8] *Leviathan*, Part I, chap. 13.

continually varying and occasionally passing below a certain threshold, in which case they may be described by the term "war,"
whether or not other states recognize the situation as juridically a
"state of war," and whether or not the precise form of conflict which
sociologists designate "war" has developed. Concretely there might
be war, although abstractly there might not be.[9]

Qualitative analysis of abstract ideas has thus revealed war in the
legal and sociological senses as a state of law or a form of conflict,
while quantitative analysis of concrete circumstances has revealed
war in the technical and psychological senses as a degree of violence
or of animosity. The same differentiation of conception, here illustrated, respectively, by quotations from Grotius, Cicero, Clausewitz, and Hobbes, is illustrated in Appendix III by extracts from
Grotius, Cruce, Machiavelli, and Erasmus. They, respectively, look
at war from the ideological, sociological, technological, and psychological points of view.

Whatever point of view is selected, war appears to be a species of
a wider genus. War is only one of many abnormal legal situations.[10]
It is but one of numerous conflict procedures.[11] It is only an extreme
case of group attitudes.[12] It is only a very large-scale resort to violence.[13] A study of each of these broader categories when applied to
the specific characteristics of war—abnormal states of law between
equals, conflict between social groups, hostile attitudes of great intensity, and intentional violence through use of armed force—may
throw light upon the phenomenon of war, although war itself does
not exist except when hostility and violence contemporaneously pass

[9] The distinction between war in the material sense and war in the legal sense was
emphasized by the United States Supreme Court in *The Three Friends*, 166 U.S. 1
(1897), accepting the distinction in Justice Nelson's dissent in *The Prize Cases*, 2
Black 635 (1863). Wright, "Changes in the Concept of War," *op. cit.*, pp. 761 ff.

[10] Of which proclamation of martial law, suspension of the writ of habeas corpus, and
state of siege are others.

[11] Of which negotiation, conciliation, mediation, intervention, arbitration, and adjudication are others (see above, n. 2).

[12] "Alliance," "entente," "friendship," "strained relations," and "breach" are words
for other international attitudes.

[13] Defense, reprisals, military expeditions, pacifications, insurrections, police action,
and executions usually involve smaller quantities of violence.

beyond a certain threshold producing a new situation which law and opinion recognize as war.

Combining the four points of view, war is seen to be a state of law and a form of conflict involving a high degree of legal equality, of hostility, and of violence in the relations of organized human groups; or, more simply, the legal condition which equally permits two or more hostile groups to carry on a conflict by armed force.

It is to be observed that this definition implies sufficient social solidarity throughout the community of nations of which both belligerents and neutrals are members to permit general recognition of the behaviors and standards appropriate to the situation of war. While war manifests the weakness of the community of nations, it also manifests the existence of that community.

2. FRAME OF REFERENCE

War in the narrower sense is a form of social behavior, and it appears that very few of the essential conditions affecting human behavior are entirely beyond human control given sufficient time. Social philosophers have vainly sought unchangeable conditions as points of departure or frames of reference. For this purpose they have utilized such concepts as the intention of God or the laws of nature; the influence of geography or climate; the evolution of social, economic, or political institutions; the biological nature, needs, or instincts of human beings; the characteristics of sovereignty or of technology; the processes of social integration, adaptation, conflict, assimilation, or imitation. Civilized man, however, has failed to conform to the assumption that any of these concepts are fundamental. He has shown himself capable of changing his gods, of inventing new uses for his physical habitat, and of transcending climate by heating or refrigeration. He has enormously varied the rate of change of his own institutions and has frequently altered the social manifestations of his primitive instincts. He has organized a baffling variety of societies, utilizing different devices for integration and adaptation, and he has interested himself in an extraordinary variety of values.[14]

[14] John Dewey emphasizes the modifiability of human nature and of institutions, including war and competitive economy, and insists that whatever limits there are to this modifiability must be "arrived at by experimental observation" which at any time

Thus the selection of a frame of reference for any study in the social sciences is in large measure artificial, and the expediency of any particular frame depends on the long- or short-run objective of the study or on the particular end in view. One may assume, although it is always a doubtful assumption, that certain conditions in a given society will remain fixed for a considerable time, others for a less time; but there is always danger that the study itself may have influence. The direction of social attention toward conditions which might otherwise have persisted for centuries may lead to their rapid change. Consequently, a writer's attitude, in fact, is often influenced less by an objective judgment of probable permanence than by subjective preferences. He assumes those conditions to be permanent which he wants to be permanent and does his best to persuade his readers that they are permanent. If his eloquence is sufficient, they will be permanent until a more eloquent prophet arises. Whatever may be true of the natural sciences, it seems likely that the social sciences will be obliged continually to revise their assumptions.

This study attempts to cover a sufficient variety of organic and human experience to transcend narrow institutional limitations. It does, however, assume, except in the chapter on animal warfare, persistence of the biological characteristics of the human species, the physical laws and general physical characteristics of the world as known to contemporary science, and the isolation of human society and social contacts within this planet. The problem is set within a definite biological, geological, and astronomical milieu. Within this frame there is room for very great social, psychological, legal, and technological variation. There have been great changes in history. There is opportunity for much human control in the future.

3. PERSPECTIVE

The social sciences have found it useful to distinguish studies of particular events or limited periods or areas from studies of general trends and relationships. Historic, geographic, or practical studies

---

is subject to the possibility of future improvements in "our technique for effecting change" ("Human Nature," *Encyclopaedia of the Social Sciences* [New York, 1935], VII, 536). See also Pitirim Sorokin, *Social and Cultural Dynamics* (New York, 1937), I, 17 ff.

of the former type are obliged to accept existing conventions and traditions as to the type of data and classes of relationship pertinent to a given subject unless, indeed, such studies are undertaken in order to verify propositions elaborated from broader surveys. On the other hand, economic, political, sociological, geographic, and historical studies may cover broad areas and long periods, in which case there is a possibility, not always realized, that novel ideas as to the pertinent types of data and relationships may be suggested, although the very breadth of such surveys usually precludes sufficiently detailed examination of events or a sufficiently extensive application of conclusions to verify such suggestions.[15] War has been studied by both of these methods. Particular battles and wars and diplomatic transactions have been dealt with in great detail, and there have also been broad generalizations based upon a comparison of wars in widely separated periods and under great varieties of conditions. The present study seeks generalization and does not attempt to trace the facts of particular wars, though it realizes that only studies of the latter type can provide the verification for its propositions. There are, however, many distances from which this subject may be observed and many levels at which it may be analyzed.

The journalist, military man, and diplomat are so absorbed by the requirements of the time- and space-limited situation in which they are interested observers or workers that they cannot get outside of it to discover the handle which might, if properly turned, change that situation. Valuable as is internal acquaintance with the situation, for keeping it going and locating one's self within it, it is only by getting outside of the situation, either in fact or in thought, that one can understand it as a whole, perceive the possibilities of fundamental change and identify factors, the manipulation of which might bring such change about. The journalistic and practical levels of analysis are guides for handling particular situations as they arise, but guides the object of which can never transcend that of preserving the fundamental nature of war and society as it has been.

The philosopher and theologian, on the other hand, are so thor-

[15] See Robert E. Park, "Sociology and the Social Sciences," *American Journal of Sociology*, XXVI (1920), 401 ff.; *ibid.*, XXVII (1921), 1 ff., 169 ff., reprinted in Park and Burgess, *op. cit.*, chap. i.

oughly outside of the immediate situations in which war and peace recur that they can seldom give advice as to the precise point at which practical men might take hold of a particular situation to get results. These levels of analysis suggest that war is related to many fundamental values of society for good or for evil, according to the particular philosophy or theology; but, though they may suggest action, their prescriptions are likely to be too general to be effective.

The social scientist, seeking to retain contacts with both the practical and the theoretical workers, centers attention upon the isolation of measurable or at least recognizable factors, useful for predicting or capable of manipulation for controlling the future. The historian, dealing both with the peculiarities of the concrete and with the broad tendencies of a long past, maintains an awareness of the exceptions, contingencies, and drifts to which such conclusions are liable in the complexities of social change.

These middle levels are the ones most emphasized in this study, Part II attempting to maintain a historical, and Part III a scientific, perspective.

4. ORGANIZATION

In the physical sciences it has been found useful to distinguish the pure from the applied sciences. The first organizes knowledge to facilitate the discovery of new relationships and the prediction of events without human intervention. The second organizes knowledge to facilitate the control of events by human intervention and may have the effect of creating vested interests opposed to discovery. In the social sciences this distinction is difficult to apply. There can be no human society without human intervention. Thus, to state social conditions which cause phenomena deemed undesirable is to direct attention to a program of reform. The causes of war might, therefore, be stated in terms of conditions or circumstances which have existed, or they might be stated in terms of the absence of structures or policies which human ingenuity might bring into existence. The causes of war are the absence of conditions of peace. But though cause and prevention are inseparable, attention may be directed more toward one than the other. In this study Part II will deal with the factors which have conditioned the form and occurrence of war in past epochs, Part III will attempt to analyze such factors now operative and efforts to modify their operation, and Part IV will attempt to evaluate measures of the latter type in the present stage of human history.

The artificiality of any classification of the causes or preventives of war must be kept in mind. A war, in reality, results from a total situation involving ultimately almost everything that has happened to the human race up to the time the war begins. To make study possible, however, it is necessary to abstract from this total reality the fields which seem most profitable to cultivate at the moment. This can be done, first, by drawing boundaries to delimit blocks of time and space which are sufficiently isolated so that, without unreasonable negligence, attention can be confined to circumstances within each. This process constitutes the writing of history. Second, the total situation may be analyzed within these blocks so as to identify the factors and to describe the interactions which produce the oscillations of war and peace. Finally, the methods of observation and manipulation can be described by which these oscillations can be controlled in the present epoch. Parts II, III, and IV of this study, respectively, attempt to do these three things.

5. POINTS OF VIEW

The meaning of the historical, analytic, and practical points of view will be elaborated in the initial chapters of each of the following parts of this study, but those discussions may be briefly anticipated here.

a) Historical.—With respect to the historical treatment of the subject in Part II it is important to have in mind that the rise of communication and transportation in the present period has enlarged the block of time and space which must be considered. Adequate explanation of warfare among a group of Australian aborigines might be found in the materials of a small area and a brief history, but today the politics and economy of the civilized states are so intertwined that materials from all over the world and from a long history are relevant. From the point of view of our study the world is a unity because wars or disturbances anywhere immediately modify the situation everywhere, and, as men base their action upon tradition, custom, ancient ambitions and resentments, and assumed analogies from the past, the history of centuries or even of millenniums is part of the living present. The historical part of this study deals with the characteristics of war in each of the great emergencies of organic history—warfare of animals, of primitive man, of civilized man, and of states equipped with modern technology. In each the techniques, theories, functions, and drives of war are considered.

By technique is meant the art by which methods or instruments are consciously adapted to ends or purposes. A technological explanation of war states the influence of the existing military technique upon the decision of a person or government to resort to war and upon the results of war in a given situation.[16]

By theory or law is meant a general proposition stating verified or enforced relationships. A theoretical or ideological explanation of war states general rules concerning the actual or required relations of groups or states, justifying, or accounting for, the occurrence or form of war in a given circumstance.[17]

By function is meant the relation of an entity or activity to the changing values of the whole of which it is a part or to which it is subordinate. A functional or sociological explanation of war states the role of war in the life of the group or nation which wages it and in the life of the higher group or family of nations within which it occurs.[18]

[16] Ralph Barton Perry (MacIver, Bonn, and Perry, "The Roots of Totalitarianism," *Annals of American Academy of Political and Social Science* [Philadelphia, 1940], pp. 28 ff.) and Emil Lederer ("Technology," *Encyclopaedia of the Social Sciences*) warn against an overemphasis upon technologism and technological interpretations of history.

[17] Rationalism implies a preference for theoretical explanations. According to Groethuysen ("Rationalism," *Encyclopaedia of the Social Sciences*), it is a "theoretical or practical tendency which aims to interpret the universe in terms of thought." Josef Kunz urges more attention to theory in international law ("The Theory of International Law," *Proceedings of the American Society of International Law, 1938*, pp. 23 ff.).

[18] The word "function" (from the Latin *functio*, "performance," "execution") refers in mathematics to the relation of a dependent to an independent variable ("$x =$ function y"); in physiology to the service of an organ to the body ("The function of the heart is to pump blood"); in medicine to the activity as distinct from the structure of a part of the organism ("His liver did not function properly, but the trouble was merely functional not structural"); in anthropology to the contribution of a ceremonial, activity, or object to the culture and life of the group ("Among the Murngin, war

By drive is meant a characteristic of an organism or personality which accounts for its specific reaction to a given situation. A psychological explanation of war states the war-producing tendency of the drives and other psychological traits of individuals or peoples in different situations.[19]

The word "cause" is used to apply to any of these or other types of explanation.

b) Analytical.—With respect to the analytical treatment in Part III, it has been decided to take as points of departure four different conceptions of the entities whose behavior may at the present time constitute war: (1) the government, (2) the state, (3) the nation, and (4) the people. These distinctions are related to a philosophical analysis[20] because the government, as the organization of political

---

functioned to maintain the sex ratios essential to group stability"); in political science to the duties of an office ("The function of the courts is to apply the law"); and in sociology to the relation of an activity or entity to the changing values of the society ("The trend in government has been from purely traditional to functional organization"). These various meanings are involved in the term "functionalism" in philosophy which "sums up and designates the most general of the many consequences of the impact of Darwinism upon the sciences of man and nature. This was to shift the conception of 'scientific thinking' into a temporal perspective; to stress relations and activities as against terms and substances, genesis and development as against intrinsic character, transformation as against continuing form, dynamic pattern as against static organization, processes of conflict and integration as against formal composition out of unchanging elements. In short, the shift was from 'structure' to 'function' as the principal tool of scientific explanation and interpretation" (H. M. Kallen, "Functionalism," *Encyclopaedia of the Social Sciences*, VI, 523).

[19] See Appen. VIII. "Psychologism" implies a preference for psychological interpretations of epistemology and history.

[20] An analysis may proceed by induction, leading the reader from concrete instances to abstract ideas or generalizations. It may proceed by deduction, leading from abstract propositions to their concrete consequences or verifications. It may proceed by rhetoric or persuasion, starting with the reader's subjective sentiments and proceeding to their objective realizations or manifestations. Finally, analysis may proceed by exposition or practical instruction from the objective observation or act to its subjective meaning or consequences. These four methods of analysis may be, respectively, compared to the physical, mechanistic, behavioristic, and operational formulations of scientific method (see Leonard Bloomfield, *Linguistic Aspects of Science* ["International Encyclopedia of Unified Science," Vol. I, No. 4 (Chicago, 1939)], p. 13) to the economic, religious, artistic, and political periods of history (see below, chap. vii, n. 42); and perhaps (with addition of observation) to the medieval division of the liberal arts—dialectics, rhetoric, and grammar.

power, is the warmaker viewed concretely and objectively; the state, as the organization of law, is the warmaker viewed abstractly and objectively; the nation, as the organization of culture, is the warmaker viewed abstractly and subjectively; while the people, as the organization of population and habitat, is the warmaker viewed concretely and subjectively.[21] These four concepts, therefore, lead us, respectively, to the (1) technological, (2) ideological, (3) sociological, and (4) psychological approaches to the problem.[22] Respectively, they attempt to answer the questions: How is war fought? How is war thought? Why is war thought? Why is war fought?

c) *Practical.*—With respect to the practical problem of controlling war dealt with in Part IV, consideration will be given (1) to the factors within contemporary states which tend to make them belligerent, (2) to the circumstances in the relations of pairs of states which tend to bring them into conflict with each other, (3) to the conditions in the world as a whole which tend to make all states belligerent at certain times, and (4) to the process which typically eventuates in war at the present time. This discussion of the problems of the aggressive state, the international feud, the international crisis, and the incipient war will provide the basis for a consideration of the way in which the world-community as a whole should develop if war is to be controlled.

War might be treated from points of view other than those here mentioned. It has, in fact, been most commonly treated from the artistic or literary point of view. Writers have sought to induce in

[21] Some writers have included all objective aspects of the social entity (government and state) in the concept *state* which they distinguish from all its subjective aspects (people and nation) in the concept *society:* Hans Speier, "Society versus the State," *Social Research,* III (August, 1936), 320; Leon Duguit, "The Law and the State," *Harvard Law Review,* XXXI (1917), 1 ff.; E. M. Borchard, "The Relation between State and Law," reprinted from *Yale Law Journal,* XXXVI (1927), 112; H. E. Cohen, *Recent Theories of Sovereignty* (Chicago, 1937), pp. 38 ff.; Talcott Parsons and George H. Sabine, articles, respectively, on "Society" and "State," in *Encyclopaedia of the Social Sciences.* Others have distinguished all the concrete aspects of the social entity (people and government) by the concepts *group* or *aggregate,* which they distinguish from all its abstract aspects (nation and state) by the concepts *community* or *association:* see articles by E. C. Lindeman, Edward Sapir, and Morris Ginsburg, respectively, on "Community," "Group," and "Association" in *Encyclopaedia of the Social Sciences.*

[22] See Appen. III.

their readers a subjective realization of war more frequently than they have sought to state what war has been, to distinguish its elements, or to control its incidents. Some of the factors accounting for different interpretations of war have been alluded to in the first chapter, and some of the influences of such interpretations upon the control of war are mentioned in the last. It is not the object of this study, however, to induce an attitude toward war in the minds of the readers, or to explain the variety of attitudes which have been and still are held on the subject, but rather to state what war has been in the past, what it is in the present, and what it may be in the future.

PART II

THE HISTORY OF WAR

CHAPTER III

HISTORY AND WAR

A HISTORY of war may suggest to the reader a narrative of the incidents of a battle, of a war, or of all the wars in the life of a nation, epoch, or civilization. None of these things will be attempted here. The history of war as a whole is to be attempted. Polybius wrote:

> Some idea of a whole may be got from a part, but an accurate knowledge and clear comprehension can-not. Wherefore we must conclude that episodical history contributes exceedingly little to the familiar knowledge and secure grasp of universal history.[1]

What, then, is a history of war as a whole? Consideration of the meaning of history and the meaning of war may suggest the answer.

I. MEANING OF HISTORY

The word "history" means, on the one hand, the happenings in a given time and space or during the life of a given whole and, on the other hand, a written or oral presentation of such of those happenings as are deemed important to a comprehension of the period or the whole dealt with. History in the first sense is the data of history in the second sense. The historian, however, is not a passive recorder of this data. He must react positively toward it by finding exactly *what happened*, exactly where and exactly when; by selecting for presentation that which is *important;* and by presenting those selected happenings in a manner to indicate their *significance.*

All writing, whether practice, science, literature, or history rests upon history in the first sense. Every writer must find some facts from the data of the past, employing for that purpose some conceptions of evidence, method, and logic. The varieties of writing differ, however, in the principles of selection employed and in the relations deemed significant.

[1] Evelyn S. Shuckburgh (ed.), *The Histories of Polybius*, I (London, 1889), 5.

25

Thus professional practitioners and men of affairs tend to select events which will contribute to *current utility* and to treat relations of value and cost, of means and ends, as especially significant. They prefer technological explanations which go directly to the point of practical accomplishment.

Scientists tend to select events which will contribute to *verifiable generalizations* and to treat relations of measurable quantities, of origin and development, of cause and effect as especially significant. They prefer theoretical explanations which contract the broadest verifiable generalization into the briefest phraseology.[2]

Orators and literary men tend to select events which the *general public whom they address* deem important and to treat relations of symbol and reality, of personality and motivation, as significant. They usually prefer psychological explanations, as these are most comprehensible to the average audience.

Historians, however, tend to select events which the public of the time and place *written about deemed important* and to treat relations of proximity, of continuity, of part and whole, as especially significant. They, therefore, prefer functional explanations which interpret the event or happening in terms of the whole of which the history is being written. Only those happenings are narrated which can be thus interpreted. But a fair sampling of such happenings or of coordinated groups of them must be presented. Polybius continued:

It is only by the combination and comparison of the separate parts of the whole,—by observing their likeness and their difference,—that a man can attain his object: can obtain his view at once clear and complete; and thus secure both the profit and the delight of History.[3]

If war as a whole is to be dealt with, its vast history must be divided into a relatively small number of parts which can be compared.

2. MEANING OF WAR

War has been defined as a violent contact of distinct but similar entities.[4] One could not carry in mind or compare all such contacts of all such entities since time began. Even if the narrower sociologi-

---

[2] William of Occam's razor—"essentia non sunt multiplicanda praeter necessitatum" —together with the development of scientific method as the criterion of truth has been the guide of science.

[3] See above, n. 1.　　　　　　　　　　[4] See chap. ii, sec. 1.

cal conception of war is employed, one could not consider together all the battles, campaigns, or wars which have occurred between social groups. Each of these war-manifesting events, however, pertains to a warring entity, and it is possible to group these entities. If we exclude purely physical entities, warlike behavior appears to be comprehensively divisible into that pertaining to animals, to primitive man, to civilized man, and to man using modern technology.

In comparing the warfare of each of these great entities, it must not be lost sight of that each is an outgrowth of its predecessor. Thus, there is a continuity from the belligerent behavior of the most primitive animals to that of the most modern state. The change from each of those entities to its successor was, however, so great as to constitute a new form of warfare—an emergence rather than an evolution.[5]

Each of these great groups of fighting entities manifests temporal and local variations in the character of its fighting, thus suggesting subgroups and further divisions of the fighting populations.

3. FACTORS IN HISTORY

While the history of war consists primarily in a presentation of the distinctive warlike behavior of each of these groups and subgroups, that history cannot be complete without a suggestion of the relationships which, by inducing oscillating, sporadic, or persistent changes, have led to those differences.

Oscillation, for example, may result from astronomical phenomena causing the succession of day and night, of winter and summer, and perhaps of long-time climatic variations;[6] from biological phenomena, such as the stages of individual development, the succession of generations, and perhaps a natural rise or decline of populations;[7]

[5] See chap. iv, n. 22.

[6] Ellsworth Huntington has presented evidence of climatic oscillations of some five centuries in various parts of the world (*The Pulse of Asia* [Boston, 1907]; *Palestine and Its Transformation* [New York, 1911]; *Civilization and Climate* [New Haven, 1915]; *World Power and Evolution* [New Haven, 1919]), but this evidence has been considered inadequate by some historians with respect to the Near East (see A. T. Olmstead, "Climatic Changes in the Near East," *Bulletin of American Geographic Society*, XLIV [1912], 432 ff.; Huntington's response, *ibid.*, pp. 440 ff.; and Olmstead's reply, *ibid.*, XLV, 439 ff.; F. J. Teggart, *Rome and China* [Berkeley, 1939], pp. 234 ff.).

[7] See Corrado Gini, "The Cyclical Rise and Fall of Population," in *Population* ("Harris Foundation Lectures" [Chicago, 1930]).

from sociological phenomena, such as economic cycles and political periods;[8] and from ideological phenomena, such as successions in the forms of human interest and institutions.[9]

Perhaps more significant than oscillations, fluctuations, and cycles in the history of war has been the influence of sporadic events, such as pestilence, famine, and war itself; technical and social inventions; scientific and geographic discoveries; and the occurrence of religious and political leaders.[10]

The hypothesis of continuous change in the same direction whether called evolution or progress, retrogression or decay, must also be considered, as must the hypothesis that every trend is in reality but a segment of a long oscillation.[11]

War has unquestionably made history in the first sense of the word, but it is also true that history in the second sense of the word has often been a contributing factor toward the making of war. History has, in fact, as often been the handmaid of statesmanship as of scholarship. The following chapters do not purport to be a complete history of war but only a setting-forth of some of the outlines for such a history. If, however, the history of nations has at times contributed consciously or unconsciously to war, perhaps the history of war may contribute to peace.

[8] See A. H. Hanson, *Business Cycle Theory* (Boston, 1927); *Economic Stabilization in an Unbalanced World* (New York, 1932).

[9] See chap. vii, n. 42. The distinction between biological, sociological, and ideological sources of change resembles Pitirim Sorokin's distinction between external, functional, and logical sources of cultural integration and change (*Social and Cultural Dynamics* [New York, 1937], I, 10 ff.).

[10] Given sufficient time and space, however, such apparently sporadic events may, by the law of large numbers, exhibit statistical regularity and persistent patterns.

[11] Many writers have contended that evolution involves eventual dissolution, that progress involves eventual retrogression, and, consequently, that evolution and progress merely refer to exceptionally long oscillations (see Herbert Spencer, *First Principles*, final chapter; Books Adams, *The Law of Civilization and Decay* [New York, 1910]; Gini, *op. cit.;* see also A. J. Todd, *Theories of Social Progress* [New York, 1918], pp. 143 ff.). The idea of descent from, or more rarely progress toward, a superior or "golden age" characteristic of Indic, Mesopotamian, Syriac, Classical, and Western civilizations usually tended toward the idea of oscillations (see Arthur A. Lovejoy, Gilbert Chinard, George Boas, and Ronald S. Crane [eds.], *A Documentary History of Primitivism and Related Ideas*, I [Baltimore, 1935], 4, 426–29, 433).

CHAPTER IV

ORIGIN OF WAR

I. STAGES IN THE HISTORY OF WAR

WARS, in the broadest sense of the word, have occurred between physical entities,[1] but this study is limited to organic history which began perhaps a billion years ago. The organic population or symplasm first penetrating the oceans, later covering the land and invading the air, has gone through evolutionary changes so rapid as to be revolutionary during the transitions from one major geologic age to the next. The relative biological stability of the long intervening periods has been characterized by the continuous dominance of a particular biological form. Thus, ages of trilobites, of fishes, of amphibians, of reptiles, and of mammals have succeeded one another. These ages have each been divided into epochs separated by lesser biological transitions, probably resulting from the periodic geological catastrophes. Within these epochs in the various areas of the earth's surface definite zones of biologic forms have been distinguished, separated by catastrophic changes of climate and terrain. These changes have occurred in the order of every million years and have destroyed many species and genera.[2]

The human species was probably biologically united in its origin and will probably be socially united before its end, but, from the wandering of the first group of men from the ancestral home, sometime in the late Miocene or early Pliocene,[3] to the modern era of

[1] Periods of mountain-building and continent elevation seem to have occurred at intervals of some twenty million years as a result of disequilibriums among masses within the earth (T. C. Chamberlain, "Certain Phases of Megatectonic Geology," *Journal of Geology*, XXXIV [January–February, 1926], 25; "Geology," *Encyclopaedia Britannica* [14th ed.], X, 158, 171).

[2] See Pirsson and Schuchert, Table, 1915, printed in *Encyclopaedia Britannica* (13th ed.), "Palaeontology," III, 15; Ellsworth Huntington, *World Power and Evolution* (New Haven, 1919), p. 110; A. S. Romer, *Man and the Vertebrates* (Chicago, 1933), p. 8.

[3] This was probably about 1,000,000 years ago (G. Elliot Smith, *Human History* [London, 1930], p. 499), although recent estimates vary from 500,000 to 4,000,000 years ago. Keith ("New Discoveries Relating to the Antiquity of Man," diagram reproduced in

world-communication, human evolution has moved in a number of separate channels. These separations were so complete in prehistoric times as to produce distinctive races. The less complete separations of historic times produced the distinctive civilizations. Such separations as have existed in modern times account for the distinct nations. The history of war can, therefore, be divided into four very unequal stages dominated, respectively, by animals, primitive men, civilized men, and men using modern technology. Whether these stages are abstractions from a continuous evolution or indications of radical mutations will be discussed later. In any case the evidences available for studying war are very different for each of these stages.

For the first or prehuman stage evidence is confined to the structure of the few paleontological remains of man's prehuman ancestors and the behavior of contemporary animals. The latter are not in the direct line of human descent, and their behavior merely suggests what may have been the nature of war among man's actual ancestors.[4]

The second stage, that of primitive man, began with the emergence of primates, able to communicate with one another by a definite language, a million to a half-million years ago.[5] The later

---

H. E. Barnes, *The History of Western Civilization* [New York, 1935], p. 5) estimates the Pleistocene and Pliocene at about 250,000 each; Osborne ("Men of the Old Stone Age," diagram reproduced in Huntington, *op. cit.*, p. 126) at 500,000 each; and Romer, (*op. cit.*, p. 8) at 1,000,000 each. Keith places the branching of the prehuman from the anthropoid stream in the Middle Oligocene which, according to these various estimates, would have been from 1,000,000 to 4,000,000 years ago. Older geological estimates originated man from 100,000 to 500,000 years ago, while biblical estimates placed the creation at 5,000 to 8,000 years ago (F. Müller-Lyer, *The History of Social Development* [New York, 1921], pp. 332–35). Roland B. Dixon (*The Racial History of Man* [New York, 1923], pp. 503 ff.) argues that the human race originated from the crossing of several originally isolated prehuman types. The more generally held theory, that man originated from a single stock, is presented by L. H. Dudley Buxton (*The Peoples of Asia* [New York, 1925], p. 16). On controversy as to whether man originated in the grasslands of northern Asia or the tropical forests see H. F. Osborne ("Is the Ape Man a Myth?" *Human Biology*, I [1929], 4–9) and W. K. Gregory ("Is the Pre-dawn Man a Myth?" *Human Biology*, I [1929], 153). See Appen. V, Fig. 9.

[4] See Charles Letourneau, *La Guerre dans les diverses races humains* (Paris, 1895), chap. i; J. Sageret, *Philosophie de la guerre et de la paix* (Paris, 1919), chap. iii.

[5] The distinction of man from animals by ability to convey objective ideas by speech is recognized by R. M. and A. W. Yerkes (*The Great Apes* [New Haven, 1929], p. 303);

developments of this stage continues in limited areas of Africa, Asia, Oceania, and America down to the present time. Evidence of the condition with respect to war and peace in this stage is to be found in archeological remains of the ancestors of the civilized communities[6] and in the observations of contemporary primitive peoples,[7] although the latter type of evidence must be used with caution.[8] Contemporary primitive men have in most cases borrowed much from neighbors of a higher culture. In some instances their present culture may be a degeneration from a higher civilization.

The third or historic stage began in the valleys of the Nile and Euphrates, six or perhaps even ten thousand years ago, in the valleys of the Indus and Yellow rivers four or five thousand years ago, and in Peru and Mexico perhaps three or four thousand years ago. Whether

---

S. Zuckerman (*Functional Affiliations of Man, Monkey and Apes* [New York, 1933], p. 156); W. T. Hornaday (*The Minds and Manners of Wild Animals* [New York, 1922], pp. 25 ff.). Müller-Lyer (*op. cit.*, pp. 45, 304 ff.), though recognizing speech as essential to progress, insists that "its origin . . . . presupposes a community, a social life." See also L. C. Marshall, *The Story of Human Progress* (New York, 1928), pp. 165 ff.; F. W. Blackmar, *History of Human Society* (New York, 1926), pp. 121 ff.; A. H. Keane, *Ethnology* (Cambridge, 1916), pp. 160, 195 ff. G. Elliot Smith distinguishes man rather by certain improvements in vision and the co-ordinating centers of the cortex. "Man," he writes, "is the ultimate product of that line of ancestry which was never compelled to turn aside and adopt protective specialization, either of structure or mode of life, which would be fatal to its plasticity and power of further development" (*The Evolution of Man* [Oxford, 1924], p. 35). See below, n. 23, and Appen. VII, n. 56.

[6] See H. F. Osborne, *Men of the Old Stone Age* (3d ed.; New York, 1924).

[7] L. T. Hobhouse, G. C. Wheeler, and M. Ginsburg, *The Material Culture and Social Institutions of the Simpler Peoples* (London, 1915). These data have been differently presented and interpreted by writers of the evolutionary school (W. G. Sumner, *War and Other Essays* [New Haven, 1911]; M. R. Davie, *The Evolution of War* [New Haven, 1929]), of the diffusionist school (W. J. Perry, "An Ethnological Study of Warfare," *Memoirs of Manchester Literary and Philosophical Society*, Vol. LXI, No. 6 [1917]; G. Elliot Smith, *The Evolution of Man*), and of the functional school (A. R. Radcliffe-Brown, *The Andaman Islanders* [Cambridge, 1922]; B. Malinowski, "Culture as a Determinant of Human Behavior," in *Factors Determining Human Behavior* ("Harvard Tercentenary Publications" [Cambridge, Mass., 1937]), pp. 133-68.

[8] H. J. Spinden (in G. Elliot Smith *et al.*, *Culture, the Diffusionist Controversy* [New York, 1924], p. 94, n. 12) writes that most primitive men today are "safely neolithic." Assuming that Neolithic culture nowhere goes back over 10,000 years, we have little direct evidence of man's way of life back of the last 1 per cent of his history. In the earlier 99 per cent of this history man underwent biological as well as cultural changes. Since Neolithic times there is no evidence of important biological change.

this stage which, except in Peru, can best be dated from the use of writing[9] originated autochthonously at several points or by transmission of major elements from a single or small number of centers is debated.[10] It continues in many places to the present time. Evidence of the nature of war in this period is to be found in contemporaneous and older writings, in inscriptions of a descriptive, chronological, and analytical character, and in archeological remains. Studies of the contemporary culture of civilized peoples is also of great value for interpreting earlier civilizations.[11]

The fourth stage, that of world-contact, may be said to have begun with the invention of printing in the fifteenth century, soon followed by the voyages from western Europe establishing continuous contacts between the centers of civilization in Europe, the Near East, America, and the Far East.[12] Since that time nearly all areas of

[9] That written language is essential for much advance in civilization has been widely recognized, although the Peruvians developed a civilization without any writing other than the mnemonic device of the quipu (see A. H. Keane, *Man, Past and Present* [Cambridge, 1900], p. 25; Max Schmidt, *The Primitive Races of Mankind*, trans. A. K. Dallas [London, 1926], p. 155; Marshall, *op. cit.*, p. 172; Clark Wissler, *Man and Culture* [New York, 1923], p. 81). The "earliest attempt . . . . at writing which is not simply pictorial" occurred in Egypt about 3400 B.C. (J. H. Breasted, *Ancient Times* [Boston, 1910], p. 42; G. Elliot Smith, *Human History*, pp. 334, 443). Even with language the growth of civilization may require a challenge, neither too severe nor too light, from the environment (A. J. Toynbee), whether that challenge is provided by marshes or wildernesses to be subdued (Toynbee), a stimulating climate (Huntington), contact with different or hostile groups (Gumplowicz, Müller-Lyer), or an intimate mixture of races (Flinders-Petrie). It may also require conditions favorable to invention, of which leisure is probably more important than necessity (Müller-Lyer), and to provide this leisure division of labor, the practice of agriculture, and an environment favorable to agriculture are all important (J. H. Breasted, *The Dawn of Conscience* [New York, 1933], pp. 94 ff.; G. E. Smith, *The Evolution of Man;* W. J. Perry, *op. cit.;* Morris Halperin, "Cereals and Civilization," *Scientific Monthly*, April, 1936, p. 355). See below, n. 23.

[10] See G. E. Smith, *et al.*, *Culture, the Diffusionist Controversy*, Appen.

[11] Hans Delbrück, *Geschicht der Kriegskunst* (6 vols.; Berlin, 1900–1929); O. E. Spaulding, H. Nickerson, J. W. Wright, *Warfare* (London, 1924); C. Oman, *History of the Art of War in the Middle Ages* (2 vols.; London, 1924); Letourneau, *op. cit.;* see below, chap. vii.

[12] Printing, it has been claimed, "is the medium which turned the darkness of the middle ages into light; which secured to posterity the intellectual achievements of the past; and which furnished to civilization a means of recording all future progress" (J. R. Riddel, "Printing," *Encyclopaedia Britannica* [14th ed.]). Its importance in creating a world-civilization is emphasized by Marshall, *op. cit.*, p. 179, James Westfall

the world have been brought within the orbit of continuous world-contact through printed communication. Such contacts have become notably more intense with the steam and electrical inventions of the nineteenth and twentieth centuries. Evidence with respect to the history of war and peace in this period is to be found in descriptive writings, much more voluminous than those available for the earlier historic period, and, in addition, in a wealth of legal, economic, and statistical materials, contemporaneously organized for the purpose of political, economic, and sociological record and analysis. The existence of this type of material, especially with respect to developments in the nineteenth and twentieth centuries, makes possible much more detailed analysis of the processes of group life and culture than was true of earlier times. Furthermore, the fact that we live in this culture makes it possible to test conclusions by contemporary observation of processes and of the effects of changes.[13]

2. RELATION OF THE ORIGIN TO THE MEANING OF WAR

Before dealing with the history of war in these four epochs, we should justify the assumption that war is to be found in all of them. It has been contended that war originated at a certain stage of civilization and that, in so far as war exists among primitive peoples, it has been learned by them from their civilized neighbors or has been retained by them, while in other respects they degenerated from

Thompson, *The Medieval Library* (Chicago, 1939), p. 630, and J. B. Scott, *The Spanish Origin of International Law* (Oxford, 1934), Vol. I, chap. i. There has been some reaction from the nineteenth-century tendency to emphasize the transition in civilization at the Renaissance, as illustrated by J. A. Symonds ("The Renaissance in Italy, 1875–88," in art. "The Renaissance," *Cambridge Modern History*, Vol. I, and *Encyclopaedia Brittanica* [14th ed.]). Certain historians like H. O. Taylor (*Thought and Expression in the Sixteenth Century* [New York 1920]), J. T. Shotwell ("Middle Ages," *Encyclopaedia Britannica* [11th ed.], see extract in Davis and Barnes, *Readings*) and A. J. Toynbee (*A Study of History* [Oxford, 1934]) emphasize the continuity of Western history from the time of Charlemagne to the present. See below, n. 23, and chap. viii.

[13] For history of war in the recent period see G. Bodart, *Militär-historisches Kriegs Lexikon (1618–1905)* (Leipzig, 1908); F. A. Woods and A. Baltzley, *Is War Diminishing? A Study of the Prevalence of War in Europe from 1450 to the Present Day* (Boston, 1915); Sir G. Butler and S. Maccoby, *The Development of International Law* (London, 1928); Col. J. F. C. Fuller, *War in Western Civilization, 1832–1932* (London 1932); Pitirim Sorokin, *Social and Cultural Dynamics* (New York, 1937); and chap. xii below.

civilization to savagery. This theory is supported by the extreme "diffusionist" or "historical" school of anthropology represented by W. H. R. Rivers[14] and G. Elliot Smith[15] and has been most elaborated by W. J. Perry.[16] These writers contend that war was invented in predynastic Egypt, along with agriculture, social classes, and human sacrifice. This "archaic" civilization was diffused by widespread travels of the Egyptians during the pyramid-building age. The nomadic barbarians on the outskirts of this civilization learned war from it and developed war methods in attacks upon its centers.

The majority of anthropologists decline to accept this theory. They do not find it necessary to accept either the theory that every culture trait, however widespread, must have had a single historic origin from which variations have diverged or the theory that all peoples tend to invent similar culture traits at the appropriate stage of their development and thus that all cultures tend to converge, whatever their origins. Borrowing and independent invention both occur, and evidence must be adduced to explain the presence of each particular trait in each particular group. The evidence of contemporary primitive cultures, of contemporary apes, and of the remains of prehistoric man suggest that forms of violence have always been widespread among men, though there has always been much variation both among individuals and among groups. No general golden age of peace existed at any stage of human history nor did any general iron age of war. Neither the Rousseauan nor the Hobbesian

[14] *History and Ethnology* (London, 1922).

[15] *The Evolution of Man; Culture, the Diffusion Controversy;* and *Human History.*

[16] "An Ethnological Study of Warfare," *op. cit.;* "The Peaceful Habits of Primitive Communities," *Hibbert Journal,* October, 1917; *The Children of the Sun* (London, 1923). The theory is set forth in its most complete form in *The Growth of Civilization* (New York, 1923). W. C. MacLeod (*The Origin and History of Politics* [New York, 1931]) follows Perry in denying the universality of human belligerence, although he admits the probability of blood revenge in very ancient societies and considerable losses, proportionate to the size of the groups from such quasi-warlike violence (pp. 61 ff.). He also, like Perry, emphasizes the role of diffusion and, while pointing out that with diffusion the conquest theory of the origin of the state requires the assumption of only one conquest, denies the primary function in state building ascribed to war by Gumplowitz, Ratzenhoffer, Lester Ward, and Oppenheimer (pp. 47 ff., 70 ff.). H. F. Cleland (*Our Prehistoric Ancestors* [New York, 1928]) states that, though Neolithic man fortified villages and sometimes fought, warfare in the modern sense did not exist until the age of metals (pp. 131, 216, 338).

concept of natural man is adequate. Man was and is a complex compound of inherited tendencies and social conditionings, crystallizing at different times and places into numerous cultures exhibiting varying forms and degrees of violence.[17]

To decide, therefore, whether war was spontaneously practiced by human groups everywhere or was borrowed from one or a few societies, it is necessary to study the evidence from many groups. In order to do that, it is necessary to consider in what sense war is meant.

If by war is meant the use of firearms to promote the policy of a group, it must be admitted that the contemporary primitive peoples borrowed warfare from people of modern civilization. The dispersion of many modern war techniques—weapons, formations, tactical movements, and strategic ideas—can be demonstrated from historical evidence. Doubtless, in this technological sense, war was invented in Europe only about five centuries ago and subsequently diffused throughout the world.

If, however, by war is meant the reaction to certain situations by resort to violence, the assumption of borrowing seems more doubtful. Animals of the same species quarrel, and quarrel violently, and many of the things they quarrel about—food, territory, females—are the things men quarrel about. In this psychological sense war is a mode of behavior which belongs to most men and animals and probably to all children.[18] It does not seem likely that children acquired this trait in imitation of their parents, who in turn acquired it from their civilization which came indirectly from Egypt.

If by war one has in mind a period of time, initiated and ended according to law, during which, and during which alone, violence may be legitimately resorted to as an instrument of group policy,

[17] See Appen. VI.

[18] Susan Isaacs has presented numerous observations of aggressive behavior among young children (*Social Development in Young Children* [London, 1933]); William McDougal lists "pugnacity" as one of the human instincts (*An Introduction to Social Psychology* [Boston, 1918]); Freud emphasizes "aggression" as one of the primitive drives of human nature (letter to Einstein on "Why War?" International Institute of Intellectual Cooperation, *Correspondence* [Paris, 1933]); and E. L. Thorndike describes "fighting reactions" in his book on *The Original Nature of Man* (New York, 1913), pp. 68 ff.

doubtless animals and many primitive men do not practice it, although there are primitive peoples with highly formalized belligerent practices. It appears to be in this sense that Perry uses the term "war," and anthropologists of other schools admit that war as a legitimate instrument for plunder or conquest was little known among primitive peoples.[19] In this legal, political, and economic sense war probably originated among civilizations, accompanying the development among them of political organizations involving subordination, property, dense populations, and codified law. It then diffused to their less civilized neighbors.[20]

Finally, war may mean a social custom utilizing regulated violence in connection with intergroup conflicts. In this sociological sense war appears to have originated with permanent societies. Such societies are found among the social insects and were probably characteristic of man from the beginning. War in this sense is found in nearly all existing human groups, however primitive.[21]

There are thus senses in which war is an organic phenomenon, others in which it is a human phenomenon, others in which it is a phenomenon of civilization, and others in which it is an achievement of very recent times. We must be careful to define precisely what we mean by war, before we can hope to locate its origin.

3. EMERGENCE OF THE VARIOUS ASPECTS OF WAR

While our study of animal, primitive, civilized, and modern war in the following chapters will indicate more precisely the sense in which war has existed in these successive stages of organic and social history, we may here anticipate the conclusions to be there supported.

It is believed that the transitions from each of these stages to the next marked real changes or breaches in the continuity of history. Each began by the emergence[22] of a new type of dynamic equilib-

[19] See Radcliffe-Brown, *op. cit.*, pp. 85–87; Malinowski, *op. cit.* Letourneau (*op. cit.*, p. 530) points out that war for economic ends began with the development of a pastoral or agricultural economy.

[20] See above, nn. 14–16.

[21] Camilla H. Wedgewood, "Some Aspects of Warfare in Melanesia," *Oceania*, I (April, 1930), 5–33; Radcliffe-Brown, *loc. cit.*

[22] W. M. Wheeler, *Emergent Evolution and the Development of Societies* (New York, 1928). The tendency for evolutionary stages, deemed of equal importance to become

rium, was characterized by a new trend of evolution, and can be studied by a new type of evidence. Each of these transitions appears to have resulted from the rapid cumulation of changes tracing back to certain fundamental inventions, most important of which have been the successive improvements in the means of communication. Speech, writing, and printing initiated, respectively, the ages of man, of civilization, and of the world-community.[23]

War in the psychological sense began with organic nature. The most primitive protozoa were endowed with drives adapted for obtaining food, for reproduction, and for self-preservation, and these drives, when stimulated by circumstances arising more or less frequently in the animal's environment, resulted in violent behavior of the organism as a whole. While among the more specialized animals the circumstances causing violent behavior have varied greatly in type and frequency, and on the whole violence between animals of the same species has not been common, yet it is doubtful whether there are any animals which cannot be provoked into fighting by some stimuli. There are rudiments of war in the sociological sense,

---

shorter, i.e., for the rate of progress to accelerate, has been emphasized by Kant, by Henry Adams, and by Müller-Lyer (*op. cit.*, pp. 336 ff.). Whether there is objective evidence for this generalization or merely an illustration of the tendency to rate importance according to proximity to the rater in time and space is difficult to say.

[23] These three inventions, like most others, were gradual achievements resulting from the combination of several independent inventions. Spoken language combined the use of imitative and ejaculatory sounds, of symbolic sounds or words properly so called, and of relationships suggested by the ordering or modification of words in sentences (Wissler, *op. cit.*, p. 81). Thus the invention does not mark a point in time but a long period during which opinions might differ whether or not spoken language existed. So also writing combines the use of conventionalized pictures, or symbolic pictures, and of phonetic symbols. Certain written languages developed the latter very inadequately, and some "preliterate" tribes use the first (Wissler, *op. cit.*, pp. 84 ff.; H. E. Barnes, *op. cit.*, I, 103 ff.). Printing involves the combination of the invention of paper, block printing, and movable type. The total achievement occupied more than a thousand years in China and the Western world (Barnes, *op. cit.*, p. 839; see also E. Sapir, *Language* [New York, 1921], chap. i; Leonard Bloomfield, *Language* [New York, 1933], chap. ii, and *Linguistic Aspects of Science* [Chicago, 1939], p. 6). Müller-Lyer identifies these three epochs marked by changes in the means of communication (*op. cit.*, p. 244) with epochs marked by fundamental transportation changes: (1) man-power without mechanical assistance, (2) artificial transport using animals, carts, and ships; (3) steam and electrical transport initiating "the epoch of world commerce" (p. 244); and with epochs marked by fundamental changes in the mode of economic exchange: (1) natural

especially among the social insects and among some of the higher mammals; but, on the whole, war does not exist among animals other than man, except in the sense of violent behavior by the individual animal induced by the appropriate stimulus to an organic drive.

War in the sociological sense could not exist as a distinct phenomenon before the emergence of human societies, permanently constituted through communication by language and the accumulation of traditions. Under these conditions it was first possible for the individual to identify himself with a group represented by a symbol and to distinguish his group thus represented from other groups like it but bearing a different relationship to himself. Thus, morals began, and they generated a conscience in the individual and the possibility of belligerent behavior in response not to organic drives but to tribal mores, to the demands of the superego. While there are tribes that fight rarely, as there are animals that fight rarely, it seems probable that this is because of environmental circumstances which seldom stimulate the belligerent mores which exist. No tribes have been adequately described that will not fight as units under certain circumstances, and in most tribes the mores prescribe violent behavior in a variety of circumstances connected with tribal solidarity, religion, magic, marriage, and sport. War as a regular means of live-

---

economy without exchange, with simple barter or "natural" money, such as animals, shells, or weights of metal; (2) money economy with coined money; and (3) credit economy with token money (p. 242). He even associates these epochs with changes in dress: (1) natural or tropical dress, (2) national or subtropical dress, and (3) dress of fashion or northern dress (p. 142); with changes in economic organization: (1) clan organization, (2) industrial organization, and (3) capitalistic organization (p. 198); (cf. N. S. B. Gras, [1] collectional, cultural, nomadic and settled village economy, [2] town economy, [3] metropolitan economy [*An Introduction to Economic History* (New York, 1922), p. 317]); with changes in division of labor: (1) differentiation between the sexes, (2) differentiation among men, and (3) differentiation among women (p. 232); and with changes in the dominant factor in production (1) nature, (2) labor, and (3) capital (Roscher) (p. 249 and table, p. 252). Müller-Lyer seems to regard changes in the modes of economic exchange as fundamental, but it seems to the present writer that these and other changes have followed those in the means of communication. The appreciation of the artistic impulse seems to have been greatly affected by these communication inventions. Primitive man decorated his body, civilized man used art also to form and adorn his buildings, and modern man pays especial attention to the adornment of his books. Prints are the characteristic art of today (Carl Zigrosser, *Six Centuries of Fine Prints* [New York, 1937]).

lihood, however, to get food, slaves, or booty or to expand hunting grounds, seems to exist among the food-gatherers mainly through borrowing from peoples of a higher culture, although these types of war have been developed among a few of the social insects.

War in the sense of a legal situation equally permitting groups to expand wealth and power by violence began with civilization.[24] Not until the arts of writing, agriculture, and animal husbandry had developed was it possible to organize a permanent human group or state larger than the primary or man-to-man-contact group, with a distinction of ruler and ruled, a clear conception of property, and a body of law, distinct from the mores, to regulate these relationships, to preserve internal order, and to formulate social interests.[25] Only under these conditions could war become institutionalized as a rational means to political and economic ends. War as a legitimate procedure for acquiring territory, cattle, slaves, and political prestige has existed among civilized peoples and has been transmitted by them to their more primitive neighbors. Only among civilized people has war been an institution serving political and economic interests of the community, defined by a body of law which states the circumstances justifying its use, the procedures whereby it is begun and ended, and the methods by which it is conducted.

War in the modern technical sense began with the period of world-

[24] Letourneau (*op. cit.*, pp. 104, 530) points out that primitive warfare was more juridical than civilized war in the sense that its purpose was the sanction of existing law, but as an institution for creating new law and new rights war began with civilization. "The violent appropriation of labour power and commodities, although it is usually an accompaniment of warlike actions among native races, is not the real object of war. Unfortunately, ethnologists have too often overlooked the fact that war as such is entirely a conception of international law, and certain prerequisites are necessary before human contests can be called war" (Max Schmidt, *op. cit.*, p. 171).

[25] Breasted interprets what is perhaps a copy of the oldest extant Egyptian inscription (from the First Dynasty, 3400 B.C.) to indicate that great importance was then attributed to "understanding" and "command." These qualities of personality were identified with origins, thus anticipating the doctrine of the logos, "In the beginning was the word." "Loved" and "hated" conduct are associated with such commands rather than with custom (*The Dawn of Conscience*, pp. 37 ff.). Thus, the dynamic idea that society and law are creations of personality sharply distinguishes even the earliest stages of Egyptian civilization from primitive cultures. The Pyramid texts (2475–2625 B.C.) suggest that this idea led to royal cannibalism as a means of acquiring the virtues of the personality of the deceased (*ibid.*, pp. 88 ff.).

civilization. All belligerent entities—animals, primitive peoples, and the historic civilizations of the past—have, of course, had war techniques—weapons, tactics, and strategic ideas—but in the modern sense war means the use of firearms and chemicals for striking and of steam, gas, and electrical engines for military movement. This utilization of sources of power other than those of man and beast in hostile operations has transformed the character of such operations and made them war in the modern sense. It is true that human power had been converted in form and direction in the past by mechanical devices such as the bow, arquebus, and siege engine, but the force of these instruments was limited by the power of the human arm to bend the spring upon which the device depended. Until recent periods man had no reliable methods for releasing power stored by other than human or animal muscle for the purpose of advancing toward or striking an enemy.[26] This change has made war more destructive, more likely to spread, and consequently of more general interest. Resort to war anywhere has tended to become a matter of concern to all governments, and consequently the use of this technique must be justified in terms of the world-order, whether to sanction international law as it is or to effect revisions of that law deemed to be desirable.[27] Animals have fought from inherited drives, primitive men have fought from group custom, people of historic civilization have fought for group interests, but people of contemporary world-civilization fight for a better world-order.

Thus, according to the definition of war we have in mind, we can place its origin at the beginning of any of the four stages which we are about to consider. Animal war resembled modern war only in the

[26] The sailing vessel was about the only such device useful in war at all, and it was so unreliable before the modern period that oared vessels were preferred in war.

[27] "War in our time is neither a lawful resort to force for the legitimate enforcement of rights, as the classical apologists for the 'just war' described it, nor an antisocial or criminal outbreak precipitated by wicked leaders, as a certain type of contemporary pacifist is prone to regard it. . . . . War today is essentially international revolution. It is revolt against some part of the international order which has become intolerable to a nation or to a group of nations. It is an attempt to accomplish readjustment of that order by risking the desperate hazards of an appeal to arms. It is the last recourse of those who are determined to accomplish change" (Edwin D. Dickinson, "The Law of Change in International Relations," *Proceedings of the Institute of World Affairs, 1933,* XI, 175).

psychological sense. War among primitive people, untouched by civilized neighbors, resembled modern war only in the psychological and sociological senses. War among the historic peoples resembled modern war in the psychological, sociological, and legal senses. Only since the advent of continuous world-cultural contacts in the fifteenth century has war existed in the modern technological sense.

In all its stages war can, of course, be approached from the sociological, legal, and technical points of view as well as from the psychological. In each of these four stages violent behavior has served superindividual functions, has exhibited formal regularities of recurrence and conduct, and has proceeded by describable techniques as well as from understandable psychological drives. Even animal warfare has functions, a theory, and a technique, but they are not the functions, theory, and technique which characterize modern human warfare. While the history of modern psychological drives goes back to the animals, that of modern sociological institutions goes back only to primitive man, that of modern law only to early civilizations, and that of modern technology only to the inventions of the late Middle Ages. Animal sociology rests on different foundations from human sociology, primitive law rests on different foundations from civilized law, and modern technology rests on distinctive foundations. War has changed its character with each of these great transitions.

CHAPTER V

ANIMAL WARFARE

THE study of animal warfare may contribute toward understanding the organic bases and social tendencies of war and the influence of particular military techniques and of war in general upon the survival of societies and races. Human beings are but a small element of the organic population of the earth. The great symplasm, whose history began in pre-Cambrian times, is composed of protoplasmic cells, each adapted to a definite environment but similar to one another in origin, chemical composition, organization, and behavior; in exhibiting reactions of movement, repetition, response, and irritability; in engaging in activities of nutrition, reproduction, rivalry, and protection; and perhaps in experiencing feelings of hunger, affection, dominance, and fear.[1]

1. DRIVES

The psychological causes of war lie ultimately in the characteristics of protoplasm,[2] and study of the simpler animal forms gives

[1] See excellent definition of "organism" and description of seven types of organisms from unicellular animals to human societies in W. M. Wheeler, "An Ant Colony as an Organism," *Journal of Morphology*, Vol. XXII (1911), reprinted in *Foibles of Insects and Men* (New York, 1928), pp. 130 ff. See also A. E. Emerson, "Social Coordination and Superorganism," *American Midland Naturalist*, XXI (January, 1939), 183. Other activities such as quiescence, restlessness, and investigativeness with their accompanying feelings of satisfaction, nostalgia, and curiosity may be as universal characteristics of protoplasm as those mentioned, but they are harder to discriminate as definite behavior patterns. S. Zuckerman finds that social behavior among the primates is mainly related to sex (*The Social Life of Monkeys and Apes* [London, 1932], pp. 29, 235). H. E. Howard finds the same to be true of birds (*An Introduction to the Study of Bird Behavior* [Cambridge, 1929]), and Freud finds it to be true of men. Recent experiments, however, have tended to emphasize the importance of a distinct dominance drive in birds and mammals (A. H. Maslow, "The Dominance Drive as a Determiner of Social Behavior in Infrahuman Primates," *Psychological Bulletin*, XXXII [1935], 714–15).

[2] George W. Crile, *A Mechanistic View of War and Peace* (New York, 1915), pp. 4, 52; W. M. Wheeler, *Emergent Evolution and the Development of Societies* (New York, 1928), p. 46. Emerson suggests that the assumed "psychic correlations, particularly

42

better evidence of the basic pattern of these characteristics than the study of such a complex form as man. Such a study suggests a classification of fundamental drives, in terms of the end object, as food, sex, dominance, self-preservation, home territory, activity, independence, and society.[3]

Among individual animals violence is motivated most commonly by the drives for food when between animals of different species and by the drives of sex, territory, dominance, and activity when between animals of the same species. All animals have means of self-defense, but flight is more common than hostile action against the aggressor. Animals with highly organized societies, like the bees and ants, fight primarily from the societal drive. The society as a whole is driven to aggressive hostilities by the needs for food or territory and in some instances by the urge for migration or parasitic dominance. Such societies often have specialized members or castes to defend them when attacked. The need of defense has played an important role in developing animal aggregations and societies.[4]

Among the animals biologically nearest to man, the drive for dominance is usually at the root of fighting, though frequently the drives of activity and sex play a part in such incidents. Because of the relatively weak social organization of apes, the dominance and activity drives in combination may lead to alliances against the dominant leader, especially when the capacity of the latter is declin-

---

between human societies and human personality" is "probably the result of a dualistic philosophy and may therefore break down through the modern study of biological psychology" (*op. cit.*, p. 183). "The body is a federation of organs and tissues, living in symbiosis, but there is still some hostility or selfishness in parts. A compromise is established, but the control is not perfect, and there may be disorder. Malignancy means imperfect control. Epithelium and connective tissue, according to Roberts (Morley Roberts, *Warfare in the Human Body*, pp. 40–43), control each other, and their failure to do so is the real cause of malignancy. But all we wish here is the idea of a struggle of parts as a natural incident in an evolving body which has not attained to perfect integration" (J. Arthur Thomson, *What Is Man?* [New York, 1924], p. 266).

[3] Drives should strictly be distinguished in terms of the need felt rather than the object or situation striven for, but the two classifications are parallel and the latter terminology is less ambiguous (see Appen. VIII).

[4] See Appen. VII, "Animal Warfare," sec. 1.

ing with age. These occasionally result in balance-of-power wars like those among sovereign states.[5]

Detailed studies of group behavior of monkeys and apes in captivity and of young children indicate that the situations precipitating fights were similar. The aggression precipitating a fight usually involved several drives, and fighting once begun tended to spread throughout the group. Aggressive behavior usually arose from rivalry for *possession* of some external object, from *intrusion* of a stranger in the group, or from *frustration* of activity.[6]

Possessiveness may be manifested in respect to food, territory, objects of curiosity such as toys, or another member of the species, especially of the opposite sex. Among children this may be an adult. Jealousy from possessiveness of the latter type leads to fighting more often than does rivalry for food.[7] The desire for possession seems often to be increased among both apes and children by awareness that another of the group desires the same thing.[8] Hostility against an intruder may arise from apprehension that a stranger may interfere with the satisfaction of other drives, particularly that he may become a rival for valued possessions. It may therefore be considered a hypothetical form of possessiveness or perhaps possessiveness toward the existing group situation as a whole. Rage, aggressiveness, and fighting may arise from frustration of the normal activity associated with any drive and may be directed against any person or object believed, often erroneously, to be guilty of the interference. This type of aggression involves more inference than does aggression arising from possessiveness and is less characteristic of fighting among apes than among children. Among the latter the

[5] A. H. Maslow, "The Role of Dominance in the Social and Sexual Behavior of Infrahuman Primates," *Journal of Genetic Psychology*, XLIX (1936), 197; Zuckerman, *op. cit.*, pp. 221-22; E. F. M. Durbin and John Bowlby, *Personal Aggressiveness and War* (New York, 1939), p. 56.

[6] Durbin and Bowlby, *op. cit.*, pp. 8-11, 51-72; Zuckerman, *op. cit.;* Susan Isaacs, *Social Development in Young Children* (London, 1933).

[7] "What evidence is available points to sexual rivalry as the sole cause of serious fighting among baboons" (Durbin and Bowlby, *op. cit.*, p. 58, quoting Zuckerman, *op. cit.*, p. 235). Maslow ("The Role of Dominance in the Social and Sexual Behavior of Infrahuman Primates," *op. cit.*, p. 262) thinks that Zuckerman exaggerates the role of sex and underestimates that of dominance.

[8] Durbin and Bowlby, *op. cit.*, pp. 8, 64.

frustration may even be attributed to the child's own incapacity, leading sometimes to self-punishment.[9]

2. FUNCTIONS

The animal world exhibits not only less evolved forms of protoplasmic organization than man but also more evolved forms of individual and social specialization. Ants and termites maintained highly complex societies in the Oligocene fifty million years before the origin of man.[10] These societies have, therefore, had time to develop specializations and modes of maintaining social equilibrium superior, in some respects, to those of human society. If we could assume that diverse organic forms tend, under similar conditions, to evolve behavior and social adaptations toward a common goal, as suggested by the hypothesis of convergent evolution, then these societies, of which no less than twenty-four forms have been independently evolved among the insects alone, might show us the possibilities of human communities in future geologic ages.[11]

The sociological causes of war are to be found by analyzing the function of war in the life of the larger whole. Among colonial insects, fighting habits of certain members of the society function to preserve the society, as among men; but among animals in general, fighting habits, though varying in intensity among individuals, are characteristic of the entire species. Animal fighting, therefore, must ordinarily be interpreted functionally in relation not to a society or a culture but to a race or species. A tendency toward deadly intraspecific fighting would be a serious disadvantage for the race and would usually be eliminated by natural selection. For this reason intraspecific fighting among animals is seldom lethal. Differing from human war, which is always intraspecific and is often most serious

[9] *Ibid.*, pp. 10, 68.

[10] Wheeler's study of ants preserved in Baltic amber indicates that there have been no important structural changes since the Lower Oligocene and that all the important castes then existed (*Social Life among the Insects* [New York, 1923], p. 7).

[11] See W. M. Wheeler, *Demons of the Dust* (New York, 1930), a study in insect behavior emphasizing the great resemblance of behavior in the ant lion and the ant worm, although structurally and genetically the two insects are very different. Both construct pitfalls and throw dust in the face of approaching prey. The ants and termites also show great resemblances in behavior and social organization, although belonging to two remote orders of insects. See also Wheeler's *Social Life among the Insects*.

between peoples of the same race, animal fighting declines in deadliness with closeness of genetic relationship of the combatants. The
really deadly animal violence is between widely separated species, as
the lion and the antelope, and resembles human operations in the
hunt or the slaughter-house rather than in war. The competition for
a limited food supply among animals of the same species results not
in lethal conflict and combat but in dispersion and starvation of the
least fit. It usually takes the form of aggressiveness by the male,
sometimes aided by the female in defending the home territory, the
nesting and feeding area, from others of the species. Its human analogy is economic competition between individuals or firms rather than
warfare.[12]

Animal individuals and species in a neighborhood exhibit widespread dependencies upon one another. Unmitigated predaciousness
and parasitism usually have a suicidal effect. Survival of the species
depends upon wise maintenance of the balance of nature, and natural
selection has shown a persistent tendency to limit parasitism and
predaciousness even between unrelated species. The species with the
largest number of individuals and the widest range usually has
neither of these characteristics. Both ant and human societies have
gone through hunting, pastoral, and agricultural stages, and the
latter has proved to have the greatest survival value. The trend of
evolution has been toward symbiotic relations and perhaps toward
vegetarian diet.[13]

3. TECHNIQUES

The modes of attack and defense—the specializations in mobility,
striking power, armor, co-operation, and mass attack—are so diverse
and extreme among animals that it is easier to see their relations to
the incidence of fighting, and their effects on the preservation of
species, than in the less extreme variations found in human history.

Among individual animals specialization in mobility, as among
birds, deer, and monkeys, makes for a war of maneuver and is particularly favorable to intraspecific war, which, however, results in
dispersion rather than in death. Tenacity, making for a war of at-

---

[12] A. M. Carr-Saunders, "Biology and War," *Foreign Affairs*, VII (1929), 430 ff.
[13] See Appen. VII, sec. 2.

trition, as among boa constrictors and bears, is particularly unfavorable to intraspecific war as it invariably results in the death of the victim and, consequently, is disadvantageous to the species. Specialization in striking power, as among lions and cobras, making for a war of pounce, is also unfavorable to intraspecific war, though it acts as an incitement to aggression against weaker species. Specialization in protective armor, as among tortoises, armadillos, and clams, makes war unlikely, unless the armor is accompanied by considerable striking power and moderate mobility, as in the elephant, rhinoceros, and swordfish. In that case a war of shock may occur even within the species, though more rarely than in the less heavily protected and more mobile animals. Genetic lines specializing in heavy protective armor tend to increase in size and to decrease in mobility and adaptability, sometimes to a suicidal extent, as in the dinosaurs.

The advantage of an animal in battle depends upon the particular combination of all these types of military equipment. It appears that genetic lines specializing in mobility and tenacity have prospered most, although the first has maximized and the second has minimized the frequency of intraspecific hostilities. Clumsiness, resulting from specialization in protective armor, and predaciousness, resulting from specialization in striking power, have not characterized the most numerous species, especially among the higher animals.

Certain animals, like ants, termites, and buffalo herds, have developed collective military techniques, but these are more often for defense than for aggression. Animal societies which specialize in striking power and mobility, like the driver and slave-taking ants, tend to be predacious and parasitic, characteristics not favorable to rapid multiplication. Specialization in protective walls, as among the termites, while avoiding intraspecific war, stunts the possibilities of adaptation to changing conditions. On the other hand, specialization in protective group loyalty, as among the ants, tends to maximize intraspecific war. The great body of ant colonies, however, with fifty million years of social experience behind them, generally keep to their own nests and feeding areas and engage in hostilities only when attacked by the parasitic or predacious minority of the ants.[14]

[14] See Appen. VII, sec. 3.

A study of these techniques suggests that long survival of a species has resulted from a balance between the efficiency, which comes from integration of the entire structure and behavior of the animal about a specialized technique, and the flexibility, which comes from avoiding such complete specialization and integration that adaptation to new conditions becomes difficult or impossible. Violent changes of climate, food supply, or habitat have resulted in the elimination of the narrowly specialized species and genera, particularly those specializing in size, armor, and predaciousness.

4. THEORY

The theory of animal war is the theory of organic evolution—the nonsurvival of the unfit.

The balance of organic nature is maintained principally through the process of one species preying upon another, especially upon the young, and of one species crowding another out of an area which forms for it a suitable habitat. These modes of elimination are, of course, counterweights to reproduction, which, when sexual, permit a tremendous multiplication of combinations from gene mutations arising in an individual.[15] Climatic, geologic, and geographic change may at times suddenly alter the balance and exterminate populations or even species and genera; but, in a constant physical environment, being preyed upon and being crowded out of a food supply are the modes of eliminating the superabundant population provided by the extraordinary fertility of most species—fertility such that almost any species would, if all survived and reproduced, occupy the world or the solar system in a short time.[16] Only the social insects which confine reproduction to a single female in the society, the workers being made sterile, have adopted a process of limitation through birth control.[17]

[15] On the normal racial advantage of sexual reproduction see R. A. Fisher, *The Genetical Theory of Natural Selection* (Oxford, 1930), pp. 121 ff.; Sewall Wright, "The Roles of Mutation, In-breeding, Cross-breeding and Selection in Evolution," *Proceedings Sixth International Congress of Genetics, 1933*, I, 356.

[16] A. M. Carr-Saunders, *The Population Problem* (Oxford, 1922), chap. ii. P. Kropotkin, *Mutual Aid, a Factor of Evolution* (London, 1910), pp. 68 ff.; Charles Letourneau, *La Guerre dans les diverses races humains* (Paris, 1895), p. 8.

[17] Wheeler, *Social Life among the Insects*, p. 13. Alfred J. Lotka (*Elements of Physical Biology* [Baltimore, 1925]) suggests that it is a plausible if not inevitable supposition

The normal modes of elimination may, at times, be greatly exaggerated or decreased through invasions of an area, especially by man;[18] but in nature their adjustment to reproduction is often so precise that from year to year the population of each species in a given area may vary very little. However, these populations usually undergo gradual quantitative changes, sometimes of a cyclical character.[19] Such quantitative changes of populations are accompanied by evolutionary changes of type, the speed of which depends upon the balance of such factors as random variation, mutation, migration, cross-breeding of different races of the species, and the intensity of selection measured by the proportion between those destroyed and those surviving from year to year.

The rate of evolution of a biological community or biocoenosis will be augmented by intense selection among its constituent species, and such selection will be intensified by radical change in the physical environment or encroachment of neighboring biological communities. The rate of evolution of a species, however, is not determined by the intensity of selection among individuals of the species, as suggested by some interpretations of Darwinism, but by selection among comparatively isolated races which have drifted apart as a result of local inbreeding. As an evolutionary factor, selection must operate upon communities, races, subspecies, or species rather than upon individuals.[20] But, whether between individuals or groups, the struggle for existence is not a conscious conflict resembling war but an unconscious competition for food supply.

---

that some adjustment of the birth rate to the food supply takes place in many species (p. 129).

[18] Theodore Roosevelt estimated that, in killing a dozen lions, each of which would have killed a buck, pig, or zebra every five or six days, or in all 700 or 800 a year, he disturbed the balance to the advantage of the "harmless game" in spite of the fact that he killed a hundred or more of them himself (*African Game Trails*, p. 168).

[19] Herbert Spencer assumed a rhythmical variation in the population of a species (*First Principles*, chap. xxii, sec. 173), and Lotka confirmed this assumption by an analytic consideration of equilibrium conditions (*op. cit.*, pp. 61–62).

[20] Sewall Wright, "Evolution in Mendelian Populations," *Genetics*, XVI (March, 1931), 97 ff., and review of R. A. Fisher's *The Genetical Theory of Natural Selections*, in *Journal of Heredity*, XXI (August, 1930), 349 ff.; Kropotkin, *op. cit.*, p. 65. Fisher shows that the probability of any change in the behavior or structure of a species bene-

Among colonial insects and perhaps other species mutual aid, co-operation, and specialization of function appear to be of significance for regulating the survival and evolution of the group. All animals live in groups, using that term in the broadest sense to include biocoenoses consisting in symbiotic relations among different species in the same area, aggregations or close masses of animals of the same species, families united by sex and parental relations, as well as societies of every degree of integration and duration. Relatively few animals have developed social co-operation and specialization of function within the group smaller than the biocoenosis and larger than the family. The societies of ants, bees, and termites are really large families. Beavers, rooks, and apes exhibit germs of extrafamilial co-operation. While the propriety of identifying subhuman with human societies is controversial,[21] the influence of symbiotic and aggregational relations among animals upon both reproduction and elimination is emphasized by ecologists.[22]

With respect to the survival of individual animals the role of war is indeterminate. Among the carnivores the most skilful in the use of violence will survive. Among the herbivores the most speedy and alert will survive. With respect to species, the gregarious herbivores have had an advantage over the predacious carnivores. Skill in lethal violence has not been a characteristic of the most numerous species. Aggressiveness, especially of males, to defend the family and home territory against intrusion by others of the species has been common among both birds and mammals. This type of warlike behavior has

---

fiting it (in the sense of increasing its population) diminishes in proportion as the change is great and as the species is well adapted. Thus, in proportion as species have become adapted to a fixed environment, the rate of evolution diminishes (*op. cit.*, p. 46). To promote survival, a well-adapted species or society ought to be conservative, while a poorly adapted one ought to be liberal, but radical changes will probably be bad for either.

[21] Zuckerman, *op. cit.*, pp. 206 ff.; Durbin and Bowlby, *op. cit.*, pp. 51 ff.

[22] Victor E. Shelford, *Animal Communities in Temperate America* (Chicago, 1913), pp. 8 ff.; W. C. Allee, *Animal Aggregations: A Study in General Sociology* (Chicago, 1931), chap. xx; see also Alfred Espinas, *Des sociétés animales* (Paris, 1878); Kropotkin, *op. cit.;* Wheeler, *Social Life among the Insects;* Hermann Reinheimer, *Symbiosis: A Socio-physiological Study of Evolution* (London, 1920); E. G. Boulenger, *Animal Mysteries* (New York, 1927), pp. 103 ff.

been of value to the species in dispersing its members over a wide area and preventing their extinction. Animals lacking this characteristic, like the American bison and carrier pigeon, tended toward excessive aggregation and were at a disadvantage when confronted by new enemies. With respect to biological communities, interspecific hostilities, preying and being preyed upon, is a major factor in preserving equilibrium among the numerous species composing the community. If most species were not the natural food of others, the great variety of animal life, valuable for the stability of such a community, could not continue. A few species would soon crowd all the others out. Thus, while herbivorous species are at an advantage in the interspecific competition for a living, from the standpoint of a biological community the existence of predacious species is important.

War has played an important role in the preservation of the societies of many species of colonial insects. Among some such societies it may have been an agency for promoting internal solidarity, and it has undoubtedly served for external defense and for acquiring food. Animal societies relying mainly upon devices not involving lethal violence or parasitism have apparently been the most successful in multiplying and spreading over the earth.[23]

The study of animal war has much to contribute to an understanding of the psychology of human war, and in this respect the role of dominance, activity, and sexuality among the primates, man's nearest relatives, is most instructive. The greatest difference lies in man's superiority in communications through his possession of language and, as a result, his vast superiority in social organization. In the latter respect the ants most resemble man, and the analogy of their wars for predation and defense with those of nations has often been insisted upon. There are, however, great differences. The members of a human society can communicate at a distance and so the society may expand over ever increasing areas. While ant societies are composed of the children of one queen, human societies are genetically heterogeneous, assuring them a greater variability and duration of life. The members of a human society, moreover, lack the degree of hereditary and structural specialization, differen-

[23] Appen. VII, sec. 4d.

tiation, and stratification characteristic of ants. Human society thus compensates for its difficulties in maintaining internal social order by the possibilities of progress and of eventual universal co-ordination of the species. While the problem of civil war will always be more serious in human than in ant societies, the problem of external intra-specific war is soluble among men but not among ants.

It is to be anticipated that man, having organized his societies toward intellect and progress, will not converge toward the ant's "societies" emphasizing instinct and stability, though despotic totalitarianism would lead in that direction. The mechanism of formic social solidarity throws light, however, upon the irrational foundations of human societies. The history of both types of society indicates that there is survival value in minimizing predation, parasitism, and other forms of violent behavior. In this respect convergent evolution of the human and insect types of society may be expected.[24]

[24] Appen. VII, sec. 4d.

CHAPTER VI

PRIMITIVE WARFARE

PSYCHOLOGISTS and sociologists seldom deal with the subject of war without at least a preliminary chapter on primitive war,[1] and sometimes they seem to feel that the subject of war has been adequately treated without getting beyond the primitive stage. Davie writes at the end of his study of primitive war:

> In our study of the evolution of war in early societies, we have surveyed the greater portion of the whole history of the institution, for civilization is as yet in its infancy as compared with the vast expanse of primitive times. In the light of the perspective which we have acquired, what may be predicted about the future? The underlying causes and motives of war were present at the beginning and for the most part still exist.[2]

Strategical writers and jurists, on the other hand, do not deal with primitive war at all or introduce merely decorative, inaccurate, and unconvincing illustrations from the field. The official code of the United States Army (art. 381) refers to the "internecine war of savages" as the unspeakable condition to which unjust or inconsiderate retaliation, by removing the belligerents farther and farther from the mitigating rules of regular war, will by rapid steps bring civilized belligerents. Strategical writers insist on the need of "more brutal" methods in dealing with savages who do not observe "the individual decencies of civilized regular soldiers."[3] Even when dealing with the specialized topic of "small wars," that is, operations of civilized against uncivilized people, such writers do not properly consider

[1] See, e.g., Charles Letourneau, *La Guerre dans les diverses races humains* (Paris, 1895), chaps. ii–viii; Jean La Gorgette, *Le Rôle de la guerre* (Paris, 1906), pp. 32 ff., 403 ff.; W. G. Sumner and A. G. Keller, *The Science of Society* (4 vols.; New York, 1927), I, 16 ff., 354 ff.

[2] M. R. Davie, *The Evolution of War* (New Haven, 1929), p. 232.

[3] Capt. Elbridge Colby, "How To Fight Savage Tribes," *American Journal of International Law*, April, 1927, pp. 280, 283, 284.

53

primitive warfare but only the technique and rules which have been or should be used by civilized peoples in such operations.[4]

This difference among writers suggests that, if a study of primitive war has anything to contribute to knowledge of contemporary war, it is to its psychological foundations and sociological functioning rather than to its law and technique. Yet primitive peoples have usually observed rules in the initiation and conduct of war and have utilized a variety of technical and strategical methods.

Primitive war, like animal war, has been evolving through a vastly greater period of time and among a much greater variety of social organizations than has civilized war. Thus, if the data were on hand, it would present superior opportunities for comparison, for correlation of the incidence of war with varying social and material conditions, and for estimating the variability or persistence of the elements of warfare. Unfortunately, the data with respect to any primitive group do not extend far back in time. People without writing do not leave adequate records. Even at the present time, however, there are probably over a thousand distinct primitive peoples,[5] whereas there are only about seventy independent civilized states. Apart from the historical record, the opportunity for observing warfare under varying conditions is greater among the primitive than among the civilized peoples.

I. THE CONCEPTION OF PRIMITIVE WARFARE

The study of primitive warfare at once confronts two formidable difficulties: Who are primitive people? and What part of their behavior is warfare?

It is difficult to distinguish primitive man from civilized man. There are very few of the present "primitive," "preliterate," "sim-

---

[4] Col. C. E. Callwell, *Small Wars: Their Principles and Practice* (3d ed.; London, 1906); Lieut.-Col. W. C. G. Heneker, *Bush Warfare* (London, 1907).

[5] See L. T. Hobhouse, G. C. Wheeler, and M. Ginsburg, *The Material Culture and Social Institutions of the Simpler Peoples* (London, 1915), pp. 30–45, listing 650 distinctive primitive peoples. Each of these peoples is divided into many sovereign groups; thus there may be 50,000 to 100,000 primitive sovereign groups in the world. Clark Wissler says there are seven cultural provinces and six hundred distinctive Indian cultures in the United States (*Man and Culture* [New York, 1923], p. 14).

pler," "nature," or "savage" people[6] who have not received some elements of their culture from civilized people.[7] It appears that war practices, weapons, and techniques are among the first things to be borrowed by primitive people, although the rapidity of such borrowing varies greatly among different primitive tribes.[8] It cannot be assumed, therefore, that the war practices of any contemporary primitive people have any close resemblance to the war practices of man in the hundreds of thousands of years before there was any civilization—if, indeed, there were any war practices during that period.[9]

As a convenient even if rather arbitrary rule, primitive people may be defined as human beings that live in self-determining communities which do not use writing.[10] The absence of writing and of recorded history usually involves other features of culture. The community is usually confined to a group which can be reached for purposes of administration and leadership by general assemblies addressed by word of mouth or by runners carrying the message in memory.[11] The absence of writing also limits early education to that which the family and neighbors can pass on to the child from memory. Law is limited to customs carried in memory and passed by tradition from generation to generation. Scientific generalization is limited to that which can be developed from evidence within one man's memory of his own experience, of the experience of his acquaintances orally and uncontrollably repeated to him, and of the even less reliable tradition of the group passed orally from generation to generation. This process usually results only in empirical rules for dealing with frequently repeated concrete situations and in logical extensions of these rules by "magic." The latter purports to

[6] Each of these terms is subject to some objection (see R. R. Marett, *Psychology and Folklore* [London, 1920], pp. 29–30, quoting Von Luschans' remark: "The only 'savages' in Africa are certain white men" [*Papers on "Inter Racial Problems*," ed. G. Spiller, p. 22]). Contemporary anthropologists seem to prefer the term "simpler people" or people of "simpler culture" in distinction from people of "more complex culture," but the term "primitive" is probably more commonly used.

[7] Hobhouse, Wheeler, and Ginsburg, *op. cit.*, p. 28.

[8] See below, n. 121.   [9] See above, chap. iv, sec. 2.

[10] See above, chap. iv, sec. 1.

[11] The Incas, who alone developed a culture, which might be called civilization, and a long-lived empire without writing, developed this practice and also a mnemonic device, a knotted whip called quipu.

control things at a distance through their identification with symbols, fetishes, and formulas associated with the distant object or person either by resemblance or by past contact.[12] Only limited knowledge about many phenomena of nature can result from this inadequate method of investigation. Consequently, many infrequent occurrences such as death, illness, storms, and eclipses appear capricious or acts of will. They are attributed to the malignity of men of other tribes or to supernatural manlike beings. Revenge may be sought against the former and religious observances may be devised for propitiating or otherwise influencing the behavior of the latter. In the absence of techniques for the accumulation of knowledge from wide areas and over long periods of time, the methods, tools, utensils, and machines for carrying on practical affairs of life are limited to those which have been invented by a trial-and-error process without aid of general ideas. Some primitive people use domesticated animals, but, except for the dog, such use has been borrowed from civilized people in historic times. The plains Indians, for example, did not use the horse until the Spaniards had introduced it to America.[13] Most preliterate people are limited to instruments operable by manpower.

To summarize: in addition to the absence of writing and of recorded history, primitive people are as a rule politically integrated in relatively small clans, villages, or tribes which speak a common language. Blood relationship plays a major part in their organization. They form the pattern of life by relatively fixed tribal customs and attempt to control their environment through magic ritual, through propitiation of supernatual beings, through hostility against neighbors, and through practical techniques utilizing mainly the power of the human individual.[14] Because of the inefficiency of

[12] Sir James Fraser (*The Golden Bough* [New York, 1923]) describes these, respectively, as homeopathic and contagious magic.

[13] Clark Wissler, "The Influence of the Horse in the Development of Plains Culture," *American Anthropologist* (N.S.), Vol. XVI (1914).

[14] See Hobhouse, Wheeler, and Ginsburg, *op. cit.*, chap. i. Most primitive people had the dog and some used it for transportation. A primitive people is ordinarily united by a distinctive language, heredity, culture, and technology, but, with progress, these characteristics tend to unite different overlapping or concentric groups (see L. Bloomfield, *Language* [New York, 1933], chap. iii).

these controls, they are in the main bound to adapt their way of life to the surrounding physical, animal, and especially vegetable environment.[15] Thus the group customs manifest great variety according to the differences in this environment, but within each group the behavior patterns are more uniform and less complex than among civilized people.

Less than ten thousand years ago all people were primitive in this sense. However, the total number of the human race, though scattered over all the continents, may then have been less than that of a moderate-sized city of today. Civilization began in the Nile Valley and in Mesopotamia, later in the valleys of the Indus and of the Yellow River, in Mexico, and in Peru; but it affected only a minority of the world's population for thousands of years. At the beginning of the Christian Era probably half of the world's population was still "primitive." At the time of the discovery of America a quarter was probably in that condition. Civilization, however, has spread rapidly in the recent era, and today probably less than 5 per cent of the world's two billion people is still primitive.[16] In a sense, even these are not primitive within our definition because they are nominally subject to states where writing is used. But, in so far as they still enjoy practical autonomy, they may be classified as primitive. Under the influence of missionaries, administrators, and traders, however, they are rapidly becoming eliminated, assimilated, civilized, or deprived of all autonomy. Anthropologists are aware that studies of primitive man must be made immediately because in another century he may be extinct.

Anthropological writers have divided primitive people into a

---

[15] See Appen. VII, sec. 4c. H. T. Buckle wrote: "Looking at the history of the world as a whole, the tendency has been, in Europe to subordinate nature to man; out of Europe to subordinate man to nature" (*History of Civilization in England* [London, 1869], chap. iii, p. 152 [quoted in Marett, *op. cit.*, p. 31]).

[16] These changes in ratios are due in part to a dying-out of primitive people through contact with civilization (see G. H. Pitt-Rivers, *The Clash of Cultures and Contact of Races* [London, 1927]); in part to the racial amalgamation of civilized and primitive peoples and the diffusion of civilization to primitive peoples, but more to the rapid numerical and geographic expansion of civilized peoples during this period (see W. F. Willcox, *International Migrations* [New York: National Bureau of Economic Research, 1929–31]; W. Woytinsky, *Die Welt im Zahlen* [Berlin, 1925], Vol. I; R. R. Kuczynski, "Population," *Encyclopaedia of the Social Sciences*).

thousand or so groups, each with a definite geographical situs and manifesting common racial, sociological, cultural, and linguistic characteristics. Each of these groups is called "a people" and is given a name such as the Andamanese, the Angami Nagas, the Igorots, the Iroquois, the Murngin, the Wintun. Some of these peoples number millions of individuals; others, only a few hundreds. Some constitute a single political unit; others are divided into numerous independent tribes or villages. The consciousness of the existence of "the people" may or may not exist in the minds of all the constituent members. Thus "the people" is often a conception developed through anthropological observations and studies rather than an integrating symbol operating within the group itself. Anthropologists are not always agreed upon the limits of a particular people or upon its distinctive characteristics.[17]

Added to the difficulty of identifying primitive peoples in general and in particular is the difficulty of identifying their wars. Primitive peoples only rarely conduct formal hostilities with the object of achieving a tangible economic or political result. Their hostilities are seldom conducted by a highly organized professional military class using distinctive instruments and techniques regulated by an intergroup law applicable only during periods of "war" and designed to render war an efficient instrument of policy. These elements which go to make up the concept of war today are products of civilization, and only their rudiments can be found among primitive peoples.[18]

Though broader than the concept of civilized war, the concept of

[17] Hobhouse, Wheeler, and Ginsburg, *op. cit.*, p. 13, and above, n. 5.

[18] Hostilities among the Trobriand Islanders was "rather a form of social duel in which one side earned glory and humiliated the other, than warfare conducted to obtain any decisive advantage, economic or other" (B. Malinowski, "War and Weapons among the Natives of the Trobriand Islands," *Man*, No. 5, January, 1920, pp. 10-12; see also A. R. Radcliffe-Brown, *The Andaman Islanders* [Cambridge, 1922], pp. 85-87, and below, n. 24). These statements of field anthropologists may be compared with those of students with less firsthand information: "Savage hordes fought openly for the possession of hunting- and fishing-grounds" (W. S. Thompson, *Danger Spots in World Population* [New York, 1930], p. 4); "The prospect of booty and reprisal for theft are among the foremost reasons why primitive men fight" (Davie, *op. cit.*, p. 81). Instances of predatory warfare can be found among primitive people but they seem not to be common except after contact with civilization (see n. 63 below).

primitive war is narrower than that of animal warfare. Primitive war does not include violence against animals of other species, violence against other human beings unsanctioned by the group, and violence against members of the group sanctioned by that group.[19] These three types of violent behavior—the hunt, crime, and punishment—although considered "war" among animals, are among all primitive groups so distinct from violence sanctioned by the group as a whole against other human beings external to the group that they can be excluded. The line between privately initiated external violence sanctioned by the group, such as feuds and head-hunting, from action for which the group as a whole is responsible is less easy to draw. In most cases these two types of activity, which may be denominated, respectively, "reprisals" and "war," can be distinguished. They are, however, closely related, and it seems advisable to include all external, group-sanctioned violence against other human beings in the conception of primitive war. These distinctions are well stated by Marett:

Taking, then, the average community of savages who, thanks mostly to the custom of exogamy, have reached the tribal stage of society, we can represent its moral relationships by three concentric circles. That which immediately surrounds the centre stands for the consanguine group, or kin, which, whether it counts descent in the mother's or the father's line, restricts this veritable home-circle to that one side of the family. The intermediate zone contains the rest of the tribe, and marks what is roughly the outer limit of the criss-cross of affinities which exogamy produces. A tribesman as opposed to a kinsman by blood is thus any possible connexion by marriage who does not happen to be a pure stranger. There remains the vast outer circle of those who are neither kith nor kin, neither acquaintances nor birth-mates, but live beyond the bounds of tribal law and religion. Correspondingly, then, there are three degrees of moral responsibility severally involving an intense solidarity, a half-hearted neighbourliness, and an utter aloofness.

Hence there will be as many different ways in which fighting and killing may come about, namely, through intestine strife, through feud, or through downright war. These distinctions are by no means arbitrary, since they are based on a real and well-recognized departmentalization of the social life. The stupidest savage is not likely to confuse in his mind the occasions on which he is liable to commit the abominable sin, to become implicated in an affair of honour, and on

[19] Punishment often takes the form of group-tolerated private retaliation or of group-regulated compensation or combat rather than of group-conducted punishment in the strict sense (see Hobhouse, Wheeler, and Ginsburg, *op. cit.*, pp. 54 ff.).

behalf of home and country to take up arms against foreign devils. There are bound to be marginal cases, of course, as when duty towards the mother's clan begins to include the father and his people as well, or, again, when distant or disaffected members of the tribe rank as hardly better than sworn foes. On the whole, however, there stand out in sharp contrast to each other three spheres of conduct, to which entirely separate commandments apply as follows: to the first, Thou shalt commit no murder; to the second, Thou shalt compound with thy neighbor on the principle that a life for a life is fair give-and-take; and to the third, Thou shalt utterly destroy the destroyer.[20]

Limitations applicable to these three relations are derived, respectively, from group customs (civil law), intergroup custom (international law), and human nature (natural law); but it seems convenient to group the second and third types of relationship together, thus distinguishing war in the wider sense from crime and punishment.[21]

2. GENERAL CHARACTERISTICS OF PRIMITIVE WAR

Primitive peoples may be classified racially, geographically, culturally, and sociologically. There are relationships between these classifications. Peoples in the same area are likely to be racially and culturally similar, and peoples of similar race and culture are often similarly organized.[22] But there are numerous exceptions, and correlations cannot be assumed. All these classifications may provide evidence with respect to the evolution or diffusion of particular cultural traits such as war, but great caution is necessary in generalization.[23]

[20] R. R. Marett, *Sacraments of Simple Folk* (Oxford, 1933), pp. 47–48. See also Camilla H. Wedgewood, "Some Aspects of Warfare in Melanesia," *Oceania*, I (April, 1930), 5; Hobhouse, Wheeler, and Ginsburg, *op. cit.*, p. 228; Sumner and Keller, *op. cit.*, IV, 115–18.

[21] The Murngin, a people of northern Australia, have distinctive names for six types of warfare: (1) fight within a camp, (2) secret interclan killing, (3) night raid on a camp, (4) general open fight, (5) pitched battle, and (6) ceremonial peace ordeal. Nos. 2, 3, and 5 are the bloodiest (A. W. Lloyd Warner, "Murngin Warfare," *Oceania*, II [1931], 457).

[22] W. C. MacLeod, *The Origin and History of Politics* (New York, 1936), pp. 109 ff. See above, n. 14.

[23] G. H. Pitt-Rivers (*op. cit.*, p. 3) distinguishes and describes the relation between the first three of these classes: "Human history in its totality is therefore a tripartite record which should refer to (*a*) the history of populations—considered according to their regional organization, inter-related to (*b*) the history of races considered in relation to changes in, and migrations of, stocks, which, again, is related to (*c*) the history

While the functions, drives, techniques, and formalities of war vary greatly from tribe to tribe, it will be convenient, first, to classify primitive war according to the general degree of its development as an institution. There are primitive people who fight none at all or rarely and in an unorganized and unpremeditated manner. War is not a definite institution of the mores. There are others who fight frequently in well-recognized circumstances and with well-established rules and techniques. War is definitely within the mores. There are, of course, line cases. Most peoples can, however, be rather definitely divided into the warlike and the unwarlike.[24] The familiar distinction between industrial and military types of political

---

of culture and its evolution." He also suggests that the evolutionary (Tylor, Westermarck, Frazer), climatological (Huntington), and historical (Rivers, Elliot Smith) schools of anthropology emphasize, respectively, these successive classifications. The functional school (Malinowski, Radcliffe-Brown, Lowie, Thurnwald), in which he places himself, emphasizes particularly the sociological classification of peoples (pp. 8, 12; see Appen. VI). The distinction between animal species, communities, and societies (chap. v, sec. 4) corresponds to a racial, geographical, and sociological classification of animals. It is difficult to speak of the culture of animals. "Culture," writes Malinowski, "introduces a new dimension in the plasticity of instincts" (*Sex and Repression in Savage Society* [New York, 1927], p. xi).

[24] Marett, *Psychology and Folklore*, pp. 32–33. Herbert Spencer (*Principles of Sociology* [3d ed.; New York, 1896], II, 578 ff., 615 ff.) describes the characteristics of tribes of each type. W. J. Perry ("An Ethnological Study of Warfare," *Manchester, Lit. and Phil. Soc., Proceedings*, Vol. LXI, No. 6 [1917]) considers the theoretical and historical implications of this difference. Sumner and Keller (*op. cit.*, IV, 129 ff.) and Davie (*op. cit.*, pp. 244–64) give numerous specific instances of mild and serious warfare. Hobhouse, Wheeler, and Ginsburg (*op. cit.*, p. 228) attempt to classify various characteristics of warfare in all primitive peoples. As an illustration of unwarlikeness, I quote from Radcliffe-Brown, who found that from 1872 to 1902 inclusive the Jarawa made eight attacks on camps of Friendly Andamanese in which two Friendly Andaman men and one girl were killed, three men and one boy wounded, and, in addition, there were two or three chance meetings in which killings occurred, but apparently the total war and feud casualties in thirty years could be counted on the fingers of one hand. "Such a thing as fighting on a large scale seems to have been unknown amongst the Andamanese. In the early days of the Penal Settlement of Port Blair, the natives of the South Andaman combined in large numbers to make an attack on the Settlement, but this seems to have been an unusual course of action in order to meet what was to them an altogether unusual contingency, their territory having been invaded by a large force of foreigners. Their only fights amongst themselves seem to have been the brief and far from bloody skirmishes described above, where only a handful of warriors were engaged on each side and rarely more than one or two were killed. Of such a thing as war in which the whole of one tribe joined to fight with another tribe I could not find any evidence in what the natives were able to tell me of their former customs" (*op. cit.*, pp. 86–87).

organization, emphasized by Herbert Spencer, T. H. Buckle, and others in comparing civilized as well as uncivilized states, conforms in some degree to this distinction.[25] Among primitive peoples the distinction is more emphatic, since all civilized people have war to some degree in their mores. For purposes of correlation this dual classification has been refined by distinguishing the most unwarlike peoples who fight only in defense; the moderately warlike who fight for sport, ritual, revenge, personal prestige, or other social purposes; the more warlike who fight for economic purposes (raids on herds, extension of grazing lands, booty, slaves); and the most warlike of all who, in addition, fight for political purposes (extension of empire, political prestige, maintenance of authority of rulers).[26] Is this classi-

[25] "Excluding a few simple groups such as the Esquimaux, inhabiting places where they are safe from invasion, all societies, simple and compound, are occasionally or habitually in antagonism with other societies; and, as we have seen, tend to evolve structures for carrying on offensive and defensive actions. At the same time sustentation is necessary; and there is always an organization slight or decided, for achieving it. But while the two systems in social organisms, as in the individual organisms, co-exist in all but the rudimentary forms, they vary immensely in the ratios they bear to one another. In some cases the structures carrying on external actions are largely developed; the sustaining system exists solely for their benefit; and the activities are militant. In other cases there is predominance of the structures carrying on sustentation; offensive and defensive structures are maintained only to protect them; and the activities are industrial. At the one extreme we have those warlike tribes which, subsisting mainly by the chase, make the appliances for dealing with enemies serve also for procuring food, and have sustaining systems represented only by their women, who are their slave-classes; while, at the other extreme we have the type, as yet only partially evolved, in which the agricultural, manufacturing, and commercial organizations form the chief part of the society, and, in the absence of external enemies, the appliances for offence and defence are either rudimentary or absent. Transitional as are nearly all the societies we have to study, we may yet clearly distinguish the constitutional traits of these opposite types, characterized by predominance of the outer and inner systems respectively" (Spencer, *op. cit.*, I, 556–57; cf. *ibid.*, III, 568 ff.). Buckle (*op. cit.*, pp. 190–95) identifies military and industrial states with uncivilized and civilized states respectively. Benjamin Kidd (*Social Evolution* [London, 1895]) identifies military and industrial states, respectively, with states where competition, considered a necessary condition of progress, is between the group as a whole and between the individual members of the group. Adam Smith (*An Inquiry into the Nature and Causes of the Wealth of Nations* [1776, ed. 1838], Book V, pp. 318 ff.) identifies the industrial state with the state that has specialized its defense by creating a professional army instead of relying upon the less expensive and less efficient militia. See also Auguste Comte, *Philosophie positive*, IV, 418, 713; VI, 68, 424–36.

[26] See Appen. X.

fication of peoples according to their peaceableness or warlikeness correlated with any other ways of classifying primitive peoples?

Geographically, people may be divided according to the continent in which they live. Among primitive people war as an instrument toward rational ends has been least developed in Australia and most developed in Africa.[27] European civilization seems to have sprung from very warlike primitive peoples.[28] America and Asia exhibit both very warlike and very unwarlike people.[29]

More significant geographical classifications can be made according to the climatological and topographical environment of peoples. Primitive peoples in extremely cold and extremely hot climates tend to be unwarlike, although the very warlike Bering Sea Eskimo lives in as cold a climate as the very unwarlike Greenland Eskimo, and the warlike Bantus and unwarlike Pygmies both dwell in the tropics of Africa. In general, however, a temperate or warm, somewhat variable, and stimulating climate favors warlikeness. However, it also favors civilization.[30] These favored regions have developed civilization or have been occupied by civilization, leaving the primitive people only the less satisfactory environments.[31] Among contemporary primitive people the largest proportion of the warlike live in hot regions of medium climatic energy.[32]

Primitive people inhabiting deserts or the seashore are more likely to be warlike than those in forests and mountains, and those in the

---

[27] Davie, *op. cit.*, pp. 52, 55, 255.

[28] Marett, *Psychology and Folklore*, p. 39; Davie, *op. cit.*, pp. 5 ff. See also James Baikie's lively description of the routing of the peaceful Mousterians by the warlike Cro-Magnon's and Aurignacians, the latter probably being the first races whose blood survives in modern Europe (*Peeps at Men of the Old Stone Age* [London, 1928], chap. viii). The warlike character of the later Mediterranean, Alpine, and Nordic invaders of Europe is attested by the historic tradition these peoples formulated in such epics as the *Iliad* and the *Aeneid* and in such histories as Tacitus' *Germania*.

[29] See Table 5, Appen. IX.

[30] Ellsworth Huntington, *World Power and Evolution* (New Haven, 1919), p. 230.

[31] "The world as it is now constituted consists of the piratical nations, thickly and firmly established in the world's great areas of intercommunication and characterization, with dwindling folk of no importance scattered about in the odd corners, and lucky to be even there" (Marett, *Sacraments of Simple Folk*, pp. 59–60).

[32] See Tables 6 and 8, Appen. IX.

grasslands are the most warlike of all.[33] Warlikeness appears to be related to the stimulating character of the climate and to the lack of barriers to mobility rather than to the economic difficulty of the environment. The primitive nomad of desert and steppes has a hard environment to conquer, but he may have a stimulating climate. His terrain, adapted to distant raids and without natural defenses, leads him to institutionalize war for aggression and defense. The seashore dweller, because of easy opportunities to travel, is encouraged to piracy as the nomad is encouraged to raid. The Eskimo of the north, with an equally difficult economic problem but with too severe a climate and with the protection of isolation and impediments to travel, is often but not always peaceful. The hunters of forest and mountain, protected by natural barriers, tend to be peaceful. But where the climate is stimulating as with the eastern American Indian, they may be warlike. The forest dwellers of the Andaman Islands, Africa, Malaya, and Indonesia, with a less stimulating climate, are more peaceful.

Physical anthropologists, on the basis of head, hair, nose, pigmentation, blood group, and other measurements divide the contemporary human species into races. While the subject is controversial, a grouping into eight races and twenty subraces seems as widely accepted as any other. Apart from historically recorded migrations, these races and subraces have had their habitat as follows: (1) the Pygmies including the Negritoes in Malaya, Indonesia, and perhaps Tasmania and the Bushmen, Hottentots, and Batwa in Africa; (2) the Australoids including the Australians inhabiting the Australian continent and the Pre-Dravidians of southern India; (3) the Negroids including the Negroes and Bantus in South and Central Africa

---

[33] See Table 7, Appen. IX. If the genus *Homo* first differentiated on grassland and steppe, as held by H. F. Osborn and others ("Is the Ape Man a Myth?" *Human Biology*, I [1929], 4–9; Morris Halperin, "Cereals and Civilization," *Scientific Monthly*, April, 1936, p. 355), warlikeness may have been an original human characteristic. With this view the unwarlike character of the modern aborigines of tropical forest and arctic sea cannot be taken as typical of earliest man but rather as a modification induced by the peculiar environment of certain offshoots from the main human stem. J. R. Marett ("War, Food and Evolution," *Nineteenth Century and After*, April, 1936) attempts to relate the aggressiveness of the steppe dwellers to the superior development of the anterior pituitary, the larger size and general masculinity arising from the abundance of carbon, sodium, and phosphorus in the diet provided by the environment.

and the Papuans or Oceanic Negroids in parts of Indonesia and Melanesia; (4) the Hamitoids including the Hamites of North East Africa and the Dravidians of India; (5) the brown race including the Arctics in North Asia, the Indonesians in India, Malaya, and Indonesia, and the Polynesians in the Pacific Islands; (6) the Red Indians including the Paleoamerinds and the narrowheaded Indians of the periphery of the American continent, the typical broadheaded American Indian, and the Eskimo of the American Arctic; (7) the yellow race including the Mongols of North Asia, the Chinese, and the southern or Oceanic Mongols of South Asia, Malaya, and parts of Indonesia; and (8) the white race including the Alpines in central and eastern Europe, central Asia and northern India, the Mediterraneans in North Africa, East Asia, and southern Europe, and the Nordics in northern Europe.[34] Civilized as well as primitive peoples are today to be found among all these races except the Pygmies and Australoids. Very few primitive peoples remain among the various branches of the white race. Among the primitives it cannot be said that race is very closely related to war practices, although Pygmies and Australoids seem to be the least warlike; Negroes, Hamites, and whites the most warlike; with the red, yellow, and brown races occupying an intermediate position. Certain of the subraces belonging to these more warlike races, however, such as the Papuans, Dravidians, Arctics, and Eskimos, are quite unwarlike.[35]

Culturally, primitive peoples have often been divided into those who make their living by collecting shellfish, fruits, and nuts; by hunting animals; by herding domestic animals; or by agriculture. Those who ascribe an evolutionary significance to these stages regard the herdsmen, agriculturist, and higher hunters and fishers as paral-

[34] There are, of course, no sharp lines between these races or between their habitats—there are simply variations in the frequency of certain physical characteristics in the designated areas (see A. S. Romer, *Man and the Vertebrates* [Chicago, 1933], pp. 269 ff.). See Appen. XI.

[35] See Table 9, Appen. IX. Letourneau (*Sociology* [London, 1881], pp. 199, 509; *La Guerre*, pp. 212–13, 244) and Davie (*op. cit.*, pp. 53, 55) find the most peaceable people in the Mongolian race, and the latter regards the Negro as the most warlike race, although both recognize the great variations with respect to warlikeness within all races. J. R. Marett seeks to explain the warlikeness of negroes by endocrinal characteristics resulting from dietary and sexual relations ("War, Food and Evolution," *op. cit.*).

lel developments from the lower hunting and agricultural cultures.[36] The picture is not, therefore, one of continual progress but of a tree with different types of culture developing above a certain point. It seems clear that the collectors, lower hunters, and lower agriculturalists are the least warlike. The higher hunters and higher agriculturalists are more warlike, while the highest agriculturalists and the pastorals are the most warlike of all.[37]

Sociologically, primitive peoples may be classified into those who are integrated in primary (clan), secondary (village), tertiary (tribe), and quaternary (tribal federations or states) groups.[38] In general, the first are the least and the latter the most warlike.[39]

Primitive peoples may also be classified sociologically into those who utilize division of labor only between the sex and age groups,

[36] See Hobhouse, Wheeler, and Ginsburg, op. cit., chap. i; F. Müller-Lyer, The History of Social Development (New York, 1931), pp. 324 ff.; Adam Smith, op. cit., Book V, pp. 311 ff. This assumes that culture is determined primarily by economy or material culture. Value systems or religions might constitute a better basis of cultural classification, but no such classification seems to have been developed. Primitive people have been classified on the basis of linguistic type and linguistic affiliation but there appears to be no direct correlation between such classification and culture (see E. Sapir, Language [New York, 1921], chap. x; H. Petersen, Linguistic Science in the Nineteenth Century [Cambridge, Mass., 1931], pp. 99-102).

[37] See Table 10, Appen. IX.

[38] Hobhouse, Wheeler, and Ginsburg, op. cit., pp. 46 ff. Spencer (op. cit., Part II, chap. x, secs. 256, 257) considers societies organized as clans or villages as "simple societies" and those in which the clans or villages are organized into tribes as "compound societies." His "doubly compound societies" correspond to tribal federations and states, above which are the "trebly compound" modern nations and empires. Additional complications in respect to degree of stability of headship and sedentary or nomadic character are also introduced. N. S. B. Gras (An Introduction to Economic History [New York, 1922], p. 317) also declines to recognize the village as a political group composed of clans, thus classifying primitive political organizations as the clan, the tribe, and the territorial state, above which are the national state and the imperial state which, however, appear only after civilization. These five political types he correlates, respectively, with the collecting, cultural nomadic, settled village, town, and metropolitan types of economic organization. Among nomadic peoples, clans may be directly united into tribes which would thus be "secondary groups," but ordinarily primitive people are settled in permanent or temporary hordes or villages combining several clans and themselves grouped into tribes. The customs with respect to totemism, exogamic blood relationships, and age groupings introduce infinite complications (see, e.g., Radcliffe-Brown's detailed account, "The Social Organization of Australian Tribes," Oceania, I [1930], 37 ff.; see also below, nn. 51 and 52).

[39] See Table 11, Appen. IX.

between involuntary classes (castes, serfs, slaves, nobles, etc.), and between voluntary, professional, or occupational groups (farmers, herdsmen, various types of artisans, soldiers, priests, and rulers).[40] The latter type of specialization is little developed among primitive peoples, although it appears that voluntary specialization may develop in groups that have never known compulsory classes. Professional soldiers, except as an age and sex group, exist only among semicivilized and civilized people. In general, the more the division of labor, the more warlike, the groups with compulsory classes being the most warlike of all primitive people.[41]

Finally, primitive peoples may be classified sociologically according to the abundance of extra-group contacts with societies of a widely different culture. Some peoples are isolated by natural barriers or the frugality of the food supply; others are in continuous communication with civilized or semicivilized people; others are on highroads of migration and in frequent close contacts with such people. In general, the groups with the most varied and frequent contacts are the most warlike.[42] Hoijer concludes a detailed study of the causes of primitive war with this statement:

The presence of many groups within a certain area offers—providing natural barriers do not interfere—opportunities for numerous cultural contacts. In striving to remain a tribal entity and to preserve itself physically, the group must perfect a strong social organization and a powerful war machinery. Needless to say, these strivings are unconscious. If they fail, they lose their group identity, if, indeed, they are not annihilated altogether. Those who succeed, establish strong tribal organizations whose lives can only be maintained by hostility—warfare becomes the necessary means of preserving group identity, in primitive society.[43]

[40] Müller-Lyer (op. cit., pp., 232–33) recognizes three stages characterized, respectively, by occupational specializations between the sexes, among men, and among women, the last two being stages of civilization. MacLeod (op. cit., pp. 77 ff.) emphasizes the importance of age groups and gerontocracy among many primitive people.

[41] Adam Smith, however, believes that professionalization of armies makes for industrial society (see above, n. 25). See Table 12, Appen. IX.

[42] See Table 13, Appen. IX.

[43] Harry Hoijer, "The Causes of Primitive Warfare" (manuscript in University of Chicago Library), p. 111. W. G. Sumner (Folkways [Boston, 1906], p. 12, quoted by Davie, op. cit., p. 17) writes: "The closer the neighbors, and the stronger they are, the intenser is the warfare, and then the intenser is the internal organization and discipline of each." MacLeod (op. cit., p. 128) insists that "the form of a people's state is a function of the people's contacts."

It would appear that the seriousness and degree of institutionalization of war among primitive peoples is related more closely to the complexity of culture, political organization, and extra-group contacts than with race or physical environment, although a warm but stimulating climate and an environment favorable to mobility over wide areas seem also to be favorable to warlikeness.

These conclusions with respect to the static circumstances of warlikeness and unwarlikeness among primitive peoples suggest the following generalizations with respect to the dynamics of the situation.

Unwarlikeness has been the result of prolonged opportunity of neighboring groups to achieve equilibrium in relation to one another and to the physical environment. This opportunity has only been offered if the physical environment has been stable and if peoples of different culture have not interfered. The latter has resulted from natural barriers, lack of means of travel, or inhospitableness of climate.

Reciprocally, warlikeness has resulted from frequent disturbances of the equilibrium of a group with respect to its physical environment or its neighbors. The first has usually resulted from climatic changes, migrations, or the invention or borrowing of new types of economic technique. The second has usually resulted from migrations, invasions, or other influences bringing a group into continuous contact with a very different culture.

Among primitive peoples borrowing or invention of means of mobility or more efficient weapons promoting migration, invasion, or expansion of contacts increases warlikeness.[44] Such borrowing or invention proceeds very slowly among primitive groups unless forced by contact with much more civilized peoples.[45] Thus, the more primitive the people, the less warlike it tends to be.

As in the case of animal warfare, we shall deal successively with the functions, the drives, the techniques, and the laws of primitive warfare.

[44] H. F. Cleland (*Our Prehistoric Ancestors* [New York, 1928], pp. 217, 338) thinks warlikeness was greatly stimulated by the use of metal, which necessitated expeditions to get ore and created a differential in military efficiency, making exploitation of the nonmetal users by the metal users practicable. Wissler comments on the influence of the horse, borrowed from Spaniards in the seventeenth century, in stimulating predatory warfare ("The Influence of the Horse in the Development of Plains Culture," *op. cit.*).

[45] See below, n. 121.

3. FUNCTIONS

Warfare functions among primitive peoples primarily by maintaining the solidarity of the political group. Social solidarity implies that the social milieu is compatible with the requirements of human personality; consequently, war, in maintaining group solidarity, must as an institution accommodate itself to the latter. The way in which it has done so will be examined in considering the drives and the laws of war.

Social solidarity also implies that the economic goods, procurable with the techniques available to the group, are adequate for the physical sustenance of its members and that the women available are adequate to accommodate the men whose demands are often controlled by mores supporting polygyny. Among animals, war, if regarded as including interspecific preying, is a major factor in preserving the balance within biological communities,[46] but among primitive human communities abstention during prolonged lactation, abortion, and infanticide are usually more important devices for keeping the population of a group within the food supply.[47] Primitive war, however, does have a population-eliminating tendency, sometimes as important as civilized war;[48] and, in so far as this tendency reduces the occurrence of socially disrupting famines and epidemics, it makes for social solidarity. Since primitive war usually eliminates men more than women, it renders polygyny easier and reduces the socially disrupting rivalry for women. Such rivalry is often at the root of killings which lead to feud and war, but the killings consequent upon the latter tend to remedy the situation which starts them, and social solidarity is maintained.[49]

[46] See above, chap. v, sec. 4.

[47] A. M. Carr-Saunders (*The Population Problem* [Oxford, 1922]) assembles much evidence to support this conclusion. The data, however, are inadequate clearly to establish the magnitude of the components of the population equilibrium among primitive groups. See Appen. XII.

[48] Carr-Saunders expresses the opinion that there has been relatively little loss of life from primitive warfare (*op. cit.*, p. 150), but among certain peoples this loss has undoubtedly been great (A. L. Kroeber, "Native American Population," *American Anthropologist* [N.S.], XXXVI [1934], 10–12). There have been few accurate estimates of the actual war losses of primitive peoples. See Appen. XIII.

[49] "If war were abolished, the percentage of men would increase, and the pressure would probably be too strong on the social structure by men looking for mates for the present form of polygyny, with its attendant mechanisms, the levirate and sororate, to

The political group among a particular primitive people may be a primary group as a clan or a large family; a secondary group as a village; a tertiary group as a tribe, composed of several villages; or even a quaternary group such as a federation of tribes, or a primitive state.[50] Among every primitive people, however, there is some group which constitutes the *political* unit, thus characterized because it is the group which sanctions the use of force internally and externally. It punishes crime, authorizes retaliation, and makes war. Most commonly, it is a village or group of neighboring villages. War serves to distinguish this group as the center of social organization. Where war does not exist, this political unit may be difficult to identify, although ordinarily it can be identified as the authority for punishing internal offenses against the mores.[51]

Intermarriage under the practice of exogamy, peaceful trade and other contacts with neighbors, and ceremonial gatherings tend to amalgamate neighboring groups into larger but looser units. War tends to counteract this process. Thus Warner writes of the Murngin, a people of northern Australia:

> Warfare is in direct opposition to ceremony. It tends to destroy the larger solidarity, and ultimately to reduce the people who are at peace with each other to the clan unit, since it is only within the clan where there is absolute assurance that fighting can-not take place. . . . . The great ceremonies tend to enlarge the group solidarity both in numbers and in extent of territory and provide a smoothly functioning unit out of a large number of clans, but warfare destroys this and reduces the limits of solidarity down to the clan.

> Since both traits are necessary to the tribe's social organization a nice periodical balance has been struck; at one period ceremonialism controls the people's activities, and later war is uppermost in the relations of the local groups.[52]

---

survive. Since these latter mechanisms do much toward strengthening the society and preventing chaos attendant to the transfer of a woman from one clan to another, it will be seen that warfare, while destroying one type of solidarity [ceremonial], is partly responsible for the solid foundation of the kinship structure in Murngin society" (Warner, *op. cit.*, p. 482). R. L. Buell (*The Native Problem in Africa* [New York, 1928], II, 571) comments on the demoralizing influence upon the population of the Congo of polygyny, coupled with an excess of males over females resulting from white administration.

[50] See above, n. 38.

[51] Hoijer, *op. cit.*, p. 2. In Australia it is the horde, a group of families occupying a common territory (Radcliffe-Brown, "The Social Organization of Australian Tribes," *op. cit.*, p. 37; see also Hobhouse, Wheeler, and Ginsburg, *op. cit.*, pp. 46–49).

[52] Warner, *op. cit.*, pp. 480–81.

In respect to its function, therefore, primitive warfare differs from animal warfare. Except among the social insects, the latter functions primarily to preserve the species and secondarily to preserve the individual. Primitive warfare functions primarily to preserve the social group and secondarily to satisfy certain psychic needs of human personality.

Warfare assists in preserving social solidarity by keeping alive the realization of a common enemy who will destroy the group if it is not prepared to resist;[53] by strikingly symbolizing the group as a unit in a common enterprise;[54] by creating a certain discipline and subordination to leadership;[55] by providing an outlet for anger in activities not hostile to the harmony of the group;[56] by preventing the

[53] "The exigencies of war with outsiders are what make peace inside, lest internal discord should weaken the in-group for war" (Sumner, *op. cit.*, p. 12, quoted by Davie, *op. cit.*, p. 16). "When it was a question of an attack or defense against other tribes, the Akamba (Eastern Bantu) were always united. But when no external danger threatened or prospects of booty did not bring about a union, perpetual internal quarrels and feuds prevailed" (G. Lindblom, *The Akamba in British East Africa, 1916*, p. 201, quoted by E. Torday, *Descriptive Sociology, African Races* [London, 1930], p. 139).

[54] "When a group engages in a fight with another it is to revenge some injury that has been done to the whole group. The group is to act as a group and not merely as a collection of individuals, and it is therefore necessary that the group should be conscious of its unity and solidarity" (Radcliffe-Brown, *The Andaman Islanders*, p. 252).

[55] "We have had ample proof that centralized control is the primary trait acquired by every body of fighting men, be it horde of savages, band of brigands, or mass of soldiers. And this centralized control, necessitated during war, characterizes the government during peace" (Spencer, *op. cit.*, p. 557). "Their social organization [the warlike tribes of Borneo] is firmer and more efficient, because their respect for and obedience to their chiefs, and their loyalty to their community, are much greater; each man identifies himself with the whole community and accepts and loyally performs the social duties laid upon him" (W. McDougall, *An Introduction to Social Psychology* [Boston, 1918], p. 289, quoted by Marett, *Psychology and Folklore*, p. 38). "Moreover, duly sublimated, it [hate] provides a basis for patriotism, however ridiculous it may be that hating one set of men should provide an excuse for loving another; yet, as it is, war has proved the chief nurse of what Bagehot calls the preliminary virtues. Courage, loyalty, and obedience, the threefold outcome of its tutelage, furnish the state with a backbone for which economic interest offers but a feeble substitute" (Marett, *Sacraments of Simple Folk*, p. 60). The suppression of native fighting by Europeans has weakened the authority of the chiefs among the Pondo (Monica Hunter, *Reaction to Conquest* [London, 1936], pp. 410, 427).

[56] Marett, referring to wars of revenge as "safety valves for the emotions," writes: "We must recognize it, in fact, as originally no more than a quite blind and undirected act of baffled rage, following hard upon the heels of an unmeasured grief. . . . . It is as

amalgamation of neighboring groups into units too large and heterogeneous to function unitedly with the available means of communication and civic education;[57] by sanctioning the tribal mores;[58] and
sometimes by limiting population, particularly the male population,
to a figure adapted to the economy and mores of the group.[59] Most
of these functions have been excellently explained by Camilla H.
Wedgewood in her study of warfare in Melanesia:

One of the important functions of war is to increase the social solidarity of
the opposing communities. . . . . Each individual member of a tribe or district
owes a double loyalty, first to his clan or village, and second to the larger unit of
which these form a part. These loyalties do not necessarily conflict, but events
may occur which make them do so. . . . . The social structure of Melanesia is for
the most part one in which the clan is all-important, a man's loyalty to his clan
must outweigh other loyalties and the recognized practice of clansmen joining in
in defense of a fellow member serves to reaffirm and thereby strengthen the
bonds which exist between them. At the same time, in order that such conflicts,
while strengthening the clan, may not prove disruptive to the larger unit, these
are regulated and controlled and no acts of vindictive hostility such as cannibalism are permitted. The wider unity is never wholly lost sight of, while the
strength of the bonds of kinship is intensified.

When we consider conflicts between people who are normally hostile, the
unifying force of war becomes more apparent. The men are made conscious that
they are fighting for their tribe or district. This is effected in part by the rituals

---

if the demented mourners thought to discharge their random weapons at death itself,
and thereupon some wretched mortal intercepted the blow. . . . . Just as he would not
himself go down before death without a struggle, so through the sympathy of his kins-
men he continues to challenge the force that would annihilate him, and reaches a happy
release for himself in and through their relief at finding a vent, however inappropriate,
for their desire to maintain the fight against the common enemy" (*Sacraments*, pp. 52–
54). War, if followed by a proper peace, may even improve the relations between the
belligerents. "The purpose of the [peace] ceremony is clearly to produce a change in the
feelings of the two parties towards one another, feelings of enmity being replaced
through it by feelings of friendship and solidarity. It depends for its effect on the fact
that anger and similar aggressive feelings may be appeased by being freely expressed.
Its sole function is to restore the condition of solidarity between two local groups that
has been destroyed by some act of offense" (Radcliffe-Brown, *Andaman Islanders*, pp.
238–39).

[57] See n. 52 above.

[58] "Warfare also helps to prevent the breaking of tribal laws by the threat of retaliation by other social groups. Finally, it acts as the ultimate police power in the functioning of Murngin society. It is the threat of its force which ultimately prevents flagrant
breaking of tribal taboos" (Warner, *op. cit.*, p. 482).

[59] See above, n. 49.

preliminary to war. . . . . The "official" war ceremonies are essential, and have the effect, as do all ceremonies performed in unison, of making all the fighting men conscious of their common interest in a single enterprise. Nor are those who are left behind permitted to take up a passive attitude towards the expedition. For them there are tabus to be observed, often of a stringent nature, and thus the whole community, combatant and noncombatant, is united. Added to the force of these ritual preparations for war is the sense of a common danger which, until it becomes so excessive as to create panic, has always and among all peoples the power to submerge individual antagonisms and unite men. If the expedition is successful then this fear is replaced by a sense of social well-being that creates amity within the group; but even those who have been defeated will, through their common action in a common danger, have benefited to some extent, unless the damage inflicted upon them has been very severe, and, as we have seen, their loss in men and prestige is in part made good at the rites of peace-making. In the olden days, before the white man introduced fire-arms into Melanesia, the evidence shows that the mortality arising from wars of whatever kind, was not great. With the coming of the gun the number of casualites increased considerably, and war became therefore a disintegrating rather than a unifying force.

In earlier times, the very fact of fighting, therefore the mere display of hostility, rendered the people of a group more aware of themselves as members one of another. But wars were not undertaken without some cause, such as murder by physical or by magical means, insult to an important person, damage to gardens, etc. They were, in fact, entered upon when the community had in some way suffered and needed some other people on whom to vent its anger for the injury which it had received. The expression of this anger, in fighting, relieved it; the discomfort and irritation which was disquieting the community was brought to an end, and thus a sense of well-being was restored.

We see now, that war serves the double purpose of enabling a people to give expression to anger caused by a disturbance of the internal harmony, and of strengthening or reaffirming the ties which hold them together. Further, it is a means whereby a community can express itself as a unit and emphasize its distinction from all other units.[60]

The utility if not indispensability of war as an instrument for performing these social services among primitive people is suggested by its existence in some form among most of them. Even the small groups inhabiting remote Pacific islands were usually divided into mutually hostile moieties which fought periodically but not too destructively without economic or political objectives or consequences.[61]

[60] *Oceania*, I (1930), 32–33.

[61] Wedgewood (*op. cit.*, pp. 8–9, 16) reports such a condition in the Trobriand Islands (see also Malinowski, "War and Weapons among the Natives of the Trobriand Islands," *op. cit.*), San Cristóbal, New Caledonia, Lifu, Southwest Melekula, New Hebrides, New

The larger and more complex the group, the more necessary has war appeared to be as an instrument for its integration. Thus, warlikeness has been correlated with high cultural and social organization. On the other hand, high culture and social organization develop greater mastery of nature and greater powers of destruction in war. Consequently, after a certain stage it is to be expected that the disintegrating effect of overdestructive war would render warfare no longer functional.[62] This stage, however, does not arise among primitive peoples but only after civilization is well developed.

War also serves social solidarity among the more advanced primitive peoples as the instrument of group enlargement and group prosperity, although neither territorial conquest nor seizure of slaves nor plunder of economic goods is characteristic of primitive warfare. These consequences are in the main limited to groups which are culturally on the threshold of civilization and are in such geographical relation to civilized peoples that borrowing is probable.[63] More important than these economic consequences are the contributions to group solidarity made by the psychological functioning of war. In providing an outlet for certain natural human drives and certain commonly developed sentiments which might otherwise manifest themselves in disturbances to the internal solidarity of the group, war has preserved social harmony within many primitive groups.[64]

4. DRIVES

All the drives considered in connection with animal war—food, sex, territory, activity, self-preservation, society, dominance, and independence—can be observed among primitive peoples.[65]

Britain, Loyalty Islands, remarking that these "apparently meaningless displays of force" in reality "were socially important and helped to preserve a vigorous society" (p. 33).

[62] This thought is developed in detail by La Gorgette, *op. cit.*, see also Davie (*op. cit.*, p. 233), Spencer and Buckle (above, n. 25), Marett (*Psychology and Folklore*, pp. 44–45), and Max Schmidt (*The Primitive Races of Mankind*, trans. A. K. Dallas [London, 1926], p. 171). See also below, n. 174.

[63] Wedgewood (*op. cit.*, p. 11), Perry (*op. cit.*), Hoijer (*op. cit.*, pp. 63, 64, 69). The latter notes that among primitive peoples the economic motive of warfare was most important in Africa (p. 77). See also above, n. 18.

[64] See above, n. 56.

[65] The motives of primitive warfare in all parts of the world are discussed by Davie, Hoijer, Sumner and Keller, and Perry.

a) Food.—Primitive nomads raid their neighbors when pasturage is short and take their cattle for food.[66] Among the collectors and hunters, war for robbery of food occurs, although rarely.[67] Cannibalism, although known as a motive for war, is usually associated with ritual rather than with the dining-table.[68] If acquisitive motives play a part in primitive war, the commodity sought is likely to be an object of magic, ritual, or prestige value rather than of food value.[69] On the whole, with primitive man, as with animals, violence for food is generally directed against organisms of wholly different species (the hunt), not against other men.

b) Sex.—Fighting for women among exogamous tribes is common.[70] Sex is closely linked with the entire social organization of primitive people in which blood relationship plays an important role; thus war for maintaining the solidarity of the group is, among the most primitive people, hardly distinguished from war in defense of the family.[71] Breaches of the sex mores—rape or adultery—by nonmembers of the group are perhaps, together with murder of a group member, the most common causes of feuds and wars.[72] Among many

[66] Ellsworth Huntington, *The Character of Race as Influenced by Physical Environment* (New York, 1924); Davie, *op. cit.*, pp. 84 ff. Cattle-raiding is the commonest course of war among the Pondo of South Africa (Hunter, *op. cit.*, p. 414).

[67] Hoijer, *op. cit.*, p. 71.

[68] Wedgewood, *op. cit.*, pp. 12–13; Davie, *op. cit.*, pp. 65 ff.; E. M. Loeb, "The Blood Sacrifice Complex," *Memoirs of American Anthropological Association*, No. 30, 1923, pp. 6 ff.

[69] Perry, *op. cit.*, p. 11; Hoijer, *op. cit.*, p. 76. Only among the higher cultures is plunder of weapons or other material artifacts important (see Davie, *op. cit.*, pp. 81–83; Sumner and Keller, *op. cit.*, I, 363). Davie exaggerates the role of economic acquisitiveness in primitive war (see E. F. Durbin and John Bowlby, *Personal Aggressiveness and War* [New York, 1939], pp. 112–17).

[70] J. R. Marett emphasizes the influence of primitive war in selecting for parentage large men of developed anterior pituitary and aggressive disposition adapted to arid regions and to changing environmental conditions ("War, Food and Evolution," *op. cit.*). Davie, *op. cit.*, pp. 96 ff.; Sumner and Keller, *op. cit.*, I, 364, IV, 121 ff. These writers seem to exaggerate when they say that "some question of food or of women lies at the root of most of their hostilities" (*op. cit.*, I, 369, citing Jenness and Ballentyne, *D'Entre casteaux*, p. 202). A Maori proverb is said to assign women and land as the chief cause of warfare (Hoijer, *op. cit.*, p. 56). See also above, n. 49.

[71] See below, nn. 87 and 88.

[72] "The causes for warfare [among the Murngin] are the killing of a member of a clan by a man belonging to another clan, and interclan rivalry for women. This latter cause is usually the primary reason for most killings" (Warner, *op. cit.*, p. 478). See also

people successful warriors and head-hunters acquire prestige without which they are frequently ineligible to marriage. These types of war are often directly encouraged by the women.[73]

c) *Territory.*—All primitive people live in defined territories which supply their economic needs, but among the collectors and hunters boundaries are usually so well recognized by neighbors, and population growth is so well adjusted to the food supply available in the area, that occasions seldom arise necessitating territorial expansion or defense of one's own.[74] The encroachments of civilized man, however, demonstrate that practically all primitive people will fight to defend their territory, if necessary.[75] In practice, however, wars seldom have the object of territorial aggression or defense until the pastoral or agricultural stages of culture are reached, when they become a major cause of war.[76] Territory provides both a source of livelihood and the home of the family; the drive for its acquisition or defense is, therefore, closely related to the drives of food and sex.

d) *Activity.*—War for adventure or sport is common among primitive people. Primitive peoples often distinguish different types of war. Among the Melanesians there is a very mild form of war between related clans, seldom resulting in casualties, fought with clubs only, in the spirit of a game. With more habitual enemies there is a form of pitched battle which, while resulting in casualties, is surrounded by elaborate formalities and rules limiting its destructiveness and distinguishing it from the most serious type of war—am-

---

Hoijer, *op. cit.*, pp. 29, 30. "If, however, there was a time when human society was matricentral, and its chief mystery, because the very secret of its corporate identity, was the mother's blood, it is easy to conceive how her natural function as a peacemaker might be reinforced by a conditional curse issuing from the blood itself, sole fountainhead of vitality alike physical and spiritual. To shed it unlawfully by killing man or violating woman would thus poison the social life at its very source" (Marett, *Sacraments*, pp. 50–51).

[73] Davie, *op. cit.*, p. 101; Sumner and Keller, *op. cit.*, I, 364. Pondo women accompanied the army and encouraged the warriors, whom they watched from neighboring hills, by singing salacious songs and tucking their skirts around their waists, thus exposing themselves (Hunter, *op. cit.*, p. 408).

[74] Carr-Saunders, *op. cit.*; Wedgewood, *op. cit.*, p. 11; Hoijer, *op. cit.*, p. 63.

[75] Radcliffe-Brown, *Andaman Islanders*, pp. 85–87.

[76] Davie, *op. cit.*, pp. 78 ff.; Sumner and Keller, *op. cit.*, I, 361, IV, 119 ff.; Hoijer, *op. cit.*, p. 63; Hunter, *op. cit.*, p. 412.

bushes or early-morning raids with the object of annihilating the village. Certain Australian tribes occasionally send out expeditions, ostensibly to procure medicinal plants and minerals such as red ocher hundreds of miles away. They usually have to fight their way through tribes on whose territory they trespass and return with thrilling tales of adventure rather than with valuable commodities. These milder forms of war give an opportunity for working off aggressive impulses without danger to the social solidarity or economic welfare of either of the contending parties.[77]

e) Self-preservation.—All men, like all animals, will defend themselves if attacked and no means of escape presents itself; but individual self-defense cannot originate violence, and the most primitive people, unless engaged in war, will usually prefer flight to fight.[78] Conventional rules often mitigate the severity of war in the interest of the individual's desire for self-preservation. War to revenge the death of a relative or a member of the group or to defend the group's mores and integrity is closely related to the drive of self-preservation because of the ease with which the individual identifies himself with his family or his group.[79]

Elliot Smith has emphasized the search for supposedly "life-giving substances" as a motive for aggression,[80] but he attributes this activity to the stage in which civilization originated. While raids for objects of ritual or prestige value are common among primitive people, they do not often seem to be directly related to the drive of self-preservation but rather to that of sex.[81]

f) Dominance.—Wars for political domination, so important among civilized people, hardly exist among the primitive collectors.

[77] A. W. Howitt, *The Native Tribes of South-East Australia* (London, 1904), pp. 710 ff.; Wedgewood, *op. cit.*, pp. 9–11, 13–14; Hoijer, *op. cit.*, p. 14. Malinowski writes of the Trobriand Islanders (*Man*, January, 1920, p. 10): "The mere fact of fighting as a sport, and the glory derived from a display of daring and skill, were an important incitement to warfare." Sumner and Keller (*op. cit.*, I, 363) emphasize the importance of war for glory and vanity, as does Davie (*op. cit.*, p. 147). See also above, n. 73, and for varieties of war among the Murngin (northern Australia), above, n. 21.

[78] "A great many natives will not fight at all unless they can choose their own positions" (Heneker, *op. cit.*, p. 45).

[79] Above, n. 72.

[80] G. Elliot Smith, *Human History* [London, 1930], pp. 33 ff.

[81] Above, nn. 69 and 73.

It may be that the continued primitiveness of these peoples is due in part to the feebleness of the dominance drive in their heredity and the consequent lack of a spirit of emulation in their societies.[82] Where chieftainship arises, however, with more complex social organization, and usually a pastoral or agricultural way of life, fights among rivals to obtain the chieftainship and wars initiated by the chief to augment his prestige or to check internal disaffection are common.[83] In advanced primitive groups where division of labor and social classes have developed, wars serve to maintain the dominant position of the ruling class as well as to preserve the sense of social solidarity of the group as a whole. Even where there is not a division of classes, group leadership depends on the acquisition of individual prestige, and among the warlike people success in warlike activities is the surest road to prestige. Among the head-hunters not only marriage but dominance and leadership in the group depends upon the number of heads secured.[84]

g) Independence.—Wars of independence are unknown among the most primitive people because slavery, subjection, and class stratification are unknown. Slavery, social classes, empires, and minorities are phenomena of civilization and of the most highly developed of the primitive people.[85] Even where wars are made for slaves, class oppression, or conquest, as they are among a number of African tribes, the slaves, the oppressed classes, or the subjugated people very rarely revolt.' The Zulu conquered a number of tribes, forming an empire, and, although they armed some of these subject people, including the Thonga, to continue their conquests, these people did not revolt.[86]

h) Society.—The maintenance of social solidarity is the normal function of primitive war. The sense of group loyalty constitutes a war drive among the members of the group and springs from their

[82] A. H. Maslow notes the great variability of this drive among individuals and groups ("Dominance, Feeling, Behavior and Status," *Psychological Review*, XLIV [July, 1937], 404 ff.).

[83] Hoijer, *op. cit.*, pp. 49 ff.; Davie, *op. cit.*, pp. 160 ff.; Hunter, *op. cit.*, p. 411.

[84] Above, n. 73.

[85] Davie, *op. cit.*, pp. 164 ff.

[86] *Ibid.*, p. 168; Walter Dyk, "A Study of the Effect of Change of Technique upon the Warfare of Primitive People" (manuscript at University of Chicago), pp. 18–20.

education rather than from their primitive impulses. The capacity of men to develop and observe customs and traditions which subordinate them to the group gives to warfare in obedience to the group mores the character of war in response to a human drive.[87] Primitive man fights whenever in accordance with his mores and religion the occasion is appropriate. He gives little consideration to the consequences but fights whenever to do so accords with the behavior pattern learned in youth. The occasions which the mores point to as appropriate for warlike activity differ from tribe to tribe, but the primitive idea of justice, an injury for an injury, a man for a man, is always important. War to revenge murder, adultery, or insult injurious to the tribe or one of its members, war for a sacrificial victim or a head necesssary to fulfil the requirements of religious ceremonial, war to punish a neighbor for injurious magic operations—all these emphasize the group mores and present vividly to the individual the reality of the ties of blood, religion, and custom which make the human aggregate a psychic unity.[88] On the other hand, war to proselyte others to their religion is unknown among primitive peoples. The beliefs and practices of the group are considered its peculiar heritage incapable of extension to others.[89]

In general, among primitive people war is a function of group mores rather than of human instinct, although the development of the mores has been influenced by the natural drives of man. Impulses of sex, adventure, and social sympathy receive satisfaction in or from war, but the occasion and the form of the war response are

[87] These artificial drives developed by education and habit may be in conflict with natural drives existing from heredity. The effort at reconciliation leads to the psychological and sociological peculiarities which constitute culture (see Malinowski, *Sex and Repression in Savage Society*).

[88] Davie, *op. cit.*, pp. 103 ff.; Hoijer, *op. cit.*, pp. 87 ff. Warner finds that among the Murngin the principle of reciprocity dominates the war and, in fact, all other mores: "If a harm has been done to an individual or a group, it is felt by the injured people that they must repay the ones who have harmed them by an injury that at least equals the one they have suffered" (*op. cit.*, p. 462). The primitive belief in animism which attributes all disasters to human or para-human agencies and the human tendency to displace hostility to the loved and to project self-guilt upon a scapegoat combine to suggest identification of an unfriendly out-group as the agent responsible for disasters. Any death or other disaster in a tribe is likely to be the occasion for a war of revenge (Durbin and Bowlby, *op. cit.*, pp. 14, 19, 94, 110, 117; Fraser, *op. cit.*, p. 547).

[89] Sumner and Keller, *op. cit.*, I, 366.

among primitive people sociological rather than psychological problems.[90]

5. TECHNIQUES

The technique of primitive warfare, as of animal warfare, consists,
on the one hand, of the preparation of military weapons, material,
and organization and, on the other, of the process of mobilizing and
and of utilizing such instruments to the best tactical and strategic
advantage. While, in respect to animals, the process of preparing
military instruments is mainly morphological and unchangeable except by organic evolution, in respect to primitive people, weapon
type, material, and organization are matters of behavior no less than
are the tactical and strategic utilization of these instruments.

Naked man is among the least specialized of the animals for defense and attack. His fists, fingernails, and jaws provide little striking power compared with that which many of the animals, even of
much smaller bulk, possess in their anatomical structure. With respect to mobility, he cannot run as rapidly as the antelope or swim as
well as the seal. He has the wings neither of the bird nor of the bat,
and, while his hands assist in climbing, he is less at home in the trees
than are the apes and monkeys. He has no shell or carapace. He
lacks even fur, feathers, or scales, his skin being particularly vulnerable. He has the tenacious holding power of neither the bulldog
nor the boa constrictor.[91]

[90] Durbin and Bowlby (*op. cit.*, p. 12) suggest that adult war differs from the fights
of animals and children in that it is a group activity and is supported by elaborate theories. "In the first place the aggressions of adults is normally a group activity. Murder and assault are restricted to a small criminal minority. Adults kill and torture each
other only when organized into political parties, or economic classes or religious denomi-
nations, or nation states. A moral distinction is always made between the individual
killing for himself and the same individual killing for some real or supposed group interest. In the second place, the adult powers of imagination and reason are brought to the
service of the aggressive intention. Apes and children when they fight, simply fight.
Men and women first construct towering systems of theology and religion, complex
analyses or racial character and class structure, or moralities of group life and virility
before they kill one another. Thus they fight for Protestantism or Mohammedanism,
for the emancipation of the world proletariat or for the salvation of the Nordic culture,
for nation or for king. Men will die like flies for theories and exterminate each other
with every instrument of destruction for abstractions."

[91] See word pictures of the life of tool-less men in L. C. Marshall, *The Story of Human
Progress* (New York, 1928), chap. i; Baikie, *op. cit.*, p. 35. See also Lewis Mumford,
Technics and Civilization (New York, 1934), p. 83.

This weakness in physical instruments, however, has been more than compensated for by the psychological equipment which has made it possible for man to develop weapons and organization outside of his body, to modify the utilization of them with extraordinary flexibility in accord with the exigencies of the occasion, and to keep to his purpose with a tenacity and morale unprecedented in the animal kingdom.

Although in these traits of weapon-making, organization, strategy, and morale the most primitive men were superior to all other animals, yet, compared with the achievement of civilized men in these regards, they resemble more the apes and the ants who manifest rudiments of these qualities.

The striking weapons of primitive peoples are confined to arm-, foot-, or mouth-propelled instruments. These include war hammers, battle-axes, and swords; thrusting spears; and missile weapons, such as the hurled spear, or javelin, the arrow propelled by arm- or foot-drawn bow, or the blowpipe. The striking edge or point of these weapons is of hard wood, stone, bone, or metal, and occasionally poison is used on the tip of arrow or spear.[92] Among collecting and hunting people these weapons are usually not differentiated from those used in the hunt.[93] The warrior is merely a hunter, for the moment, attacking other men. Ordinarily the men alone engage in war as they do in hunting, although occasional tribes utilize women as warriors.[94] The protection of primitive warriors consists of wood or leather shields and an occasional head or body armor of skin, feathers, textiles, or wood. For mobility they are limited to hands and feet, which, however, are capable of traversing rugged terrains, dense underbrush, trees, and mountains without noise. The holding power is limited to the tactical ability of the individual with his weapon. Except among the highest of primitive people, such as the warlike Zulus and other pastoral tribes of East Africa, who have been in rather continuous contact with civilization, there is no professional

[92] For description and illustration of primitive weapons see Lieut.-Gen. A. Lane-Fox Pitt-Rivers, *The Evolution of Culture and other Essays* (Oxford, 1906), pp. 45 ff.; Lieut.-Col. L. A. D. Montague, *Weapons and Implements of Savage Races* (London, 1921); see also Torday, *op. cit.*, pp. 366–71.

[93] Radcliffe-Brown, *The Andaman Islanders*, p. 418; Max Schmidt, *op. cit.*, p. 159.

[94] Davie, *op. cit.*, pp. 23 ff.

military class.[95] There is little of mass organization or group tactics. War is usually conducted by sudden sallies or ambushes followed by individual duels and an inclination to retreat at the first reverse. Primitive man appears to be flighty and lacking in morale compared to civilized man.[96]

In general, it may be said that primitive man in fighting relies mainly on striking power, particularly striking power at a distance, with bow and arrow, and on mobility, utilizing the stratagem of surprise from ambush or darkness. His war is one of pounce and maneuver. Only after contact with civilization does he organize a mass charge and complicated tactics. He seldom builds elaborate fortifications,[97] and war of attrition is rare.[98] Man was a hunter before he was a warrior, and in devising his artificial weapons of the hunt he imitated the strategy and tactics of such hunting animals as the lion, tiger, and wolf, who hunted the same game as he did but were better equipped by nature. In the detailed construction of his weapons he imitated horns, claws, and tusks. When he fought men, he used the same weapons and tactics that he was familiar with in the hunt.[99] There was little differentiation until the higher stages of primitive culture, and even today weapons of the hunt and of war are similar.[100]

[95] Specialization begins with a pastoral or agricultural way of life requiring the bulk of the population to continue economic pursuits while the war is in progress (Sumner and Keller, *op. cit.*, I, 374). See quotation under "Military Organization," in Torday, *op. cit.*, pp. 138 ff.

[96] Sumner and Keller, *op. cit.*, I, 378; Davie, *op. cit.*, pp. 244–50; below, n. 113.

[97] Stone forts in the Rhodesian hills are believed by Perry to be the work of early Arab gold miners (*op. cit.*). For description of stockades and other village defenses used by the more advanced peoples of Africa see Torday, *op. cit.*, pp. 138–50; and Max Schmidt, *op. cit.*, p. 161. Neolithic men in Europe fortified villages (Cleland, *op. cit.*, p. 131).

[98] A siege is said to have taken place among Indians at "Starved Rock," Illinois.

[99] Lieut.-Gen. A. L.-F. Pitt-Rivers, *op. cit.*, pp. 55, 94 ff.; Radcliffe-Brown, *Andaman Islanders*, p. 418.

[100] Note the difficulty in distinguishing "arms of war" and "arms capable of use both for military and other purposes" in recent arms trade conventions. See St. Germain Convention, 1919, art. 1; Geneva Convention, 1925, art. 1; "Draft Convention on Trade in and Manufacture of Arms Proposed by the United States," *Munitions Industry* (73d Cong.; 2d sess. [Senate Committee Print No. 1 (Washington, 1934)]), pp. 73, 81, 97.

This general description distinguishing techniques of primitive war from those of animal and civilized warfare is not intended to minimize the great differences in respect to war techniques which exist among different primitive groups. As has been noted, among primitive people the most important function of warfare is the preservation of the solidarity of the fighting group; consequently, the techniques of warfare are adapted to the special situation of each group. While a group may borrow new weapon types, tactics, and maneuvers, and may improve those it has by experimentation, and while doubtless such changes actually occur much more frequently than do changes in fighting instruments and behavior in the process of organic evolution among animals, yet the fighting techniques of primitive tribes are extremely persistent. Pitt-Rivers writes:

> Throughout the entire continent of Australia the weapons and implements are alike, and of the simplest form, and the people are of the lowest grade. The spear, the waddy, and the boomerang, with some stone hatchets, are their only weapons; but amongst these it has been noted that, like the implements of the drift, there are minute differences, scarcely apparent to Europeans, but which enable a native to determine at a glance to what tribe a weapon belongs. This, whilst it proves a tendency to vary their forms, shows at the same time either an incapacity, or, what answers the same purpose, a retarding power or prejudice, which prevents their effecting more than the smallest appreciable degree of change.[101]

Primitive life as a whole is guided by relatively inflexible custom, and fighting techniques are no exception to this rule. War is not an economic instrument with most primitive people, and, unless they come in contact with civilized people who employ war for economic or political purposes, there is little reason for changing their war techniques. Where plunder, territory, or the expansion of power are sought by war, there is a motivation for steady improvement of its technique. This motivation, however, does not exist when the object of war is sanction of the tribal mores and symbolization of group solidarity. For these purposes the traditional methods are as good as new ones.

That this persistence of a war technique among primitive people is a product of stable conditions rather than of inability to invent or

[101] *Op. cit.*, p. 51.

adopt is, however, indicated by (1) the great diversity of fighting techniques which exists among the primitive people, showing that in past times tribes have adopted their fighting techniques to new conditions, and by (2) the historic record of borrowing and rapid change in tribes subjected to drastic modification of conditions, particularly to contact with civilization.

Anthropologists emphasize the tenacity with which primitive groups insist on weapons of precisely the form they are accustomed to, even when a better material is provided, and their unwillingness to accept from traders equally useful or even superior weapons of novel character.[102] Yet archeological remains and contemporary weapons of primitive people exhibit a great diversity, but with gradations and distributions suggesting continuous improvement and borrowing in the past.[103] The bow and arrow is one of the most widely distributed weapons, although detailed differences in construction and method of holding the arrow are very persistent.[104] Side by side with the bow-and-arrow users, however, people using only the spear are to be found.[105] Poison is used in many places as widely separated as Malaya and South America, but in many intervening places it is not found.[106]

No less diverse than the forms of weapons are the forms of organization. Although women are very rarely fighters, among the Dahomey a female warrior corps is important.[107] Among some tribes all men fight on occasions;[108] among others certain age groups alone

[102] Ibid.

[103] Ibid., pp. 89 ff. Pitt-Rivers applied the Darwinian idea of "unconscious selection" to this problem as early as 1868 (p. 96).

[104] Edward S. Morse, "Ancient and Modern Methods of Arrow Release," Bulletin of the Essex Institute, Vol. XVII (October–December 1885); Additional Notes on Arrow Release (Salem, Mass.: Peabody Museum, 1922).

[105] As the Massai and Akikuyu in the early phase of their contact (see below, n. 117).

[106] The local presence of poisonous plants is, of course, a factor in this distribution (A. L.-F. Pitt-Rivers, op. cit., p. 78; Sumner and Keller, op. cit., IV, 140 ff.).

[107] Davie, op. cit., pp. 25 ff. Women seem occasionally to have engaged in fighting in Angola, Canary Islands, Valley of the Amazon, Patagonia, Central America, Hawaii, Australia, Tasmania, Arabia, and Albania and among the Ainu and Apache (ibid., pp. 30–34).

[108] As in Melanesia (Wedgewood, op. cit., p. 20).

fight;[109] and among others fighting is by a few champions.[110] Only among the pastoral and agricultural peoples is there anything like a professional military class.[111] Some have permanent war chiefs; some do not.[112]

Tactics and strategy also show wide variations. The surprise attack or ambush, with a brief period of fighting, and then withdrawal is commonest, although within this type of fighting there are considerable variations in the bloodiness and destructiveness to property.[113] Pitched battles on the field are relatively uncommon and less bloody than the surprise attack, although they are sometimes utilized under certain circumstances by people who under other circumstances employ the surprise attack.[114] The discipline necessary for group tactics and strategic movement is most developed among the pastoral people.[115]

To summarize, it appears that, as general culture advances, the size of the fighting group tends to increase; the warrior class tends to become more specialized; missile weapons (the hurled stone or javelin, blowpipe, bow and arrow) tend to be superseded by piercing or striking weapons (the thrusting spear, battle-ax, or sword); discipline and morale tend to increase; and the battle of pounce and retreat tends to give way to the battle of mass attack and maneuver. With these changes the casualties and destructiveness of war tend to become greater.

[109] As among the Masai and other East African tribes (*ibid.*). See MacLeod, *op. cit.*, pp. 216 ff.

[110] This seems often to occur in Papua and Australia and among the Eskimos (Wedgewood, *op. cit.;* Davie, *op. cit.;* pp. 177, 244–49). See Hobhouse, Wheeler, and Ginsburg, *op. cit.*, p. 123, for account of regulated fights of champions and expiatory exposures of persons guilty of certain offenses in Australia.

[111] Davie, *op. cit.*, p. 167; Wedgewood, *op. cit.*, p. 20; see above, n. 95.

[112] Davie, *op. cit.*, pp. 285 ff.; Hoijer, *op. cit.*, pp. 49 ff.

[113] For description of methods used see Radcliffe-Brown, *Andaman Islanders*, p. 86; Davie, *op. cit.*, pp. 285 ff.

[114] Wedgewood, *op. cit.*, pp. 13 ff.; Malinowski, "War and Weapons among the Natives of the Trobriand Islands," *op. cit.*, p. 11; MacLeod, *op. cit.*, pp. 62–63.

[115] Such as the Zulu and the Masai of East Africa (Davie, *op. cit.*, pp. 168–69, 255 ff.) and the Pondo of South Africa, who have a territorial military organization including all able-bodied men (Hunter, *op. cit.*, pp. 401 ff.).

In spite of their usual slowness in accepting weapons differing in form from those with which they are familiar, primitive people have on occasion accepted radically different weapons of unquestionable superiority such as the thrusting spear, the horse, and the gun.[116] The bow-and-arrow-using Akikuyu, coming into East Africa from the south, after being driven back by the invading Masai, who came from the north and used the thrusting spear or assegai, finally adopted the weapon and tactics of their enemy, defended themselves, and even drove their enemy back in places. Walter Dyk says of this history:

A warring pastoral nation with a distinctive and efficient military organization and a weapon very effective in open warfare appeared on the scene among peaceful agriculturalists. In spite of continuous, courageous and often successful opposition, and in spite of natural defenses and the deadly poison arrow, the warrior group over-ran the territory and dominated it, conquering some of the inhabitants, remaining a constant menace to others. At first the Akikuyu relied for protection from the ravages of their foes on the geographical features of their country, ravines, deep bush in which the Masai were at a decided disadvantage. They built defensive works and hid their villages in the most unexpected places. They then used only the bow and arrow, no spear, and made no offensive attacks on the Masai. As the protective stretch of impenetrable forest rapidly diminished, and they were faced with the prospect of annihilation, or of being driven from their homes, they proceeded to take over Masai customs and the weapon which had proved so invincible. Though they attempted to introduce the Masai military organization, they were but mildly successful, for as Rutledge writes, "they had no idea of military organization, drill, and obedience." As the forest gave way to fields they found means of keeping cattle, and following their better success in the field of battle with the imported assegai, they began making raids. In 1890 when rinderpest decimated the Masai cattle, and internal discontent and civil war undermined their military organization, we can only guess at what might have happened had not the British been on the scene. The power of the Masai was waning, and a new power, that of the Akikuyu, seemed in the ascendant; for a once peaceful agricultural tribe had become a warring one, losing its native culture in exchange for a pastoral and foreign one. It is unquestionable that in this change the borrowed assegai proved a main and impelling factor. A more efficient weapon taken over, at first, as a means of self-preservation became in turn an impetus to a new field of endeavor, acquisition by means of conquest.[117]

[116] H. Peake and H. J. Fleure, *The Horse and the Sword* (New Haven, 1933). The natives' ability to utilize firearms is demonstrated by the anxiety of colonizing states to prevent the traffic in arms in certain barred zones of Africa (see treaties mentioned in n. 100, above).

[117] *Op. cit.*, pp. 16–17, where C. W. Hobley, *Ethnology of the Akamba*, and W. S. Rutledge, *With a Prehistoric People*, are cited.

The Zulu adopted the formations and tactics of the British in South Africa and applied it successfully, even teaching it to some of their subject peoples, such as the Thonga, who however utilized it in behalf of their masters rather than of themselves.[118]

The Hawaiians acquired arms and knowledge of European military methods from stranded sailors, with the result that a military empire over all the Islands was soon established by Kamehameha, "the Napoleon of the Pacific," in the early nineteenth century.[119] The horse and the gun introduced by the Spaniards soon spread among the plains Indians in America and changed their whole culture, especially their fighting tactics. After noting the relatively sedentary life of the eastern and western Indians of North America, Powell writes:

When, however, the interior portions of the country were first visited by Europeans, a different state of affairs was found to prevail. There the acquisition of the horse and the possession of firearms (indirectly from the Spaniards in Mexico) had wrought very great changes in aboriginal habits. The acquisition of the former enabled the Indian of the treeless plains to travel distances with ease and celerity which before were practically impossible, and the possession of firearms stimulated tribal aggressiveness to the utmost pitch. Firearms were everywhere doubly effective in producing changes in tribal habitats, since the somewhat gradual introduction of trade placed these deadly weapons in the hands of some tribes, and of whole congeries of tribes, long before others could obtain them. Thus the general state of tribal equilibrium which had before prevailed was rudely disturbed. Tribal warfare, which hitherto had been attended with inconsiderable loss of life and slight territorial changes, was now made terribly destructive, and the territorial possessions of whole groups of tribes were augmented at the expense of those less fortunate. The horse made wanderers of many tribes which there is sufficient evidence to show were formerly nearly sedentary. Firearms enforced migration and caused wholesale changes in the habitats of tribes, which, in the natural order of events, it would have taken many centuries to produce. The changes resulting from these combined agencies, great as they were, are, however, slight in comparison with the tremendous effects of the wholesale occupancy of Indian territory by Europeans.[120]

[118] Dyk, *op. cit.*, pp. 8 ff.

[119] R. S. Kuykendall and H. E. Gregory, *A History of Hawaii* (New York, 1926).

[120] J. W. Powell, "Indian Linguistic Families North of Mexico," *Seventh Annual Report of the Bureau of Ethnology to the Secretary of the Smithsonian Institute, 1885–86* (Washington, 1891), p. 32; see also Wissler, "The Influence of the Horse in the Development of Plains Culture," *op. cit.*

While the primitive military techniques are relatively persistent under normal primitive conditions, these illustrations suggest that, upon contact with new instruments of obvious utility, many primitive peoples have changed their fighting techniques with relative rapidity. It is to be noted, however, that the warlike peoples borrow new fighting techniques far more rapidly than do the nonwarlike. If war is an institution in the mores, improved techniques are easily appreciated and adopted; but if war is not in the mores, military instruments and methods will hardly be noticed and will be borrowed only after long contact with those who use them. "The rapidity with which the Polynesians accepted firearms and appreciated their worth in battle is almost unbelieveable." On the other hand: "The Bushmen to this day have not been noticeably affected either by the gun or the horse or the military activities of the British and Dutch. The Papuans of New Guinea are only now showing signs of unrest and possible change after one hundred and fifty years of contact with the guns and powder of the whites."[121]

It cannot be overlooked, however, that eventually the introduction of new techniques may convert nonwarlike into warlike people. These changes, however, arising in the main from the contact of primitive with civilized and semicivilized peoples, hardly belong in the subject of primitive warfare. With such contacts, the primitive people change not only the techniques but also the functions, drives, and laws of their wars. War ceases to be a function of tribal mores serving to perpetuate the *status quo* and becomes a struggle for existence, a characteristic it seldom has among uncontaminated primitive groups.

6. THEORY AND LAW

Among primitive peoples the law of war does not consist of hereditary behavior patterns, as among animals,[122] nor does it consist in rules for the rational adaptation of means and ends as among civilized peoples;[123] but it consists of group customs or behavior pat-

---

[121] Dyk, *op. cit.*, pp. 5, 35. [122] See Appen. VII, sec. 4.

[123] According to the U.S. Rules of Land Warfare, 1917, art. 9, "the development of the laws and usages of war is determined" primarily by the principle of military necessity that "a belligerent is justified in applying any amount and any kind of force which

terns of the members of the group acquired through education and discipline to which each generation is subjected. The rules of primitive warfare differ from those of animal war in that they are within the consciousness of the participants; but they differ from civilized war in that the reason for the rule is not. Primitive man takes the mores as facts to be observed and conformed to without question. He has, it is true, explanations or rationalizations which he uses in educating the next generation but which, in the opinion of the scientific anthropologist, may or may not be related to either the historical or the functional reason for the custom in question.[124]

Among animals the law of war, existing in the genetic constitution of the species, is necessarily the same for all members of the species, subject to the usual margin of individual variation; but among primitive men, although all of the same species and psychologically much alike,[125] the law existing in the group mores may vary greatly from group to group. Having persisted because of the function it serves in preserving a particular sovereign group, whether clan, village, tribe, or tribal federation, from internal dissolution and external destruction, the law does not necessarily extend beyond that group, although similar rules may be practiced by neighbors who have borrowed them, by other groups of common origin who have inherited them, or by groups with similar problems who have independently developed them.[126] Because of the secondary psychological and international functions which primitive war practices serve, many groups do have similar problems. The rules are, however, related primarily to the situation of the particular group and only secondarily to the situation of the individual, of the human species, or of the larger community of which the group is a part.

Among civilized people, on the other hand, war has ordinarily been an instrument of national policy justified by reason of state, however that may have been rationalized in universal terms of justice,

---

is necessary for the purpose of the war; that is, the complete submission of the enemy at the earliest possible moment with the least expenditure of men and money" only secondarily by the principles of humanity and chivalry.

[124] Radcliffe-Brown, *Andaman Islanders*, p. 235.

[125] Marett, *Psychology and Folklore*, p. 70; *Sacraments*, p. 20.

[126] Appen. VI.

authority, or evolutionary utility;[127] and the basic rules for its conduct have arisen from military necessity. Among civilized peoples, therefore, reason has tended continuously to co-ordinate the detailed rules of war acquired by tradition into a system logically deducible from a few principles.[128] Among primitive peoples, on the other hand, the co-ordination, in so far as it exists, has resulted from the more or less unconscious evolution of the mores.[129]

Because of the great variability of the law of primitive war from tribe to tribe, it is difficult to deal with the subject in general terms—as difficult as it is to generalize the law of animal war for all species. In fact, there is here a close analogy. As the carnivorous animal survives by aggression, and the herbivorous by peaceful aggregation, so some primitive groups survive by warlikeness and others by nonwarlikeness; as some carnivores leap on their prey in silence, while others give tongue on starting the quarry, so some warlike peoples attack from ambush, others only after formal declaration.[130]

The customs of primitive war may be classified by a number of criteria. Some rules have an objective import such as those exempting certain individuals, times, or places from violence, while others such as war dances have a merely subjective import. They create an attitude in the participants. In primitive war, as in civilized and modern war, there are rules and ceremonials relating to the initiation and termination of war as well as to the actual conduct of hostilities. Most primitive groups observe different war practices toward a related group with which friendship normally exists and toward a wholly alien group. Hostilities of the first type, although group sanctioned, are usually of the nature of a feud to secure revenge, reprisal, or glory for a particular individual or family within the group.[131] The significance of the rules and ceremonials of primitive war can best be understood by considering whether they have developed to

---

[127] See Sturzo, *The International Community and the Right of War* (New York, 1930).

[128] See above, n. 123. [129] See Sumner, *op. cit.*

[130] See chap. v, sec. 3; Appen. VII, sec. 3.

[131] Wedgewood, *op. cit.*, pp. 9–11, 13–20; see above, n. 20. For detailed description of war practices of primitive tribes see Wedgewood, *op.cit.*, p. 31; Davie, *op.cit.*, pp. 176–95; 292–96; Sumner and Keller, *op. cit.*, I, 383–95, IV, 115 ff.; H. Spencer (ed.), *Descriptive Sociology*, especially revised edition (1930), on *African Races*, by E. Torday, pp. 138 ff.

serve a psychological need of the individual, a social need of the group, or a need of the international community of which the group is a member. This distinction corresponds to the distinction in modern international law between rules founded on natural law (*jus naturale*), civil law (*jus civili*), and the law of nations (*jus gentium*).[132]

With the advance of culture and contact, several sovereign groups of one period tend to be integrated into a larger sovereign group of the age to come; primary groups unite to form secondary groups, secondary to form tertiary, and tertiary to form quaternary.[133] During the transition of sovereignty from one group to the next, rules of international law mediating between the sovereignty which is going and that which is coming are important. Primitive peoples, however, differ from civilized in their resistance to progress. Their societies are relatively static; consequently, such transitions are rare, and the rules and ceremonials of war are usually rooted primarily in the social needs of the sovereign group and secondarily in the psychological needs of the individual. They are rules of civil or of natural law rather than of true international law.[134]

The psychological need for rules of war springs from the natural[135] dislike of man either to be killed or to kill one of his own species. That most individuals have an urge for self-preservation in spite of

[132] Grotius distinguishes natural law, defined in the larger sense, as that which proceeds from "the essential traits implanted in man," from the civil laws of each state which "have in view the advantage of that state," and from the law of nations which functions for "the advantage, not of particular states, but of the great society of states" (*De jure belli ac pacis*, Proleg., secs. 12, 17). For him the law of war was derived from natural law and the law of nations (secs. 25–28).

[133] See above, nn. 38 and 52.

[134] Wedgewood (*op. cit.*, p. 31) points out, however, that the mutual risk of exhaustion or annihilation and sometimes the mutual need arising from economic interdependence of neighboring groups requires some international law to moderate fighting among all primitive people. "Thus between the international laws of Europe and those of Melanesia, there is no difference in kind, but only in complexity; the functions of both are the same."

[135] "Natural" is used to distinguish hereditary from acquired traits with full realization that the latter necessarily have a genetic foundation. Acquired traits might be called "artificial" in that they are the intended consequence of an educational procedure. In the Freudian terminology natural traits are those which the equilibrium between the aggressive and the libidinous drives of the id establish in the average human personality (ego) apart from influences of the superego.

the occasional occurrences of suicides, of self-sacrifice, of masochistic behavior, hardly needs emphasis. On the other hand, the rarity of serious intraspecific hostilities among animals[136] and the general opinion of psychologists that cruelty is abnormal[137] suggest the general existence of hereditary patterns against intraspecific killing in all organisms. The generally accepted theory that organic evolution tends to shape individuals with behavior patterns not unfavorable to survival of the species provides an explanation for this phenomenon.[138] That even among men destruction of his kind is unnatural is suggested by the general abhorrence of murder by people of all cultures, though the powerful in-group-out-group sentiment, especially among primitive peoples, may greatly moderate and sometimes wholly eliminate this abhorrence with respect to others.[139] Doubtless there are individuals to whom brutal and sadistic behavior is "natural," and doubtless most individuals can be stimulated to such behavior by suitable circumstances, but such individuals and such circumstances are abnormal. This abhorrence of murder is evidenced by the practice of almost all groups in severely punishing killing within the group. Among primitive people this rule is so sanctioned that intragroup murder seldom occurs, and, if it does, the taboo sometimes prevents retaliation upon the murderer. He is simply ostracized, which, however, usually results in his suicide or flight.[140] Primitive people, even though warlike, often retain the

[136] See above, chap. v, sec. 2

[137] See art. "Cruelty," *Encyclopaedia Brittannica* (14th ed.), but see Durbin and Bowlby, *op. cit.*, p. 12.

[138] See above, chap. v, sec. 4.

[139] Such criminologists as Garofalo have classified murder as a crime against "natural law" (see art. "Criminology," *Encyclopaedia of the Social Sciences*). William Seagle, however, writes that "a horror of homicide is a modern phenomenon" and points out that the "mental elements as well as external circumstances" rendering homicide punishable have varied greatly among both primitive and civilized peoples. He does not, however, deny that every society punishes homicide in some circumstances ("Homicide," *Encyclopaedia of the Social Sciences*). Marett points out that a "taboo bears witness to nature but to education" but at the same time he emphasizes the "grief and indignation and sheer horror" aroused at the killing of a relative or tribesman, augmented when the killer is also a tribesman. It seems probable that natural horror and social expediency have conspired to produce the universal taboo against murder (*Sacraments*, pp. 49, 51). See also Davie, *op. cit.*, pp. 18–20; Durbin and Bowlby, *op. cit.*, p. 108.

[140] Marett, *Sacraments*, pp. 50, 51.

taboo against murder with respect to blood relations. As these groups are usually exogamous, this means that certain members of a hostile group may be barred from killing certain of the enemy who happen to be blood relations.[141] This in part accounts for the usual rule which minimizes the violence of hostilities between groups bound by marital ties.[142] If further evidence is necessary to prove the unnaturalness of human killing, it may be found in the fact that the most primitive people, isolated and uncorrupted by contact with higher cultures, often have neither war nor brutality in their mores.[143]

It is therefore unnatural for men, as for other animals, to want to be killed or to kill others of the species, but people who engage in war necessarily both risk their lives and seek to kill other men. Thus devices are necessary to create conditions in which this unnatural behavior will seem to be natural. The suicidal and cruel impulses latent in most human beings and perhaps in most animals but normally submerged by the dominant drives of self-preservation and sympathy toward others of the species must be released. In normal personalities the self-preservative and sympathetic drives direct the aggressions to animals of a wholly different kind, as in the hunt, or to symbols, as in games or social activities. For purposes of war, however, this normal direction of the aggressions must be modified. The warrior must canalize his aggressions so as to prepare himself for self-sacrifice and for the human hunt.[144]

It may be for this reason that among primitive people the initiation of war usually involves decking the warrior in paint and garments which modify his normal personality. War dances, songs, and fastings subordinate his personality to the mob. Exaggeration of the enemy's unnatural behavior alienates him from all sympathy.[145]

Equally necessary is it to restore the normal personality of the

[141] Hoijer, *op. cit.*, pp. 8 ff.   [142] Wedgewood, *op. cit.*, pp. 9–11.

[143] See Table 10, Appen. IX, and chap. iv, sec. 2.

[144] Freud has briefly expounded his theory of the normal personality as the result of an equilibrium between the aggressive and libidinous instincts in the article "Psychoanalysis," *Encyclopaedia Britannica* (14th ed.).

[145] Marett, *Sacraments*, pp. 59 ff.; Primitive people often employ elaborate war medicines to render the warrior invulnerable and to assure victory (see Hunter, *op. cit.*, pp. 409 ff.).

warrior and other members of the group after the war is over. Thus there are ceremonials of peace which give vivid recognition to the idea that, after all, the former enemies are human beings and that, in spite of their recent offense, the perpetuation of unnatural slaughter is not necessary.[146] Even more significant, in this connection, is the common behavior of sorrow rather than rejoicing displayed by the group toward the returning war party, thus described by Marett:

> The avenging party, conscious of a disagreeable duty faithfully accomplished, might well expect to be greeted with grateful acclamation on its return. On the contrary the women, whose weakness does not, consist in overdoing logic, greet them with a doleful cry, "Why did you kill our friends?" . . . . Nay, so far is it from being a triumphant ending to a dashing adventure, that, until the taboo is lifted, not a word must be said concerning a task that from first to last was sacramental, in that it raised a blind impulse to hit back to the level of a solemn and inspired duty.[147]

As Marett suggests, deception of the ghosts of the slain enemies may be the natives' rationalization of this behavior, but its reason may lie deeper in the human need to restore the normal dominance of sympathy over cruelty among members of the group.

A similar function may be served by the chivalric practice not infrequent among primitive people of insistence upon equal advantage in combat. The warrior will withhold his hand until the enemy is equally armed.[148] Thus the unnatural character of the killing about to take place is veiled by the sympathetic and even noble gesture toward the intended victim. In such performances, however, the gesture is as adverse to the self-preservative impulses of the warrior as it is favorable to his sympathetic impulses, and therefore this chivalry occurs only if the individual has so sublimated himself in the service of his group that the personal risks of his position are not present in his mind. The rules of primitive war do not ordinarily manifest much fairness to the enemy. Attacks are from ambush or at night when the victims are at every disadvantage, and usually, if un-

---

[146] Radcliffe-Brown describes the peace ceremonies among the Andamanese (*Andaman Islanders*, p. 238).

[147] *Sacraments*, pp. 58–59; see also Warner, *op. cit.*, p. 463.

[148] Marett, *Psychology and Folklore*, pp. 40 ff. Sumner and Keller, *op. cit.*, IV, 144. Declarations of war may sometimes have this motive (see Davie, *op. cit.*, pp. 292 ff.).

expected resistance develops, the attackers beat a hasty retreat.[149] The spirit of self-sacrifice stimulated by the war dances and preliminary harangues cannot long hold the self-preservative impulses in check.

Rules of the kind just considered, while contributing to the individual's need to rationalize military behavior, contribute also to the group's need that war shall function in the interest of its solidarity. The maintenance of group solidarity requires that the population of the artificial group be substituted for the population of the natural species as defining an entity to which the disposition of sympathy shall be habitually extended. War is obviously a useful device for this purpose, because, in its practice, it becomes clear to the dullest members of the in-group that they are treating one another with sympathy and other human beings with the utmost brutality. Thus, preparatory ceremonials of war, overtly manifesting the group character of the expedition and the sanction and support extended to the warriors by all members of the group, and also emphasizing the unnatural and despicable behavior and character of the enemy, while orienting the individual's personality to his task, drive home to all members of the group the symbolic significance of the war—the distinctiveness of the group from the rest of the human species.[150] Furthermore, in spite of the lack of acclaim which, among some tribes, immediately greets the returning warrior,[151] in general the

---

[149] See above, n. 113.

[150] Radcliffe-Brown thus states the hypotheses underlying the theory that ceremonial serves the function of maintaining and transmitting sentiments (defined as "organized systems of emotional tendencies centered about some object") deemed necessary to the group: "(1) A society depends for its existence on the presence in the minds of its members of a certain system of sentiments by which the conduct of the individual is regulated in conformity with the needs of the society. (2) Every feature of the social system itself and every event or object that in any way affects the well-being or the cohesion of the society becomes an object of this system of sentiments. (3) In human society the sentiments in question are not innate but are developed in the individual by the action of the society upon him. (4) The ceremonial customs of a society are a means by which the sentiments in question are given collective expression on appropriate occasions. (5) The ceremonial (i.e. collective) expression of any sentiment serves both to maintain it as the requisite degree of intensity in the mind of the individual and to transmit it from one generation to another. Without such expression the sentiments involved could not exist" (*Andaman Islanders*, pp. 233–34). See above, n. 139.

[151] See above, n. 147.

mores of the group extend honors and rewards to him.[152] The virtues essential to tribal solidarity—courage, self-sacrifice, loyalty, obedience, and discipline—are exalted by the war mores;[153] in fact, so successful are these mores in overruling nature that, as we have noticed, most contemporary primitive people can be characterized as warlike.[154] The educational influence of the group has been so potent that to the stranger its members appear "naturally" to have not only the social virtues mentioned but also to be naturally vainglorious and insensible to human suffering. The "savage" who, etymologically, is a "silvaggio" or "woodlander," becomes the symbol of cruelty.[155]

The military mores are, therefore, an effective civic training by which the natural man, timorous for his life and sympathetic to humanity, is converted into a member of a group, courageous in the pursuit of its customs and brutal to the rest of the human race.[156]

The group, however, is never wholly isolated. The borders of its hunting grounds are contiguous to those of other groups in times of peace as well as in times of war. Marriage may take place outside; in fact, it may be necessary under exogamy, which usually characterizes all but the most primitive people. The normal sympathy and curiosity of human beings establish contacts of friendship, exchange of gifts, and economic barter with neighbors. The economic and cultural values of intergroup co-operation are perceived. Consequently, the claims of a larger community embracing the neighboring communities supplement the claims of human sympathy in developing rules of war to minimize both the duration of fighting and its rigor.

---

[152] Hoijer writes: "The career of a warrior is the one most highly regarded and best rewarded in primitive society everywhere" (*op. cit.*, p. 16).

[153] Marett, *Psychology and Folklore*, pp. 36–38.

[154] See Table 10, Appen. IX.

[155] Marett, *Psychology and Folklore*, pp. 30, 41. "Against outsiders it is meritorious to kill, plunder, practice blood revenge, and steal women and slaves, but inside the group none of these things can be allowed" (Davie, *op. cit.*, p. 18).

[156] The animal moral dogma, "Thou shalt love thyself and thy species," is changed into the primitive human dogma formulated by Sir Edward Tylor, "Thou shalt love thy neighbor, and hate thine enemy" (*Contemporary Review*, XXI, 718, quoted by Marett, *Psychology and Folklore*, p. 36).

It is frequently understood that blood relatives,[157] certain diplomatic and religious personalities,[158] certain places, as the sea or the trees,[159] and certain times, as night,[160] are exempt from destructive activities; that poisoned weapons should not be used[161] and that fighting should cease after a certain number of casualties;[162] that peace, once made, should not be broken without cause.[163] Among the more advanced people, women and children or even men captured from the enemy are spared, usually, to be made slaves.[164] The common requirement for pecuniary compensation for casualties and wounds, often paid by the victor to the loser, is a means of securing the peace and of ending feuds.[165] Sometimes the usual rule of a life for a life is carried out by a process of intergroup arbitration by which the tribe whose member is responsible for the original murder turns over to the tribe of the victims one of its less desirable members on which the injured group may wreak vengeance.[166]

These rules are most extensive in the relations of neighboring groups which are normally friendly.[167] They may develop into even more far-reaching rules of peaceful relationship obligatory within alliances by which tribes join forces in war, particularly in wars to end war,[168] or even into rules binding within a permanent federation, by

[157] See above, n. 141; Hoijer, *op. cit.*, pp. 8 ff., 90.

[158] *Ibid.*, p. 93; Wedgewood, *op. cit.*, p. 14; Sumner and Keller, *op. cit.*, IV, 143.

[159] Hoijer, *op. cit.*, p. 89; Wedgewood, *op. cit.*, p. 14.

[160] Wedgewood, *op. cit.*, p. 14.

[161] Sumner and Keller, *op. cit.*, IV, 140.

[162] *Ibid.*, p. 15.

[163] Radcliffe-Brown, *Andaman Islanders*, p. 238; Davie, *op. cit.*, pp. 186–90.

[164] Sumner and Keller, *op. cit.*, IV, 143; Hobhouse, Wheeler, and Ginsburg, *op. cit.*, p. 232.

[165] Marett, *Sacraments*, p. 57; Wedgewood, *op. cit.*, p. 25. Attempts to end Murngin feuds by payment of Wergeld are usually unsuccessful (Warner, *op. cit.*, p. 477).

[166] Warner, *op. cit.*, p. 477. This practice existed among the Arab tribes of Iraq in 1926 (see Q. Wright, "The Government of Iraq," *American Political Science Review*, XX [November, 1926], 765).

[167] Wedgewood, *op. cit.*, pp. 9–10.

[168] *Ibid.*, pp. 21 ff.; see also below, n. 173. Such wars occur no more than once a decade among the Murngin and are called "gaingar" (Warner, *op. cit.*, p. 473).

which the original sovereign groups gradually become units in a larger sovereign group.[169] Outside of this circle there may be sworn or habitual enemies with which there is no peace and few limits to the rigors of war.[170] Where head-hunting is an important part of the mores, the maintenance of peace even among neighbors is difficult to achieve. Intergroup retaliation, feuds, and war are practically continuous.[171]

Primitive international law is therefore at best rudimentary and lacking in universality. The comity of the intergroup community is less important in determining war practices than is the custom of the particular group or the demand of human nature. Taken as a whole, however, illustration can be found in the war practices of primitive peoples of the various types of international rules of war known at the present time: rules distinguishing types of enemies; rules defining the circumstances, formalities, and authority for beginning and ending war; rules describing limitations of persons, time, place, and methods of its conduct; and even rules outlawing war altogether.[172] Wars to end war, which sometimes occur in Australia after minor wars have become abnormally frequent and destructive, usually are so destructive and exhausting, sometimes resulting in losses to each of the federated groups of belligerents of as many as a dozen or two men, that the peace outlawing war which follows is observed for a considerable period.[173]

Primitive warfare was an important factor in developing civilization. It cultivated the virtues of courage, loyalty, and obedience; it

[169] The Union of the Six Nations of the Iroquois were such a federation.

[170] Wedgewood, *op. cit.*, pp. 13 ff.

[171] Hoijer, *op. cit.*, pp. 18 ff., 33 ff.; Perry, *op. cit.*, pp. 4 ff.; Davie, *op. cit.*, p. 252. The Indians of eastern United States waged war for status within the group with the result that it was "insane, unending, continuously attritional, from our point of view and yet it was so integrated into the whole fabric of eastern culture, so dominantly emphasized within it, that escape from it was well nigh impossible" (Kroeber, *op. cit.*, p. 10).

[172] See W. B. Ballis, *The Legal Position of War: Changes in Its Practice and Theory from Plato to Vattel* (The Hague, 1937).

[173] A. R. Radcliffe-Brown has drawn the writer's attention to this practice. See also n. 168 above.

created solid groups and a method for enlarging the area of these groups, all of which were indispensable to the creation of the civilizations which followed. It must, however, be emphasized that primitive warfare was very different from warfare in historic civilization and differed even more from contemporary warfare among the advanced peoples. Recognition of the progressive tendencies of primitive war (assuming that the movement from savagery to civilization is progress), does not imply that warfare at later stages is progressive. As primitive society developed toward civilization, war began to take on a different character. Civilization was both an effect and a cause of warlikeness. The custom of war provided a basis for wider aggregation and more secure defense. The rise of wider aggregation and division of labor, division of ruler and ruled, created conditions favorable for the development of war in the interests of the ruling class. The value of war in developing social virtues and social organization was more and more offset by its evils in eliminating human sympathy, in preventing co-operation beyond the warmaking group, and in increasing destructiveness; but, on the whole, among primitive people its advantages for progress outweighed its disadvantages. Marett writes:

It is a commonplace of anthropology that at a certain stage of evolution—the half-way stage, so to speak—war is a prime civilizing agency; in fact, that, as Bagehot puts it, "Civilization begins, because the beginning of civilization is a military advantage." The reason is not far to seek. "The compact tribes win," says Bagehot. Or, as Spencer more elaborately explains, "from the very beginning, the conquest of one people over another has been, in the main, the conquest of the social man over the anti-social man."[174]

With primitive groups as with animal species, the survival value of war utilization has varied with the particular situation of the group or species; but with animals, on the whole, adaptations based upon peace and co-operation have proved more favorable to multiplication of the type than adaptations based upon predation and parasitism.[175]

Among primitive people, on the other hand, the warlike groups

[174] *Psychology and Folklore*, pp. 36–37; see above, n. 62.
[175] See above, chap. v, sec. 2.

have multiplied both in individual and in type. The peaceful groups could not organize to a size sufficient for extensive division of labor without the military virtues and the sense of group solidarity created by the fear of an external enemy, and they could not protect wealth, herds, or agricultural lands from warlike neighbors unless they institutionalized war themselves. Out of the warlike peoples arose civilization, while the peaceful collectors and hunters were driven to the ends of the earth, where they are gradually being exterminated or absorbed, with only the dubious satisfaction of observing the nations which had wielded war so effectively to destroy them and to become great, now victimized by their own instrument.

CHAPTER VII

HISTORIC WARFARE

FROM the first organisms of archaic times to the nationally and internationally organized human race of today, history has been a seamless web; but, in studying the role of warfare in this history, it is convenient to recognize three great transitions when certain inventions initiated such rapid, cumulative changes that the resulting condition constituted a new emergence.[1] These were the transitions from animals to man, from primitive culture to civilization, and from civilization to a world-order.

The study of animal and primitive warfare throws light on the function of conflict in a living system and on the nature of the drives toward lethal conflict among the entities which compose this system. Only indirectly or by analogy do these studies aid in understanding the influence of changing military techniques and of changing theories or rationalizations upon the incidence and character of contemporary war.

A study of historic war, by which is meant warfare within or between the literate civilizations from Egypt and Mesopotamia down to the age of discovery in the fifteenth century—a span of over six thousand years—may give a more direct understanding of these latter influences.

Efforts have been made to tabulate the military events of history and to study their trends and fluctuations over long periods of time.[2]

---

[1] See chap. iv, n. 22.

[2] See F. A. Woods and A. Baltzly, *Is War Diminishing? A Study of Europe from 1450 to the Present Day* (Boston, 1915); Gaston Bodart, *Militar-historisches Kriegslexicon (1618–1905)* (Leipzig, 1908); J. S. Lee, "The Periodic Recurrence of Internecine Wars in China," *China Journal of Science and Arts*, XIV (March and April, 1931), 111–15, 159–63; Pitirim Sorokin, "Indices of the Movements of War in the History of Ancient Greece, the Western Roman Empire and Eight Other European Countries from 500 B.C. to 1925 A.D.," a résumé presented to American Association for the Advancement of Science, December, 1933, and printed in *Social and Cultural Dynamics* (3 vols.; New York, 1937), III, 543 ff.; James C. King, "The Periodicity of War, 1625–1925" (manuscript for Causes of War Study, University of Chicago, 1934).

These efforts, however, have not been particularly rewarding for a number of reasons.

The historic record is, except for the most recent times, extremely fragmentary. A fair record is available of the wars of Western Europe and of the Classical Mediterranean civilization since the fifth century B.C., but for an adequate statistical base the wars of the Egyptian, Mesopotamian, Syriac, Indian, Chinese, Mayan, and other civilizations should be available for comparison. Much of this material exists, but it has not as yet been made easily usable for any but specialized historians. Furthermore, even when records of the battles and wars exist, data as to the number of participants and casualties are unreliable.[3]

Furthermore, no class of military incidents has the same significance in all periods of history. The battle has been the most persistent type of military incident. It has meant a concentrated military operation between armed forces on a limited terrain for a limited time, usually a day or less. At some periods, however, battles have been isolated events from which flowed important political consequences. At other times a battle has been but an incident in a campaign consisting of complicated strategic operations over a season or in a siege or maritime blockade. In such circumstances political consequences cannot be attributed to the single battle but only to the whole campaign. Campaigns themselves have sometimes been but incidents in a war waged on many fronts with a number of distinct armies over a series of years. Neither the battle, the campaign, nor the war is entirely satisfactory as a unit for statistical tabulation.

It is difficult to rate the relative importance of any of these incidents. Sir Edward Creasy's *Fifteen Decisive Battles of History*[4] suggests the danger of any objective scheme of rating, such, for instance, as duration, number of men engaged, number of casualties, etc., em-

---

[3] Commenting on Herodotus' statement (vii. 186) that the Persian army had 5,283,-220 men, Hans Delbrück (*Geschichte der Kriegskunst* [6 vols.; Berlin, 1900–1929], I, 10) calculates that its tail would have been at Susa beyond the Tigris when its head was engaged at Thermopylae (see O. L. Spaulding, H. Nickerson, and J. W. Wright, *Warfare: A Study of Military Methods from the Earliest Times* [London, 1924], p. 33; see also Samuel Dumas and K. O. Vedel-Petersen, *Losses of Life Caused by War* [Oxford, 1923], pp. 21 ff.).

[4] 1st ed.; London, 1851.

phasized by Bodart, by Wood, and by Sorokin.[5] Creasy's list contains Joan of Arc's victory at Orléans and the French Revolutionary Battle of Valmy, in each of which the casualties were only a few hundred, as well as Marathon, Syracuse, the destruction of the Armada, and Saratoga, where they were only a few thousand. In the rest of his battles—Arbela, Metaurus, Arminius' victory over Varus, Châlons, Tours, Hastings, Blenheim, Pultova, and Waterloo—the casualties reached tens of thousands, but he included none of the bloodiest battles with casualties asserted to reach hundreds of thousands in ancient, medieval, and modern history.[6] Creasy's rating was based on a subjective judgment of the political and social consequences of the battle, a sort of criteria unsuitable for a general statistical study of military incidents.

Military events have varied greatly with respect to the purposes and nature of the combatants. Should one place in the same category civil wars between factions in the same state, international wars between states of the same civilization, and imperial wars between groups from different civilizations? Should the objectives (wars, interventions, reprisals), the legal characteristics (just or unjust, formal or informal), and the technical characteristics (battles, sieges, naval battles, blockades) of military events be distinguished?

Finally, what time and space limitations should be adopted in a statistical tabulation of military incidents? The data are lacking for a single tabulation of all battles or wars between civilized peoples since civilization began, and it is doubtful whether a tabulation which lumped together Egyptian, Mesopotamian, Chinese, Indian, and Mayan wars would be illuminating. If there are regular trends or fluctuations of war and peace, it seems probable that they are relative to groups of people in more or less continuous contact with one another, i.e., to a civilization.

I. NATURE OF CIVILIZATION

Arnold J. Toynbee has set forth cogent reasons for considering a civilization rather than a state, a nation, a population, or a race as the unit about which a history may best be written.[7] He has identi-

---

[5] Above, n. 2.

[6] See Figs. 1, 2, and 8.   [7] A Study of History (3 vols.; Oxford, 1934).

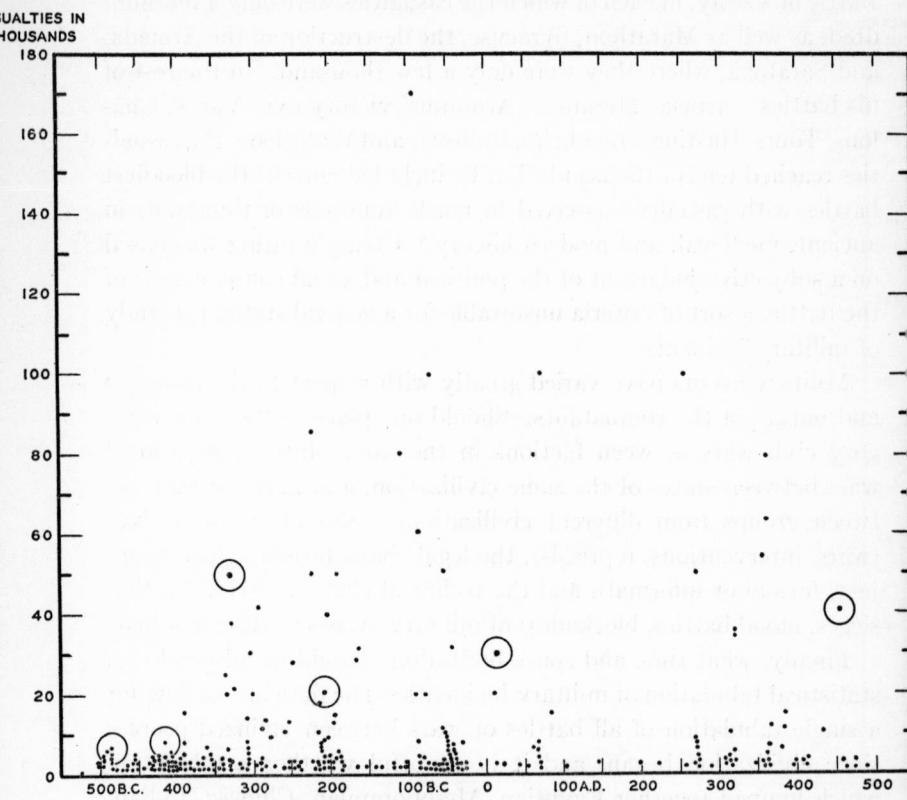

FIG. 1.—Dates and casualties of battles of Classic civilization, 550 B.C.–A.D. 500. The data are from Thomas B. Harbottle, *Dictionary of Battles from the Earliest Date to the Present Time* (London, 1904). The circles indicate the battles listed by Edward Creasy, *The Fifteen Decisive Battles of the World* (London, 1851).

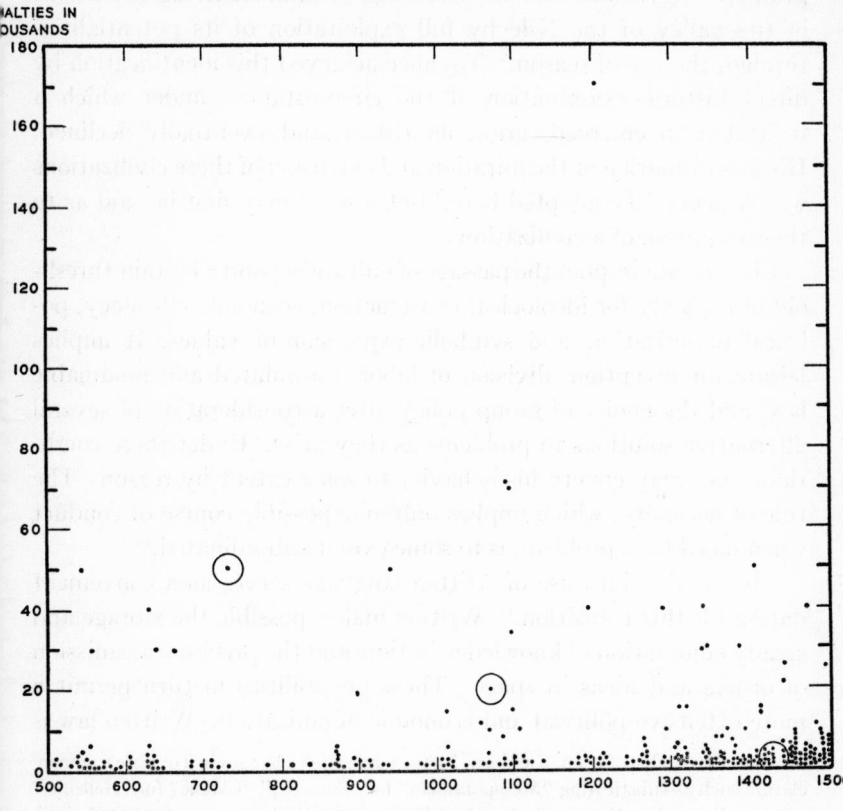

FIG. 2.—Dates and casualties of battles of Western civilization, A.D. 500–1500.
Data from Harbottle, *op. cit.* The circles indicate the battles listed by Creasy, *op. cit.*

fied twenty-one civilizations which developed to maturity and five others which failed to do so. The earliest civilization began when primitive Egyptians met the challenge of difficult living conditions in the valley of the Nile by full exploitation of its potentialities through the use of reason.[8] Toynbee achieved this identification by direct historic examination of the circumstances under which a fruitful faith emerged, grew, flourished, and eventually declined. His determination of the duration and extension of these civilizations will in general be adopted here,[9] but a word may first be said as to the conception of a civilization.

Civilization implies the passage of culture beyond a certain threshold of capacity for ideological construction, economic efficiency, political organization, and symbolic expression of values. It implies leisure for invention, division of labor, formulated and modifiable law, and the choice of group policy after a consideration of several alternative solutions to problems as they arise. Under these conditions man may govern his behavior to some extent by reason. The rule of necessity, which implies only one possible course of conduct when faced by a problem, is to some extent subordinated.[10]

The coming into use of written language serves as a convenient dating for this transition.[11] Writing makes possible the storage and steady cumulation of knowledge in time and the precise transmission of orders and ideas in space. These possibilities in turn permit a more extensive political and economic organization. Written law is

[8] See above, chap. iv, nn. 9 and 25. I have made a few changes in Toynbee's nomenclature such as substituting "Mesopotamian" for "Sumeric," "Classic" for "Hellenic," "Chinese" for "Far Eastern." Toynbee discusses the Eskimos as an "arrested civilization," though they would usually be considered a primitive people. Toynbee does not include in his list the Germanic or Germano-Gallic civilization with the distinctive Hallstatt and La Tène cultures, during the first millennium B.C., and utilizing writing during the later period. A. de Gobineau (L'Inegalité des races humaines [Paris, 1853], I, 362–65) identifies ten civilizations.

[9] See Appen. V, Figs. 12 and 13, for duration and extension of civilizations.

[10] See Toynbee, op. cit., I, 147, III, 243 ff. "The idea of progress, of development, appears to me the fundamental idea contained in the word civilization" (F. P. G. Guizot, The History of Civilization in Europe [1828], trans. William Hazlitt [New York, n.d.], p. 11). Clark Wissler thinks primitive and higher culture can only be distinguished by the degree of complexity and richness of content of cultural complexes (Man and Culture [New York, 1923], p. 78).

[11] See chap. iv, nn. 9 and 25.

more precise and uniform in time and space than customary law, but it also is more susceptible to change by conscious legislation. Thus its use makes possible the transition from customary to progressive culture. A particular group may not for a long time avail itself of the opportunities which writing gives it, but the potentiality is there. Challenges will in time be presented by the physical or social environment, and, if the response utilizes the advantages of writing, civilization may be realized.

A civilization does not, necessarily, imply general literacy of the population but only that writing is available to the group and has enabled it to pass the cultural threshold, above which major group decisions are frequently the result of rational weighing of alternatives in the light of steadily cumulating knowledge and below which such decisions are usually the result of unreflecting obedience to the mores. Choice of alternatives implies reference to fundamental values, either as articulate or as inarticulate major premises in every act of choice. Primitive cultures also have such values, but they are merely the principles implicit in the concrete mores themselves and are, consequently, incapable of serving to improve the mores. When the mores are observed, the values are achieved. In civilization the fundamental values are subjective aspirations, above particular rules or rituals, and so able to serve as criteria for changing the latter.

How are different civilizations to be distinguished from one another in time and space? Historians commonly speak of Egyptian, Mesopotamian, Chinese, Classical, and Western civilization, but few have developed criteria by which the birth and death of a civilization can be dated and its geographical boundaries at any time marked on a map.[12]

The problem is obviously more difficult than that of distinguishing primitive peoples from one another. While anthropologists differ in some cases, there is an approach to agreement upon the geographical limits and linguistic, racial, sociological, and cultural characteristics of most of the thousand-odd primitive peoples which exist today.[13]

---

[12] See Toynbee, *op. cit.*, I, 26 ff.

[13] See chap. vi, sec. 1. As a culture area is really only the center of distribution of particular traits which fade out on the periphery and mingle with foreign traits, there is room for difference of opinion even here (Wissler, *op. cit.*, p. 62).

Furthermore, the date, if not of the birth, at least of the death of
several such peoples which have ceased to exist, as the Tasmanians
and the Natchez Indians, can be precisely stated.[14]

The members of a civilization may at a given time belong to a
variety of races, speak a variety of languages, and participate in a
variety of political, economic, social, and cultural institutions and
values. The very progressiveness, implicit in the definition of a civilization, means that its laws, techniques, and institutions are undergoing continuous change in time. These changes do not necessarily
affect the whole civilization simultaneously. Furthermore, a civilization is capable of expanding much more rapidly than is a primitive
people. The latter expands by natural growth of its population, by
the gradual interpenetration of adjacent cultures, and, to a limited
extent, among the higher primitive people, by conquest and cultural
imposition. A civilization, on the other hand, may spread very rapidly in a disintegrating culture through the sowing of seeds by a few
traders, missionaries, soldiers, or writers.[15] In a dozen years Alexander Hellenized much of Asia, and in a similar time Caesar Roman-
ized much of Gaul.

Each civilization is distinguished by a unique complex of fundamental values in which its members believe and which to some extent
guides their choices. Usually this belief is manifested by the general
acceptance of a religion, but sometimes the forms of the same religion
conceal fundamental differences in the substance of the values it
supports in different areas of its realm. On the other hand, two formally different religions may be so similar in substance that they
constitute but one civilization. The extremely subjective character
of the criteria which set the limits to a civilization has been noted by
Spengler, Toynbee, Wissler, Sorokin, and others who have dealt with
the subject.[16] It is difficult to assemble precise evidence of the real

[14] See J. A. Swanton, *Indian Tribes of the Lower Mississippi* (Smithsonian Bull. 43),
pp. 193 ff. The date of the death of some civilized speech communities can be stated, as
Cornish speakers in 1777 and Dalmatian speakers in 1898 (see H. Pedersen, *Linguistic
Science in the Nineteenth Century* [Cambridge, Mass., 1931], pp. 55, 93).

[15] Wissler (*op. cit.*, pp. 176 ff.) thinks conquest more often follows than causes spread
of culture.

[16] See Toynbee, *op. cit.* Oswald Spengler (*The Decline of the West*) distinguishes the
civilizations of antiquity, the Orient, and the modern world by their respective posses-

beliefs of individuals. Furthermore, such beliefs may change rapidly. Thus the limits of a civilization will always be vague and founded upon historic judgment, buttressed by a variety of evidences, not upon a limited number of precise criteria.

Among the usable evidences for determining the geographical limits of a civilization are barriers to the freedom and frequency of personal movements and of intermarriage, barriers to trade and the transmission of economic techniques, barriers to the spread of religious and scientific information and propaganda, and barriers to political recognition and diplomatic intercourse. Within an area where there are few such barriers there is usually a single civilization. Clearly, however, the barriers may be at different points in

sion of the "Appolonian," "Magian," and "Faustian" spirits. Guizot thinks that a civilization may be studied from "the heart of the human mind" or "in the midst of the world" (*op. cit.*, Lecture I, pp. 20–21), but he actually distinguishes civilizations— Egyptian, Syrian, Indian, Phoenician, Ionian, Greek, Roman, Western, etc.—by their "principles" (Lecture II, p. 26). "It is a core of ideas and beliefs, actuating a people and in a large measure controlling their career, that forms the backbone, or at least the unifying element, in the culture-complex" (Wissler, *op. cit.*, p. 3). That distinctive attitudes have characterized and differentiated the civilizations is not denied by the "environmentalists" and "economic interpreters" who emphasize the importance of a distinctive topography, climate, flora, fauna, or other types of economic resource in creating those attitudes (see E. Huntington, *Civilization and Climate* [New Haven, 1915]; G. Taylor, *Environment and Nature* [Chicago, 1936]; N. I. Vavilov, "Asia, Source of Species," *Asia*, February, 1937; see also below, nn. 28 and 33). Lewis Mumford, like Karl Marx (*Capital* [London, 1902], Vol. I, chap. xv), gives due weight to the influence of technology upon culture and disparages both the Spenglerian "absolute isolationism" which conceives each civilization as an evolution of basic ideas and Elliot Smith's "unconscious imperialism" which conceives all civilizations as the consequence of diffusion from a single source (*Technics and Civilization* [New York, 1934], pp. 108, 470; see also below, Appen. V). Elsewhere Mumford emphasizes the influence of ideals (*The Story of Utopias* [New York, 1922]). Sorokin (*Social and Cultural Dynamics*) denies that all cultures have a "functional" unity (I, 41 ff.). Some may be mere spatial congeries of accumulated traits, others may be unified by such external influences as climate, geography, vegetation, others may manifest a causal or functional relation between the various elements, but in the most advanced cultures or civilizations every trait is logically related to and acquires meaning from the "central principle" of the civilization (I, 32). He does not, however, attempt to state the central principles of the various civilizations but to measure through time the relative role of the "ideational" and "sensate" principle in the arts, philosophies, and social relationships of each civilization, apparently assuming that the civilization is distinguished by this profile of its life-history. He deals especially with the Greco-Roman and Western civilizations but pays some attention to the Egyptian, Babylonian, Hindu, Chinese, and Arabic civilizations.

different fields of human activity. The area continuously affected
from a given center by travelers and migrants may be different from
the area affected by trade and economic techniques proceeding from
that center. Again the area affected by cultural influences and by
political controls may be broader or narrower. Furthermore, the
efficiency of barriers to various forms of contact changes in time.
At any time the efficiency of a barrier is not absolute but relative.[17]

Determination of the beginning and end of a civilization is even
more difficult because a civilization is always changing. There is
seldom any complete breach in the continuity of a population, although the population density of a region does usually increase with
the rise of a civilization and decline with its disintegration.[18] The
problem is one of determining when the disintegration of one body of
beliefs and acceptance of another has been so rapid as to constitute a
relative cultural discontinuity. The historic accompaniments of the
transition from one civilization to another have often been described
—political and social disintegration, decline in production and trade,
famine, pestilence, and decline in population, invasion, conquest, and
large-scale migrations.[19]

While one civilization is disintegrating, however, the germs of a
new civilization may be developing within the same area, and the
process of coexistence and compromise may go on for a considerable
time until eventually the new one triumphs—a process illustrated by
the growth of Teutonic Christianity, which eventually became Western European civilization, within the Roman Empire.[20] Doubtless

---

[17] See Appen. V.   [18] See Fig. 15, Appen. V.

[19] See G. H. Perris, *A Short History of War and Peace* (New York, 1911), pp. 104 ff.;
Toynbee, *op. cit.*, Vol. I, sec. 1.

[20] Gibbon wrote in the final chapter of *The Decline and Fall of the Roman Empire* that
he had "described the triumph of barbarism and religion" over civilization (Vol. VI,
chap. lxxi). A historian a thousand years hence might describe the sixteenth to the
twenty-first centuries as the triumph of nationalism and science over civilization (Ferdinand Schevill in W. H. C. Laves [ed.], *The Foundations of a More Stable World Order*
[Chicago, 1941]). This attitude is taken somewhat by Carlton J. H. Hayes (*The Historical Evolution of Nationalism* [New York, 1931]) and Ralph Adams Cram (*The Substance
of Gothic* [Boston, 1917]). The Renaissance to the present has marked the gradual transition to world-civilization, first in Europe and then in other parts of the world (below,
n. 23). Sorokin attempts to distinguish all civilizations mainly by the proportion of
"sensate" and "ideational" elements in their arts, philosophies, and institutions. These
two elements rise and fall like the themes of a fugue, the transitional periods being

there have been many incipient civilizations which did not triumph but were destroyed by or integrated in the dominant civilization within which they were born. Toynbee regards far eastern or Nestorian Christianity and far western or Irish Christianity as illustrations of such abortive civilizations.[21]

If a civilization differs from a primitive culture in being characterized by more subjective criteria, it differs from a nationality in being less self-conscious. As the anthropologist distinguishes one primitive people from another by observation of individual and group characteristics and behaviors, so the historian distinguishes one civilization from another by study of the records giving evidence of individual and group attitudes. A Greek or Roman of the third century B.C. was hardly aware of the entity which the modern historian calls Classical civilization. He was aware of his city, or of a portion of the civilization, such as the Greek cities participating in the Olympic games or the Amphyctionic council, but he was not aware of Classical civilization as a whole until a later stage of its development, when it was politically integrated in the Roman Empire.

A nation, on the other hand, exists not as a discovery of science or history but as a dynamic symbol in the minds of its members. For this reason, a nation becomes integrated into a single state much more rapidly than does a civilization. The existence of a nation is therefore dependent upon continuous and general communication throughout a considerable population—a condition seldom fulfilled until the rise of democratic institutions, general literacy, and vernacular literature in the modern period, particularly in the nineteenth century.[22]

There is ground for saying that in the contemporary world there is only one civilization—the civilization of humanism, liberalism, scientific method, and relativism formed, after the invention of printing, the Renaissance, the discoveries and the reformation, from a blend of Western, Classical, Syriac, Arabic and other civilizations.

---

marked by the dominance of neither (*Social and Cultural Dynamics*, I, Part I, esp. 190, and above n. 16; below, Fig. 31, Appen. XVII).

   [21] *Op. cit.*

   [22] J. C. King, "Some Elements of National Solidarity" (manuscript, University of Chicago, 1933).

This civilization has gradually destroyed, or incorporated with some adaptations, the civilizations of America, the Far East, India, and Islam, adapting itself to this digestive feat by differentiation into a hundred distinctive nationalities. It is, of course, true that the ghosts of several old civilizations still mediate between the nations and the world-community, but these ghosts are in process of evaporation.[23]

2. HISTORY OF CIVILIZATION

There has been a transition in something over six thousand years from a world divided into thousands of distinctive, isolated, and relatively unchanging primitive peoples to a community comprising the entire human race, grouped into a hundred self-conscious nationalities, most of which are organized into states, and a rapidly diminishing fringe of primitive peoples on the outskirts. This is the field of history in the narrow sense of the term. The momentous changes which history records are related both to the succession of civilizations and to the life-history of particular civilizations.

a) *Succession of civilizations.*—The twenty-six completed, abortive, and arrested civilizations include ten primary civilizations which arose in relatively isolated parts of the world among primitive peoples from the fourth to the second millennium B.C., eight secondary civilizations each of which grew out of one or more primary civilizations from the second millennium B.C. to the first millennium A.D., and eight tertiary civilizations which have grown out of the secondary civilizations in the last fifteen hundred years. The accompanying diagram[24] dates these civilizations from the time they became sufficiently distinctive to figure in history to the time they disintegrated, were absorbed by another civilization, or came into continuous contact with the contemporary world-civilization. From

[23] Toynbee believes that while there is a world-wide economic and political system there is not a world-wide civilization today but at least five distinctive civilizations (*op. cit.*, I, 150 ff.).

[24] Fig. 12, Appen. V. "In all history and prehistory in Europe there have been only two great crashes and two periods of retrogression. The first in the Aegean (1500–1200 B.C.), the second involved the whole ancient world (400–700 A.D.)" (Stanley Casson, "Progress and Catastrophe," *Harper's Magazine*, February, 1936, p. 327). It will be noted that these periods conform in the main to the transitions from primary to secondary and from secondary to tertiary civilizations in the Near East and the Mediterranean.

the diagram, from a mapping of the approximate area of each civilization at its maximum,[25] and from general historical information, it appears that the civilizations in these three successive groups have tended to become shorter lived, broader in area, less homogeneous, more progressive, more in contact with one another, and separated from one another less by physical barriers than by artificial or social barriers.[26]

This is but to say that the primary civilizations had many of the characteristics of primitive peoples—cultural homogeneity, a long, relatively isolated, and unchanging life in an area narrowly restricted by natural barriers.[27] The tertiary civilizations, on the other hand, have had many of the characteristics of the contemporary world-

[25] Fig. 13, Appen. V.

[26] The extreme contrast can be seen by comparing the long-lived, confined, isolated, homogeneous, and stable Egypt with the short-lived, expansive, crusading, heterogeneous, and dynamic Europe of the Middle Ages. A similar shortening of the distinctive periods of art is indicated by the chart of "Periods of Art" from 6000 B.C. to A.D. 1900 printed in the *Encyclopaedia Britannica* (14th ed.), XVII, 522–26. The chart indicating the connections in the arts of the different civilizations of the Eastern Hemisphere, and the tendency for art to develop synchronously in these separate civilizations, even in the earliest times, contains a warning against too easy an assumption of the isolation of the early civilizations (see also *Independence, Convergence, and Borrowing* ["Harvard Tercentenary Publications" (Cambridge, Mass., 1937)]). The continuity of the direction of change through successive civilizations, toward the conquest of geographic barriers and of social inertia, has induced many to envisage history from primitive man to the present as an evolution or progress, only temporarily halted by occasional catastrophes. To them there has been not many but one civilization. The steps in the achievement of civilization, from this point of view, have been the inventions and discoveries in science and technology. Man has progressed through rough and smooth stone ages, through bronze, copper, and iron ages, through eo-, paleo-, and neotechnic ages, each an improvement on its predecessor (H. G. Wells, *The Outline of History* [New York, 1920]; George Sarton, *Introduction to the History of Science* [Washington, 1927–31]). Lewis Mumford (*Technics and Civilization*), while emphasizing the continuous progress of techniques, is not certain that this progress has continuously advanced society (see above, chap. iii, n. 11, and below, Appen. V).

[27] Clark Wissler states that primitive communities seldom live over five hundred or a thousand years (*An Introduction to Social Anthropology* [New York, 1929], p. 38). Toynbee (*op. cit.*, I, 147) also suggests that primitive groups are normally short lived. Wissler and Toynbee may have drawn their conclusions from observation of primitive people in contact with civilization. Studies of kitchen middens suggest that, before such contacts, primitive people may have normally continued with little change for tens of thousands of years. This opinion was expressed to me by Lloyd Warner, from his study of northern Australian peoples.

civilization—broad area, cultural heterogeneity, frequent changes, some of them so radical that they might be considered the end of one and the beginning of a new civilization. It may be added that certain of these tertiary civilizations such as the Irish, Scandinavian, and Nestorian did not establish themselves in very wide areas and perhaps could be regarded as nationalities of the Western Christian civilization rather than as distinct civilizations.

b) History of a civilization.—Many theories have been offered to explain the rise and fall of civilizations. Some regard this phenomena as a consequence of climatic pulsations. A stimulating climate develops civilization, and change to a depressing climate causes civilization to collapse.[28] The influence of malaria, plague, and other diseases in suddenly reducing population and demoralizing society has also been suggested as a cause for the decline of civilization.[29]

Others have suggested that racial mixture resulting from immigration or conquest produces a stimulus both biological and cultural, which eventually wears off as the two races become assimilated. Stagnation and decay follow.[30] Others emphasize the conflict-producing effect of mixture of very different races and the peaceful influence of an approximation to race purity.[31] Somewhat similar is the theory which emphasizes the challenge resulting from rapid population growth upon a biologically fertile people—a characteristic which the upper levels of the society lose with the enervating influence of luxury produced by the rising civilization itself. This progressive infertility of the upper classes gradually penetrates down, unless there

---

[28] Ellsworth Huntington, *World Power and Evolution* (New Haven, 1919), chap. xi; *Civilization and Climate.* Toynbee gives a good account of the relation of climatic change to invasions from the nomads (*op. cit.*, III, 404 ff.). See maps illustrating similarity of climatic optima and height of civilization (below, Figs. 16 and 17, Appen. V). But compare Wissler's map of the diffusion of "Western European Civilization" (below, Fig. 18, Appen. V) as a warning that Huntington's measure of the height of civilization may give too much weight to the Western conception of "civilization."

[29] Hans Zinzer, *Rats, Lice and History* (Boston, 1935); W. H. S. Jones, *Malaria: A Factor in the Decline of Greece and Rome* (London, 1909).

[30] W. M. Flinders-Petrie, *The Revolutions of Civilization* (3d ed.; London, 1922).

[31] G. T. Wrench, *The Causes of War and Peace* (London, 1926), pp. 14–15.

is a steady influx of migration of a younger race at the lower levels, and the civilization collapses.[32]

Others think the opportunities of abundant nature, to an energetic migrant group, for leisure and opportunity to invent, to discover, and to develop agriculture and industry brings the growth of civilization.[33] Presently, however, the growth of population exceeds the capacity of the economic techniques to provide. The primitive checks upon population growth—infanticide, abortion, and prolonged lactation—have been forgotten, with the result that famine, pestilence, and war occur; population declines; social disintegration and collapse proceed.[34] Others emphasize the social, economic, and political degeneracy arising from the advance of civilization itself in increasing centralization and augmenting wealth and leisure, on the one hand, poverty and pauperism, on the other, creating class differences and fomenting dissipation, degeneracy, discontent, and civil strife.[35] Some emphasize particularly the corrupting influence of

[32] Corrado Gini, "The Cyclical Rise and Fall of Population," in *Population* ("Harris Foundation Lectures" [Chicago, 1930]); J. R. Seeley, *Roman Imperialism* (Boston, 1871), pp. 54 ff.

[33] Morris Halperin ("Cereals and Civilization," *Scientific Monthly*, April, 1936, p. 355), Vavilov (*op. cit.*, p. 113), and many others emphasize the importance of agriculture to civilization. See Vavilov's work indicating the areas in which the leading cultivated plants were developed and compare with map indicating the areas occupied by the civilization (E. D. Merrill, "Plants and Civilization," in *Independence, Convergence, and Borrowing*, p. 22; see below, Figs. 13 and 14, Appen. V). F. Müller-Lyer (*The History of Social Development* [New York, 1921], p. 345) suggests that leisure to think rather than necessity is the mother of invention and progress, a hypothesis given some support by J. Rossman's study of *The Psychology of the Inventor* (Washington, 1931), p. 40. Rossman points out, however, that formulation of a social need is usually the first step in inventions (p. 57) and that favorable social conditions are more important than individual genius in accounting for inventions (p. 3). See also S. C. Gilfillan, *The Sociology of Invention* (Chicago, 1937), pp. 60, 67; Mumford, *Technics and Civilization*, chap. i.

[34] R. Malthus (*An Essay on the Principle of Population* [1st ed., 1798]) implies this. See also V. G. Simkovitch, "Hay and History," *Political Science Quarterly*, XXVIII (1913), 385; "Rome's Fall Reconsidered," *ibid.*, Vol. XXXI (June, 1916).

[35] G. Ferrero, *The Ruin of the Ancient Civilization and the Triumph of Christianity* (New York, 1921); Brooks Adams, *The Law of Civilization and Decay* (New York, 1896).

new ideas on the decline of a civilization;[36] others emphasize the disintegrating effect of war and militarism.[37]

Again there are those who think that no one physical, biological, or social cause applicable to all civilizations is to be expected. They search for the explanation of the rise and fall of particular civilizations in historical incidents, accidents, and contingencies. At times success in foreign wars, wise social experiment, and a series of good crops may advance civilization; while at times invasion, civil war, bad crops, and unwise legislation may cause it to decline. In time a prolonged conjunction of unfavorable conditions is almost certain to occur sufficient to destroy the civilization altogether.[38]

Probably there is some truth in all these theories, inconsistent as certain of them appear to be. All of them emphasize the stimulating influence of challenge and response arising from a conflict situation in the more or less intimate relations of individuals. They also generally emphasize the demoralizing influence of too complete an adaptation.[39] The tendency toward a certain regularity in the rise and

[36] Gibbon implied that as barbarism and Christianity had triumphed, Roman civilization had declined (above, n. 20).

[37] "Improvement in military technique is usually, if not invariably, the symptom of a decline in civilization" (Toynbee, op. cit., III, 167; see also ibid., p. 145). Wissler believes the power of militarism has been overrated. "Ultimately strife and blood will come again, with dissolution into smaller units, only to begin the long tragic struggle all over again" (Man and Culture, p. 180). "The war system was doubly injurious to the arts of peace, both in the robbery of enemies and in crushing out by wholesale competition the honest industries at home. This was the fundamental weakness of antique society, and ultimately was responsible, more than any other factor, for its downfall" (James T. Shotwell, War as an Instrument of National Policy [New York, 1929], p. 11).

[38] "I hold myself that history is quite as much cataclysmic as evolutionary; that it is not a mere logical stream of events, but a series of happenings, affected in the most inscrutable fashion by incalculable things—natural phenomena, the appearance of outstanding human personalities, new inventions and discoveries, not unfrequently by a mere chance of war" (Sir Charles Oman, "A Defence of Military History," in Aston, The Study of War [London, 1927], pp. 27–28). Historians like Gibbon, Ferrero, and Toynbee, though each emphasizes the influence of a favorite type of phenomena, usually have this point of view. See a summary of various philosophies of history in Frederick Adams Woods, The Influence of Monarchs (New York, 1913), pp. 16–18.

[39] Toynbee emphasizes this point of view. It is clear that the continuous existence of a stimulating climate, a superior race (even if such races exist as asserted by Gobineau, Madison Grant, Hitler, et al.), or abundant resources cannot per se account for the continuous development of civilization. There must be changes of such conditions or con-

fall of civilizations suggests that the process, in part at least, is inherent in the nature of civilization and is not entirely dependent upon external physical changes, upon biological changes, or upon historical accidents.

It does not appear, however, that civilizations have had a normal life-span similar to the three score and ten allotted to man. They have ranged in life from over four thousand years to a few hundred, although the shorter lived, such as the Irish, Nestorian, Aztec, and Yucatec civilizations, appear to have been cut off young by conquest. The tendency for the average life, even of those dying a natural death, to shorten as history has advanced, suggests that no regular climatic pulsation has been mainly responsible. There may, however, have been a normal life-span for civilizations existing at the same period due to the tempo of social change at a given technological level—a span which has shortened as civilizations have succeeded each other with the cumulative growth of science and technology.[40]

There is evidence of a tendency for a civilization to progress through four typical stages. (1) A civilization begins with a new social ideal created in response to a challenge of adverse environment, invasion, or civil war. The struggle of this ideal with the *status quo* creates a *heroic age* of travel and migration, bold experiment, daring leadership, artistic, religious, and military enthusiasm. (2) Conflicts among the many movements started in this period leads to a *time of trouble* full of civil dissension, economic collapse and rebuilding, intra- and extra-civilization wars. (3) The economic distress of this period often leads to political activity and a more complete integration of the civilization in a stable balance of power or perhaps in a *universal state*. (4) The suppression of individual freedom and of local autonomy, the absence of the stimulus resulting at other times from

flicts within them, otherwise the result will be an approximation to perfect adaptation which, as Toynbee points out in the case of the Eskimos, the Nomads, and other "arrested civilizations," colonial insects, and utopias, means stagnation (*op. cit.*, II, 88 ff.; see also *ibid.*, I, 207–71).

[40] Clark Wissler refers to the tendency of cultural change to accelerate as the culture gets older (*The Relationship of Nature to Man in Aboriginal America* [New York, 1926], pp. 201 ff.). Henry Adams refers to acceleration in history in his "Letter to History Teachers," printed in his *The Degradation of Democratic Dogma* (New York, 1919). See also above, n. 26.

internal conflict, leads to boredom, degeneracy, loss of faith, frequently compensated by the growth of art and luxury in the upper classes and of new religions among the internal or external proletariat who do not share in the benefits of the civilization. To arrest this disintegration, the universal state often adopts one of these religions. This *universal church*, however, proves to be out of harmony with the genius of the ancient civilization. Disintegration continues until eventually the civilization is overrun by the internal and external proletariat who initiate a new heroic age and a new civilization on the roots of the new religion.[41]

These four stages of enthusiasm, trouble, stability, and boredom have tended to be characterized, respectively, by a dominant interest in religion, politics, economics, and art—a succession similar to that noted by Plato[42] and often exhibited in shorter fluctuations of more recent times. For instance, America was dominated by religious interest in the Colonial period, by political interest in the revo-

[41] This in general follows Toynbee, though he regards the "heroic age" or *Volker-wanderung* not as the beginning of a civilization but as the end of its predecessor. The barbarians " 'Heroic Age' was an epilogue to Hellenic History, not a prelude to ours. Their epic was a swan-song" (*op. cit.*, I, 62). He points out that the barbarian states which succeeded the Roman Empire in the fifth century were not ancestors of the medieval states which did not arise until Christianity was firmly established among the "Barbarians." But was it not out of the interaction of the barbarian states, the church, and the tradition of Rome that the new civilization arose? (see n. 67 below; see also Henry Osborn Taylor, *The Medieval Mind* [London, 1911]). The first of these periods may be dominated by what Sorokin calls "ideational" philosophies, the third by "sensate" philosophies with a transitional time of trouble or decline between (below, n. 42). Changes in the intensity of war, in the characteristics of military strategy and organization, and in the law and ideology of war which influenced and were influenced by these social and economic changes are considered later in the chapter.

[42] Plato thought aristocracy or the balanced republic in which the gods are respected becomes corrupted and degenerates into the ambitious republic full of contention and political maneuvering. This leads to oligarchy, the rule of the rich, under which the pursuit of gain colors all activities; and this to democracy with liberty and equality and a great variety of interests but no discipline, ending in the slavery and wretchedness of tyranny and the beginning of a new cycle, when that is overthrown (*Republic* viii, ix). Aristotle recognized this cycle but questioned its inevitability (*Politics* v. 12). He thought tyranny was more likely to supervene between oligarchy and democracy than between democracy and the free state (iii. 15). Plato and Aristotle were both influenced by the conception of a succession of gold, silver, bronze, and iron ages, popularized by Hesiod. See A. O. Lovejoy *et al.* (eds.), *History of Primitivism* (Baltimore, 1935), I, 25 ff., 162 ff., 173 ff.; see above, chap. iii, sec. 3; below, chap. viii, sec. 3; Appen. IV.

lutionary and constitution-building period, by economic interest in the post–Civil War period, and perhaps by a rising interest in art and literature since World War I. Probably a similar sequence may be noted in the artistic Renaissance of fifteenth-century Europe, the religious conflicts of Europe from the Reformation to the Thirty Years' War, the political wars and revolutions of the seventeenth and eighteenth centuries, the economic developments after the Industrial Revolution of the nineteenth century, and perhaps a new Renaissance of modern art since World War I.[43] Thus, though the European cycle began over a century earlier, the two have become synchronous.

This sequence has a certain logic. Religious enthusiasm induces attempts at a variety of ideal ways of life, the incompatibility of which leads to conflict and trouble. These divert attention to the problem of political adjustment, eventuating in stability which provides the milieu for practical invention and the pursuit of prosperity. This creates wealth, with which luxury and the arts may be patronized, and also the desire to patronize them, as a compensation for the sordid pursuit of gain. Art, however, may lead, on the one hand, to an interest in fundamental values and, on the other, to neglect of the practical requirements of life resulting in human misery, both circumstances inducing a new interest in religion. In the successive periods the characteristic forms of conflict have been, respectively, argument, violence, competition, and propaganda, though conflicts originating in any of these forms may eventuate in war.

3. RELATION OF WAR TO CHANGES OF CIVILIZATION

What has been the relation between changes in civilization and changes in war? No precise correlation is possible. Statistical data concerning war are available for only a few of the civilizations.[44] Even descriptions of the character of war and armies are incomplete with respect to many of the civilizations.[45] Furthermore, a civiliza-

---

[43] Sorokin presents evidence for a relative increase in the ideational element in the art of Western countries since the late nineteenth century (*ibid.*, I, 400, 404).

[44] See above, n. 2; below, Appen. XVI and Figs. 1 and 2.

[45] See above, n. 3; below, Appen. XV.

tion has not been a simple thing. Each civilization has been, through most of its life, composed of many states which have been in ceaseless process of alliance, federation, union, disunion, or disintegration and each state has usually been composed of factions and groups which also continually coalesce and separate. A model of history would be a time dimension rising above a map. This three-dimensional space would be divided into civilizations with fluctuating time and space boundaries within which are vaguely bounded states composed of vaguely bounded factions.

A complete history of civilized war would involve identification of all these units and description of the characteristics of war in each. In this chapter, however, historic units smaller than a civilization will not be considered. While civil wars and interstate wars have occurred in all civilizations, intercivilization wars have been commonly regarded as most important and have figured most in history. For example, the bulk of the battles before 1500 in Harbottle's *Dictionary of Battles*[46] occurred in wars of this category, as did eight of Creasy's fifteen battles, including each of the seven before Hastings.[47] Inquiry will, therefore, be confined to the variations of military activity with respect to successive civilizations, with respect to types of civilization, and with respect to the stages in the development of a civilization.

Military activity has varied with respect to the intensity of war, to the character of armies, to the character of operations, to the relations of belligerents, and to the objectives and justifications of hostilities. The following description is based upon appended tables indicating the fluctuations of some of these characteristics.[48]

a) *Successive civilizations.*—The magnitude of war has oscillated in long waves during the historic period. In the Western world armies were bigger and major wars more frequent in antiquity and modern times than in the Middle Ages, although it is generally accepted that there has been much exaggeration in the descriptions of the size of armies engaged in battles among ancient oriental nations.[49] Furthermore, every civilization tends to rise to a maximum of military activity in its time of trouble and then to sink down until there is a

---

[46] T. B. Harbottle, *Dictionary of Battles* (London, 1904).

[47] Creasy, *op. cit.*   [48] See Appens. XIV and XV.   [49] See above, n. 3.

new high of military activity at its decline and fall.[50] With allowance for these oscillations, however, it appears that, comparing successive civilizations, armies have tended to become larger absolutely and in proportion to the population,[51] war has tended to become absolutely and relatively more costly in life and wealth,[52] and military activity has tended to be more concentrated in time with longer peace intervals between wars.[53] War has tended to become more extended in space with fewer places of safety and more inconvenience to the civilian.[54] War has ideologically and legally become more distinct from peace and has tended to be regarded as more abnormal and more in need of rational justification.[55] The changes in war have on the whole tended to favor defensive rather than offensive operations.[56] Consequently, war has tended to be less rapidly decisive and, relative to other institutions, less influential upon world-politics.[57]

These trends exhibit a movement toward the present situation of enormous armies and great war costs; of alternating periods of concentrated military operations over the entire world and relatively peaceful intervals between; of extensive rules for justifying, condemning, and restricting military operations; and of strategy tending toward protracted stalemates, the use of mutual attrition, and relatively indecisive results.[58]

[50] See Appen. XVI and Figs. 1 and 2.

[51] "Taken as a whole, and allowing for possible exceptions, the aggregate fighting power of mankind has grown immensely, and has been growing continuously since we knew anything about it" (W. Bagehot, *Physics and Politics* [London, 1903], p. 46). See also Q. Wright, *The Causes of War and the Conditions of Peace* (London, 1935), p. 40; G. F. Nicolai, *The Biology of War* (New York, 1918); Sorokin, *Social and Cultural Dynamics*, III, 543 ff.; see below, chap. ix, sec. 3.

[52] Q. Wright, *op. cit.*, p. 43; see Appen. XVI; see below, chap. ix, sec. 4.

[53] Q. Wright, *op. cit.*, pp. 41–42; see Appen. XVI; see below, chap. ix, secs. 2d, 3b.

[54] This is the natural result of increased means of mobility (see below, chap. ix, sec. 3d).

[55] See below, nn. 187–91.

[56] Q. Wright, *op. cit.*, p. 51, and below, chap. xii, sec. 3b; Table 16, n. 25, Appen. XIV.

[57] J. Holland Rose, *The Indecisiveness of Modern War* (London, 1927), chaps. i and ii; Q. Wright, *op. cit.*, pp. 69–71.

[58] The characteristics of modern war were envisaged by the Polish banker, Ivan Bloch, in 1899 (*The Future of War* [Boston ed., 1914]). See also Interparliamentary Union, *What Would Be the Characteristics of a New War?* (London, 1931).

b) Types of civilizations.—Because of the great variations in the military characteristics of each civilization during its long life, it is not easy to relate military characteristics to the geographic, economic, or other characteristics of the civilization as a whole. As all civilizations have tended to become less aggressive as they have become older, civilizations must be compared at the same stage of their development.

If warlikeness is regarded as a compound (1) of habituation in cruelty arising from bloody religious rites, sports, and spectacles, (2) of aggressiveness manifested by frequency of active invasions in imperial or interstate wars, (3) of military morale indicated by discipline of armies and reserves, and (4) of political despotism manifested by completeness of territorial and functional centralization of authority with absence of constitutional and customary limitations,[59] it appears that the most warlike civilizations were the Classic, Tartar, Babylonic, Syriac, Iranic, Japanese, Andean, and Mexican. The moderately warlike were the Hittite, Arabic, Germanic, Western, Scandinavian, Russian, and Yucatec. These lists appear to exhibit no high correlation with chronology, geography, or economy. The more warlike civilizations include primary, secondary, and tertiary civilizations; large and small populations; steppe, arable, maritime, and plateau environments; grazing, dry farming, and commercial economies. There was a tendency, however, for civilizations in a plateau or mountainous environment, civilizations dependent on grazing, and civilizations with a heterogeneous population and with close intercivilizational contacts to be warlike.[60]

By the same criteria, the most peaceful civilizations were the Egyptian, Minoan, Orthodox (Byzantine), Mesopotamian (Sumerian), Nestorian, Irish, Indian, Hindu, Sinic, Chinese, and Mayan. These also are distributed among the chronological, population, geographic, and economic types, although it appears that homogeneous and isolated civilizations and those on rivers and dependent on irrigation agriculture tended to be peaceful. The isolated Japanese, perhaps, owed their warlikeness to their heterogeneous racial composition.[61]

---

[59] Cf. Appen. X.   [60] Appen. XIV, Table 16, cols. 2, 3, 5, and 6.

[61] *Ibid.;* see also Wrench, *op. cit.*, chap. iii.

There was perhaps a tendency for secondary civilizations, such as the Babylonic, Syriac, Classic, Hindu, and Mexican to be more warlike than the primary civilizations from which they sprang—the Egyptian, Mesopotamian, Minoan, Indian, and Mayan—and for tertiary civilizations, such as the Western, Arabian, Iranian, and Russian to be the most warlike of all. This may have been due to the fact that each successive civilization began as a barbarian or external proletarian group seeking to gain the advantages of the established civilization by warlike activity. If it was eventually successful, having been born in military success, it usually continued warlike.[62] Furthermore, the later civilizations with better means of communication were less isolated while their greater inventiveness made them less homogeneous. Both of these factors tended toward warlikeness.[63]

It is possible that maritime civilizations like the Scandinavian and nomadic civilizations like the Tartar and Arabic tended to be more warlike than agricultural civilizations such as the Egyptian, Mesopotamian, and Mayan because of greater mobility and more immediate responsiveness to climatic changes. This relationship, however, is far from clear.[64]

It has been said that civilizations in cold climates have tended to aggress against those in hot climates, as illustrated by the raids of Mongols, Aryans, Achaians, Gauls, and Germans upon the civilizations to the south of them. It appears, however, that such aggressions have really proceeded from the steppes in many directions as a result of drought, of administrative collapse in the invaded area, or of trade stoppages.[65]

[62] "The ancient civilizations were not allowed to remain long unassailed. Before long a warlike people would appear from somewhere or other, and would attempt to displace the existing ruling family, the attempt sometimes being successful" (W. J. Perry, *The Growth of Civilization* [New York, 1923], p. 128). See Fig. 19, Appen. V. "On a stationary military frontier between a civilization and a barbarism, time always works in the barbarians' favor; and, besides this, the barbarians' advantage increases . . . . in geometrical progression at each arithmetical addition to the length of the line which the defenders of the civilization have to hold" (Toynbee, *op. cit.*, II, 283). See Appen. XIV, Table 17, col. 1.

[63] See chap. vi, sec. 2.

[64] E.g., the maritime Minoans were very peaceful (Appen. XIV, Table 16, col. 2).

[65] See above, n. 28; chap. iii, n. 6; F. J. Teggart, *Rome and China* (Berkeley, 1939), p. 240.

There is perhaps some support for the suggestion that martial character has come from mountains and passivity from plains when one considers the relatively warlike disposition of the Hittites, Iranians, Andeans, and Mexicans. Such exceptions as the peaceful Nestorians may be due to the early stage at which that civilization was destroyed by conquest.[66]

A civilization, however, has seldom been dominated by any one factor. Warlikeness has resulted from a conjunction of circumstances in the internal composition and external relations and conditions of a particular civilization. Its peculiar combination of social, religious, political, and military institutions and external contacts has been an adaptation to a variety of circumstances in its environment and basic economy and not a consequence of any limited set of conditions.

c) Stages of a civilization.—The intensity of war measured by the frequency of battles and the number of participants has usually increased through the heroic age (the swarming period) when war has characteristically been utilized either for aggression against or for defense from other civilizations. Its intensity has continued to increase through the time of troubles, but during this period war has often been interstate and civil as well as imperialistic and defensive. The period of stability which follows has usually been more peaceful, though the size of armies has not greatly decreased. As this period has progressed, aggression from the outside has often occurred. Barbarians, or another civilization in the swarming stage, have assaulted the civilization with increasing capacity as their armies have learned more of the art of war from contacts with the older civilization. This was illustrated by the assaults of the Hyksos against Egypt (1760 B.C.), of the Aryans against the Hittites and the Babylonians (1780 B.C.), of the Scythians against Persia (500 B.C.), of the Achaeans against the Minoans (1200 B.C.), of the Gauls and Germans against Rome in the fourth century B.C., and again with more success in the fourth and fifth centuries A.D., and of the Scandinavians against Western and southern Europe in the ninth and tenth centuries. The intensity of war has thus increased in the final stage. External attacks, often successful, have led to internal revolts until the civiliza-

[66] Perris, *op. cit.*, p. 14. See Appen. XIV, Table 17, col. 2.

tion has disintegrated under joint pressure from outside and from within.[67] These variations in the intensity of war have been typically accompanied by changes in the character of armies and of military operations.[68]

4. FUNCTIONS

The frequency and character of historic wars have varied primarily with the stages of a civilization, secondarily among the different civilizations and, to a limited degree, among the political groups within the civilization. Such wars have functioned to promote change rather than stability and, in the long run, to disintegrate rather than to integrate civilization.[69]

Among animals the characteristics of belligerent activity are correlated primarily with species. Lions, wherever or whenever living, tend to exhibit the same type of belligerent behavior. The same is true of buffaloes, red ants, goldfinches, and gorillas, although the normal behavior of an animal may be considerably modified by extreme conditions such as domestication, extraordinary climate, etc. Although animal war does assist in maintaining the balance of nature, its long-run tendency seems to be to promote change. Territorial war within the species, especially developed among birds, spreads the geographical range of the species. This results in competition which eliminates some species and increases others. Sexual combats have an evolutionary influence by assuring that the germ plasm of the most powerful males shall increase in the next generation. These dynamic effects of war mean that, if a long-run, evolutionary point of view is taken, the belligerent characteristics of the race do change. The Paleozoic ancestors of Mesozoic dinosaurs were less belligerent, and the Mesozoic ancestors of lions and tigers were very mild.[70]

Among primitive men belligerent activity is not closely correlated with race or biological differences, but its character differs for each

---

[67] Perry, *op. cit.*, chap. vii. H. M. Chadwick (*The Heroic Age* [Cambridge, 1912], p. 460) emphasizes the extent to which the attacking "barbarians" acquired their arts of war from the civilization they were attacking. See Figs. 12 and 19, Appens. V and XVI.

[68] See below, sec. 6.

[69] See Shotwell, *op. cit.*, p. 11; Toynbee, *op. cit.*, III, 167.

[70] See above, chap. v, sec. 2; below, Appen. V.

people. All the sovereign political groups belonging to a particular primitive people manifest the same peculiarities of belligerent behavior; sometimes it is head-hunting, sometimes cattle raids, sometimes formal battles, sometimes revenge feuds. There may be some differences among different villages or tribes of the same people, but these are not usually more significant than are the differences in belligerent behavior between different animals of the same species. The influence of war, however, differs from that among animals in being static rather than dynamic. Primitive war preserves the solidarity of the existing political group. It guards it from sedition within and from union or conquest without. Among the more advanced primitive peoples war may exert a dynamic influence by amalgamating tribes in federations or kingdoms and in spreading the culture traits of the conqueror. But among the majority of primitive people, this function is negligible. War is essentially conservative, preserving the organization and customs of the society as it is.[71]

Civilized war has resembled both animal war in that its influence has been dynamic rather than static and primitive war in that its influence has been social rather than biological. The dynamic influence of civilized war, however, has been marked on a much shorter time scale than that of animal war. While animal war has required hundreds of thousands of years to register important evolutionary changes, civilized war has produced marked changes in the course of centuries—changes which have been registered in the stages of the civilization. These changing stages caused by war have reciprocally influenced the character of war. Thus civilized war has been correlated primarily with the stages of the civilization in which it takes place. All civilizations have indulged in similar types of war when young, when middle aged, and when old. The primary function of war has apparently been to assure these successions in the life of a civilization.[72]

There have, however, been some differences in the warlike characteristics of different civilizations. War has, therefore, played a dynamic part in the competition of civilizations. It has spread the culture of some at the expense of others. Here, again, there is a resemblance to the dynamic function of animal war, that of giving a wider

[71] See above, chap. vi, sec. 3.　　　　[72] Shotwell, *op. cit.*, p. 15.

geographical distribution to organic species. The more belligerent civilizations have been most successful in distributing their culture widely. The conquests of Alexander, of Caesar, of Islam, and of the sixteenth-century discoverers distributed Greek, Roman, Arabic, and Western civilization over wide areas.[73]

Although all the political groups within a civilization have usually had war practices and methods of similar type at the same stage in the history of the civilization, there have been some differences. The military characteristics of Sparta, Athens, and Rome all differed in Classical civilization; as did the military characteristics of France, Great Britain, and Germany in medieval Western civilization. These differentials have tended to spread the influence of the cultures of the more belligerent groups throughout the civilization. It must be emphasized, however, that within a civilization other methods of cultural expansion, such as trade, education, travel, have been relatively more important than they have been between civilizations. Within a civilization the military techniques of all states have tended to approximate one another through the process of military competition and imitation with the result of a military balance of power. Even if the balance is broken and one eventually conquers all the rest, creating a universal state, the culture of the defeated state has sometimes prevailed in large areas as did much of Greek culture in the Roman Empire.[74]

The importance of this dynamic influence both between civilizations and within a civilization has differentiated civilized from primitive war. Civilized war has, however, resembled primitive war in performing also a conservative function, that of preserving the political and cultural solidarity of existing political groups against internal sedition and external aggression. Observed over such short periods as decades, this function of war has usually seemed most important. Statesmen have often believed that resort to war is necessary to prevent or resist invasion and to preserve the *status quo*. With a longer

[73] See Appen. V.

[74] On different military characteristics of Athens, Sparta, Thebes, Macedonia, and Rome in Classic civilization see Spaulding, Nickerson, and Wright, *op. cit.*, chaps. iv, v, vi. On differences of England, France, Spain, Switzerland, and Italy in the later Middle Ages see C. Oman, *History of the Art of War in the Middle Ages* (London, 1924), Vol. II; Spaulding *et al.*, *op. cit.*, chap. viii.

view such beliefs have frequently proved erroneous. The internal and external advocates of change have usually gained more from war than have the advocates of stability.[75] The result of war has seldom been completely predictable, so stability has immediately been jeopardized when it begins, because no one has been able to predict the result.[76] The more prolonged and destructive has been the war, the more changed has been the world after it is over. On the other hand, revolutionists and aggressors have had little to lose and have frequently won glory and achieved the political changes they sought by war. With such expectations they have worked at war with more single-mindedness and eventually have usually won. Even if their first effort has resulted in a deadlock or in victory for the forces of the *status quo*, the destructiveness of the war itself has often created a more fertile field for the future activities of the advocates of change.[77] Thus wise defenders of the *status quo* have usually preferred propaganda, economic controls, or argument as methods for settling controversies, avoiding violence and war to the utmost. In diplomacy and in popular thinking the function of war in a given stage of a civilization has been the achievement of ideals, the reform of the *status quo*.[78]

If civilized war has been dynamic favoring change, has it in the entire life of a civilization favored integration or disintegration? Has it favored the insurgent who wished to divide political structures or the imperial conqueror who wished to combine them? While vast empires have been built by war, they have only been preserved by organizing peace. As the destructiveness of wide external conquest has typically brought internal discontent and sedition in parts at least of the new empire, it has not provided a suitable milieu for con-

[75] Pre–World War I international law regarded war as a necessary instrument both for sanctioning international law and for changing it (see Josef Kunz, "The Law of Nations, Static and Dynamic," *American Journal of International Law*, XXVII [October 1933], 634).

[76] All generals affirm that "the outcome of an encounter cannot be predicted and has no appearance of being predetermined, but arises, in the likeness of a new creation, out of the encounter itself" (Toynbee, *op. cit.*, I, 301).

[77] See above, n. 62.

[78] The philosophic advocacy of violence as a political method has been more common among radicals than among conservatives.

stitutionalism. Conquest has provided the material for civil war. Thus war in the long run has favored political disintegration rather than political integration.

Three related processes have conspired to this result. (1) Superiority of the attack over the defense has favored political unification by war,[79] but a lengthening record of the experience of a particular civilization with war has resulted in a steady increase of knowledge of the defense for all modes of attack known to that civilization and at the same time in a steady decrease in the range of possible surprises. Thus the power of defense has increased and that of attack has diminished. Local units have more and more been able to resist centralization, and political structures have disintegrated.[80] (2) This reduction of war to a process of mutual attrition through perfection of the arts of defense has also increased the destructiveness of war with an increasingly disintegrating effect upon social morale and the stability of political institutions. (3) Furthermore, the importance of success in war in the survival of states has tended to spread military discipline and organization by conquest and imitation throughout the civilization. Militarism, however, discourages imagination, inventiveness, cultural and scientific progress. It produces a rigidity and inflexibility of social and political structures. "Militarism" paradoxically proves hostile to military skill and augments the trend toward the defensive within the civilization. The civilization as a whole becomes unable to adapt itself to the complaints of the internal proletariat crying for social reform and the external proletariat hungry for plunder.[81] As a consequence of these three processes,

[79] "If it be true that centralization hinges on the preponderance of the attack in war, the surest way of measuring the advance toward civilization of rude peoples must be by military engineering" (Brooks Adams, *op. cit.*, p. 96; see also pp. 79, 80, 354, 362). See also Oman, *History and Art of War in the Middle Ages*, II, 52 ff., and Perris, *op. cit.*, pp. 98–100, on the political consequences of the superiority of the defense in the late Middle Ages. Bertrand Russell generalizes: "Broadly speaking, when the defensive is strong, civilization makes progress, and when the offensive is strong, men revert towards barbarism" (*Which Way to Peace* [London, 1936], p. 16). This needs qualification.

[80] See above, n. 56.

[81] Toynbee sets forth in detail the operation of this principle within the historic civilizations in his chapter on the "Failure of Self-determination" (IV, 119 ff.) under the suggestive section heads, "The Mechanicalness of Mimesis," "The Intractibility of Insti-

when a civilization has passed beyond a certain threshold in its military development, the power of arms to integrate political units has so declined, the power of arms to destroy political morale has so increased, the dependence of institutions upon arms has become so general, and the inability of arms to adapt themselves to new conditions has become so manifest that the balance between the constructive and destructive influence of war has become permanently adverse, and the civilization, which in human experience has never been able to get rid of war altogether, has disintegrated.[82]

States and civilizations have been built up by war but have eventually disintegrated through war. Realization of this may in part account for the frequent decline in warlikeness of states and civilizations as they get older. But because all old civilizations of the past have had younger civilizations beside them or within them, they have not been able to escape war altogether, and their inflexibility has made it difficult to cope with attacks effectively.

The paradox set forth in connection with primitive war may be recalled. Moderate war is socializing, whereas too much and too destructive war is disintegrating.[83] With primitive man war makes for stability and gradual progress. With civilized man the threshold is passed. A rising civilization develops war too much and seals its own doom. The time of trouble, as Toynbee points out, marks the beginning of the end of a civilization.[84] Those civilizations in which war

---

tutions," and "The Nemesis of Creativity," especially under the latter, "The Suicidalness of Militarism" (p. 465). For his discussion of the development of internal and external proletariats which, however, he regards as manifestations of more fundamental "schisms in the soul of a civilization," see V, 58 ff. Alfred Vagts emphasizes the difference between "militarism" and the "military way" (*A History of Militarism* [New York, 1937]).

[82] See Wissler, *Man and Culture*, p. 180. This tendency of war in the life of a civilization can be observed also in the course of a particular war. At first the aggressor, better prepared, may wage a successful offensive and expand his political structure as did Napoleon and Germany in World War I, but if the war continues for any length of time, it tends toward stalemate, attrition, and general disintegration. Differentials in the operation of this tendency in warlike and peaceful civilizations may account for some of the differences in their longevity (see below, n. 155).

[83] Above, chap. vi, sec. 6. G. F. Nicolai, *The Biology of War* (London 1919), pp. 420–21; Toynbee, *op. cit.*, IV, 647 ff.

[84] Toynbee, *op. cit.*, III, 145 ff.; VI, 315–20.

has been a relatively unimportant political instrument, such as those of ancient Egypt, of Sumeria, of ancient China, have lasted the longest. The military civilizations of Babylonia, Classical antiquity, Western Europe, Arabia, and Turkey have been relatively short lived.[85]

While war has had the function of insuring change in civilization, its ultimate effect has been to produce oscillations in the rise and fall of states and civilizations. What persistent evolution there has been in human history is not due to war but to thought. The Alexanders, Caesars, and Napoleons have produced oscillations; the Aristotles, Archimedes', Augustines, and Galileos have produced progress. Yet it must be emphasized that it is the very persistence of progress in the art of war within each civilization and in the succession of civilizations that has induced these oscillations, continuously increased their amplitude, and shortened their length.[86]

5. DRIVES

The drives to war discussed among animals and primitive people have existed also among civilized people, although their relative importance has been very different. Food and sex have been of relatively little importance in the consciousness of civilized people when they make war, though their unconscious influence may be important. While dominance and independence play little part in warfare among animals other than the primates, they have been generally operative in wars during the historic period. Territory, adventure, defense, and society have all figured in historic as they have in animal and primitive war. The drive toward societal union and toward independence has often been manifested among the civilized people in wars for abstract social symbols, representing forms of religion, culture, or justice. The drives for territory and defense have usually figured in legal rationalizations for war. Political motives often combine drives for dominance, territory, and adventure.

It must be emphasized that a study of drives, or basic behavior patterns of the individual, provide a less satisfactory explanation of civilized than of animal or primitive war. Animals fight when an ex-

---

[85] See Fig. 12, Appen. V; Toynbee, *op. cit.*, IV, 465 ff.

[86] See above, n. 26, and Casson, *op. cit.*, pp. 324 ff.

ternal stimulus activates one of these patterns inbred in the animal. Primitive men fight when such a stimulus activates a pattern to which they are habituated by the group mores. Such a pattern, while sometimes complex, is usually rather closely related to one of these basic drives. Civilized man, however, is less guided by such necessities. The drives are frequently combined by the individual's experience to form complex dispositions or behavior patterns.[87] These behavior patterns provide the fuel which political leadership may kindle to create a war spirit. But each individual's behavior patterns are continuously being modified by new experience, and political leadership is influenced to take such steps by a variety of circumstances including the leaders' own attitudes and, in addition, rational considerations of policy, law, and technical preparedness.[88] Among civilized people, therefore, there is seldom an immediate causal relationship between any one drive and a war. The drives do not account for the war; they originate the behavior patterns of the people, which in turn provide the materials out of which war may be made. But why someone wishes to make it at a particular time and place, and whether his propaganda skill is such that he can do so, can be answered only by a detailed historical analysis of the particular situation.[89]

[87] Graham Wallas (*The Great Society* [New York, 1917], p. 27) distinguishes simple and complex "dispositions." He illustrates the latter, which involves both "instinct" and "intelligence," by mother love, acquisitiveness, and curiosity. E. F. M. Durbin and John Bowlby (*Personal Aggressiveness and War* [New York, 1939], pp. 8–9) emphasize frustration, possessiveness, and intrusion as the dispositions most involved in war. They assume a "natural" tendency to resort to violence to fulfill any of these dispositions (p. 25). The punishment of the child causes repression of this tendency and develops an unpleasant ambivalence or mixture of love and hate for the punishing parent. To escape the anxieties arising from this condition, aggressive impulses are displaced and guilty feelings are projected upon some other person or thing. This very complex disposition, resulting from the infantile experiences of nearly all people, is made use of by governments to solidify the internal order by inducing their people to displace their aggressions and project their guilt feelings upon another state. In such a situation any incident can be made the occasion for war upon the scapegoat (pp. 16 ff.).

[88] See Ellsworth Faris, "Of Psychological Elements," *American Journal of Sociology*, XLII (September, 1936), 159 ff.

[89] The mixture of motives leading to historic wars has been a major theme of history. An excellent illustration is provided by Ernest Barker's account of the "Crusades," *Encyclopaedia Britannica* (14th ed.), VI, 773 ff. The clergy wished (1) to assist penitentiary pilgrimages to the Sepulcher; (2) to divert the fighting instincts from private

With these considerations in mind, we may suggest some of the ways in which these drives have been an influence in historic wars.

a) Food.—Civilized people have seldom sought directly for food, although the part which cattle raids played in the war drives of the

---

war, which was disintegrating Christendom, and which the church was trying to curb by the truce and peace of God into channels which would benefit the church; and (3) to establish the rule of the church in the Holy Land; but (4) the Norman princes and younger sons like Bohemund were affected primarily by the ambition and adventure of carving a principality in the east, while (5) the Italian towns were "anxious to acquire the products of the East more directly and cheaply, by erecting their own emporia in the Eastern Mediterranean." "So far as the crusades led to permanent material results in the East, they did so in virtue of these [latter] two forces. Unregulated enthusiasm might of itself have achieved little or nothing; enthusiasm caught and guided by the astute Norman, and the no less astute Venetian or Genoese, could not but achieve tangible results. The principality or the emporium, it is true, would supply motives to the prince and the merchant only; and it may be urged that to the mass of the crusaders the religious motive was all in all." (6) "To thousands the hope of acquiring spiritual merit must have been a great motive. . . . ." But, in addition, (7) "famine and pestilence at home drove men to emigrate hopefully to the golden East," and finally (8) the Crusades made a peculiar appeal to the Norman French because of the rise in France of the Cluniac movement and chivalry, the recent suffering of France from battle, murder, pestilence, and famine from which any escape was welcome and the continuance of the old Norse instinct for wandering, for religiosity, and for territory. Pope Urban's appeal, "Let the truce of God be observed at home; and let the arms of Christians be directed to conquering the infidel in an expedition which should count for full and complete penance" activated many of these motives.

Compare with this P. T. Moon's analysis of the motives of modern imperialism (*Imperialism and World Politics* [New York, 1926], chap. iv) and Thucydides' brief statement of the causes of the Peloponnesian War: "The real cause I consider to be the one which was formally most kept out of sight. The growth of the power of Athens, and the alarm which this inspired in Lacedaemon, made war inevitable. Still it is well to give the grounds alleged by either side, which led to the dissolution of the treaty and the breaking out of the war" (i. 1. 24). These may be contrasted with the more individual motives emphasized in Polybius' analysis of the "causes, pretexts and first actions" of the Second Punic War. The causes he considers to have been Hannibal's oath to fulfil his father's, Hamilcar's, desire for revenge, shared by the Carthaginian people, because of Rome's victories resulting in the loss of Sicily and Sardinia and in the payments of tribute; and in addition the confidence inspired by the Carthaginian success in Spain (iii. 6–13). An equal emphasis upon personal motives is given in Hume's description of the Hundred Years' War: (1) Edward's claim to the succession to the French throne through his mother, (2) the animosity between Edward and Philip arising from the support which they, respectively, gave to Robert of Artois and David Bruce of Scotland, and (3) Edward's success in getting support from enemies of Philip, from friends of Robert, from his own relatives, and from groups on the Continent vulnerable to British gold (*History of England*, chap. xv).

forebears of civilized man is indicated by the importance of this drive in the warfare of the highest contemporary primitive people[90] and by such verbal survivals as the Vedic word for war which means "desire for cows."[91] Desiccation producing shortage of pasturage has undoubtedly induced many movements of nomads using war to conquer new lands and instituting periods of general warfare.[92] Economic objectives have undoubtedly existed for war among agriculturalists also—to secure slaves, raw materials, trade routes, opportunities for migration.[93] Even when leaders have had other purposes, such objectives may have sometimes been useful for interesting the population in the enterprise.[94] Economic rewards to the fighters—prizes, booty, land in the area to be conquered, and relief from debts at home have generally been promised and often given.[95]

It seems doubtful, however, whether among agricultural civilizations immediate economic expectations have been so important among leaders who initiate military activity as political considerations. Leaders may think that increase of political power will indirectly increase economic opportunity, but the immediate objective

[90] See above, chap. vi, sec. 46. See account of Arab wars for plunder (Gibbon, op. cit., V, 87) and E. Huntington, Character of Races (New York, 1927).

[91] "India," Encyclopaedia Britannica (14th ed.), XII, 184.

[92] Wrench, op. cit., p. 470; M. Sprengling, "Moslem North Africa," in Berthold Laufer (ed.), The New Orient (Chicago, 1933), II, 379 ff.; Owen Lattimore, "China and the Barbarians," in Joseph Barnes (ed.), Empire in the East (New York, 1934), pp. 3-39; see above, n. 28.

[93] Perris, op. cit., p. 30. "The search for new and more direct connections with the routes of oriental trade is one of the motives underlying the crusades" (Barker, op. cit., p. 772b). "The wars of the decaying [Roman] Republic were in well-nigh every instance wars of mere plunder" (T. A. Walker, History of the Law of Nations [Cambridge, 1899], p. 56).

[94] Alexander and Caesar were not so free in popularizing expeditions of conquest by unreal economic arguments as have been their modern followers, Hitler and Mussolini.

[95] The Crusaders were promised relief from debts (C. Bemont and G. Monod, Medieval Europe [New York, 1903], p. 652). It was the practice in Greece and Rome to distribute prize and booty to the soldiers (Grotius De jure belli ac pacis iii. 6. 12, 14, 123; C. Phillipson, International Law and Custom of Ancient Greece and Rome [London, 1911], II, 237; Walker, op. cit., p. 41). This was also the practice in the Middle Ages (T. Twiss, Introduction to the Black Book of the Admiralty ["Rolls Series," No. 55 (London, 1871)], I, 76; H. G. Marsden, "Early History of Prize Jurisdiction in England," English History Review, XXIV, 675).

is usually power rather than prosperity. If one runs through Creasy's *Fifteen Decisive Battles*, it is difficult to find an immediate economic objective in any with the possible exception of Attila's invasion of Europe at Châlons and the Norman conquest of England at Hastings.

Economic factors operate less as a direct pull to war among civilized people than as an indirect push. Difficulties in making a living, overpopulation, and hard times render a people vulnerable to radical propagandas which, whether in the name of religion, culture, or government, advocate war as an instrument. Thus food may sometimes be a concealed drive for war when the conscious motive is different.[96]

  b) Sex.—War to secure women is known among civilized people, as the Roman rape of the Sabine women in the eighth century B.C.,[97] and the legitimacy of this cause of war is discussed by Grotius.[98] The opportunity for free play to sexual passion has been considered a perquisite of soldiers, especially in the taking of a besieged city.[99]

[96] W. F. Ogburn, "The Psychological Basis for the Economic Interpretation of History," *American Economic Review*, IX (Suppl., 1919), 291–308. It appears, however, that economic factors effect migration more by the pull of anticipated conditions in the new home than the push of those in the old home (Harry Jerome, *Migration and Business Cycles* [New York, 1926]).

[97] M. R. Davie (*The Evolution of War* [New Haven, 1929], p. 100) cites woman-stealing as a common cause of war among the Egyptians, Hebrews, Greeks, Arabs, and Nordics. The Byzantine emperor Alexius is said to have held out the bait of the beauty of Greek women in certain of his appeals for aid before the First Crusade (*Encyclopaedia Britannica*, VI, 773*b*). Durbin and Bowlby (*op. cit.*, p. 115) disagree with Davie and agree with Letourneau in holding sex gratification more important than economic interest in this practice.

[98] *Op. cit.* ii. 2. 21; 22. 7.

[99] Walker (*op. cit.*) comments on the brutality of the practices in taking besieged places among the Greeks (p. 41), Romans (pp. 48, 60), Carthaginians (p. 57), Teutons (p. 65), Franks (p. 72), and Crusaders (p. 124). The Saracens apparently were better (pp. 76, 127), but the British during the Hundred Years' War (p. 132), the states of the Renaissance (p. 191), and those of the Thirty Years' War (pp. 194, 195) were equally bad. Throughout, apparently Sully's comment was applicable: "Les violences contre le sexe, qui sont les malheureux droits de la guerre" (*Memoirs* [Paris, 1822], I, 124, and Walker, *op. cit.*, p. 192). In the eighteenth century places taken by assault could be sacked for twenty-four hours. This applied to loot. Theoretically to slay or rape was forbidden (J. W. Wright, "Sieges and Customs of War at the Opening of the Eighteenth Century," *American Historical Review*, July, 1934, p. 632).

A more legitimate expectation of feminine favor for the military hero may also have played its part in maintaining the war system.[100] Leaders as well as followers may also have been anxious to fight or to institute bold policies tending to war as a compensation for sexual impotence or as an escape from distressing matrimonial conditions.[101]

War in revenge for the stealing of women has figured among civilized peoples since the incident of Helen of Troy.[102] Attila's gallantry in rescuing Honoria, who had offered to be his bride, from imprisonment by her brother, the emperor Theodosius, has been given as one reason for his invasion of Europe. The attack upon German women by the Roman legionnaires is said to have been a major cause of the revolt under Arminius leading to the massacre of Varus' legion in the time of Augustus.[103] Dynastic claims to territory may be based on royal marriages but frequently can only be realized by war.[104]

Sex has played an important role in civilized war, often lying behind economic, social, and political motives. Rear Admiral Fisk notes that men have done most of the fighting and writes: "If the earliest cause of fighting was to obtain and retain the means wherewith to support women and children, it probably has been the fundamental cause ever since, even though this fundamental cause has been overgrown with others more apparent."[105]

---

[100] Aristotle (*Politics* ii. 9) wrote that "warlike races are prone to the love of women." Brooks Adams notes that "in martial ages, women are idealized" (*op. cit.*, p. 366). E. Westermark (*History of Human Marriage* [London, 1921], II, 1–4, 33) believes that women "instinctively prefer strong and brave men to feeble and cowardly ones" (see Davie, *op. cit.*, p. 101; Mumford, *Technics and Civilization*, pp. 96 ff.; and above, chap. vi, sec. 4b). Against this assumption one may recall the feminine pacifism in Aristophanes' *Lysistrata* and the significance of peace movements among contemporary women. Dr. Bernhard Bauer suggests an explanation. Women in most civilizations have been able to exercise power through the use of sexual charms rather than through intelligence. The success of this method can be most clearly manifested by influencing masculine rulers in warlike activity. He credits Mme de Pompadour with Louis XV's attack on Austria which led to the Seven Years' War (*Women and Love* [New York, 1934], p. 127).

[101] H. D. Lasswell, *Psychopathology and Politics* (Chicago, 1930).

[102] Gentili cites a number of such cases (*De jure belli, libri tres*, I, 20, 153, 158).

[103] Creasy, *op. cit.*, pp. 116, 146.   [104] Perris, *op. cit.*, p. 116.

[105] Bradley A. Fiske, *The Art of Fighting* (New York, 1920), p. 16. The Freudians emphasize the role of sexual jealousy in creating the anxieties which can be remedied by displacing aggressive impulses upon an out-group (Durbin and Bowlby, *op. cit.*, pp. 8, 127; above, n. 87).

c) Territory.—Conflicting claims to territory have very frequently figured in civilized war. Civilized, like primitive, men when politically organized will generally fight to defend from invasion territory to which they regard the political organization as clearly entitled; but because civilized man is more dynamic and less habituated to respect the territory of others than is primitive man,[106] and also because his rational habits make him more fertile in devising legal, dynastic, economic, or political claims to territory which he wants, war has arisen over this cause more frequently among civilized than among primitive groups.[107]

While the drive for territorial expansion has sometimes had an economic background, it has often been immediately based upon strategic considerations or upon the general supposition that the acquisition of any territory augments political prestige because it signifies political success. Civilized statesmen go after territory as civilized businessmen go after money, without direct consideration of what they are going to do with it when they get it.[108]

d) Adventure.—Among civilized people the adventure spirit has played a larger part as a war drive in the earlier than in the later stages of a civilization. The heroes of Homeric Greece, the knights of King Arthur and Charlemagne, and the adventurous followers of

[106] See above, chap. vi, sec. *3c.*

[107] Civilized agricultural societies recognize more precise boundaries than do the nomads and, whether feudally or nationally organized, regard land as a good in itself. Their systems of international law recognize its defense as a justification for the use of force, and their foreign politices often consist in efforts to expand territory (Walker, *op. cit.*, pp. 82, 113). C. A. Beard emphasized the traditional proclivity of agricultural aristocracies to use war for territorial expansion ("Prospects for Peace," *Harper's Magazine*, February, 1929).

[108] The Crusades "appealed to that desire to gain fresh territory upon which Malaterra remarks as characteristic of Norman princes" (Barker, *op. cit.*, p. 774*a*). After examining all the transfers of territory in Europe during the nineteenth and twentieth centuries, Rogers Churchill considers that, of the 129 cases, 51 were motivated by considerations of nationality or desire of the inhabitants, a consideration probably of little importance prior to the fifteenth century; 32 by a desire for expansion, 23 by strategic considerations, 16 by economic needs, and 15 by historic claims (in some cases more than one factor was ascribed). He adds "for states to take territory from the vanquished after wars . . . . was natural, customary, traditional. . . . . Size did [in former times], and still does, denote greatness; and greatness seemingly indicates power; and power in turn inspires fear, or at least caution in others" (manuscript prepared for Causes of War Study, University of Chicago), Part V, secs. 2 and 5.

Cortez, Drake, and Raleigh were primarily interested in adventure if the traditions of these early days of the Classical, Western, and world civilizations are to be believed. At times, when the technique of war and the rules governing its conduct are of a type to make it relatively innocuous, as in the days of knight-errantry and of the *condottieri*,[109] the adventure spirit may often be the mainstay of army recruiting. When changing techniques make actual war more serious, this spirit is given an outlet in tournaments, games, hunting, and exploration.[110]

e) Self-preservation.—War for individual self-preservation has seldom figured among civilized men who are normally protected by political and legal institutions. Defense of the home or the fatherland from invasion, while perhaps more appropriately classed under the territorial or even the sexual drive, has always been related to self-preservation among civilized people and has usually constituted an important item in domestic war propaganda and legal justification. Declarations of war have often referred to the necessity of resistance to aggression, and such resistance, frequently referred to as self-defense or self-preservation, has usually been accepted as a just cause of war.[111]

[109] "Winter operations, work which involved strain, the infliction of heavy casualties, were avoided by the condottieri, as tending to reduce the common stock of trained soldiers—the currency on which was based their political and economic stability" (F. L. Taylor, *The Art of War in Italy, 1494–1529* [Cambridge, 1921], p. 6). See also Machiavelli, *The Prince*, chap. xii; Oman, *History of the Art of War in the Middle Ages*, Book XII, chap. ii; Spaulding *et al.*, *op. cit.*, p. 418.

[110] These activities seem to have been developed in Greece even in the time of Homer but especially during the long period of the Olympic games from 776 B.C. to A.D. 389; in Rome from the third century B.C. to A.D. 404; in the Middle Ages from 1066 to 1559; and in modern times especially since the seventeenth century. Their history can be surveyed in the *Encyclopaedia Britannica* (14th ed.) under the titles "Games, Classical"; "Gladiators"; "Tournament"; "Hunting"; "Big Game Hunting"; "Geography, Progress of Discovery"; "Arctic Regions, Exploration." Doubtless the adventure spirit plays an important part in the motivation of volunteers for foreign legions in recent wars in Morocco, Spain, China, etc.

[111] Defense was one of the recognized "just causes of war" in the Middle Ages (John Eppstein, *The Catholic Tradition of the Law of Nations* [Washington, 1935], pp. 60, 93), and it has continued as a formal justification for war (J. von Elbe,"The Evolution of the Concept of the Just War," *American Journal of International Law*, XXXIII [1939], 685). See list of formal reasons for war in declarations of 1914–18 in United States Naval War College, *International Law Documents, 1917* (Washington, 1918), p. 262.

f) Domination.—The desire of an individual to gain or maintain political power or domination over a population,[112] the desire of a class to acquire or maintain a dominant position in society,[113] the desire of a population to dominate over a colony or people of "lower culture,"[114] and the desire of a state to be in a position to dominate in controversies with other states[115] may all be grouped as manifestations of the political motive in internal and external government, and all have figured prominently in the causation of civilized war.[116]

[112] Caesar "never for a moment forgot that in fighting the battles of Rome he was maintaining in his service an army devoted to himself, which would give him strength and prestige in fighting his own political battles; and the time came when he needed it and used it" (Spaulding *et al., op. cit.*, p. 158). "A prince ought to have no other aim or thought, nor select anything else for his study, than war and its rules and discipline; for this is the sole art that belongs to him who rules, and it is of such force that it not only upholds those who are born princes, but it often enables men to rise from a private station to that rank. And, on the contrary, it is seen that when princes have thought more of ease than of arms they have lost their states" (Machiavelli, *op. cit.*, chap. xiv.).

[113] "From the very moment that the institution of private property had arisen and the various human societies gradually split into classes, the interests of the dominating social groups became the main stimulus of wars" (M. Pavlovitch, *The Foundations of Imperialist Policy* [London, 1922], p. 21). "Politically, war is a weapon employed by ruling classes as a means of protecting and extending their interests" (Scott Nearing, *War* [New York, 1931], p. 10). "From the disturbed and warlike times, when the Aryans were establishing themselves as the superior race, and in some degree blending their blood with the conquered, occurred the events later sung in the two great epics of India, the 'Mahabharata' and the 'Ramayana' " (Wrench, *op. cit.*, p. 58). Karl Liebknecht, *Militarism* (New York, 1917), p. 38. See also views of W. J. Perry, discussed in Appen. VI, below.

[114] The Roman Republic, "the nation which had bred up its successive generations to the task of subduing mankind, which, by unrivalled firmness of cohesion, by enduring tenacity of purpose, by methodic study and science of destruction, had crushed all the surrounding nationalities, not with a temporary prostration merely, but with utter and irretrievable dissolution—now found its work done and its occupation gone" (Seeley, *op. cit.*, p. 22).

[115] See Thucydides' and Polybius' respective explanations of the Peloponnesian and Second Punic wars (above, n. 89). "That international politics is a struggle for power is recognized in popular parlance more frequently than in the erudite tomes of jurists or in the idealistic pleas of pacifists. States are habitually spoken of as 'Powers.' This usage is based upon the assumption that the State is an embodiment of power and that its relations with other states are determined by power considerations" (F. L. Schuman, *International Politics* [New York, 1933], p. 503).

[116] "Dominance rather than fear seems to be largely responsible for the existing unsatisfactory world situation. For nations take on the character of the dominant men who make them great. In establishing and maintaining world dominance they impose fetters on other nations that arouse opposition which eventually becomes a struggle to

Dominance, hegemony, prestige, power, control, authority, and influence, all imply unequal relations, though each suggests a distinctive form in which inequality is manifested. Successful war, or a generally recognized capacity to make such a war, has in all civilizations been regarded as an important instrument for attaining and maintaining these positions in the field of politics. Among civilized people war has generally been regarded as an instrument of politics.[117] The successful military leader has often become king or dictator.[118] The ruler has prevented internal sedition by making external war.[119] The landowner, the townsman, the peasant, and

overthrow that dominance. Dominance was a prime cause of the World War" (Rear Admiral Charles L. Hussey, U.S.N., *The United States and Great Britain* [Chicago, 1932], pp. 166–67).

[117] "War is nothing but a continuation of political intercourse, with a mixture of other means" (Von Clausewitz, *On War* [London, 1911], III, 121). "It is evident therefore that the business of war is to be considered as commendable, not as a final end, but as the means of procuring it" (Aristotle *Politics* vii. 2). "Blood and iron have been not only the historical instruments of every state for the assertion of its will among its neighbors, but they have been as well the instruments within the state by which political institutions have come into life and maintained themselves throughout the centuries" (Shotwell, *op. cit.*, pp. 9, 13, 14; see also Schuman, *op. cit.*, pp. 512–18).

[118] Studies of the characteristics of rulers suggest that (1) rulers throughout the history of civilization have tended to belong to an interrelated class or caste characterized particularly by military ability (Perry, *op. cit.*, chapter on "Coming of the Warriors"; see Appen. V, below; Frederick Adams Woods, *op. cit.*, pp. 13, 271); that (2) within this caste the actual rulers are continually selected from those most capable of military leadership (Woods, *op. cit.*, pp. 272–73); and that (3) when a person not belonging to this caste achieves political power, it is usually because he has (like Cromwell, Washington, or Napoleon) remarkable military ability. This is emphasized by Aristotle in discussing the characteristics in which tyrants differ from kings (*Politics* v. 11) and by Machiavelli in discussing the differences in the methods appropriate to new and hereditary princes (*op. cit.*, chaps. ii and vi). See also above, n. 112. The tendencies of democracy have made these generalizations less true in certain countries during the past century.

[119] Foreign war as a remedy for internal tension, revolution, or insurrection has been an accepted principle of government, perhaps illustrated by the Jugurthine and Mithridatic wars of Marius and Sulla at a time of incipient internal revolution in Rome; by the Crusades as a cure for private feudal war (see above, n. 89); and in recent times by the wars of Austria against Serbia (1914) and of Japan against China (1931). Secretary Seward advised President Lincoln to get into trouble with Great Britain or France in order to prevent the incipient Civil War (Carl Russel Fish, *American Diplomacy* [New York, 1923], pp. 106–7). The American minister at Madrid sent a dispatch in April, 1898: "They want peace if they can keep peace and save the dynasty. They prefer the chances of war with the certain loss of Cuba, to the overthrow of the dynasty" (*U.S. Foreign Relations, 1898*, p. 665).

the urban worker have looked upon civil war as the ultimate means for improving the conditions of their class,[120] and the class in power has looked upon international war as the means for preserving the threatened *status quo*.[121] Successful war has often brought to a state diplomatic recognition in the family of nations; rising armaments have preserved this status; and conquest, power, and prestige have given states hegemony or empire over other states or peoples in a region and recognition as a "great power."[122]

Within certain civilized communities, individuals, groups, or the government have sought to utilize other devices such as superstition and religion, law and constitutionalism, wealth and economic organization, civic education, propaganda, art, literature, and science, as instruments for making and maintaining political prestige and power. Such devices have, in certain situations, proved of practical value, but usually among the civilized people they have been combined with war and threats of war.[123]

g) *Independence.*—Where some are dominant, others provide material for independence movements. Civilized peoples, because of

[120] Sometimes an independence movement may demand only freedom from oppression (see below, nn. 124–29), but "the rejection of an inferior status may be associated with outright demands for supremacy through the total destruction of rivals, as in proletarian socialism" (H. D. Lasswell, *World Politics and Personal Insecurity* [New York, 1935], p. 94).

[121] Liebknecht, *op. cit.*, pp. 13 ff.; see above, nn. 113 and 119.

[122] State independence, even in most recent times, has rarely been recognized except as a result of success in arms (see Q. Wright, "The Proposed Termination of the Iraq Mandate," *American Journal of International Law*, XXV [July, 1931], 436 ff.). On the Great Powers see J. Westlake, *Chapters in the Principles of International Law* (Cambridge, 1894), pp. 92 ff.; T. J. Lawrence, *Principles of International Law* (7th ed.; New York, 1923), sec. 113; James Lorimer, *Institutes of the Law of Nations* (Edinburgh, 1883), Vol. I, Book II, chaps. xv and xvi; Heinrich Triepel, *Die Hegemonie, ein Buch von führenden Staaten* (Stuttgart, 1938).

[123] "New implements of power now begin to emerge; among these . . . . are: (1) skills in mass organization, (2) the use of symbolism, (3) the growth of new types of social controls through the developing science of human behavior; through education, preventive medicine, mental hygiene, medical treatment, social work, guidance of leisure time, eugenics, semicustodial care and like methods far reaching in their implications for the social and political order. As compared with the older situations in which armies, wealth, fear, custom, superhuman sanction played so large a part, the new world, politically speaking, displays quite a different form of power possibilities" (C. E. Merriam, *Political Power* [New York, 1934], pp. 304–5). On criteria for evaluating states see Lorimer, *loc. cit.*

their literacy and consequent greater ease of communication, secretly and at a distance, have found such movements more feasible than have primitive people oppressed by empires. Propaganda has usually been the first instrument of such movements. Even large populations cannot fight the armies of established authority with bare hands, but they may reach directly the mind of the soldier behind the gun.

Civilized history, however, records military revolts of slaves,[124] of religious and national minorities,[125] of colonies,[126] of peasants,[127] of townsmen,[128] and of other oppressed classes.[129] Independence, like dominance, is a drive peculiarly characteristic of civilization.[130] While it has often inspired groups and has been at the root of nationalist and isolationist movements, it has also inspired individuals to struggle for power with the hope that it will emancipate them from the power of others.

h) Society.—While booty, sex, adventure, and preservation of the home are all appealed to in arousing a war spirit, the social group has proved the most useful symbol for this purpose among civilized men, and of all social groups the political has been most important.[131] Civilized men have usually been taught from earliest youth that it is

[124] As that led by Spartacus in Italy, 73-71 B.C., and by Nat Turner in Virginia, 1831.

[125] As that of Rim Sin in southern Babylonia against Samsu Iuna, 2072 B.C. (A. T. Olmstead, "The Babylonian Empire," *American Journal of Semitic Languages and Literatures*, XXXV [1919], 95); that of Gauls under Vercingeterix in 52 B.C.; those of the Irish against England in the times of Edward III, Elizabeth, Cromwell, and in 1798 and 1919; that of the Dutch against Spain in 1568; and those of various Balkan states against Turkey in the nineteenth century.

[126] As Britain against Rome in A.D. 120, United States against Great Britain in 1775, and Latin America against Spain after 1810.

[127] As the peasant revolt in England under Wat Tyler and John Ball in 1381 and in Germany in 1524.

[128] As the revolts of the Hanseatic League, Rhine League, and Swabian League against the princes in the thirteenth and fourteenth centuries.

[129] As the Parisian proletariat against France in 1792 and 1871, and the Russian workers and peasants in 1917.

[130] See chap. vi, sec. 4g.

[131] The political group may have various forms—city-state, empire, feudal domain, kingdom, or national state—but in all cases it claims a unique competence over the lives of its people. It is the state that kills internally by criminal justice and externally by war. Lasswell writes: "That subjective event which is the unique mark of a state

noble to die for their state, and, when they are told that its needs and security require war, they have usually been ready to fight.[132]

Primitive man has the same drive, but it is usually expressed as defense of the tribal mores.[133] It is among civilized men that group loyalty particularly requires campaigns of aggression and conquest. The civilized state is dynamic, sometimes more, sometimes less, but usually it is anxious to grow. Consequently, patriotism may be appealed to in support of imperialism.[134]

This happens whenever the state is thought of not merely as a community and a population but also as an idea and a culture, the spreading of which is a blessing to those forced to receive it.[135] Aggression and imperial expansion have, under such circumstances, assumed the guise of a duty and a responsibility.[136] The social drive has been enlisted for wars of religious[137] and cultural proselytism[138] and for wars to sanction international law and the international

---

is the recognition that one belongs to a community with a system of paramount claims and expectations" (*Psychopathology and Politics*, p. 245; *Politics: Who Gets What, When, How* [New York, 1936], p. 229).

[132] Lasswell, "Nations and Classes: The Symbols of Identification," chap. ii in *World Politics and Personal Insecurity*. After discussing the rival groups competing with the state for the individual's loyalty—the region, race, religion, economic class— C. E. Merriam discusses the techniques utilized for promoting loyalty to the state and concludes: "There is no indication that the power of these ideologies tends to decline in recent times, for they still hold sway over men's minds and serve as the basis of political idealism and allegiance. There can be no doubt that they will continue to do so, for a long period of time" (*The Making of Citizens* [Chicago, 1931], p. 278).

[133] See above, chap. vi, sec. 4h.

[134] F. L. Schuman (*op. cit.*) discusses briefly the dynamic and belligerent characteristics of oriental city-states (p. 8); the oriental empires (p. 10); Greek city-states (14); Rome (p. 23); medieval feudal states (p. 38); Renaissance states (p. 54); and modern national states (p. 292).

[135] On changing conceptions of sovereignty see Q. Wright, *Mandates under the League of Nations* (Chicago, 1930), p. 279; "National Sovereignty and Collective Security," *Annals of the American Academy of Political and Social Science*, July, 1936.

[136] P. T. Moon, "Why Europe Shouldered the White Man's Burden," chap. iii in *op. cit.*

[137] As the wars of Islam, of the Crusades, and of Protestants and Catholics in Europe after the Reformation.

[138] As the imperial wars of Egypt, Babylonia, Assyria, Macedonia, Rome, and modern states.

order.[139] To be so utilized, however, the social drive must be converted into an idea.[140]

While animal war is a function of instinct and primitive war of the mores, civilized war is primarily a function of state politics. It seldom springs spontaneously from the behavior patterns of the masses but from the calculations of the leaders. The drives of the masses as organized into behavior patterns at a given time are significant because they may be worked upon to create an army and a war spirit in the civilian population. While the drives for dominance and for independence often motivate the leaders, they are usually combined with other drives and may be subordinated to the drive for social service.

6. TECHNIQUES

"As general culture advances, among primitive peoples the size of the fighting group tends to increase; the warrior class tends to become more specialized; missile weapons (the hurled stone or javelin, blowpipe, bow and arrow) tend to be superseded by piercing or striking weapons (the thrusting spear, battle-ax, or sword); discipline and morale tend to increase; and the battle of pounce and retreat tends to give way to the battle of mass attack and maneuver. With this progress the casualties and destructiveness of war tend to become greater."[141]

The end of the tendency here suggested indicates the characteristics which have distinguished civilized war from primitive war. There is a specialized military class of some size, equipped with swords, spears, or similar weapons, disciplined in group tactical maneuvers. Fortifications and siege operations assume new importance, as, among certain civilizations, do naval operations.[142] Civilized armies have through most of history relied mainly upon the soldier's legs for mobility, the soldier's shield for defense, the soldier's

---

[139] As the medieval wars between the imperial and papal parties and modern coalitions against Napoleon (1815), Germany (1917, 1939), and Italy (1935, 1940).

[140] See below, n. 184. [141] See above, chap. vi, sec. 5.

[142] "At the time of the earliest monuments, the art of war is so highly developed that relatively little progress is manifest in succeeding centuries, save in the size of the armies employed and in their engineering supports. Through ages men fought with practically the same weapons till gunpowder came into use" (Perris, op. cit., p. 23).

arm for striking, and bruising, cutting, or piercing weapons for attack. Certain animal and physical aids have, however, appeared fairly early in most civilizations.[143]

The horse was introduced to Egyptian, Mesopotamian, Hittite, and Greek civilizations by the invasion of nomadic Aryans after the twentieth century B.C. Indian and Chinese civilizations probably utilized the horse as early, and it has been utilized as a war instrument by all subsequent civilizations except those in America which first saw the horse after it was introduced by the Spanish conquerors. The sedentary civilizations usually hitched the horse to a chariot for war purposes, while the nomads rode on his back. Other animals have been used to increase war mobility, particularly the elephant in India and Carthage.[144]

The more advanced primitive peoples used hedges, wooden palisades, and earthworks to protect their villages; but civilization, with the control it gave over great quantities of servile labor, introduced walls of masonry and rubble on a large scale such as the great wall of Nineveh built before 2000 B.C., fifty miles in perimeter, 120 feet high, 30 feet thick, and equipped with 1,500 towers.[145] Civilized armies also often added to the body protection of the shield various types of armor and helmets.[146]

Civilized man began with the knowledge of the bow and arrow contributed to him by his primitive ancestors. The principles of mechanical elasticity, torsion, and momentum have been developed and utilized by most civilizations in siege instruments which have added greatly to the hurling and battering power of human muscles. Roman siege engines were built to throw stones weighing up to 600 pounds distances up to a thousand yards. Archimedes is said to have made a machine for the siege of Syracuse which could throw stones

---

[143] For details of the techniques used in different civilizations see Appen. XV.

[144] See H. Peake and H. J. Fleure, *The Horse and the Sword* (New Haven, 1933); Spaulding *et al., op. cit.*, p. 23; Wissler, "The Influence of the Horse in the Development of Plains Culture (in the United States)," *American Anthropologist* (N.S.), Vol. XVI January–March, 1914.

[145] See "Fortification and Siegecraft," *Encyclopaedia Britannica*, IX, 524.

[146] See B. Laufer, *Prolegomena on the History of Defensive Arms* ("Field Museum Anthropological Series," Vol. XII, No. 2, Pub. 177 [Chicago, 1914]); C. H. Ashdown, *British and Foreign Arms and Armour* (London, 1909).

weighing 1,800 pounds, and there seems to be some weight to the tradition that he constructed mirrors which burned the Roman fleet by focusing the rays of the sun.[147]

Many primitive peoples built canoes which they utilized in war as well as in peace. The Egyptian and Mesopotamian civilizations utilized in war river boats, designed primarily for peaceful purposes, but as early as 2000 B.C. Sesostres of Egypt is said to have had a fleet of four hundred long ships. It was not, however, until the first millennium B.C. that specialized navies began. The Phoenicians became the great sea power in the seventh century B.C. and the Athenians in the fifth century. The Greeks, Romans, and Carthaginians constructed vessels of special design built with high walls for defense and banks of oars and sails for speed and maneuver. A navy would have vessels of several types specializing, respectively, in speed, carrying capacity, ramming, and boarding.[148]

Most civilizations took from their primitive forebears bronze swords and spears, though the Mexican civilization had no metal and utilized obsidian or natural glass set in wood for war purposes. Iron was used for weapons in Egypt by 2000 B.C.; in Mesopotamia, by 1500 B.C.; in Europe and China, by 700 B.C. Primitive people also sometimes utilized fire in war. Civilized people improved the temper and quality of metal weapons, and, with the rise of fortification and siegecraft, boiling pitch, Greek fire, starvation, and flooding were utilized for defense and also for attack.[149]

The cumulative effects of these animal and physical aids to mobility, protection, striking power, and attack made civilized war very different from primitive war even in its early stages, and the dynamic and progressive character of civilization produced continuous improvement in instruments both of attack and of defense. Civilizations in contact with each other employed similar instruments. Ani-

[147] "Fortification and Siegecraft," *Encyclopaedia Britannica*, IX, 525.

[148] P. A. Silburn, *The Evolution of Sea Power* (New York, 1912), chap. ii; W. L. Rodgers, *Greek and Roman Naval Warfare* (New York, 1937); "Navy and Navies," *Encyclopaedia Britannica*, XVI, 175; C. G. Starr, Jr., "The Ancient Warship," *Classical Philology*, XXXV (October, 1940), 353–74.

[149] W. H. Prescott, *Conquest of Mexico* (Philadelphia, 1876); H. J. Spinden, "The Population of Ancient America," *Geographical Review*, XVIII (October, 1928), 645; "Fortification and Siegecraft," *Encyclopaedia Britannica*.

mals could be bred and designs could be imitated by handworkers from materials which were generally available. Knowledge of a military invention once acquired would soon spread to neighboring civilizations and would seldom be forgotten, although the military value of devices varied greatly according to the tactical and strategic skill of those who used them. Even primitive people of warlike character have rapidly appreciated the utility of new military instruments with which they have come in contact. Civilized people have all been more or less warlike, have been less bound by custom than primitive people, and have been under steady pressure from expanding neighbors and their own aggressive policies to improve their military potentialities. Consequently, the diffusion of military inventions among them has been much more rapid than in the case of primitive people. Furthermore, the art of writing makes the transmission and preservation of information about new devices more easy.[150]

Civilized history as a whole, up to the modern period, has presented a picture of uniform and continuous evolution with respect to military instruments. There were, it is true, differences, particularly in the technological backwardness of the isolated American civilizations; but differentials in the animal and physical aids to war available to the different civilizations did not develop in six thousand years of history comparable to those which have developed in the last few centuries.[151] The new instruments developed in the modern period were of a type which could not be produced in quantity except in highly industrialized areas with access to quantities of certain raw materials to be found only in a few places. The tremendous differentials in military power which developed as a result between different groups of civilized people have been one of the outstanding characteristics of history during the past few centuries.

The relatively uniform and continuous evolution of military instruments through the historic period was not paralleled in the history of military organization, strategy, and morale. Here, consider-

---

[150] See above, chap. vi, sec. 5. Laufer (*Prolegomena on the History of Defensive Arms*) discusses the spread of certain types of arms, armor, and tactics from Persia to China and elsewhere.

[151] Oman, *History of the Art of War in the Middle Ages*, Vol. II: "Conclusion," esp. p. 436, and *A History of the Art of War in the Sixteenth Century* (London, 1937).

able differences appeared between civilizations and even greater differences in the stages of a single civilization. These traits depend on the genius of the general and the training of the soldier. They are more easily forgotten and spread less rapidly than mechanical military devices.

The early Mesopotamian civilization developed the phalanx. Babylonia developed a large standing army and close-order tactics. Persia utilized horse archery with a rigorous discipline and high morale as did the nomadic Tartars, the Arabs, and the Turks. The Greeks relied on the phalanx with a disciplined infantry of high morale. The Romans used the more open and flexible legion of soldiers equipped with hurling javelin and sword. Western Christian civilization employed cavalry with lance and sword and developed heavy body armor and fortifications. The Phoenicians and Scandinavians used navies. Chinese and Indian civilizations tended to be peaceful, though sometimes maintaining very large armies without rigorous discipline. Chandragupta, who initiated the Maurya empire immediately after the time of Alexander the Great, is said to have had an army of 600,000 infantry, 30,000 horsemen, 36,000 men with elephants, and 24,000 men with chariots.[152] The Japanese have always maintained a high military morale. The American civilizations had large armies accustomed to bloody religious rites, without horse, and more disciplined in Peru than in Mexico.[153]

The differences between civilizations in respect to warlikeness was considerable. The warlike civilizations of Babylonia, Persia, Rome, Turkey, Japan, and Peru centralized political and military authority and often utilized conscription, rigorous discipline, and military propaganda to sustain morale; while the more peaceful civilizations of Egypt, Sumeria, India, and China had less centralized government through much of their histories and more frequently relied on the use of volunteer or militia armies.[154]

There was a tendency for the more warlike civilizations to have

[152] "India," *Encyclopaedia Britannica*, XII, 186c.

[153] See Appens. XIV and XV. Nearing (*op. cit.*, pp. 119 ff.) gives some figures on the size of armies in Egypt and Rome.

[154] Appen. XV. These characteristics were among those chosen as indices of warlikeness in Table 16 in Appen. XIV.

superior archery and hand weapons. Other military techniques seem to have no direct relationship to warlikeness. Civilizations fall, however, into rather distinct classes with respect to the relation between offensive and defensive power. Certain warlike civilizations developed powerful methods of attack but in their period of maturity developed a great superiority of defense, thus they remained invulnerable to external invasion until disintegrated from within because of the capacity of revolting internal groups effectively to resist central authority through the use of these defensive methods. The Babylonic, Classic, Western, and Russian civilizations were of this type. Other warlike or moderately warlike civilizations, however, such as the Hittite, Tartar, Germanic, Andean, Mexican, and Yucatec, though developing a powerful attack, never created effective means of defense. After a rapid expansion they were overwhelmed by external enemies. The Japanese tended to this type but were protected from annihilation by their isolation and adaptability. They have to date succeeded in preserving a certain distinctiveness as a nationality in the developing world-civilization.

The Peaceful civilizations also were of two types. The Orthodox Christian, Sinic, Chinese, Indian, and Hindu developed powerful defensive methods and were never completely annihilated. The remaining peaceful civilizations (Egyptic, Minoan, Mesopotamian, Mayan) relied mainly on isolation for defense and succumbed after a long existence when invaded by warlike peoples. The Irish and Nestorian civilizations were of similar type but, existing at a much later period, could not preserve their isolation as long and were destroyed by warlike invaders before they had achieved maturity.[155]

The differences between civilizations in respect to military organization, strategy, and morale have been less significant than the differences between the various stages of the same civilization. Every civilization has usually been warlike at one stage of its development and not at another. In fact, every civilization has tended to follow a definite order of change in its military as in its political, social, economic, and ideological history, with a general tendency to become less aggressive as it gets older.[156]

[155] Appen. XIV, Table 17, cols. 18, 19, 25, 26. See also below, nn. 187–89.
[156] Appen. XV. This does not mean it has fewer wars (above, n. 67).

The heroic age which has initiated each civilization has usually been characterized by many small armies, consisting of leaders with private retainers, relying upon rapidity of movement, sudden paralyzing pounce, and rapid withdrawal, like the strategy of a lion. Military operations have been frequent, brief, and relatively inexpensive.[157]

The time of troubles has usually been characterized by the evolution of larger, better-disciplined, and better-equipped citizen or militia armies, with the royal army as a nucleus, inspired by the morale of patriotism, and employing the strategy of mass attack by phalanx, legion, or cavalry, like the charge of a buffalo herd. The state that has originated this type of army has had initial successes and has often embarked upon expansionist wars; but the method has spread, and, when it has been employed by most of the states of the civilization, wars have tended to become very severe, destructive, and relatively indecisive. The spirit of militarism and of cynicism has often developed and has marked the beginning of the decline of the civilization.[158]

Such a military situation has usually been reflected in political practices within the civilization based on the balance of power and in rules of international law regulating war and neutrality and aimed at preserving the independence of the states with a minimum of international friction. Civilizations, however, have never been able to maintain rules of international law capable of preserving such an equilibrium. Instead the military balance of power and the military spirit have stimulated military inventors and strategists to busy themselves with the art of war. Better-disciplined, more maneuverable professional armies have superseded the citizens' army which, however, has usually remained as a reserve to be called on in emergency. With such powerful armies, equipped with new technical, tactical, and strategic inventions, ambitious statesmen have made

[157] The data in support of this and the following paragraphs are contained in Appen. XVI, dealing with the frequency of battles in certain civilizations, and Appen. XV, describing military organization and methods in the stages of all civilizations.

[158] Toynbee (op. cit., III, 167 ff.) notes the great military advances in the Babylonic and Sinic times of trouble when in each case the chariot gave way to the man on horseback. He suggests that both war and agriculture, based on slavery, improve in technique as civilization declines (see also above, n. 37).

repeated efforts to break the balance of power. Such an effort has often been successful and has opened the way for extensive conquests by one state. These conquests have sometimes expanded the area of the civilization itself at the expense of neighboring civilizations or primitive peoples. It has sometimes resulted in politically organizing the whole civilization in a "universal state." In that case there has sometimes been a period of peace and stability in which the professional army is engaged only in defending the frontiers against barbarians and suppressing occasional revolutionary movements or insurrections.

Under such conditions the willingness to endure military hardships has tended to decline among the citizens, and the professional army has degenerated into a mercenary army recruited from colonials or foreigners interested in safety and pay rather than victory. Military operations have tended to rely on mechanisms, fortresses, or trenches and to end by attrition of one or perhaps both sides rather than by pounce, charge, or maneuver. When new discontents or ambitions have arisen among the internal or external proletariat, the army, which lacks loyalty to the civilization to which it no longer really belongs, has frequently proved unreliable, particularly as wars of attrition are costly and wearying to the soldier. Presently the civilization has collapsed from internal disintegration and external invasion. This period of collapse, like the time of trouble, has frequently been characterized by many costly wars.

The history of the technical aspects of civilized war suggests that there has been continuous improvement of military techniques, first to strengthen the offensive and then, in response, to strengthen the defensive; that there have been typical differences in the characteristics of war in the different stages of most civilizations; and that there have been some differences between civilizations with respect to warlikeness and military technique. These latter differences, however, have not been clearly related to any single characteristic of the civilization's composition, organization, or environment, although a civilization which is homogeneous and isolated is less likely to be warlike than one with a heterogeneous population and close intercivilization contacts.[159]

[159] Above, nn. 60–66.

7. LAW

a) General characteristics.—Primitive people have had law, but the rules of this law have not been very clearly distinguished from the rules of morals and religion, science and magic, and the practical arts. All the rules were prescriptions of the mores, not integrated into logical systems, and hardly subject to conscious change by the community.[160]

Civilizations have been characterized by an emphasis upon rational as distinguished from customary behavior patterns, and, as a result of this emphasis, there has been in all civilizations a tendency toward the recognition of certain distinctive classes of rules, each of which tends to become logically integrated—to constitute an ideological system.[161]

Civilizations have not immediately cast off the primitive conceptions of eternal rules beyond human control, but they have distinguished certain rules which are subject to conscious manipulation and adaptation to new needs from others which are not. This distinction between natural law and voluntary law was manifested in early Greek philosophy,[162] registered in the usual linguistic distinctions between *jus et lex, droit et lois, Recht und Gesetz,* justice and law, and emphasized in the promulgation of codes in the early history of most civilizations. Such codes initiated most systems of civilized jural law and distinguished it from primitive custom which is necessarily unwritten.[163] These codes, such as the twelve tables of Rome, were not looked upon as legislating the substance of right, which was still thought of as immutably fixed by nature or custom. They stated the customs and prescribed procedures and penalties. Once the substantive rights were committed to writing, procedures began

---

[160] Chap. vi, sec. 6.

[161] The tendency is augmented through the development of specialized classes—the priests, lawyers, doctors, warriors, engineers, etc.—each of which applied one of these systems—law, religion, science, and the various practical arts. There seems to be little evidence of specialized professional education until organization of the medieval universities about faculties of "divinity, law and physics" and of the guilds about the various practical arts ("Professions," *Encyclopaedia of Social Sciences,* XII, 476).

[162] Sophocles *Antigone* i. 450; Aristotle *Nichomachian Ethics* v. 7; James Bryce, *Studies in History and Jurisprudence* (Oxford, 1901), II, 565 ff.

[163] Henry Sumner Maine, *Ancient Law* (4th ed.; London, 1870), chap. i.

to develop for changing them through the use of fictions, interpretations in accord with general moral principles, and legislation. Eventually most of the civilizations achieved a situation in which a large part of the rules covering human behavior lay in the field of man-made jural law. This jural law was distinguished from the general rules prescribed by religious revelation or discovered by scientific investigations and deemed to be beyond human control.[164]

Another distinction early recognized by most civilizations was that between rules concerning human relations and rules concerning nonhuman phenomena. The Greek philosophers recognized two varieties of "natural law" dealing, respectively, with the immutable aspects of human relations and of natural phenomena. The first came to include formulations of moral doctrines deemed necessary implications of human nature or of the nature of society, while the second came to include formulations of physical and biological observations, such as Euclid's laws of space and Archimedes' law of buoyancy. A similar distinction, however, was applicable to voluntary law, that between jural law and the practical arts. Rules designed to assure stable human relations were distinguished from rules designed to accomplish more precise and immediate practical ends. Instructions for steering a boat, healing the sick, raising crops, and conducting military operations were deemed subject to continuous experiment, invention, and improvement by the individual or leader in charge of the operation and were distinguished from rules of jural law, which, while subject to change, involved to so great an extent the interest of the society as a whole that they could only be changed by prescribed public procedures. In the one case the only sanction for the rule was success in achieving the end aimed at, while in the other the rule, until changed by proper procedure, was sanctioned by social pressures and penalties.[165]

After jural law had become clearly distinguished from scientific, moral, and practical law, the distinction between public law and private law began to be recognized within it. The germs of this dis-

---

[164] *Ibid.*, chap. ii; Q. Wright, "Article 19 of the Covenant of the League of Nations and the Doctrine Rebus sic Stantibus," *Proceedings of the American Society of International Law, 1936*, pp. 55 ff.

[165] Bryce, *op. cit.*, p. 561.

tinction were to be found in many primitive communities which recognized the difference between offenses injuring the group as a whole, to be dealt with by collective action, and those which injured only a member of the group, to be dealt with by private vengeance.[166] With the growth of civilization, however, states, claiming a monopoly of the use of violence and the enforcement of law, claimed also authority to change law by accepted procedures or even to change those procedures. The claims of a state could only be expressed through its law. Consequently, rules concerning crime, public administration, legislative procedure, and constitutional change assumed a distinctive character and distinguished the state as a public corporation with a personality of its own from the individuals which composed it. The idea of the corporate state, however, was not easy to grasp, and most civilizations for long periods went through feudal stages where the state was confused with the ruler or with a hierarchy of rulers whose private property and public jurisdictions were scarcely distinguished.[167]

Finally, the distinction between municipal law governing internal relations and international law governing relations between equal political units was recognized. At first, when the corporate character of the state was not clearly perceived, international law concerned the relation of princes. Since their public and private characters were not clearly distinguished in their internal administration, their external relations resembled that of private individuals in a society.[168] With the growth of the corporate conception of the state, clearly distinguishing public and private law, international law came to have the unique character of law between equal public sovereignties, but none of the historic civilizations achieved a systematic exposition of international law thus conceived. Such an exposition has been the contribution of the modern period since 1500.[169]

[166] Maine, op. cit., chap. x, p. 385; A. R. Radcliffe-Brown, "Law, Primitive," Encyclopaedia of the Social Sciences, IX, 202.

[167] Q. Wright, Mandates under the League of Nations, p. 279; "National Sovereignty and Collective Security," op. cit., p. 3.

[168] Roscoe Pound, "Philosophical Theory of International Law," Bibliotheca Visseriana (Leyden, 1923), Vol. I.

[169] Walker, op. cit., pp. 158 ff.; G. Butler and S. Maccoby, The Development of International Law (London, 1926); C. Van Vollenhoven, The Law of Peace (London, 1936), chap. i.

b) *Law concerning war.*—A law of war, rationally defining the circumstances under which resort to war is legitimate and the activities which are legitimate during war, cannot exist, as Grotius clearly perceived,[170] without an international law systematizing all the values and relations of sovereign states. As most civilizations have never achieved such a systematization, they have not had a law of war in this sense. That achievement has been reserved for the contemporary period, and even now the manifest inconsistencies between legitimate violence and a reign of law, between sovereignty and subjection to law, between neutrality and membership in a jural community, between rules of municipal law and rules of international law, have been by no means ironed out.[171]

The historic civilizations, therefore, have not had a law of war in the full sense, but most of them have had a body of doctrine reconciling the religious, ethical, and economic values of the civilization and the political and legal values of the particular state with the practices of war. This body of doctrine has characteristically consisted of two branches, one of which has been international but not law, the other of which has been law but not international. The first has contained rules drawn from religion, ethics, and philosophy and to a limited extent from international practice, defining the circumstances under which war may be resorted to (*ius ad bellum*) and of practices which ought not to be indulged in during war toward friends or even toward enemies (*jus in bello*).[172] The second body of

[170] *De jure belli ac pacis* i. 1. 1.

[171] Q. Wright (ed.), *Neutrality and Collective Security* (Chicago, 1936); W. H. C. Laves (ed.), *The Foundations of a More Stable World Order* (Chicago, 1941); see above, n. 167; below, chap. xiv.

[172] F. M. Russell (*Theories of International Relations* [New York, 1936]) presents a general survey. For China see R. S. Britton, "Chinese International Intercourse before 700 B.C.," *American Journal of International Law*, XXIX (October, 1935), 616 ff.; W. A. P. Martin, "Traces of International Law in Ancient China," *International Review* (New York), XIV (January, 1883), 63 ff.; E. D. Thomas, *Chinese Political Thought* (New York, 1927); C. P. Sui, *Le Droit des gens et la chine antique* (Paris, 1926). For India see P. Bandyopadhyay, *Law and Custom in Ancient India* (Calcutta, 1920); S. V. Visawanatha, *International Law in Ancient India* (London, 1925). For Classic civilization see W. B. Ballis, *The Legal Position of War: Changes in Its Practice and Theory from Plato to Vattel* (The Hague, 1937); Walker, *op. cit.,*; Phillipson, *op. cit.* For medieval civilization see A. Vanderpol, *La Doctrine scolastique du droit de guerre* (Paris, 1919); R. Regout, *La Doctrine de la guerre juste* (Paris, 1935); Eppstein, *op. cit.*; L. Sturzo, *The International Community and the Right of War* (New York, 1920); Ballis, *op. cit.*; Walker, *op. cit.*; Van Vollenhoven, *op. cit.*

doctrine has contained rules drawn from legislation, decrees, or judicial precedents of the state designed to preserve the ruler's monopoly in warmaking by restricting private war, piracy, reprisals, or assistance to belligerents and designed to promote military efficiency by regulating the private emoluments of military activity and specifying the authority for acts initiating or conducting war.[173]

It is clear that these two types of rules differ from the law of war forming a chapter in the systematic body of contemporary international law. They also differ from the law of war recognized among primitive peoples.

The latter consists of rules developed in the mores of each tribe from three sources: the psychological need of individuals about to embark upon war to acquire an attitude of readiness to die and to kill; the sociological need of the group for an overt manifestation of its unity and solidarity in the war enterprise; and the international need of the group for peaceful relations with its present enemy after the war is over. Through trial and error each group developed in its mores rules, distinctions, and rituals to serve these purposes more or less adequately in its particular situation. In most cases the function of the rule was not clearly appreciated by the participants. They were observed because they were the custom, not because their utility was appreciated.[174]

Among civilized people, on the other hand, the object of rules of war has been to relate the activities of war to a consciously perceived end. War has been characteristically a means to political ends, but political ends have not been the only ends which people have deemed important in most stages of most civilizations. Consequently, before war can be embarked upon wholeheartedly, it has been necessary that the rulers who initiate it and, in lesser degree, the soldiers and civilians whose vigorous co-operation is essential to success be convinced that it is a means to a desirable political end and that it will not frustrate other more important ends.

[173] Grover Clark, "The English Practice in Regard to Reprisals by Private Persons," *American Journal of International Law*, October, 1933; A. F. Hindmarch, *Force in Peace* (Cambridge, Mass., 1933), chap. iii; Q. Wright, "Prize Money" (manuscript, University of Illinois, 1913); Richard Lewinsohn, *The Profits of War through the Ages* (London, 1936), pp. 300 ff.

[174] See above, chap. vi, sec. 6.

The law of war has served these two functions. The desirability of a given political end might be proved by mere assertion by the supreme political authority, but such assertions have proved more convincing when supported by general principles to which the public has become habituated. Only in ages of accepted despotism has "reason of state" been asserted as sufficient grounds for war even from the political point of view.[175] Ordinarily need of self-defense, preservation of group interests, expansion of a superior culture or religion, enforcement of justice, realization of dynastic claims, or similar objectives have been asserted, and the assertion of any such end has implied a body of doctrine in which objectives are evaluated and a particular one given a position of importance. Such a doctrine might be elaborated from internal sources, but, if elaborated from sources more broadly accepted in the civilization, its persuasive value has been greater.[176]

Such sources become almost indispensable for solving possible conflicts between the stated political objectives of the war and other objectives commanding the individual's loyalty. When the state says you must go to war for reason of state, but the church says, "Thou shalt not kill," or "The meek shall inherit the earth," a body of doctrine becomes necessary to reconcile the two commands, and this must be drawn from sources as broad as the religion. Since the fundamental ethical norms are usually as broad as the civilization, rules to serve this function must be deduced from these norms. In other words, a rationalization of civilized war requires that deductions be developed from the fundamental principles of the civilization capable of justifying war and war activities in the circumstances in which the political rulers wish to resort to it.

This was done for Classical civilization in the philosophies of war set forth by Plato, Aristotle, and Cicero[177] and for western European civilization by the Catholic theory of just war initiated by Augustine in the fourth century and developed by Isadore, Hostiensis, and Aquinas during the succeeding millennium.[178]

Most civilizations have been based on principles with which war

[175] Sturzo, *op. cit.*   [176] Above, n. 172.

[177] See Ballis, *op. cit.;* Phillipson, *op. cit.*

[178] See Vanderpol, *op. cit.;* Regout, *op. cit.;* and Eppstein, *op. cit.*

is easily reconciled, and so rules of war have been mainly formal prescriptions relating to the initiation and conduct of war and scarcely distinguished from strategic wisdom.[179]

Where, however, the principles of a civilization have been on their face hostile to war, more elaborate argumentation has become necessary. Thus in the Indian, Chinese, and Western civilizations, which accepted the values of peace and harmony as fundamental, the doctrine of war became somewhat elaborate and controversial. Particularly was this true of the Christian civilizations in view of the pacifism and nonresistance of the earliest Christian communities.[180] After Christianity had become the official religion of Rome and the Roman Empire was pressed on all sides by non-Christian barbarians, such Christian writers as Augustine perceived practical reasons of state for war.[181] To reconcile this with the pacific duty of a Christian, they elaborated the doctrine that war is justified if it is the only means to justice. It is such only if there is a just cause, i.e., if injustice has been or is about to be committed which war may rectify or prevent; if no peaceful means for accomplishing this end is available or adequate; if the injuries to be anticipated from the war do not outweigh the injustices which have been or may be endured; if a proper political authority, after due consideration of these conditions, has sanctioned the war; and if the motives of that authority for making war are solely the promotion of justice. If all these conditions are fulfilled, the war is just according to the Catholic doctrine, and a Christian may engage in it.

[179] For ancient Jewish law of war see Deut. 20 : 19, 20; Walker, *op. cit.*, p. 36; for Greek see Walker, *op. cit.*, p. 42; Roman, *ibid.*, p. 47.

[180] They sometimes, but rarely, continued to serve in the Roman army after baptism (Eppstein, *op. cit.*, chap. ii). C. J. Cadoux (*The Early Christian Attitude toward War* [London, 1919]), on the basis of a careful examination of the writings of Tertullian, Lactantius, Origen, Cyprian, the Hippolytian Orders, and other sources as well as the interpretations of later controversialists, concludes that the early church was definitely against war; that no baptized Christian enlisted until the time of Marcus Aurelius (A.D. 174); and that, though Christian opposition to war weakened in the third century, the church continued to oppose war until Constantine accepted Christianity and attributed his victory at Saxa Rubia to its influence in A.D. 312. Even after this the church's attitude remained doubtful until the time of Augustine, a century later. See also Grotius, *op. cit.* i. 2. 9; Gibbon, *op. cit.*, chap. xv (ed. Boston, 1851), I, 551; W. Cunningham, *Christianity and Politics* (Boston, 1915).

[181] Eppstein, *op. cit.*, p. 65.

The writers conceded that a Christian should subordinate his judgment as to the justice of the war to that of the political authority in doubtful cases. Only if it was clear to him that the war was unjust could he decline to "render unto Caesar."[182] While the writers recognized that objectively a war could only be just on one side, the later ones, at least, realized that "invincible ignorance" might result in the party in the wrong thinking he was in the right.[183]

Such rationalization as this indicated that, as civilization has advanced, it has become more and more necessary that wars should be fought for ideas. Civilized war, like primitive war, has been a conflict between two armies, between two populations, and between two societies, but it has also been a conflict between two ideas. When each of the belligerents has been a unit of the same civilization, the ideas at war have sometimes been deductions from the same fundamental idea. War in such cases has been a conflict between rival interpretations of the same idea. Both sides have been fighting for justice, for Christianity, for security, for progress, etc. Ideas at war have not always been distinguished from one another by logic. Christianity has fought Islam, Protestantism has fought Catholicism, democracy has fought autocracy, without much consideration of what the logical difference, if any, between the ideas represented by these several symbols may be. It has been assumed that a logical distinction exists because the words which symbolize these different social myths are distinct. Again, in periods when loyalties have been concentrated upon the state, the ideas at war have been assumed to be represented by the symbols of the belligerent societies themselves. Athens has fought Sparta, Rome has fought Carthage, France has fought England. The fighting idea and the fighting societies have been the same, but usually some broader ideological war has developed, if for no other reason, to assist in getting allies. No other state can be expected to assist in a war for England or for France, but in a war for liberty allies may be available. The idea for which an army struggles is nearly always broader than the army itself. Where

---

[182] For an excellent summary see *ibid.*, pp. 92, 122.

[183] Francis de Vitoria, *De jure belli*, sec. 32; Regout, *op. cit.*, pp. 206 ff.

the fight is only to obtain booty, prize, or adventure for the fighters the enterprise is hardly war at all but piracy or robbery.[184]

The presence of an ideological conflict, a struggle for values be yond the immediate interest of the participants—values which may be achieved even though all the combatants die—has distinguished civilized war from animal and primitive war and from other forms of civilized violence.[185] This characteristic has also made it possible for war to develop extremes of destructiveness. War mores have developed among primitive people to reconcile individual psychological needs, group solidarity, and intergroup contacts. Consequently, they have not tolerated wars so severe as to assure the death of the participants, to threaten the existence of the group, and to destroy intergroup relations. But when war is for an idea, especially a very broad one deemed fundamental in the civilization, the necessary limits to destructiveness have not been evident. If one fights for democracy, it may be appropriate to destroy all the states and most of the individuals so that a clear field will remain in which democracy can grow. If it is Christianity against Islam, each may be prepared to destroy all the adversaries if only a few of its side can remain to perpetuate the true faith.

The law of war, particularly that part dealing with the conduct of war (the *jus in bello*), has sought to counteract this tendency by setting limits to the methods which may be used in order to reduce destructiveness and to make future reconciliation possible. When war is fought for broad, ideological objectives, such rules have tended to break down because the end is thought to justify all means and war has tended to become absolute. Though the development of civilization has tended to the emphasis upon such objectives in war, it has also tended to the development of sentiments of humanity and a more longsighted expediency. Consequently, the rise of a civiliza-

[184] See C. E. Merriam (*The Making of Citizens*, pp. 5 ff.) on the varying objectives of political and nonpolitical loyalties and H. D. Lasswell (*World Politics and Personal Insecurity*, chap. ii) for general theory of symbols of identification in world-politics.

[185] "The phenomena of war, slavery, sub-, super-, and co-ordination are of course a commonplace of life among ants and many other types of animal aggregations. The philosophies and their accompanying hypocrisies appear only when the life stream has thrust its way farther down the drift of time" (Merriam, *The Making of Citizens*, p. 4).

tion has meant more legal regulation of war but also more appeal to military necessity as a grounds for evading such rules in practice.[186]

Has there been any trend in the ideology of war through the six thousand years of civilized history? It seems clear that the later civilizations have emphasized the ideological conflict more than have earlier civilizations. There is not much evidence that the ancient oriental and American monarchies fought for ideas other than the avenging of injury or the expansion of empire. In the secondary civilizations of the Mediterranean, China, and India, however, wars for the spread of civilization against barbarism, for preventing injustice, or for remedying injuries are known. In the tertiary civilizations of Europe and Asia such broad ideas as the propagation of the true faith, defense against barbarian invasions, and enforcement of just claims are usually the declared objects of war.[187]

With this development, there has been a continuous trend toward the elaboration of laws of war. The older civilizations recognized rules to mitigate atrocities during war, especially when the enemy was of the same civilization, but they do not appear to have elaborated the *jus ad bellum* until the fifth century B.C., when in Greece, India, and China the justice of going to war began to be discussed. Principles on this subject may have been embodied in the Roman *jus fetiale*.[188] These rules were elaborated in much more detail by the theologians and canonists of Christian Europe.[189] The later civilizations also elaborated rules for the conduct of war such as the Roman *jus belli* and the medieval treatises on chivalry embodying Saracen ideas.[190]

[186] See Lueder's argument for military necessity (*Kriegsraison*) in Holtenzendorff, *Handbuch des Volkerrechts*, IV, 254–56, 484, quoted and criticized in Westlake, *op. cit.*, pp. 238–44. Clausewitz (*op. cit.*) thought civilization tended to absolute war. This seems to have been the opinion of Bloch (*The Future of War* [Boston, 1914], pp. xvi) and of J. F. C. Fuller (*The Dragon's Teeth* [London, 1933], p. 161) who, however, see stalemate and mutual attrition as the result, perhaps stimulating a new emergence either of war elimination or of a new civilization (Fuller, *op. cit.*, pp. 273–99).

[187] See references above, nn. 111 and 172.

[188] Walker, *op. cit.*, p. 47.   [189] Epperstein, *op. cit.*

[190] Walker, *op. cit.*, pp. 48, 129 ff. Vollenhoven (*op. cit.*, p. 35) notes that medieval books on war may be divided into two classes: those of the theologians, like the Italian Legnano, the Dutchman Henri de Gorcum, the Spaniard Juan Lopez, and the Zealander Guillelmus Matthaei, and those of the admirers of chivalry, like Honoré Bonnet and Christine de Pisan.

Within this general trend toward a development of both the *jus ad bellum* and the *jus in bello*, there were fluctuations in the theory of war during the life of each civilization. In discussing these fluctuations it will be convenient to utilize the distinction between the body of doctrine developed from the internal law of the state and that developed from international sources.[191]

c) *Internal law and violence.*—The internal law of states began where the law of primitive peoples left off, with the distinction between acts of violence against public interests—crime and war—to be dealt with as special events by the authorities of the tribe, and acts of violence against private interests left to private vengeance.[192] Civilized peoples, however, soon began to realize the contradiction between law and violence, at least within the state, and the law of the state, in successive stages, sought to control violence.

During the heroic age the law usually attempted to forbid private internal violence, at first by permitting some authority to intervene as arbitrator and to award blood money to the injured party in order to prevent feuds.[193] Then there were efforts to suppress such violence by a local voluntary police, "the hue and cry." Enforcement of the "king's peace" was the next step. At first the king's peace extended over only the place where the king was or over the areas directly controlled by him. Later it extended throughout the entire realm which he claimed,[194] sometimes with certain exceptions such as the duel for offenses involving honor.[195]

With the characteristic anxiety to solidify the authority of the state during the many wars in the time of trouble, an effort was often

---

[191] See above, nn. 172 and 173.

[192] Above, n. 166.   [193] Maine, *op. cit.*, pp. 374 ff.

[194] F. W. Maitland and F. C. Montague, *A Sketch of English Legal History* (New York, 1915), pp. 66–67; D. J. Medley, *English Constitutional History* (2d ed.; Oxford, 1898), pp. 384–92.

[195] The duel did not exist in Classic civilization but seems to have been known by the Germans of Tacitus. It was expecially developed in Western civilization as a legal procedure (trial by battle) and later a settlement of honor ("Duel," *Encyclopaedia Britannica*, VII, 711 ff.). The judicial duel was introduced into Italy by the Lombards in the seventh century and began to decline in the twelfth century, at which time the duel of honor began to develop, attaining great importance in the sixteenth and seventeenth centuries. Marco Polo reported that the duel of honor had existed in Malabar (see F. R. Bryson, *The Sixteenth-Century Italian Duel* [Chicago, 1938], Introd.).

made to control private external violence by regulating or forbidding reprisals and private military expeditions which might involve the sovereign in war against his will, and which would, in any case, dissipate his military resources. Sovereigns have expended great efforts to realize their claim to a monopoly of violence.[196]

The period of stabilization and the universal state has usually witnessed efforts of the state to limit its own internal violence. Constitutional guaranties have sometimes limited arbitrary methods in the suppression of crime, mob violence, and rebellion.[197]

Finally, as the civilization went into decline, efforts were sometimes made by the state to limit its own external violence. Formalities like the Roman *jus fetiale*, or the medieval declaration of war, were occasionally insisted upon before the state went to war, and laws attempted to curb irregularities of privateers and mercenaries, who in this period constituted much of the armed forces, by limiting their economic perquisites from captures and successful sieges. Extensions of law into the conduct of war sometimes proved so contrary to the nature of the latter that armies, so hampered, were at a disadvantage in contests with the rising heroes of a new civilization recognizing fewer restrictions in warfare.[198]

d) International law and violence.—Parallel with these changes in municipal law were changes in the international conception of legitimate war.

In heroic ages war was regarded as natural. It seemed self-evident that the group could go to war to acquire slaves, territory, or trade. The group was a law unto itself. Its neighbors constituted merely an environment to be plundered at will except as immediate expediency might suggest the contrary. Such an attitude appeared among the Homeric Greeks[199] and the barbarian invaders of the Roman Empire.[200]

In the time of trouble, ideas of justice were resorted to in support

---

[196] See above, n. 173.

[197] Maine (*op. cit.*, p. 381) finds that a law of 149 B.C. for the first time provided for dealing with certain crimes by a regular judicial procedure in Rome.

[198] See above, n. 186.　　　　　　　　　　[199] See the *Odyssey*.

[200] "In the Dark Ages between 476 and 800 A.D. international law reached its nadir in the West" (Walker, *op. cit.*, p. 64).

of war, but they were subjectively interpreted. Wars were made at this stage to prevent invasion, to recover seized property, and to punish crime against citizens.[201] Even when reasons of mere expediency were urged, as in the Athenian conversation with the Melians in Thucydides, their elaboration showed that the idea of justice was sufficiently important to require argument.[202] Opposing philosophies of pacifism and militarism tended to develop during this period.[203]

The period of stability which usually followed led to emphasis upon the need of proper authority to initiate war and upon the distinction between public war thus initiated and private war not so initiated. There were efforts to eliminate the latter as in the Roman *jus fetiale*[204] and the medieval truce and peace of God.[205] When a universal state developed, this idea led to the conception of a single authority on earth, or at least within the civilization, competent to make or authorize war. In the Roman Empire war was never legitimate unless authorized by the emperor, and Dante sought to revive this idea in the late Middle Ages.[206]

The decline of the historic civilizations was usually marked by a wide separation of theory and practice. While the theorists elaborated the *jus ad bellum*, in practice political rulers dispensed with efforts to determine the justice of war by appeal to principle or accepted authority and assumed that *de facto* power constituted a suffi-

[201] See, e.g., medieval concepts of just war, above, nn. 181–83.

[202] *History of the Peloponnesian War* v. 5. 16.

[203] See Russell's comparison of the pacifist Mencius and the militarist Shang Yang in the period of warring states in China, fourth century B.C. (*op. cit.*, pp. 20, 32); of the pacifist emperor Asoka and the Machiavellian *Arthasastras* probably written by Kautilya in the early Maurya period of India, third century B.C. (pp. 40, 44); of the pacifist Aristophanes and militarist expositions of Athenian policy by Thucydides during the Peloponnesian War in the fourth century B.C. (pp. 59, 60); of the pacifist Dante and more militant Legnano in the fourteenth century (p. 99); and in the early fifteenth century the pacifist Erasmus and the militarist Machiavelli (pp. 119 ff., 128 ff.). The defense of pacifism by the Christian Origen against the defense of war by the Platonist Celsus in the third century may also be mentioned, though this occurred during the period of the universal state in Classical civilization (see Cadoux, *op. cit.*).

[204] Walker, *op. cit.*, p. 47.

[205] A. C. Krey, "The International State of the Middle Ages, "*American Historical Review*, October, 1922. Vollenhoven (*op. cit.*, p. 32) takes a less favorable view.

[206] *De monarchia.*

cient credential for making war. War was frankly made for "reasons of state" during this period. Any policy for the augmentation of power was sufficient reason, and any authority capable of making war was a state.[207] Such a system marked the conflict between the old civilization which was passing away and the new civilization in its heroic age.

To trace the relation between changes in the legal position of war, on the one hand, and changes in the frequency and destructiveness of war, on the other, would require a detailed historical narrative. The relation was probably reciprocal. New material techniques and conditions of war gave birth to new theories, which in turn affected the disposition to wage war and the persistence and morale with which it was waged. The theory which, at any given time, would do most for peace depended, therefore, upon the material conditions of war at the moment.[208]

Civilized society was distinguished from primitive society by the greater influence of ideas upon the internal and external behavior of the group. Civilized men used ideas to improve the technique of war, and they used war to spread ideas. War created and expanded states and then destroyed them. It unified civilizations and then disintegrated them.[209] The constructive and destructive potentialities of war went hand in hand, with the result that successive civilizations, measured by major fluctuations in population, culture, and social organization, became larger, less homogeneous, and less enduring. Within each civilization wars became less frequent and more destructive. The human race as a whole tended to more homogeneity, greater rapidity of social change, and more synchronous fluctuation in all its parts.

[207] Sturzo, op. cit.

[208] There has been no persistent trend in civilizations toward a general acceptance of either pacifism or militarism. Rather there has been a tendency toward increasingly sharp cleavages of opinion. Schools of pacifism and militarism often arose in the time of troubles and continued in conflict with each other through the civilization (see above, nn. 186 and 203).

[209] See Toynbee, op. cit., III, 145 ff., 167 ff.

CHAPTER VIII

CHARACTER OF MODERN CIVILIZATION

MODERN anthropologists interpret and evaluate each trait of a culture by reference to its function in the culture as a whole, that is, by reference to its service or disservice in supporting the changing values of the culture as manifested by the totality of its practices, customs, ideas, and sentiments and their interrelationships at any moment.[1] An attempt has been made in earlier chapters to state the role of war in the functioning of animal life, of primitive societies, and of historic civilizations. To appreciate the role of war in the modern world, the nature of that world must be kept clearly in mind. The complexity of the modern world, the fact that we live in it, and the absence of any other contemporary world, with which it can be compared and from which it can be differentiated, make it difficult to grasp it as a whole, more difficult than is the case with an animal species, a primitive people, or a historic civilization.

It has, therefore, seemed advisable to digress from the direct consideration of war to examine in this chapter the emergence, the spirit, the development, and the changes of modern civilization. This digression will be followed by chapters in which the characteristics of modern war and its relations to the various aspects of modern civilization will be studied.

1. EMERGENCE OF MODERN CIVILIZATION

The period of the Renaissance marked the emergence of a new type of dynamic equilibrium and initiated a new trend in history comparable to the emergence of civilized from primitive societies and of men from animals.[2] Statistical series, relating to population growth; gold, silver, and coal production; wheat prices; wages and

---

[1] A. R. Radcliffe-Brown, *The Andaman Islanders* (Cambridge, 1922), p. 230. For conception of function see chap. ii, sec. 5a above; Appen. V, n. 11, below.

[2] See chap. iv, sec. 1.

166

hours of labor; inventions and scientific discoveries; and forms of art, literature, and philosophy exhibit movements of unprecedented magnitude during this period.[3] The importance of this transition has been recognized by natural scientists,[4] philosophers,[5] literary and artistic critics,[6] economists,[7] anthropologists,[8] internationalists,[9] and historians.[10]

[3] John U. Nef, *The Rise of the British Coal Industry* (London, 1932), pp. 20, 123; George F. Warren and F. A. Pearson, *Gold and Prices* (New York, 1935), pp. 156, 297, 322, 324, 436; Thorold Rogers, *Work and Wages* (ed. 1890), pp. 73, 135; W. F. Ogburn (ed.), *Recent Social Trends* (New York, 1933), I, 126; Pitirim Sorokin, *Social and Cultural Dynamics* (New York, 1937), I, 382, 400, 483, 576, 633; II, 137, 168, 170, 189, 630; III, 231, 236. See also Appen. XVII, Figs. 28–34.

[4] W. C. Dampier-Whetham, *A History of Science* (New York, 1930), p. 111; Benjamin Ginzburg, "Science," *Encyclopaedia of the Social Sciences* (New York, 1935), XIII, 598.

[5] "Protestantism is in essence ecclesiastical modernization. Scientific method in religion, higher criticism, humanitarian passion and the like started and grew to strength in the Protestant world" (H. M. Kallen, "Modernism," *Encyclopaedia of the Social Sciences*, X, 565). See also Walter Lippmann, *A Preface to Morals* (New York, 1929), pp. 73, 94.

[6] W. H. Pater, *Studies in the History of the Renaissance* (London, 1873). Henry Hallam begins his *Introduction to the Literature of Europe* (London, 1839) with the revival of learning about 1400, and Anne C. L. Botta states in her *Handbook of Universal Literature* (New York, 1896) that a new period in the literature of Italy, France, Spain, Germany, and England began about 1500 (pp. 194, 243, 297, 407, 457).

[7] "The period centering about the year 1500 was marked by changes so rapid and so extensive that they deserve the name of revolution" (Clive Day, *A History of Commerce* [New York, 1907], p. 128). See also H. M. Robertson, *Aspects of the Rise of Economic Individualism* (Cambridge, 1933), p. 45; Nef, *op. cit.*, I, 124, and "Industrial Europe at the Time of the Reformation," *Journal of Political Economy* (1941), pp. 1 ff., 221 ff.; Alfred Marshall, *Principles of Economics* (2d ed.; London, 1891), p. 28.

[8] Clark Wissler, *An Introduction to Social Anthropology* (New York, 1929), p. 43.

[9] J. B. Scott, *The Spanish Origins of International Law* (Oxford, 1934), pp. 4 ff. International lawyers have always emphasized the importance of the transition from the orthodox medieval conception, expounded in Dante's *De monarchia* (and common to many historic civilizations) of a universal community of individuals organized in a universal church or state (see A. J. Toynbee, *A Study of History* [3 vols.; Oxford, 1934]), to the modern conception of a universal community of sovereign states. See T. A. Walker, *A History of the Law of Nations* (Cambridge, 1899), chap. ii; J. Westlake, *Chapters on the Principles of International Law* (Cambridge, 1894), chaps. ii and iii; L. Oppenheim, *International Law* (5th ed.; London, 1937), Vol. I, chap. ii; J. L. Brierly, *The Law of Nations* (2d ed.; Oxford, 1936), chap. i; F. M. Russell, *Theories of International Relations* (New York, 1936), chaps. vii–ix; Q. Wright, "National Sovereignty and Collective Security," *Annals of the American Academy of Political and Social Science*, July, 1936. The latter conception which regards the sovereign state as the indispensable mediator

Among the significant developments of the century from 1450 to 1550 were the effective use of explosives, of clocks, and of printing; the discoveries of America and of new routes to the East; the rise of vernacular literatures, the rediscovery of ancient literatures, and the renascence of art; the fall of the Eastern empire, the reformation of Western Christianity, and the rise of strong national dynasties in England, France, and Spain; and the acceptance by the European leaders of the ideas of critical scholarship, of science, of territorial sovereignty, and of business accounting. Western civilization came into contact with ten living and dead civilizations as well as with many primitive cultures. Institutions and methods, values and ideas, were compared and exchanged by the rising élites. The geocentric, anthropocentric, religiocentric, hierarchical order, established by revelation and tradition in Western Christendom and in most of the other civilizations, confining the human mind and spirit to a static economy and immutable truths, became infected by fevers of in-

---

between the individual and the world-community is the characteristic contribution of modern international law. The historians of the concept do not disagree with this, though they differ in their emphasis upon the relative importance of practice and theory in the origination of the concept. Julius Goebel (*The Equality of States* [New York, 1923], pp. 25–29, 58) attributes most influence to the growing practice of treaty-making and arbitration among later medieval monarchs, though he does not deny the importance of theoretical expositions, especially those of Bartolus, on the distinction between corporations which do and do not recognize a superior. E. D. Dickinson (*The Equality of States in International Law* [Cambridge, Mass., 1920], pp. 30–31, 68 ff.) emphasizes the influence of the theories applying the Stoic and patristic conception of the natural equality of men in a state of nature, by analogy to sovereign states. This analogy was inherent in the organic theories of the state developed by such medieval writers as John of Salisbury, Marsilius of Padua, and Nicholas of Cues but was first made explicit by Hobbes and Pufendorf in the seventeenth century (see review by Q. Wright in *American Journal of International Law*, XVIII [1924], 386 ff.). C. Van Vollenhoven (*The Law of Peace* [London, 1936]) emphasizes the ruin by 1500 of hopeful world-institutions created in the main by commercial interests in the late Middle Ages (pp. 55–70) and the novelty of the system of sovereign states in a balance of power which originated in Italy and gradually spread over Europe and the rest of the world after this time.

¹⁰ J. A. Symonds, *The Renaissance in Italy* (London, 1875–88), and "Renaissance," *Encyclopaedia Britannica* (14th ed.), XIX, 122 ff. "The age of the Cathedral had passed. The age of the Printing Press had begun" (W. E. H. Lecky, *History of the Rise and Influence of the Spirit of Rationalism in Europe* [London, 1870], I, 259). See also Henry Adams, *Mont St. Michel and Chartres* (New York, 1913); J. W. Draper, *History of the Conflict between Religion and Science* (New York, 1875), pp. 290 ff.; Harry Elmer Barnes, *The History of Western Civilization* (New York, 1935), I, 810–17; II, 3–6.

quisitiveness and skepticism which would eventually prove fatal. In the West pioneers were by 1550 looking out upon vast unknown realms of nature, art, and opportunity, confusing and bewildering, but perhaps capable of being ordered by human energy, especially if that energy could be directed by new methods of observation, experiment, analysis, and representation, and could utilize new techniques of expression, communication, persuasion, and control.

These changes were so momentous that the civilization of Europe in the seventeenth century was wholly different from that in the fifteenth. Some of the institutions of medieval Christendom, it is true, survived. Some survive even in the twentieth century, but their spirit is as feeble as was the spirit of classical institutions in the sixth century. A new civilization, inspiring new states, new churches, new corporations, and new universities had turned its back on the European Middle Ages and was advancing to occupy the hitherto uncivilized lands of America, the Pacific, and Africa and to penetrate and gradually to supersede the ancient civilizations of Mexico and Peru; Russia, Turkey, and the Arab countries; India, China, and Japan.

2. SPIRIT OF MODERN CIVILIZATION

This pluralistic civilization, which emerged from Western Europe in the fifteenth century, gradually spread over the world through the influence of travelers, traders, missionaries, soldiers, administrators, immigrants, books, newspapers, telegraphs, and radios. Has this civilization been characterized by a unique complex of fundamental values?[11] The values of modern civilization have not been organized in the form of a universal religion nor have they as yet superseded entirely the beliefs which characterized the civilizations which the world-system has gradually engulfed. Belief in humanity, in liberty, in science, and in tolerance has, however, become characteristic of the leaders of thought whether they spring from a Christian, Jewish, Moslem, Confucian, Buddhist, or Hindu tradition. This philosophy may be expressed by the words "humanism," "lib-

[11] See Appen. XVIII. Speaking for China as a new convert to world-civilization, Lin Yu Tang writes: "The position should be bravely taken that the modern world has a spiritual unity and that modern culture is the common heritage of the world" (*My Country and My People* [rev. ed.; New York, 1939], p. 362).

eralism," "pragmatism," and "relativism,"[12] or collectively by the word "modernism."[13]

It is not intended by these terms to denote any precise philosophical system but to suggest attitudes which have been exemplified to an increasing degree in modern thought and behavior.[14] The connotations of these four words seem to have become more favorable, especially in the past century,[15] although the terms or the ideas which they symbolize were associated with the most characteristic Renaissance tendencies. These ideas also provide a synthesis of many of the apparently conflicting post-Renaissance philosophical systems and seem adapted to the conditions which have developed in modern civilization.

a) Humanism.—Humanism asserts that the source of values is human insight, particularly the insight that every man is an end, that institutions and arts exist for man, and that every member and section of the human race is worthy of consideration in social planning and action. In 1495 Queen Isabella urged that the newly discovered Indians be treated with humanity. In 1542 Francis of Vitoria recognized that the Indians had rights under natural law. Missionaries proceeded to the Americas and Asia on the assumption that all human souls were equally valuable. Vigorous societies la-

[12] These words or ones of similar meaning have been used by numerous writers of diverse schools of thought in characterizing modern civilization and have frequently figured in the titles of influential associations, especially in the nineteenth century (see Appen. XVIII).

[13] "Modernism" was used by Rousseau in a letter to M. D., January 15, 1769, to describe the humanitarianism, rationalism, and tolerance of the philosophs. It has been recently described as "the endeavour to harmonize the relations between the older institutions of civilization and science" (Kallen, *op. cit.*, p. 565). The cumulative growth of science tending toward universalism and rapid change (see George Sarton, *Introduction to the History of Science* [Washington: Carnegie Institution, 1927], Vol. I, introductory chap.), associated with the static tendency of institutions and beliefs, creates conditions favorable to violent conflict if the gap is allowed to become too great. A philosophy and method to make adjustments continuous is needed, and this need has dominated modern history. Human action must be based on what is anticipated rather than on what has been. The difficulty of doing this has always been the major cause of war (see above, chap. vi, sec. 2; chap. vii, sec. 4). Modernism has sought to provide the remedy.

[14] Quantitative studies of trends of attitude, philosophic analyses of modern thought, and popular oratory in support of these propositions are cited in Appen. XVIII.

[15] See Appen. XVIII.

bored in most Western countries for the protection of natives and eventually succeeded in eliminating the slave trade and, in most sections of the world, the status of slavery. Revolutions in England, United States, France, and Russia proclaimed the equality of man. Governments more and more accepted the thesis that they were created for the good of the governed not only at home but in their colonies. Reforms designed to ameliorate the conditions of slaves, serfs, natives, women, children, laborers, and others who appeared to be oppressed or underprivileged proceeded apace by legislation, both national and international.[16]

The progress of such legislation, it is true, was often delayed, halting, or ill conceived, and powerful privileged groups—slaveholders, landlords, capitalists, imperial administrators, aristocrats, nationalists, racialists, Fascists, Nazis—have resisted such movements by force and by rationalizations, asserting that particular classes, groups, nations, or races are entitled to special consideration;[17] but those excluded have less and less accepted the discriminations either in theory or in practice. The permission to dominate over someone else has proved less and less acceptable as a compensation for being dominated over, especially for those at the bottom of the social, economic, or racial ladder with nothing left to dominate over except their own sentiments. Law, both municipal and inter-

---

[16] Q. Wright, *Mandates under the League of Nations* (Chicago, 1930), chap. i. See also B. Kidd, *Social Evolution* (London, 1895), pp. 300 ff. J. C. Faries (*The Rise of Internationalism* [New York, 1915], pp. 198 ff.) lists 150 conferences on "social interests" from 1839 to 1913. Much of the work for human melioration is now co-ordinated officially through the League of Nations and the International Labor Organization, though private international organizations on such subjects continually increase in numbers (see brief account of mandates, minorities, health, social, humanitarian, and labor work of these institutions, Secretariat of the League of Nations, *The Aims, Methods and Activity of the League of Nations* [Geneva, 1935], pp. 108–20, 147–91; this volume states that there are 800 international bodies in the field [p. 195]).

[17] A number of such theories are summarized by C. E. Merriam and H. E. Barnes, *A History of Political Theories, Recent Times* (New York, 1924), chap. xiii; and texts are printed by Alfred Zimmern, *Modern Political Doctrines* (Oxford, 1939). See also articles in the *Encyclopaedia of the Social Sciences* on such topics as "Fascism," "National Socialism," "Nationalism," "Imperialism." For attacks on the humanitarian-liberal tradition among English writers see J. F. Stephen, *Liberty, Equality, Fraternity* (New York, 1873); C. H. Pearson, *National Life and Character* (London, 1893); W. H. Mallock, *Aristocracy and Evolution* (New York, 1898).

national, originally based upon prescriptive privilege, has, through the influence of fictions, conceptions of natural rights, equity, and legislation, more and more realized that justice must assume not only equal protection of the laws but equality of status and opportunity.[18]

The word "humanism" has been associated with great figures of the revival of learning—Petrarch and Boccaccio in the fourteenth century and in the fifteenth century More, Montaigne, Rabelais, and particularly Erasmus. The latter was interested not only in the interpretation for general human consumption of classical and biblical literature but also in ameliorating human conditions generally, especially by the prevention of war. Montaigne's humanism was of a more contemplative type, viewing objectively the variations in human manners and morals in America and elsewhere as do modern anthropologists, but with the result, and perhaps with the intention, of reducing confidence in the unique claim of any particular moral or religious system.[19] Interest in the learning, desires, conduct, and welfare of all human beings characterized these men, and that interest has continued in Europe and has penetrated to other lands as illustrated by the growth of internationalism[20] and humanitarianism[21]

[18] H. S. Maine, *Ancient Law* (4th ed.; London, 1876), esp. chap. ii. His famous generalization concerning a tendency of law to move from status to contract appears on p. 170. For confirmation of this by modern anthropology see R. R. Marett ("Law, Primitive," *Encyclopaedia Britannica* [14th ed.], XIII, 782), who notes the inequalities and limitations of freedom imposed by law in primitive societies and points out that "in the modern democratic State [civic rights of the individual] tend to be created as equal for all concerned." See also Dickinson, *op. cit.*, chap. ix, and Q. Wright, "Article 19 of the League of Nations Covenant and the Doctrine Rebus sic Stantibus," *Proceedings of the American Society of International Law*, April, 1936, pp. 55 ff. Ellery Stowell (*Intervention in International Law* [Washington, 1921]) emphasizes the increasing tendency to justify interventions for "humanitarian" reasons (pp. 51 ff.). See, however, Philip Jessup, "The Defense of Oppressed Peoples," *American Journal of International Law*, XXII (January, 1938), 116 ff.

[19] Scott, *op. cit.*, pp. 8, 48–49; Robert Adams, "The Pacifist Idealism of the Oxford Humanists Reformers" (manuscript, University of Chicago, 1936); Montaigne, *Essays* (Cotton trans.), "Of Cannibals," I, 169.

[20] Faries, *op. cit.*; P. B. Potter, *An Introduction to the Study of International Organization* (4th ed.; New York, 1935), chap. iii.

[21] The tendency of charity and social work to move from relief to prevention, from spontaneous giving to professional standards, from private to public control, from local to national and then international administration can be traced in the articles on "Char-

within all countries. Stimulated by such movements, spontaneous aid is usually forthcoming to distant people suffering from the results of earthquake, flood, famine, or other serious disasters. Sometimes this human sentiment has been quite distinct from political sentiment. There is no more remarkable characteristic of modern civilization than that illustrated by the outpouring of American and Western European charity to the aid of famine-stricken Russia after World War I, while the governments of those countries were making every effort to hamper the political success of the Soviets.[22]

Humanism, however, has not been excluded wholly from the field of politics. It contributed through the ideas of Vitoria, Gentili, Grotius, and others to the development of international law,[23] through the ideas of Crucé, Sully, St. Pierre, Kant, and others to the development of international organization,[24] through the ideas of Erasmus, More, Penn, Ladd, and others to the movement for peace and disarmament,[25] and through the ideas of the physiocrats and utilitarians, Quesnay, Franklin, Adam Smith, Mill, Say, Bastiat, Cobden, and others to the movements for free trade and economic internationalism.[26]

Thus, today, a considerable number of persons are spread throughout the world who, though bearers of particular national cultures, are

---

ity" and "Social Service" or "Social Work" in the *Encyclopaedia Britannica* and the *Encyclopaedia of the Social Sciences*. The official international organization of remedial humanitarianism is illustrated by the International Relief Union Convention (M. O. Hudson, *International Legislation* [Washington, 1931], III, 2090) and the Nansen Commission on Refugees and of preventive humanitarianism by the International Labor Organization and the Social Work of the League of Nations.

[22] H. H. Fisher, *American Relief Administration in the Russian Famine* (New York, 1926), John Dewey has pointed out that care for the sick and wounded, even of the enemy, is just as "natural" as the waging of war ("Does Human Nature Change," *The Rotarian*, February, 1938, p. 8).

[23] Scott, *op. cit.;* Geoffrey Butler and Simon Maccoby, *Development of International Law* (London, 1928).

[24] Butler and Maccoby, *op. cit.*, chap. i; Lord Phillimore, *Schemes for Maintaining General Peace* ("British Foreign Office Peace Conference Handbooks," No. 160, No. 20 [London, 1920]); W. E. Darby, *International Tribunals* (London, 1904).

[25] C. F. Beales, *A History of Peace* (New York, 1931); Merle Curti, *Peace or War: The American Struggle, 1636–1936* (New York, 1936).

[26] J. K. Ingram, *A History of Political Economy* (New York, 1893), chap. v; Henry Higgs, *The Physiocrats* (London, 1897).

also humanists[27] in the sense that they are interested in considering what human interests demand both in general, as have in earlier civilizations only persons of great religious insight,[28] but also in particular situations and emergencies, and the opinions of such persons have sometimes been followed by actions supported by the general masses.[29]

The condition which has made belief in humanism possible to more than a very few has been the development of communication, travel, and transport. These changes have so reduced the isolation of groups that both sympathy and self-interest have urged a steadily increasing fraction of the human race to give attention to the condition of others even in distant regions. It is to be noted, however, that a new improvement in means of communication seems at first to intensify contact in the neighborhood more rapidly than it expands the area of contact.[30] Thus while printing circulated news of ancient and distant civilizations and provided the great thinkers with a basis for belief in humanism, it developed vernacular languages and stimulated even more contacts within the nation. The initial effect of this invention was, therefore, to break down the isolation of classes oc-

[27] Humanism has been expressed through internationalism rather than through cosmopolitanism (see Nicholas Murray Butler, *The International Mind* [New York, 1913], p. 102; I. Nitobe, *Lectures on Japan* [Chicago, 1938], p. 343; A. Zimmern, "The Development of the International Mind," in *Problems of Peace* [Geneva: Institute of International Studies, 1925], Lecture I). Salvador de Madariaga (*The World Foundation* [Oxford, 1936], p. 7) has urged the need of extending understanding of "world unity" without implying "world uniformity." See also Madariaga, *The World's Design* (London, 1938), final chap. on "World Citizenship."

[28] According to Walter Lippmann, "humanism takes as its dominant pattern the progress of the individual from helpless infancy to self-governing maturity," thus replacing the traditional religion's "conception of man as the subject of a heavenly king." The former, he thinks, has always been the concept of the great religious teachers. "Their concern was not to placate the will of God but to alter the will of man. This alteration of the human will they conceived as good not because God commands it, but because it is intrinsically good for man, because by the test of experience it yields happiness, serenity, whole-heartedness." Religion was therefore, as Whitehead puts it, "the art and the theory of the internal life of man, so far as it depends on the man himself and on what is permanent in the nature of things" (Lippmann, *op. cit.*, pp. 175, 195).

[29] See above, nn. 21 and 22.

[30] M. M. Willey and Stuart A. Rice, "The Agencies of Communication," in Ogburn (ed.), *Recent Social Trends*, I, 217.

cupying the same area and speaking the same language, and to emphasize national cohesion and exclusiveness.[31]

The same seems to have been true of the railroad, newspaper, postal service, telegraph, telephone, and radio. Statistical compilations indicate that national communication greatly exceeded the international communication, by these means, in all the countries where statistical data made study possible, and, furthermore, the services in these countries were nucleated in national centers usually controlled by government. Consequently, these inventions tended to intensify the sentiment of nationalism.[32] The radio, for example, appears to have been very important in promoting the extreme forms of nationalism in fascist Italy and Nazi Germany. Lasswell writes:

> The initial effect of expanding secondary contact may be to increase the danger to peace in world affairs, since insecurity reactions are easily aroused when new adjustments are required, and numerous local interests can profit by propagating insecurity. . . . . The long-run effect of expanding contact may reverse the initial results. New devices for the prevention of conflict may be developed as reactions against the heightened danger; but to generalize from this to the expectation of world unity is a doubtful operation. . . . . Thus far in the history of the world changing zones of conflict have both widened and restricted the area of peace.[33]

The great communication inventions created the potentiality of a wider acceptance of humanism at the time of the Renaissance, but they assisted in the development of nationalism immediately. The result was that the boundaries of the old civilizations became more and more attenuated, those of the nation-states became more and more defined, while the world-culture of humanism developed among

[31] J. C. King notes that especially in the nineteenth century "various forces—the increase in mobility, the growth of newspapers and books, conscription, and free public education—have tended to spread and unify the national languages" ("Some Elements of National Solidarity [manuscript, University of Chicago, 1933], p. 181). He emphasizes the contribution this has made to the spirit of nationalism, although national linguistic uniformity is by no means achieved in most of the states even yet (*ibid.*, chap. vii: "Nationalism and Language").

[32] *Ibid.*, chaps. ii and iii.

[33] H. D. Lasswell, *World Politics and Personal Insecurity* (New York, 1935), pp. 203–6. The invention of the airplane has probably immediately increased national insecurities because of the vulnerability of cities to air bombardment, but the ultimate effect may be otherwise (see chap. xii, sec. 1*d*, below).

limited groups in all countries. Will these latter groups develop and be able to control the future of the human race in its own interest? Graham Wallas raises the question in *The Great Society*.

Men find themselves working and thinking and feeling in relation to an environment, which, both in its world-wide extension and its intimate connection with all sides of human existence, is without precedent in the history of the world. . . . . The Greek thinkers, with all their magnificent courage and comprehensiveness, failed in the end either to understand or to guide the actual social forces of their time. Our own brains are less acute, our memories less retentive than those of the Greeks, while the body of relevant facts which we must survey has been increased ten-thousand-fold. How are we to have any chance of success?[34]

Only, he answers, if we more adequately organize the great society in adaptation to the facts of human psychology. Some form of universal federation adjusting a great variety of cultures to the unity of humanity is clearly suggested.

b) *Liberalism.*—Liberalism asserts that every individual should have an opportunity to develop his own personality.[35] Leonardo revolted from the authority of artistic tradition; Luther, from the authority of the church; Galileo, from the authority of Aristotelian science; Adam Smith, from the authority of mercantilist economics. Some of these, in asking liberty for particular groups, were ready to diminish the liberties of others. The "liberties" referred to in Magna Carta may have implied the liberty of the baron or freeman to oppress those under him as well as to be free from oppression by those above him. Sir Edward Coke, however, expresses the aspiration of seventeenth-century England in reading a more general guaranty of liberty into that instrument.[36] More and more the maximizing of freedom for every individual became the ideal of law guaranteed by constitutional bills of rights, protected by constitutional checks and balances, administered by judicial procedures, enlivened by the slo-

[34] New York, 1917, pp. 3, 15–16. See also p. 235.

[35] See Appen. XVIII.

[36] See Edward Coke, *Institutes* (London, 1628), II, 50 ff.; W. S. McKechnie, *Magna Carta* (Glasgow, 1905); C. H. McIlwain, *The High Court of Parliament* (New York, 1910); *Lochner* v. *New York*, 198 U.S. 45 (1905); R. E. Cushman, *Leading Constitutional Decisions* (1925), pp. 93 ff.; Rodney L. Mott, *Due Process of Law* (1926), chaps. iii and xxvi; H. J. Laski, "Liberty," *Encyclopaedia of the Social Sciences*.

gans of popular oratory, and justified by philosophers as different in other respects as Locke, Kant, Spencer, and Mill.[37]

There have been periods in the life of most of the modern states when tyranny, regimentation, and totalitarianism have been practiced and philosophies have been created to justify the subordination of the individual. Changing technical and industrial conditions have required variations of the field in which individual freedom must be restricted in the interests of others and of the community as a whole. The trend, however, has been toward the expansion of the areas in which liberty is the ideal and toward improvement in the procedures for defining and applying the law for securing those liberties.[38]

[37] H. J. Laski, *The Rise of Liberalism* (New York, 1936). Certain political philosophers like Buckle and De Tocqueville have insisted that the intervention of local, regional, and functional liberties between the individual and the community as a whole is essential for individual liberty—that equality of individuals in the great community implies the negation of liberty. Although local home rule and local option is still often desired, liberty has tended to be less a demand for local organization and authority and more a demand for individuals or classes of individuals, as the process of centralization, necessitated by the space- and time-reducing inventions has emphasized the functional rather than the geographical aspects of political, economic, and social organization. This process of functionalizing larger and larger areas has not halted at the sovereign state, although in law the sovereign state is still an essential mediator between the individual and the world-community. The "liberty" or "sovereignty" of the state is still freedom to oppress its subjects as well as to protect them from other sovereigns, but the development of international administration has tended to create some guaranties for the liberty of the individual at the expense of the liberty of the state (see C. Eagleton, *The Responsibility of States in International Law* [New York, 1928], pp. 220 ff.; Q. Wright, *Mandates under the League of Nations*, pp. 267–77; "National Sovereignty and Collective Security," *op. cit.*). A. D. Lindsay writes: "All modern political theory, except the theory of Bolshevism and Fascism, is in this sense individualistic in that it seeks to find room for and encourage the individual moral judgment and is based on toleration and the maintenance of a system of rights" ("Individualism," *Encyclopaedia of the Social Sciences*, VII, 677). Even the Soviet constitution of 1936 has a bill of rights.

[38] See "Liberalism," "Liberty," "Individualism," *Encyclopaedia of the Social Sciences*. Walter Lippmann (*An Inquiry into the Principles of the Good Society* [Boston, 1937]) finds government through impartial application of a common law rather than through administration to achieve given goals to be a necessary condition of liberalism, which in the economic field he distinguishes from laissez faire, on the one hand, and from collectivism, on the other. He considers the trend toward the latter since 1870, and especially since World War I, as an eddy in the general current of modern thought and government due to the failure to distinguish liberty under law from the license of laissez faire and to the failure to perceive that planning for a whole society presumes a capacity to

While the great figures of the Renaissance nearly all sought practical liberty from one authority or another, and one aspect of liberalism was illustrated in the political writings of the monarchomachs who asserted definite limits to political obedience sanctioned by the right of violence, it was not until the seventeenth century that philosophical exposition of liberalism began. During this century Crucé laid the foundations of economic liberalism; Althusius and Locke, of political liberalism.[39]

While Hobbes could hardly be called a liberal, his exposition of the foundations of obedience provided a basis upon which English utilitarians and German Kantians developed a philosophy of liberalism in the eighteenth and nineteenth centuries. Hobbes insisted that men could only be brought to associate in peace in so far as their interests would be better served by that association. Thus human psychology became the foundation of ethics and politics. The Hobbesian theory of psychology emphasized security or freedom from fear as the main drive of human nature, superior even to the drives of greed and dominance. Consequently, it assumed that men were prepared to sacrifice all liberty and permanently to yield full obedience to a dictator who could keep the peace.[40] Hobbes's successors,

---

predict wants and desires with some precision for some time in advance. Such prediction for the whole of a society is not possible by statistical extrapolation in a free society with sufficient economic surplus and sufficient emancipation from the rule of custom to permit individual choices and rapid fluctuations of fashion. Adequate prediction requires, therefore, a central control of opinion and of economic wants, which, in turn, requires a militarization of the society both to coerce internally and to create acquiescence in such coercion by developing the need for military preparation against an external enemy. "A directed society must be bellicose and poor. If it is not both bellicose and poor, it can not be directed" (p. xii). See also *ibid.*, pp. 89 ff.; Friedrich A. von Hayek, *Freedom and the Economic System* ("Public Policy Pamphlet" No. 29 [Chicago, 1939]). Pitirim Sorokin interprets "liberalism" as an effort to maximize "sensate" freedom, distinguished from the maximization of "ideational" freedom which may be facilitated by authoritarian regimes (*op. cit.*, III, 168 ff.). On inconsistency between different "freedoms" see E. P. Cheyney (ed.), *Freedom of Inquiry and Expression* (*Annals of the American Academy of Political and Social Science*, Vol. CC [1938]), and review by Q. Wright, *Bulletin of the American Association of University Professors*, XXVI (April, 1940), 255 ff. For temporal variations in acceptance of liberalism see below, n. 44.

[39] See articles with bibliography on each of these names, *Encyclopaedia of the Social Sciences*.

[40] See "Hobbes," *ibid.*; "Individualisn," *ibid.*, VII, 177, and Theodore de Laguna, *Introduction to the Science of Ethics* (New York, 1914), pp. 177 ff.

however, took a different view of human nature. They convinced themselves that human personality had more facets than Hobbes allowed it and that so great a sacrifice as Hobbes demanded was not necessary for peace. Locke thought that certain natural rights were inalienable.[41] Mill thought that too great curtailment of liberty would prevent progress.[42] Spencer formulated the proposition that "every man has freedom to do all that he wills, provided he infringes not the equal freedom of any other man."[43] Sir Henry Maine, at about the same time, detected a historical inevitability in the enlargement of liberty expressed through his famous formula that "the movement of the progressive societies has hitherto been a movement *from Status to Contract.*"[44] The attempt to guarantee the liberty of members of minority or colonial groups by international legislation and institutions is the most recent development of this movement.[45]

The degree of liberty actually enjoyed has always been to some extent contingent upon varying conditions of peace and war, tranquillity and tension. In times of war, disorder, and tension the demand for security has generally superseded the demand for freedom. People have been willing to submit to tyranny and regimentation as necessary in defense against external or internal violence, but in times of peace and tranquillity the demand for freedom has gradually asserted itself. These fluctuations have been particularly notable in the history of post-Renaissance states.[46] During this period the demand for freedom has, on the whole, increased and remained at a continuously higher level than in any past civilization, probably due to the influence of printing, education, and literacy. These have made the individual more conscious of his autonomy, of his desires, and of the possibility of attaining them. Consequently, the older controls of custom, superstition, and coercion have been less avail-

[41] *Of Civil Government*, secs. 23, 131, 190. For discussion of the physiological need for a certain minimum of freedom in both animals and men see Sorokin, *op. cit.*, III, 173 ff.

[42] *On Liberty.*

[43] *Social Statics* (London, 1880), p. 121.   [44] *Op. cit.*, p. 165.

[45] Secretariat of the League of Nations, *op. cit.*, pp. 108–20; Q. Wright, *Mandates under the League of Nations*, chap. i.

[46] See Lindsay Rogers, *Crisis Government* (New York, 1934); Lasswell, *op. cit.*, p. 221, and above, n. 29.

able.[47] In this connection, Draper notes the anxiety which the development of the press aroused among the ecclesiastical authorities. This led to the Lateran decree of 1615 which established an ecclesiastical censorship under penalty of excommunication.

But these frantic struggles of the powers of ignorance were unavailing. Intellectual intercommunication among men was secured. It culminated in the modern newspaper, which daily gives us contemporaneous intelligence from all parts of the world. Reading became a common occupation. In ancient society that art was possessed by comparatively few persons. Modern society owes some of its most striking characteristics to this change.[48]

It is probable that in the long run the principle of authority will succumb before easy, general access to knowledge. It appears, however, that early liberals overestimated the rationalism of men and underestimated the powers of propaganda, especially with the modern instruments of communication—the press, movie, and radio. There are many people who do not know their interests in the complicated world and desire to be told. There are others who prefer security to freedom and desire to be protected. Furthermore, no education can protect against continued suggestions from a controlled press or radio when no countersuggestions are available.[49]

The first effect of literacy, therefore, was to make people more vulnerable to propaganda because secondary contacts could reach a broader area, and consequently emotional control from an interested élite with a monopoly of the means of communication became more practicable.[50] This also seems to have been the first effect of other

[47] C. E. Merriam, *Political Power* (New York, 1934), pp. 296 ff., 305.

[48] Draper, *op. cit.*, pp. 293–94. Hallam finds instances of ecclesiastical censorship of printed books as early as 1480 (*op. cit.*, I, 257). The more subtle controls of the press which exist even in the freest countries are discussed by R. W. Desmond (*The Press and World Affairs* [New York, 1937]), who concludes: "The Press can do much more than it has done toward the attainment of the ideal. But public education comes first. More people must want to be well and truly informed. It is above all the readers choice" (p. 378).

[49] Merriam, *op. cit.*, pp. 307 ff.; F. L. Schuman, *The Nazi Dictatorship* (New York, 1935), pp. 78 ff., 360 ff.

[50] "Propaganda is a concession to the rationality of the modern world. A literate world, a reading world, a schooled world prefers to thrive on argument and news. It is sophisticated to the extent of using print; and he that takes to print shall live or perish by the Press. All the apparatus of diffused erudition popularizes the symbols and forms of pseudo-rational appeal; the wolf of propaganda does not hestitate to masquerade in

new communication inventions, notably the radio.[51] The long-run effect, however, may be opposite. As Lippmann points out, elucidations of what the good is may eventually percolate where literacy and means of communication exist, and efforts to induce men blindly to follow a leader or exhortations to follow a traditional good may be foiled by a mass reaction of skepticism.[52] This, at least, is the faith of liberalism as expressed by Justice Holmes, dissenting in the Abrams case.[53] Men like certainty, security, and direction, but throughout most of modern history they have tended to insist even more on freedom and the opportunity to make up their own minds.

  c) *Pragmatism.*—Pragmatism, which means the general application of scientific method, diverts men from the quest for certainty by denying that certainty is possible. It asserts that the only test we

---

the sheepskin. All the voluble men of the day—writers, reporters, editors, preachers, lecturers, teachers, politicians—are drawn into the service of propaganda to amplify a master voice. All is conducted with the decorum and the trappery of intelligence, for this is a rational epoch, and demands its raw meat cooked and garnished by adroit and skillful chefs" (H. D. Lasswell, *Propaganda Technique in the World War* [New York, 1927], p. 221).

  [51] See Willey and Rice, *op. cit.*, in Ogburn (ed.), *Recent Social Trends*, I, 215; William A. Orton, "Radio," *Encyclopaedia of the Social Sciences*, XIII, 62. W. F. Ogburn ("The Influence of Invention and Discovery," in Ogburn [ed.], *Recent Social Trends*, I, 155–58) finds that radio has had the rather inconsistent results of increasing "executive pressure on legislatures," acting as "a democratizing agency," and "spreading rumors and propaganda of nationalism." He also suggests that it tends to make campaign speeches "more logical and cogent," though "some political broadcasters have not caught up with the times and still try oratorical effects." These observations were based on American experience. In Europe, while radio has potentialities for peace, its actual use has made for the accomplishment of national ends and for international friction (see Thomas Grandin, "The Political Use of the Radio," *Geneva Studies*, X [August, 1939], 86).

  [52] Lippmann, *A Preface to Morals*, p. 318, and above, n. 38. See also C. K. Ogden, "Words, Thoughts, and Things," *Bentham's Theory of Fictions* (New York, 1932), p. lxii; Q. Wright, "National Sovereignty and Collective Security," *op. cit.*, p. 103.

  [53] "To allow opposition by speech seems to indicate that you think speech unimportant, as when a man says that he has squared the circle, or that you do not care wholeheartedly for the result, or that you doubt either your power or your premises. But when men have realized that time has upset many fighting faiths, they may come to believe even more than they believe the very foundations of their own conduct that the ultimate good desired is better reached by free trade in ideas—that the best test of truth is the power of the thought to get itself accepted in the competition of the market, and that truth is the only ground upon which their wishes safely can be carried out" *Abrams* v. *U.S.*, 250 U.S. 616, 630 [1919]).

have for judging the truth of any proposition is confirmation by experience of its concrete consequences. It assumes that, with the recording of new experiences, every truth will in time be discarded or
limited in its scope.[54]

Machiavelli assumed that what had worked in history and in his
own observation was the test of political wisdom.[55] Leonardo and
Vesalius dissected human bodies to improve the anatomy of Galen.[56]
Erasmus studied original texts to improve traditional interpretations.[57] Copernicus observed the heavenly bodies "much and long"
to improve Ptolemaic astronomy.[58] Bacon formulated the inductive
tests of truth and emphasized the idola or biases from which induction can never be wholly free.[59] Descartes developed analytic meth-

[54] See F. S. C. Schiller, "Pragmatism," *Encyclopaedia Britannica* (14th ed.). In his
excellent article on "Pragmatism" in the *Encyclopaedia of the Social Sciences*, H. M.
Kallen relates its formal development by Pierce, James, Dewey, and Schiller (1) to experience with the changeableness of life on the American geographic and business frontier, where men were not born good but "made good," and which had already shaken the
Calvinistic tradition in the thinking of Emerson and Walt Whitman, and (2) to the growing realization by scientists like Darwin, Mach, and H. Poincaré, that scientific concepts "depend for their validity on verification by piecemeal experiments, each yielding
a concrete, specific, sensory experience" and that they "are not revelations of nature,
only a device for handling her" (XII, 307–11). Pragmatists insist that procedures and
means are the test of the validity of conclusions and ends. Belief in any abstract proposition or social goal should, therefore, be subordinate to belief in the procedures, tested
by experience, for attaining abstract truths and social objectives of the type in question.
Criticism should pay more attention to the methods of discovering, inventing, and creating the true, the good, and the beautiful than to formulations and embodiments of
these values to date. Constitutions should pay more attention to procedures for formu-
lating and administering justice than to definitions of social, political, and economic
justice. The definitions change more rapidly than the procedures. Reforms achieved by
wrong methods prove not to be reforms at all (Q. Wright, "The Munich Settlement and
International Law," *American Journal of International Law*, XXXIII [1939], 31). See
below, chap. xiv, sec. 3.

[55] In the dedication of *The Prince* to Lorenzo the Magnificent, he says that he has
digested into the little volume the results of "reflection with great and prolonged dili-
gence" upon "knowledge of the actions of great men, acquired by long experience in contemporary affairs, and a continued study of antiquity" ("Everyman's" ed., p. 1).

[56] Dampier-Whetham, *op. cit.*, pp. 117, 128.   [57] *Ibid.*, p. 108.

[58] *De revolutionibus orbium celestium* i. 10 (trans., in Dampier-Whetham, *op. cit.*,
p. 121).

[59] Though his experimental attempts contributed little to knowledge or to the activities of contemporary experimenters, "he was the first to consider the philosophy of inductive science, and he profoundly influenced the French Encyclopaedists of the eight-

ods for finding the concrete consequences of propositions which could be tested.[60] The development of mathematics and of scientific instruments, the telescope and the microscope, suggested the artificialities intervening between abstract propositions and immediate experience. Hobbes, Locke, Berkeley, Hume, and Kant showed that nothing can be experienced except through the medium and subject to the aberrations of human psychology.[61] Bentham emphasized the suggestion of Locke that nothing can be formulated except through the medium and subject to the coloring of language or symbolic systems which necessarily often represented fictional entities.[62]

The scientific study of psychology, language, and logic since Kant and Bentham has rendered these aberrations and colorings more calculable in a given environment but not more deducible from immutable principles.[63] Recent thinkers on these subjects—evolutionists,

---

eenth century" (Dampier-Whetham, *op. cit.*, p. 138). His idola seem to have been borrowed from "the causes of human error" specified by his namesake of 350 years earlier, Roger Bacon (*ibid.*, p. 99), though this was doubted by Hallam (*op. cit.*, I, 131).

[60] Dampier-Whetham, *op. cit.*, p. 148.　　　　　[61] *Ibid.*, pp. 151, 206-13.

[62] *Ibid.*, p. 207; C. K. Ogden, "Bentham's Theory of Fictions and the Magic of Words," *Psyche*, XIV (1934), 9-87. H. Vaihinger (*Philosophie des als Ob* [Leipzig, 1911; trans. London, 1924]) independently developed the same idea. See Morris R. Cohen, "Fictions," *Encyclopaedia of the Social Sciences*.

[63] The contrast between the medieval certainty of truth and the present uncertainty cannot be better illustrated than by comparing the subject matter of the medieval trivium—rhetoric, grammar, and dialectic (taken from the Roman educational curriculum [see "Education," *Encyclopaedia Britannica*, VII, 974-75])—with contemporary theories of psychology, language, and logic. In the Middle Ages the student learned certain principles from Aristotle informing him how to express himself persuasively, accurately, and truthfully (see R. M. Hutchins, "What Is a General Education?" *Harper's Magazine*, November, 1936, pp. 602 ff.). It is no less important today for persons to learn these things, and perhaps they can be learned but not by deduction from accepted principles. The sciences of psychology, language, and logic would seem the modern repositories, if any, of the principles, respectively, of rhetoric, grammar, and dialectic, but the articles on these subjects in the *Encyclopaedia of the Social Sciences*, and on their histories in the *Encyclopaedia Britannica*, display no unified body of doctrine on any of them. There is an abundance of theories, mostly emphasizing the contingency of propositions and the number of unsolved problems. Joseph Jastrow comments on the "shifting scope" of psychology (*Encyclopaedia of the Social Sciences*) and G. S. Brett on the growing importance of "the problem of personality" in that field (*Encyclopaedia Britannica*). Edward Sapir emphasizes the need of an international language (*Encyclopaedia Britannica*), and the *Britannica* article on language comments on the difficulty of defining "the meaning of meaning." John Dewey ends his discussion of

behaviorists, psychoanalysts, psychophysical measurers, gestaltists, social anthropologists, orthologists—are together in asserting that there is nothing certain or immutable in human nature, language, or logic.[64]

---

logic with the statement that a working logic requires that "concepts and facts should be elements in and instruments of intelligently controlled action" (*Encyclopaedia of the Social Sciences*), while the *Britannica* authors (H. W. Blunt and Abram Wolff) end with a statement of the pragmatic position which they criticize, asserting that "truth works and is economic, because it is truth" without explaining how they know it is truth except from the fact that it works and is economic. This development of uncertainty may be attributed to the introduction into systematic thought and education of observation and experiment, i.e., thought proceeding from the particular to the universal which figured to some extent in the medieval quadrivium (geometry, arithmetic, music, and astronomy) but was not much emphasized until the post-Renaissance development of science, with roots rather in medieval magic, alchemy, and astrology (see Lynn Thorndyke, *A History of Magic and Experimental Science* [New York, 1929]). Emphasis on this method both supplemented and modified the older methods proceeding from the universal to the particular (dialectic, logic), from the objective to the subjective (grammar, language), and from the subjective to the objective (rhetoric, psychology).

[64] Darwin, Spencer, and James insisted that psychological processes spring from physiological functions and that both are subject to evolutionary change. Weber and Pavlov, from studies of neural physiology, and Binet and Thurstone, from studies of attitude expression, attempted to analyze psychological processes into measurable elements. The social anthropologists, however, insisted that the elements were the product of an ever changing social milieu (Ellsworth Faris, "Of Psychological Elements," *American Journal of Sociology*, XLII [September, 1936] 174–75), and the Gestalt school insisted that the appreciation of their relations in the total situation continually modified the significance of these elements. Watson and Freud, utilizing the methods of observation and the prolonged interview, respectively, found that behavior patterns were not the direct consequence of inherited drives or instincts but of the specific organization of those drives in the individual's history. To the behaviorists all states of consciousness were but conditioned responses to stimuli or to behavior, especially of the larynx and the ductless glands, with no explanatory value. To the Freudians they were "rationalizations" which buttressed attitudes mainly dependent upon the unconscious functioning of wishes and repressed memories. The psychologists thus all tended to the view that states of mind—emotions, observations, reasons, and desires—were consequences as much as causes of behavior. The approach from the standpoint of language and logic exhibited a similar trend. Max Müller emphasized the continual evolution of languages; Ogden and Richards emphasized that because a thing can be said without violating rules of grammar does not prove it true, that the meaning of words may change with context and with social change and is to be tested by the effect of using the word in a given milieu. Nonpragmatic logicians, like Bradley and Bosanquet, tended to regard the truth of their absolute systems as only to be tested by more of itself, which is little more than to acknowledge, as do the mathematicians and symbolic logicians, that the truth of any part of the system is dependent upon its basic assumptions (see articles referred to, above, n. 63).

After the certainties of authority had been rejected, the certainties, which Leonardo and other Renaissance thinkers had anticipated from observation, also evaporated. The tendency was to reject as criteria of truth the absolutism of revelation, of authority, of ideas, of words, of the senses, of the instincts. The dependence of the process of truth-finding upon artificial instruments—hypotheses, fictions, symbols, words, mathematical systems—which are themselves the product of a particular social milieu, became more and more accepted and was finally formulated in the philosophy of James, Dewey, Pierce, Schiller, and Mead, known as pragmatism but always associated by them with the general progress of scientific method. "Pragmatism," writes Morris, "involves, first, the complete acceptance of the scientific attitude and method as the attitude and method of philosophy."[65]

The modern world with its rapid succession of new inventions, new fashions, and new wants, with its uncertainties of the future and its rapid changes in modes of life and standards of behavior, is adapted to such a philosophy. Chesterton complains that "heresy has become a term of praise"; Wilenski calculates that during the past century a new movement in painting has been inaugurated in Paris every ten years. Lippmann adds that "in the advanced and most emancipated circles" new philosophies have been born and have died with equal speed.[66] Constitutional, legislative, and political changes

---

[65] Charles W. Morris, *Pragmatism and the Crisis of Democracy* ("Public Policy Pamphlet," No. 12 [Chicago, 1934]), p. 9; George H. Mead, *Movements of Thought in the Nineteenth Century*, ed. Merritt H. Moore (Chicago, 1936), p. xi. The relation of pragmatism to the experimentalism, nominalism, utilitarianism, and hypotheticalism of the scientific tradition from Roger Bacon and William of Occam, through Leonardo, Francis Bacon, and Descartes to Galileo, Newton, Laplace, and Darwin is illustrated by the following quotations from Kallen's article on "Pragmatism" (*Encyclopaedia of the Social Sciences*, XII, 307–11): "A theory is preferred over an alternative one because it is simpler and more convenient when judged by its experiential consequences. . . . . As the consequences fall out, so things are judged—true, false; good, evil; right, wrong; beautiful, ugly. . . . . All systems of ideas, metaphysical and non-metaphysical alike, are relative to the situation in which they arise and the personalities they satisfy, and are subject to continuous verification of consequences. . . . . Pragmatism dissolves dogmas into beliefs; eternities and necessities into change and chance; conclusions and finalities into processes." Ralph Barton Perry points out the danger that "instrumentalism" may seem to lend support to "technologism" which maintains the "sophism" that "whatever is done with the use of perfected scientific means is good" (R. M. MacIver, M. J. Bonn, and R. B. Perry, *The Roots of Totalitarianism* [Philadelphia, 1940], p. 29).

[66] Lippmann, *Preface to Morals*, pp. 5, 111.

seem to occur no less frequently in all states. People who live under these conditions may find it comforting not to anticipate certainty.

Change has been especially rapid in China, Turkey, Mexico, Russia, and other countries affected by the rapid penetration of Western ideas. Pragmatism has been widely accepted in these countries.[67] The pragmatic point of view has been more obviously characteristic of Confucianism than of other religions,[68] though it does not require sophistication in science and psychology to conclude that all religions must rest on a pragmatic foundation. When Whitehead says that Aristotle "does not lead him very far toward the production of a god available for religious purposes," when Kirsopp Lake says it was the Neo-Platonist conception of god which "made Christianity possible for the educated man of the third century," and when Walter Lippmann admits the wisdom "of adopting a policy about God," it is clear that God has become an instrument for establishing truth rather than the truth itself or, as Whitehead says, "God is not concrete, but He is the ground for concrete actuality."[69]

The initial effect of the pragmatic attitude has probably been to increase strife. Elimination of absolute truth creates the impression that all is whirl. The only proof of the value of an end is success in achieving it. There is no way of judging one objective better than another in advance, but any objective may be pursued with the expectation that it may be achieved, hence be proved of value. This seems to be the concept of pragmatism in W. Y. Elliott's *The Pragmatic Revolt in Politics*, which groups all movements of revolt from syndicalism to fascism under that head.[70] This, however, is the very attitude which the defenders of pragmatism hope a general understanding of it may eliminate. To deny absolute truth is not to deny that certain truths are the best at a given moment. Pragmatism, according to its advocates, does not hold that truth emerges from the application of any method but only from the application of those methods which have, in experience, yielded results which were pre-

[67] Kallen, "Pragmatism," *op. cit.*, p. 310.

[68] Hu Shih, "The Civilization of the East and the West," in C. A. Beard (ed.), *Whither Mankind?* (New York, 1929), pp. 25 ff.

[69] Lippmann, *Preface to Morals*, pp. 26, 28, 29.

[70] New York, 1928. See also confusion with "technologism" (above, n. 65).

dicted and were consistent with the general body of truths. It is notorious that violent methods such as war and revolution have seldom yielded results which were predicted or were consistent with the body of social values which had been tested by experience. In fact, war aims and peace terms are not often closely related to each other. Resort to war or to violent revolution, as distinguished from the employment of an overwhelmingly powerful police force, is resort to chance, not the application of scientific method and is, consequently, the reverse of pragmatism.[71] It cannot be said that the consequences flowing from the initiation of violent methods have often proved to have value. Schiller wrote that "das Weltgeschichte ist die Weltgericht"; but the pragmatist would say that history is not a judgment but merely a record of what happened.

Peace, say the pragmatists, is menaced, on the one hand, by the transcendentalists who, certain that truth can be made by willing it firmly enough, fight to prove their infallibility, and, on the other hand, by the skeptics who, convinced of the futility of any other argument, fight to preserve their existence. The pragmatists hope to contribute to the discomfiture of both by substituting the opinion that some truths are easier to demonstrate than others but that all situations present numerous choices of formulation and procedure.[72]

There have been reactions against the pragmatic attitude in the interest of certainty and permanence[73] or of particular power constructions,[74] but it does not seem likely that the world, either of sciences, of arts, or of affairs, will in any discernible future present a

[71] Morris, op. cit., p. 5; A. E. Murphy, International Journal of Ethics, XXXIX (1928), 239 ff.

[72] "The deepest characteristic of science is that, while it renounces the pretension of finality at any time, the very social nature of its enterprise secures for it that relative stability which provides the via media between dogmatism and individualistic anarchy" (Morris, op. cit., p. 12).

[73] Kallen doubts whether pragmatism can ever be a popular philosophy because "men have invented philosophy precisely because they find change, chance and process too much for them, and desire infallible security and certainty" ("Pragmatism," op. cit., p. 311). Albert Schinz (Anti-pragmatism, trans. from French [Boston, 1909]) thinks pragmatism may have a place in the field of ethics, but "there exists a conflict between intellectual truth and moral truth, a conflict that all the ratiocination of the world will not suppress" (p. xx). See below, n. 88.

[74] Morris, op. cit., pp. 3 ff.

milieu offering much substantiation for such philosophies. All cultures have tended to accept the pragmatic methods of science and law which insist, on the one hand, that concrete problems be solved by the application of valid generalizations and, on the other, that any generalization is valid in proportion to the excellence of the procedures by which it was formulated.[75]

d) *Relativism.*—Relativism, asserting that no experience is real except in relation to a frame of reference, has been demolishing what little of certainty pragmatism has left.[76] For relativism, there is no being apart from our knowledge about it, and that knowledge always proceeds from postulates which are themselves continually changing. It thus leaves the entire field of philosophy to pragmatism[77] and cultivates an attitude of tolerance. Tolerance, it is true,

[75] Above, n. 54. Societies in rapid transition tend to substitute "the revolutionary conscience" for law and "party loyalty" for technical expertness, but they very soon get over this in modern times (see J. N. Hazard, "In the Soviet Law School," *Asia*, October, 1939, p. 565; Joseph Stalin, "Report on the Work of the Central Committee of the Communist Party of the Soviet Union, January, 1934," *International Conciliation*, No. 305, December, 1934, pp. 445 ff.).

[76] Bertrand Russell, dealing with "Relativity, Philosophical Consequences" (*Encyclopaedia Britannica*, XIX, 100), points out that, in relativity, "bodies become far more independent of each other than they were in Newtonian physics: there is an increase of individualism and a diminution of central government, if one may be permitted such metaphorical language," and that, while the importance attributed to the point of view of the observer by relativity does not imply Berkleyian idealism, it does imply that reality means only that "those respects in which all observers agree when they record a given phenomenon may be regarded as objective, and not as contributed by the observers." Thus it tends toward pluralism and democracy in the sense that reality grows from opinion.

[77] Philosophers have apparently always been relativists. If arguing by the method of analysis and deduction, as did Aristotle, Euclid, Aquinas, Descartes, and Kant, they realized that a priori forms for analysis (transcendental essences) or assumptions for deduction (axioms and postulates) were necessary and had to be taken on faith or intuition, the only test of their validity being the pragmatic one that their use yielded satisfactory results (see "Transcendentalism," *Encyclopaedia Britannica*). If arguing by the method of induction and synthesis or dialectic as did Plato, Erigena, Spinoza, and Hegel, they realized that a priori assumptions for induction (the continuity of nature, the laws of probability) or hypotheses for synthesis (perfect forms, absolute ideas, or rational principles which constituted the goal of argument or the direction of investigation) must be believed in without demonstration. Each school of transcendentalists thought the pragmatic argument for adopting a particular brand of a priori reality was adequate. The British epistemologists (Hobbes, Locke, Berkeley, Hume, Mill, Spencer) realized that such arguments would not be conclusive without support by a theory of

grew from liberalism rather than from relativism. It began in the modern period as a recognition of the individual's freedom—to choose his religion. But its tendency was to cast doubt on the objective reality of the postulates of the religion chosen. When different people in the same community could and did accept different religions, it was difficult to believe that any religion was absolute.[78] Each was relative to the personality which accepted it or to the culture within which it flourished.

Ellsworth Faris writes:

The history of the thought of the last three hundred years could almost be written as the passage in one realm of life and another from fixity and absoluteness to change and relativity. . . . . It was Woodrow Wilson in the twentieth century who, voicing what was in the minds of his people, expressed the ultimate consequence of this long movement when he declared that the reign of law, based on the consent of the governed, was to be sustained by the "organized opinion of mankind." In this statement, opinion, with its tides and currents, was changed from an object of scorn to the final court of appeal in political life.[79]

Copernicus wrote in 1540: "First and above all lies the sphere of the fixed stars, containing itself and all things, for that very reason immovable; in truth the frame of the Universe, to which the motion and position of all other stars are referred."[80] Mathematicians and logicians had long realized that their systems rested on ultimate postulates or axioms which could not be proved but could only be

---

knowledge; and, since no theory of knowledge could pull itself up by its own bootstraps, they early abandoned the problem of ontology as hopeless. They consequently attributed "necessary assumptions" to custom, as did Hume, or relegated their demonstration to "the unknowable," as did Spencer. The only real absolutists have been the dogmatists who believed in revelation (the authority of the word), the intuitionists who were confident that introspection was an unimpeachable source of truth, and the scientists who originally were no less confident of the reality of the results of sensory observation. The position of the dogmatists has been shattered by the religious criticism of the modern period, intuitions have been shown to vary with social and personal history by the anthropologists and psychologists, and scientific relativity has been forcing the scientists to be less naïve about their assumptions which had already been weakened by the phenomenology of Ernst Mach and Karl Pearson.

[78] Guido de Ruggiero, "Religious Freedom," *Encyclopaedia of the Social Sciences;* John M. Mecklin, "Freedom of Speech for Clergymen," in Cheyney (ed.), *op. cit.*, p., 188.

[79] Faris, *op. cit.*, pp. 174–75; Dampier-Whetham, *op. cit.*, pp. 484–85.

[80] Dampier-Whetham, *op. cit.*, p. 121.

accepted on faith.[81] The same was found to be true of all the sciences and philosophies and also of the things with which they dealt.[82] The relativity of space was demonstrated by astronomers from Copernicus and Bruno to Einstein, Eddington, and Jeans. They pushed the frame of reference from the earth to the fixed stars and then to the universe of visible galaxies and finally to the type of time-space postulated.[83] The relativity of time was suggested by the geologists as they pushed back origins from the Book of Genesis to longer and longer geologic epochs; of language by the philologists, logicians, and orthologists; of organic forms by the evolutionists; of law and morals by the anthropologists; of attitudes and beliefs by the psychologists and historians; of social laws and institutions by the Marxists; of truth by the philosophers and pragmatists; and of God by the metaphysicians.[84] A frame of reference must be assumed upon which the existence of anything depends, and that frame only exists in relation to another in infinite regression, the final frame at which any discourse stops being a matter of faith or opinion.[85]

The conditions of the contemporary world, unfavorable to absolutistic theories of knowledge, equally militate against absolutistic theories of being, particularly when relativism offers a harborage for most of the past ontologies by according them a relative truth. The monists, dualists, pluralists, idealists, materialists, realists, nominalists, conceptualists, phenomenalists, and others can live in harmony under relativism if each will confine its validity to its own frame of reference. As ideologies, empires, and churches, claiming to be uni-

[81] Above, n. 74. In the Middle Ages the postulates of faith which philosophy must accept were enforced by the church.

[82] The critical writing of the epistemologists from Hobbes to Kant contributed to this result (above, n. 77) and was carried on in the nineteenth century by the phenomenalism of Ernst Mach and Karl Pearson (see Dampier-Whetham, *op. cit.*, pp. 316–17, 343, 445).

[83] Sir James Jeans, "Relativity," *Encyclopaedia Britannica*, XIX, 98 ff.; Dampier-Whetham, *op. cit.*, p. 422; Mead, *op. cit.*, p. 413.

[84] A. N. Whitehead, above, n. 69.

[85] See Mortimer Adler, *Dialectic* (New York, 1927). Mr. Adler has subsequently assumed an absolutistic position (see address to Conference on Science, Philosophy, and Religion and comments thereon, University of Chicago, *Daily Maroon*, November 14, 1940).

versal, have found themselves at war but have eventually subsided to sovereignty within prescribed jurisdictions, so many philosophies can find spheres of peaceful and useful activity within the frame of appropriate limiting conditions.

The continued existence of attitudes apparently inconsistent with the trend of modern thought is therefore to be expected, but it is also to be expected that efforts will be made to integrate these attitudes with the trend. Philosophies which emphasize the reality of social groups have been exaggerated in some populations to assertions of the absolute value of that group. Few people would deny the historical vitality of many groups and the utility of certain groups to human welfare and individual liberty at the present time and perhaps for a long future. An increasing number of people, however, insist that the philosophical justification for the existence of any particular group must lie in proof of its contribution to the welfare of the individuals which compose it or of humanity as a whole.[86] Political leaders find it increasingly expedient to assume that society is for the benefit of man, that man is not to be sacrificed for the perpetuation of any particular society.[87]

Philosophies and theologies which assume the universal and eternal applicability of certain dogmas continue to engage in vigorous missionary and propaganda efforts. Religious leaders, however, have tended to justify belief in the absolutism of their doctrines by insisting that the dogma must be assumed to be absolute to make it of value to the believer.[88] Nevertheless, they often admit certain qualifications in the application of the dogma in view of the special cir-

---

[86] Gierke seems to have recognized this (*Das deutsche Genossenschaft*, Vol. I, chap i; Lewis, *op. cit.*, p. 113).

[87] Lincoln's "Gettysburg Address"; Lippmann, *The Good Society*, pp. 375 ff.

[88] "While all the ideal values may remain if you impugn the historic record set forth in the Gospels, these ideal values are not certified to the common man as inherent in the very nature of things. . . . . The orthodox believer may be mistaken as to the facts in which he believes. But he is not mistaken in thinking that you cannot, for the mass of men, have a faith of which the only foundation is their need and desire to believe. . . . . Without complete certainty religion does not offer genuine consolation. Nor can it sanction the rules of morality" (Lippmann, *A Preface to Morals*, pp. 32, 33, 49, following a discussion of Protestant Fundamentalist and Catholic justifications of their positions). See above, n. 73.

cumstances of a particular time and place.[89] Modern religion thus tends to find a pragmatic justification both for its absolutistic statement of dogma and for its relativistic application of dogma, a situation which the law has long recognized in the maxims *dura lex sed lex*[90] and *summa jus summa injuria.*[91]

e) Modernism and war.—Humanism, liberalism, pragmatism, and relativism are becoming the faith of the contemporary world-civilization,[92] and, viewing their long-run effect, it seems that conditions are not unfavorable to an even more intensive and extensive acceptance of these attitudes, though it is the essence of pragmatism and science, of relativism and toleration, to acknowledge the possibility that these or any other attitudes will eventually change. It is also to be noted that these attitudes constitute frames of reference of the broadest type. Their general acceptance is not incompatible with a wide variety of laws, customs, and institutions in different parts of

---

[89] "Our belief as Christians, or Churchmen, that divorce and re-marriage after divorce are inconsistent with the principles laid down by Christ and accepted by the Church, cannot preclude us as citizens from the right or even the duty to improve the existing law where it demands improvement, or to remedy abuses which have been disclosed" (speech by Archbishop of Canterbury in the House of Lords, June 24, 1937, explaining his refusal to vote against the pending divorce bill [*Parliamentary Debates, House of Lords*, Vol. CV, col. 745]).

[90] Justinian *Digest* xl. 9, 12. 1.   [91] Cicero *De officiis* i. 10. 33.

[92] Since writing this I have examined Sorokin's tables illustrating the fluctuations in the relative importance of various philosophies from 600 B.C. to A.D. 1930. As these tables deal only with Greco-Roman and Western civilizations, they do not adequately indicate the world-tendencies in the modern period, nor do Sorokin's categories exactly correspond to mine. His method consists in a classification of all important philosophers, weighted for importance and counted for each twenty-year period. "Singularism," the social exemplification of nominalism, has increased in importance since 1400 (*op. cit.*, II, 279). This attitude is related to liberalism but is not identical with it, because liberalism is interested in evaluating the individual's wants and in satisfying them (see Appen. XVIII) as well as in proving the existence of the individual. "Universalism," the social exemplification of "realism," corresponds somewhat to humanism, but it tries to answer an ontological rather than an axiological problem. Universalism declined in the thirteenth and seventeenth centuries but has risen since (*op. cit.*, p. 279). "Empiricism" and "temporalism" may have some relation to pragmatism and have been rising since 1500 (pp. 32, 226). "Relativism," according to Sorokin, has fluctuated greatly since 1300 but with a tendency to rise since 1450 (p. 516). Sorokin's own treatment of all philosophical systems and of causality, time, space, and number is an exemplification of relativism (see graph of trends in sixteen types of thought, *ibid.*, II, 629 and 630).

the world and among different social groups. General acceptance of these attitudes would not provide a basis for predicting the forms of world-civilization in any concrete detail, although it might suggest some of its broadest outlines.

Can this faith, which suggests processes rather than achievements, probability rather than certainty, variety rather than unity, balance rather than hierarchy, continuous adjustment rather than permanence, provide the inspiration and stimulus which the development of civilization requires?[93] The pragmatists insist that the very uncertainty of their philosophy provides "the wild-game flavored universe which moral action" especially in the Faustian West demands[94] and eliminates the inevitability which has cramped the spirit of earlier civilizations. A truly world-civilization must have within itself a promise of continuous conflict from which alone the new can emerge because such a civilization cannot get this stimulus from external relations.[95] Conflict, however, must be conducted by methods which do not threaten destruction, and within a world-civilization this is peculiarly important because humanity, having put all its eggs in one basket, would be in a serious situation if the basket were dropped. There is a possibility, however, that a universal civilization may learn how to keep internal conflicts from degenerating into the destructiveness of war—a possibility which hardly exists in the case of intercivilization conflicts. The uncertainties of pragmatism and relativism may assure flexibility for adjustment. The numerous autonomous and competing centers of action preserved by liberalism may maximize the opportunities for experiments in adaptation, if subject to the restraining ideal of humanism.

This is not the place to consider in detail the relation of these attitudes to each other or the consequence of their growth and accept-

[93] Doubts have been expressed by Horace Kallen (above, n. 73); Walter Lippmann (above, n. 88); Dampier-Whetham (*op. cit.*, pp. 486 ff.); Carl J. Friedrich, *Politica methodice digesta of Johannes Althusius* (Cambridge, 1932), Preface, p. x; and Raymond L. Buell, *Isolated America* (New York, 1940), pp. 297 ff.

[94] Morris, *op. cit.*, p. 15.

[95] John Dickinson, "Social Order and Political Authority," *American Political Science Review*, XXIII (May, 1929), 299; Q. Wright, *Causes of War and Conditions of Peace* (London, 1935), pp. 2–3, 86.

ance.[96] The object of this discussion has been to state the nature of these attitudes, their origins, the degree of their acceptance during the last three centuries, and their relevance to the conditions of the contemporary world. Though in the twentieth century modernism seems to have contributed to war, its characteristic attitudes originated in a desire for peace. The creative, if not the originating, minds with respect to each of these attitudes—the humanist Erasmus, the liberal Crucé, the pragmatist Dewey, the relativist Einstein—were all pacifists.[97] Kant, whose philosophy certainly approached relativism and pragmatism, recognized humanism and liberalism as essential elements in an organization of peace.[98] Modernism in seeking a continuous adjustment of pluralistic and monistic tendencies, a synthesis of variety and unity, of change and stability, of science and religion, recognizes each as necessary to the other. Liberty is necessary to peace, peace to liberty, and both to prosperity and progress.[99] The failure to maintain modernism, not modernism itself, has been the cause of recent conflicts.

The general acceptance of modernism would offer the possibility for the peaceful solution of every controversy by dialect. There is no limit to the process of synthesizing apparently irreconcilable ideals when both parties believe that all ideas are relative to some higher universe of discourse and that rational procedures can be developed for discovering new universes of discourse.[100]

[96] See below, chap. xiv.

[97] See Erasmus, *Antipolemus, or the Plea of Reason, Religion, and Humanity against War* (1518) (London, 1794); Emeric Crucé, *Le nouveau cynee, ou discourse d'estat representant les occasions et moyens d'establir une paix générale, et la liberté du commerce par tout le mond* (Paris, 1623), trans. T. W. Balch (Philadelphia, 1909); Albert Einstein, exchange of letters with Sigmund Freud on "Why War?" (July, 1932), in International Institute of Intellectual Cooperation, *Correspondence* (Paris, 1933); John Dewey, articles on "The Outlawry of War," *New Republic*, March 21, 1923; April 25, 1923; October 3 and 24, 1923; March 23, 1932; *Christian Century*, December 23, 1926.

[98] Immanuel Kant, *Eternal Peace* (1795) (Boston, 1914).

[99] W. E. Dodd, "The Dilemma of Modern Civilization," in Q. Wright (ed.), *Neutrality and Collective Security* (Chicago, 1936), pp. 93–108. The same idea is expressed in Walter Lippmann's *The Good Society*.

[100] Adler, *Dialectic*. Lasswell points out the psychological difficulty in the "approach to world politics which undertakes to sentimentalize procedures" because men spontaneously regard "justice" as a higher value than "order" (*World Politics and Personal Insecurity*, p. 249). But justice also may be interpreted as a procedure.

Threats of war and war itself have constituted a major obstacle to the advance of modernism. While the latter implies continuous response to challenges of the new,[101] it implies that responses shall be intelligent and humane. The conduct of war requires the suppression of the humanistic attitude and the suppression of liberty. It also requires acceptance of authority and of the thesis that the purposes for which the war is being fought have an absolute value irreconcilable with the purposes of the enemy. Its results are indeterminable and its costs are excessive. A world safe for modernism seems to be both a consequence and a cause of a relatively warless world.

Peace is today menaced by the idealists, who consider their causes so valuable that they justify the sacrifices even of war, no less than by the realists who think, because war has a long history, it is inevitable and must be prepared for. A general opinion that the value of any cause is relative to its cost, which may vary in accord with the speed of realizing it, and that the inevitability of any future is relative to the potentialities which are overlooked or excluded, especially when the future in question is a somewhat distant one, may assist in eliminating both of these menaces to peace.

The movement toward world-civilization, which began in Europe at the period of the discoveries, is today manifested by a high degree of economic, political, and social interdependence among all sections of the world and by a widespread acceptance of common attitudes on fundamental problems. For the first time in world-history the foundations have been laid for a civilization without a periphery. All previous civilizations were surrounded by barbarians or by alien civilizations with which any relation other than that of war of defense or aggression was inconceivable. When for the first time men could at least conceive of the human race as a whole, the international problem assumed a new form.[102] Ideologies of international

---

[101] A. J. Toynbee's *Study of History* sustains the thesis that civilization is the consequence of successful responses to new challenges. If challenges are lacking or if responses are not successful, civilization declines.

[102] Evidence that such a change has taken place in the post-Renaissance period is to be found in the fact that no previous utopia has contemplated the possibility of a warless world. Pacifists like the early Christians had looked for peace only in the world to come or, like Dante, within an empire defended from external attack. Since the Renaissance, Erasmus, Crucé, Penn, Kant, Ladd, Wilson, and many others have contemplated the possibility and traced some of the characteristics of a warless world.

law and international organization developed on a world-scale, philosophies of humanism and liberalism, and common attitudes with respect to the nature of truth and reality spread to all sections of the world. "Soon after the world had been circumnavigated," writes Clark Wissler, "when it was certain that the world was round, and that all the important lands had been discovered, scholars began to sense a world unity, or to see it as a whole."[103] The world, however, is still divided into many states which have often been at war. There have been periods when material contacts and spiritual understanding seemed reciprocally to stimulate each other. There have also been times when material contacts have been utilized to promote armed conflict as a means toward the individualization of particular groups. If a world-civilization is in process of creation, it is clear that it is and may remain a process, not an achievement.[104]

3. PERIODS OF MODERN CIVILIZATION

Historians generally agree in dividing the post-Renaissance epoch into four periods characterized, respectively, by (a) wars of religion, 1520–1648; (b) political absolutism, 1648–1789; (c) industrialism, democracy, and nationalism, 1789–1914; and (d) World War and its consequences.[105] The last period is so little advanced that it has not yet been characterized.

The Renaissance itself from 1480 to 1520 compressed into a short space of time intensive artistic, cultural, scientific, and social activity and invention.[106] The first three of the succeeding periods of

[103] Op. cit., p. 43. Though he regards modern history as but the continuance of the history of Western civilization which began with the fall of Rome, A. J. Toynbee recognizes that the world has achieved a certain political and economic unity and that because of this international relations have entered a new phase. His criticism of the conception of "the unity of history" seems to be directed against the frequent assumption that "Europe has expanded" and subjugated all "native" cultures. With this criticism the present writer agrees, but, in his opinion, Toynbee gives inadequate weight to the sources of the culture of the élite in all sections of the contemporary world (op. cit., I, 30 ff., 149 ff.). Cf. above, chap. vii, sec. 2b.

[104] See C. A. Beard (ed.), Whither Mankind? (New York, 1929); Toward Civilization (New York, 1930).

[105] See, e.g., F. Schevill, A Political History of Modern Europe (New York, 1907); Carl Ploetz, Manual of Universal History, trans. W. H. Tillinghast (New York, 1915).

[106] See Appen. XVII, sec. 5. Alfred Marshall (op. cit., p. 1) regards the religious, economic, military, and artistic spirits as "the great forming agencies" of world-history, the first two being the most important.

about a century and a quarter each have been not only recognized as distinctive but have also been characterized as dominated, respectively, by religious, political, and economic interests. The contemporary epoch may be characterized by a new florescence of invention and change.[107]

The dates here noted are somewhat arbitrary and have in fact been contested by some historians. Some regard the end of the first period as 1630, when the Thirty Years' War ceased to be dominantly religious and became political.[108] Others have placed it at 1661, when France had finally made peace with Spain and Louis XIV had begun to rule in person.[109] So also some would end the second period as early as 1776, when Jefferson and his colleagues wrote the American Declaration of Independence, Adam Smith published *The Wealth of Nations*, Gibbon published the first volume of *The Decline and Fall*, Bentham published *A Fragment on Government*, and Watt began the manufacture of steam engines for the general production of power.[110] Others would postpone this transition to 1815, when the In-

[107] Butler and Maccoby divide their book on the *Development of International Law* (p. viii) into three periods termed, respectively, those of the Prince, the Judge, and the Concert. "In the first period, the scholar is still in the age of the dissolving Holy Roman Empire: in the second, commercial and dynastic wars . . . . dominate the scene: in the third and last, it is the voice of some force other than that of pure nationalism which, whatever be the reason, reasserts itself." For discussion of normal succession of social interests see above, chap. vii, n. 42; Appen. IV.

[108] Ploetz, *op. cit.*, p. 308.

[109] A. H. L. Heeren, *History of the Political System of Europe* (Northampton, Mass., 1829), I, 16.

[110] G. R. Putnam, *Handbook of Universal History* (New York, 1916), p. 176. The definite dating of the "industrial revolution" in England from about 1760, emphasized in Arnold Toynbee's *Lectures on the Industrial Revolution* (London, 1890), is not generally accepted by modern economic historians who find that "industrialism" was very incomplete until after the Napoleonic period but its roots go back to the sixteenth century (see Herbert Heaton, "Industrial Revolution," *Encyclopaedia of the Social Sciences*). J. T. Merz (*A History of European Thought in the Nineteenth Century* [London, 1907]) notes that at about this time the nationalism of thought which had resulted from the supercession of Latin by vernaculars as the language of learning began to suffer attrition from the cross-fertilizing influences of foreign travel and education in foreign vernaculars by the writers (I, 16). This doubtless reacted to make the nations more self-conscious of their nationalities. Van Vollenhoven, writing from the point of view of international law, begins this period, which he characterizes as that of "the law of war and of peace," with the armed neutrality of 1780 which he thinks first attempted definite sanctions against war (*op. cit.*, p. 113). He groups the preceding periods since 1492 together under the title "The Reign of War." The period following the creation of the League of

dustrial Revolution began to manifest itself definitely on the continent of Europe.[111] The periods were not in reality separated by precise dates but by several years of transition. This was inevitable because new formulations and attitudes would arise in one place and would require some time to diffuse over the entire area covered at the time by world-civilization. The periods in America, for example, lagged considerably behind those in Western Europe.[112]

a) Wars of religion (1520–1648).—Religious interests arose in the German and Genevan reformations. They soon spread to the Netherlands, the Scandinavian countries, England, and France. The countries less affected by the Reformation—Spain, Austria, and Italy—were presently stimulated to renewed interest in religion by the Counter Reformation. During this period wars, while not unrelated to political or even economic interests, were ostensibly fought for religion.[113] Great thinkers on political and social questions— Luther, Calvin, Hooker, Barclay, Bellarmin, Althusius, Grotius, and, to a lesser extent, Bodin—proceeded from religious premises. In the thought of the time religious values were basic. War and politics were regarded by the masses as instruments of religion.[114]

b) Political absolutism (1648–1789).—The Thirty Years' War completed the secularization of politics begun by the Renaissance. Europe agreed that Protestant and Catholic states could dwell together in a system. This was to recognize that religion had ceased to

---

Nations, which provided for more comprehensive sanctions against war, he describes as "The Law of Peace and of War."

[111] F. Schuman, *International Politics* (New York, 1933), p. 76.

[112] See Appen. XIII, sec. 6.

[113] Especially the French Huguenot wars (1562–94), the Dutch Wars of Independence (1568–1648), the German Thirty Years' War (1618–48), and the English Civil War (1642–48), but Elizabeth's wars in Ireland, Scotland, and Spain, Maximilian's "Holy League" war against France, and Charles V's wars in Mexico, Peru, France, and Turkey had ostensibly religious motives.

[114] "With a few exceptions (such as Machiavelli and the Politiques) religion or the interests of some religious body gave the motive of the political thought of the period" (J. N. Figgis, *From Gerson to Grotius, 1414–1625* [Cambridge, 1907], p. 31). "To this cause [the Reformation] is due the fact that the politics of two centuries turns so largely on questions religious and ecclesiastical" (C. H. McIlwain, *The Political Works of James I* [Cambridge, Mass., 1918], p. xvii).

be of supreme importance—a fact emphasized by the willingness of most states to give a measure of religious toleration within their territories.[115] But if men would no longer fight for religion, they would for reasons of state or political principle. During the next period wars were fought to expand the frontiers of states in Europe or to acquire overseas dominions; to defend frontiers or to preserve the balance of power; to establish independence or particular types of political institutions.[116] The great thinkers—Hobbes, Locke, Hume, Montesquieu, Rousseau, Pufendorf, Bynkershoek, Wolff, Vattel, and Blackstone—approached social problems from a political or juristic point of view.[117]

c) *National industrial democracy (1789–1914).*—These political problems did not cease to be of interest nor did they entirely cease to

[115] "Only gradually was this idea [*cujus regio, ejus religio*] undermined by the more realistic theory, represented for instance by the French *politiques*, that an attempt to enforce religious unity would end not in political cohesion but in political disintegration." The Edict of Nantes (1598) was a recognition of this "opportunistic principle" (Ruggiero, *op. cit.*, p. 243). There have been political controversies over religion in most of the states since 1648, but they have not led to war and they have not often concerned "questions of doctrine and salvation." Rather they have concerned the authority of church or state in such matters as education, marriage, and social direction. The growth of religious toleration, especially since the French Revolution, has really meant the decline in loyalty to the church and substitution therefor of loyalty to the nation (King, *op. cit.*, pp. 156, 170). This change in the general attitude toward religion is typical. The great controversies over which groups have fought in one period have not usually been settled. New ideas which synthesize the old conflict arise and the old controversy ceases to be of major importance (see above, n. 53, and below, n. 136).

[116] The wars of expansion of Louis XIV, Charles XII, Peter the Great, Frederick the Great, and Catherine the Great, the colonial wars of England and the Netherlands, and the American War of Independence are typical. The balance of power suggested by Lisola in 1667 was considered the proper basis of international politics by Sir William Temple and King William III, was specifically referred to in the Treaty of Utrecht (1713), and was rationalized by the philosopher Hume (*Of the Balance of Power* [1752], *Philosophical Works* [Boston, 1854], III, 364 ff.). J. R. Seeley writes: "Competition for the New World between the five western maritime States of Europe; this is a formula which sums up a great part of the history of the seventeenth and eighteenth centuries" (*The Expansion of England* [London, 1883], p. 98).

[117] International law and politics became systematic sciences during this period, developed, respectively, from the works of Grotius (utilizing the less systematic works of Victoria and Gentili) and Hobbes (utilizing the less fundamental expositions of Machiavelli, Bodin, and Filmer) (see Sir Frederick Pollock, *An Introduction to the History of the Science of Politics* [London, 1908], pp. 55–92).

provide causes of war, but economic problems which had not been absent in the causation of the colonial wars of the eighteenth century became more important. Such problems occupied an important place in the ideologies of the American and the French revolutions[118] and in the wars of nationalism and economic imperialism of the nineteenth century.[119] The economic spirit had become firmly established in England as early as the time of Elizabeth, and the dominant position acquired by Great Britain, as a result of priority in the Industrial Revolution, contributed greatly to the diffusion of the economic spirit in the late eighteenth and nineteenth centuries.[120] Writers such as Adam Smith, Bentham, Hamilton, Jefferson, the Mills, Ricardo, Buckle, Spencer, Sismondi, Bastiat, Marx, Proudhon, and Liszt emphasized this spirit, and some who deplored it, like De Tocqueville, recognized its growing importance.[121] The German transcendentalists—Kant, Fichte, and Hegel—and the Italian nationalist Mazzini were less economically minded, but they were a minority.[122] Popular thinking conceived of war, if justified at all, as an instrument of economic progress.[123]

d) World-wars and internationalism (1914———).—In the period after World War I social theorists tended to emphasize psychological

---

[118] Economic grievances were included in the declarations of both these revolutions (see W. E. Dodd, "When Washington Tried Isolation," *American Mercury*, IV [March, 1925], 344 ff.).

[119] See John Bakeless, *The Economic Causes of Modern War* (New York, 1921).

[120] Nef, *The Rise of the British Coal Industry*, I, 165.

[121] Economics first became a systematic science during this period, developed from the work of the physiocrats and Adam Smith (see J. K. Ingram, *A History of Political Economy* [New York, 1893]; L. H. Haney, *History of Economic Thought* [New York, 1913], p. 132). Alexis de Tocqueville was convinced that democracy tended to exaggerate the economic spirit (*Democracy in America, 1840* [New York, 1862], Vol. II, chap. x). Buckle and Spencer considered the development of "industrial" as distinct from "military" societies a sign of progress (see Ernst Barker, *Political Thought in England from Herbert Spencer to the Present Day* ["Home University Library" (London, n.d.)], chaps. iii, iv, and viii).

[122] Barker, *op. cit.*, chap. ii.

[123] This is indicated by the fact that pacifists such as Norman Angell (*The Great Illusion* [New York, 1910]) considered it a sufficient attack on war to show that it was economically inefficient.

rather than technological or historical factors.[124] Graham Wallas,[125] A. L. Lowell,[126] Walter Lippmann,[127] C. E. Merriam,[128] and H. D. Lasswell[129] have dealt with the relation of opinion to politics, and psychological interpretations of war, like those of Nicolai,[130] Crile,[131] Freud,[132] Waelder,[133] and Russell,[134] have been common. It seems

[124] The change in economics wrought by the psychological emphasis of the marginal utility school is indicated by the shift, since the war, in the common analysis of the subject from production, distribution, exchange, and consumption to value and distribution. E. R. A. Seligman writes ("Economics," *Encyclopaedia of the Social Sciences*, V, 348) that "at the present time marginalism together with its variant known as mathematical economics has probably the largest following among economists," and F. H. Knight, dealing with marginal utility, concludes that goods and services are of economic interest only as they represent "values or sacrifices. These cannot be treated as physical things but must be defined in the same vague and shifting terms as the human impulses, successes and failures which the scientific mind finds such unsatisfactory material" (*Encyclopaedia of the Social Sciences*, V, 363). See also article and bibliography on "Economic Incentives," *Encyclopaedia of the Social Sciences*. Herman Heller, dealing with "Political Science" (*ibid.*, XII, 209, 305), writes: "Present day political science revolves primarily around the problem of the attainment, consolidation and distribution of political power . . . ." which today involves manipulation of "the manifold instruments of mass appeal and mass exploitation." Thus the science must rest on a more detailed psychology than the abstractions identifying human nature with greed, sympathy, fear, ambition, or other such qualities which were adequate for early political scientists. The sociologists and anthropologists have also tended to base their work on a realistic psychology, notably in the works of W. I. Thomas, L. L. Bernard, and B. Malinowski. See "Social Psychology," *Encyclopaedia of the Social Sciences*, XIV, 15–16. Psychology became a systematic science in this period, developed from the work of Wundt, James, Freud, and others, thus providing a basis for this newer trend of the social sciences (see "Psychology," *Encyclopaedia of the Social Sciences*).

[125] *Human Nature in Politics* (London, 1908); *The Great Society* (New York, 1917).

[126] *Public Opinion and Popular Government* (New York, 1914); *Public Opinion in War and Peace* (New York, 1922).

[127] *A Preface to Politics* (New York, 1913); *Public Opinion* (New York, 1922).

[128] *The Making of Citizens* (Chicago, 1931); *Political Power* (New York, 1934).

[129] *Propaganda Technique in the World War* (London, 1927); *World Politics and Personal Insecurity* (New York, 1935); *Politics: Who Gets What, When, How* (New York, 1936).

[130] *The Biology of War* (New York, 1918).

[131] *A Mechanistic View of War and Peace* (New York, 1915).

[132] Letter to Einstein, "Why War?" International Institute of Intellectual Cooperation, *op. cit.*

[133] Institut International de Cooperation Intellectuelle, *Lettre sur l'étiologie et l'évolution des psychoses collectives* (Paris, 1933).

[134] *Why Men Fight* (New York, 1930).

probable that the present period will be less dominated by the economic spirit than the last and that the psychological spirit manifested in such interests as art, education, and propaganda will play a larger role.[135]

4. CHANGES IN MODERN CIVILIZATION

These transitions in the general interest dominating modern civilization have been accompanied by changes (a) in basic values, (b) in science and technology, (c) in population and health, and (d) in political organization and institutions. In these matters there have been persistent trends.

a) *Values.*—As noted in section 1, there has been a general trend of ideas away from privilege, authority, absolutism, and dogmatism and toward humanism, liberalism, pragmatism, and relativism, with, however, local and temporary setbacks, particularly in the periods following great wars. It would appear, however, that consciousness of these four attitudes did not develop simultaneously but consecutively. Each attitude became defined in efforts to synthesize attitudes of a different type in conflict with one another in the successive periods of modern history.[136]

Humanism, in the sense of devotion to humane letters, arose with the revival of learning, but as an ethical principle it developed during the period of religious controversy when "humanists" were confronted by the competing claims of Catholics and Protestants to be the only elect of God. The humanists' effort to synthesize these claims contributed the universal ideas of international law, the family of nations, human rights, and social reform.[137] While on the whole humanism has grown in acceptance, it has always been opposed by claimants to unique privilege, such as, in recent times, the advocates of extreme nationalism, tribalism, and class domination. The application of humanism has always been in large meas-

---

[135] Sorokin, *op. cit.*, I, 687.

[136] Each, therefore, was a synthesis resulting, according to the Hegelian dialectic, from the opposition of thesis and antithesis in the respective fields of religion, politics, economics, and science.

[137] Which permitted the peaceful coexistence of the religions on the principles either of Erastianism or of toleration and even the peaceful coexistence of Christians and infidels.

ure suspended between groups at war with each other but not wholly, as evidenced by the existence of laws of war seeking to compromise military necessity with the claims of humanity.[138]

Liberalism, while implicit in the thought of the great men of the Renaissance and manifested in movements for religious toleration at the end of the sixteenth century, was not formulated until the political period, when the autocratic policies of sovereigns, claiming to rule by divine right, aroused opposition from groups which considered themselves oppressed. The contract theory of society, the concept of natural rights, and the principle of toleration were revived and elaborated by the liberals. These ideas subsequently secured institutional recognition in constitutions and treaties, sanctioned by checks and balances, or balances of power, ideas derived from the Newtonian physics. These guarantees, however, were often subject to suspension in time of emergency and have been less generally applied in times of war, revolution, and high tension, such as the period since World War I, when group security seems more precious than individual liberty, group solidarity more valuable than toleration. The nonobservance of the principles at such times has sometimes been a stimulus to their more precise formulation later.[139]

Pragmatism was first definitely formulated during the economic period as a consequence of the increasing opportunities for individual and social choice offered by expanding frontiers of knowledge, technology, and society and was stimulated by the idea of organic evolution. Its protagonists were impressed by the inadequacy, especially in America, where social change was most rapid, of theories, of religious and racial predestination, of political and legal absolutism, and of scientific and economic determinism.[140]

Relativism was formulated by Einstein in the scientific field in the

[138] Butler and Maccoby, *op. cit.*, p. 193; J. Westlake, *International Law* (Cambridge, 1913), Part II, p. 61; IV Hague Convention, 1907, Preamble (A. P. Higgins, *The Hague Peace Conferences* [Cambridge, 1909], p. 207).

[139] Constitutional bills of rights were formulated as a consequence of abuses which led to the British (1628–88), American (1776–89), and French (1792) revolutions, and treaty guaranties to natives and minorities were formulated as a consequence of the abuse of Christians in the Near East, natives in the Congo Basin, and of minorities in eastern and central Europe before World War I.

[140] See above, n. 54.

early twentieth century as a result of refined physical measurements made by Michelson and Morley in the 1880's. It has been extended into philosophy from reflection upon the most advanced knowledge of biological, psychological, social, and ideological change which had thrown all forms of dogmatism into confusion.[141]

Both pragmatism and relativism were inherent in the scientific methods applied during the entire modern period, though their premises had frequently been contradicted by scientific formulations. They have always been opposed by dogmatic theologies or philosophies claiming to possess avenues to certainty or insight, and their popularity has waned in times of tension when groups have demanded dogmatic assurance of the correctness of their positions.[142]

b) Science and technology.—There has been a tendency for the annual number of inventions in pure and applied science to increase. These inventions not only have increased man's power over nature but also have increased his power to make new inventions. The compass, clock, gunpowder, and printing, which ushered in the modern period, were followed in the seventeenth century by the telescope, microscope, and the calculus; in the eighteenth century by the steam engine and textile machinery; in the nineteenth century by steam navigation, the railroad, the telegraph, telephone, electric motor, electric light, internal-combustion engine, rifle and machine gun; in the twentieth century by the submarine, airship, automobile, moving picture, and radio, to mention only those inventions having a direct relation to economic and political activities.[143] Technology has proceeded from the period of eotechnics, dependent on wooden construction and the power of wind and water, through the period of paleotechnics, dependent on iron and steel construction and the power of coal, to the present neotechnic period, dependent on alloys for construction and the power of electricity.[144]

---

[141] See above, n. 76.   [142] See above, n. 65.

[143] See Ogburn (ed.), *Recent Social Trends*, Vol. I, chap. iii; Ploetz, *op. cit.*, pp. 279, 485. T. H. Buckle (*History of Civilization in England* [London, 1869], I, 199 ff.) argues that the war spirit in Europe was reduced by the invention of gunpowder, political economy, and steam power. See also E. E. Free, "Inventions and Discoveries," *Encyclopaedia Britannica*, XII, 545 ff., and above, Appen. XVII.

[144] Lewis Mumford, *Technics and Civilization* (New York, 1934), pp. 109 ff.

While man has always been an inventor, the acceleration of inventive activity has been a phenomenon which sets the modern period apart. In fact, one of the manifestations of the pragmatic attitude characterizing this period has been the invention of devices for facilitating invention, particularly the propagation of pure science, the systematic concentration and dissemination of objective knowledge by scientific journals, encyclopedias, and libraries, the co-ordination of research by scientific societies, research endowments, and research institutes attached to industrial and educational institutions, and the enactment of patent laws.[145]

A plotting of the rate of increase in the number of inventions in each twenty-five-year period over the number in the preceding twenty-five-year period indicates a rise from 1475 to 1525 and then a continuous drop until 1660. A phenomenal rise at this period during which scientific societies were being rapidly created followed by a drop until 1725. After this the rate of increase was high until 1850, when it dropped, although the absolute number of inventions in each twenty-five-year period continued to increase.[146]

Paralleling this increased inventiveness has been an increased use of coal and other fuel;[147] greater division of labor;[148] industrialization

[145] "The role of invention in the form of technical and social change in modern Europe is, however, as unique in the history of mankind as is the contemporary advent of "capitalistic" economy; the two may be taken as different aspects of the same great transformation of the western world. . . . . This changed attitude, which conceives of science as an instrument for making and remaking a universe of one's own, seems to contain the secret of the European's ultimate political ascendency over the older civilizations of Asia" (Carl Brinkman, "Invention," *Encyclopaedia of the Social Sciences*, VIII, 248). See also Free, *op. cit.*, p. 547; Ogburn (ed.), *Recent Social Trends*, I, 164.

[146] There is a similar drop since 1850 in the rate of increase by twenty-five-year periods in the number of patents given in the United States and Great Britain, and there has been a drop in the rate of increase in the physical discoveries reported from France, England, and Germany since 1815 (see table in Ogburn [ed.], *Recent Social Trends*, I, 126, and below, Appen. XVII, Figs. 32, 33.

[147] Nef, *The Rise of the British Coal Industry*, I, 123; see Table 19, Appen. XVII. Warren and Pearson (*op. cit.*, p. 47) present graphs showing a rise in the index of coal production in the United States from 1839 to 1914 of 6.22 per cent on the average per year and 3.86 per cent per capita per year but a decline since 1914 of 0.25 per cent per year and 1.69 per cent per capita per year.

[148] "Between the end of the sixteenth century and the beginning of the nineteenth the vocational division of labor failed to bring about any real progress in industrial

of larger proportions of the population;[149] a growing dominance of money economy and capitalism;[150] an increase in the amount and speed of trade, travel, and communication;[151] an increase in the economic interdependence of often widely separated groups;[152] a per

methods. But with the industrial revolution a new and powerful development set in under the influence of capitalism" (Arthur Salz, "Specialization," *Encyclopaedia of the Social Sciences*, XIV, 281). This writer distinguishes professional or social division of labor, technical division of labor within an enterprise, and geographical division of labor (*ibid.*, p. 279).

[149] Herbert Heaton ("Industrial Revolution," *Encyclopaedia of the Social Sciences*) traces the course of industrialization in the principal countries. The ratio of the industrial to the total population has been estimated for various countries at different times (see "Occupation," *Encyclopaedia of the Social Sciences*, XI, 433). For progress of industrialization in far eastern countries see S. Nasu, in Corrado Gini *et al.*, *Population* ("Harris Foundation Lectures" [Chicago, 1930]), pp. 191, 194; J. B. Condliffe (ed.), *Problems of the Pacific, 1929*, pp. 65 ff. In the United States the proportion of the occupied population engaged in agriculture declined from 72.3 per cent in 1820 to 21.3 per cent in 1930, while the proportion in industry, commerce, and clerical services rose from 14.9 per cent in 1820 to 59.5 per cent in 1930 (Mordecai Ezekiel, "Population and Unemployment," p. 238, in L. I. Dublin [ed.], *The American People* [*Annals of the American Academy of Political and Social Science*, Vol. CLXXXVII (November, 1936)]).

[150] Werner Sombart ("Capitalism," *Encyclopaedia of the Social Sciences*, III, 206) distinguishes the periods of early capitalism (1250–1750), of high capitalism (1750–1914), and of late capitalism since 1914 characterized by an increase of socialism and government regulation.

[151] Eugene Staley presents isochronic maps to indicate these changes (*World Economy in Transition* [New York, 1939]).

[152] Franz Eulenberg ("International Trade," *Encyclopaedia of the Social Sciences*, VIII, 194) presents a table showing the growth of the world's total international trade from 2.8 billion dollars in 1840 to 66.7 billion in 1929 shared at the first date by United Kingdom, United States, Germany, and France in the ratios 32, 8, 0, 10, respectively, and at the later date in the ratios 14, 14, 10, 6. There was a material diminution of this trade from 1929 to 1934. The relative importance of international trade to different countries is illustrated by the following table (*ibid.*, p. 197):

PER CAPITA FOREIGN TRADE TURNOVER, 1929

Country	Dollars	Country	Dollars
Denmark	266	Germany	100.0
Netherlands	243	United States	79.0
Switzerland	228	Japan	32.0
Great Britain	219	British India	6.5
France	103	Russia	5.7

After commenting on the economic dependence of all countries, he thinks it "not . . . . open to doubt that the drive for national economic self-sufficiency is inspired by political considerations rather than by economic logic" (p. 200). For a detailed analysis of the

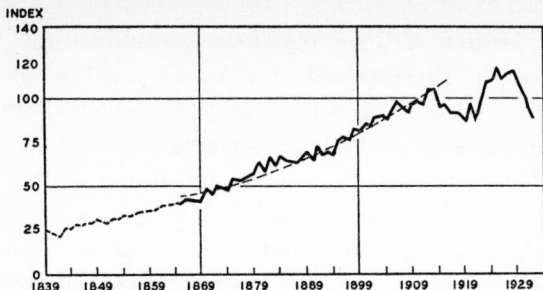

FIG. 3.—Increase in world's production per capita, 1840–1932 (1910–14 = 100). From 1865 to 1914 the world's physical volume of production per capita increased 1.91 per cent per year. During the World War I period it was strikingly decreased. This shows that man cannot fight and produce at the same time. (From George F. Warren and Frank A. Pearson, *Gold and Prices* [New York, 1935], p. 57.)

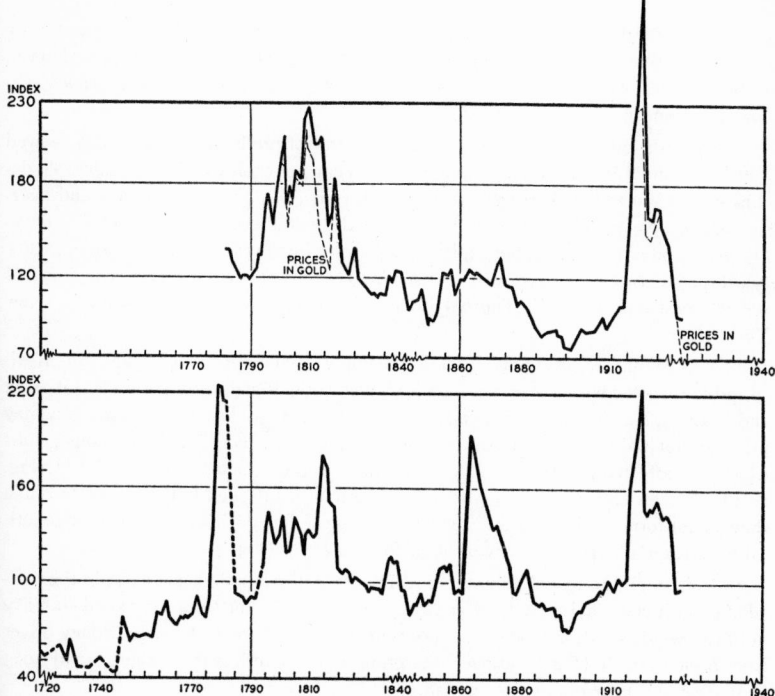

FIG. 4.—Changes in wholesale prices in currency in the United States (*below*) and in England (*above*), 1720–1930 (1910–14 = 100). Prices were high during war periods and declined afterward. (From Warren and Pearson, *op. cit.*, p. 16.)

capita increase in wealth and real income;[153] and a great increase in money prices.[154] These trends have not all been continuous. Nef estimates that the rate of increase of coal production and trade in England rose rapidly in the latter sixteenth century, then declined in the eighteenth century. Even in the nineteenth century it did not exceed the rate of increase of Elizabeth's time, and there has been a falling-off since 1915.[155] The trend, however, has been toward an acceleration of the rate of change and a shrinking of the world in terms of the time to transfer things, persons, information, or ideas from one place to another.

c) *Population and health.*—There has been a rapid and apparently continuous growth of population especially in Europe and in the areas touched by European civilization, though since 1870 the rate of increase of Western countries has begun to decline.[156] There has

---

factors contributing to the movement for national economic self-sufficiency or autarchy since World War I and especially since the depression of 1929 see Alvin H. Hansen, *Report of the Commission of Inquiry into National Policy in International Economic Relations* (Minneapolis, 1934), pp. 103 ff.

[153] Snyder's index of the world's physical volume of production, 1840–1932, showed a normal annual increase of 3.15 and 1.91 per cent per capita with a considerable decline during World War I, 1915–20, and after the depression of 1929 (Warren and Pearson, *op. cit.*, p. 57). This means a doubling of the world's wealth about every twenty-five years and of the world's per capita wealth every forty years during the past century (see Fig. 3). From the sixteenth to the nineteenth centuries, however, the trend of wages was down (see J. E. Thorold Rogers, *Six Centuries of Work and Wages* [New York, 1890], p. 73).

[154] This change, resulting mainly from the importation of precious metals from Mexico and Peru, is the most notable economic change at the Renaissance period (see Warren and Pearson, *op. cit.*, pp. 436 ff., and Appen. XVII, Fig. 30, below). Changes in money prices are related to changes in the commodity purchasing power of the precious metals which are affected by the world's production of these metals (Appen. XVII, Fig. 29); to changes in the monetary price of the precious metals; and to the degree to which they do not form the basis of the currency because of demonitizing legislation or practical utilization of paper currency or other form of credit (Fig. 4).

[155] Nef, *op. cit.*, p. 123. Estimates of real wages in England indicate a rise in the period of great inventional activity after 1650, followed by decline before 1700 and stability until the rapid rise after 1800 of 1.61 per cent per year (Rogers, *op. cit.*). Money prices have been variable (Fig. 4, above). See graph of wheat prices in England, 1259–1933 in Warren and Pearson, *op. cit.*, p. 438.

[156] R. R. Kuczynski, "Population," *Encyclopaedia of the Social Sciences*, XII, 241 ff., and in Gini *et al.*, *op. cit.*, pp. 283 ff.; see below, Appen. V, Fig. 15; Appen. XVII, Fig. 28; and Figs. 5 and 6.

also been a tendency for population to concentrate in large cities.[157] The figures available for estimating the rate of population growth are

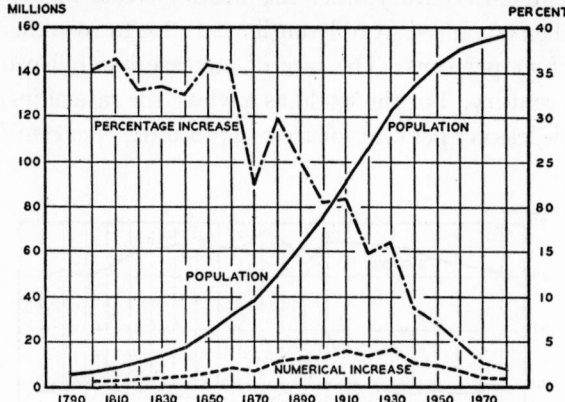

FIG. 5.—Population growth and rate of increase of population in the United States, 1790–1980, estimated after 1940. (From W. F. Ogburn [ed.], *Recent Social Trends in the United States* [New York, 1933], I, 2.)

FIG. 6.—Population growth and rate of annual increase in the United States, 1910–31. (From Ogburn [ed.], *op. cit.*, I, 3.)

liable to serious error especially with respect to extra-European areas.[158] These estimates, however, indicate that European popula-

[157] "Population," *Encyclopaedia Britannica*, XVIII, 232–33. For a graph of these trends in the United States see Ogburn (ed.), *Recent Social Changes*, I, 8.

[158] Kuczynski, *op. cit.*

tion increased some 11 per cent from 1450 to 1500 and continued to
increase at this rate in succeeding half-centuries until the second half
of the seventeenth century, when the rate of increase was 18 per cent.
The rate then advanced steadily until from 1850 to 1900 there was an
increase of 51 per cent. The rate of increase has fallen off in the
twentieth century. For the world as a whole the rate of increase has
been a little less (17 per cent for 1650–1700 and 42 per cent for 1850–
1900).[159]

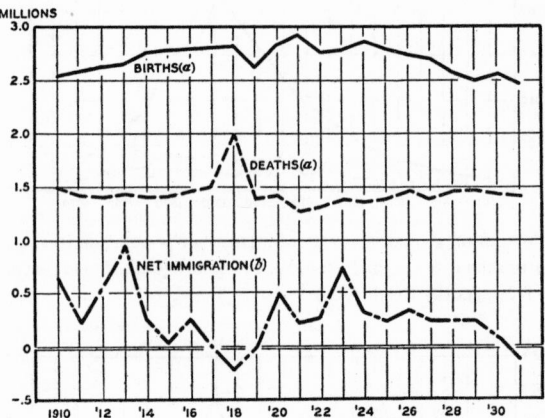

Fig. 7.—Annual births, deaths, and immigration in the United States, 1910–31. $a =$
Contains allowance for estimated number of births and deaths not registered; $b =$ The
excess of aliens and citizens arriving in, over those departing from, continental United
States. (From Ogburn [ed.], *op. cit.*, I, 38.)

Great advances have been made in medicine, sanitation, and accident prevention. These have kept pace with the conditions favorable to epidemics such as congested population, rapid travel, and
transportation from all sections of the world and to accidents from
increasing use of rapidly moving machinery and means of transportation.[160] Without these advances in preventive medicine such con-

---

[159] The average annual rate of increase in Europe was 9.1 per 1,000 from 1870 to 1900
and only 7.8 from 1900 to 1930. This low rate was in part due to the war period when
population actually declined in Europe. The annual average rate of increase from 1920
to 1930 was 10.4, a long-time high for Europe (see *Encyclopaedia of the Social Sciences*,
XII, 243, 245, and below, Appen. V, Fig. 15.

[160] See Hans Zinsser, *Rats, Lice and History* (New York, 1935); "Preventive Medicine," "Plague," "Industrial Accidents," "Industrial Welfare," *Encyclopaedia Britan-*

ditions would have rendered human life extremely precarious. With these advances the trend apparently has been toward a reduced and less fluctuating mortality rate in most sections of the world.[161] The plagues which made grave inroads upon European population for two hundred and fifty years after the Black Death of 1346 became less and less violent until now the annual death rate in most parts of the world approaches constancy from year to year apart from epidemics now caused in the main by war.[162]

---

nica; "Public Health," "Industrial Hazards," "Industrial Hygiene," *Encyclopaedia of the Social Sciences.*

[161] "Death Rate," *Encyclopaedia Britannica*, L. I. Dublin, "Mortality," *Encyclopaedia of the Social Sciences*, XI, 24. The death rates fell from 12 to 50 per cent in the principal countries in the fifty years from 1880 to 1930 and in the latter year ranged from 8.6 per 1,000 in New Zealand to 11.3 in the United States, 18.2 in Japan, and 23.7 in Chile. For table of average annual increase of populations in most European countries and in Europe as a whole since 1800 see Kuczynski, *op. cit.*, pp. 243–44. Decreasing birth and death rates has meant that the population has tended to be older. For recent changes in the age composition of the population of various countries see "Population," *Encyclopaedia Britannica*, XVIII, 234, and discussion by Ogburn (*Recent Social Trends*, pp. 26 ff.), who points out that from 1820 to 1930 the median age of the population of the United States advanced from 16.7 to 26.4 years. For fluctuations of birth and death rates in the United States see Fig. 7. For recent trends in birth and death rates see A. J. Lotka and John Collins in L. I. Dublin (ed.), *The American People*, 1 ff., 84 ff. Finkelstein estimates that the average length of life in the sixteenth century was nineteen years; in the eighteenth century, thirty years; and in the twentieth century, thirty-nine years (see A. J. Todd, *Theories of Social Progress* [New York, 1918], p. 122).

[162] William Farr, *Vital Statistics* (London, 1885), pp. 253, 310, 318. The periodical inroads of plague can be studied in the seventeenth-century bills of mortality printed by J. Graunt, *Natural and Political Observations* (London, 1676), and William Heberden, *Collection of Yearly Bills of Mortality, 1657 to 1758* (London, 1759). See also W. F. Ogburn, "Malthusian Theory and the Population of Iceland, 1750–1920," in *Constato italiano per la studio dei problemi della populazioni* (Rome, 1932); Friedrich Prinzing, *Epidemics Resulting from Wars* (Oxford, 1916). For effect of Civil War and World War I on rate of population increase in the United States see Figs. 5, 6, and 7. If the causes of death are divided between those which exhibit marked temporal fluctuations in a given population such as famine, pestilence, disaster (vulcanism, earthquake, storm, flood, fire), and hostilities, and those which do not, such as infant and maternal mortality, suicide, homicide, and execution, industrial, transportation, and other accidents, nonepidemic disease, and old age, it is certain that the relative number of deaths attributable to the first list as a whole had diminished during the modern period, but this is not true of all the items. Thus there has probably been some increase in the proportion of deaths from hostilities and from accidents, but the main increase has been in deaths from old age and nonepidemic diseases. A rough comparison based on estimates for the

d) Political organization and institutions.—No less striking than the ideological, technical, and population changes has been the course of political organization in modern civilization. Four movements have gone on, not entirely simultaneously, dealing, respectively, with (i) the expansion and (ii) integration of the family of nations and with (iii) the territorial definition and (iv) institutional organization of the nation-states.

(i) The civilization which started in Western Europe at the Renaissance and developed a family of European Christian nations including Spain, England, France, Austria, the many principalities of Italy and Germany, the Scandinavian countries, Poland, and the Baltic countries steadily spread in area to include Russia and the American countries in the seventeenth and eighteenth centuries; the Near East, the Far East, and India in the nineteenth century; and Africa and the Pacific in the twentieth century. A precise fixing of the dates when successive states entered this civilization is necessarily arbitrary. The rise of a national political sovereignty on a definitely secular basis, inspired by the complex of Renaissance ideas and minimizing the influence of feudalism, may be taken as the criteria for Western Europe.

With this criteria modern civilization may be said to have begun in Spain in 1479 with the union of Castille and Aragon; in England with the advent of the Tudor monarchy in 1485; in Italy with the ad-

---

percentage of deaths from causes thus classified in the seventeenth and twentieth centuries in Western countries follows:

SPORADIC CAUSES OF DEATH	CENTURY		CONTINUOUS CAUSES OF DEATH	CENTURY	
	Seventeenth	Twentieth		Seventeenth	Twentieth
Famine.............	3	0	Infant and maternal.....	20	8
Epidemic...........	20	7	Disease and old age......	45	71
Disaster............	2	1	Accident...............	5	7
Hostilities..........	2	3	Suicide and homicide....	3	3
Total...........	27	11	Total.............	73	89

(See *Encyclopaedia of the Social Sciences*, "Mortality" [with statistics for United States, 1929, 1930], "Disasters," "Epidemics," "Famines," "Accidents," "Floods," "Fires," "Suicide," "Homicide," "Child Mortality," and books by Graunt and Heberden, above.)

vent of the secular pope, Alexander VI, in 1492; in France with the advent of the Orleanist dynasty in 1498; in western Germany with the death of Maximilian I and the rise of Luther in 1519; in eastern Germany with the proclamation of Albert of Brandenberg as Protestant hereditary duke of Prussia in 1525; in Austria with the accession of the Protestant-inclined Maximilian II as emperor and king of Bohemia and Hungary in 1554; in the Scandinavian countries, with the accession of Gustavus Vasa in Sweden and of Frederick I in Denmark in 1523.

Poland entered modern civilization in 1573 when the Compact of Warsaw was issued providing for religious toleration. The monarchy was converted into a republic with an elected king, and Henry of Valois, a French prince, was invited to the throne, soon followed, however, by the great Stephan Bathori, who came to the throne in 1575. Russia may be said to have entered modern civilization when Peter the Great began his policy of Westernization after 1700. The Balkan States cannot be said to have entered modern civilization until Turkish control was eliminated by the recognition of independence and admission of these states to the family of nations after 1828.[163]

Extra-European areas may be said to have entered Western civilization when a European élite, with the ideas of modern civilization, achieved a definite leadership, or when a non-European élite was able to gain the admission of the state to full membership in the family of nations through recognition, exchange of diplomatic relations, or participation in the treaty system. With this criterion the North American seaboard entered modern civilization in the seventeenth century, although not admitted to the family of nations until 1783. The Latin-American countries entered modern civilization even earlier with conquests of Columbus, Cortez, and Pizarro, although not admitted as independent members of the family of nations until after 1822. The British Dominions entered modern civilization with the progress of British, French, and Dutch settlement in Canada, South Africa, Australia, and New Zealand from the seventeenth to the nineteenth

---

[163] See W. W. White, *The Process of Change in the Ottoman Empire* (Chicago, 1937); Van Vollenhoven, *op. cit.*, pp. 82, 83.

century although not admitted as independent members of the family of nations until the twentieth century.

Turkey was admitted formally to participation in the "law and concert of Europe" by the conference at Paris which ended the Crimean War in 1856. It had, of course, long before this been in military and some diplomatic contact with Europe. India came definitely within world-civilization with the British annexation in 1858. China entered into regular diplomatic and treaty relations with the West in 1858 and Japan in 1867.[164] The Arab countries have only been establishing such relations in the twentieth century. It may be said, however, that all sixty-seven states which were invited to become parties to the Pact of Paris and most of which were at one time members of the League of Nations have become participants in modern civilization. The homelands together with the hundred-odd territories under the sovereignty, protection, and influence of these states constitute practically the whole world.[165]

(ii) This expanding civilization has been to an increasing extent integrated, though with setbacks in periods of war, by economic and religious ties developed through the centralized administration of commercial corporations and missionary enterprises; by political ties developed through imperial administration, diplomatic, and consular services; and by legal and administrative ties developed through treaties, international unions, the League of Nations, the International Labor Organization, the Permanent Court of International Justice, all governed by and administering a general system of international law.[166]

(iii) The political units of this modern world-civilization have tended, through the processes of coalition and self-determination, to

[164] Q. Wright, *Diplomatic Machinery of the Pacific Area* (Institute of Pacific Relations, 1936), pp. 9 ff.

[165] For list of members of the family of nations see Oppenheim, *op. cit.*, Vol. I, Part I, chap. i, sec. 12; Manley O. Hudson, "The Members of the League of Nations," *British Year Book of International Law, 1930*, pp. 130 ff. Several of these states were occupied after 1935. Classifications of all political areas of the world may be found in League of Nations, *Estimated World Requirements of Dangerous Drugs in 1934* (Geneva, 1933), pp. 8–9; United States Department of State, *Admission of Aliens into the United States* (Washington, 1935), map, p. 64.

[166] See Clyde Eagleton, *International Government* (New York, 1932); Pitman B. Potter, *Introduction to the Study of International Organization* (4th ed.; New York, 1935).

form themselves or to be formed into national states. Feudal principalities in England, France, and Spain had been in large measure absorbed by the kingdoms before the modern period began. The consolidation of the Netherlands and of Switzerland was recognized in the Conference of Westphalia. The consolidation of Germany and of Italy together consisting of over two thousand feudal domains in 1600, and some three hundred such domains at the Peace of Westphalia, was not effected until the nineteenth century.[167]

New states have also been formed by the process of recognition both of communities not formerly in close contact with Western Europe, such as those of Eastern Europe and the Orient, and by the self-determination of communities formerly parts of empires, as the United States and the Dominions from the British Empire; the Latin-American countries from the Spanish and Portuguese empires, the Balkans and the Arab states from the Ottoman Empire, the Successor States from the Hapsburg Empire, and the Baltic States from the Russian Empire. More than a hundred states are today recognized as having sovereign or quasi-sovereign status under international law. They vary greatly in homogeneity and in size, several have been militarily occupied, and doubtless the process of coalescence and self-determination will continue.[168]

The process by which national states have been formed may be regarded as manifestations of the spirit of nationalism. In the earlier period the state, ruled by a powerful government, took the initiative in creating nations by manipulating the opinion of the population which it could control, while in the more recent period the nationalities, united by private propaganda often centered in a foreign country, quickly took the initiative in breaking up states which existed. Before the press had thoroughly developed, established governments apparently had an advantage over dissident nationalities, but with the development of the press the situation changed. Perhaps the radio, which is becoming the main instrument of propaganda, will again change the situation to the advantage of governments. At present the two processes—nationalization programs initiated by the

[167] Butler and Maccoby, *op. cit.*, chap. i; G. N. Clark, *The Seventeenth Century* (Oxford, 1929), p. 82; C. V. Wedgwood, *The Thirty Years' War* (New Haven, 1939), p. 34.
[168] See above, n. 164.

governments and self-determination programs initiated by minority groups—are striving against each other in many sections of the world,[169] and both conflict with the trend toward world-integration.[170]

(iv) There has been a tendency for the national states to assume a certain similarity of internal organization and law. All have a foreign office and an executive head. All claim internal sovereignty of their territory and nationals. Most have some division of executive, judicial, and legislative authority and a functional division of the administration into offices for foreign affairs, war, navy, finance, commerce, etc. All assume responsibilities for defense of the national frontiers and for the maintenance of internal law and order, and most conduct other services of general interest such as the post office and the collection of statistics and often many types of economic and social regulation. There are, of course, variations, which have assumed dominant importance since World War I, in the ideology and the symbolic structure by which authority is preserved and also variations in the extent to which the administration regulates or administers economic, religious, and social activities. But there is a general similarity of structure and function.[171]

The process of developing constitutional organization toward a common type has been characteristic of the political and economic periods of modern history. In general, the foreign affairs, military,

[169] "Before the advent of democracy the state had tended to mold nationality in its own image. It had tended toward the cultural unification of all its inhabitants. With the awakening of the political and social consciousness of the masses, the cultural group, the nationality, began to rival the state and each nationality began to demand a state of its own. Before the French Revolution the state hammered the nationalities into its own form. In the nineteenth century the nationality began hammering the state. In those regions where the state had long been strong it had so reduced the minorities that they were too feeble to bring about its dissolution. But where the state had not had the same long and powerful history, the nationalities began carving up the states or consolidating them in order to produce coincidence of political organization and nationality" (J. C. King, *op. cit.*, pp. 227–28). Cf. L. P. Mair, *The Protection of Minorities* (London, 1928).

[170] See chap. xiv, below.

[171] For various classifications of forms of government and constitution see J. W. Garner, *Introduction to Political Science* (New York, 1910); W. J. Shepard, "Government," *Encyclopaedia of the Social Sciences;* and J. T. Shotwell (ed.), *Governments of Continental Europe* (New York, 1940).

financial, and judicial organizations of the major European states approximated their present form during the late seventeenth and eighteenth centuries. The legislative and internal administrative organizations developed during the nineteenth century. The American and Asiatic states have lagged somewhat behind the European states in the development of similar constitutional structures.[172]

It appears that important changes in opinions, interests, and ideas; in inventions, technology, and economy; in population, medicine, and social conditions; and in government, law, and international organization have all taken place in modern civilization with a trend toward a world-order based on the consent of autonomous nationalities maintaining universal standards of social amelioration, individual liberty, rational procedures, and religious tolerance.[173] The rate of change, however, has been neither continuous nor synchronous in all regions, phases, and periods of this civilization. Europe has in general led other regions. Science and technology has in general led other phases. In Europe the period from the Renaissance to the Peace of Utrecht was marked by rapid but violent advance in the direction of the trend. The eighteenth century was a period of co-ordination, stabilization, and overseas expansion. The nineteenth century witnessed the most rapid and, on the whole, peaceful advances. The twentieth century, in marked contrast, has been characterized by violent conflict resulting from growing awareness of inconsistencies between different assumptions of the civilization itself and the emergence of movements in definite opposition to the trend. War has had an important role in this process of change, both as cause and as consequence.[174]

[172] For seventeenth-century states see Clark, *op. cit.*, p. 82, and for twentieth-century states see Q. Wright, *Mandates under the League of Nations*, p. 276, and E. D. Dickinson, *op. cit.*, chap. vi: "International Limitations upon the Equality of States."

[173] Most of the trends here noted were emphasized in the report of the Special Committee of the League of Nations on the Development of International Cooperation in Economic and Social Affairs, *Monthly Summary of League of Nations, Special Supplement*, August, 1939, p. 7. See below, chap. xv, n. 58.

[174] See chaps. x and xiv.

CHAPTER IX

FLUCTUATIONS IN THE INTENSITY OF MODERN WAR

THE intensity of war may be measured by the frequency of battles, of campaigns, or of wars.[1] These military incidents may be weighted according to the absolute number of combatants engaged, to the number engaged relative to the supporting population, to the absolute number of battle casualties of various types (killed, wounded, prisoners), or to the number of casualties relative either to the number of combatants or to the number of the supporting population.[2]

The intensity of war may also be measured by the absolute or relative losses of life attributable to it in the military and civil population during a given time or to the absolute or relative losses of wealth attributable to it. In estimates of this type there is always a ques-

---

[1] For distinction between these three words see below, sec. 2. Study of the changes in the attitude of one group toward another or of changes in the tension level within the group composed of two or more states might provide more refined measurements of war intensity, but the materials for such studies exist only in respect to limited areas and in very recent times (J. T. Russell and Q. Wright, "National Attitudes in the Far Eastern Controversy," *American Political Science Review*, XXIII [1933], 555 ff.; Q. Wright and Carl J. Nelson, "Attitudes in the United States toward China and Japan, 1937–38," *Public Opinion Quarterly*, III [1939], 46 ff.; Q. Wright, *The Causes of War and the Conditions of Peace* [London, 1935], pp. 109–12).

[2] S. Dumas and K. O. Vedel-Petersen (*Losses of Life Caused by War* [Oxford, 1923], chap. i). Dumas comments on the difficulties because of absence of records, errors of estimation, and falsification in compiling such statistics. In illustration he cites four estimates of French losses in the Battle of Novi (August 4, 1797) which vary from 20,600 to 9,500 with respect to total losses and from 7,000 to 1,500 with respect to killed. The Berlin bureau of statistics of January 26, 1871, reported the Prussian losses in the assault of Perches before Belfort as 41 killed, 154 wounded, 96 missing, while Col. Deupert-Rocheau, military governor of Belfort, says 225 Prussian prisoners were brought back to the town. The present writer was informed by Arabs on the spot two weeks after the event that at least 5,000 had been killed by the French bombardment of Damascus in October, 1925, while General Sarrail reported a total of 137 killed (*American Journal of International Law*, XX [April, 1926], 264). See also Pitirim Sorokin, *Social and Cultural Dynamics* (New York, 1937), III, 265.

tion as to the extent to which indirect losses should be counted. The population suffers not only from casualties in battle but also from disease in the army, from war-induced famine and epidemics in the civilian population, and from decline in the birth rate and increase in the death rate from causes more or less related to the war.[3] Prosperity suffers not only from direct destruction of property and workers by military action but from dislocations of production and trade which may cause serious depressions long after the war is over.[4]

To give proper weight to all these considerations in estimating the intensity of war at a given time and place would involve general demographic and economic studies of the countries concerned not only during the war but afterward. Due consideration should be given to the influence of the war upon the character and energy of the productive population during the war and after it is over and to the post-war demographic tendencies which may tend to compensate for war losses.[5]

[3] These factors, for the principal wars from 1792 to 1914, are discussed by Dumas (*op. cit.*, pp. 25–59 [military losses], 115–23 [civil losses]), and for World War I by Vedel-Petersen (*op. cit.*, pp. 137–45 [military losses], 146–82 [civilian losses]); L. Hersch, "Demographic Effects of Modern War," in Interparliamentary Union, *What Would Be the Character of a New War?* (London, 1931); E. L. Bogert, *Direct and Indirect Cost of the Great World War* (New York, 1919), pp. 269–84.

[4] Bogert (*op. cit.*, pp. 265–68, 284–99) estimates the direct economic costs of World War I at $186 billion, the indirect costs at $152 billion, a total of $338 billion. "Whatever the intervening secondary causes may have been, the ultimate cause of the great depression that has lasted since 1929 is to be found in the impoverishment and economic dislocation caused by the War which began in 1914. . . . . When the war ends, however, all the peoples—belligerents and neutrals, victors and vanquished—become involved in the ultimate costs inherent in the destruction of trade, the demoralization of moneys, the dissipation of reserves, and the accumulation of debts. There is no victor in a modern war, nor any real gain to the neutrals. All nations are involved in the collapse of their common economic welfare" (J. B. Condliffe, *War and Depression* ["World Affairs Pamphlets" (Boston, 1935)], pp. 5–6, 9). See also Q. Wright (ed.), *An American Foreign Policy toward International Stability* ("Public Policy Pamphlets," No. 14 [Chicago, 1934]), pp. 50–51, and *Report of the Commission of Inquiry into National Policy in International Economic Relations* (Minneapolis, 1934), pp. 110 ff., 281 ff.

[5] These factors seem to have been inadequately considered in such estimates as that by Bogert (above, n. 4). They are considered by Francis W. Hirst (*The Consequences of War to Great Britain* [London, 1934], p. 305), who, after quoting from John Stuart Mill on the rapidity with which populations often recover from war (*Political Economy*, Book I, chap. 5), writes: "I am inclined to think that the moral evils due to the losses and miseries endured by our men at the front are still in operation, and that economic in-

No such general studies will be attempted here. Our present interest is not in ascertaining the consequences of war but in comparing the intensity of military activity at different times and places. For this purpose intensity must be measured by units of military activity occupying as limited a time and space as possible. The frequency of battles seems to conform more closely to this requirement than any other of the readily available indices. The number of casualties and other immediate consequences of military activity will sometimes be taken into consideration.

Attention will be given to (1) spacial and (2) temporal variations in the intensity of war and to general trends with respect to (3) the quantity and (4) quality of war during the modern period.

1. SPACIAL VARIABILITY

The spacial variability of war may be considered by comparing the warlikeness of states and by ascertaining the local concentration of warlike activity.

a) Warlikeness of states.—Countries differ greatly in the frequency with which they have been at war. From 1480 to 1940 there were about twenty-six hundred important battles involving European states. Of these twenty-six hundred battles France participated in 47 per cent; Austria-Hungary in 34 per cent; Germany (Prussia) in 25 per cent; Great Britain and Russia each in about 22 per cent; Turkey in 15 per cent; Spain in 12 per cent; the Netherlands in 8 per cent; Sweden in 4 per cent; and Denmark in 2 per cent. These percentages are for the whole period of four hundred and sixty years. When tabulated by fifty-year periods, it appears that the percentage of participation by France, Austria, Great Britain, and Turkey has been relatively constant, that by Prussia and Russia has tended to increase, and that by Spain, the Netherlands, Sweden, and Den-

---

efficiency, political ineptitude, and a certain measure of social degeneracy must be traced to this cause, which contributes along with war debts, war taxes, war tariffs, and quotas to an abnormal mass of demoralizing unemployment." Some of the comparisons which he quotes between pre-war and post-war conditions seem less pessimistic. Some of these emphasize higher standards of living and of intelligence, more independence and initiative, less rigid class and sex distinctions, among the post-war generation (Hirst, *op. cit.*, pp. 64 ff.). The 134 volumes on the *Economic and Social History of the World War*, edited by James T. Shotwell, of which Hirst's book is one, deals with the consequences of the war in all the principal countries. See below, n. 69.

mark has decreased in the last three centuries.[6] The results are similar if participation in wars rather than in battles is taken as the criterion, though the differentiation between great and small states is less extreme.[7] Clearly the great powers have been the most frequent fighters.

The same conclusion is suggested by an analysis of the proportion of war years in the history of states. F. A. Woods concludes such an analysis with the statement: "It is the stronger nations since 1700 that have devoted the most time to war. Moreover, the lesser na-

---

[6] See Appen. XIX, Tables 22 and 23, and Fig. 37. Efforts were made to estimate the warlikeness of the various primitive peoples and of the past civilizations and to relate these estimates to certain environmental and social factors (see above, chaps. vi, sec. 2, vii, sec. 3, and below, Appens. IX and XIV). Modern states have varied so much in respect to warlikeness in relatively short historic periods that an effort to relate the warlikeness of these states to persistent factors does not promise to be rewarding. Attribution of a persistently warlike character to certain states, such as that implied by De Lapradelle's emphasis in December, 1914, upon Vattel's reference to the peculiarly warlike character of "the various German tribes of whom Tactitus speaks" (Introduction to Vattel, *The Law of Nations* [Carnegie ed.; Washington, 1916], pp. xxv ff.), seems not to have been based upon a comparison of any objective criteria of warlikeness. The Germans, like most modern peoples, have been very warlike in certain periods of their history and unwarlike in other periods. At times when Prussia was warlike, other German states were unwarlike. The extreme variability in the number of battles and in the proportion of war years at different periods in the history of the same state is indicated in Appen. XIX, Tables 22 and 23, and Appen. XXI, Table 46. The averages in the final columns of these tables are made of elements with such a wide deviation from the mean that they convey little information. Thus in Table 26 the averages vary from Spain, with 66 per cent of its time devoted to war (although Sorokin's indices makes Spain one of the least warlike of states [Table 49]), to Denmark, with 23 per cent of its time devoted to war. But in the first half of the sixteenth century Denmark was at war nearly half the time and in the second half of the eighteenth century Spain was at war only a third of the time. Furthermore, Prussia, which is certainly not among the least warlike of states (in fact, the average of Sorokin's index makes it nearly three times as warlike as its nearest rivals, France and Russia), has averaged a smaller proportion of war years than most of the states on the list. It is, of course, possible that indices based upon the actual amount of fighting are not the best indices of "warlikeness." See also Sorokin, *op. cit.*, III, 348–49.

[7] Of the 278 wars involving European states during this period, the percentage of participation by the principal states was: England, 28; France, 26; Spain, 23; Russia, 22; Austria, 19; Turkey, 15; Poland, 11; Sweden, 9; Netherlands, 8; Germany (Prussia), 8; Italy (Savoy-Sardinia), 9; and Denmark, 7. During most of the period Prussia and Sardinia ranked as small states, but their percentage of participation has markedly increased as they grew in power. The proportional participation of the Scandinavian states and the Netherlands, on the other hand, has declined. See Table 44, Appen. XX.

tions were once the great powers. Spain, Turkey, Holland, and Sweden were active in warfare at the same period that they were politically great."[8] His figures indicate that the powers which could be classed as great during the whole modern period had averaged twice as many wars as the smaller states, though the wars of the latter often were of longer duration. Dutch wars, for example, averaged 5.4 years each and French only 1.8. The French, however, had fought 147 wars compared to only 29 by the Dutch. Consequently, the French had been engaged in fighting a much larger proportion of the period.[9]

The fighting propensity of the great powers at the present time is illustrated by an analysis of all the military campaigns (wars, interventions, suppression of insurrections) of all the states from 1900 to 1930. This analysis indicates that the seven great powers had averaged 46 campaigns each during these thirty years and that each campaign averaged fourteen months. Eight secondary powers of Europe and Asia had averaged 19 campaigns each of an average duration of eight months. The Balkan, Latin-American, and minor African and Asiatic states averaged 10 campaigns each of an average duration of six months. The remaining states, nine noncolonial small powers of northern Europe, average only one campaign each of five months' average duration. Several of these—Denmark, Sweden, Norway, Switzerland, Estonia—had not fought any campaigns at all in this period.[10]

[8] F. A. Woods and A. Baltzly, *Is War Diminishing?* (Boston, 1915), p. 31. See also *ibid.*, pp. 103–5, and below, Table 46, Appen. XXI. Gaston Bodart (*Losses of Life in Modern Wars, 1618–1913* [Oxford, 1916], pp. 4, 75) differs somewhat from Woods in estimating Austrian and French war years since 1600. Pitirim Sorokin arrives at similarly high indices for the great powers (see Table 49) and comments: "In the life history of nations, the magnitude of war, absolute and relative, tends to grow in the periods of expansion—political, social, cultural, and territorial—of the nations at least as frequently as in the periods of decline" (*op. cit.*, III, 364).

[9] See Table 47.

[10] See Table 48. The data on which this is based were prepared by Mr. William T. Fox, using the following studies in manuscript in the University of Chicago library: Mary Jane Brumley, "Minor Wars and Interventions of the British Empire, 1900 to 1924" (1928); Edna Wallace, "French Military Operations in the Western Sahara and Morocco" (1931); Lula Caine, "Minor Wars and Interventions of the United States" (1936); Ruby Garrick, "Use of Military Force in the Pacific Area" (1930); and Wilbur W. White, "Wars in Arabia, 1900 to 1926" (1929).

b) Geographic concentration of battles.—A plotting of the geographic location of battles during this period indicates that throughout the period battles have tended to concentrate in three highway areas between regions otherwise separated by natural barriers—Flanders, the Po Valley, and Egypt. Points of geographic contact between great powers have also been areas of battle concentration: Alsace-Lorraine, the contact point of France and Germany, and the northern Balkans, the contact point of the Austrian, Russian, and Turkish empires. Battles have also concentrated in areas of unstable political organizations: in Germany prior to the middle of the nineteenth century, in Spain during the early nineteenth century, and in the Balkans during the nineteenth and twentieth centuries.[11]

2. TEMPORAL VARIABILITY

A temporal plotting of belligerent activities indicates certain periods and fluctuations.

a) The battle period.—One characteristic period is that which results from the revolution of the earth on its axis. Warfare at night has not been common. The rotation of the earth on its axis has, through most of history, marked the length of one of the most characteristic phenomena of war, the battle.[12] This limitation upon the period of continuous fighting is doubtless due primarily to the technical difficulty of fighting at night, but the physiological and psychological fact that soldiers get tired of fighting after a few hours may also be significant.[13] This limitation has been less true in more recent wars, owing to changes in military technique. Land battles in World Wars I and II often continued during the night and air-raiding upon civilian centers tended to become nocturnal because of the greater security of the attacking forces in spite of the greater difficulty of finding and hitting targets. While in the seventeenth century 96 per cent of the battles lasted for a day or less, in the eighteenth century

[11] Manuscript and series of maps prepared by James C. King for Causes of War Study, University of Chicago, indicating location of battles in Europe by fifty-year periods, 1625–1925.

[12] A battle consists of the operations during a period of time in which hostile forces are uninterruptedly in contact with each other.

[13] See "A. L. C.," *The Military Historian and Economist* (1916), I, 297 ff.; Ivan Bloch, *The Future of War* (Boston, 1914), pp. 50–52, 340.

the figure was 93 per cent, in the nineteenth century 84 per cent, and in the twentieth century only 40 per cent. Sieges constituted an important proportion of war operations in the seventeenth and eighteenth centuries, a less proportion in the nineteenth century, and almost none at all in the twentieth century (unless we consider trench warfare, mass air attacks, and continental blockades as continuous sieges). Sieges are, of course, excluded from these computations. The object of the siege is to starve the garrison into submission, and that always takes more than a day. Sieges have, however, tended to increase in length. While there have been long sieges in all centuries, in the seventeenth and eighteenth centuries less than 10 per cent lasted over a hundred days, while in the nineteenth and twentieth centuries, 21 per cent lasted longer than that period.[14]

b) *The campaign period.*—Another striking period in war is that of the seasons caused by the revolution of the earth about the sun. Wars in the North Temperate Zone have ordinarily begun and been fought most intensely in the spring or summer. The campaign has lasted until winter, and then the armies have hibernated. This also has tended to change. In the Middle Ages 90 per cent of the European battles were waged from April to November inclusive; in the seventeenth and eighteenth centuries, 87 per cent; in the nineteenth and twentieth centuries, only 78 per cent.[15] During World War I the men stayed in the trenches all winter. The war on the western front was a continuous campaign, and the campaign was almost a continuous battle.[16]

It is interesting to note that the antipathy both to night fighting and to winter fighting has been less marked in the case of Japan than in that of most European countries. Japan has often started battles

[14] See Tables 24, 25, 26. Commandant J. Colin, *France and the Next War* (London, 1914), pp. 151 ff.

[15] See Table 27.

[16] The average duration of the campaigns of the major belligerents was 2.2 years and of the wars of the major belligerents 4.4 years (regarding a legal state of hostilities with each enemy as war). The difference is due to the long period of negotiation after hostilities had stopped before legal peace was restored and to the rapid ending of campaigns in certain areas by defeat of one side while the war continued in other areas. The military histories have divided World War I into battles, but on the major fronts these divisions are often rather artificial (see below, n. 45).

in the middle of the night. It started the Russian war of 1904 and the Jehol operations of 1933 in the middle of winter. Its operations begun in China in 1937 did not diminish in vigor during the winters. Perhaps the novelty of these actions gave a surprise advantage. There are technical advantages in night and winter fighting, such as ease of approaching the enemy and of dragging artillery over frozen swamps, rivers, and lakes, available to a highly disciplined belligerent.[17] Russia doubtless calculated on these advantages in opening its campaign against Finland in December, 1939.

Most countries, however, have started wars in the spring or summer. The United States began the Revolution, the Civil War, and the wars against Spain and Germany in April, the Mexican War in May, the War of 1812 in June, and the naval hostilities against France in July, 1798. War was declared in December, 1917, upon Austria, but this was simply a phase of the existing war against Germany. A list of 64 French wars of the seventeenth and eighteenth centuries indicates that only 13 began in the five months October through February and that 32 began in the five months March through July. For the ending of these wars the seasons were reversed. Twenty-five terminated October through February, and 21 March through July.

The British war of 1803 against Napoleon began in May. Austria, Russia, and Prussia joined in September, January, and October of 1805 and 1806, respectively. The war was renewed after the Peace of Tilsit in April; the Russian campaign began in June, 1812; the war of liberation in August, 1813; and the Hundred Days' War in March, 1815.

England began the Crimean War in March, 1854. The Austrian-Sardinian War began in April. Bismarck's wars against Austria and France began in June and August, respectively. The Russo-Turkish War began in April, 1878; the Italo-Turkish War in September, 1911; the Balkan Wars in October and July, respectively; World War I in August, 1914. Hitler chose March for his rearmament (1935) and

---

[17] Friedrich Bernhardi (*On War of Today* [New York, 1914], II, 129) refers to the Japanese practice of continuing artillery fire through the night during the Russo-Japanese War. See also Lt.-Col. Tovey, *Elements of Strategy* (2d ed.; London, 1906), chap. xi; Dumas and Vedel-Petersen, *op. cit.*, p. 81; Colin, *op. cit.*, pp. 44 ff., and above, n. 13.

Rhineland remilitarization (1936) declarations and for the seizure of Austria (1938) and Czechoslovakia (1939), any of which might have precipitated war.[18] But the Sudeten demands (1938) and the Polish invasion (1939), the latter of which actually precipitated general war, were made in September.

c) *The war period.*—Another less definite period is that of the duration of a war, a period of four or five years. Many wars have been shorter because of the defeat of one side. The average duration of participation in a war by the eleven principal European powers from 1450 to 1930 was 2.5 years. The average varied little from the fifteenth through the eighteenth century (2.5), but participations in war were exceptionally short in the nineteenth century (1.4) and exceptionally long in the twentieth (4).[19] The average length of the 278 wars from 1450 to 1930 was 4.4 years.[20] It is true that wars have in the legal sense often lasted longer than five years. There has been a Hundred Years' War, a Thirty Years' War, and a Seven Years' War. A study of these wars, however, discloses that it is very unusual for a continuous series of campaigns to go on for more than five years. These long wars were actually broken by long truces, or vigorous fighting was not carried on at one or both ends of the legal war period. The typical war, in which the belligerents are fairly equally balanced, is likely to last for four or five years, as did the American Civil War and World War I. Perhaps four or five years of the strain of war is as much as people can stand without resting. Signs of break in internal morale are almost certain to appear in one or both of the belligerents after that period. Siege warfare has gone on longer. In the latter part of the Hundred Years' War, after the time of Joan of

[18] The exact date of beginning and ending of wars is not easy to determine. Woods and Baltzly (*op. cit.*) list the principal wars from 1450 to 1900 but merely give the years of beginning and ending as does Gaston Bodart, who lists wars from 1618 to 1905 (*Historisches Kriegslexicon* [Leipzig, 1908], pp. 602 ff.), and Sorokin, who prints a list of 967 wars of ancient Greece and Rome and of the principal European states since the eleventh century, giving duration, estimates of the army strength, and casualties in each (*op. cit.*, III, 543 ff.). J. F. Maurice discusses the precise date of origin of many wars from 1700 to 1870 (*Hostilities without Declaration of War* [London, 1883]). See also A. L. MacFie, "The Outbreak of War and the Trade Cycle," *Economic History*, III (February, 1938), 91. The writer has utilized these and other materials collected by Mr. Clifton Utley and Mr. James C. King (see Appen. XX, Tables 1–10).

[19] Table 47, Appen. XXI.   [20] Table 45, Appen. XX.

Arc, the French spent almost twenty-five years recapturing the fortresses which had been taken by the British.

d) Political oscillations.—In addition to these three periods—the normal battle period of a day, the campaign period of a season, and the war period of four or five years—a longer period may be detected. There appears to have been a tendency in the last three centuries for concentrations of warfare to occur in approximately fifty-year oscillations, each alternate period of concentration being more severe. This period is not discernible in the sixteenth century and is scarcely noticeable in the seventeenth century. The War of the Spanish Succession (1701–14) occurred less than a century after the Thirty Years' War (1618–48), but there were several important wars initiated by Louis XIV between these two great wars. The War of the Spanish Succession was followed in about a century by the Napoleonic Wars, which were followed in about another century by the World War (1914–18, renewed in 1939). In the mid-eighteenth century a concentration of wars centered about the Seven Years' War (1756–63) and in the mid-nineteenth century about the Crimean War and the wars of Italian and German nationalism.

In the history of the United States a similar periodicity is suggested. The United States has fought a major war, then for fifteen or twenty years it has let its navy and army deteriorate while it has developed its domestic economy. After that it has again built up the army and navy. When this process has reached a certain point, the perfected instrument has been tried in a minor war which, after another fifteen or twenty years, has been followed by another major war, completing the period in about fifty years. The American Revolution, a major war, was followed by a period of vigorous attempts to maintain neutrality, finally breaking down in a minor war against France in 1798, a further development of the navy, and then a second major war with England in 1812. After a period of quiescence for fifteen or twenty years, military interests began to revive in the 1830's, leading to the imperialistic war against Mexico in 1846. This whetted the country's appetite for war during the "roaring fifties" until the Civil War (1861–65) produced a satiety of fighting and was followed by a rather complete degeneration of both the army and the navy. In the late 1880's naval building was again begun and the

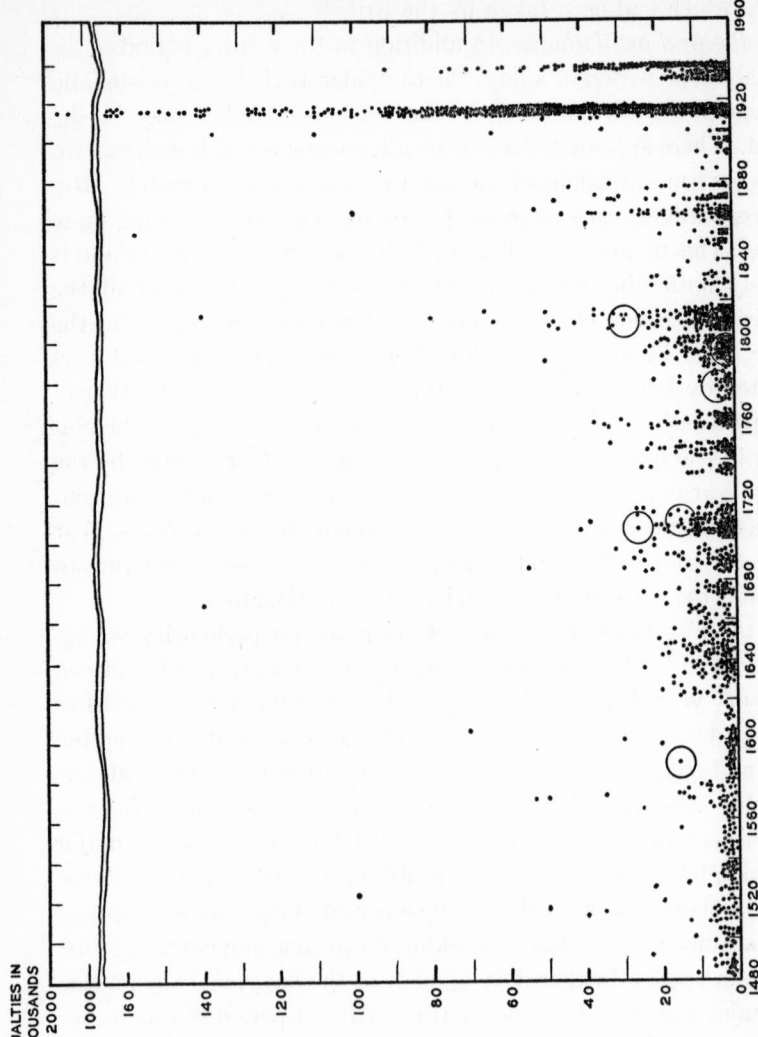

Fig. 8.—Dates and casualties of battles of modern civilization, 1480–1940. The data are from Har-bottle, *op. cit.*; Gaston Bodart, *Militar-historisches Kriegslexicon (1618–1905)* (Wien and Leipzig, 1908); and from other sources. The circles indicate the battles listed by Creasy, *op. cit.*

white fleet developed during the nineties. Theodore Roosevelt, in 1896, voiced the popular sentiment that "this country needs a war." The war came against Spain in 1898. After this, military and naval preparations developed rapidly, and the country came into World War I in 1917. There have thus been three periods of 37, 49, and 56 years each from the beginning of one major war to the beginning of the next. The first period was short, perhaps because the United States began its wars out of synchrony with the European war fluctuations.

A similar periodicity appears in British history. Tabulation of the dates at which battle honors have been given to British regiments shows a remarkable fifty-year fluctuation in the frequency of such battles. Concentrations appear during the wars of Marlborough, the Seven Years' War, the Napoleonic Wars, the Crimean War, and World War I. The American Revolution did not contribute to English regiments any battle honors. It is interesting to notice that, as in the case of the United States, there has usually been a minor imperial war, but one yielding several battle honors, preceding each major war.[21]

Tabulations of the important battles of modern civilization indicating dates and casualties[22] or decennial frequency[23] disclose this fifty-year periodicity of battle concentration, particularly in the last two centuries. Each period of battle concentration of fifteen to thirty years' duration—1618–48, 1672–90, 1701–15, 1740–63, 1789–1815, 1854–78, 1914–41—is broken by one or more truces of a year or two so that continuous fighting for over four or five years seldom occurred. A tabulation based not upon the number of battles but upon the number of war casualties in ten-year periods shows this fluctuation even more clearly in the cases of England, France, and the United States.[24] The data are inadequate for such a compilation for other countries.

---

[21] C. B. Norman, *Battle Honors of the British Army* (London, 1911). See Table 28 and Fig. 36, Appen. XIX.

[22] Fig. 8. The periods of greatest battle concentration do not precisely correspond with the periods of the great transitional wars noted in chap. xiv.

[23] Fig. 35 and Table 22, Appen. XIX.

[24] Figs. 38–40 and Tables 53, 54, 55, Appen. XXI.

A fifty-year war period has often been noticed. Spengler attributed it to the passage of two generations. The warrior does not wish to fight again himself and prejudices his son against war, but the grandsons are taught to think of war as romantic.[25] Others have attributed the cycle to business. After the activity of building up from the losses of a great war, heavy industries find it possible to induce armament-building at an increasing rate and for this purpose mobilize demands first for imperialistic expeditions, then for defense from reported aggressions. In the interim they may seek to augment their sales by stirring up war in a "Balkan" region.[26] After a careful statistical study of this subject, Dr. James C. King concludes:

> Battles have tended to become concentrated in periods of a few years instead of being more or less equally distributed in each year. This has meant an increase in the proportion of years free from battles but also an increase in the oscillations between peace years and war years. Finally, for the eighteenth and the nineteenth centuries great wars seem to occur about one hundred years apart and a somewhat less period of belligerent activity appears about mid-way between the great wars. This cyclical movement seems to be characteristic of the relations of European states and is most marked for those states at the center of the European system.[27]

This periodicity is not sufficiently regular to justify prediction, nor is there reason to attach mystical importance to the fifty-year period

[25] Oswald Spengler, *The Decline of the West*, I, 109–10, citing R. Mewes, *Die Kriegs und Geistes perioden im Volkerleben* (1896). Sorokin presents Mewes' data suggesting a 56-year oscillation but does not find it supported by his own data (III, 356). He also questions Giuseppa Ferrari's finding (*Teoria del periodi politici* [Milan, 1874]) that revolutions occur every fourth generation (120 years) (III, 483). Walter Millis (*The Martial Spirit* [Cambridge, Mass., 1931], pp. 35, 66) calls attention to an interpretation by the *Journal of Commerce* attributing the military enthusiasm in the United States in 1898 to the lapse of a generation since the Civil War, and to the attitude of Civil War veterans in the House of Representatives against the Cuban independence resolution. Margaret Mitchell comments on the tendency to imitate grandparents (*Gone with the Wind* [New York, 1936], p. 680).

[26] Ralph H. Stimson, "The War System," *Conferences on the Cause and Cure of War* (New York, 1933), pp. 22 ff. The United States Senate, Special Committee Investigating the Munitions Industry, 1936 (Nye Committee), recorded some evidence in its voluminous hearings indicating an active interest of certain American munition manufacturers in creating an atmosphere favorable to sales both in the United States and in foreign countries. This was also indicated in the earlier investigation of the activities of William G. Shearer in connection with the Geneva Disarmament Conference of 1927 (see H. C. Engelbrecht and F. C. Hanighen, *Merchants of Death* [New York, 1934]).

[27] "The Periodicity of War" (manuscript, Causes of War Study, University of Chicago, 1935), pp. 14–15.

as did the Mayan and Jewish calendars. On the other hand, it is not impossible that biological, psychological, economic, and political conditions may at times have tended to stabilize the fluctuations of war and peace about such a period. Certain economists have noticed a long economic cycle of about fifty years,[28] and it appears that in England and the United States a political party has tended to dominate for about fifty years.[29] A fifty-year fluctuation has been especially evident during the last three centuries, although it can also be detected in the Hellenistic period between Alexander and Augustus.[30] Each of these periods was characterized by rapid economic progress, by a rising influence of political propaganda, and by balance-of-power politics.

Fluctuations in the intensity of war in the history of a state would tend to assume a definite periodicity if the international system exerted a persistent pressure toward war and if the economic and technological period necessary to recover from a severe war and to prepare for another were identical with the psychological and political period necessary to efface the anti-war sentiment after such a war and to restore national morale. The economic period of recovery and preparation is very short under primitive conditions but lengthens with increasing capitalization of production and of military activities. The political period after a very severe war may, on the other hand, approximate two generations if social attitudes are largely formed by parental transmission, but it becomes shorter with the development of effective methods of centralized propaganda by the government. With the progress of civilization, these two periods

[28] Alvin H. Hansen (*Economic Stabilization in an Unbalanced World* [New York, 1932], pp. 93 ff.) quotes Kondratieff, who located the lows of the long waves in 1789, 1842–51, 1893–97, and 1930 and the highs in 1810, 1870–75, and 1914–21. He attributed these waves to differential rates of technological progress in production of goods and gold and believed the upswing bred wars and the downswing revolution. Referring to Sir Walter Layton's familiar periods of rising prices, 1849–74 and 1896–1914, preceded and separated by periods of falling prices, MacFie (*op. cit.*, p. 97) writes: "Wars of the last hundred and twenty years have shown a predominating tendency to break out in the second stage of the prosperity phase of the trade cycles, that specially suggestible stage of the cycles as we know them; but only in those which occur in prosperous long periods."

[29] See A. N. Holcombe, *The Political Parties of Today* (New York, 1924).

[30] The Punic Wars of Rome were spaced about fifty years apart (see Spengler, *op. cit.*).

should, therefore, become identical at some duration of less than two generations.

Such a periodicity, resulting from processes within the state, would, moreover, tend to become generalized throughout the family of nations if extensive international trade rapidly diffuses techniques and transmits economic fluctuations from one state to another. Furthermore, such a periodicity might be expected to persist as long as international politics is organized as a balance of power which extends and intensifies wars among the great powers and assures the defeated of future opportunities for revenge and reacquisition of prestige by maneuvering power politics. The alternating periods of predominant war and predominant peace have varied in length, but there has been a tendency for each to approximate twenty-five years during the two periods of Western history when the conditions here suggested have been most nearly realized.[31]

3. QUANTITATIVE TRENDS

Has war manifested a persistent trend through these fluctuations in its modern history?

a) Magnitude.—The size of armies has tended to increase during the modern period both absolutely and in proportion to the population.[32] In the sixteenth century the mercenary armies seldom reached over twenty or thirty thousand. In the seventeenth century armies began to be nationalized and often reached fifty or sixty thousand. The European population during this century attained about the level it had reached in the Roman Empire and about as large a proportion of the population was under arms, some three in a thou-

[31] The major wars have divided modern history into distinct periods (see chap. viii, sec. 3, and chap. xiv). The Thirty Years' War marked the transition from dominantly religious to dominantly political interests, and the Napoleonic period marked a transition to dominantly economic interests. World Wars I and II may also mark a transition. For a suggestion that these periods have each been divided into characteristically different halves see Appen. IV, n. 34; chap. vii, n. 42.

[32] Adam Smith's penetrating discussion of the "Expense of Defense" (*Wealth of Nations*, Book V, chap. i, Part I) suggests a diminution of the proportion of the population engaged in war from practical unanimity in hunting and pastoral societies, through 20–25 per cent (all able-bodied men between seed time and harvest) among simple agriculturalists, to only 1 per cent in the industrial society of the time at which he wrote (1776). He, however, made no precise estimates for the period from 1500 to 1776, and was, of course, unaware of the developments destined to occur afterward, but he did realize that the expense increased with civilization (see below, n. 34).

sand. From then on there has been a steady rise in the size of European standing armies, absolutely and relatively. In the eighteenth century Marlborough, Prince Eugene, and Frederick the Great had armies of eighty or ninety thousand men. Napoelon had as many as two hundred thousand men in certain battles, and at times he may have had a million men or 5 per cent of the French population mobilized.[33]

There was some diminution in the size of armies in the period of tranquillity after 1815, but after 1870 there was, among the great powers, a steady growth in the size and cost of armies and navies. Before the nineteenth century was over the eight great powers averaged five hundred thousand men each in the army and navy, and before the outbreak of World War I another one hundred thousand had been added. The military establishments did not increase, however, much faster than national populations and national budgets. On the average about five in a thousand of the population was in the military services and about a third of the national budget was spent for their maintenance. Budgets, however, increased more rapidly than did populations so the per capita cost for the army and navy advanced on the average from $1.03 per year in 1870 to $2.31 in 1914. After World War I the military and naval establishments diminished under the influence of poverty and disarmament agreements, but the state of tension which prevailed after 1931 soon carried them to new heights.[34]

[33] Tables 29, 30, and Fig. 41, Appen. XIX, and n. 37 below. Bodart (*Kriegslexicon*, p. 785) calculates the normal size of armies in the Thirty Years' War at 19,000; the wars of Louis XIV at 40,000; the wars of Frederick the Great at 47,000; the Napoleonic Wars at 84,000; the Franco-Prussian War at 70,000; and the Russo-Japanese War at 110,000. He also lists the actual size of the armies commanded by the principal generals during the period (pp. 787–91). Somewhat different figures on this subject are given by Engelbrecht and Hanighen (*op. cit.*). See also Sorokin, *op. cit.*, III, 547 ff.

[34] See Table 58, Appen. XXII. F. W. Hirst (*The Political Economy of War* [London, 1915], pp. 81 ff.) gives figures for the standing armies of European states in 1858, totaling 2,675,000, and in 1898, totaling 3,562,000, which he compares with the 300,000 of the Roman Empire of the time of Augustus. For estimates of the total strength of forces in certain nineteenth-century wars see Bloch, *op. cit.*, p. 345, and W. L. Woytinsky, *Die Welt in Zahlen* (Berlin, 1928), VII, 118. Estimates of number mobilized by various belligerents in World War I are given by Dumas and Vedel-Petersen, *op. cit.*, pp. 140 ff., and Woytinsky, *op. cit.*, p. 115. Adam Smith concludes his chapter on the "Expense of Defense" (*op. cit.*) with the statement: "The first duty of the sovereign, therefore, that of defending the society from the violence and injustice of other independent societies,

In 1937 the world as a whole had about eight million men in its standing armies, or four to one thousand of the population—considerably above the ratio maintained by the Roman Empire of Augustus. Immediately mobilizable reserves would add two million more and trained reserves some thirty million more. Of the soldiers in standing armies more than half were in Europe, which, however, had less than one-quarter of the world's population. Europe in 1937 kept nearly three times as large a proportion of its population under arms as it did in the days of Augustus. France, with less than half the population of the Roman Empire, maintained almost twice as big an army, some nineteen to every one thousand of her European population.[35]

Furthermore, modern states enlarge their armies far more in times of war than was formerly the case, and in addition the bulk of the adult civilian population is mobilized for some war work.[36] The relative size of the war army has, therefore, increased even more rapidly than that of the peace army. While in the seventeenth century countries rarely mobilized 1 per cent of their population for war, the original belligerents of World War I mobilized 14 per cent of their populations.[37] It is clear that during the modern period there has

---

grows gradually more and more expensive, as the society advances in civilization. The military force of the society, which originally cost the sovereign no expense either in time of peace or in time of war, must, in the progress of improvement, first be maintained by him in time of war, and afterwards even in time of peace. The great change introduced into the art of war by the invention of firearms, has enhanced still further both the expense of exercising and disciplining any particular number of soldiers in time of peace, and that of employing them in time of war. Both their arms and their ammunition are become more expensive." The writer has utilized a study of the growth of naval tonnage and naval and military expenditures in the principal countries since 1870 by Nathan Reich, studies of military legislation in Germany and France since 1870 by A. F. Kovacs and Max Swearingen, and a study of British naval legislation since 1870 by Alice M. Christenson, all prepared for the Causes of War Study at the University of Chicago. See also F. M. Anderson and A. S. Hershey, *Handbook for the Diplomatic History of Europe, Asia and Africa, 1870–1914* (Washington, 1918), pp. 468–74.

[35] See League of Nations, *Armament Year Book.* The figures for 1930 are summarized in D. P. Myers, *World Disarmament* (Boston, 1932), pp. 356 ff. Annual figures are given for each country in the *Statesman's Year Book.*

[36] Hans Speier, "Class Structure and 'Total War,'" *American Sociological Review,* June, 1939, pp. 370 ff.

[37] See Tables 52–57, Appen. XXI. Hoffman Nickerson (*Can We Limit War?* [Bristol, 1933], pp. 111 ff.) attributes the tendency to rely on huge masses resulting in increased

been a trend toward an increase in the absolute and relative size of armies whether one considers the peace army, the number mobilized for war, the number of combatants engaged in battle, or the number of the military and civil populations devoting themselves to war work.

b) Discontinuity.—Another general trend has been toward a decrease in the length of wars and in the proportion of war years to peace years.

While major wars from the sixteenth to the nineteenth centuries often lasted over ten years, there were many short minor wars. The average duration of a war during these centuries was about five years compared with three years in the nineteenth century. The average for the first forty years of the twentieth century has been 2.6 years.[38]

In the sixteenth and seventeenth centuries the major European states were formally at war about 65 per cent of the time. In the three succeeding centuries the comparable figures were 38 per cent, 28 per cent, and 18 per cent, respectively.[39] This refers only to recognized wars. If the colonial expeditions and interventions in America,

---

destructiveness of war to the growth of democracy. The average size of armies in all the battles in the modern period are listed by fifty-year periods in Tables 29 and 30 and Fig. 41, Appen. XIX. This indicates that the size of armies tended to increase in the seventeenth century, to drop slightly in the eighteenth century, and to rise rapidly in the nineteenth and twentieth centuries. They also show that after 1600 the victorious armies averaged considerably larger than the defeated. From 1475 to 1600 the defeated armies averaged larger, probably because of the large number of instances in which smaller European armies defeated very large Turkish, Mexican, Peruvian, or Indian armies in this period. The size of these non-European armies during this period accounts in part also for the rapid increase in the size of the battle armies from 1500 to 1650. Changes in the average size of the army engaged in battles give no evidence of changes in the average size of the army mobilized for war because, even in the modern period of mass mobilization, many battles have been fought between small contingents. The figures are, of course, affected by the definition of a battle. Bodart included in his list land engagements in which the total losses of both sides in killed, wounded, and prisoners was over 1,000 and sea engagements in which such losses were over 500 (see Table 24, Appen. XIX). For difficulties of applying such a criteria to World War I because of the different scale of operations in different theaters see *Report of the Battle Nomenclature Committee as Approved by the Army Council* (Great Britain, Parl. Pap. 1921, Army, Cmd. 1138), p. 6.

[38] See Table 45, Appen. XX. If a war is counted for each pair of states, while there was a diminution in duration in the nineteenth century, the twentieth-century wars were exceptionally long (see above, n. 19).

[39] See Table 46, Appen. XXI.

Asia, and Africa, were counted, most of the great powers would have been "at war" a large proportion of the time even in the past century. The United States, which has, perhaps somewhat unjustifiably, prided itself on its peacefulness, has had only twenty years during its entire history when its army or navy has not been in active operation during some days, somewhere.[40] In the modern period the distinction between legal states or war, on the one hand, and reprisals, interventions, or military expeditions, on the other, has been recognized in international law.[41] This distinction was sharpened in practice in the two centuries before 1920 but has more recently fallen into abeyance. While in the earlier and most recent parts of the period it has not always been easy to distinguish recognized wars from other hostilities, it seems clear that there has been a steady decline in the frequency of war in the European area. Whereas there were over fifty European wars in the sixteenth and in the seventeenth centuries, there were only one-half as many in the eighteenth and in the nineteenth centuries, and there have been only eleven in the first forty years of the twentieth century.

c) *Intensity*.—A third trend has been toward an increase in the length of battles, in the number of battles in a war year, and also in the total number of battles during a century. Reference has been made to the increasing number of battles over a day's duration in recent centuries.[42] The number of battles in a war has also tended to increase. In the sixteenth century less than two important battles occurred on the average in a European war; in the seventeenth century, about four; in the eighteenth and nineteenth centuries, about 20; and in the twentieth century, over 60.[43] The number of war years per century has declined but the number of battles per war year has increased more rapidly. As a result, the total number of battles fought in a century has tended to increase. Harbottle lists 106 battles in the sixteenth century. Bodart lists 231 battles in the seventeenth century, 703 in the eighteenth, and 730 in the nineteenth. There had

[40] See Table 48, Appen. XXI, and manuscript by Lula Caine (above, n. 10).

[41] See Q. Wright, "Changing Concepts of War," *American Journal of International Law*, Vol. XVIII (October, 1924).

[42] See above, n. 14, and Table 26, Appen. XIX.

[43] See Table 45, Appen. XX. Bodart gives the number of battles per month in the 38 principal wars from 1618 to 1905 in *Kriegslexicon*, p. 612. See also Fig. 8 above.

already been 882 battles in the twentieth century by 1940.[44] The intensity of war measured by frequency and duration of battles has certainly increased.[45]

This conclusion is confirmed by Sorokin, who has compared by centuries the number of wars weighted to take account of duration of war, size of fighting force, number of casualties, number of countries involved, and proportion of combatants to total population. His indices for the principal European wars during the last nine centuries are:

12th	13th	14th	15th	16th	17th	18th	19th	20th
18	24	60	100	180	500	370	120	3,080

The intensity of war seems to have been exceptionally high in the seventeenth and exceptionally low in the nineteenth century. Apart from these two centuries the index rises continuously, and extraordinarily in the twentieth century.[46]

d) Extensity.—A fourth trend has been toward an increase in the number of belligerents in a war, in the rapidity with which a war spreads, and in the area covered by a war.

[44] See Fig. 35 and Table 22, Appen. XIX.

[45] See Nickerson, *op. cit.* This has meant that battles and campaigns have tended to lose their distinctiveness. The division of the action on the western front in World War I into "operations," "groups of battles," "battles," "tactical incidents," and "actions" is more or less artificial. "The extension of the period covered by the so-called battles in Europe from days to weeks, and even to months, has introduced an entirely new factor, and the term 'battle' in the ordinary pre-war application of that word is obviously no longer sufficient" (*Report of Battle Nomenclature Committee*). See above, n. 37.

[46] See Table 46, Appen. XXI, and note similarity of variations with those in Table 23, Appen. XIX. See also chart by G. F. Nicolai, *The Biology of War* (New York, 1918). In his *Social and Cultural Dynamics* Sorokin does not attempt to combine these indices. His figures for the relative size of armies and of casualties indicate similar variations but with a less marked increase (Tables 50 and 51, Appen. XXI). Sorokin's method was to multiply the estimated average size of the army by the length of the war and to divide this by the estimated population. The casualties were found by applying to this figure the percentage of casualties to the size of the army as estimated for the century. As the older wars were longer and less concentrated, this method gives them an exaggerated weight. A comparison of Sorokin's figures with J. C. King's figures, found by adding the army size or casualties in all the battles as given for France and England by Bodart, indicates that Sorokin's figures are two to four times larger for the seventeenth and early eighteenth centuries. King's figures are too small, particularly for World War I, because the battles listed by no means include all the war casualties. The comparison, however, suggests that Sorokin's method does not give proper weight to the highly concentrated wars of the late eighteenth, nineteenth, and twentieth centuries. See Table 2, Appen. XXI.

Bodart lists 83 wars from 1618 to 1905 in which major battles were fought. Some of these occurred simultaneously among overlapping powers and can be combined, reducing the list to 71. There appear to have been 45 wars of this type in the modern period before 1618 and 10 since 1905, making a total of 126 major wars from 1475 to 1940.[47] A war usually terminates by the conclusion of a formal peace, often in more than one treaty, and the states which participate in that peace may be considered the participants in the war, although in a few cases surviving belligerents did not participate in the peace negotiations. This was the case with Russia in the peace of 1919 which ended World War I. The number of states participating in a peace may be different from the number which began hostilities, as some states may disappear or be divided during the war.[48]

Of these 126 wars, the 42 which began in the late fifteenth and in the sixteenth centuries averaged 2.4 participants each; the 22 which began in the seventeenth century averaged 3.5 participants each; the 19 which began in the eighteenth century averaged 4.8 participants each; the 32 which began in the nineteenth century averaged 3.1 participants each; and the 11 which began in the twentieth century averaged 5.6 participants each. Utilizing the list of 278 wars in Appendix XX (Table 45), the corresponding figures are 2.4, 2.6, 3.7, 3.2, and 4.8. Thus, apart from the nineteenth century, in which there was a large number of imperial and civil wars, the trend was toward an increase in the number of participants. Wars between great powers involving the balance of power have had the largest number

[47] At least 278 wars have occurred during the modern period, but only 126 seem to have contained important battles (see Appen. XX and Tables 1–9).

[48] For legal purposes each pair of states at war with each other may be regarded as constituting a distinct war. This conception of war was used in Table 47, dealing with the duration of wars. In this sense the World "War," 1914–20, consisted of 76 "wars." The hostilities were ended by four armistices by the Allied and associated powers with Turkey, Bulgaria, Austria-Hungary, and Germany, respectively. There were, however, five treaties of peace—Versailles (Germany), St.-Germain (Austria), Trianon (Hungary), Neuilly (Bulgaria), and Lausanne, superseding the abortive Treaty of Sèvres (Turkey). In addition to these were special armistices and treaties of peace, later superseded, made by the Central Powers with Russia and Rumania, and separate treaties of peace made by the United States with Germany, Austria, and Hungary and by China with Germany. It would, therefore, be possible to regard World War I as constituting 76, 4, 5, or some other number of wars, but it seems best to follow the usual practice and to regard World War I as a unity concluded by several interrelated treaties of peace (see Table 42, Appen. XX).

of participants. Hitherto wars between non-European states or imperial wars of European powers overseas have frequently involved only two powers, and this type of war was especially prevalent in the nineteenth century. Experience in the twentieth century suggests that in the future even those types of war are likely to spread.[49]

Wars have often begun as civil wars or bilateral wars. Consequently, the fact that they have, in increasing degree, ended with a larger number of participants indicates the increasing tendency of wars to spread. Except for the nineteenth century, the position of nonbelligerency has become increasingly difficult to maintain.

This seems to be a consequence of the increasing interdependence of states with respect to commerce, opinion, and politics and of the development of techniques which have made possible an extensive interference in these fields by the belligerents. More and more belligerents have tried to destroy or regulate enemy and neutral commerce by naval and other means; to control enemy and neutral opinion by propaganda; and to influence the foreign policy of nonbelligerent governments by appeals to alliances, the balance of power, or collective security. This has developed to such a point that today, if the great powers are involved in a war, all states find their commercial interests seriously injured, their publics excited and often divided by propaganda, their mortality increased by war-spread diseases, and their security menaced by immediate aggression or by changes in the balance of power which may result from the war. The burdens of neutrals have increased.[50]

Small states have usually preferred to endure these evils rather than to enter a war which would probably make their situation worse and to whose result they could contribute little. They have, however, succeeded in doing so only if they were distant from the scene of battle or if both belligerents preferred to have them remain neutral. The great powers, on the other hand, have generally, if the war lasted long, considered it to their advantage to enter the war. They have believed that they could defend their frontiers and contribute

[49] The Boxer affair involved many states, and there was serious danger that the "Manchukuo" and Ethiopian wars would involve other states (see Table 41).

[50] See Q. Wright, *The United States and Neutrality* ("Public Policy Pamphlet," No. 17 [Chicago, 1930]); Charles Warren, "Troubles of a Neutral," *Foreign Affairs*, April, 1934, pp. 377 ff.

to the results of the war and that, if participants, they would have an opportunity to exert influence at the peace conference.

Since the Thirty Years' War there have been fourteen periods in which war existed with a great power on each side for over two years. There were only three of these major war periods—those containing the War of the Polish Succession (1733–38), the American Revolution (1775–83), and the Crimean War (1854–56)—in which a single one of the great powers remained at peace throughout the period.[51] A closer analysis indicates that the difficulty of a great power maintaining neutrality has become progressively greater during these three centuries.

In each of the four major war periods in the seventeenth century all the great powers became belligerents before the initial war was over, but in no case did they all become involved in the same war. It was at that time possible for powers to be belligerents in one war and to be neutral in respect to another war going on at the same time.[52] Of the seven major war periods in the eighteenth century, this was true of five, but in two of the periods—those containing the Seven Years' War and the French Revolutionary War—all the great powers became belligerents in the same war. Furthermore, the eighteenth-century major wars were on the average shorter (seven years each instead of fourteen each as in the seventeenth century), and they drew in the originally neutral great powers much more rapidly.

In the nineteenth century there were only two major war periods. In the Napoleonic period all the great powers were involved against France during a period of ten years but not in all cases continuously. England was at war the whole ten years (1805–15); Austria in 1805, 1809, 1813–14, and 1815; Russia in 1805, 1806–7, 1812, and 1815; Prussia in 1805, 1806–7, 1812, 1813–14, and 1815; the Netherlands in 1805, 1813–14, and 1815; Spain in 1807–14, and 1815; Portugal in 1807–14; Denmark in 1813–14; and Sweden in 1805–10 and 1813–14. During this period Russia was drawn into special wars with Turkey and Sweden, and the United States into a war with England. The

---

[51] See Table 43, Appen. XX.

[52] G. N. Clark, "Neutral Commerce in the War of the Spanish Succession and the Treaty of Utrecht," *British Year Book of International Law, 1928*, pp. 69 ff.; Philip Jessup, *Neutrality: Its History, Economics and Law* (New York, 1935), I, 82, 145.

Crimean War period did not actually last for two years, but all the great powers except Prussia and Austria became involved in it.

In the twentieth century the World War of 1914 spread within a year to all the European great powers and Japan, and to the United States in two and one-half years. Thirty-three states, half those of the world, including several from Asia, Latin America, and Africa, eventually became belligerents. Others became quasi-belligerents and also participated in the peace conference.[53] The war was renewed in 1931 with spasmodic and relatively isolated hostilities in China, Ethiopia, Spain, Czechoslovakia, Lithuania, and Albania, but, with the German attack on Poland in September, 1939, the war showed signs of becoming general. France, Great Britain, and the Dominions except Ireland entered immediately. Before the end of 1940 Russia attacked and made peace with Finland; Germany invaded Denmark, Norway, Netherlands, Belgium, Luxemburg, and Rumania; Italy entered the war, attacking Egypt and Greece; and Japan, already fighting China, joined the axis, threatening the United States.

The tendency of wars to spread can also be illustrated by charting the distribution of battles in these wars.[54] The battles of the Thirty Years' War were all concentrated in central Europe; those of the War of the Spanish Succession in the Low Countries, central and western Europe, and America; those of the Seven Years' War in various parts of Europe, India, and America; those of the Napoleonic Wars in all sections of Europe, the Near East, and America; those of the World War in all sections of Europe, the Near East, the Far East, Africa, and the waters of America and the Pacific.

The tendency of the war system of modern civilization to be less localized may also be statistically indicated by noting that Bodart's list of battles, deemed important for this system, includes no battles outside of Europe prior to 1750 and only 13 from 1750 to 1800. From 1800 to 1850, 11 extra-European battles are listed; and from 1850 to 1900, 78. From 1900 to 1940, 228 such battles seem to have occurred.

---

[53] See Table 42, Appen. XX.

[54] See maps of distribution of battles by twenty-five-year periods prepared by J. C. King for the Causes of War Study, University of Chicago.

Since 1600 the percentages of extra-European battles in succeeding centuries were 0, 2, 13, and 25.[55]

e) Cost.—A fifth trend has been toward an increased human and economic cost of war, both absolutely and relative to the population. The human cost of war is a difficult problem to get data upon. The proportion of persons engaged in a battle who are killed has probably tended to decline. During the Middle Ages 30–50 per cent of those engaged in a battle were often killed or wounded. In the sixteenth century 40 per cent of the defeated side might be killed or wounded and about 10 per cent of the victors. The latter cut down the members of the defeated army as they ran away. Thus at the beginning of the modern period the average casualties in battle were probably about 25 per cent of those engaged. In the three succeeding centuries the proportion has been estimated as 20, 15, and 10 per cent, respectively, and in the twentieth century about 6 per cent.[56] Prior to 1900 about a quarter of the battle casualties died, and in World War I about a third; thus the proportion of those engaged in a battle who die as a direct consequence of the battle seems to have declined from about 6 per cent to about 2 per cent in the last three centuries.[57]

The proportion of the population engaged in the armies, however, has tended to become larger,[58] and the number of battles has tended to increase.[59] As a result, the proportion of the population dying as a direct consequence of battle has tended to increase.[60] The losses from

[55] Note also the increasing proportion of extra-European and imperial wars indicated in Table 45, Appen. XX.

[56] Bodart, *Losses of Life in Modern Wars*, pp. 14 ff., 83 ff. The casualty rate for war years has tended to increase from 3 or 4 to 8 or 10 per cent because of the much greater concentration of battles (see Sorokin, *op. cit.*, III, 299).

[57] Bodart, *Losses of Life in Modern Wars*, pp. 18 ff. Table 56 indicates that 13 per cent of those mobilized in World War I were killed. As most of those mobilized fought in more than one battle, the proportion killed in a battle would be less. The officer casualties have usually been 50 per cent higher than the average casualties (see Dumas and Vedel-Petersen, *op. cit.* pp. 61 ff.). The improved medical and sanitary services have greatly reduced the proportion of deaths among those wounded and surviving the battle, but modern arms have greatly increased the proportion of the casualties killed outright on the battlefield; thus, of the total battle casualties, a large proportion die (Bogert, *op. cit.*, p. 273).

[58] See above, n. 32.

[59] See above, n. 43; Bodart, *Losses of Life in Modern Wars*, pp. 9, 10.

[60] Bodart's statement (p. 14) that "the percentage of casualties suffered by armies in war has varied widely in the last four hundred years, and in spite of the progressive im-

disease in armies has declined. Dumas gives figures of the Napoleonic period suggesting that 80 or 90 per cent of the total army losses
were from disease.[61] Bloch states that in the nineteenth century this
proportion averaged 65 per cent.[62] In World War I, while disease
accounted for 30 per cent of the losses in the Russian army and 26
per cent in the American army, in the German army only 10 per cent
of deaths were from this cause.[63] It has been estimated that, of 1,000
deaths in the French population in the seventeenth century, about
11 died in active military service. The corresponding figure for the
eighteenth century is 27; for the nineteenth, 30; and for the twentieth, 63. For England the corresponding figures for these four centuries are 15, 14, 6, and 48.[64] The exceptionally heavy losses of the

---

provement in weapons, shows a tendency to *decrease*," seems not to be supported by his
own figures, if the greater frequency of battles is taken into consideration (see above,
p. 56).

[61] Dumas and Vedel-Petersen, *op. cit.*, pp. 29 ff. The disease losses in earlier centuries
may have been even greater. Zinsser thinks that army typhus and other epidemics have
had more influence on the results of war than generalship (*Rats, Lice, and History* [New
York, 1935]). See also F. Prinzing, *Epidemics Resulting from War* (Oxford, 1916).

[62] Bloch, *op. cit.*, p. 345. See also Woytinsky, *op. cit.*, VII, 118 and his Diagram 4
facing p. 128; Dumas and Vedel-Petersen, *op. cit.*, p. 31.

[63] Woytinsky, *op. cit.*, p. 118. Leonard Ayres shows that, while direct battle deaths
in the American army in wars of the past century have tended to go up (Mexican War,
1846–48, 1.5 per cent per year of men in army; Civil War, 1861–65 [North], 3.3 per cent;
Spanish War, 1898, 0.5 per cent; World War I, 1917–18, 5.3 per cent), disease deaths
ended sharply downward (Mexican War, 11 per cent; Civil War, 6.5 per cent, Spanish
War, 2.6 per cent, World War I, 1.9 per cent). The proportion of disease deaths to total
deaths in these wars was, therefore, Mexican War, 88 per cent; Civil War, 66 per cent;
Spanish War, 84 per cent; World War I, 26 per cent (*The War with Germany: A Statistical Summary* [Washington, 1919]).

[64] Adding Bodart's figures for battle losses (*Kriegslexicon* and Table 53, Appen.
XXI), it appears that French casualties (killed and wounded) were 269,357 in the seventeenth century, 713,067 in the eighteenth century, and 1,010,150 in the nineteenth.
Bodart says (*Losses of Life in Modern Wars*, p. 18) that one-fourth of the total casualties
died on the battlefield or of wounds later; thus the total battle deaths in the successive
centuries would be 67,339, 178,267, and 252,287. The same method of estimating made
the British battle deaths during these centuries 22,612, 31,429, and 27,322. These figures, however, are much too low. Dumas and Vedel-Petersen (*op. cit.*, pp. 27 ff.) and
Bodart himself (*Losses of Life in Modern Wars*, p. 156) present figures suggesting that
French army losses in the nineteenth century were over 2,500,000 and British army
losses during that century 300,000, or ten times the estimates above. These estimates
include army losses from disease and from minor engagements not listed among Bodart's
battles. If we apply this factor to Bodart's figures for the successive centuries, and take
World War I losses from Bogert (*op. cit.*, p. 272) and estimate death rates on the suppo-

seventeenth century because of the civil wars and the exceptionally
light losses of the nineteenth century because of the dominance of
British sea power obscure the trend in this last case. Adequate figures were not obtainable for other Continental powers, but indications are that they would disclose an upward trend as does France,
although, because of the Thirty Years' War, German losses in the
seventeenth century were exceptionally heavy and, because of their
relative frequent participation in war, the military service losses of
France and England were probably above the general average for
European countries in both centuries.[65]

The civilian losses from the direct ravages of war[66] were much less
than the service losses until World War II. Furthermore, until that
war, civilian losses have tended to decrease since the seventeenth
century. Air raids were serious during World War I, but they did not
kill as large a proportion of the civilian population as were killed in
the Thirty Years' War when sieges sometimes resulted in the slaughter
of all the inhabitants of the city.[67] The civilian losses from air bom-

---

sition that in Western Europe they have halved in the last three centuries (see A. J. Todd,
Theories of Progress [New York, 1918], p. 112), we get the result indicated in Table 57,
Appen. XXI. Sorokin's relative casualty figures (our Table 51), though roughly similar,
were arrived at in a wholly different way.

[65] See above, sec. 1a.

[66] Omitting losses from declining birth rate and war-spread epidemics (see below,
nn. 69 and 70).

[67] Total British civilian losses from air raids during World War I were 1,117 killed
and 2,886 injured. The most serious civilian loss at sea was the sinking of the "Lusitania," with 1,198 casualties (F. W. Hirst, *The Consequences of the War to Great Britain*,
pp. 302 ff.). Compare these with the massacre of 30,000 civilians on the capture and
sacking of Magdeburg during the Thirty Years' War. The population of Bohemia is said
to have been reduced from 4,000,000 to 800,000 by this war (see Dumas, *op. cit.*, pp.
116 ff.). J. B. Moore estimates that the population of Germany as a whole sunk from
16,500,000 to 4,000,000 during the Thirty Years' War; that of France from 19,000,000
to 16,500,000 during the War of the Spanish Succession; and that Prussia lost 6 per cent
of her population as a result of the Seven Years' War. He does not state the source of
these estimates, except that relating to the War of the Spanish Succession, which is from
Levasseur (*International Law and Some Current Illusions* [New York, 1924], pp. 10 ff.).
C. V. Wedgwood (*The Thirty Years' War* [New Haven, 1939] p. 516) states that German population sank from 21,000,000 to 13,500,000 during the Thirty Years' War.
Moore's implication that World War I, which he estimates cost Germany and France
only 5 or 6 per cent of their populations (in military not civilian losses), was less de-
structive than these earlier wars is not supported by such military writers as Hoffman
Nickerson (*op. cit.*). While recognizing the great destructiveness of the religious wars in

ardment greatly increased, however, in the Ethiopian, Spanish, Chinese, Polish, and Finnish hostilities of the 1930's and reached a high point in the battle of Britain in 1940. Taking all factors into consideration the proportion of deaths attributable to military service and to hostilities has probably increased among European countries from about 2 per cent in the seventeenth to about 3 per cent in the twentieth century.[68]

War has always resulted in serious losses to the civilian population from decline in the birth rate, and this has probably increased because of the increased proportion of the population engaged in war. Death rates reached absolute maximums and birth rates reached absolute minimums in most of the belligerent countries during World War I.[69] In the past, wars have assisted in spreading epidemics among the civilian population. Whether the superior preventive medicine of modern times has decreased these losses is difficult to say. The influenza epidemic of 1918 made serious ravages in all countries, belligerent and neutral. It has been estimated that during World War I these losses of population were as great as the direct losses in Europe. Each was about ten million. Outside of Europe the indirect losses were much greater because of the ravages of influenza in Asia and America. The total deaths from military action and war-distributed disease attributable to World War I have been estimated as over forty million.[70] It is probable that the total of deaths indirectly due to war have been three times as great as direct war deaths in twentieth-century Europe and that the proportion of such losses outside Europe and in Europe in earlier centuries has been greater.

---

cluding the Thirty Years' War (p. 97), Nickerson thinks the wars of the Roman Empire, of the Middle Ages, and of the eighteenth century were effectively limited (p. 106). He compares the British losses of 5,000 a year in the War of the Spanish Succession (estimated by G. M. Trevelyan, *England under Queen Anne* [London, 1930], I, 433) with the losses of 200,000 a year in World War I (p. 126). Democracy and mass massacre began with the American Revolution and has not abated since (p. 214). For other references on the subject see Q. Wright, "Changes in the Conception of War," *American Journal of International Law*, XVIII (October, 1924), 766, and Prinzing, *op. cit.*

[68] See above, chap. viii, n. 162.

[69] Hersch, *op. cit.*; K. O. Vedel-Petersen, in Dumas and Vedel-Petersen, *op. cit.*, pp. 46 ff.

[70] Hersch, *op. cit.*

Probably at least 10 per cent of deaths in modern civilization car
be attributed directly or indirectly to war.

While it is difficult to be certain of the increase of war's destruc
tiveness in regard to the quantity of population, there is little doub
but that war has been progressively more detrimental to the qualit
of population. Vernon Kellogg, continuing the arguments of Her
bert Spencer, David Starr Jordan, and John Bates Clark, has demon
strated the race-deteriorating influence of modern war by studies o
the statistics concerning the recruiting of soldiers, by study of th
measurable physical effects of the Napoleonic Wars upon the Frencl
population, and by study of the influence of war upon the spread o
race-deteriorating diseases.[71]

Closely related to the racial cost of war but even less susceptibl
to objective measurement are the social and cultural costs of war ii
the deterioration of standards. Wars of large magnitude have beer
followed by anti-intellectual movements in art, literature, and philos
ophy; by waves of crime, sexual license, suicide, venereal disease, de
linquent youth; by class, racial, and religious intolerance, persecu
tion, refugees, social and political revolution; by abandonment o
orderly processes for settling disputes and changing law; and by
decline in respect for international law and treaties. The standard
of some people and groups have, however, been stimulated by wa
in the opposite direction. The measurement and evaluation of sucl
post-war movements is highly subjective, but probably standard
have tended seriously to deteriorate.[72]

There is also little disagreement respecting the increasing eco
nomic cost of war in direct burdens on the government and indirec
losses from maldirection of productive forces. War has become s
thoroughly capitalized that it is necessary to mobilize the entire re
sources of the country. Debts of astronomical magnitude are ir

[71] Vernon Kellogg in Gaston Bodart and Vernon Kellogg, *Losses of Life in Moder
War* (Oxford, 1916), pp. 159 ff. See also D. S. Jordon, *The Blood of the Nation* (Bostoi
1910); H. R. Hunt, *Some Biological Aspects of War* (New York, 1930); Raymond Pean
"War and Population," *Science*, LI (1920), 553–56; *ibid.*, LIII (1921), 120–21; Holmel
Trend of the Race, pp. 205 ff.

[72] See H. C. Engelbrecht, *Revolt against War* (New York, 1937), chaps. xi–xv; W. I
Hall, *International Law*, Preface to 3d ed. (1889); Q. Wright, *Research in Internation
Law since the War* ("Carnegie Endowment for International Peace, Pamphlet Series
No. 51 [Washington, 1930]); see above, n. 5.

curred, so great that they cannot be paid. The resulting default and the readjustments necessary because of the malapplications of capital during the war bring depressions long after the war.[73]

It is true that some military experts think the progress in utilizing expensive machines for war may limit war destructiveness because of the anxiety the high command will be under to safeguard these devices which are so expensive that they cannot easily be replaced. The modern battleship costing $40,000,000 is not lightly risked, and similar considerations, it is said, will apply to expensive tanks and airships.[74] This moderating influence of military capitalization, however, has not yet been demonstrated in practice; instead, increasing capitalization has increased the destructiveness of war.

From the standpoint of the loss of human life, the deterioration of racial stock, and the loss of economic wealth, the trend of war has been toward greater cost, both absolutely and relative to population. It is to be observed that these trends are most obvious if data are confined to strictly international wars. Civil wars such as the French Huguenot wars of the sixteenth century, the British War of the Roses of the fifteenth century and the Civil War of the seventeenth century, the Thirty Years' War from the standpoint of Germany, the Peninsula War, from the standpoint of Spain, the American Civil War, and the Chinese Taiping Rebellion were costly both in lives and in economic losses far in excess of contemporary international wars. This fact is not surprising when it is considered that a single country bears all the loss, that both sides usually employ the same techniques, that large levies of untrained troops usually figure on both sides, and that defenses have not been prepared, with the result that campaigns cover large areas of territory, making the civilian losses exceptionally heavy. This observation, of course, applies only to civil insurrections reaching the stage of recognized war. Many

---

[73] Estimates of the economic costs of World War I are given in n. 4 above. See also J. T. Shotwell (ed.), *Social and Economic History of the World War* (134 vols.), especially volumes on Great Britain and the United States by F. W. Hirst and J. M. Clark, respectively.

[74] Hoffman Nickerson, *op. cit.;* J. V. N. Fuller, *The Reformation of War* (New York, 1923); J. Holland Rose, *The Indecisiveness of Modern War* (London, 1927). See Appen. XXIII.

rebellions, revolutions, and insurrections are suppressed before going to such extremes.[75]

4. QUALITATIVE TRENDS

Some of the most important trends in the character of war are not easily measured. Changes in the functions, drives, techniques, and law of modern war will be dealt with in the next chapters.

War has during the last four centuries tended to involve a larger proportion of the belligerent states' population and resources and, while less frequent, to be more intense, more extended, and more costly. It has tended to become less functional, less intentional, less directable, and less legal. In the most recent period the despotic states have attempted a more efficient utilization of war as an instrument of policy and have led the nations to a more complete organization of the states' resources, economy, opinion, and government for war even in time of peace. States have become militaristic and war has become totalitarian to an unparalleled extent.[76]

That these trends of war are related to the ideological, economic, social, and political trends of modern civilization indicated in the preceding chapter can hardly be doubted. The accelerating speed of technological and social change in the modern world, the more rapid geographical diffusion of ideas and methods, the increasing economic and political interdependence of separated areas, the growth of population and standards of living, the rise of public opinion and popular initiative in politics, have together tended to concentrate military activity in time and to extend it in space; to make it less easy to begin, to localize, and to end; to make it materially more destructive and morally less controllable; to make it appear psychologically more catastrophic and less rational; to make it more difficult for any state to isolate itself from militarization in time of peace and from hostilities in time of war, once the controls of international law and organization have been successfully defied.

[75] The French and the Russian revolutions seem to have been less destructive of life through military operations than those mentioned, though the French losses in the Vendee were considerable, and Russia suffered greatly from famine during and after the revolution. For discussion of military characteristics of the principal popular uprisings since the French Revolution see Freytag-Loringhoven, *A Nation Trained in Arms or a Militia* (New York, 1918), chaps. vii–viii. Sorokin prints a comprehensive list of internal disturbances since the time of ancient Greece (*op. cit.*, III, 578 ff.).

[76] Hans Speier and A. Kähler, *War in Our Time* (New York, 1939); Nickerson, *op. cit.;* and G. Ferero, "Forms of War and International Anarchy," in *The World Crisis* (London: Graduate Institute of International Studies, 1938), pp. 85 ff.

CHAPTER X

FUNCTIONS OF MODERN WAR

Whave been the function of war in modern civilization? Wars have been initiated in the modern period by national governments or national parties and not by world-institutions or world-parties. They have been intended to serve sovereign states or lesser groups rather than the world-community. Should we not, therefore, ask, "What has been the function of war in French history? in British history? in German history?" These questions are undoubtedly relevant to a history of war, and they have been dealt with in numerous national histories. The function of an activity may, however, be broader than its intention. This history of war treats modern civilization as a whole. It must, therefore, consider the effect of war in maintaining existing values or in achieving new values in that civilization. To do so, it will be necessary, however, to give some consideration to the function of war in the history of particular nations because, if war has favored some nations or types of nations at the expense of others, it will thereby have affected the values dominant in the civilization as a whole.

Modern civilization has not become either uniform or unified, although it has at times manifested a tendency toward both uniformity and unity. It has changed continuously, and these changes have proceeded at different rates in different areas. The characteristics of war have also changed greatly during the past few centuries, especially during the past century. The relationship between war and political, economic, social, and cultural change has, therefore, been extremely variable in modern history. This variability continues to the present time among different nations and regions. War among the great powers has functioned differently in the sixteenth, the eighteenth, and the twentieth centuries. War has functioned differently in Europe, in the Far East, and in the Americas, in Great Britain, in Germany, in Poland, in Italy, and in Japan.

Because of this variability, the most obvious generalization about the function of war in modern civilization is that it is difficult to ascertain. There is, however, a more widespread opinion than in any other period in history that war has not functioned well in the twentieth century. From being a generally accepted instrument of statesmanship, deplored by only a few, war has, during the modern period, come to be generally recognized as a problem.[1]

I. HISTORICAL USES OF WAR

War has been the method actually used for achieving the major political changes of the modern world, the building of nation-states, the expansion of modern civilization throughout the world, and the changing of the dominant interests of that civilization.[2]

The monarchs in the fifteenth, sixteenth, and seventeenth centuries used war to compel small feudal principalities to accept a common rule,[3] and, having established their authority in the following centuries, they created nations by the power which military control gave them over civil administration, national economy, and public opinion.[4] They were not, however, always successful in creating and

---

[1] See chap. i above.

[2] Chap. viii, sec. 3d. Scott Nearing (War [New York, 1931], chap. ix) has collected quotations from Ferrero, Lester Ward, Steinmetz, Admiral Fiske, Walter Bagehot, Field Marshal Roberts, and others which support the proposition which he quotes from J. T. Shotwell (War as an Instrument of National Policy [New York, 1929], p. 15): "War . . . . has been the instrument by which most of the great facts of political national history have been established and maintained."

[3] Charles Oman, The Sixteenth Century (London, 1935); G. N. Clark, The Seventeenth Century (Oxford, 1929); J. C. King, "Some Elements of National Solidarity" (manuscript, University of Chicago, 1933), p. 223, citing W. Mitscherlich, Der Nationalismus West Europas (Leipzig, 1920), pp. 117–58. The role of armies and arms-traders in the making of states from the sixteenth to the nineteenth century is discussed in H. C. Engelbrecht and F. C. Hanighen, Merchants of Death (New York, 1934).

[4] King, op. cit., pp. 225 ff. The sentiment of nationality having been instilled into the populations by the monarchs and the aristocracies, the nations sometimes dispensed with both, and the role of military coercion and military symbolism was sometimes subordinated to other means of civic education. Charles E. Merriam (The Making of Citizens [Chicago, 1931], summarizing nine volumes of studies on civic education in various countries) compares the systems of national civic training in Great Britain, France, Germany, United States, Soviet Russia, Italy, Switzerland, and Austria-Hungary with special reference to the use of the schools, government services, political parties, patriotic organizations, traditions, symbolisms, vehicles of communication (language, literature, press, radio, movies), and love of locality as instruments of political cohesion. While the military services and symbols figure as such an instrument in all instances, in some cases other instruments have been more important.

maintaining a national sentiment in the entire population subject to their rule. In fact, they sometimes maintained that rule by promoting local division of sentiment.[5] As a result dissident minorities and nationalities sometimes developed and occasionally achieved statehood, very seldom without war, often with the military assistance of outside states, never without the passive assistance of some. Such separatist movements have required centers, out of the reach of the government attacked, within which propaganda might be organized and arms assembled. The American colonists established such a center under Franklin in Paris. The Greeks had such a center in England and the Irish in the United States. The Cubans had a *junta* in New York, the Czechoslovaks in Pittsburgh, and the Syrians in Cairo.[6] Out of these war-supported movements, whether of union or of separation, beginning in England and France in the Middle Ages and spreading to central and eastern Europe, America, and Asia in the following centuries, developed the sixty-odd nation-states of the present world.

The expansion of the culture and institutions of modern civilization from its centers in Europe was made possible by imperialistic war. This proved a relatively easy process as long as European powers continued to enjoy a great superiority in war techniques over extra-European peoples and as long as there was enough extra-European territory for all. Quarreling between Spain and Portugal, it is true, marked the first discoveries; and imperial expansion has never since been unaccompanied by diplomatic and sometimes mili-

---

[5] Divide and rule was the policy of the Hapsburg Empire (see Oscar Jászi, *The Dissolution of the Hapsburg Monarchy* [Chicago, 1930]), of the Ottoman Empire, and perhaps at times of the French mandate in Syria and the British Empire in India.

[6] Theodore Ruyssen ("The Problem of Nationality," *International Conciliation*, No. 118, September, 1917, p. 3) distinguishes four methods by which nationalities have altered their condition—separation, agglomeration, emancipation, and autonomy within the framework of a larger state. See also *International Conciliation*, Nos. 109 and 112; W. W. White, *The Process of Change in the Ottoman Empire* (Chicago, 1937), pp. 262 ff.; W. H. Ritsher, *Criteria of Capacity for Independence* (Jerusalem, 1934); Q. Wright, "The Proposed Termination of the Iraq Mandate," *American Journal of International Law*, XXV (July, 1931), 436 ff.; C. R. M. F. Cruttwell, *A History of Peaceful Change in the Modern World* (London, 1937), pp. 90 ff., 121; A. J. Toynbee "Lesson of History," *Peaceful Change: An International Problem*, ed. C. A. W. Manning (New York, 1937), p. 31.

tary quarreling. But the colonially ambitious had opportunities to seize land still unappropriated by a European power down to the post–World War I seizure of Abyssinia by Italy.[7] The opportunities, however, have narrowed, and at the same time the populations of the territories still unappropriated by European powers began to adopt European military techniques. The Turks always had these techniques. The Turkish Janissaries in fact taught Europe the disciplined use of firearms, cavalry, and other methods which subsequently became characteristically European.[8] But at first the American Indians, East Indians, Chinese, and Japanese, though usually able to present forces much more numerous than the expeditions sent against them from the European countries, lacked firearms and tactical organization and were often divided among themselves. Cortez, with four hundred men, sixteen horses, three cannon and muskets, and a tactful stimulation of the Tlascalans against their Aztec oppressors, conquered eight million Mexicans. Pizarro was similarly successful in Peru and Clive in India.[9] Later the British and Americans opened China and Japan by only moderate uses of force.[10] It is true missionaries and traders had their share in the work of expanding world-civilization, but always with the support, immediate or in the background, of armies and navies.

War has, furthermore, contributed to the historic transitions of human interest and ideas during the modern period. It has usually accomplished this through facilitating a synthesis of conflicting opinions rather than the victory of one. The Thirty Years' War resulted in victory for neither Protestant nor Catholic but for the sovereign state and the family of nations. The Napoleonic Wars resulted in

[7] See Parker T. Moon, *Imperialism and World Politics* (New York, 1926); H. E. Barnes, *World Politics in Modern Civilization* (New York, 1930), chap. ii. The economic value of unappropriated colonies continually declined. Those most recently acquired have made no economic return to the possessing state commensurate with costs of administration and defense (see Grover Clark, *A Place in the Sun* [New York, 1936]; *The Balance Sheets of Imperialism* [New York, 1936]).

[8] O. L. Spaulding, H. Nickerson, and J. W. Wright, *Warfare* (London, 1924), p. 442.

[9] William H. Prescott, *Conquest of Mexico; Conquest of Peru;* Bernal Diaz del Castillo, *The Discovery and Conquest of Mexico*, trans. A. P. Maudslay (London, 1928).

[10] In the British "opium wars" of 1839 and 1858 and the American expedition to Japan under Perry in 1854.

victory for neither hereditary absolutism nor revolutionary democracy but for constitutional nationalism. World War I resulted in
victory for neither agrarian nationalism nor industrial imperialism
but for new political structures, the precise character of which is still
undetermined.[11]

War has also had a role in maintaining the established status of
nations and the established international order. It has served the
state by protecting its frontiers, symbolizing its unity, and recalling
to the population the necessity of political loyalty as the price of immunity from invasion.[12] This function of war has been more impor-

[11] Above, chap. viii, sec. 4a. Whether the League of Nations, Continental unions, or
totalitarian states will prove to be the dominant form precipitated by World War I,
it is still too early to say. The ideological struggle between autocracy and democracy
which began in 1792 and was emphasized in 1914 was again emphasized in 1939. This
ideological struggle resembles the religious struggle of three centuries earlier, and the
"Second Thirty Years' War" may end it by diverting attention to new issues (see Peter
F. Drucker, *The End of Economic Man* [New York, 1939]).

[12] It is doubtful whether the thirteen colonies would have united except through fear
that otherwise they would be one at a time reconquered by Great Britain (John Fiske,
The Critical Period in American History, 1783–1789 [Boston, 1892], p. 56). When that
fear was first removed by the peace of 1783, serious controversy and even hostilities developed among several of the states, and when it was again removed by the peace of
1815, processes of disunion began which culminated in the Civil War of 1861, to prevent
which Secretary of State Seward urged the familiar expedient of foreign war (Carl Russel Fish, *American Diplomacy* [New York, 1923], p. 305). Fear of invasion from the
United States created the Dominion of Canada in 1867 (R. C. Trotter, *Canadian Federation* [London, 1924], pp. 45 ff.). Opposition to France created the German Empire; opposition to white armies and foreign interventions created Soviet Russia; opposition to
Japanese invasion appears to be creating a nationally united China. These are modern
instances of a device which has almost always been employed in state-building. The
British invasion in the Hundred Years' War was the beginning of French nationalism;
Napoleon's invasion rejuvenated German nationalism. "People do not unite but unite
against specific collective groups. . . . . Large organized areas in recorded history have
been sustained by threats from the periphery." H. D. Lasswell (*World Politics and Personal Insecurity* [New York, 1935], p. 239) explores the psychological assumptions of this
proposition, and André Maurois (*The Next Chapter: The War against the Moon* [Lon-
don, 1927]) explores its political applicability in case interplanetary hostilities could be
instituted. Hoffman Nickerson (*Can We Limit War?* [London, 1933], pp. 20, 45) appears to have given it inadequate consideration in proposing the formula: "Moral dissension produces discontent, discontent equals potential war, therefore, the degree of
moral dissension within any society will equal the potential war within that society."
If intense moral union can only be achieved by actual or imminent external war, it would
perhaps be more accurate to say that "the degree of moral union within any society will
measure its external war potential."

tant in some states than in others, but there is none in which war or war preparations have not to some degree at some time been used as an instrument of national stability and order.

War has been one means for maintaining the balance of power upon which the political and legal organization of the world-community has in large measure rested. The balance of power is a system designed to maintain a continuous conviction in every state that if it attempted aggression it would encounter an invincible combination of the others. The manifest willingness of menaced states to go to war has assisted in maintaining that conviction. When any state has developed its armaments too little or too much, and when alliances have not been made promptly to rectify the balance, war has usually ensued. In a world expectant of violence, the maintenance of a constant relationship in the military potential of all has been the price both of state independence and of peace. Because of the variety of factors affecting military potential, of the difficulty of measuring their changes accurately, and of compensating variations promptly, the balance has hitherto been maintained with insufficient delicacy to preserve the peace. But with all its crudity the system has prevented any one of the modern states from getting sufficiently powerful to swallow or dominate all the others, as Rome swallowed the states of its time.[13]

War or the danger of war has, therefore, contributed toward building the modern nation-states, toward spreading and developing modern civilization, toward preserving peace and stability within the states, and toward maintaining the international system of independent states. These results, however, are not entirely consistent with one another. Furthermore, war has at times contributed toward destroying nations, civilization, stability, and the international system.

The dynamic function of building new nation-states and of spreading and changing cultural ideas has often been incompatible with the static function of preserving the nation-states and the world-system which has existed at a given time. The divergence between the ad-

[13] Lasswell, *op. cit.*, pp. 54 ff.

vocates of change and the advocates of stability has been continuous, and the fact that each has, on occasion, found war a useful instrument accounts, in some measure, for the continuance of war.[14]

The advocates of change have not all wished the same changes. Some have wished to unify political institutions and cultural ideas, usually by expanding those established in a given place into larger areas, while others have wished to diversify institutions and ideas, usually by breaking up or discrediting those dominant in a given area at a given moment. It is often difficult to distinguish integrating from disintegrating movements because a movement, the immediate effect of which is to disintegrate existing institutions and customs, may be supported on the ground that this is necessary in order to realize a more perfect integration in the long run. The two types of movement can, however, usually be distinguished sufficiently for practical purposes if attention is limited to a moderate time span, say a generation.

The actual policy of governments in initiating war has not usually been concerned with integration in general but with a particular from of integration—with the preservation or development in a particular area of the kind of civilization embodied in the nation. While each of the nations has distinctive characteristics, certain types of integration have been especially significant. Thus the despotic type integrated by *coercive* central authority may be distinguished from the democratic type integrated by general and freely given consent. The traditional type integrated by *custom* may be distinguished from the progressive type integrated by a mobile public opinion.[15]

Let us, therefore, consider whether on the whole war has functioned during the modern period to promote stability or change, to integrate or to disintegrate the world-order, to promote despotic or democratic nations, to promote traditional or progressive nations.

[14] John Foster Dulles, *War, Peace and Change* (New York, 1939), pp. 138 ff.

[15] Combinations of these two criteria indicate four familiar types of states: (1) the despotic-traditional monarchies of the eighteenth century; (2) the democratic-traditional monarchies and republics of the nineteenth century; (3) the despotic progressive totalitarian states; and (4) the democratic progressive nations of the twentieth century (see n. 32, below).

2. STABILITY AND CHANGE

This is not the place to analyze the various forms of stability in the long view.[16] In the short view stability is the absence of sudden change. Stability is compatible with gradual changes, even though in cumulation they may be very important and even though in a distant and unpredictable future they may result in violent reaction. Evolution may be a prelude to eventual revolution, and revolution may be a step in an evolution if a sufficiently long view is taken; but in a short view the two can be distinguished—revolution manifests instability and evolution manifests stability. Nor is this the place to consider the relation of stability in one aspect of civilization to that in another. Political stability may assist or it may hamper religious, economic, cultural, or social stability. Here we are concerned only with political stability.

In this sense the stabilizing influence of war during the modern period appears to have been in inverse relation to its intensity. Wars of great intensity have destroyed existing political values, institutions, and standards, opening the way for radical changes. The destruction and hardships resulting from such wars have provided a suitable ground for revolutionary movements.

The statistical data presented in chapter ix indicate that the intensity of war increased through the fifteenth, sixteenth, and seventeenth centuries, then declined in the eighteenth and nineteenth centuries, with a marked increase in the twentieth century. A. J. Toynbee, from general historical information, comments on the remarkable ferocity of the wars of religion in the sixteenth and seventeenth centuries and of the even greater violence of the recent wars of nationalism.[17] While no precise correlation between these variations in the intensity of war and variations in the degree of political instability can be made, it would appear that the political order of Europe changed most radically and rapidly in the seventeenth and twentieth centuries when war reached greatest intensity. The seventeenth century witnessed the supercession of feudalism and the Holy Roman Empire by the secular sovereign states as the dominant political institutions of Europe. The twentieth century appears to be witness-

[16] See below, chap. xv.

[17] A. J. Toynbee, *A Study of History* (Oxford, 1934–39), VI, 318.

ing the supercession of the secular sovereign states by something else. Exactly what cannot yet be said.

Important changes took place, it is true, during the less warlike eighteenth and nineteenth centuries. Science and technology developed; many areas were industrialized; international trade, international communication, and population increased, but these changes, though sometimes referred to as revolutionary and involving occasional violence, proceeded by such gradual steps that they could better be described as evolutionary. The significant political changes of these centuries—the expansion of modern civilization overseas and the rise of democracy and nationalism—often proceeded with revolutionary speed, but such revolutions were usually closely associated with wars. The Seven Years' War marked the apex of colonial expansionism. The French revolutionary and Napoleonic wars signalized the advent of democracy in Europe. The Bismarckian wars marked the rise of nationalism.

Thus, while it cannot be said that there was less change in world-civilization during periods of comparative tranquillity than during periods of war, it appears that political institutions were more stable during such periods and that changes of a revolutionary character usually occurred in periods when war was intense.[18] The direct relation between political revolution and war, whether as cause or as effect, is in fact such a historical commonplace as to need no elaboration.[19]

3. INTEGRATION AND DISINTEGRATION

Among the earlier civilizations war, in the long run, favored political disintegration rather than political integration. States and civilizations have been built up by war but have been eventually destroyed through war. This has been attributed to the tendency of experience with war to augment the power of the defensive over the

---

[18] The American, French, and Spanish revolutions preceded, and the Russian, German, Austrian, and Turkish revolutions followed, world wars. Kondratieff suggests that revolutions appear at the bottom and war at the top of the long economic cycles but adduces inadequate evidence (see A. H. Hansen, *Economic Stabilization in an Unbalanced World* [New York, 1932], pp. 93 ff.; Pitirim Sorokin, *The Sociology of Revolution* [London, 1925], pp. 376 ff.).

[19] Lyford P. Edwards, *The Natural History of Revolution* (Chicago, 1927).

offensive, thus making the revolt of local groups possible, to increase the destructiveness of hostilities, thus promoting political instability, and to militarize all states, thus promoting inflexibility and incapacity to adapt political and social organization to new conditions.[20]

The present world-civilization is still in its early stages, and, because of its universality and the superiority of its mastery of science, it is markedly different from earlier civilizations. The tendency of this civilization to date has, on the whole, been toward political integration. The thousands of feudal principalities of Europe made independent by the disintegration of the medieval church and empire and the numerous native states of America, Asia, Africa, and the Pacific have been integrated, in large measure through the agency of war, into sixty-odd nation-states and empires.

There has, however, been a countertendency. Beginning with the American Revolution, there has been a tendency for the modern empires to disintegrate with increasing acceleration as nationalism has spread from modern Europe. The Spanish, Portuguese, French, Ottoman, Hapsburg, Russian, Chinese, British, and American empires have given birth to new nation-states, dominions, or commonwealths. By the end of the nineteenth century the process of disintegration became more rapid than that of integration, so that the number of independent political entities increased. At the same time political integration on a world-scale was proceeding through international unions and leagues. More recently Japan, Italy, Germany, and Russia have attempted to integrate a number of formerly independent states into empires by conquest. Twenty-one states were occupied and several of them were declared annexed from 1935 to 1941.[21]

Economic integration, until the recent autarchic movement, proceeded even more rapidly than political integration under the influence of inventions, speeding and cheapening communication, travel and transportation, of industrialization, and of geographic division of

[20] See chap. vii, sec. 4; chap. viii, sec. 4d. Among primitive peoples the influence of war was mainly static in contrast to the dynamic influence of ceremonial. War prevented the union of the existing political units into larger wholes (chap. vi, sec. 3).

[21] Ethiopia, Albania, Austria, Czechoslovakia, Danzig, Poland, Denmark, Norway, Netherlands, Belgium, Luxembourg, Estonia, Latvia, Lithuania, Jugoslavia, Greece, and much of China, France, Rumania, Hungary, and Bulgaria. The birth and death of states is indicated in the table of wars in Appen. XX, Tables 1–10.

labor.[22] There has also been a tendency toward religious and intellectual integration. The characteristic values of modern civilization, originating in Europe, especially in England,[23] have become more widely accepted through the development of literacy, communication, missionary activities, and international conferences. The ideas of sovereignty and nationalism, however, have not been in complete harmony with these values, and recent extreme forms of these movements—totalitarian despotism—have developed outright contradictions.

World-civilization has been in its heroic age. The military offensive has on the whole had an advantage over the defensive. Hostilities, while very destructive in the seventeenth and twentieth centuries, were on the whole moderate during the eighteenth and nineteenth centuries. Militarization of states did not become general, largely because of the influential position of Great Britain, defended by sea power and defender of humanism, liberalism, science, and tolerance. The variety of interpretations of the meaning of modern civilization among the nations has, moreover, assured a capacity of modern civilization to adapt itself to new conditions.

There are, however, signs that civilization may be entering upon a time of troubles. Considering the modern period as a whole, there has been a tendency for military operations to become more concentrated with longer gaps of peace between. War and peace have alternated in oscillations of increasing amplitude. Viewing the progress of military technique in 1899, Ivan Bloch, Polish banker, wrote:

We have had many opportunities for conversing with military men of different nationalities, and everywhere we were met with the conviction that in a future war few would escape. With a smokeless field of battle, accuracy of fire, the necessity for showing example to the rank and file, and the rule of killing off all the officers first, there is but little chance of returning home uninjured. . . . . It is notable that the younger and the better educated they are, the more pessimistically do officers look on war. . . . . As the popularity of war decreases on all sides, it is impossible not to foresee that a time will approach when European governments can no longer rely on the regular payment of taxes for the covering of military expenditure. . . . . These changes tend to make the economic convulsions caused by war far greater than those which have been experienced in the past. . . . . But even if peace were assured for an indefinite time, the very prepa-

[22] Eugene Staley, *World Economy in Transition* (New York, 1939).

[23] See George Catlin, *Anglo-Saxony and Its Tradition* (New York, 1939).

rations made, the maintenance of armed forces, and constant rearmaments, would require every year still greater and greater sacrifices. Yet every day new needs arise and old needs are made clearer to the popular mind. These needs remain unsatisfied, though the burden of taxation continually grows. And the recognition of these evils by the people constitutes a serious danger for the state. . . . . The exact disposition of the masses in relation to armaments is shown by the increase in the number of opponents to militarism and preachers of the Socialist propaganda. . . . . Thus side by side with the growth of military burdens rise waves of popular discontent threatening a social revolution. Such are the consequences of the so-called armed peace of Europe—slow destruction in consequence of expenditure on preparation for war, or swift destruction in the event of war—both events convulsions in the social order.[24]

Bloch's suggestion, that actual or potential war had become costly beyond any value either to national states or to world-civilization, was supported by economists such as Norman Angell and Francis Hirst before World War I and was widely indorsed after that war. It was commonly accepted that another general war might destroy civilization, but the unwillingness of states to modify their economic, political, and legal sovereignty sufficiently to create an adequate world-organization led to new tensions between the states favorable to the *status quo*, on the one hand, and, on the other, those insistent that territorial revision was necessary to their economic requirements in a world of increasing economic barriers. The immediate result was the organization of despotism and totalitarianism within the revisionist states.

After 1930 the new despots became convinced that certain recent inventions, especially the bombing airplane, the submarine, and the tank might again make war profitable to the more efficient and the better prepared. They achieved rapid conquests by *Blitzkrieg* methods in countries with inferior equipment and efficiency, such as Ethiopia, Albania, Poland, and Denmark.[25] Less rapid successes were registered in China, Spain, Finland, and Greece, where the disparity was not so great. Against equally industrialized powers, large-scale preparation of these weapons[26] and threats of ruthlessness gave the

[24] *The Future of War* (Boston, 1914), pp. 352–56. Captain Liddell-Hart comments on the superiority of Bloch's judgment on the trend of war compared with most generals (*Europe in Arms* [New York, 1936], p. 210).

[25] See Henry J. Reilly, "Blitzkrieg," *Foreign Affairs*, January, 1940, pp. 254 ff.

[26] See T. P. Wright, "Winged Victory," *Aviation*, XXXIX (April, 1940), 33.

aggressors a nuisance value which they were able to exploit diplomatically in the cases of Spain, Austria, and Czechoslovakia, but
when general war eventuated success was doubtful. Sociological observers had already amplified Bloch's pessimistic outlook.

Thus war has assumed a totalitarian character. Every technological improvement applied to the machinery of destruction tightens the grip which modern
war has on the common man's life. The scope of war has become as large as that
of peace, or indeed even larger, since under modern conditions it is the interest of
efficient warfare to militarize peace. Hence, it is possible to conjecture certain
social implications of a future war. The techniques of preparedness as they are
being developed in the dictatorial countries today indicate at least the direction
into which democracies will be forced to move when war comes. Not the economics of preparedness nor the propaganda of national honor nor the regimentation of labor will remain an exclusive concern of dictatorship. They are of the
substance of modern war, whether it be socially anticipated or actually waged;
it is the timing rather than the magnitude of the national effort that can be said
to depend on a particular form of government. War always concentrates and
reveals the potential forces of collective life as they are embodied in the given
social organization.

Under modern social and economic conditions once it is resolved to settle
international controversies by force there remains virtually no domain of life
which cannot be said to require fortification for the sake of increased efficiency.
Upon work and recreation alike must be imposed the relentless laws of preparedness. The mobilization plans must include the manipulation of sentiments and
opinions, for minds as well as cellars have to be made bombproof. . . . .

The present preparation for war necessitates disastrous sacrifices of human
values. It is indeed one of the main inferences to be drawn from this book that
those sacrifices are by no means restricted to the men living in the totalitarian
countries. In the organization of the world today there prevails an economic and
moral interdependence of the national units that compose it. Totalitarian preparation for war in one country is bound to affect the life of the common man in the
most distant lands.[27]

Judged by the standards of modern civilization, war has tended to
increase in costs and to decline in value. One would expect an increasing reluctance of statesmen to resort to it. The general increase
in the length of time between wars[28] as well as the utterances of
statesmen themselves suggest that this expectation has been realized. Yet it has taken only one state to start a war, and there have

[27] Hans Speier and Alfred Kähler, *War in Our Time* (New York, 1939), pp. 13, 14.
[28] Above, chap. ix, sec. 3b; Table 46, Appen. XXI.

been enough new inventions and rash statesmen to assure that eventually a war would be begun, and once begun war has tended to spread and to be difficult to end. It may very well be that modern civilization has reached a stage at which wars of increasing severity will initiate the process of disintegration. In his monumental *Study of History* Arnold J. Toynbee, discussing the points at which modern Western history conforms to the patterns of a disintegrating society in its time of trouble, writes:

This later cycle of ferocious Western wars which began in the eighteenth century, and which has not ceased in the twentieth, has been keyed up to an unprecedented degree of ferocity by the titanic driving power of demonic forces—Democracy and Industrialism—which have entered into the institution of War in our Western World in these latter days where that world has now virtually completed its stupendous feat of incorporating the whole face of the Earth and the entire living generation of Mankind into its own body material. Our last state is worse than our first because in this vastly expanded house, we are possessed today by devils more terrible than any that ever tormented even our seventeenth century and sixteenth century ancestors.[29]

4. DICTATORSHIP AND DEMOCRACY

The disintegration of one civilization may, however, be the beginning of another. If, as Gibbon believed, Christianity and barbarism were responsible for the fall of Rome,[30] these two, in combination with elements of Classical civilization, created Western civilization.[31] Even if internal contradictions and total war should be fatal to civilization as modern man has known it, there are local variations in that civilization, some of which may survive and originate a more viable civilization.

Spencer and Buckle distinguished between military and industrial nations according as political solidarity was based on military discipline and coercion or upon consent arising from benefits conferred or anticipated.[32] Others have distinguished between autocratic and

[29] VI, 319.

[30] "I have described the triumph of barbarism and religion" (Gibbon, *Decline and Fall of the Roman Empire* [ed. 1851], Vol. VI, chap. lxxi, p. 523; see also Vol. III, final chapter).

[31] Henry Osborn Taylor, *The Medieval Mind* (3d ed.; New York, 1919).

[32] Above, chap. vi, n. 25. Sir Alfred Zimmern's distinction between "welfare-seeking states" and "power-seeking states" is similar (*Neutrality and Collective Security*, ed. Q. Wright [Chicago, 1936], pp. 58 ff.), as is Charles E. Merriam's distinction between

democratic nations according as policy develops from the governing few or from a crystallization of opinion originating in numerous independent groups or individuals. These distinctions are different. The first concerns the sanctions and the second the sources of group policy. In practice, however, they are similar. Military discipline requires centralized authority, and voluntary consent is given more readily to institutions and policies which have developed from a democratic public opinion. Opinions have differed as to which of these types of nations is more prone to war,[33] but continuous war undoubt-

---

the organization of consent and the organization of violence (*Prologue to Politics* [Chicago, 1939]). Alfred Vagts's (*A History of Militarism* [New York, 1937]) distinction between the peaceful way and the "military way" is also similar. On the other hand, the distinction between "civilianism" and "militarism" is quite different. By the latter term Vagts, Speier, and others refer to "social structures in which political power and social esteem are distributed in favor of the military class" (Hans Speier, "Militarism in the Eighteenth Century," *Social Research*, III [August, 1936], 304). The "military state" refers not to the class benefited by the social structure but to the type of control most responsible for group solidarity and is, as Speier notes, "equally applicable to primitive tribes of warriors, to feudalism, and to the regime of the absolute state" (*ibid.*, p. 304). "Militarism" might exist in "industrial states." There was, for example, considerable militarism in the eighteenth-century European absolutisms in which the military leaders were a small class enjoying a privileged status, though the main bond of social solidarity in the population consisted in the reciprocal economic and cultural activities of the bourgeois who were quite separate from and contemptuous of the noble military officers, the proletarian soldiers recruited from the dregs of society, and the military virtues and concepts of honor. Militarism and the military state come together, however, in their extreme forms, "when the distribution of power and esteem assumes the form of centralization of control, an attendant state monopoly of raising, controlling and equipping armies, and a universality of military mores." The modern totalitarian despotism, child of a union between French revolutionary democracy and the absolutism of the ancient regime, is an extreme type both of militarism and of the military state (*ibid.*, pp. 305 ff.). On the other hand, a genuine liberal democracy which might result from a union of French revolutionary democracy and British liberalism, though hardly realized as yet, might present an extreme type both of "civilianism" and "the industrial state." Cf. n. 15 above.

[33] "Autocratic regimes" fight for "dynastic policies," but democracies are often "swayed by prejudice and blinded by passion" (E. Root, "The Effect of Democracy on International Law," *Proceedings of the American Society of International Law*, 1917, p. 7). See also *Foreign Affairs*, I (September, 1922), 56; Q. Wright, "Conference on Social Studies," Harvard Summer School, August, 1923; Imanuel Kant, *Eternal Peace* (Boston, 1914), pp. 78–79. In his war message of April 2, 1917, President Wilson said: "A steadfast concert for peace can never be maintained except by a partnership of democratic nations." Nickerson (*op. cit.*, p. 111), on the other hand, writes: "Among the impudent claims for democracy, perhaps the most impudent is that it is a peaceful

edly favors despotism. Democratic procedures of deliberation and respect for law must often be abandoned during war; and, if war recurs too frequently, they may not be re-established. A particular despotism, it is true, may succumb to war even more rapidly than its democratic enemy, whose morale may be superior provided it accepts authority during the war, but the military and despotic type of nation gains in the long run by war and threats of war. Industrial and democratic nations have, on the other hand, flourished in long periods of comparative peace.

An actual nation is seldom either a pure despotism or a pure democracy, but in every nation the control of military and foreign affairs has tended to be more concentrated than the control of domestic affairs. In military affairs the more democratic states have insisted upon civilian control of army and navy with parliamentary control of appropriations, of military organization, and of the major uses of force. In the despotisms, on the other hand, the military have been in large measure independent or in a position to control the civil branches of government.[34] In foreign affairs the executive has re-

form of government." Machiavelli (*Discourses*, Detmold trans., I, 59) and Kant thought republics more trustworthy than autocracies. Undoubtedly forms of government have some influence on foreign policy, but broad generalization on the subject is treacherous. Detailed studies of the operation of the governments of Japan and France in crises of the last fifty years suggest that, in both, the foreign policy of the state has in the main been determined by circumstances other than the constitutional organization. But in France, so far as constitutional institutions have had an influence, they have checked warlike activities, while in Japan they have more often acted as a spur to such activity (see Tatsuji Takeuchi, *War and Diplomacy in the Japanese Empire* [New York, 1935], p. xix; James Q. Reber, "War and Diplomacy in the German Reich" [manuscript thesis, University of Chicago Library, 1939]; Fred L. Schuman, *War and Diplomacy in the French Republic* [New York, 1931], p. xvi; D. P. Heatley, *Diplomacy and the Study of International Relations* [Oxford, 1919], pp. 51 ff., 270 ff.; D. C. Poole, *The Conduct of Foreign Relations* [New York, 1924], pp. 165 ff.; Paul S. Reinsch, *Secret Diplomacy* [New York, 1922], pp. 185 ff.; Q. Wright, *The Control of American Foreign Relations* [New York, 1922], pp. 360 ff., and "Domestic Control," in C. P. Howland [ed.], *Survey of American Foreign Relations* [New York, 1928], pp. 83 ff., 91 ff.; Lieut.-Col. J. S. Omond, *Parliament and the Army, 1642-1904* [Cambridge, 1933]; Francis R. Flournoy, *Parliament and War* [London, 1927]; Major-General Sir Frederick Maurice, *Governments and War* [London, 1926]).

[34] See Omond, Vagts, Takeuchi, Schuman, and Reber, above, nn. 32 and 33, and Lindsay Rogers, "Civilian Control of Military Policy," *Foreign Affairs*, January, 1940, pp. 280 ff.

tained the initiative in all countries, but in the more democratic nations executive freedom of action has been hampered by an active and independent public opinion, by indirect checks on the control of appropriations, by certain direct checks, such as legislative participation in treaty-making and general responsibility of the executive to parliament or to the electorate. These limitations have seriously affected the capacity of the more democratic nations to conduct foreign policy efficiently when that policy must be conducted within a balance-of-power system. Secrecy and dispatch in decision, continuity and positiveness in policy, priority of foreign over domestic considerations, all maxims of autocratic diplomacy and conditions of success in the game of power politics, present difficulties to ministers who are dependent for their lives or their budgets upon legislative bodies. The latter have usually been most interested in domestic issues, have often changed their policies, especially when elections bring in new parties, and have always been anxious to investigate and to delay by long debates. Democratic public opinion, moreover, does not easily change international friendship and hostility as the exigencies of balance-of-power politics require.[35]

In a world where states have maintained and advanced themselves mainly through the use of war or threats of war, the democracies have found themselves at a disadvantage when dealing with despotisms. Consequently, they have usually professed a desire to increase the role of law and discussion in international affairs and to reduce the role of war and threats to a minimum.[36] The reluctance of democracies to curb the sovereignty of the nation, their distrust of other nations and of distant authorities, their frequent incapacity to perceive the international repercussions of measures undertaken for domestic purposes, has often thwarted the realization of these pro-

[35] Carl J. Friedrich, *Foreign Policy in the Making* (New York, 1939); Q. Wright, *Control of American Foreign Relations*, pp. 363–65; De Tocqueville, *Democracy in America* (New York, 1862), I, 254.

[36] Root, *op. cit.* Oppenheim thinks the history of international law demonstrates that its progress is bound up with the triumph of democracy and nationalism (*International Law* [3d ed.], sec. 51, pars. 3, 4), and Kant set forth as one of the conditions of eternal peace that "the civil constitution in every State shall be republican" because only thus could law prevail among independent nations, though he distinguished a "republican constitution," designed to assure government by law, from democracy (*op. cit.*, pp. 76 ff.).

fessions in practice. The despotisms, however, realizing their relative advantage in the game of power, and aware that war itself will be less dangerous to their basic principles and ideals than to those of the democracies, have exerted their efforts to diminish the role of law and discussion and to increase that of violence and menace.[37] To them war has continued to be useful both for internal and for external policy; in fact, as the number of democracies has increased, the value of war to the despotisms has increased. The greater the number of sheep, the better hunting for the wolves.

Periods of general war and tension have, therefore, tended to increase the number of despotisms and to increase the influence in world-civilization of the standards appropriate to such regimes. The long periods of peace, especially those in the eighteenth and nineteenth centuries, have, on the other hand, witnessed a remarkable development of the idea and practice of democracy.

Probably all people prefer liberty and prosperity to discipline and preparedness if they can do so safely. When, however, security depends mainly on the balance of power, the advantages of dictatorship have been so manifest that periods of developing peace and democracy have been rare in civilized history. The trend of the eighteenth and nineteenth centuries in this direction can be accounted for by the entry into the European balance of power of a state defended by sea power. Because of geography and a dominant navy, Great Britain could defend itself and greatly influence Europe and the world without militarizing. As a result, constitutionalism, liberalism, and a form of democracy could and did develop in Great Britain, and under the *pax Britannica*, which Britain was able to maintain because of its navy, its world-empire, its industrial and financial strength, and its prestige, these characteristics of government could and did spread widely. The decline in the relative power position of Britain in the twentieth century as a consequence of the industrialization of Germany, the United States, and Japan; of the development of aerial and submarine war; and of the rise of the labor party and more thoroughgoing democracy in Britain itself led naturally to a revival of the initiative of military despotism in the game of power

[37] Marcel Hoden, "Europe without the League," *Foreign Affairs*, October, 1939, pp. 13 ff.

politics and the spread of the standards and practices appropriate to such states.[38]

While nations like Britain defended by maritime or other natural barriers have often felt free to develop liberty and democracy, nations with extremely vulnerable frontiers, especially when accompanied by memories of past invasions, have tended in the opposite direction.[39] The population of such nations has habitually preferred discipline to liberty. Military preparation has come to occupy more attention than popular welfare, with a consequent trend toward dictatorship and totalitarianism. Germany, vulnerable to invasions on two frontiers, and late in achieving national unity, has sacrificed civil liberty for military preparedness. The varying influence of military vulnerability, of national traditions, of the infiltration of liberal ideas, of industrial development and economic progress, has produced different degrees and forms of constitutionalism, liberalism, and democracy among the great powers. The smaller states, defended by the jealousy of their great neighbors rather than by their own defenses, have found it easier to abandon militarization and to accept democracy.

Modern nations, like animals and primitive tribes, have in the evolutionary process differentiated their constitutional and military structures, each adapting its ideals and traditions to the defensive necessities of its geographical and economic position.[40] These defensive necessities must, by the law of survival, take precedence over considerations of either welfare or civilization so long as those interested in the latter neglect to universalize the rule of law through organization.

The latter effort has commanded no more than halfhearted allegiance even from the democratic nations who would profit most from it, because few of them and none of the great ones have been pre-

---

[38] Zimmern, *The League of Nations and the Rule of Law* (London, 1936), pp. 87 ff.; Rushton Coulborn, "A Farewell to Leadership: Britain and the World, 1919–39," in W. H. C. Laves (ed.), *International Security* (Chicago, 1939).

[39] Pitman B. Potter, *The Freedom of the Seas* (London, 1924), pp. 171 ff.; Zimmern, *op. cit.*, chaps. iii and iv.

[40] See Q. Wright, "The Government of Iraq," *American Political Science Review*, XXVI (November, 1926), 743 ff., and Introduction to F. L. Schuman, *War and Diplomacy in the French Republic* (New York, 1931), p. xvi.

pared to sacrifice independence and sovereignty for security and welfare. While political values have differed with forms of government and geographical position, all the great powers have considered the maintenance of their power position of primary political value. As a result, world-politics have continued to be power politics. The great powers have continued to subordinate considerations of welfare, political tradition, and national ideals to the diplomatic and military requirements of power.

The acquisition of the status of a "great power" has depended primarily upon military prestige, military potential, and military achievement. The great powers have been the great fighters,[41] not only because power has made for belligerency and successful belligerency has made for power, but also because the great powers have had a better chance of surviving war than have the little powers. Hundreds of small states have ceased to exist in the last three centuries,[42] and those that have survived have done so because they have enjoyed a situation of natural isolation, have served as a buffer between mutually jealous powers, or have had the support of a powerful ally.

It seems probable that international relations might be so organized that war would be eliminated or greatly reduced in violence and frequency. But the existence of peaceful small states does not prove that this is possible in a system of power politics, any more than the continued existence of salaried clerks proves that competitive profits can be eliminated in a free enterprise system. In the recent world the balance of power and the mutual jealousies of the great states have been the major factors in preserving the independence of the little states and in making it possible for them to organize liberty and democracy, although the caution and peacefulness of the latter and a limited sense, even among the great powers, of a common interest in preserving respect for law and treaties, have been contributing factors.[43]

[41] Above, chap. ix, sec. 1a; Fig. 37, Appen. XIX.   [42] See chap. viii, sec. 4d.

[43] Collective security through the League of Nations, antiwar and nonaggression treaties, and general principles of international law may have added to the security of the small states at times, but these institutions were rather the evidence of a temporarily stable balance of power than the cause of it. Oppenheim (*op. cit.*, Vol. 1, sec. 51) writes: "The first and principal moral [to be drawn from the history of international law] is that

Power politics has in history tended toward the dominance of great powers and has discouraged the growth of democracy among them. Organization of the world under the dominance of a single powerful democratic state in a relatively invulnerable position, or, for brief periods after general wars, under the dominance of a powerful league supported by all or most of the states, gave sufficient general confidence in security during nearly two centuries of modern history to counteract this natural trend and to permit a wider spread of liberty and prosperity than the world had ever known. In the absence of some such general organization the modern shrinking world cannot be safe for democracy and no state can be completely democratic. All must preserve large elements of authority and decision in the conduct of military and foreign affairs, and all will be in occasional peril from the threats of despotisms. War in the modern world has favored despotism and thwarted the development of democracy.

a Law of Nations can exist only if there be an equilibrium, a balance of power, between the members of the Family of Nations. If the Powers can not keep one another in check, no rules of law will have any force, since an overpowerful State will naturally try to act according to discretion and disobey the law. . . . . The existence of the League of Nations makes a balance of power, not less but all the more necessary, because an omnipotent State could disregard the League of Nations." Kant also realized that international order had rested on "mutual antagonisms" (*op. cit.*, p. 14), a "kind of equilibrium" to regulate the "really wholesome antagonism of contiguous States as it springs up out of their freedom," and that states have not desisted from their purposes by argument alone, "even though armed with testimonies" of Grotius, Puffendorf, and Vattel, but the very practice of appealing to law encouraged him to think that eventually a world-federation based on reason would supersede the balance of power (pp. 17, 83). Bertrand Russell (*Which Way to Peace?* [London, 1936], chap. viii) was optimistic when he advocated that Great Britain save itself from war and remove a stimulus to foreign militarism by getting rid of its empire, imitating Denmark in unilateral disarmament, and announcing a policy of national nonresistance on the theory that the harmlessness and indigestibility of states like Denmark deter their militaristic neighbors from attacking them. Military preparation by a state has doubtless invited attack by the state threatened, but so also has a high degree of vulnerability. Russell's policy might lead to the absorption not only of Great Britain but also of Denmark, Belgium, and other states which have in the past survived because of Britain's power. The question whether even such a result would be less disastrous to civilization than resistance to invasion raises issues both of fundamental values in civilization and the probability of the populations actually refraining from resistance in the crisis. Russell advocated this policy only to gain time and considered that "a single supreme world government, possessed of irresistible force, and able to impose its will upon any national State or Combination of States" as "the political condition for permanent peace" (p. 173).

5. TRADITIONALISM AND PROGRESS

War has frequently been characterized as always destructive and never constructive.[44] Doubtless war in itself has never constructed new political, economic, social, or cultural institutions or practices, and it has often destroyed old organizations and customs. By doing the latter, however, it has sometimes cleared a field in which the new could develop if the creative intelligence of man was present. War has been like a fire which, if not too severe, may facilitate the growth of new vegetation by removing accumulations of dead grasses, brush, and logs. If too intense, however, fire may destroy the roots, the seeds, and even the fertility of the soil. Perhaps better, war may be compared to the wrecking crew which facilitates the growth of the city by destroying obsolete buildings so that new ones may be built in their place. Such analogies, as also the analogy to the catabolic and anabolic processes in the organism, both of which are essential to its life, may lead to unwarranted conclusions.

War as here defined is not the only method of eliminating the obstacles to progress. Education and legislation may each be used to destroy the old as well as to build the new, and they are less likely than war to get out of hand and become dangerous and destructive. They maintain a continuous relationship between the consuming and producing aspects of sound political progress.

War has been a factor contributing to unanticipated historical results, some of which were subsequently regarded as good and others as bad. It has also been an instrument employed to bring about expected historical results, sometimes at more and sometimes at less cost. These are facts of history, and they suggest that war in general cannot unequivocally be considered wholly destructive or wholly constructive. An evaluation of war in general, however, means little. War should be evaluated in a particular historical milieu. In evaluating it today one should consider not only its effect in recent history but also the economy of its use compared with other processes which might be used.[45] Our present problem, however, is not one of evaluation but one of relating historical causes and consequences.

It has been pointed out that war contributed to the building of the modern nation-states, to their organization in a European system, to

[44] A. J. Toynbee, *A Study of History*, IV, 640 ff.　　[45] See Vol. II, Part IV.

the development of ideas, sometimes inconsistent, peculiar to that system, and to the planting of the seeds of those ideas all over the world. These contributions, however, were made largely in the fifteenth, sixteenth, and seventeenth centuries.

In the eighteenth and nineteenth centuries war was less intense in Europe, but the European states by means of war or threats of war extended their dynamic civilization at the expense of the traditional cultures of America, Africa, and the Pacific and injected the virus of their civilization into the ancient civilizations of China, Japan, and India. Traditionalism was in this period destroyed by war and progressivism profited by war, though there was a considerable give-and-take among the occidental and oriental states in which the latter contributed much to the world-civilization initiated by the former. War contributed to the rapid augmentation of world-contacts and thus to the spread of European ideas of humanism, liberalism, science, and tolerance as well as to the spread of European ideas of strategy, imperialism, and nationalism.

In the past half-century the economic and propaganda aspects of war technique have so gained in importance that the diplomatic and military advantage of highly centralized and militarized states appears to have increased. This may in part account for the decline in liberalism and the growth of state socialism during this period.[46] Most states tended to increase armaments, to subject their populations to more discipline, and to organize their national economy and opinion in the interest of efficient war, although this tendency was more manifest in some states than in others. The result, however, was a shaking of general confidence in the standards of world-civilization as they had been understood in the mid-nineteenth century. These standards were dealt severe blows by World War I. They, however, survived and appeared to achieve a wider extension and acceptance than ever before in the years immediately following.[47] This phase, however, was short lived. Even more shattering blows were

---

[46] See Walter Lippmann, *The Good Society* (Boston, 1937).

[47] "The World War not only played havoc with democracy from 1914 to 1918 but seriously jeopardized its subsequent development. At the same time . . . . the World War promoted and exalted the ideals of democracy as no event in the history of mankind had ever done before" (W. E. Rappard, *The Crisis of Democracy* [Chicago, 1938], p. 83). See also E. Bourquin, *The World Crises* (London, 1938), p. 67.

dealt by the great depression and the totalitarian aggressions of the 1930's. Departures from what have been considered civilized standards were notable not only in the totalitarian states but everywhere. Whether the new forms of despotism, rejecting humanitarianism and suppressing freedom, can survive, whether if they do they can avoid the rigidity and unadaptability characteristic of such regimes in the past, and whether if they fail the remaining democracies can reorganize progress according to their traditional ideals remains to be seen. War has been hostile to blind traditionalism in recent history, but, if individual liberty is a major constituent of progress, it cannot be said that war in its present form has promoted progress.

The preceding survey suggests that in the most recent stage of world-civilization war has made for instability, for disintegration, for despotism, and for unadaptability, rendering the course of civilization less predictable and continued progress toward achievement of its values less probable.[48]

[48] "Only with the formation of independent political units where military power is maintained as a means of tribal policy does war contribute, through the historical fact of conquest, to the building up of cultures and the establishment of states. In my opinion we have just left this stage of human history behind and modern warfare has become nothing but an unmitigated disease of civilization" (B. Malinowski, "Culture as a Determinant of Behavior," in *Factors Determining Human Behavior* ["Harvard Tercentenary Publications" (Cambridge, Mass., 1937)], p. 141).

CHAPTER XI

DRIVES OF MODERN WAR

DRIVES to war among men in the modern world-civilization have been little different from those in earlier civilizations, though the new techniques which have been introduced and the new circumstances of life in the modern nation-state, with its highly mechanized and specialized ways of living, have further emphasized the gap between the objectives of a war and the drives of the people which support it.[1]

With the rise of constitutionalism, first in England and during the nineteenth century in most other countries, the initiation of war tended to become a matter of policy decided by procedures in which many functionaries of the state participated—diplomatic officers, army and navy authorities, the chief executive, and sometimes the legislature,[2] with a trend toward an increasing influence of legisla-

[1] See above, chap. vii, sec. 5.

[2] See Takeuchi, Schuman, Poole, Wright, Reber, and Flournoy (above, chap. x, n. 33) for procedures utilized by various modern states to reach decisions during international crises. Popular control in foreign affairs has in most states lagged behind such control in domestic affairs. "A democratic constitution may be held to be necessary in domestic government in a modern State, but may without inconsistency be condemned, or in essentials curtailed, in its application to international policy. . . . . In seeking to shape and control foreign policy the politically enfranchised majority of a people are passing beyond the concerns of one nation—their own—to those of others. In these others the methods adopted may not be in consonance with freedom of discussion and unrestrained publicity" (D. P. Heatley, *Diplomacy and the Study of International Relations* [Oxford, 1919], p. 56). See also *ibid.*, p. 67; John Locke, *Treatise of Civil Government*, secs. 144–48; Q. Wright, *The Control of American Foreign Relations* (New York, 1922), pp. 141, 363–65, quoting Locke, Montesquieu, Blackstone, Hamilton, Jay, Washington, *et al.* on this point. The hampering effect of the operation of the system of checks and balances under the American Constitution has led to pessimism in some quarters as to the effectiveness of that system for handling international relations under modern conditions (D. C. Poole, "Cooperation Abroad through Organization at Home," *Annals of the American Academy of Political and Social Science*, July, 1931; Q. Wright, "Domestic Control of Foreign Relations," in C. P. Howland [ed.], *Survey of American Foreign Relations* [New York, 1928], pp. 87, 111; George W. Wickersham, "The Senate and Our Foreign Relations," *Foreign Affairs* [New York], II [December, 1923], 177 ff.) a situation which has led the Supreme Court to attribute wider and wider powers to the

tures and electorates[3] and a declining influence of professional military men.[4] Before important decisions are reached in a constitutional democracy, alternatives of policy are discussed, and the choice finally made is influenced by many considerations, such as conceptions of national interest and of the course of events; the state of alliances, of military preparedness, of public opinion, and of public finance; traditional national policies; and justifications under international law.[5] Under such conditions the spontaneous drives of individuals appear to be unimportant.

It cannot be denied, however, that a vigorous personality with a predisposition to use the "big stick" or the *fait accompli* rather than peaceful modes of settlement has sometimes had a great deal of influence, even in a constitutional country and, in a despotism, that influence has often been determining. The personality of high officials has, therefore, been important.[6] Types that overcompensate

---

president in this field. See *U.S. v. Curtiss-Wright Export Corporation et al.*, 299 U.S. 334 (1936) and *U.S. v. Belmont*, 301 U.S. 324 (1937), in which Justice Sutherland reiterates the views he had earlier expressed in public lectures (*Constitutional Power and World Affairs* [New York, 1919], chap. ii). Nevertheless, there has been a tendency toward the broader participation of popular agencies of government in foreign affairs (Paul Reinsch, *Secret Diplomacy* [New York, 1922]; George Young, *Diplomacy Old and New* [London, 1921]; D. C. Poole, *The Conduct of Foreign Relations under Modern Democratic Conditions* [New Haven, 1924]). On the technical changes resulting see C. K. Webster, "Lord Palmerston at Work, 1830–41," *Politica* (London), August, 1934; S. H, Bailey, "Devolution in the Conduct of International Relations," *Economica* (London). November, 1930; H. K. Norton, "Foreign Office Organization," *Annals*, Suppl. Vol. CXCIII (May, 1929). Differing from the assumption of most modern states that foreign affairs is an essentially executive function, Aristotle associated it with the "deliberative department" of government which he distinguished from the executive and judicial (*Politics* ii. 14).

3 See Carl J. Friedrich, *Foreign Policy in the Making* (New York, 1938).

4 See Charles E. Merriam, *The New Democracy and the New Despotism* (New York, 1939), pp. 132 ff.

5 See, e.g., considerations entering into the Japanese decision to make war on Russia in 1904 (T. Takeuchi, *War and Diplomacy in the Japanese Empire* [New York, 1935], pp. 137 ff.).

6 Poole, *Conduct of Foreign Relations*, pp. 23 ff. The degree of influence exercised by leading personalities on American entry into World War I has been highly controversial (see Walter Millis, *Road to War* [Boston, 1935]; O. W. Riegel, "The Pattern of an Unneutral Diplomat," *Southern Review*, summer, 1936, pp. 1 ff.; Charles Seymour, *American Neutrality, 1914–1917* [New Haven, 1935]; Newton D. Baker, *Why We Went to War* [New York, 1936]).

inferiority complexes by belligerency, that achieve success through domineering, or that escape a sense of guilt through finding a scapegoat, have had much influence in starting wars in the modern period.[7]

Such persons, however, have found it progressively more necessary to give close attention to the state of public opinion. In the modern period war has demanded a wider participation of the population than ever before. The state of the public mind has come to be an important element in preparedness for war. If the public wants war, or can be brought to want war, the technical requirements for conducting operations may be produced by utilization of the skills and materials available in the modern state. Such improvisation may, it is true, be inefficient and costly, but with a will the way may be found. If, however, opinion is against war, no amount of technical preparedness will assure military success.[8]

In the earlier stages of modern civilization armies were composed of mercenaries or professionals, and the general population was little involved. Consequently, skill in military discipline and diplomacy and enough cash to pay the soldiers and foreign agents were the main requirements.[9] With the rise of nationalism, large conscript armies, and highly mechanized warfare, this condition changed. Government funds and credit adequate to stimulate the managers of mine, farm, and factory to full activity became a major consideration.[10] In very recent times there has been another change. Govern-

[7] H. D. Lasswell, *Politics: Who Gets What, When, How* (New York, 1936), pp. 181 ff.; E. F. M. Durbin and John Bowlby, *Personal Aggressiveness and War* (New York, 1939), pp. 134 ff.

[8] Charles E. Merriam, *Political Power* (New York, 1934), p. 305; J. W. Dafoe, "Public Opinion as a Factor in Government," in Q. Wright (ed.), *Public Opinion and World Politics* (Chicago, 1934), p. 6. "Modern conditions of war are gradually extending the domain of morale and increasing its influence. For among belligerent nations, war affects a greater number of people and does so with methods of increasing violence" Marshal Ferdinand Foch, "Army—Morale in War," *Encyclopaedia Britannica*, II, 413).

[9] This was one reason for the "bullionist" economic doctrine of the seventeenth century (Jacob Viner, *Studies in the Theory of International Trade* [New York, 1937], p. 25). See also Hans Speier, "Militarism in the Eighteenth Century," *Social Research*, III (August, 1936), 304–36.

[10] It has been said that Germany felt unable to go to war over the Moroccan crisis of 1911 because of the credit situation. F. M. Anderson and A. S. Hershey, Handbook for the Diplomatic History of Europe, Asia and Africa, 1870–1914 (Washington, 1918), p. 404.

ments have been able so to energize the population that the human and material resources of the nation may be mobilized for war with only limited recourse to the coercions of military discipline and the persuasions of economic reward. Money and foreign credit are not necessary if sufficient men, materials, and skill exist within the territory which government can continue to control during military operations and if the morale of the population can be maintained by propaganda.[11]

While military, diplomatic, economic, and propaganda activities have all been necessary in preparing for and waging war in all stages of human history, in the modern period there has been a progressive increase in the relative importance of the latter.[12] It is therefore pertinent to ask why the modern man is susceptible to war propa-

[11] F. L. Schuman (*The Nazi Dictatorship* [New York, 1935]) describes the method used in Nazi Germany to create such a morale. While the persecution of scapegoats, dramatization of external threats, and propaganda were primarily relied upon, violence and the distribution of loaves and fishes to strategic persons or groups were not wholly neglected. There has been a great deal written on the use of propaganda to maintain morale in wartime (see H. D. Lasswell, *Propaganda Technique in the World War* [New York, 1927]; Philip Davidson, *Propaganda and the American Revolution* (Chapel Hill, 1941), chaps. xvii, xix; Hazel Benjamin, "Official Propaganda and the French Press during the Franco-Prussian War," *Journal of Modern History*, June, 1932; Luella Gettys, "Reports on Propaganda Activities during All Wars of the United States" [Causes of War Study, University of Chicago, 1929]). The use of propaganda in the fascist states to create a war spirit in peacetime is but an extension of its use in the national states since the French Revolution, to "fanaticize national patriotism" (Hoffman Nickerson, *Can We Limit War?* [London, 1933], p. 114); to gain support for military legislation intended to "encourage the development of a warlike individuality" through the population (Baron Freytag Lorenhoven, *A Nation Trained in Arms or a Militia* [New York, 1918], p. 218); to "change popular sentiment" so that it will support a "strong military policy" (Major-General Emory Upton, *The Military Policy of the United States* [2d ed.; Washington, 1907], p. xv); to create a general recognition that war has become a "national business" demanding a "national effort" (Stephen King-Hall, *Imperial Defence* [London, 1926], pp. 30, 168, 191). See Karl Liebknecht, *Militarism* (New York, 1917), chap. iii; see also Hans Speier and Alfred Kähler, *War in Our Time* (New York, 1939).

[12] This is suggested by the study by Luella Gettys (*op. cit.*) of the relative importance of the use of violence (coercion, punishment), habituation (administration, discipline), rewards (orders, wages, pensions, bonuses, prizes), and symbols (propaganda, education) for securing the necessary soldiers, military materials, money, and morale in wars of the United States. For general description of these four methods see Lasswell, *Politics*, Part II, and *Propaganda Technique during the World War*, pp. 5 and 214.

ganda. Why is it that so many men like war or can be brought to like it?[13]

The question could only be completely answered by an analysis of each human personality and the circumstances to which it must adapt itself. There is no single instinct which if stimulated will send any man to war.[14] But most men acquire some notions which tend to pull them into war, and many endure circumstances which tend to push them into war. These notions and circumstances are different for each individual, but they may be classified, and for many classes there is an appropriate appeal which may pull or push the individual over the threshold of war.[15]

This is not the place to describe the psychological mechanisms of modern personality, to classify personality types, to trace the experiences which contribute to building each type, nor to analyze the process by which each adjusts itself to changing conditions.[16] Each personality combines in a distinctive manner drives of self-preserva-

---

[13] Leo C. Rosten, "Men Like War," *Harper's Magazine*, July, 1935, pp. 189 ff.; John Carter, *Man Is War* (New York, 1926). H. C. Engelbrecht (*Revolt against War* [New York, 1937], chap. iv) has assembled psychological analyses, anthropological reports of primitive pacifism, historical accounts of resistance to conscription, military disaffection and desertion, and escapes through fetishism, alcoholism, and conscientious objection to sustain the thesis "man is not war."

[14] Of the 528 members of the American Psychological Association, 378 replied to the question "Do you as a psychologist hold that there are present in human nature inerradicable instinctive factors that make war between nations inevitable?" The answers were: "No," 346 (91 per cent); "Yes," 10 (3 per cent); unclassified, 22 (6 per cent) (John M. Fletcher, "The Verdict of Psychologists on War Instincts," *Scientific Monthly*, XXXV [August, 1932], 142–45). Some writers recognize a primitive "pugnacity" drive (below, Appen. VIII), but the majority find that individual fighting occurs in a variety of situations usually involving several drives (above, chap. v, sec. 1).

[15] See H. D. Lasswell, *World Politics and Personal Insecurity* (New York, 1935). Charles K. A. Wang ("A Study of Attitudes on Patriotism and War" [manuscript for Causes of War Study, University of Chicago]), applying attitude measurement scales prepared under the direction of L. L. Thurstone to 1,872 individuals in academic and professional groups, found, among other things, that men who fought frequently in childhood are more favorable to war than those who did not; that people with education beyond the high-school level are less favorable to war; that people are favorable to war in proportion to the amount of military eduation and military service they have had; that people are more favorable to war between the ages of thirty-five and forty-four than at any other ages; that men are more favorable to war than women.

[16] See Lasswell, *Psychopathology and Politics* (Chicago, 1930) and *Politics*, pp. 181 ff.

tion and territory, food and activity, sex and society, dominance
and independence. These pairs of drives are respectively exemplified, though with overlapping and complication, in the (1) political,
(2) economic, (3) cultural, and (4) religious motivations and interests which modern civilization tends to distinguish.[17]

1. THE POLITICAL MOTIVE

The politician or statesman often has an interest in war as a means
of maintaining his position or augmenting his power.[18] In time of
war or threat of war people tend to support those in authority provided destruction is not too great. Successful war augments the prestige of the government and usually increases the territory and resources from which the government draws its power.[19] During modern history, but especially in its early stages, this interest among the
governing classes has constituted an important political motive for
war.

[17] See above, chap. v, sec. 1; chap. vi, sec. 4; chap. vii, sec. 5; and Appen. VIII below.
These motives correspond to the interests which have dominated successive stages of
modern civilization, though the somewhat broader term "cultural" is substituted for
the term "artistic" (above, chap. vii, n. 42; below, Appen. IV). It seems to be recognized
that political motives have to do primarily with security and territorial power (George
E. G. Catlin, *The Science and Method of Politics* [New York, 1927]; *A Preface to Action*
[New York, 1934]; Charles E. Merriam, *Political Power*) and economic motives with
sustenance and utilization of resources, although acquisition of all articles and services
of human interest measurable in terms of money (wealth) and even some things not so
measurable have been included (E. Z. Dickinson, *Economic Motives* ["Harvard Economic Studies," Vol. XXIV (Cambridge, 1922)]; "Acquisition," "Economic Incentives," *Encyclopaedia of the Social Sciences*). Cultural motives include nonutilitarian and
"refining" activities such as pursuit of the fine arts, pure science, and polite society (see
"Culture," *Encyclopaedia of the Social Sciences*), and also motives related to the family,
education, and social amelioration. A broader definition of culture would include all the
motives which maintain social groups or institutions, thus covering the three other types
of motives considered. Religious motives relate to the propitiation of and adjustment
to supernatural persons or forces believed to be responsible for life and death, natural
order and disaster, social justice and inequality, and other human experiences which in
a given society are considered mysterious and uncontrollable by direct manipulation.
The contrast between the subjective sense of the independence of personality and the
objective awareness of the subordination of the personality to conditions may be at its
root ("Conversion, Religious"; "Religion," *Encyclopaedia of the Social Sciences*).

[18] Above, chap. vii, sec. 5f.

[19] N. S. Timasheff (*The Sociology of Law* [Cambridge, 1939], pp. 171 ff.) analyzes the
constituents of power as dominance and prestige of the rulers, subordination and obedience of the ruled, and suggests numerous devices by which these attitudes are created
and maintained (see also Merriam, *Political Power*).

The ruled have also had political motives favorable to war. The individual's security depends, under modern conditions, upon the maintenance of law and order. The first condition of law and order, however, has been a government with power to command general obedience within its territory.[20] The loyalty upon which the power of government has rested has been to a considerable extent dependent upon general apprehension of war. There has, therefore, been a relation between law and order within a given territory and the war system.

Loyalty to the demands of the government is, furthermore, a satisfaction to the individual once he has identified himself with the state in whose name the government acts. Patriotism and nationalism are the names given to the attitude of the individual in identifying himself, respectively, with the fatherland and with the nation.[21] Since

[20] Timasheff (*op. cit.*, p. 191) regards the following statement by Ortega y Gasset (*The Revolt of the Masses* [New York, 1932], p. 155) as "probably correct": "As long as there is any doubt as to who commands and who obeys, all the rest will be imperfect and ineffective. Even the very conscience of men, apart from special exceptions, will be disturbed and falsified." This is reminiscent o iHobbes's statement (*Leviathan*, chap. xvii): "The final cause, end or design of men, (who naturally love liberty, and dominion over others,) in the introduction of that restraint upon themselves, (in which we see them live in Commonwealths,) is the foresight of their own preservation, and of a more contented life thereby; that is to say, of getting themselves out from that miserable condition of war, which is necessarily consequent to the natural passions of men, when there is no visible power to keep them in awe, and tie them by fear of punishment to the performance of their covenants, and observation of those laws of nature. . . . . The only way to erect such a common power . . . . is to confer all their power and strength upon one man, or upon one assembly of men, that may reduce all their wills, by plurality of voices, unto one will. . . . . He is called sovereign, and said to have sovereign power; and every one besides, his subject." Merriam points out some necessary correctives to this absolutism of authority: "Central control is one fact in organization, but difficult as it is for authoritarians in many cases to recognize the opposite principle, it has equal validity. A place for noncontrol, for irresponsibility, is as important as central control. The function of initiative and criticism and opportunity for a free hand within certain limits is just as essential to a successful system, as is central control and unquestioned command in a crisis moment, and general control at all times" (*Political Power*, p. 291).

[21] Carlton J. H. Hayes (*Essays on Nationalism* [New York, 1926], pp. 5–6) points out that nationalism also may mean the historical process of nation formation, the doctrine urging that state and nation should be coterminous, and the policy of forming a new national state. "Nations, classes, tribes and churches have been treated as collective symbols in the name of which the individual may indulge his elementary urges for supreme power, for omniscience, for amorality, for security" (Lasswell, *World Politics and Personal Insecurity*, p. 39). Patriotism is somewhat broader than nationalism because it may apply to the sentiment of the population of a city-state or a feudal state which does

the French Revolution the opinion has developed that order and
justice could best be maintained if these sentiments were accepted
throughout the population of the state. The state should, therefore,
also be a nation. Modern governments have made extraordinary
efforts to develop patriotism and nationalism among the people subject to their control through popular education, commemorative
festivals, popular participation in political activities, patriotic organizations, fostering of national art and literature, and bestowal of
honors upon strategic individuals.[22] These methods have usually
been so effective that a large percentage of the adult population has
come to feel a powerful disposition to support war when the symbols
of the nation-state are affronted. The maintenance of the security,
honor, prestige, and power of the nation have become dominant
values in the minds of most modern populations. The conviction
that readiness for war and, on occasion, war itself are necessary to
realize these values has probably occupied first place among the motives which have induced peoples in the recent stage of modern history to accept war.[23] The popularity of war is similar to the popularity which the duel has enjoyed at times when personal honor has been

---

not constitute a nation. But if patriotism is sufficiently general and intense in a considerable population, the population might be said to constitute a nation (see F. W. Coker,
"Patriotism," Encyclopaedia of the Social Sciences).

[22] Charles E. Merriam, The Making of Citizens (Chicago, 1931). "The false doctrine
that patriotism is a narrow and provincial trait incompatible with our duty to mankind
in general should never again be permitted to go without vigorous challenge. Patriotism
is something far older than our institutions and far stronger than any impulse to individual preservation; for men in all ages have willingly sacrificed themselves in untold numbers in response to its appeal. It is the sentiment which binds the people of a country
together for the common good and the common defense, without which they would perish; and so clearly necessary is it to their continued existence as an independent unit of
society that if it were not an instinctive attribute of the soul, it would be necessary to
develop it by artificial means" (George Sutherland, United States senator from Utah
and later associate justice of the United States Supreme Court, Constitutional Power an
World Affairs [New York, 1919], p. 176).

[23] There is considerable variation in the degree of nationalism in modern states. J. C.
King, defining nationalism as the "extent of persistent resistance which the country
would offer to disruption of national unity," concluded from ratings given by experts
and from a study of communication, geographic, historic, literary, religious, linguistic,
and racial indices that among certain states in 1933 France had the most nationalism,
after which ranked Great Britain, United States, Germany, Switzerland, Italy, and
Spain ("Some Elements of National Solidarity" [manuscript, University of Chicago],
p. 246).

regarded as a major value which can be maintained only by manifestation of willingness to risk life for honor.[24]

The political motive for war has, therefore, changed during the modern period from a dominantly dynastic or governmental loyalty of the few to a dominantly national loyalty of the many. From the wish of the governing class to maintain its position of dominance and prestige in the state, it has become the wish of the population of the nation to maintain and improve the position of the state in the family of nations. Both types of political motive, however, continue to operate with varying relative importance in different states.

2. THE ECONOMIC MOTIVE

Economic advantage implies increased capacity to command the necessities for sustaining life and the conveniences permitting freedom of activity. Particular groups or organizations can gain an economic advantage from war through selling war supplies, securing advancement in the military profession, augmenting the sales of newspapers or other means of public information, or contributing various services to the conduct of war.[25] Entire populations frequently believe that they will gain an economic advantage from war even though competent economists do not indorse this opinion.

The value of war as a means to solve group economic problems of overpopulation, shortage of raw materials or foodstuffs, and industrial depression is at best dubious. Victory is always uncertain, and the possibility of using victory to solve such problems is not clear if existing property rights are respected. Under conditions which pre-

[24] Henry IV of France is said to have granted 14,000 pardons to duelists (the duel had been formally abolished by Henry II in 1547), and it is estimated that in his time (1589–1607) 4,000 gentlemen were killed in affairs of honor in France ("Duelling," *Encyclopaedia of the Social Sciences*). "Honor is an open acknowledgment of external demand but an acknowledgment which through pride has become enthroned in the very citadel of the self. . . . . Honor can not be arbitrated because 'when honor's dead the man is dead' " (T. V. Smith, "Honor," *Encyclopaedia of the Social Sciences;* see also Lasswell, "Chauvinism," *World Politics and Personal Insecurity;* J. A. Hobson, *The Psychology of Jingoism* [London, 1901]). See Frederick R. Bryson (*The Sixteenth-Century Italian Duel* [Chicago, 1933]), who distinguishes (1) state duel, a war by champions; (2) judicial duel, a stage in settlement of disputes by courts; (3) duel of honor. With some overlapping these prevailed respectively in ancient, medieval, and modern times.

[25] H. C. Engelbrecht and F. C. Hanighen, *Merchants of Death* (New York, 1934); Richard Lewinsohn, *The Profits of War through the Ages* (London, 1936); Philip N. Baker, *The Private Manufacture of Armaments* (London, 1936).

vailed, until the German mass deportations and confiscations in conquered areas in World War II, war was seldom economically rational from the standpoint of the general welfare of even a victorious people.[26] The belief, however, that war might be generally profitable to the victor persisted. Before the period of international capitalism, war had been traditionally regarded as an economic instrument, and the complex conditions of capitalistic economy, which made it no longer such, were difficult for the average man to understand.[27] Furthermore, even if war was unlikely to solve economic ills, such ills created frustrations from which war might offer an escape. Those enduring bad and deteriorating conditions were receptive to the propaganda of philosophies of violence, however unlikely such philosophies might be to yield practical results.[28]

By altering the relative command of resources, war might add to the military power if not to the economic welfare of the victor. As a consequence, war to acquire the economic sinews of war and to withhold them from a potential enemy might be reasonable in a world of power politics, but such a war would proceed not from economic but from political motives.[29]

Political and economic motives cannot, however, be easily sepa-

[26] Norman Angell, *The Great Illusion* (New York, 1910); *Raw Materials, Population Pressure and War* ("World Affairs Books," No. 14 [New York, 1936]; J. H. Jones (*The Economics of War and Conquest* [New York, 1915], p. 160) finds that Angell in some respects overstated the case for the economic futility of war but defends the following proposition: "Although a war of conquest is likely to bring some return of wealth, and *may*, over a long period, bring a return commensurate with the outlay, the *chance* of a gain equal to or greater than the cost is never adequate compensation for the outlay itself. . . . . In almost all international questions which endanger peace in the West it is probable that economic questions do occupy a subordinate position." See also Jacob Viner, "Interdependence," *League of Nations Society in Canada Fourteenth Annual Conference*, XIII (1936), 218–31; Lionel Robbins, *The Economic Causes of War* (London, 1939), pp. 72–76; Q. Wright, "Population and International Relations," *Annals of the American Academy of Political and Social Science*, CLXXXVIII (November, 1936), 318 ff.

[27] Above, chap. vii, sec. 5a. Benjamin Williams, *The United States and Disarmament* (New York, 1931), pp. 45 ff.

[28] H. C. Engelbrecht, *Revolt against War*, pp. 247–48.

[29] R. G. Hawtrey, *Economic Aspects of Sovereignty* (London, 1930), pp. 25 ff. Sir Arthur Salter, "The Future of Economic Nationalism," *Foreign Affairs*, October, 1932, p. 18; Eugene Staley, *Foreign Investment and War* ("Public Policy Pamphlet," No. 18 [Chicago, 1935]), p. 11.

rated. A war may be fought to increase political power but with an eye to the ultimate economic advantages of such power. Furthermore, even if conditions are such that war cannot yield economic resources useful for either welfare or power, readiness for war may give prestige and relative political power. The power of the government may contribute to internal stability and to the accomplishment of diplomatic objectives, both of which may have an economic utility. In an age when personal honor is generally regarded as of high value, the individual who is ready to avenge his honor with his sword may gain certain economic advantages from the prestige arising from general knowledge of that fact. Potential challenges may have a nuisance value to the "man of honor" when dealing with the economically minded, although in the long run he may suffer compensating disadvantages because of the inclination of the peaceful merchant to avoid all contact with his type.[30] So also the concealed costs of the political method of economic advancement has often eliminated all profits.[31]

The fighting of war itself may provide immediate profit, glory, ideological fulfilment, or political advantage for certain privileged persons. Such persons, who want a war for special reasons, have sometimes found it useful to "rationalize" it in terms of general economic welfare in order to create a favorable public opinion. This was particularly true in the economically minded century which preceded World War I.[32]

[30] It may be worth recalling that, in the Middle Ages, wealth tended to pass from the fighters to the Jews, who did not fight duels. Similarly in the Ottoman Empire wealth tended to pass from the fighting Turks to the nonfighting Jews and Armenians. It is true that in these instances the natural economic flow was sometimes suddenly reversed by plunder or massacre.

[31] Jones, op. cit., pp. 143 ff. There is no evidence that states which cannot use threats in diplomacy, such as Switzerland, the Netherlands, and the Scandinavian countries have had less per capita wealth than the great powers which can and do. These states, however, may owe their security in part to the balance-of-power situation among the great powers. See above, chap. x, secs. 1, 4, n. 43.

[32] It has been common to attribute economic motives to modern wars (see John Bakeless, The Economic Causes of War [New York, 1921]), and the Marxists have developed an elaborate theory in support of such attribution (see M. Pavlovitch, The Foundations of Imperialist Policy [London, 1922]; Engelbrecht, Revolt against War, pp. 238–48). Scott Nearing (War [New York, 1931], p. 88) writes: "Wars of conquest and colonization are fought for land, food areas, resources, raw materials, trade routes, bul-

The relative importance of the various economic motives for war has varied in the modern period. At first the political influence of the masses was so slight that their depression or ambition had little influence, and the main economic factor in war was the desire of rulers to acquire wealth for their own enjoyment or to increase the power of the state. War was made to augment the power to make war.[33] While this motive continues, particularly among the totalitarian regimes, the influence of depression of the masses as a war-engendering factor has increased with the progress of democracy and the expectation of continuing economic improvement. Motives of escape from domestic depression, coupled with dubious theories concerning the economic value of protectionism and of the political control of markets and sources of raw materials, have created demands for *Lebensraum*, colonies, and conquest. Such demands, together with rising barriers to international economic intercourse, have induced a rational reluctance on the part of all states to be wholly dependent on international trade. This has resulted in a downward spiral toward war as international trade has been subjected to more and more artificial barriers.[34]

The Marxian theory, attributing imperialist war to the steady pressure for colonial, commercial, and financial expansion by the cap-

---

lion, plunder, tribute. These wars probably make up the bulk of the wars recorded in histories." Of the other two types of war which he distinguishes, he attributes "domestic or civil wars" to class economic exploitation and "competitive wars" to rivalry for power as an instrument of economic advantage. The search for economic motives for American entry into World War I was evident in the investigation of the munitions trade and the bankers by the Special Senate Committee investigating the Munitions Industry, 1936 (Nye Committee). Some senators attributed their votes for the war resolution of April 6, 1917, to economic causes, and Japanese and Italian statesmen emphasized economic reasons for their respective campaigns in Manchuria and Abyssinia. Careful studies, however, have shown that competent economists, bankers, and merchants have usually been against imperialistic war (below, n. 34) and that other than economic motives have played a large part in most modern wars. See Parker T. Moon, *Imperialism and World Politics* (New York, 1926), p. 74, who writes: "Altruism, national honor, economic nationalism, surplus population, self-protection—such are the principles or ideas which nerve nations to valiant feats of empire-building. The initiative, to be sure, is taken by interests; but the support is given by ideas." Bertrand Russell writes: "The true cause [of World War I] must be sought for outside the economic sphere" (*Why Men Fight* [New York, 1930], p. 40).

33 Above, n. 29.   34 See Robbins, *op. cit.*, pp. 77–85.

italists, because of the declining internal market and the increase of productive capacity, has not been generally sustained by detailed historical studies. The pressure of capitalistic interests, investors, arms-traders, and concessionaires has been a factor in some instances of colonial and international war, but not in most. Investors have more frequently been the unwilling instruments of a politically motivated imperialism than the concealed drivers of diplomatic or military expansionism.[35]

3. THE CULTURAL MOTIVE

The culture of all societies has recognized war as the appropriate response to certain breaches of the mores. In modern states attacks upon the homeland, upon government officials and agencies, and upon citizens and their property have been regarded as breaches of law justifying war. Traditional policies of many states have added other injuries to this category as, for example, attacks on protected or neighboring territory. The average man has accepted war as "natural" when its initiation has been reasoned or rationalized in such juridical or traditional concepts, but he does so because he regards such concepts as the wall which protects the distinctive and precious values of his culture and way of life. These values center around the pattern of intimate family and social relations and activities of recreation, creativeness, and artistic appreciation, giving a zest to life.

Modern man may also accept war as an escape from the limitations of humdrum existence, as an adventure offering the variety which his way of life has failed to provide. In even the best-regulated modern cultures there have been persons who have desired to escape from boredom, petty annoyances, or frustrations. In most populations the proportion of individuals who are unhappy is probably large in normal times, and in times of depression much larger. The impersonalization and mechanization of modern society has

[35] Eugene Staley, *War and the Private Investor* (New York, 1935); Jacob Viner, "Political Aspects of International Finance," *Journal of Business of the University of Chicago*, April and July, 1928, *Southwestern Political and Social Science Quarterly*, March, 1929; Robbins, *op. cit.;* above, n. 32.

probably exaggerated this condition.[36] The great human wishes, according to W. I. Thomas, have been for new experience, for response, for recognition, and for security.[37] It is doubtful whether the augmented wealth, the more rapid communication, and the more effective control of nature, which modern society has been able to give only by the impersonalization, mechanization, complication, and broadening of human relations, contributes to the average man any but the last of these, even in time of peace, in as great measure as did earlier societies.[38] Unless modern states can diffuse the first three of these values in larger measure, there will always be many persons within their populations who want relaxation, adventure, excitement, or escape, actually or vicariously, through identification with a hero, no matter what the character of the fire into which they are invited to jump. They will not believe it worse than the frying pan in which they find themselves.[39]

In the early stages of the modern period, the cultural motive for war was confined to a limited upper class, but democracy, rising standards of living, and the mechanization of life have increased the prevalence of this motive in all ranks of the population.

4. THE RELIGIOUS MOTIVE

Crusading for religion, for nationalism, for reform, or for other socially approved symbols has been an element in most wars. Identification of the personality with a cause, which dominates all the participants and at the same time provides an opportunity for voluntary activity by each, satisfies the common desire of men at the same time

[36] "As long as men work as addressing clerks or attendants to bolt no. 264, without pleasure, without dignity, without meaning, war offers individual redemption and personal glory" (Rosten, *op. cit.*, p. 192).

[37] R. E. Park and E. W. Burgess, *Introduction to the Science of Sociology* (Chicago, 1924), p. 489.

[38] See Lyford Edwards, *The Natural History of Revolutions* (Chicago, 1927); G. T. W. Patrick, *The Psychology of Relaxation* (New York, 1916).

[39] See Lewis Mumford, *Technics and Civilization* (New York, 1934), pp. 309 ff. The considerable number of foreign volunteers in wars where there is no obligation of patriotism as a stimulus gives evidence of this. The motives of some foreigners serving in the Spanish civil war are indicated in a series of letters, *From Spanish Trenches*, ed. Marcel Acier (New York, 1937).

to be free, to be leaders, and to be led.[40] Identification of a war with such a cause serves as a reason to the sincere and as a rationalization to others. The growing mechanization and impersonalization of modern societies, particularly of their economic processes, continually increases the incompatibility between social requirements and individual drives. Consequently, there is an increasing demand for an opportunity such as war is thought to provide, for the release of normally suppressed antisocial dispositions without a sense of guilt. While some wish to escape an unpleasant or cramping environment, others hope to escape from the conflicts within their own personalities.[41]

Most social systems subject children to parental discipline resulting in ambivalent feelings of hate and love for the parent. Such conflicting attitudes are most easily solved by displacing aggressions upon an external person or group. Furthermore, personal faults or guilty feelings may often be removed from consciousness by projecting them upon someone else. Anthropologists have emphasized the conflict between natural human desires, especially those of sex and

[40] Above, n. 17.

[41] Above, n. 36. "In the collective psychosis, a part of the aggressive instinct is released and directed against the enemy of the moment, among a great number of individuals who are neither mentally ill nor criminals, and of whom, each, taken individually is normal, is well adapted to reality. . . . . One asks, how is this release effected— how can it happen that the human conscience, elaborated through thousands of years and recreated by each individual in the course of his childhood, permits it. Two mechanisms especially contribute to this result. . . . . To this mechanism of a general order (subordination to leadership) which operates in every crowd is added participation in the ideal offered to the man in a crowd. . . . . This ideal in the course of history has had several different names. God, loyalty, patriotism, a future society, etc. Always the aggressions may be released for the greater glory of an elevated conception. The conscience is thus reassured and men can enjoy at the same time the joy of having satisfied their instincts, ordinarily so laboriously restrained, and of having attained one of their ideals" (Robert Waelder, "Lettre sur l'étiologie et l'évolution des psychoses collectives," in Institut international de cooperation intellectuelle, Correspondence [Paris, 1934], pp. 96–102). "To people fraught with uncertainties the huddling together in the mass rhythm of war-time brings a momentary resolution of many doubts and the sense of fulfilment. In this respect, despite its ghastly incongruity, war constitutes an increasingly deceptive way out for a world living by contradictions" (Robert S. Lynd, Foreword to H. C. Engelbrecht's Revolt against War, p. x). See also Bertrand Russell, op. cit., p. 13; Sigmund Freud, letter to Einstein on "Why War?" in International Institute of Intellectual Cooperation, Correspondence (Paris, 1933).

dominance, and the requirements of social existence among primitive people.[42] They have also emphasized the very common utilization of attack upon a scapegoat as the method of solving individual and group ambivalences.[43]

Conflicts within individual minds have been important factors in fights among children and among primitive people. Such conflicts have been even more severe in the minds of adults in modern civilization. The more complex society becomes, the more it requires that natural drives be suppressed or expressed only in conventional or sublimated form. Normally man submits because of the pressure of social sanctions, but he longs for an opportunity to give himself free reign with full social approval. The religion of nationalism encourages the individual to identify a potentially hostile nation as the scapegoat, against which he can express his animosities. Such expression may become open and active in time of war. The soldier in the early stages of war senses to the full and with moral satisfaction his participation in the group's great task, but at the same time he is free, without inhibitions of conscience, to satisfy his individual aggressions against the persons and property of the enemy. Observers have often reported on the elation of the soldiers at the front in the early stages of war.[44] This elation has been attributed to the complete reconciliation apparently offered to these conflicting motives. The unreality of this adjustment, however, gives it the character of a "collective psychosis" and renders its participants impervious to rational appeal until the illusion is dissipated, which in modern war it generally is before the war has advanced very far.[45] In earlier wars where the group task was symbolized in terms of a religious or national demand and the risks were not so great, the fighter's crusading zeal might persist longer.

5. THE SOURCES OF MOTIVES

Motives may be classified according to the phase of the personality from which they spring. The terms "conscience," "reason," and

[42] B. Malinowski, *Sex and Repression in Savage Society* (New York, 1927).

[43] James Frazer, *The Golden Bough* (New York, 1923); Durbin and Bowlby, *op. cit.*

[44] Nickerson, *op. cit.*, p. 19; above, n. 41.

[45] Waelder, *op. cit.*, p. 90; *Psychological Aspects of War and Peace* ("Geneva Studies," Vol. X [Geneva, 1939]), p. 44.

"impulse," roughly equivalent to the Freudian terms "super-ego," "ego," and "id," provide such a classification.[46]

Motives sanctioned by the conscience derive from ideas highly valued by the culture or "mores" and accepted by the individual at so early an age that he has forgotten their source. These ideas seem to exist apart from the individual. Motives which spring from impulse also have an unconscious source which may, however, be in conflict with the conscience. In that case the motives constitute the "countermores." Such an internal conflict may be so unpleasant as to precipitate suicide. This suggests that the motives associated with conscience and impulse may be adequate to induce great risks to life, especially when these two varieties of motive are in conflict. On the other hand, motives springing from "reason" or the individual's concept of his self-interest as integrated in the ego could hardly do so. As self-preservation usually ranks highest among those interests, for the individual to sacrifice his life in behalf of such interests would be unreasonable. One may go to war to preserve one's state, one's culture, one's idea of justice, or one's honor but only rarely to preserve one's own life.

It thus appears that, while appeals to self-interest may be suitable to stir up an aggressive spirit and even a willingness to assume considerable risks for a suitable reward, only appeals to ideals or impulses can create the abandoned spirit of self-immolation which may be necessary for certain military undertakings in modern war.[47] For this reason economic motives which in the nineteenth century were treated as the major interests, and which have been adequate to induce the mercenary or professional soldier to undertake the risks of his calling, have not been able to create a genuine willingness of the modern masses to die in battle. To a man of reason war is a thing to be avoided. *Dulce bellum inexpertis.*[48]

[46] Lasswell, *World Politics and Personal Insecurity*, pp. 63 ff.

[47] "Imperialism, nay, all history, is made by the dynamic alliance of interests and ideas" (Moon, *op. cit.*, p. 74). See also above, chap. vii, n. 89.

[48] Erasmus, 1515, cited by Van Vollenhoven, *The Law of Peace* (London, 1936), p. 59. "The psychic attitude which the cultural process forces upon us opposes war in the strongest way. . . . . Everything which favors the development of culture also works against war" (Freud, *op. cit.*, p. 9).

To create a spirit ready to participate in the mass massacre characteristic of the most recent wars, cultural, religious, and political motives have been especially enlisted. These motives are directed to such ideals as the family, the church, and the nation—ideals which modern culture stamps with supreme value. *Dulce et decorum est pro patria mori.*[49] Such a sentiment cannot spring from reason but only from the unconscious depths of the personality manifested in conscience or impulse. The appeal to these fundamental drives has been necessary to induce men to engage in modern war and has also played a part in giving to modern war its peculiarly unrestrained character.[50]

[49] Horace *Odes* iii. 2. 14; Homer *Iliad* xv. 583.
[50] Nickerson, *op. cit.*, pp. 114 and 198.

CHAPTER XII

TECHNIQUE OF MODERN WAR

THE technique of war concerns, on the one hand, the instruments (weapons and organizations) with which war is carried on and, on the other hand, the utilization of these instruments (operations and policies) to achieve the objects of war.[1]

Weapons are material or mechanical devices for use in war. A weapon usually combines striking power, mobility, protection, and holding power in varying degrees. None of these characteristics, however, particularly the last, can be wholly dissociated from the skill of the individual or organization which uses the weapon.[2]

Military organizations are organized groups of individuals equipped with weapons and disciplined to co-ordinate action on command in order to forward the purposes of war. A military organization resembles a great weapon. It functions, however, on the word of command, not on some mechanical pressure or application of muscular power.

Military operations consist of the consciously directed internal and external movements of military organizations on land, on sea, or in the air. The management of military operations in direct contact with the enemy in order to win battles is called "tactics." The manage-

---

[1] Cf. concept of technique of animal (Appen. VII, sec. 3), primitive (chap. vi, sec. 5), and historic (chap. vii, sec. 6) warfare. "Military instrument" is defined with reference to animal warfare in Appen. VII, sec. 3. That definition, rephrased to apply to modern civilization, would read: "A military instrument is a material or social entity used by a government to destroy or to control by threats or violence another government or to ward off such destruction or control."

[2] Rear Admiral Bradley A. Fiske writes: "If used to guard or attack, an implement becomes a weapon—a weapon is merely a tool for a warlike purpose" (*The Art of Fighting* [New York, 1920], p. 12). Some writers confine the word "weapon" to an instrument with striking power. Thus Colonel Fuller does not consider the tank and the airplane weapons, but only vehicles—means of carrying weapons. He, however, regards will or tenacity, movement toward the enemy, hitting the enemy, and preventing one's self from being hit as the elements of war and emphasizes the close relation of the power to hold, to move, and to protect with the power to hit (*The Reformation of War* [New York, 1923], pp. 25, 26, 120).

ment of operations so as to effect such contact under maximum advantage in order to win campaigns is called "strategy." The management of operations so as to determine the times, areas, and results of campaigns in order to win the war is called "grand strategy." The object of war is usually to bring about the complete submission of the enemy, but limited wars may have special territorial or other objectives.[3]

Military policy consists of the objectives, principles, methods, and rules which guide the preparation and direction of military operations under given conditions.[4] Military policy is subordinate to national policy. The government decides when military operations shall be employed in preference to diplomacy, economic pressure, propaganda, invocation of international procedures, or other methods for promoting the nation's foreign policy.[5]

Throughout the long history of war there has been a cumulative development of military technique. Invention of defensive instruments has usually followed close on the heels of the invention of offensive weapons. This balance of technology has tended to support a balance of power, but the balance has not tended toward increasing stability. Consequently, the political effect of military invention has not been continuous. There have been times when inventions have given the offensive an advantage, and conquerors have been able to overcome the defenses of their neighbors and build huge em-

[3] According to the U.S. Rules of Land Warfare, 1914, "the object of war is to bring about the complete submission of the enemy as soon as possible by means of regulated violence" (art. 10). Clausewitz emphasized the tendency of war to become absolute (*op. cit.*, I, 2). G. Ferrero emphasizes the advantage of limited war which always measures costs in terms of specific objectives ("Forms of War and International Anarchy," in W. E. Rappard *et al.*, *The World Crisis* [London, 1938], pp. 85 ff.). See also Hans Speier, "Class Structure and 'Total War,' " *American Sociological Review*, IV (June, 1939), 370 ff.

[4] The United States War Policies Commission reported on March 12, 1932, that "under the direction given the Commission by Congress there appeared to be almost no subject directly or indirectly connected with the conduct of war which was not included in the scope of the Commission's authorized investigations" (*Documents by War Policies Commission* [72d Cong., 1st sess.; House Doc. No. 271 (Washington, 1932)], p. 1). See also *War Policies Commission Report, December 10, 1931* (72d Cong., 1st sess.; House Doc. No. 163 [Washington, 1931]), pp. viii–ix.

[5] Carl von Clausewitz, *On War*, I (London, 1911), 86; Fuller, *op. cit.*, p. 214; Fiske, *op. cit.*, pp. 62, 365.

ires. At other times the course of invention and the art of war have avored the defensive. Local areas have been able to resist oppression, to revolt, and to defend themselves from conquest. Empires have crumbled, local liberties have been augmented, and international anarchy has sometimes resulted.

During the last five centuries military invention has proceeded more rapidly than ever before. Important differentials in the making and utilization of such inventions have developed. In general, the inventions have favored the offensive, and there has been a tendency for the size of political units to expand. This tendency was, however, arrested during much of the nineteenth century by inventions favoring the defensive, and many self-determination movements were successful.

I. DEVELOPMENT OF MODERN MILITARY TECHNIQUE

"Until within the last few years," wrote Rear Admiral Bradley A. Fiske in 1920, "the most important single change in the circumstances and methods of warfare in recorded history was made by the invention of the gun; but now we see that even greater changes will certainly be caused by the invention of the airplane."[6] Modern civilization began in the fifteenth century with the utilization of the first of these inventions and has witnessed the steady improvement of this utilization through development of accuracy and speed of fire of the gun itself; penetrability and explosiveness of the projectile; steadiness, speed, and security of the vehicle which conveys it over land or sea toward the enemy; and adaptation of military organizations to such utilization.

While the airplane continued this development by providing an even swifter vehicle for carrying the gun, it also introduced the third dimension into warfare. This made possible the use of gravitation to propel explosives, more extensive and accurate scouting, and military action behind the front, over vast areas, and across all barriers of terrain. Both of these inventions, after their use was thoroughly understood, greatly augmented the power of the offensive, though, in the case of the gun, the defense immediately began to catch up, and the general trend of war between equally equipped belligerents was

---

[6] *Op. cit.*, p. 361. See also Lewis Mumford, *Technics and Civilization* (New York, 1934), p. 87.

toward a deadlock.[7] A similar tendency is already observable in the
case of the airplane.

These two inventions are but the most striking of the numerous
applications to war of the technical advances characteristic of modern civilization. In historic civilizations men and animals provided
the power for military movement and propulsion. In the modern
period wind and sail, coal and the steam engine, petroleum and the
internal combustion engine, have successively revolutionized naval,
military, and aerial movement, as gunpowder, smokeless powders,
and high explosives have successively revolutionized military propulsion. The history of modern military technique falls into four
periods, each initiated by certain physical or social inventions and
leading to certain military and political consequences: the periods
of experimental adaptation of firearms and religious war (1450–
1648), of professional armies and dynastic wars (1648–1789), of industrialization and nationalistic wars (1789–1914), and of the airplane and totalitarian war (1914——).

a) *Adaptation of firearms (1450–1648)*.—During the period of discoveries and wars of religion medieval armor was being abandoned,
pikemen, halberdiers, and heavy cavalry were going. The organization of the Turkish Janizary infantry, well disciplined, equipped
with cutlass and longbow, and supported by light cavalry and artillery, was being copied throughout Europe. Heavy artillery had begun to reduce feudal castles in the early fifteenth century and the
Wagenburg revolutionized field tactics. Hand firearms first used by
Spaniards, Hussites, and Swiss in the fifteenth century were adopted
by all in the general wars of the early sixteenth century. The experience of the Thirty Years' War ended this period of experimental
adaptation of firearms by the mercenary armies, and modern armies
began to emerge.[8]

Naval architecture was greatly improved during this period. The
clumsy galleons of the Spanish Armada, differing little from those of

[7] Fiske, *op. cit.*, p. 355; see below, sec. 3*b*.

[8] C. Oman, *A History of the Art of War in the Sixteenth Century* (New York, 1937),
chap. i; *The Sixteenth Century* (London, 1936), chap. xi; O. L. Spaulding, H. Nickerson,
and J. W. Wright, *Warfare* (London, 1924), pp. 407 ff. In England, advocates of the
longbow continued through the reign of Elizabeth, though harquebus and musket were
generally used. See also Appen. XV, nn. 37, 38, below.

Columbus a century earlier, and resembling the oar-driven galleys of the Middle Ages, were superseded in the mid-seventeenth century by longer, swifter, and more heavily armed "broadside battleships" which differed little from those of Nelson, nearly two centuries later.[9]

Equipped with the new technique of firearms, Europeans had occupied strategic points in America, Africa, and Asia, readily overcoming the natives whom they found there. The tendency of this new technique was toward political integration inside and expansion outside of Europe. By increasing the relative power of the offensive, firearms made it possible for the more aggressive rulers, especially those of Turkey, Portugal, Spain, France, Britain, Prussia, the Netherlands, and Sweden, to expand their domains in Europe at the expense of feudal princes and to expand overseas at the expense of native chieftains.

b) Professionalization of armies (1648–1789).—The seventeenth and eighteenth centuries witnessed the development of the professional army loyal to the king and ready to suppress internal rebellion or to fight foreign wars if paid promptly and if the officers were adequately rewarded by honors and perquisites of victory. Louis XIV and Cromwell contributed greatly to the development of this type of army, which, however, in the eighteenth century tended to be more concerned with safety and booty than with victory. Consequently, military invention emphasized defense and fortification. The art of war prescribed elaborate rules of strategy and siegecraft. Rules also dealt with the treatment of prisoners, with capitulations, with military honors, and with the rights of civilians. The Prussian army with its vigorous discipline, aggressiveness, and new strategic ideas under Frederick the Great to some extent broke through this defensive technique and brought this type of army to the highest point.[10]

[9] S. C. Gilfillan, *Inventing the Ship* (Chicago, 1935); *The Sociology of Invention* (Chicago, 1935). The beginnings of this type were to be found in the ships with which Drake and Hawkins fought the Armada (G. N. Clark, *The Seventeenth Century* [Oxford, 1929], chap. vii).

[10] Clark, *op. cit.*, chap. vi; Spaulding, Nickerson, and Wright, *op. cit.*, pp. 464 ff.; John W. Wright, "Sieges and Customs of War at the Opening of the Eighteenth Century," *American Historical Review*, July, 1934, pp. 629 ff.; Richard Lewinsohn, *The Profits of War through the Ages* (London, 1936), pp. 28 ff.

The destructiveness of war was limited by the general exemption from the activities of land war of the bourgeois and peasants, who constituted the bulk of the population. The bourgeois were anti-military in attitude and of little influence in the politics of most states. The monarch preferred to leave his own bourgeois and peasants to production, provided they paid taxes, and to recruit his armed forces from the unproductive riffraff, officered by the nobility, whose loyalty could be relied upon. With the existing techniques the army could not easily attack the enemy's middle classes, unless his army was first destroyed and his fortifications taken. In that case such attack was unnecessary because these classes would usually accept whatever peace might be imposed. Lacking in patriotism or nationalism, they were little concerned if the territory on which they lived had a new sovereign, provided they could retain their property.[11]

Naval vessels reached the limit in size possible for wooden ships in the seventeenth century and underwent very little change until the steel ship developed two hundred and fifty years later. The problem of adequate raw materials for war instruments was sharply presented in England during the latter part of this period as a shortage of oak for the hull beams and of huge pines for the masts developed. The United States profited in the Revolution by blocking the British from their Canadian source of mast timber. The British never met this problem by a consistent policy of planting until after the Napoleonic Wars, when oaks were planted too late to become ripe until wood was superseded by steel in shipbuilding.[12]

This negligence, however, indicated no lack of naval interest in Great Britain during the period. The increasing importance of commerce, the vulnerability of the British Isles to blockade, and the invulnerability of Britain to land attack induced Britain to adopt a policy of naval superiority and to rely upon control of the seas as the main instrument of warfare. By such control, at a time when land transport by wagons over bad roads was very meager, military sup-

---

[11] Hans Speier, "Militarism in the Eighteenth Century," *Social Research*, III (1936), 304 ff.

[12] Robert C. Albion, *Forests and Sea Power: The Timber Problem of the Royal Navy, 1652–1862* (Cambridge, 1926).

plies and the raw materials for making them could be withheld from the enemy's forces, sieges could be assisted by maritime blockades, and the bourgeois, in so far as they had influence, might be induced to exert it in favor of peace in order to escape loss of property and commercial profits. The British took the lead in insisting upon the right to visit and search all vessels and to capture and condemn all enemy vessels and property and such neutral vessels and property as were found to be assisting the enemy. They were, however, ready to surround these activities with the judicial safeguards of prize-court procedure which not only preserved the king's share in prizes but also might prevent privateering from degenerating into piracy and from inflicting such hardships upon neutrals as to make them enemies.[13]

c) *Capitalization of war (1789–1914)*.—The French revolutionary and Napoleonic period developed the idea of the "nation in arms" through revolutionary enthusiasm and the conscription of mass armies.[14] The idea of totalitarian war was developed in the writings of Clausewitz, rationalizing Napoleonic methods. After these wars the issue between professional long-service aristocratically officered armies and conscript short-service democratic armies was debated on the Continent of Europe with a general relapse to the former type during the long peace of Metternich's era. The rise of nationalism, democracy, and industrialism and the mechanization of war in the mid-century re-established the trend toward the nation in arms and totalitarian war.[15]

The use of steam power for land and water military transportation developed in the first half of the nineteenth century and was given its first serious test in the American Civil War. Moltke appreciated the military value of these inventions, and his genius in using railroads for rapid mass mobilization won Bismarck three wars with extraordinary rapidity against Denmark, Austria, and France. The ironclad

[13] A. T. Mahan, *The Influence of Sea Power in History, 1660–1783* (16th ed.; Boston, 1902); Philip Jessup and Francis Deak, *Neutrality: Its History, Economics and Law* (New York, 1935), Vol. I.

[14] Hoffman Nickerson, *Can We Limit War?* (Bristol, 1933), pp. 111 ff.

[15] A. F. Kovacs, "Prussian Military Legislation" (manuscript thesis, University of Chicago, 1934). See below, n. 25.

and heavy naval ordnance were also tested in the American Civil
War. The era of military mechanization and of firearms of superior
range and accuracy progressed rapidly, adding greatly to military
and naval budgets and to the importance of national wealth and industry in war. The new methods were given a further test in the
Spanish-American, Boer, and Russo-Japanese wars.

The great nineteenth-century naval inventions—steam power, the
screw propeller, the armored vessel, the iron-hulled vessel, heavy
ordnance—were at first favorable to British maritime dominance because British superiority was more marked in iron and coal resources
and a developed heavy industry than in forests and wooden ship-
builders. But this advantage did not continue. The new battleships
were more vulnerable than the wooden ships because ordnance
gained in the race with armor, and repair at sea was impossible.
Furthermore, the mine, torpedo, submarine, and airplane added new
hazards to the surface fleet, especially in the vicinity of the enemy's
home bases. Warships, therefore, became more dependent upon
well-equipped and secure bases for fueling and repair, and approach
to even a greatly inferior enemy became hazardous. With the industrialization of other powers and their development of naval strength,
Britain found it increasingly difficult to maintain a three- or even a
two-power superiority in the ships themselves, while its distant
bases became less secure.[16]

Britain abandoned the effort to dominate the Caribbean after the
Venezuelan controversy with the United States in 1896, acquiesced
in American seizure of the Spanish islands, and agreed to an American fortified Panama Canal. It also welcomed American acquisition
of the Philippines and in 1902 made an alliance with Japan, indicating
doubt of its capacity to maintain its far eastern position by its own
forces. The entente with France indicated awareness that British
Mediterranean interests could no longer be defended single handed.

Britain thus recognized that the development of naval techniques
had tended toward a regionalization of sea power, and as a result it
reduced its commitments for unilateral sea control from the seven
seas to those seas controllable from bases on the British and Portu-

---

[16] J. P. Baxter, *The Introduction of the Ironclad Warship* (Cambridge, 1933); Bernard
Brodie, *Sea Power in the Machine Age* (Princeton, 1941).

guese isles and from Gibralter, Suez, and Singapore. The far-flung British empire, the highways of the Mediterranean, the Caribbean, the China Sea, and the Pacific, could no longer be defended by the British navy alone. They must be defended by the dominions themselves and by alliances and friendships, especially with the United States, France, and perhaps with Japan. It was clear that the British capacity to maintain reasonable order, respect for law and commercial obligations, and to localize wars by maintaining the balance of power in Europe had been greatly reduced. Naval inventions and the spread of industrialization had ended the *pax Britannica*.[17]

This situation was realized by the Continental powers. They developed their armies and navies with increasing speed after observation of the Russo-Japanese War and after the failure of the Hague conferences to achieve disarmament. They paid particular attention to the potentialities of the improved rifle, machine gun, and artillery as well as to the art of intrenchment.[18] The possibilities of the mine, torpedo, and submarine were developed, especially by France, pointing the way for German utilization of these weapons in World

[17] See above, chap. x, sec. 4; Q. Wright, "The Present Status of Neutrality," *American Journal of International Law*, XXXIV (July, 1940), 410 ff.

[18] In the middle of World War I, Lieut.-Col. Azan wrote: "The curve of tactics is ever varying, yet always continuous. Among those forces whose resultant determines its direction, two in particular have greatly increased in recent years, the destructive power of cannon, the resisting capacity of field works. A careful evaluation of the importance of these forces in the recent wars of the Transvaal, of Manchuria, and of the Balkans has made it possible to sketch this curve day by day, to note its sinuosities, and to follow its development in a new direction. . . . . Since October 1914 the tactical curve has undergone but slight modifications. The two opposing forces of artillery and field work have, perhaps, gained still further in importance, each one developing in order to overthrow the other. But the essential principles of strategy and of tactics which govern the course of the present war have really changed but little since that date, nor can they ever vary but by slow degrees" (*The War of Positions* [Cambridge, 1917], Introd.). To the same effect Admiral Fiske points out that it is a curious fact, contrary to the expectations of Bernhardi, that "although both forces, especially the Germans, endeavored continually to take the offensive, the war had in one way a more defensive character on both sides than any war in recent history, because the greater part of both sides found themselves during the greater part of the war in trenches." He, however, points out, perhaps prophetically in the light of the subsequent achievements of Mussolini and Hitler, that in the interval between the wars of Frederick the Great and Napoleon "the warfare-of-positions theory secured great vogue and this is one of the reasons for the early successes of Napoleon" (*op. cit.*, pp. 355, 359).

War I. Beginnings were made, especially by France and Germany, in the adaptation of the airplane and dirigible to military purposes. The results anticipated by the Polish banker, Ivan Bloch, in his book published in 1898 occurred. War became deadlocked in the machine-gun-lined trenches and in the mined and submarine-infested seas of World War I. This deadlock was not broken until attrition had ruined all the initial belligerents, and new recruits and resources on the Allied side from the United States made the cause of the Central Powers hopeless.[19]

d) Totalitarianization of war (1914———).—The advent of aerial war in the twentieth century ended the relative invulnerability of the British Isles to invasion. The weakening of surface control of the sea by the use of mines, submarines, and airplanes further impaired the position of Great Britain, and that country during the 1920's accepted the thesis that the integrity of the empire depended upon collective security. The possibilities of the airplane and tank, neither of them fully exploited during World War I, supported hope in some quarters and fear in others that the power of the offensive would be

[19] It cannot be said that the strength of any method of attack—military occupation, economic blockade, or propaganda technique—assured victory, or that the weakness of any element of defense—the fighting forces, the national economy, or the national morale—assured defeat. The combination of an adequate supply of the essentials of war potential and the capacity to "utilize and combine all the resources existing in the nation" could stave off breakdown from attrition the longest and so achieve victory (see Liddell Hart, "The World War," *Encyclopaedia Britannica* [14th ed.], XXIII, 775). Rumania and Russia broke first, then Turkey and Bulgaria, finally Austria and Germany. Serbia and Belgium had been overrun by the enemy and were kept formally in the fight by their allies. Italy and France had suffered military defeats which would probably have meant collapse but for the immediate aid of Great Britain and the United States. Great Britain had itself been compelled to reduce its contributions both of men and credit (see Leonard Ayres, *The War with Germany: A Statistical Summary* [Washington, 1919], p. 14). Capacity for co-ordination, which was perhaps greatest in Germany because of its discipline and the fact that it had the interior lines, and least for Russia among the great powers, accounted for the longer endurance of Germany but the quantity of resources to draw upon, which was less for Germany than for its enemies who held the exterior lines, accounted for Germany's ultimate defeat. The discouraging influence which quantitative comparisons must have had on the German command after American entry into the war can be appreciated by a study of the data in Leonard Ayres's statistical summaries (above).

increased, that mobility in war would be again possible, and that the deadlock would be broken.[20]

These possibilities encouraged aggression by Japan, Italy, and Germany after 1930. Dissatisfaction with the political results of World War I, resentment at the self-centered economic policies of the democracies, serious deterioration of the middle classes, and the spread of revolutionary ideologies engendered by the costs of war and widespread unemployment flowing from the great depression of 1929 provided motives for aggressions; but, if collective security had been better organized and the airplane and tank had not been invented, the prospects would hardly have been sufficiently encouraging to induce action. As it was, the initial success of Japan in Manchuria and the failure of the disarmament conference alarmed the Soviets into rapid rearmament and encouraged Italy and Germany to do likewise, especially in the air. Initial failure of the democracies to support the treaty structure when Germany began to rearm and re-occupied the Rhineland in violation of international obligations encouraged Germany, Italy, and Japan to consort together and to continue aggression in weak areas, utilizing aviation with rapid success, while all phases of the national life were organized for total war.[21]

This development of militarism, totalitarianism, and aggressiveness was most completely exhibited in Nazi Germany. Here the reaction from military defeat had been intense, confidence in technical

---

[20] General Douhet of the Royal Italian Air Force seems to have initiated the idea (of obvious propaganda value to a state planning to expand by military bluffs, whatever its military value) that victory can only be won by attack which under modern conditions is only possible by air; that surface defense should be only to facilitate air attack; that adequate air forces can soon gain "command of the air"; that once gained this command, if ruthlessly exploited to attack the enemy's big cities, can so break the enemy's morale that it will surrender (see R. E. Dupuy and G. F. Eliot, *If War Comes* [New York, 1937], pp. 53, 60; Capt. B. H. Liddell Hart, *Paris or the Future of War* [New York, 1925], pp. 27 ff.; Hart, *The Remaking of Modern Armies* [London, 1927], pp. 96 ff., where Marshal Foch is quoted: "The potentialities of aircraft attack on a large scale are almost incalculable, but it is clear that such attack, owing to its crushing moral effect on a nation, may impress public opinion to the point of disarming the Government and thus become decisive." See also Major R. A. Bratt, *That Next War* [London, 1930], quoted by Bertrand Russell, *Which Way to Peace* [London, 1936], pp. 18 ff.)

[21] Hans Speier and Alfred Kähler, *War in Our Time* (New York, 1939), especially "War Economics" by E. Lederer, pp. 43 ff. See above, n. 10.

ability to develop mechanized war was great, the economic situation was particularly grave, and the extreme democracy of the Weimar Constitution made government weak. In the background, however, the foundations had been laid by the historic rise of Prussia through war; the methods of the Great Elector, Frederick the Great, and Bismarck; the philosophies of Fichte, Hegel, and Nietsche; the historical interpretations of Mommsen and Treitschke, and the geopolitics of Ratzel and Haushover.[22] Similar developments had begun in England under Cromwell and in France under Louis XIV and Napoleon at times when new military techniques, the disciplined use of firearms, superior co-ordination of army and industry, and mass mobilization through nationalistic propaganda appeared to give these governments a strategic initiative. The strength of parliamentarianism and reliance upon the navy stopped the trend in England. In France this trend was stopped by military defeats, the democratic sentiment of the revolution, and the declining population of the nineteenth century. In the United States decentralized institutions, geographic isolation, and the democratic tradition formed a barrier against militarism. In Japan, Italy, and the Soviet Union, however, the circumstances of political ambition, economic frustration, imputations of racial, social, or political inferiority, post-war disorganization, and revolutionary ideas when stimulated by hopes born of new military inventions tended, in varying degrees, toward military totalitarianism similar to that of Germany.

As the development of the gun by the European great powers in the sixteenth and seventeenth centuries extended their imperial control to the overseas countries, followed by the latter's imitation of their techniques and eventual revolt, so the development of the airplane by the totalitarian states in the twentieth century first extended their empires and then compelled the democracies to adopt their techniques.[23] Thus the great powers, whether with a democratic or an autocratic tradition, whether relying on the army or navy, whether European or American or Asiatic, have in a disorganized world

[22] F. Schuman, *The Nazi Dictatorship* (New York, 1935); J. T. Shotwell, *What Germany Forgot* (New York, 1940).

[23] See above, nn. 8 and 20; below, nn. 57 and 61.

felt obliged to follow the lead of that one of their number most advanced in the art of war.

The trend toward general militarization initiated by the gun was, however, checked in the eighteenth and nineteenth centuries through the rise of the naval, commercial, industrial, and financial power of a relatively liberal and antimilitary Britain; through the increasing indecisiveness and destructiveness of war; through the professionalization of the armed forces; and through the antimilitaristic philosophies of the rising bourgeois. It is possible that the position of the United States, the philosophy of peace and international organization, the economic cost of total war, and perhaps the failure of aggression in World War II may have a similar influence in the latter part of the twentieth century. In April, 1940, in spite of the success of Hitler's *Blitzkrieg* in Poland, Denmark, and Norway, some military experts were predicting the failure of that method and the entry of World War II into a long stage of attrition in which the superior morale, control of resources, and manufacturing capacity of the democracies and the neutrals trading with them might eventually win the war.[24] It seems probable, however, that small nationalities can no longer defend themselves from powerful neighbors equipped with a vast superiority of planes. As the invention of artillery made it possible for monarchs to batter down feudal castles and to build nations, so the airplane may destroy the independent sovereignty of nations and create larger regional units. These may be empires resting on conquest or they may be confederations resting on consent.

2. CHARACTERISTICS OF MODERN MILITARY TECHNIQUE

a) Mechanization.—The outstanding characteristic in which modern war has differed from all earlier forms of war has been in the degree of mechanization. The use of long-range striking power (rifles, machine guns, artillery, gases), of power-propelled means of mobility (railroads, motor trucks, battleships, tanks, airships), and of heavy

[24] Stephen King-Hall, "On Winning the War," *News Letter* (London), Suppl. 195, April 5, 1940. E. M. Earle ("National Defence and Political Science," *Political Science Quarterly*, LV [December, 1940], 481 ff.) criticizes British publicists "whose writings contributed to the general collapse by preaching the doctrine, unwarranted by experience or reason of limited liability, superiority of the defense (psychological and moral as well as tactical) and the alleged inability of either side to 'win' a war."

protective covering (armor plate on fortresses, tanks, and warships)
has meant that the problem of war manufacture has risen to primary
importance.[25] In historic civilizations the soldier provided his own
equipment, and it generally lasted as long as the soldier. Some equipment was lost, but even arrows could usually be collected in large
numbers from the battlefield. Now a dozen men must be engaged in
production and transportation services behind the lines to keep one
soldier supplied.[26]

  b) *Increased size of armies.*—A second important change has been
in the size of the armed forces, both absolutely and in proportion to
the population. It might seem that if each soldier needs such a large
amount of civilian help there would be fewer soldiers, but this has
not proved to be the case.[27] Power transport and electrical communication have made it possible to mobilize and control from the center
a much larger proportion of the population than formerly. The men
can themselves be transported rapidly by railroad and motor lorry,
and canned food can be brought to them. Where formerly 1 per cent
of the population was a large number to mobilize, now over 10 per
cent can be mobilized, of which a quarter may be at the front at one
time. But 10 per cent mobilized requires most of the remaining adult
population to provide them with the essentials for continuing operations. Thus instead of 1 per cent engaging in war and the rest pursuing their peacetime occupations of trade or agriculture, now the en-

[25] "During the years 1914 to 1918 . . . . war definitely passed into the industrial
phase of economic history. . . . . The industry of war combines two techniques: the
technique of peace which supplies war with its resources, and the technique of destruction" (J. T. Shotwell, *War as an Instrument of National Policy* [New York, 1929], pp. 34,
35). See also Friedrich von Bernhardi, *On War of Today* (London, 1917), Vol. I, chaps.
iii and iv; H. C. Engelbrecht and F. C. Hannighan, *Merchants of Death* (New York,
1934), chap. i. Pecuniary profits of war have shifted from the direct plunder or reward
of the general, privateer, soldier, and sailor to the indirect gains of the war financier,
war trader, war manufacturer, war contractor, and war speculator (Lewinsohn, *op. cit.,*
pp. 115, 300). For discussion of the effect of mechanization upon size of armed forces
and war costs see Appen. XXIII.

[26] Adam Smith, *Wealth of Nations,* Book V, chap. i; J. M. Clark, W. H. Hamilton,
and H. G. Moulton, *Readings in the Economics of War* (Chicago, 1918), pp. 93 ff., 112 ff.
Hans Speier, "Class Structure and 'Total War,' " *op. cit.,* p. 374.

[27] See above, chap. ix, sec. 3a, and Appen. XIX, Table 30, Fig. 41; Appen. XXI,
Table 52.

tire working population must devote itself to direct or indirect war service.[28]

c) *Militarization of population.*—A third change, consequent upon the second, has been the military organization of the entire nation. The armed forces have ceased to be a self-contained service apart from the general population. The soldiers and sailors must be recruited from those men whose services can be most readily supplied by women, children, and the aged. The experts in transportation and industrial services must be largely exempted in order that they may continue their "civilian" services which, under modern conditions, are no less essential to war. Such a gearing-in of the agricultural, industrial, and professional population to the armed forces requires a military organization of the entire population. Since the perfection of such an organization after the outbreak of war has been impossible, the conditions of war have more and more merged into those of peace. The military organization of the entire population in peace has become necessary as a preparation for war.[29]

Such a militarization of the population must be distinguished from the militia system, illustrated in Switzerland. In this system the duty of military service, though considered a universal burden of citizenship, has involved only a limited training which has not withdrawn persons from normal civilian occupations for long periods. Furthermore, under the militia system the civilian activities have at all times been considered normal and the military abnormal. Both systems may be called "the nation in arms," but whereas the first has involved a militarization of the entire population, the second has involved a civilianization of the military services. The difference has depended upon the degree in which military has dominated over civilian government in peacetime, the degree in which military training has dominated over civilian activity in the life of the individual, and the degree in which preparedness for war has dominated over general welfare in national policy.

Both of these defense systems may be distinguished from the professional army system characteristic of the United States and Great

---

[28] See Appen. XXIII.

[29] Speier, "Class Structure and 'Total War,'" *op. cit.;* Frieda Wunderlich, "Labor in War Time," in Speier and Kähler, *op. cit.,* pp. 245 ff.; Earle, *op. cit.*

Britain and of most European states in the eighteenth century. In this system the army has been voluntarily recruited for long service and has existed with its own organization, discipline, law, and professional standards quite apart from the civilian population. Because of the emphasis upon professional qualifications, its size has not been greatly augmented in time of war, although as emergencies develop voluntary recruitment has often given way to conscription and the press gang.

While all three systems have played their part in the history of most modern states, the development of modern military technique has tended toward the military state.[30]

d) *Nationalization of war effort.*—A fourth change, characteristic of modern military technique, has been the extension of government into the control of economy and public opinion. The military state has tended to become the totalitarian state. Other forces of modern life have, it is true, had a similar tendency. Democracy, under the influence of nationalism, has induced the individual to identify all phases of his life with that of the state, while state socialism, under the influence of depression, has induced the state to intervene in all phases of the life of the individual, but the needs of modern war have led and accelerated the process.[31] Modern war has required propaganda to sustain morale among the civilian population which, contributing directly to the war effort, can no longer expect to be exempt from attack. Modern war has also required an adjustment of the nation's economy to its needs. A free-market system, depending on profits, has proved less adequate than military discipline for reducing private consumption and directing resources and productive energy to war requirements. Since transition from a free economy to a controlled economy would be difficult in the presence of war, prepa-

---

[30] Hans Speier, "Militarism in the Eighteenth Century," *op. cit.*, pp. 304 ff., and articles on "Militia," "Conscription," "Mercenary Troops," *Encyclopaedia of the Social Sciences.*

[31] Walter Lippmann discussed in 1937 various factors which had weakened liberalism since 1870 but concluded that "there is only one purpose to which a whole society can be directed by a deliberate plan. That purpose is war, there is no other" (*The Good Society* [Boston, 1937], p. 90). In 1884 Herbert Spencer saw collectivism leading to "militant communities organized for a state of constant war" ("The Coming Slavery," reprinted in *Man vs. The State* [New York, 1903], chap. ii).

ration for war tends toward such a change in time of peace. Furthermore, autarchy is necessary as a defense against blockade. The controls necessary to confine the nation's economic life to those regions whose resources and markets will be available in time of war must be applied before the war. The modern technique of war has, therefore, led to the autarchic totalitarian state and the elimination both of free economy and of free speech.[32]

e) Total war.—A fifth change, characteristic of modern war technique, has been the breakdown of the distinction between the armed forces and the civilians in military operations. The moral identification of the individual with the state has given the national will priority over humanitarian considerations. The civilian's morale and industry support the national will. Thus the population, manufacturing, and transport centers have become military targets.[33] Bombing aircraft and starvation blockades have made it possible to reach these targets over the heads of the army and fortifications; consequently, the principle of military necessity has tended to be interpreted in a way to override the traditional rules of war for the protection of civilian life and property.[34]

[32] Speier and Kähler, *op. cit.*

[33] In 1894 John Westlake wrote: "There are ominous signs that pity, as an operative force in the mitigation of war, has nearly reached its limit. . . . . Theoretical writers have been found to preach what at one time they had been unanimous in denouncing, the devastation of whole tracts of country for sheer terror, or in vengeance for stubborn resistance by the enemy. . . . . The pity which is effectual to work great changes is that which, in running at once through millions of men, is intensified by the enthusiasm which masses engender. But pity for suffering in war is liable in democratic times to encounter other feelings of equal extent and opposite tendency, the consciousness that the war in which the nation is engaged has been willed by it, and the national determination to triumph at any cost" (*Chapters on the Principles of International Law* [Cambridge, 1894], p. 273). Von Moltke wrote in 1880: "The greatest kindness in war is to bring it to a speedy conclusion. It should be allowable, with that view, to employ all methods save those which are absolutely objectionable. I can by no means profess agreement with the Declaration of St. Petersburg, when it asserts that the weakening of the military forces of the enemy is the only lawful procedure in war. No: you must attack all the resources of the enemy's government—its finances, its railways, its stores, and even its prestige" (letter to Professor Bluntschli, December 11, 1880, cited in U.S. Rules of Land Warfare, 1914, art. 10).

[34] Q. Wright, "The Effect of the War on International Law," *Minnesota Law Review*, V (1921), 520 ff. For general discussion of doctrine of military necessity see Westlake, *op. cit.*, pp. 238 ff.; U.S. Rules of Land Warfare, 1914, arts. 10–13.

The seventeenth-century writers on international law, while admitting that the entire population of the enemy was in strict law subject to attack, distinguished between the combatants and the noncombatants, asserting that approved usage should in general exempt the latter.[35] With the progress of modern military technique in the nineteenth century, the "armed forces" came to include numerous noncombatants such as transport workers and trench-diggers, but the civilians outside of the armed forces were in general exempted from direct attack, though their property at sea was liable, and in occupied areas they and their property were subject to requisition.[36] Military practice and the rules of war were also, to some extent, influenced by the general distinction between the political and the economic life of the state, a distinction which developed particularly as a result of the physiocratic and classical schools of economics and the increasing influence of neutrals.[37] Private property on land was gen-

[35] Grotius recognized that "those who are truly subjects of the enemy" whether women, children, captives, or hostages, may under the law of nations be attacked in person and property (*De jure belli ac pacis*, Book III, chap. iv, secs. 8-14; chap. v, sec. 1), but "it is the bidding of mercy, if not of justice, that, except for reasons that are weighty and will affect the safety of many, no action should be attempted whereby innocent persons may be threatened with destruction," especially women and children the religious, farmers, merchants, and prisoners (Book III, chap. xi, secs. 8-15).

[36] "The enemy population is divided in war into two general classes, known as the armed forces and the peaceful population. . . . . The armed forces of the belligerent parties may consist of combatants and non combatants" (U.S. Rules of Land Warfare, 1914, arts. 29, 42; Hague Regulations on Law and Customs of War on Land, 1907, art. 3). Rousseau wrote in the *Social Contract:* "War is not a relation of man to man but of state to state, in which individuals are enemies only accidentally, not as men nor even as citizens but as soldiers, not as members of their country but as its defenders. Lastly a state can only have other states for enemies and not men, seeing that no true relation can be established between things of different natures" (Book I, chap. iv). To similar effect Portales, opening the French Prize Court in 1801, said in opposition to the British insistence on the right to condemn enemy private property at sea: "War is a relation of state to state and not of individual to individual" (Westlake, *op. cit.*, p. 260). The German international lawyer, Lueder, took a similar position in 1885: "In war only states and not private persons are opposed to one another as enemies" (in Holtzendorff's *Handbuch des Volkerrechts* [Berlin, 1889], Vol. IV, sec. 69, p. 265). See also Westlake *op. cit.*, pp. 259 ff.

[37] Rudolf Littauer, "Enemy Property in War," in Speier and Kähler, *op. cit.*, p. 277 The tendency to separate economic from political policy was supported not only by the economic theorizing of Quesnay and Adam Smith in opposition to mercantilism but by the practical interests of governing classes who in the later eighteenth century wished the sources of taxation to be undisturbed by war (see Speier, "Militarism in the Eight

erally considered exempt from capture,[38] and there was a strong movement, especially in the United States, to extend this exemption to private property at sea[39]—a movement which was accepted in 1856 with respect to such property on neutral ships.[40] While the total exemption of the economic life of states from the rigors of war was not accepted, because of the opposition of Great Britain and other naval powers, the idea that war should be directed solely against the military and political life of the state had considerable influence dur-

---

eenth Century," *op.cit.*) and of commercial and agricultural classes of increasing enlightenment and influence who wished to be undisturbed in their activities by wars and alliances. This attitude, which in the nineteenth century was characteristic of the British laissez faire movement under Cobden and Bright, was manifested earlier by the policy of the United States, which was dominated by such classes. Whether for protection or free-trade, Americans wished to be undisturbed by Europe's wars and alliances, and they justified their demand for exemption of their property from such disturbances, whether the United States was neutral or belligerent, on grounds of natural right rather than utility. Washington said that "the great rule of conduct for us in regard to foreign nations is, in extending our *commercial* relations to have with them as little *political* connection as possible" ("Farewell Address"). Franklin had urged the exemption of farmers, fishermen, and merchants from war (below, n. 39), Hamilton opposed confiscation of loyalist property by the states ("Camillus Letters"), and John Marshall on the bench "did all in his power to safeguard the rights and property of individuals, citizens and enemies alike" (B. M. Ziegler, *The International Law of John Marshall* [Chapel Hill, 1939], p. 22).

[38] Chief Justice Marshall in *Brown* v. *U.S.*, 8 Cranch 110 (1814); Lord Ellenborough in *Wolff* v. *Oxholm*, 6 M. and S., 92 (1817); Hague Regulations on Law and Customs of War on Land, art. 46; Norman Bentwich, *The Law of Private Property in War* (London, 1907). "In the beginning of the twentieth century these ideas, derived variously from Grotius, Rousseau and capitalist ideology, were firmly established. All textbooks on international law could safely report it to be a settled and unchallenged rule that the private property of enemy subjects is inviolable. True, there were some older precedents to the contrary, but it seemed obvious that in view of the unanimity of treaty practice and legal literature these precedents could be considered obsolete" (Littauer, *op. cit.*, p. 278).

[39] See Naval War College, *International Law Topics and Discussions* (Washington, 1905), pp. 9 ff. Franklin wrote in 1781: "There are three employments which I wish the law of nations would protect, so that they would never be molested or interrupted by enemies even in time of war. I mean farmers, fishermen, and merchants, because their employments are not only innocent, but are for common subsistence and benefit of the human species in general."

[40] In the Declaration of Paris. See H. S. Quigley, "The Immunity of Private Property from Capture at Sea," *Bulletin of the University of Wisconsin* ("Economics and Political Science Series," Vol. IX, No. 2 [Madison, 1918]).

ing the nineteenth century, especially in countries like Germany, vulnerable to blockade.[41]

While these distinctions according extensive exemptions to the noncombatants, the civilian population, and the national economy may still be supported by reference to the sources of international law, the practice of war has tended to become totalitarian. Starvation, bombardment, confiscation of property, and terrorization have in World War II been considered applicable against the entire enemy population and territory, except in so far as practical dangers of reprisal and a desire to utilize the population of occupied areas have inhibited. The entire life of the enemy state comes to be an object of attack.[42] The modern doctrine of conquest even extends to the elimination of that population and its property rights in order to open the space it occupied for settlement.[43]

f) Intensification of operations.—A sixth characteristic of modern war technique has been a great increase in the intensity of military operations in time and of their extension in space.[44]

Operations of war have always had the object of concentrating a greater military force then the enemy at a given point, the control of which is regarded as important. Such points might be fortified places, government or commercial centers, transport and communication gateways, or a battleground selected by the enemy or one to which his forces might be lured. The belligerent with inferior forces would try to delay action while it brought up reserves and improved its trenches, but if one acquired marked superiority at any moment it would usually begin a battle or siege. This episode would end in retreat or surrender by one side after a day or, in the case of siege, after several months and would be followed by months or years of maneuver during which another point of importance would emerge, forces

---

[41] Bismarck considered political hostility compatible with economic peace and vice versa (W. B. Harvey, "Tariffs and International Relations, 1860–1914" [manuscript thesis, University of Chicago, 1938], chap. iv, sec. 3).

[42] Littauer, *op. cit.*, pp. 279 ff.

[43] Arthur Feiler, "The Economic Meaning of Conquest," in Speier and Kähler, *op cit.*, p. 153. This radically changes the assumption on which arguments, such as that by Normal Angell (*The Great Illusion* [London, 1911]) against the utility of conquest were based.

[44] Above, chap. ix, sec. 3c, d.

would be concentrated, and another battle or siege would occur. The campaigns would thus be broken into distinct and separate episodes, but, because of the slowness of communication and the difficulties of winter fighting, campaigns in separated areas or in different years would be, in considerable measure, isolated from one another. War typically consisted of a number of distinct campaigns separated by long periods and wide areas of relative peace.

The inventions in mechanization and mobility, the organization of the entire population, the increase in the number of important targets for attack, has made it possible to concentrate enormously greater forces at a given point, to supply reserves and to continue attack and resistance at that point for a much longer period, to increase the number of points being attacked simultaneously, to enlarge the theater of the campaign by mutual efforts at outflanking, and to co-ordinate operations on all fronts at all seasons for the entire course of the war. The result was that World War I tended to become a single and continuous campaign, and the campaign tended to become one long battle or a series of battles so overlapping and united as to be hardly distinguishable.[45] The pattern of war instead of a grouping of dots on a map became a large black spot of ink on the map which spread rapidly until the entire map was blackened. While this pattern was not at first duplicated in the hostilities which began in 1931, it is possible that the new *Blitzkrieg* and siege tactics may eventuate in an intense, continuous, and universal battle.[46] The continuous bombardment of London indicated such a development.

These six characteristics of modern military technique—increased mechanization and size of armed forces, more general militarization and nationalization of the people, more comprehensive, intense, and extended operations —collectively tend toward totalitarian military organization of the belligerents and totalitarian military operations during the war. Though a trend in this direction began in the sixteenth century, it has been more and more emphasized during the last fifty years, with a marked acceleration during the 1930's.

These changes have been most marked in the characteristics of weapons, less marked in that of organization and operations, and of

[45] The war of position is well described by Lieut.-Col. Azan, *op. cit.*, pp. 5 ff.
[46] Below, n. 61.

little significance in the fields of policy and strategy. The art of using superior preparedness, a reputation for ruthlessness, and threats of war for bloodless victory is as old as history and was expounded by Machiavelli. The vulnerability of civilians to bombing aircraft may have increased the effectiveness of these methods against nations which have greater potential power than the threatener.[47]

Writers on modern strategy can still draw lessons from the campaigns of Hannibal, Caesar, Frederick, and Napoleon. The importance of a clear *objective*, of seizing *offensive* opportunities, and of striving for *mobility* is still paramount. The principles of *surprise*, *concentration*, *co-operation* or team work, *economizing of forces* through flexibility and maneuver, *security* of bases and positions, continue applicable, though the conditions of their application have greatly changed.[48] The number of points on the earth's surface vulnerable to military surprise has been increased by the airplane, as has the quantity of forces which may be concentrated at a point and the possibility afforded of co-operation over a large area by electrical communication. The possibilities of maneuver, while increased in strategy, because of new means of mobility, have decreased in tactics, because of the larger forces engaged and the increased difficulties of outflanking. While all bases have become more vulnerable to surprise attack, the possibility of holding positions has not greatly changed. The arts of fortification, intrenchment, and antiaircraft defense have progressed with the progress of artillery and aviation.

Because of these changes some writers have even asserted that there has been a change in basic strategic principles. It has been said, for instance, that the general objective of war is no longer to disarm the enemy by destroying or capturing fortifications and armed forces but to evade them and to strike at the government or economic nerve centers of the enemy directly. Such a change in objectives, it has been thought, might modify the principles of concentration and security.[49] It appears, however, that recent wars do not support this

---

[47] H. Simons, "Power Politics and Peace Plans," and Max Ascoli, "Peace for Our Time," in Speier and Kähler, *op. cit.*, pp. 19 ff., 348 ff.

[48] Major-General Sir F. Maurice, *Principles of Strategy* (New York, 1930); Col. J. F. C. Fuller, *The Reformation of War* (1922), pp. 28 ff.; Rear Admiral Bradley A. Fiske, *op. cit.*, 345 ff.

[49] See above, n. 20.

theory. The old principles continue to be observed under the new conditions. The *Blitzkrieg*, using airplane and tank, still aims at disarmament of the enemy, though destruction of airdromes, communication and transportation centers, and lightning mechanized invasion are, under modern conditions, the first steps in this process.[50]

3. POLITICAL EFFECTS OF MODERN MILITARY TECHNIQUE

Contemporary war appears to have made for instability, political disintegration, despotism, and unadaptability.[51] A final evaluation of the political effects of the most recent development of military technique must await the result of World War II. The influence of these techniques upon the disposition of statesmen to threaten or to resort to war and upon the political effect of such action can, however, be already observed, and such observations seem to support the analysis of the role of war in contemporary civilization here presented. Four conclusions seem justified.

a) Imperialism.—Nations skilled in modern military techniques have an overwhelming advantage over those not so skilled.[52] This was manifested in the tremendous advantage of European nations which first began to adopt modern military techniques over the American and Asiatic states opened to them by the discoveries of the fifteenth and sixteenth centuries. The spread of European imperialism followed. With the development of these techniques in the United States, Japan, and other overseas states the European empires have been seriously shaken. The accelerating development of the modern techniques in the last ten years, however, has given rise to new differentials. Consequently, all states have felt obliged to move in the direction of totalitarianism and to equip themselves with the

---

[50] Henry J. Reilly, "Blitzkrieg," *Foreign Affairs*, January, 1940; below, n. 57.

[51] Above, chap. x.

[52] Adam Smith pointed out in 1776 that "in ancient times the opulent and civilized found it difficult to defend themselves against the poor and barbarous nations. In modern times, the poor and barbarous find it difficult to defend themselves against the opulent and civilized. The invention of fire-arms, an invention which at first sight appears to be so pernicious, is certainly favorable both to the permanency and to the extension of civilization" (*op. cit.*, Book V, chap. i, conclusion). See also Liddell Hart's conclusions on the Italo-Abyssinian war (1935) in which the Abyssinians had almost no defense against air and gas attack and his conclusions on the Spanish civil war (1937) (*Europe in Arms* [New York, 1937], pp. 251 ff., and above, sec. 1a).

latest devices or to place themselves under the protection of states so organized and equipped.

b) *Wars of attrition.*—Modern military techniques, however, have increased the probability of a deadlock and a war of attrition between powers both of which are equally skilled in the use of these methods. Experience with an inflexible technique tends to favor the defensive, and highly mechanized techniques tend to become inflexible. The success of the offensive depends in large measure upon surprise, and, as the varied applications of a given technique become known, the opportunities for surprise become less.[53] On the other hand, the defensive depends upon knowledge of the best means of dealing with the enemy's offensive, and this knowledge steadily accumulates with experience of a given technique.[54] This is true of any form of conflict, whether with a serious objective or for sport. In the hands of experts chess is far more likely to result in a draw than in the hands of amateurs, and football has shown the same tendency so that the rules have been frequently changed to favor the offensive, thus keeping the game interesting.[55] While the rapid progress of

[53] "Rapidity of movement and surprise are thus the life and soul of the strategical offensive" (Lieut.-Gen. C. F. von der Goltz, *The Conduct of War* [London, 1908], p. 34). Fiske, *op. cit.*, p. 40. Secrecy in military invention, practically unknown in the nineteenth century, partly because of the role of international armsmakers, contributed to surprise in twentieth-century wars (V. Lefebure, *What Would Be the Character of a New War?* ed. Interparliamentary Union (New York, 1933), pp. 96 ff.; B. Brodie, "Defense and Technology," *Technological Review*, XLIII (January, 1941).

[54] "The modern tendency to keep up the international status quo, arises from the great age of all European states. This sentiment naturally fits in with the spirit of the strategical defensive, the principle of which is likewise that of keeping up the status quo" (von der Goltz, *op. cit.*, p. 63). See above, chap. vii, nn. 79, 80.

[55] Q. Wright, *The Causes of War and the Conditions of Peace* (London, 1935), pp. 49 ff. "Master minds, led by 'Pop' Warner of Temple University, are complaining that their teams cannot score touchdowns against the five-man line defense, and that the football rules committee at its December meeting should legislate it out of existence. It results in too many tie games, and too little scoring. The defense must be curbed, they insist, and the balance of power restored by giving the offense more latitude. Football and warfare, it is apparent, are in the same dilemma. Despite harrowing stories of new war machines that were to annihilate armies overnight and destroy cities in the twinkling of an eye, armies continue to stand fast, and cities continue to resist sieges. Events in Spain and in China indicate that the razzle-dazzle offense is no more effective than the good old orthodox 'punt, pass and prayer' attack. This is decidedly unfair to ambitious nations" (*Chicago Daily News*, editorial, November 20, 1937).

military invention during the last fifty years has provided opportunity for new surprises, on the whole, increasing mechanization and capitalization of military technique have favored the war of attrition.

Furthermore, the masses involved in a major modern battle have become so large that they cover the entire front. No maneuver can get around the flanks of an enemy whose line extends along the entire frontier.[56] The *Blitzkrieg* of 1940, co-ordinating plane, tank, and infantry, broke through at the weakest point when assisted by the element of surprise, great superiority of material, and preparatory propaganda activity.[57] The aerial bomber with its power of hitting the enemy's nerve center directly also contributed to breaking the deadlock.[58] The airplane has made the civil population and the national economy vulnerable to attack. The fear of reprisals appeared to be the only defense of cities from general air attack.[59] But to say

[56] "After a few weeks of real warfare, the offensive *au outrance*, the high gospel of the pre-war manuals, was reduced to a wallowing defensive among mud holes and barbed wire. . . . . The one problem which now confronted them was: how to re-establish movement, for until one or both sides could move there was no possibility of a decision by arms, and famine alone must become the arbiter of peace" (Fuller, *op.cit.*, p. 86). See also J. Holland Rose, *The Indecisiveness of Modern War* (London, 1927), p. 47; Liddell Hart, "Future Warfare," *Atlantic Monthly*, December, 1936.

[57] H. F. Armstrong, "The Downfall of France," *Foreign Affairs*, XIX (October, 1940), 67; M. W. Fodor, "The Blitzkrieg in the Low Countries," *Foreign Affairs*, XIX (October, 1940), 197. For anticipations of the *Blitzkrieg* technique see Fuller, *op. cit.*, chap. viii; Nickerson, *op. cit.* Liddell Hart (*The Remaking of Modern Armies*, p. 59) writes: "Once appreciate that they [tanks] are not an extra arm or a mere aid to infantry, but are the modern form of heavy cavalry, and their correct tactical use is clear. . . . . Then not only may we see the rescue of mobility from the toils of trench warfare, but with it the revival of generalship and of the art of war, in contrast to its mere mechanics. Instead of machines threatening to become the masters of man, as they actually did in 1914–18, they will give man back opportunities for the use of his art."

[58] Above, n. 20.

[59] "We who are in aviation carry a heavy responsibility on our shoulders, for, while we have been drawing the world closer together in peace we have stripped the armor of every nation in war. It is no longer possible to shield the heart of a country with its army. Armies can no more stop an air attack than a suit of mail can stop a rifle bullet. . . . . Aviation has brought a revolutionary change to a world already staggering from changes. It is our responsibility to make sure that doing so we do not destroy the very things we wish to protect. We have moved so fast we have imposed aeronautical time upon military tactics, and we have taken away the old defense of astronomical time, which has probably been civilization's greatest safeguard in the past. . . . . When I see

that each side can destroy the other's population, property, and cities more extensively than in past history does not say that rapid victory can be won by doing so if there is comparative equality of planes and productive capacity. Under such conditions war may continue in the course which Ivan Bloch predicted and World War I demonstrated—that is, toward mutual attrition.[60] After both sides have been ruined, the coalition controlling most population, raw materials, industrial equipment, and civilian morale may win because the other has run out of one of these items.[61]

---

that within a day or two damage can be done which no time can ever replace, I begin to realize we must look for a new type of security—security which is dynamic, not static, security which rests in intelligence, not in forts" (Charles L. Lindbergh, speech in Berlin, July 23, 1936, reported in *New York Times*, July 24, 1936). British Prime Minister Baldwin said that against air attack "the only defense is offense, which means that you have to kill women and children more quickly than the enemy if you want to save yourselves" (quoted by B. Russell, *Which Way to Peace?* p. 21). "None of the belligerents was inclined to initiate air attack upon the enemy's territory. . . . . Each feared the other's *riposte* (J. M. Spaight, "The War in the Air," *Foreign Affairs*, XIX [January, 1941], 405).

[60] Bloch, *The Future of War* (Boston, 1914), pp. 347 ff.; Rose, *op. cit.*; Fuller, *op. cit.*, chap. iv. "Victor and victim may suffer a common disaster. Its effects reach even into the unformed future, and rob the savings of generations yet unborn" (Shotwell, *War as an Instrument of National Policy* [New York, 1929], p. 36).

[61] The question is still controversial (see Nickerson, *op. cit.*, and above, n. 24). Hostilities in Spain and China suggested that antiaircraft defense had progressed more rapidly than air attack. With even moderate defenses the bombers could be driven so high that they could not often hit important military objectives and their ability to kill civilians and destroy property, with the utmost use of modern explosive, incendiary, and gas bombs was not so great as to paralyze, but rather to stimulate, resistance. See carefully reasoned studies by Dupuy and Eliot, *op. cit.*, pp. 64, 101; Liddell Hart, *Europe in Arms*, preliminary chapter on "Spain" and chaps. xv and xvi; editors of *Fortune*, "Background of War," which concludes (p. 246): "The new annihilating weapon of surprise which would assure immediate success to an aggressor has not appeared. On the contrary such improvements in weapons as have been made leave the relative positions of attacker and defender about what they were and subject aggressors to the risk of stalemate and long war." The Albanian, Polish, Danish, Norwegian, Low Countries, French, and, in a less degree, the Finnish campaigns of 1939–40, however, demonstrated the possibilities of the *Blitzkrieg* (see Reilly, *op. cit.*, pp. 254 ff.; J. M. Spaight, "The War in the Air, First Phase," *Foreign Affairs*, January, 1940, pp. 357 ff.; "The War in the Air, Second Phase," *ibid.*, January, 1941, pp. 402 ff.; Hoffman Nickerson, "The New German Military Theory," *Harpers* [August, 1940], pp. 239–48; see above, n. 57). For difficulties of this type of war against an enemy of vast area and population like China see Kurt Bloch, "German Interests and Policies in the Far East," Institute of

c) Role of industrial and political management.—The skills involved in modern military techniques tend to be less the capacity to command armed forces in the field and more the capacity to manage the national economy, to sustain the national morale, to destroy the enemy's morale and economy, and to handle neutrals diplomatically— in other words, the role of strictly military operations in wars between states of equal technological development has tended to decline. Wars were formerly won through military operations in the field, and this is still true where a powerful state with the latest military techniques attacks one smaller, more backward, or less prepared. States may, however, fail to win wars over their technological equals, even though they win most of the battles. With the totalitarianization of war the cost of winning battles may make them Dead Sea fruit to the victor.[62] With this development economic strength, propaganda strength, and diplomatic strength have increased in relative importance.[63] Admiral Mahan emphasized the significance of economic warfare through the use of sea power, and later writers have considered national industrial strength as the major element in war potential.[64] H. D. Lasswell and others have emphasized the sig-

---

Pacific Relations, *Inquiry Series, 1939*, pp. 43 ff., quoting W. Schenke, "Space as an Instrument of War," *Zeitschrift für Geopolitik* (1938), pp. 705 ff. See also R. E. Dupuy, "The Nature of Guerilla Warfare," *Pacific Affairs*, June, 1939, pp. 138 ff.

[62] Above, n. 60; see also Shotwell, *What Germany Forgot*, pp. 144 ff.

[63] In distinguishing the military, economic, and propaganda fronts in war, H. D. Lasswell (*Propaganda Technique in the World War* [London, 1927], pp. 9, 214) follows Clausewitz, who wrote: "There are principal objects in carrying on war, (*a*) to conquer and destroy the enemy's armed force, (*b*) to get possession of the material elements of aggression, and of the other sources of existence of the hostile army, (*c*) to gain public opinion" (Major Steward L. Murray, *The Reality of War* [London, 1914], p. 69). The Nazis "are fighting this war by trying by nonmilitary means to paralyze the will of the enemy to resist before the actual fighting even begins. . . . . The principal nonmilitary weapon the Nazis are using is the psychological weapon. . . . . Their essential purposes always are the same—first, to encourage dissension among groups opposed to them . . . . and second to encourage personal misgivings and general unwillingness to fight in each individual" (Wallace R. Deuel, "Nazi Tactics," *Chicago Daily News*, January 10, 1941).

[64] *The Influence of Sea Power on History, 1660–1783.* See W. Mackenson, "An Analysis of Admiral Mahan's Sea Power Theory" (manuscript, University of Chicago, 1936). Mahan's theory carried out Sir Walter Raleigh's statement: "Whosoever commands the sea commands the trade; whosoever commands the trade of the world commands the riches of the world and consequently the world itself" (quoted by Rear Admiral

nificance of propaganda, especially since World War I. This significance has been illustrated in the policies of Hitler and Mussolini.[65]
Bismarck recognized the importance of the imponderables in war,
and the superior diplomatic ability of the Allies in winning neutrals
contributed greatly to their success in World War I. Rapid military
victory may in fact prove a positive obstacle to diplomatic success.
Neutrals not too close to the scene of action are likely to fear and distrust the government so well prepared that it wins initial military
successes. For this reason, as well as from sympathy to the victim of
invasion and a desire to restore the balance of power, such neutrals
may give moral or even material support to the government which
loses the first round. Neutrals near to the initial victor tend, how-

---

Charles L. Hussey, "The United States and Great Britain," *American Policies Abroad*
[Chicago: Chicago Council on Foreign Relations, 1932], p. 174). Benjamin H. Williams
(*The United States and Disarmament* [New York, 1931], pp. 37 ff.), while recognizing the
importance of sea power in the wars of the seventeenth to the nineteenth century,
thinks it is less important now because of the improvements of land communications.
This idea has also been important in the geopolitical school of Germany influencing
Hitler's efforts at Continental expansion (see "Hitler's World Revolution," *New Statesman and Nation*, August 26, 1939). Charles Kruszewski, "Germany's Lebensraum,"
American Political Science Review, XXXIV [October, 1940], 967, 972). But if the tendency of wars to become wars of attrition continues, the belligerent group with the greater
economic resources at its disposal is likely to win (unless there is a great disparity in
morale) and the belligerent group that controls the sea and so has the entire world except its enemy's territory to draw from is likely to be in that position and to win as did
the sea-power group in the Seven Years' War, the Napoleonic Wars, the American Civil
War, and World War I. The question of the influence of sea power in the American
Revolution has been controversial. Mahan claims the temporary French sea power was
decisive, but Williams (*op. cit.*, p. 17) and Admiral Ballard (*America and the Atlantic*
[New York, 1923], pp. 260 ff.) think the United States would have won without French
naval aid because they had become in a measure independent of overseas trade, and the
British were not prepared to send a sufficient land force to occupy the vast country.

[65] "Employed in conjunction with the other arms of offence, propaganda saps the
stamina of the armed and civilian forces of the enemy, and smoothes the path for the
mailed fist of men and metal. The economic blockade slowly squeezes the vitality out
of a nation, and depends for its maximum effect upon a prolonged struggle. Propaganda
is likewise a passive and contributory weapon, whose chief function is to demolish the
enemy's will to fight by intensifying depression, disillusionment and disagreement"
(Lasswell, *op. cit.*, p. 214); see also Admiral Hussey, *op. cit.*, p. 206. Military men have
always realized that "in war we have to do not so much with numbers, arms and ma-
noeuvres, as with human nature" (Henderson, *Lessons from the Past for the Present*,
quoted by Dupuy and Eliot, *op. cit.*, p. 41), but they have emphasized propaganda to increase the morale of our troops rather than to destroy that of the enemy.

ever, to jump on his bandwagon, and those suffering from isolationism may acquiesce in his conquests.[66]

While it is true that military power is important, it has tended to become relatively less important in the winning of war between states of equal technological development. This is a consequence not only of the increasing importance of the other activities and of the increasing cost of winning battles but also of the increasing interpenetration of trade and communication, creating for each state economic and cultural dependence upon and vulnerability to the outside world.[67] The totalitarian state, isolated economically and ideologically from the outside world and devoting its policy, its economy, its culture, and its religion to the augmentation of military power, has been the response to this situation, but it is not certain that this effort to create artificial isolation will be successful. If it is successful, it may be at the expense of the sanity of the isolated community.[68]

d) Nuisance value.—The utility of military power has become distinct from the utility of military victory. As an instrument of policy, war is more useful because of its nuisance value than because of its capacity for positive achievement. It is like the bomb in the hands of a bank robber, which if tossed will destroy both bank and robber

[66] Q. Wright and Carl J. Nelson, "American Attitudes toward Japan and China, 1937–38," *Public Opinion Quarterly*, III (1939), 49 ff. Governments have frequently hesitated between balance-of-power, appeasement, and isolationist policies as illustrated by Demosthenes' *Philippics* and the United States Senate debates of 1939 (see F. H. Cramer, "Isolationism: A Case History," *Journal of the History of Ideas*, I [October, 1940], 459–93).

[67] It must be emphasized that the degree of dependence and vulnerability of states has in some instances become less. As Vice-Admiral Ballard has pointed out (*op. cit.*, p. 99), the overseas colonies of Spain, Portugal, and Britain in America became less economically and culturally dependent upon the motherland as they developed internally and so were able to gain political independence. The general trend of modern history, however, has been toward greater interdependence. In recent times states planning aggression have tried to attain economic self-sufficiency or to be economically dependent only on bordering countries in order to decrease their vulnerability to blockade.

[68] See Speier and Kähler, *op. cit.* "The loss of contact with other men, isolation from the community characterizes mental malady" (Robert Waelder, "Lettre sur l'étiologie et l'évolution des psychoses collectives," in Institut international de coopération intellectuelle, *Correspondence* [Paris, 1934], p. 90).

but which when threatened may induce the cashier to comply with demands peacefully. War is still in practice, if not in law, an instrument of national policy; but other instruments such as diplomacy, commercial pressure, propaganda, or the invocation of international procedures are now available. These methods are used as auxiliaries to military attack, but they also constitute alternative methods which may be used for achieving policy.

The increasing cost of war has made it less useful and has induced a greater reluctance to resort to it.[69] Furthermore, the objectives which modern states have pursued are ones less susceptible of acquisition through war than has been true in the past. War by its nature is most suitable as an instrument for occupying and controlling territory.[70] In fact, throughout civilized history the control of territory has been the commonest immediate objective of the belligerent which starts it. In modern times, however, states often wish to acquire markets or access to raw materials in territory which they have no intention of annexing. Apart from trade in war materials it is difficult to promote trade by hostilities. The fine adjustments of normal international trade and finance as well as the total quantity of wealth are certain to be adversely affected by war. For this reason the utility of war itself as an instrument of national policy has tended to decline.[71]

The threat value of war as an instrunent of policy may even have an inverse relation to its actual value as an instrument of policy. The excessively high costs of war have added to its nuisance value in the hands of adventurous statesmen. In proportion as war means ruin for all if actually resorted to, more responsible statesmen will tend to yield to the demands of those who threaten it. The bombing air-

[69] Above, chap. ix, sec. 3b, Table 46, Appen. XXI.

[70] Above, chap. vii, sec. 5c; chap. x.

[71] Williams, op. cit., pp. 45 ff.; Shotwell, What Germany Forgot. Eugene Staley (War and the Private Investor [New York, 1935]) and Jacob Viner ("Political Aspects of International Finance," Journal of Business of the University of Chicago, April and July, 1928; and Southwestern Political and Social Science Quarterly, March, 1929) have shown that modern bankers and investors have usually favored peace for economic reasons. It has been more common for navies and governments to seek the aid of foreign investors than for foreign investors to seek the aid of navies and governments. This is also the opinion of Hoffman Nickerson (op. cit., p. 176), who links sentimentalists and financiers together as friends of peace. See above, n. 60.

plane, directly threatening civilian populations, has been particularly useful as a support for diplomacy and was doubtless largely accountable for the successes of Mussolini and Hitler in warding off intervention by England and France in the cases of Ethiopia, Spain, Czechoslovakia, and Albania. In these cases war potential rather than war itself served as an effective instrument of national policy.[72] Since, however, the diplomatic use of war potential may easily result in war itself, destuctive to the policies of all participants if not to civilization itself, there is a general interest in eliminating that use. Not only resort to war but even more a threat of war should be regarded as a crime. Hitler's threat of war at Munich in September, 1938, was no less criminal than his use of war in Poland in September, 1939.[73]

Modern military technique has centralized world-power in the few governments utilizing it most efficiently, has made war suicidal among these governments, has diminished the role of strictly military activity in war, and has augmented the nuisance value of war threats as an aid to the diplomacy of unscrupulous governments.

4. PROPOSALS FOR MODIFYING MILITARY TECHNIQUE

The state of deadlock and exceptional destructiveness manifested by World War I led to four different proposals for modifying the character or control of military technique.

a) *Professionalization of military forces.*—Military writers often favored the stimulation of military invention and the further development of offensive weapons such as the airplane and tank; the reduction of numbers while increasing the length of service and efficiency of the personnel of the armed forces; the development of rules of war and of military discipline so as to confine war to the armed forces; and in general changes to make war a more controllable instrument, less subject to the immediate influence of popular emotions. Such a program of professionalizing the military forces would have the effect of strengthening the relative power of the offensive in war and of increasing the importance of *the military way* in world-politics. Some expected it to assure more rapid decisions and more

---

[72] F. S. Dunn, *Peaceful Change* (New York, 1937), pp. 8 ff.

[73] Q. Wright, "The Munich Settlement and International Law," *American Journal of International Law*," XXXIII (1939), 12–33.

limited wars,[74] thus giving a fleeting political predominance within a flexible balance of power to the nation at the moment most efficient in militarization. Others believed it would promote conquest, eliminate small political units, destroy the balance of power, integrate continental regions under the hegemony of the most efficient, and perhaps eventually integrate these regions under a world-empire of the most efficient nation of all.[75]

b) Qualitative disarmament.—Pacifist writers and disarmament conferences often favored the general elimination of offensive weapons and the improvement of national defenses through fixed fortifications. This program, usually called *qualitative disarmament*,[76] was expected to hamper rapid invasion and to make a mutually destructive deadlock so certain, in the event of war, that no state would attempt war at all or even threaten it.[77] The smaller states, it was hoped by advocates of this theory, might defend their frontiers effectively even against great-power neighbors if the latter were deprived of the more important offensive weapons.

c) Balance of power.—"Realistic" political writers often favored a more efficient application by all states of *balance-of-power* principles both in diplomacy and in military policy. They assumed that every state, if it properly understood its interests, should always be on the

[74] See Appen. XXIII.

[75] This appears to be the view of some German theorists of the *Lebensraum* and *Geopolitik* schools (Kruszewski, *op. cit.*). See also Heinrich Triepel, *Die Hegemonie, ein Buch von fuhrenden Staaten* (Stuttgart, 1938); Herman Rauschning, *The Revolution of Nihilism* (New York, 1939).

[76] Proposals for disarmed frontier zones, neutralized areas, and "buffer states" and a general strengthening of the isolation of neutrals have sometimes been considered in this category, but the effect would probably be in the direction of the first proposal, because the localization of war would tend to increase the opportunities of the well-prepared aggressor to expand step by step. Thoroughgoing disarmament schemes, eliminating defensive as well as offensive armaments, if adopted, prior to a general change of political motivations or the establishment of a supergovernment, might have a similar effect.

[77] Victor Lefebure, *Scientific Disarmament* (New York, 1931). Quotations illustrating the argument for qualitative disarmament at the conference, 1932–33, are given in Q. Wright (ed.), *An American Foreign Policy toward International Stability* (Chicago, 1935), pp. 17 ff. See also Marion Boggs, "The Distinction between Aggressive and Defensive Armaments in Diplomacy and Strategy" (manuscript thesis, University of Chicago, 1940). It should be noticed that quantitative differing from qualitative disarmament might have the effect of increasing the possibility of maneuver, thus improving the relative position of the offensive.

alert to prevent any state from dangerously increasing its relative power. The weaker should, therefore, either form alliances and rearm to thwart successful aggression by the strongest or employ their diplomatic skill to break up that state's alliances, to isolate it morally and politically, to hamper its access to war materials, and to weaken its military potential in every way.[78] Because of the regional limitations of military force and the tendency for the weaker and less immediately interested states to be neutral, such a system has tended toward the hegemony of each of the great powers in the regions most subject to their power,[79] the balance being maintained among those powers.

d) Collective security.—"Idealistic" political writers often favored transfer of dominant military force, or at least the use of such force, to a League of Nations or a world federal union capable of assuring *collective security*. The League of Nations experimented with collective procedures for determining aggression and other violations of basic law, for making essential changes in that law, and for applying sanctions. The League's sanctions depended upon contingents voluntarily contributed by various states, and of economic pressure upon the aggressor and economic assistance to the victim. A League police equipped with specialized weapons possessed only by the League was discussed but not accepted. This program assumed that, if it were certain that a state which had had recourse to war would be speedily suppressed, states would confine themselves to nonmilitary means for carrying out their policies.[80]

[78] Neutrality and nonintervention, though usually favoring aggression (above, n. 76), may place a state in the position to "hold the balance of power," i.e., the capacity to intervene on the weaker side in major crises, thus restoring the balance (Schuman, *International Politics* [New York, 1933], pp. 54 ff.; Frank M. Russell, *Theories of International Relations* [New York, 1936], pp. 317 ff.).

[79] See Karl Haushofer, *Weltpolitik von heute* (Berlin, 1936); Triepel, *op. cit.;* Johannes Mattern, "From Geopolitik to Political Relativism," in *Essays in Honor of W. W. Willoughby* (Baltimore, 1937), pp. 125 ff.

[80] See International Institute of Intellectual Cooperation, International Studies Conference, *Collective Security* (London, 1935); Sir Alfred Zimmern, *The League of Nations and the Rule of Law* (London, 1936); James T. Shotwell, *On the Rim of the Abyss* (New York, 1936); Royal Institute of International Affairs, *Sanctions* ("Information Department Papers," No. 17 [New York, 1935]); Q. Wright (ed.), *Neutrality and Collective Security* (Chicago, 1936); Walter Laves (ed.), *International Security* (Chicago, 1939).

The weakness of a league, relying upon the good faith of sovereign states to carry out their obligations and to agree to necessary changes in the *status quo*, led to suggestions of a union or federal organization providing a central authority resting directly upon world public opinion and dealing within its sphere with individuals throughout its territory.

Some, regarding moral force as eventually more powerful than physical force, abandoned hope of solving the problem of world-organization by either military or political changes and sought to create human solidarity by modifying ideals and values through ethical and religious appeals. They hoped that the material implications of sovereignty and the utility of military force might be gradually eliminated by change of the ultimate source of political power, the opinions and ideas of the individual citizen and soldier.[81] But whether through a league, a union, or an ideal, these plans are alike in rejecting neutrality and the balance of power and in emphasizing the world-community.

These proposals differ in their assumptions as to what is easiest to change. The first proposal assumed that national sovereignty, as the focus of individual loyalties, cannot or should not be changed but that military techniques and methods can be. The remaining proposals successively manifested an increasing belief in the feasibility of modifying the present exclusive focusing of human loyalty upon national sovereignty, and a diminishing belief in the possibility of modifying the trend toward the maximum utilization of science and technology in the application of military force when force has been resorted to. It is, furthermore, clear that the first and second of these proposals looked in opposite directions. It is impossible to strengthen the relative position of both the offensive and the defensive at the same time.

5. MILITARY TECHNIQUE AND CIVILIZATION

In the past, cycles of war have tended to move from (1) the technique of agility and pounce to (2) the technique of momentum and

---

[81] See Clarence Streit, *Union Now* (New York, 1939); William P. Maddox (ed.), *European Plans for World Order* (Philadelphia, 1940).

mass charge followed by (3) the technique of discipline and maneuver which in time moves to (4) deadlock and the war of attrition.[82]

The first two of these four stages have in past civilizations been
dominated by the offensive spirit illustrated in the Classical civilization before the time of Augustus (27 B.C.) and in Western civilization before the "Babylonian captivity" of the papacy (A.D. 1309).
The last two stages have been dominated by the defensive spirit.
Rome expanded little after Augustus but defended its frontiers.
Christendom did little crusading after Boniface but defended itself
from Arabs, Turks, and Tartars.[83]

A parallelism may, however, be detected between the offensive
and defensive periods in that each began with reliance upon quality
in its armies and ended with reliance upon quantity.

The military history of modern civilization exhibits analogies to
these earlier civilizations. The highly trained but relatively small
armies of the sixteenth, seventeenth, and eighteenth centuries capable of pouncing upon and paralyzing their enemies rapidly, especially when those enemies were Americans, Asiatics, or Africans
without modern arms, grew gradually in size as population increased
and methods of transportation and communication improved. When
at war with one another they relied more and more upon defensive
fortifications and siegecraft, but their basic strategy and tactics
continued with little change until the French revolutionary period.[84]

Napoleonic doctrine, built on universal conscription and the revolutionary spirit, held that military power varies mechanically as the
product of the mass and the mobility of the army. This doctrine,
however, emphasized morale even more than material and might
have been formulated from this point of view that military strength
varies morally as the product of the zeal of the nation and the perse-
verance of the army in the strategical and tactical offensive.[85] Gen-

---

[82] Above, chap. vii, secs. 3c and 6.

[83] The dates suggested for these dividing-points are arbitrary. The end of medieval
expansion might be pushed back to the fall of Acre in 1291, extinguishing the kingdom
of Jerusalem, or forward to the Black Death in 1348, which contributed much to the
permanent elimination of the offensive spirit of medieval Christendom.

[84] See above, nn. 10 and 11.

[85] Nickerson, *op. cit.*, pp. 141 ff.; Liddell Hart, *The Remaking of Modern Armies*,
pp. 88 ff.

eral acceptance of this doctrine of the nation in arms since the mid-nineteenth century may mark the transition to the second stage of modern warfare. National self-consciousness had been developed by Fichte, Mazzini, and Treitschke,[86] and the doctrine of mass warfare had been developed by Clausewitz and his successors, especially in Germany.[87] The practice of this type of warfare was facilitated by the use of the railroad for mass mobilization and of heavy mobile artillery for battering through. Its possibilities and tendencies were illustrated by the operations of Grant and Moltke, Kuropatkin and Oyama, Hindenburg and Foch.[88]

Throughout the entire modern period the doctrine of the strategic offensive has in general dominated.[89] Modern civilization was expanding on land and sea, and by the time of World War I it had superficially covered the globe. There were still nooks and corners in Africa, the Pacific, and Asia where it had not penetrated, but in the main its task appeared to be no longer external expansion but internal reorganization and integration.[90]

The progress toward totalitarian war and the spirit of the offensive continues, but the war of 1940 differs from that of 1914 in its greater mechanization and greater reluctance to sacrifice masses of men in frontal attacks. While modern civilization, viewed in the large, seems to be passing from its "heroic age" to the "time of troubles," which in past civilization has been characterized by an extraordinary development of mass warfare, this stage may be proceeding so

[86] On the rise of modern nationalism see C. J. H. Hayes, *Essays on Nationalism* (New York, 1926); J. C. King, "Some Elements of National Solidarity" (manuscript, University of Chicago, 1933), chap. ix.

[87] See works of von der Goltz, Bernhardi, and Freytag-Loringhaven cited. "The conduct of war . . . . has generally been supposed to mean the direction of armies and navies and therefore a matter to be left to soldiers and sailors. Today at least we should be aware that it means the direction for a special purpose of the whole power and resources of the nation" (Major-General Sir Frederick Maurice, *Governments and War* [London, 1926], p. 123).

[88] See Rose, *op. cit.*, chaps. i and ii; "A. L. C. Moltke's Plans of Campaign," *Military Historian and Economist*, I (1916), 297; Fuller, *op. cit.*, pp. 75 ff.

[89] There was an exception in the eighteenth century with respect, however, only to European wars (Nickerson, *op. cit.*, pp. 114 ff.; see above, chap. ix, sec. 3).

[90] See Ramsay Muir, *The Expansion of Europe* (Boston, 1923), P. T. Moon, *Imperialism and World Politics* (New York, 1926), and F. Schuman, *International Politics*, pp. 93 ff., for description of the process by which Europe expanded over the world.

rapidly that already signs are appearing of the third stage, that is, the war of maneuver with a defensive spirit and reliance upon the quality rather than the quantity of the army.[91]

Classical and Western civilizations each made such a transition in military techniques, but the political consequences of the change were different in the two cases. Classical civilization became politically organized in the universal state of Rome, and the army became the police force of that state, efficiently defending its frontiers and preserving internal peace for over two centuries. In Western Christendom, on the other hand, Boniface's hope of a centralized control by a universal church, Dante's hope of a centralized control by a universal empire, and Dubois's hope of a centralized control by a universal federation of monarchs—all three expressed in the first decade of the fourteenth century—failed of realization.[92] The Holy Roman Empire and the Catholic church were weakened by internal dissention. Mercenary armies served to defend Christendom, efficiently in Spain and inadequately in the Balkans, but they did not constitute the policy of a centralized Christendom. They were armies of the rising national states, not all of which were satisfied to defend existing frontiers. England had been expanding at the expense of Wales, Scotland, and Ireland and was about to wage the Hundred Years' War of conquest against France and then to endure the bitter Civil War of the Roses; Switzerland and Bohemia were to struggle for independence; Italian states were to engage in a series of struggles for ascendancy in the Italian peninsula, as were Spanish states in the Iberian peninsula and German states in the empire. The *pax ecclesia* did not achieve as enduring an organization as did the *pax Romana*. Western civilization declined in ceaseless internal wars of contending states and factions and steadily lost territory to the Turks, until it began to be absorbed by the rising world-civilization, inaugurated by the discoveries, the inventions, the Renaissance, and the Reformation.[93]

[91] Such a transition is anticipated by such military writers as Fuller, Liddell Hart, Nickerson, etc. (see above, n. 28).

[92] These proposals are summarized by Russell, *op. cit.*, pp. 99 ff.; see also Appen. III.

[93] See Oman, *The Art of War in the Middle Ages* (New York, 1924), and above, chaps. vii and viii.

The proposals which have been made for a more scientific organization of peace and for a more scientific organization of war suggest the alternatives before the contemporary world. The offensive power of armies may be so much weakened through continuance of the trend, perhaps augmented by disarmament agreements and change of popular evaluations from the standards of national power to those of human welfare, that all will give up the hope of or interest in dominance, and an adequate League of Nations with an efficient police or a voluntary world-union may be able to assure both collective security and peaceful change. Such a trend may be illustrated by the federal organizations of the United States, Canada, Australia, and other states, by the change of the Monroe Doctrine from a policy of United States hegemony to the Good Neighbor and Pan-Americanism, by the change of the British Empire to a voluntary commonwealth of nations, and by the attempts at world-union at the Hague and Geneva.[94]

On the other hand, national states may modify the techniques of the armies so as to favor the offensive as suggested by the initial experience with the *Blitzkrieg* in World War II, and a period of balance-of-power wars may prevent the integration of such a collective system and tend toward a series of regional hegemonies, perhaps eventuating in world conquest and empire by one state.[95]

The trend of military history since 1932 has looked toward a third alternative. On the one hand, states adopted more extensive conscription laws, maintained larger standing armies, voted larger military appropriations, provided more efficient frontier defenses, and strove for a higher degree of economic self-sufficiency. On the other hand, they utilized centralized propaganda instruments and economic controls to develop in each population a more fanatical and aggressive national spirit. The combination of these policies precipitated World War II and may tend toward frequent general wars on a gigantic scale, with the eventual destruction of civilization.

[94] See Lord Davies, *The Problem of the Twentieth Century* (London, 1930); Russell, *op. cit.*, pp. 327 ff.; Streit, *op. cit.*; and above, nn. 77 and 81.

[95] Above, n. 75.

CHAPTER XIII

THEORY OF MODERN WAR

1. GENERAL CHARACTERISTICS OF THE LAW OF WAR

IN THE chapter on historic warfare it has been pointed out that in most civilizations theories have developed which are international but not law, defining the circumstances in which war can properly be resorted to (*jus ad bellum*) and the methods which can properly be used in waging war (*jus in bello*).[1] Each of the states in these civilizations has usually established rules which are law but not international, limiting private warmaking and regulating private profits from war.[2] The first of these bodies of doctrine has served to reconcile war with the fundamental values of the civilization and the second to promote the sovereignty and efficiency of the states.[3]

In the modern period the same two bodies of doctrine are observable. Modern states have made laws designed, with increasing comprehensiveness, to reduce or to eliminate private warmaking; booty and bounties to generals and soldiers; prizes and prize money to privateers, admirals, and sailors; war profits to traders, manufacturers, and financiers.[4] These laws have had more or less success in making war a monopoly of the state to be used only for "reason of state" and not for private profit. They have also had an influence both on the development of international law[5] and on the totalitarianization of war.[6]

International standards have in the modern period achieved a more definitely juristic character than ever before. In spite of Cic-

---

[1] See above, chap. vii, n. 172.   [2] See above, chap. vii, n. 173.

[3] See above, chap. vii, sec. 3b. Some jurists, utilizing a narrow definition of law, hold that even in modern times international law is a misnomer and that its subject matter consists of these two types of rules (see J. F. Stephen, *History of the Criminal Law of England*, II [London, 1883], 34–37, 44–58; J. K. Stephen, *International Law and International Relations* [London, 1884]; for opposing position see J. Westlake, *Chapters on the Principles of International Law* [Cambridge, 1894], pp. 11 ff.).

[4] See above, chap. vii, n. 173.

[5] See below, n. 19.   [6] See above, chap. xii, sec. 2c, d.

ero's aphorism, *inter arma leges silent,* this has been particularly true of the *jus in bello,* which has achieved a detailed exposition in adjudications of prize and other courts, army and navy regulations, bilateral treaties, and the general conventions and declarations of Paris (1856), Geneva (1864, 1906, 1929), St. Petersburg (1868), The Hague (1899, 1907, 1923), and London (1909, 1930).[7] The rules thus prescribed and the degree of their enforcement have undoubtedly influenced the frequency and characteristics of war. Far-reaching regulation of military methods and instruments, if rigorously enforced, might do away with many of the evils of war, but such a result would tend to reduce the reluctance to resort to war and so to make war more frequent. On the other hand, if rules of war are lax or unenforced, war is more severe if it comes, but tends to come less frequently.

Modern civilization, like past civilizations,[8] has tended during the past century toward an assertion of more and more rigorous rules of war but less and less observance of them in major wars. The latter result can be attributed to the decline of the conception of "military honor" with the reduction of the professional and mercenary elements in armies and the rise of universal military service; to the rise of the conception of "the nation in arms" with the growth in efficiency of propagandas of national fanaticism; to the breakdown of the distinction between combatants and noncombatants with the wide entry of the civilians into the supply services, with the increasing military regimentation of national economy and morale, and with the increasing technical possibility of attack behind the lines from the air and by blockade; and, as a result of all these, to the development of the conception of "absolute war" and of broadened interpretations of "military necessity."[9] These tendencies of modern

[7] G. Butler and S. Maccoby, *The Development of International Law* (London, 1928); P. C. Jessup and F. Deak (eds.), *Neutrality: Its History, Economics and Law* (4 vols.; New York, 1935); A. Pearce Higgins, *The Hague Peace Conferences* (Cambridge, 1909); J. B. Moore, *International Law and Some Current Illusions* (New York, 1924), chap. v; M. O. Hudson (ed.), *International Legislation* (6 vols.; 1919–34), V, 1–63, 417.

[8] See above, chap. vii, n. 186.

[9] See above, chap. xii, sec. 2. Q. Wright, *The Causes of War and the Conditions of Peace* (London, 1935), pp. 61–62.

civilization have been accompanied by a decreasing frequency and increasing seriousness of war.[10]

The *jus ad bellum* retrogressed through most of the modern period. The medieval conception of just war was abandoned in the seventeenth century, and not until the establishment of the League of Nations was serious juristic attention again given to the problem. Prior to World War I international law provided no substantive and few procedural limitations upon resort to war and only certain vague qualifications upon lesser uses of force in reprisals, intervention, and defense. While legal theory confined the latter to action necessary to prevent an immediately impending, irreparable injury to territory, government, or nationals, practice included in the concept of defense broad policies like the Monroe Doctrine and the balance of power.[11] With respect to the initiation of war itself, the absence of any legal limitations was indicated by the doctrine of neutrality which asserted that third parties could not make a judgment of law on the legitimacy of such initiation and must act with formal impartiality.[12]

Modern history, which coincides with the disintegration of Western Christendom and of other historic civilizations, and which constitutes the "heroic age" of the rising world-civilization, might be expected to be peculiarly unfavorable to an effective *jus ad bellum*, and this expectation has not been disappointed.[13] Law effectively controlling or forbidding resort to war is, however, an essential condition, though by no means the only condition, of peace.[14] The his-

[10] See above, chap. ix, sec. 3.

[11] See Q. Wright, "The Outlawry of War," *American Journal of International Law*, XIX (January, 1925), 89–94; "The Meaning of the Pact of Paris," *ibid.*, XXVII (January, 1933), 42–49; G. G. Wilson, *International Law* (9th ed.; New York, 1935), chaps. viii, ix, and xvi.

[12] See below, nn. 35 and 56.   [13] See above, chap. vii, sec. 7d.

[14] "Because they do not like the idea of an international organisation compact of prohibitions and restraints, because they cleave to the doctrine of 'love your neighbor' and practise prayer and gentleness, the thurifers of the reign of peace have warmly applauded the advent of permanent peace each time it seemed to have come—first after the war of 1870, then after the Alabama arbitration in 1872, on the occasion of the two peace conferences of 1899 and 1907, at the time of the creation of the League of Nations in 1919 and of the Pact of Paris in 1928. They have been apt to forget—nay, they have deliberately forgotten—that the contribution of law, though it be only a part of what morality enjoins, is the most essential part, the minimum part, and one which cannot exist unless it is supported by force. They have forgotten—deliberately forgotten—

tory of modern international law will be traced in an effort to ascertain the degree in which it has in fact tended to become a law of peace. For this purpose four periods separated by the terminations of the Thirty Years' War (1648) and by the initiation of the French Revolution (1789) and World War I (1914) will be considered.

2. DEVELOPMENT OF MODERN INTERNATIONAL LAW

a) *Period of religious wars (1492–1648).*—The medieval idea of chivalry and of a universal order both temporal and religious was in large measure scrapped by the *real politic* of Machiavelli, the fanaticism of religious war, and the idea of territorial sovereignty. The humane spirit could not, however, be wholly suppressed, and seaborne commerce could not continue without international law.[15] Furthermore, law was necessary for the conduct and discipline of diplomatic and military administration in the new territorial states priding themselves on their efficiency.[16] These two factors, the sentiment of humanity and reason of state, acting upon the institutions and practices developed by the maritime commerce and the interprincely relations of the later Middle Ages, created modern international law.[17]

The first formulator of this law was Francis of Victoria, a Dominican friar of Salamanca, whose humane spirit had become interested in the problem as a consequence of the conquest of Mexico by Cor-

---

that law is to charity what John the Baptist was to Christ, the lesser preparing the way for the greater. That is the reason why the nations have been compelled to choose; either to persevere in their mad career of faith, in their course of an unfounded confidence, or to tread the prudent path of international hypocrisy and armed mistrust" (C. Van Vollenhoven, *The Law of Peace* [London, 1936], p. 256). See also Q. Wright, "The Outlawry of War," *op. cit.*, pp. 102–3.

[15] T. Walker, *History of the Law of Nations* (Cambridge, 1899), pp. 188–95; Van Vollenhoven, *op. cit.*, pp. 84 ff.

[16] Walker, *op. cit.*, p. 58. "International law is seen to be a composite or mixture of three kinds of law: the rules derived from the laws of war; the rules derived from the law protecting the merchants engaged in foreign commerce; and the more recent law, in the process of making which would insure a minimum of security against inhuman treatment in all parts of the world" (Ellery Stowell, *International Law* [New York, 1931], p. 7). Perhaps a fourth kind of law that relates to the practices of diplomacy and treaty-making should be added (see below, n. 52).

[17] Van Vollenhoven, *op. cit.;* Walker, *op. cit.*, pp. 138 ff.

tez.[18] Francis of Victoria delivered his lectures in 1532, and fifty years later the second important treatise on the subject was written by Balthazar Ayala, serving as judge advocate general of the Spanish armies in the Netherlands "to keep that army in good discipline and justice."[19]

The notion that sovereign princes, though supreme in their own domains, are bound by law in their external relations was emphasized by the habits of making treaties and exchanging diplomatic officers,[20] by the mutually advantageous practices for the benefit of maritime commerce,[21] by the tradition of common Christian civilization,[22] by the conception of natural law and a state of nature,[23] and perhaps also by the personal relationship and sense of common interest among the kings themselves.[24] It was natural for them to act on the assumption that they should not become so hostile to one another that they could not assist one another in the common problem of preserving their positions against dissatisfied nobles and commoners.[25]

[18] J. B. Scott, *Francisco de Vitoria and His Law of Nations: The Spanish Origins of International Law* (Oxford, 1934), chap. iii.

[19] From commission by Philip II to Ayala, May 27, 1580 (Balthazar Ayala, *De jure et officiis bellicis et disciplina militari* [Carnegie ed.; Washington, 1912], Introduction by John Westlake, I, iv).

[20] Julius Goebel, *The Equality of States* (New York, 1923), pp. 30 ff.

[21] Van Vollenhoven, *op. cit.*, chap. i.

[22] This was emphasized by Victoria and Suarez of the Spanish school, but Grotius also emphasized the obligations peculiar to Christian princes. These writers also recognized that international law accorded certain rights to non-Christian communities, but practice was at first otherwise (see Wright, *Mandates under the League of Nations* [Chicago, 1930], p. 7; Butler and Maccoby, *op. cit.*, pp. 20 ff.).

[23] E. D. Dickinson, *The Equality of States in International Law* (Cambridge, 1920), chap. i.

[24] Roscoe Pound, "Philosophical Theory and International Law," *Bibliotheca Visseriana* (Leiden, 1923), Vol. I.

[25] This solidarity of the interests of princes was exhibited in the attempts to enforce the principle of legitimacy in the post-Napoleonic conferences. During the Dutch rebellion of the sixteenth century Ayala, as a loyal official of the Spanish sovereign, laid it down that international law forbade resistance to a legitimate sovereign (chap. ii, secs. 10–23), and the rule was repeated with some qualification by Vattel (Book III, sec. 290), though he was less ready to permit third states to intervene in behalf of the prince, victim of rebellion, than was Ayala. Charles II on several occasions considered it expedient to collaborate with Louis XIV against his parliament (see Clyde L. Grose, "The Dun-

The developing law of nations was handed on by the Spanish school and by the Italian Gentili, diplomatic and legal adviser to Queen Elizabeth, to Hugo Grotius, Dutch lawyer, theologian, and diplomatist.[26] Inspired by a humanitarian desire to ameliorate the practices he witnessed during the Thirty Years' War,[27] learned in the logic of Roman law and scholastic disputation, and aware of the characteristics of the rising state system, Grotius gave the new ideology of international law a more systematic form. His whole treatment of the law of nations sprang from his original problem of determining the justifiability of military violence.[28] He contemplated a family of Christian monarchs, each enforcing law in his own realm but ready to co-operate to punish the violator of the law of nations, especially the initiator of a war which was unjust according to the medieval conception.[29] Neutrality was thus excluded unless it was impossible to determine which side in a war was just.[30] The conduct of war itself, he realized, must be governed by military necessity, but he urged *temperamenta belli* when possible in the interest of humanity and of negotiating peace.[31]

The purpose of the developing law was, therefore, justice and peace. It regarded war as a misfortune, generally unnecessary, and never justifiable except as a handmaid of law. The practice of

---

kirk Money, 1662," *Journal of Modern History*, V [March, 1933], 1–18). The trend of modern history has been for sovereigns to prefer their subjects to their brother-sovereigns even to the extent of aiding foreign rebels when it seemed expedient, as it did to some, during the Dutch, Swiss, American, Belgian, Balkan, and other insurrections (see Butler and Maccoby, *op. cit.*, pp. 17 ff.).

[26] For a brief account of early development of the science of international law see L. Oppenheim, *International Law* (5th ed.; London, 1937), Vol. I, secs. 52 ff.; Westlake, *op. cit.*, pp. 25 ff.; Walker, *op. cit.*, pp. 244 ff.

[27] Grotius, *De jure belli ac pacis* (Carnegie ed.; Oxford, 1925), Prolegomena, sec. 28.

[28] *Ibid.*, secs. 33–35.

[29] *Ibid.*, Book II, chap. xx, sec. 40, pars. 1, 4; chap. xxv, sec. 6; Van Vollenhoven, *The Three Stages in the Evolution of the Law of Nations* (The Hague, 1919), pp. 13 ff. For Grotius' statement of just causes of war see his *De jure belli ac pacis*, Book II, chap. i, sec. 2, par. 2.

[30] *De jure belli ac pacis*, Book III, chap. xvii, sec. 3, par. 1.

[31] *Ibid.*, chaps. xii–xiv.

statesmen, however, followed the precepts of Machiavelli rather than of those of Grotius.[32]

b) Period of political absolutism (1648–1789).—The period following the Thirty Years' War has been called by recent historians of international law "the Age of the Judge,"[33] referring to the legalistic character that international relations assumed under the influence of the increasing number of text-writers on the subject, the multiplication of treaties, and the activities of diplomatic officers and occasional international conferences. The initiation and waging of war and the conduct of diplomacy became formalized, but the Grotian conception of a community of nations enforcing law was not accepted in practice.[34] Instead, the idea developed that international

[32] Van Vollenhoven probably exaggerates in writing: "It would be vapid to say that hardly any trace of primitive law of nations (the practice of the time) is found in Grotius, and, inversely, nothing essential out of Grotius passed into the primitive law of nations" (*The Three Stages in the Evolution of the Law of Nations*, p. 7; see also his *The Law of Peace*, p. 102). The influence of Grotius' system can be seen in the detailed accounts by Butler and Maccoby (*op. cit.*) and by A. P. Higgins (*Cambridge History of the British Empire* [Cambridge, 1929], Vol. I, chaps. vi and xix) of international law as practiced in the seventeenth and eighteenth centuries. Even the Grotian doctrine of sanctions against the lawbreaker was written into the Treaty of Münster (1648, art. 124), printed in F. B. Sayre, *Experiments in International Administration* (New York, 1919), pp. 173 ff., and elaborated in the peace plans of Crucé, Penn, St. Pierre, and others.

[33] Butler and Maccoby, *op. cit.*, pp. 193 ff. Higgins (*Cambridge History of the British Empire*, chap. xix) treats the period 1648–1763 as a unit (see below, Appen. III). Van Vollenhoven (*The Law of Peace*) combines Butler and Maccoby's "Age of the Prince" and "Age of the Judge" into a single period which he calls "Reign of War" (1492–1780), following the medieval period (1150–1492) and followed by the period of "the law of war and peace" (1780–1914) and the period of "the law of peace and war" (1919–31). He hoped for a future period of "the law of peace."

[34] The Grotian idea was implicit in the work of Christian Wolff (1749), who deduced his positive law of nations from the assumption that there was a *civitas maxima*, or great community of states; but practice at the time more conformed to the view of Vattel, who thus stated his dissent from Wolff (1758): "From the outset it will be seen that I differ entirely from Mr. Wolff in the foundation I lay for that division of the Law of Nations which we term voluntary. Mr. Wolff deduces it from the idea of a sort of great republic (civitas maxima) set up by nature herself, of which all the Nations of the world are members. To his mind, the voluntary law of Nations acts as the civil law of this great republic. This does not satisfy me, and I find the fiction of such a republic neither reasonable nor well enough founded to deduce therefrom the rules of a Law of Nations at once universal in character and necessarily accepted by sovereign States. I recognize no other natural society among Nations than that which nature has set up among men in general. It is essential to every civil society (civitas) that each member should yield

law is but natural law based on the agreement and convenience of sovereign princes and that international relations are essentially bilateral, thus permitting neutrality.[35] Principles of law were resorted to in staking out claims in the New World, but the rights of the natives, insisted upon by Victoria, were forgotten. The new territories were *territorium nullius*, subject to acquisition by European discovery and occupation.[36]

Treaties tended to supersede principle as the basis of the international system. Throughout this period the Treaties of Westphalia (1648) were looked upon as the constitution of Europe. These were supplemented by the treaties concluded at Utrecht (1713) and other great conferences. Policy sought to maintain the balance of power which was explicitly recognized as its proper guide in the latter treaty.[37]

The conception of war underwent changes. Instead of an instrument of justice, it came to be considered an instrument of policy. Vattel, who wrote in the middle of the eighteenth century, assumed that, while princes should satisfy themselves that they had a just cause before they initiated war,[38] no one else could pass judgment

---

certain of his rights to the general body, and that there should be some authority capable of giving commands, prescribing laws, and compelling those who refuse to obey. Such an idea is not to be thought of as between Nations. Each independent State claims to be, and actually is, independent of all the others. . . . . It is clear that there is by no means the same necessity for a civil society among Nations as among individuals. It can not be said, therefore, that nature recommends it to an equal degree, far less than it prescribes it" (*The Law of Nations* [Carnegie ed.; Washington, 1916], p. 9a). See also Van Vollenhoven, *The Three Stages in the Evolution of the Law of Nations*, pp. 78 ff.

35 Bynkershoek first clearly stated the idea of impartial neutrality in 1737, thus abandoning the Grotian conception of assisting the just side, though even he qualified impartiality by the duty to carry out pre-war treaties with the belligerents (*Quæstionem juris publici* [Carnegie ed.; Oxford, 1930], Book I, chap. ix). For influences contributing to this concept see Jessup and Deak, *op. cit.*, Vol. I, chap. i; Butler and Maccoby, *op. cit.*, pp. 229 ff.; Higgins, *Cambridge History of the British Empire*, p. 553. See also Raymond Ickes, "Impartiality and Neutrality" (manuscript thesis, University of Chicago, 1936).

36 See M. F. Lindley, *The Acquisition and Government of Backward Territory in International Law* (London, 1926).

37 Harold J. Tobin, *The Termination of Multipartite Treaties* (New York, 1933).

38 *Op. cit.*, Book II, chap. i, sec. 4; Book III, chap. vii, secs. 106 and 107.

on the matter.[39] States with no direct interest in the controversy should be neutral, although qualification of that neutrality by treaties already in existence and by consideration of national interest was permitted.[40] War was a trial by battle or duel whose results determined the merits of the controversy,[41] not the execution of a judgment made after rational consideration of the merits, as it had been in the system of Grotius.[42] The initiation of war became, therefore, for third states a question of fact, not of law. The legal interest of such states lay not in the circumstances of the war's origin but in the legal changes its initiation brought about.[43]

The existence of war brought into operation new rules of law applicable to the relations of belligerents with one another and with neutrals. The latter found not only that their trading rights at sea were considerably limited but also that they were under obligations not to render any official assistance to either belligerent or to allow their territory to be used for belligerent purposes. The United States, geographically separated from the European wars of the post-French

[39] *Ibid.*, Introd., sec. 21; Book III, chap. vii, secs. 118 and 126; see also Butler and Maccoby, *op. cit.*, p. 232. Vattel also held that, though fidelity to treaties is a sacred obligation, a state becomes exempted from the observance of a treaty if to observe it would conflict with the state's duty toward itself (*op. cit.*, Book II, chap. xii, secs. 163 and 170). See Van Vollenhoven (*The Law of Peace*, p. 146), who remarks that Vattel's book "is just as destructive of a law of peace as had been the deeds of men like Pizarro, Cortez and the Duke of Alba. It displays that other fundamental vice, by which I mean the disposition to disguise evil intentions by phrases of sublime charity." For this reason "as soon as the book appears it earns the applause of the governments" (*ibid.*, p. 107).

[40] See above, nn. 35 and 38.

[41] This concept was expressed by Bacon: "Wars are not massacres and confusions, but they are the highest trials of right when princes and states shall put themselves upon the justice of God for deciding their controversies as it shall please him to put on either side" (*Works* [Montague ed.], V, 384). See Q. Wright, "Changes in the Conception of War," *American Journal of International Law*, XVIII (October, 1924), 757, 762. See also Luigi Sturzo, *The International Community and the Right of War* (New York, 1930).

[42] Above, n. 29.

[43] Q. Wright, "Changes in the Conception of War," *op. cit.*, p. 757. The same came to be true of the belligerent's interest in the war. Wars came to be "justified retrospectively," especially after the Napoleonic period (see G. Ferrero, "Forms of War and International Anarchy," in *The World Crisis* [London: Graduate Institute of International Studies, 1938], p. 87).

revolutionary period, contributed greatly to the concept of neutral status and of the rights and duties which flowed therefrom.[44] The rules of war between belligerents tended toward a formalization of war, maintenance of the professional interests of officers, and exemption of civilians and their property from the hardships of war, both on land and on sea.[45]

c) Period of industrial nationalism (1789–1914).—The "public law of Europe" as set forth in the treaties of Westphalia, Utrecht, Paris, etc., and the customary rules of war and neutrality were given rude shocks by the enthusiasm of the French Revolution and by the absolute war of Napoleon.[46]

The post-Napoleonic period was marked by an attempt at international organization inspired, on the one hand, by the czar Alexander's idealistic Holy Alliance and, on the other, by the diplomatic agreements for sustaining the system established by the Treaty of Vienna. This system, however, lost the allegiance of Great Britain because of its inability to distinguish international from domestic questions and its policy of intervention to assist Hapsburg princes claiming to continue their authority by divine right in Spain and Italy. At the same time the United States through the Monroe Doctrine expressed its opposition to the application of the system of Europe in the New World.[47] The idea of the solidarity of the great powers, however, persisted in the "concert of Europe" to maintain the "public law of Europe" and the "balance of power." The concert dealt with revolts in the Netherlands and the Balkans and was utilized by Metternich, Austrian foreign minister, to oppose liberalism and nationalism.

The effort to preserve the *status quo* by identifying it with peace and international solidarity became progressively more difficult as

---

[44] Q. Wright, "The Future of Neutrality," *International Conciliation*, No. 242, September, 1928, pp. 357–67; W. E. Hall, *International Law* (8th ed.; Oxford, 1924), sec. 213, pp. 705 ff.

[45] See above, chap. xii, sec. 1*b*.

[46] See W. A. Phillips and A. H. Reede, *The Napoleonic Period* (New York, 1936), Vol. II of *Neutrality: Its History, Economics and Law*, ed. Jessup and Deak; Ferrero, *op. cit.*

[47] W. Alison Phillips, *The Confederation of Europe* (New York, 1920).

the memory of the Napoleonic Wars receded. The system broke down in the liberal revolutions of 1848, followed by the nationalist revolt against the system in Italy and Germany. With the success of these revolts and the creation of two new "great powers" in the center of Europe, the system of the concert and of international law was revived. Bismarck, who had recently violated all the prescriptions of this system, was now favorable to it, and its application continued in near eastern and African problems. It even sought to deal with the general balance of power through disarmament at the Hague conferences of 1899 and 1907. In the larger aim these conferences failed, although they contributed to the codification of the law of war and the development of international arbitration. Arbitration had been frequently resorted to for minor and some major problems since 1796.[48]

The dominantly economic interest of this period had naturally suggested an international system of communication and police to increase the efficiency of trade and to facilitate the exploitation of backward areas. Numerous international unions on such questions as postal, telegraphic, cable, radio, river, and railroad communications; patents, trade-marks, copyrights; slave trade, the arms trade, epidemic diseases, and the conservation of natural resources had functioned efficiently and unostentatiously.[49] The rapid development of economic internationalism, however, was due less to international law and international institutions than to the liberal commercial policy of Great Britain supported by the dominant position of British sea power and British finance.[50]

As this period advanced, the diverse tendencies of nationalism and internationalism became more and more difficult to reconcile. Bismarck thought the political and economic interests of states could

[48] Butler and Maccoby designate this period "the age of the Concert" (*op. cit.*, pp. 349 ff.). The "Alabama Arbitration" between Great Britain and the United States in 1871 was probably the most important arbitration.

[49] Paul Reinsch, *Public International Unions* (Boston, 1916).

[50] Sir Alfred Zimmern, "The Problem of Collective Security," in *Neutrality and Collective Security*, ed. Q. Wright (Chicago, 1936), p. 34; Zimmern, *The League of Nations and the Rule of Law, 1918–1935* (London, 1936), p. 87. This power acted directly overseas, indirectly in Continental Europe by stabilizing the balance of power.

be dissociated;[51] but, as the economic foundations of effective wa
came to be recognized, the nationalistic spirit more and more sough
to mobilize the internal and external economic activities of the state
for the purpose of national power.[52] On the other hand, the inter
national spirit, favored alike by humanitarians and by bankers and
businessmen who wished an opportunity for secure expansion o
their operations tended to qualify the freedom of national policy
This spirit sought to prevent war, which became more and more
threatening to social and economic life as the latter became organ
ized on a world-basis.[53]

The Grotian conception of a general law functioning for a genuine
world-community appeared to be nearer to realization during the
long periods of peace in the nineteenth century than it had ever
been before. International law, however, in spite of its solidification
and detailed development by international conferences and unions
general and bilateral treaties, international tribunals, diplomatic cor
respondence, and text-writers, had not grappled effectively with the
problem of war.[54] Although reprisals, intervention, and other form
of violence short of war were dealt with in the textbooks on interna
tional law,[55] war itself was throughout the nineteenth century looked
upon as a fact, and the propriety of recourse to it was considered
not a legal question but an ethical question or a political question.[5]
Statesmen justified a war by its success in achieving its immediate

[51] W. B. Harvey, "Tariff Policies and War in Europe, 1870–1914" (manuscript thesis
University of Chicago, 1938); E. L. Woodward, *War and Peace in Europe, 1815–187*
(New York, 1931), pp. 81, 88.

[52] R. G. Hawtrey, *Economic Aspects of Sovereignty* (New York, 1930). Eugene Staley
(*War and the Private Investor* [New York, 1935]) discusses how investments serve
diplomacy (p. 71) and how diplomacy serves investments (p. 140).

[53] Jacob Viner, "Political Aspects of International Finance," *Journal of Business o
the University of Chicago*, April and July, 1928; see also above, chap. x, sec. 3.

[54] Van Vollenhoven, *The Law of Peace*, chap. iii; Zimmern, *The League of Nation
and the Rule of Law*, chap. ix.

[55] A. E. Hindmarsh, *Force in Peace* (Cambridge, 1933).

[56] See above, n. 43. "Such matters as these [whether war can ever be just] are su
premely important, but they belong to morality and theology, and are as much out o
place in a treatise on international law as would be the discussion of the ethics of mar
riage in a book on the law of personal status" (T. J. Lawrence, *The Principles of Inter
national Law* [7th ed.; Boston, 1923], p. 311).

objectives. The old idea of just war appeared less and less in the textbooks which came to be characteristically divided into sections on peace, war, and neutrality. Thus international law condemned itself to deal only with minor controversies. The great controversies for which states were prepared to fight were in practice outside of its competence. Such a theory clearly could not assist in an institutional development for eliminating war. It could only define methods of pacific settlement in the hope that states would voluntarily use them rather than resort to the risk of using their unlimited power to convert a state of peace into a state of war.[57] The relative peace of the nineteenth century was not in fact due to the functioning of an international law of peace but to the *pax Britannica* destined to survive only as long as British sea power and British finance retained their dominant position.

d) Period of world-wars and the League of Nations (1914———).—The general wars which began in 1914 have been as disturbing to the continuity of legal development as were the wars which began in 1618 and 1789. Rules of war and neutrality were forgotten in mutual retaliations, ancient boundaries were discarded, and the doctrine of national self-determination was given legal effect by the creation of new states and of procedures for holding plebiscites, for protecting minorities, and for supervising mandatory administration.[58]

An important change in the conception of war was developed as a consequence of the general acceptance of the League of Nations Covenant and the Pact of Paris in the 1920's. These instruments, springing from American opposition to war and confidence in federalism, British appreciation that its navy could no longer enforce peace alone, and French fear of a war of revenge, were based on the conception that the initiation of war is illegitimate, until such time as the specified peaceful procedures have been exhausted, according to the Covenant or, in any circumstances, according to the Pact.

[57] Zimmern, "The Problem of Collective Security," *op. cit.*, pp. 20 ff.

[58] J. W. Garner, *International Law and the World War* (London, 1920); Q. Wright, "The Effect of the War on International Law," *Minnesota Law Review*, V (1921), 436, 515; "The Effects of the League of Nations Covenant upon International Law," *American Political Science Review*, XIII (1919), 556 ff.; "The End of a Period of Transition," *American Journal of International Law*, XXXI (1937), 604 ff.

The latter permitted war only to a state which had already had war made against it and to others coming to its assistance. A state was never justified in initiating a state of war. The primary belligerent was always an aggressor.[59]

This conception differed both from the Grotian conception, which considered war a suitable procedure for enforcing a just cause, and from the Vattelian conception, which considered war a fact, the propriety of originating which was outside law altogether. From being a right and then a fact, war had become a crime. On the basis of the latter conception definite progress was made toward the institutionalizing of procedures for defining and suppressing aggression.[60]

In the great post–World War I documents—the Covenant of the League of Nations, the Statute of the Permanent Court of International Justice, the Constitution of the International Labour Organization, and the Pact of Paris for the Renunciation of War—the notions of the world-community, the system of international law, the liberties of nationalities and minorities, the protection of human rights, the perpetuation of peace, general disarmament, and progressive international legislation were all envisaged, and procedures of collective security and peaceful change were set up to realize them. Under this system the position of nonbelligerents became very different from that of traditional neutrals.[61] Peace was thought of as indivisible; war was recognized as affecting the interests of all.[62]

This system, however, was not immediately accepted. National

[59] Q. Wright, "The Outlawry of War," *op. cit.*, pp. 76 ff.; "The Meaning of the Pact of Paris," *op. cit.*, pp. 39 ff.; "Collective Rights and Duties for the Enforcement of Treaties," *Proceedings of the American Society of International Law, 1932*, pp. 101 ff.; Sir John Fischer Williams, *Some Aspects of the Covenant of the League of Nations* (Oxford, 1934), pp. 103 ff.

[60] Q. Wright, "The Concept of Aggression in International Law," *American Journal of International Law*, XXIX (July, 1935), 373 ff.; "The Test of Aggression in Italo-Ethiopian War," *ibid.*, XXX (January, 1936), 45 ff.; "The Munich Settlement and International Law," *ibid.*, XXXIII (January, 1939), 12 ff.

[61] Q. Wright, "Neutrality and Neutral Rights Following the Pact of Paris," *Proceedings of the American Society of International Law, 1930*, pp. 79 ff.; "The Present Status of Neutrality," *American Journal of International Law*, XXXIV (July, 1940) 391 ff.

[62] Sir Alfred Zimmern (*The League of Nations and the Rule of Law, 1918–1935*) discusses the aspirations and the policies of the League.

politicians and public opinions, in greater or lesser degree, tended to resist encroachments upon national sovereignty and also upon the war system in so far as it might foster national solidarity.[63] Many national economic interests, dependent on national preference, protection, or preparedness, were not ready to give up these advantages.[64] National isolationists, imperialists, and reformers, accustomed to use the sovereignty of the state for preserving the peculiarities, spreading the blessings, or improving the character of the national cultures, often hesitated to tamper with that symbol.[65] National lawyers and logicians, learned in a professional ritual, imbued with respect for traditions, and remote from the technological con-

[63] See Q. Wright, "National Sovereignty and Collective Security," *Annals of American Academy of Political and Social Science*, July, 1936. This factor operated to some extent in all countries but especially in the dictatorially governed countries in which public opinion was in large measure controlled by the government (see Max Lerner, "The Pattern of Dictatorship," in *Dictatorship in the Modern World*, ed. Guy Stanton Ford [Minneapolis, 1935]; Frederick L. Schuman, *The Nazi Dictatorship* [New York, 1935]; R. M. MacIver, M. J. Bonn, and R. B. Perry, *The Roots of Totalitarianism* [Philadelphia: American Academy of Political and Social Science, 1940]).

[64] The nature of the special economic interests favoring exclusiveness and the method of their operation are discussed by Philip G. Wright (*Protection, Benefits and Burdens* [Freeport, Ill., 1930]; "The Objects of Protection," *Tariff Review*, March, 1927). H. C. Engelbrecht and F. C. Hannighan (*Merchants of Death* [New York, 1934]) discuss the activities of the armament interests, and Walter Millis (*The Martial Spirit* [New York, 1931]) discusses the activities of the newspaper interests in bringing on the Spanish-American War.

[65] The argument for national self-sufficiency in the interest of security, illustrated by W. B. Donham (*Business Adrift* [New York, 1931]), Samuel Crowther (*America Self-contained* [New York, 1933]), and Charles A. Beard (*The Open Door at Home* [New York, 1935]), is analyzed by Alvin H. Hansen (*Report of the Commission of Inquiry into National Policy in International Economic Relations* [Minneapolis, 1934], pp. 108 ff.). The argument for imperialism in the interest of national security, prosperity, and civilization, illustrated by J. R. Seeley (*The Expansion of England* [London, 1883], Lecture 8) and Hjalmar Schacht ("Germany's Colonial Demands," *Foreign Affairs*, January, 1937, pp. 223 ff.), is analyzed by Parker T. Moon (*Imperialism and World Politics* [New York, 1926], chaps. iv and xix); Grover Clark (*A Place in the Sun* [New York, 1936]); and a Study Group of the Royal Institute of International Affairs (*The Colonial Problem* [London, 1937]). The argument for national self-sufficiency in the interest of social reform and peace, illustrated by Bennett Champ Clark ("Detour around War," *Harper's*, December, 1935), is analyzed by Henry A. Wallace (*America Must Choose* ["World Affairs Pamphlets" (New York, 1934)]); Eugene Staley (*World Economy in Transition* [New York, 1939]); and Cornelia Groth ("The Foreign Trade Policy of the New Deal" [manuscript, University of Chicago, 1936]).

ditions of communication and war, which made the older conceptions of sovereignty, national interest, and neutrality inadequate,
offered passive and sometimes active resistance to the new ideas.[66]

With its institutions still young and not even formally ratified by
all states, with its logic inadequately appreciated even by its protagonists, the organization of the world-community found both its
power and its machinery insufficient when confronted by really dangerous crises. Political institutions, as Bagehot has pointed out, require both *dignified* parts to give them power and *efficient* parts to
direct that power to appropriate ends,[67] or in more recent terminology they need a symbolic structure to attract opinion and an administrative machine to focus it on concrete problems.[68] The League
of Nations had not been able to develop the one, which is the by-
product of venerable antiquity, or to perfect the other through long
experience in adapting institutions to changing circumstances.[69]

[66] See, e.g., J. B. Moore, "An Appeal to Reason," *Foreign Affairs*, July, 1933, and
comments upon it by Q. Wright, "The Path to Peace," *World Unity*, XIII (December,
1933), 135 ff. Edwin Borchard and William P. Lage, *Neutrality for the United States*
(New Haven, 1937) and comments upon it by Q. Wright, *Southern Quarterly*, spring,
1938.

[67] Walter Bagehot, *The English Constitution* (New York, 1893), p. 72. "Politics" and
"Administration" as distinguished by Frank J. Goodnow have to do, respectively, with
the manipulation of these two parts of the Constitution.

[68] "When the political order works smoothly, the masses venerate the symbols; the
élite, self-righteous and unafraid, suffers from no withering sense of immorality. . . . .
The ascendency of an élite partially depends upon the success of the practices it adopts.
These procedures comprise all the ways by which élites are recruited and trained, all the
forms observed in policy making and administration" (H. D. Lasswell, *Politics: Who
Gets What, When, How* [New York, 1936], pp. 29, 103). The contrast between the proc-
ess of creating and of utilizing political power may be observed by comparing C. E.
Merriam's *Political Power* (New York, 1934) with L. D. White's *Public Administration*
(New York, 1926).

[69] There is an extensive literature on reform of the League. See Zimmern, *The League
of Nations and the Rule of Law;* J. T. Shotwell, *On the Rim of the Abyss* (New York,
1936); Q. Wright, "Is the League of Nations the Road to Peace?" *Political Quarterly*
(London), January, 1934; "Political Activities of the League of Nations," *Politica*, IV
(London, 1939), 197-219; *Reform of the League of Nations* ("Geneva Special Studies,"
Nos. 7-8 [Geneva, 1934]); Wright (ed.), *Neutrality and Collective Security* (Chicago,
1936). Clyde Eagleton, "Reform of the Covenant of the League of Nations," *American
Political Science Review*, XXXI (1937), 455 ff.; S. Engel, *League Reform* ("Geneva
Studies," Vol. XI [Geneva, 1940]); W. H. C. Laves (ed.), *The Foundations of a More
Stable World Order* (Chicago, 1941).

It is not surprising, therefore, that important groups revolted from the system after the serious depression of 1929. Japan, Italy, and Germany, desirous of territorial expansion, reverted to the Machiavellian conceptions of an anarchic world and the absolute sovereignty of the state.[70]

These revolts gave an opportunity to test the new system. The definition of an aggressor as the state that refused to accept the invitation of consulting states to stop fighting was applied. The Stimson doctrine refusing to recognize the fruits of aggression was accepted as a necessary implication of the Covenant and the Pact. Moral opinion was mobilized against the aggressors. In the case of Italy, engaged in aggression against Ethiopia, economic sanctions were put into effect by most of the nations. The morale of the community of nations was not, however, sufficient to enforce the law.[71]

Furthermore, the victors of World War I, overinterested in the perpetuation of a particular *status quo*, had given inadequate attention to the development of procedures for peaceful change. Grievances providing fuel for these revolts against the international system had not been dealt with in time. It became clear that a working international polity must not only suppress aggression but must also prevent the development of political inferiority complexes.[72]

General war was renewed following the German invasion of Poland in 1939 after a series of minor conquests by the "dissatisfied powers" and of "appeasements" in neglect of their obligations by the "satisfied powers."[73] War on land, sea, and in the air was conducted with little regard for the traditional immunities of noncombatants and neutrals. Nonbelligerent governments, seeking to avoid war, exhibited little confidence in the traditional law of neutrality and

[70] For factors behind these revolts see references in n. 63 and chap. xii, sec. 1d.

[71] Above, n. 60. Other references on collective security are given in n. 59. See also *Collective Security* (Paris: International Studies Conference, 1936).

[72] Q. Wright, "Article 19 of the League of Nations Covenant and the Doctrine Rebus sic Stantibus," *Proceedings of the American Society of International Law*, April, 1936, pp. 55 ff. On the subject of peaceful change see also Williams, *op. cit.*, chap. v; F. S. Dunn, in *Peaceful Change*, ed. C. A. W. Manning (New York, 1937); and *Peaceful Change* (Paris: International Studies Conference, 1938).

[73] Q. Wright, "The Munich Settlement and International Law," *American Journal of International Law*, XXXIII (January, 1939), 12 ff.

enacted regulations which renounced the exercise of some neutral rights, accepted new duties, or discriminated against the aggressors.[74] The war, however, spread rapidly.

3. INTERNATIONAL LAW AND MUNICIPAL LAW

While international law was developing in the world-community, a system of municipal law had been developing in each state. Originally such a system was embodied in the judgments and decrees handed down under authority of the sovereign prince but presumed to be applications of the traditional mores or customs of common law. With the rise of the concept of sovereignty and the consciousness of nationality, municipal law came to be the fiat of the sovereign state. The latter was an abstract entity manifested in the union of a territory, a population, a government, and a recognized status. The monarch came to be but an agent of the sovereign state,[75] and,

[74] Q. Wright, "Rights and Duties under International Law," *American Journal of International Law*, XXXIV (April, 1940), 238 ff., 302 ff.; "The Present Status of Neutrality," *ibid.*, July, 1940, pp. 391 ff.; Georg Cohn, *Neo-neutrality* (New York, 1939); Edwin Borchard, "Neutrality," *Yale Law Journal*, XLVIII (November, 1938), 37–53; H. J. Morgenthau, "The Problem of Neutrality," *University of Kansas City Law Review*, VII (1939), 109 ff.; *American Political Science Review*, XXXIII (1939), 473 ff.

[75] The "organ theory" of the monarch appears to have superseded the "divine-right" theory by revolutions in England (1649), France (1793), Germany (1919), and Russia (1917) but has recently been prohibited by law in Japan. "On February 25, 1936, Dr. Minobe said in the House of Peers: 'If we take the governing of a country to be a right belonging to the Emperor, the power comes to exist solely for the Emperor's advantage and purposes. Is this definition suitable to our characteristics as a nation? . . . . If we define the ruling subject as the nation as a body, then the Emperor, as well as being a sovereign and the highest organ of the nation, handles every right and all the activities of the nation, i.e. legislation, administration and jurisdiction have their highest origin in the emperor. . . . . ' After the close of the session of the Diet, the Ministers of the Army and Navy asked of the authorities severe treatment of the theory. There followed an order, issued by the Education Department for the suppression (or revision) of Dr. Minobe's works. The summoning of Dr. Minobe to the procuratorial office, on complaint of lese-majeste, and his severe questioning followed. . . . . Dr. Minobe tendered his resignation as a nominated member of the House of Peers on September 18. The military authorities however, still were not satisfied, so the government was compelled to give out another official statement of October 15, and in it was the following: ' "The Organ Theory" is opposed to our sacred characteristics and shows the worst possible misunderstanding of their significance. Therefore it must be eradicated absolutely.' Though this problem has been thus settled, discussion of the right or wrong of the theory is not allowed in Japan" (*Present Day Nippon* ["Annual English Supplement of the *Asahi*," No. 12 (Osaka and Tokyo, 1936)], p. 36).

as constitutionalism developed, the process of lawmaking became more and more complicated in procedure but more and more untrammeled by the traditional mores in theory.[76] As the concept of sovereignty came to be formulated and applied with reference to the nation as a whole, the notion of legislation grew in acceptance at the expense of the older idea of natural law. The latter idea had assumed that the state could not alter but could only apply the liberal and humanitarian spirit to changing conditions. Nationalism, on the other hand, emphasized the dynamic and creative character of the sovereign state and its freedom from limitation both of custom and of nature. With Rousseau the general will of the people of the community was the ultimate source of law, and with the German transcendentalists the state was the god beyond which the citizen could not look.[77] It appeared that two elements of modern civilization—pragmatism and relativism—had contributed to the destruction of the other two—liberalism and humanism—by seeming to justify the credenda and miranda of sovereignty and reason of state. A universal absolute having been shattered, a lesser absolute was put in its place.[78]

Wide acceptance of the absolute conception of sovereignty increased the difficulty of reconciling international law and municipal

[76] E. V. Dicey, *Lectures on the Relation between Law and Public Opinion in England during the Nineteenth Century* (New York, 1905); Jethro Brown, *The Underlying Principles of Modern Legislation* (London, 1915).

[77] The growth of the concept of sovereignty is discussed by Oppenheim (*op. cit.*, I, 129 ff.) and Q. Wright (*Mandates under the League of Nations*, pp. 274 ff.; "National Sovereignty and Collective Security," *Annals*, July, 1936). See also C. E. Merriam, *History of the Theory of Sovereignty since Rousseau* (New York, 1900); H. E. Cohen, *Recent Theories of Sovereignty* (Chicago, 1937).

[78] C. E. Merriam, "The Credenda and Miranda of Power," in *Political Power*, chap. iv. The doctrine of the legislative absolutism of sovereignty has been justified by the psychobiological theory that progress comes from unmitigated group struggles for existence (Sturzo, *op. cit.*) and has contributed to the Napoleonic doctrine of absolute war (Carl von Clausewitz, *On War* [London, 1911]; Hoffman Nickerson, *Can We Limit War?* [London, 1933]). Pragmatism and relativism are, of course, just as hostile to state absolutism as to any other form of absolutism, but the human desire for an absolute is such that, when doubt was cast on the validity of one absolute, opinion readily accepted another, the vulnerability of which had not yet been demonstrated (above, chap. viii, nn. 65, 93). See Ralph Barton Perry, "The Philosophical Roots of Totalitarianism" in MacIver, Bonn, and Perry, *op. cit.*, pp. 20 ff.

law. With Grotius the prince was the personal nexus between these two laws. He realized his responsibility under international law which flowed from the agreements which he himself or his dynastic predecessors had made or from the mutual interests of princes which his personal contacts continually impressed upon his attention.[79] Because of this realization he was prepared to exert the powers which belonged to him in internal administration and adjudication to see that his subjects did not interfere with his meeting of these responsibilities.[80] But when legislation came to be the expression of the sovereign will of an abstract state, enacted by legislators with little foreign contact or knowledge of international law, and when the sources of international law came to be the highly technical expositions of numerous text-writers in all languages, basing their conclusions upon a minute study of treaties, customs, general principles, commentary of judge and jurist, all of which was rather incomprehensible to the man in the street, the possibility of conflict between international law and municipal law became obvious.[81]

The humanists were divided into two camps, one of which with an eye to the dangers of war sought to augment the authority of international law to the detriment of legislative omnipotence,[82] and the other with an eye to the needs of internal reform sought to augment the absolutism of legislative sovereignty.[83] The nationalists were

[79] Above, n. 24.

[80] Unless he *wished* to violate his obligations for "reasons of state." At least he did not violate them unwittingly. Vollenhoven writes: "When surveying the accumulation of rules, fragmentary and unsystematic, dull and scanty, casual and unfixed; rules dealing with elegant details, but leaving the main concern of war and destruction untouched, the first stage of the evolution of International Law (reckoned roughly from 1570–1770) can hardly be considered edifying. And yet, however, curious it may seem, this first stage has never provoked any resentment. Why not? Because it never pretended to greater excellence than it possessed; because people knew what it was worth. It was unlovely, pitiable, characterless; but it was honest" (*The Three Stages in the Evolution of the Law of Nations*, pp. 5–6).

[81] See Ruth D. Master, *International Law in National Courts* (New York, 1932), especially the classification of theories for settling such conflicts in the Introduction, pp. 12–13. Carl Friedrich (*Foreign Policy in the Making* [New York, 1938]) emphasizes the difficulties which democracies have encountered in applying the principles of foreign policy developed in the age of absolute monarchy. See also Pound, *op. cit.*

[82] Emerich Crucé, *Le nouveau cynee* (1625), ed. T. W. Balch (Philadelphia, 1909).

[83] J. J. Rousseau, *Le Contrat social* (1762), ed. G. D. H. Cole ("Everyman's" ed.).

also divided into two camps, one of which, fearful of war, sought to renounce the exercise of sovereignty and the pursuit of interests beyond the frontier,[84] while the other, of more ambitious mold, sought to strengthen the state's capacity steadily to expand by military means.[85] Jurists sought to solve the conflict, but they divided into three schools: the national monists who insisted upon the ultimate juristic dominance of municipal law,[86] the international monists who insisted upon the ultimate dominance of international law,[87] and the dualists who recognized the autonomy of each of the systems of law, the possibility of juristic conflict, and the necessity of adequate machinery of political adjustment to rectify such conflicts.[88] On whether that machinery should be diplomatic or international in character this school was again divided.[89]

The problem was not solved, but there was a tendency to redefine sovereignty as superiority to municipal law and subordination to international law, thus making it possible for the abstract conception of sovereignty to serve the function which was formerly served by the personality of the prince. Sovereignty was to the state what liberty under law was to the individual, that is, full discretionary power within a sphere marked by the law of the wider community. That sphere, however, was increasingly conceived as defined by jural rather than by territorial boundaries. Furthermore, the law was not conceived as static, and the jural boundaries which it established for the sphere of sovereigns was not considered immutable but was subject to continuous adjustment through political procedures of diplomacy, recognition, treaty-making, conciliation, conference, and in-

[84] The national isolationists (see above, n. 65).

[85] The national imperialists (see above, n. 65).

[86] As Philip Zorn (*Grundzuge der Völkerrecht* [Leipzig, 1903]) and Erich Kaufmann (*Das Wesen des Völkerrechts und die Clausula Rebus sic Stantibus* [Tübingen, 1911]), who regarded international law as "external state law."

[87] Including "naturalists" like Wilhelm Kaufmann (*Die Rechtskraft des international-en Recht* [Stuttgart, 1899]) and "positivists" like Hans Kelsen (*Das Problem der Souveranität und die Theorie des Völkerrechts* [Tübingen, 1920]).

[88] Heinrich Triepel, *Volkerrecht und Landesrecht* (Leipzig, 1899); Q. Wright, *Mandates under the League of Nations*, pp. 283 ff.

[89] Oppenheim distinguishes the "diplomatic" from the "legal" school of international law (*op. cit.*, Vol. I, sec. 51, par. 6).

ternational legislation as well as through judicial procedures of arbitration and adjudication.[90]

The development of the controversy with respect to the spheres of international law and municipal law has given to modern international law its outstanding characteristic.[91] It has not been, like the Roman *jus gentium* and *jus naturale*, a body of principles of universal validity governing the relations of individuals of different states. It has regarded the human individual as being subject only to the law of some state.[92] International law has confined itself to the relations of states as artificial personalities. States and, perhaps, unions of states, related to the state as, in systems of municipal law, artificial corporations are related to the individual, have been considered the only subjects of international law.[93] It has been hoped that international law might thus prove a system capable of reconciling nationalism with the world-community, sovereignty with law, progress with peace. It has been hoped that it might solve the dilemma of earlier civilizations which could find no road between universal empire and continuous war.[94]

[90] Q. Wright, *Mandates under the League of Nations*, pp. 283 ff.; "National Sovereignty and Collective Security," *Annals*, July, 1936; "Article 19 of the League of Nations Covenant and the Doctrine Rebus sic Stantibus," *op. cit.*, pp. 55 ff.

[91] This characteristic is implicit in the name "international law" which seems to have been first used in the Latin ("jus inter gentes") by Zouche in 1650 and in English ("international jurisprudence") by Bentham in 1789, although Victoria in 1532 had the conception in mind (Scott, *op. cit.*, pp. 281 ff.).

[92] This is controversial, but the view stated is the most commonly accepted (Oppenheim, *op. cit.*, I, 456 ff.; George Manner, "The Position of the Individual in International Law" [manuscript thesis, Cornell University (Ithaca, N.Y., 1940)], Part VI). For possible exceptions see E. M. Borchard, *The Diplomatic Protection of Citizens Abroad* (New York, 1919), pp. 16 ff.; Clyde Eagleton, *The Responsibility of States in International Law* (New York, 1928), pp. 44 ff.; Q. Wright, *Mandates under the League of Nations*, pp. 457, 461 ff.; *Research in International Law since the War* (Washington, 1930), p. 32. See also J. Spiropoulas, *L'Individu en droit international* (Paris, 1928) and *Théorie générale du droit international* (Paris, 1930), I, 191–216; N. Politis, *New Aspects of International Law* (Washington, 1928), p. 23; Vollenhoven, *The Law of Peace*, p. 136.

[93] Oppenheim, *op. cit.*, Vol. I, Part I. The term "artificial" is not intended to deny a sociological reality to states and other associations but merely to emphasize that they are personalities different from the biological individual.

[94] Nitobe expresses his thanks for Bentham's invention of the word "international" (*Lectures on Japan* [Chicago, 1936], p. 343), and Zimmern emphasizes the superiority of an "international" system as contemplated by the League of Nations Covenant, to a

Observation of the excesses, both internally and externally, of national sovereignty grown into totalitarianism, however, stimulated a widespread opinion that international law could not command respect in the highly interdependent family of nations unless that community moved further toward true federalism. Such a development implies the establishment of a relationship between the individual and the world-community, making the individual a subject of international law with direct access to international procedures for protecting the rights guaranteed by that law.[95]

Statesmen[96] and analysts[97] have concluded that effective federal organization must rest on the will of the people ultimately affected as well as on the will of the governments directly participating, and this conclusion has been supported by reference to the history of federal governments. Where the individual has felt himself a member of the

---

world-state as set forth by H. G. Wells (in Wright [ed.], *Neutrality and Collective Security*, pp. 10 ff.). Gierke considered the "federalistic construction of the social world" more characteristic of the Middle Ages than of the modern period. The latter tends, he thought, to the totalitarian nation based on the antique conception of state centralization and absolutism or to the liberal state based on the individualistic conception of natural law and the social contract (J. D. Lewis, *The Genossenschaft Theory of Otto von Gierke* [Madison, Wis., 1935], p. 77). Modern law, he thought, had followed Roman law in denying the legal reality of associations, *Genossenschaften*. It had conceived them either as contractual relations between real individuals (*societas*) or as fictions created for its purposes by "real" sovereign states (*universitas*) and had not adequately grasped the conception that a group may have "real personality" different from the sum of its members without being absolute (*ibid.*, chap. iv). Gierke, however, overemphasized the dominance of Roman law conceptions in modern systems of national law. The legal reality of associations, public and private, has been recognized in both public and private law of civil and common law countries, not to mention the impetus Gierke himself, following in the footsteps of Althusius and Wolff, to whom he pays tribute, gave to this tendency (*ibid.*, pp. 52, 78). Gierke gave but scant attention to the world-community. To him the national state was, for a long future, but not forever (*ibid.*, pp. 24, 25), the highest form of political organization (*ibid.*, p. 24 and chap. vi). He failed, therefore, to emphasize the strongly federalistic tendency of modern international law. Sobei Mogi (*Otto von Gierke* [London, 1932], pp. 222 ff.) overemphasizes the pluralistic aspect of Gierke's thought.

[95] Above, n. 92.

[96] Salvador de Madariaga, *Theory and Practice of International Relations* (Philadelphia, 1937), p. 82; Lord Davies, *Nearing the Abyss* (London, 1936), p. 129.

[97] H. D. Lasswell, *World Politics and Personal Insecurity* (New York, 1935), p. 237; Bertrand Russell, *Which Way to Peace?* (London, 1936), p. 84; Clarence Streit, *Union Now* (New York, 1939).

larger community, that community has been strong even though as juristically decentralized as the British commonwealth of nations.[98] Where the individual has failed to acquire or has lost that feeling, the larger community has disintegrated as did the Germanic confederation in 1866 and as the United States nearly did in 1861.[99] The problem was discussed exhaustively before, during, and after the American federal convention of 1787 with inconclusive results, until settled by the Civil War. This assured the acceptance of Webster's interpretation, that the Constitution was the will of "We the *People* of the United States" and the rejection of Calhoun's thesis that it was merely a pact among "We the People of the united *States*."[100] The full realization of the first interpretation, however, appeared to be dependent not only upon effective protection against state encroachment upon the individual's rights defined by the federal law,[101] but also upon the extension of effective guaranties of due process of law within the states.[102]

[98] P. N. Baker, *The Present Juridical Status of the British Dominions in International Law* (London, 1929), pp. 216 ff.; Sir Cecil Hurst and J. W. Dafoe, in *Great Britain and the Dominions* ("Harris Foundation Lectures" [Chicago, 1928]), pp. 52, 209.

[99] E. A. Freeman published in 1863 his *History of Federal Government from the Foundation of the Achaian League to the Disruption of the United States* to sustain the thesis that federalism tends to be a transitory form of government because it "must depend for its permanence not on the sentiment but on the reason of its citizens" which is likely to suggest either consolidation or separation when circumstances change (London, 1893, ed., p. 88). Sobei Mogi (*The Problem of Federalism* [2 vols.; London, 1931], p. 1108) surveys comprehensively the ideas and practices of federalism in modern times and finds a solution of both national and international problems in "the new federalism"—"the rationalising of the authorities and functions of the state, in a harmony of the distributive and collective systems, in order that there may be continuous exercise of the freedom of individuals and groups within the collectivity of the state" (p. 1112).

[100] John Fiske, *The Critical Period of American History, 1783–1789* (Boston, 1892), pp. 184 ff.; E. S. Corwin, "We the People," in *The Doctrine of Judicial Review* (Princeton, 1914), pp. 81 ff.

[101] As provided in Arts. III and VI of the Constitution.

[102] As provided in the Fourteenth Amendment. Emphasis in distinguishing federations from confederations has usually been upon the degree in which central authority acts on individuals directly rather than upon states as such, but it would appear that the more fundamental distinction is the degree in which the individual's loyalty is directed toward the union rather than toward the states. It is clear that, in so far as the states can restrict the individual's liberty of opinion and communications, they can prevent the development of loyalties to the union. "It should not be forgotten," wrote Hamilton in the *Federalist* (No. 31), "that a disposition in the State governments to en-

Summarizing the juristic trend of the last four centuries, it appears that the anarchic theory of international relations, assumed by Machiavelli, tended to be modified as a world jural community became manifest through a network of treaties, a system of international law, permanent diplomatic missions, frequent international conferences, and numerous international organizations.[103] The international lawyers generally assumed the existence of such a community,[104] and a succession of international humanists had sought to promote it by proposals of more adequate institutions.[105] International law was theoretically considered, not merely a convenience for solving unimportant problems or for justifying dubious policies, but a corpus of procedures and principles giving form and self-consciousness to the collectivity of varied but interdependent nations, so that the collectivity, in spite of its highly decentralized organization and its tendency to change with increasing velocity, would constitute a true community of nations.

Such a community was not fully realized in practice.[106] Some said this was because the problem of reconciling the material unity of the modern world with its political disunity was insoluble.[107] Others said it was because the established rules and procedures were inade-

---

croach upon the rights of the Union is quite as probable as a disposition in the Union to encroach upon the rights of the state governments. What side would be likely to prevail in such a conflict, must depend on the means which the contending parties could employ toward securing success. As in republics, strength is always on the side of the people, and as there are weighty reasons to induce a belief that the State governments will commonly possess most influence over them, the natural conclusion is that such contests will be most apt to end to the disadvantage of the Union." To equalize this natural advantage of the state, well illustrated in the recent success of the propagandas of extreme nationalism and totalitarianism, world-authority must guarantee basic human liberties within the states.

[103] Tobin, *op. cit.;* Q. Wright, "Article 19 of the League of Nations Covenant and the Doctrine Rebus sic Stantibus," *op. cit.*

[104] But see above, n. 34, for difference of Wolff and Vattel on this point.

[105] Such as Crucé, Penn, St. Pierre, Rousseau, Bentham, Kant, Ladd, and others. See W. E. Darby, *International Tribunals* (London, 1904), for résumé of most of these plans; see also Appen. III.

[106] Above, n. 57.

[107] This seems to be the assumption underlying suggestions for a professionalization of military forces (above, chap. xii, sec. 4a).

quate to meet existing conditions.[108] Others said it was because the peoples and governments of the world were not sufficiently aware of their interest in maintaining respect for the rules and procedures which existed.[109] Still others insisted it was because the social structure of international relations was not yet sufficiently advanced to permit international law to play a constructive role in world-organization.[110]

There can be no doubt but that grave conflicts exist both in the fundamental assumptions of traditional international law[111] and in the assumptions considered dominant in different parts of the

[108] "But the League of Nations contains the very defect which destroyed the American Confederation of States. It leaves unimpaired the complete national sovereignty of its members. Nothing else was possible in 1918. But it is this central fact, and not the weaknesses of governments or nations, which is the real cause of the breakdown of the collective system in the last few years" (Lord Lothian, "New League or No League," *The Observer* [London], August 16, 1936, reprinted in *International Conciliation*, December, 1936, p. 592). Cf. the different viewpoint of John Bassett Moore: "The most fundamental defect of the plan was the creation of the warlike devices on the fantastic assumption that the members of the League would, in making use of those devices, divest themselves of their individual interests and prepossessions, of their historic and instinctive antagonisms, and altruistically unite in enforcing the idea of impartial justice" ("An Appeal to Reason," *Foreign Affairs*, July, 1933, p. 42).

[109] "The grave crisis which the world is undergoing to-day is due to this disharmony between its inherent unity and the mental, moral, and emotional disunity which actually prevails in it. While the world community is a possibility, it is not yet a reality. To a certain extent it is already one market, albeit disorganized; one political community, albeit divided; and one public opinion, albeit misinformed and confused. But it is not able to reach a higher degree of organization and development because the men and nations that compose this world community do not yet realize its existence" (Salvador Madariaga, *The World Foundation* [Oxford, 1936], p. 6). See also above, chap. xii, n. 45.

[110] See Hans J. Morgenthau, "Positivism, Functionalism and International Law," *American Journal of International Law*, XXXIV (1940), 283–84. This seems also to be the view of N. S. Timasheff (*An Introduction to the Sociology of Law* [Cambridge, Mass., 1939], pp. 261–62), who holds that law is an ethico-imperative system and that international law can only depend for its sanction upon the auto-limitation of states because by definition it precludes a centrally organized power system. He, however, recognizes that "there are strong actual guarantees; they consist of the existence of ethical conviction concerning international relations and of the interdependence of the interests of particular States." Why may not an improved sociology of law build out of these materials more adequate international organs?

[111] As between the idea of subjection to law and current ideas of sovereignty. See Arnold Brecht, "Sovereignty" in Hans Speier and Alfred Kähler, *War in Our Time* (New York, 1939), pp. 58 ff.; Q. Wright, "National Sovereignty and Collective Security," *Annals*, July, 1936; "International Law and the World Order," in *The Foundations of a More Stable World Order*, ed. W. Laves (Chicago, 1941), pp. 126 ff.

world.[112] Furthermore, these conflicts have had increasingly serious practical results as greater interdependence of all sections of the world has been accompanied by more rapid rates of social change and greater regional differentiation of political systems.[113] Under these conditions the maintenance of international law presents grave difficulties. International law will fail in its purpose if it becomes merely a description of the behavior of states and also if it becomes merely an ideal system without influence upon that behavior.[114] It must

[112] On the divergencies of Nazi, Soviet, far eastern, and Latin-American "international law" from traditional international law see John H. Herz, "The National Socialist Doctrine of International Law," *Political Science Quarterly*, LIV (1939), 536 ff.; Virginia Gott, "National Socialist Theory of International Law," *American Journal of International Law*, XXXII (1938), 704 ff.; Lawrence Preuss, "National Socialist Conception of International Law," *American Political Science Review*, XXIX (1935), 595 ff.; John N. Hazard, "The Soviet Concept of International Law," *Proceedings of the American Society of International Law, 1939*, pp. 33 ff.; "Cleansing Soviet International Law of Anti-Marxist Theories," *American Journal of International Law*, XXXII (1938), 244 ff.; T. A. Taracouzio, *The Soviet Union and International Law* (New York, 1935); W. W. Willoughby, *Foreign Rights and Interests in China* (Baltimore, 1927); Q. Wright, *The Existing Legal Situation as It Relates to the Conflict in the Far East* (New York: Institute of Pacific Relations, 1939); L. Tung, *China and Some Phases of International Law* (London, 1940); A. Alvarez, *Le Droit international americain* (Paris, 1919); Everett Melby, "The Latin-American Attitude on Protection of Aliens" (manuscript thesis, University of Chicago, 1938); Borchard, *op. cit.*, pp. 836 ff.

[113] W. Friedman, "The Disintegration of European Civilization and the Function of International Law," *Modern Law Review*, December, 1938, pp. 194 ff.; "State Control and the Individual," *British Year Book of International Law, 1938*, pp. 118 ff.; Morgenthau, "Positivism, Functionalism and International Law," *op. cit.*

[114] H. Lauterpacht (*The Function of Law in the International Community* [Oxford, 1933]; *Private Law Sources and Analogies of International Law* [London, 1927]) emphasizes the constructive function of international law, and H. J. Morgenthau ("Positivism, Functionalism and International Law," *op. cit.*) emphasizes the need of keeping that law in harmony with existing sociological and political conditions. The general international situation greatly affects the attitude of jurists. Thus the general juristic optimism of the 1920's (see Q. Wright, *Research in International Law since the War*, pp. 2, 24) was succeeded by general juristic pessimism in the 1930's (see Friedman, *op. cit.;* Morgenthau, "Positivism, Functionalism and International Law," *op. cit.;* Thomas Baty, "The Trend of International Law," *American Journal of International Law*, XXXIII [1939], 653 ff.; Sir Alfred Zimmern, "International Law and Social Consciousness," *Transactions of the Grotius Society*, XX [1934], 25). A longer-sighted weighing of the situation is offered by Norman A. M. Mackenzie ("The Nature, Place and Function of International Law," *Proceedings of the American Society of International Law, 1938*, pp. 6 ff.), Josef L. Kunz ("The Theory of International Law," *Proceedings of the American Society of International Law, 1938*, pp. 23 ff.) and Roscoe Pound ("The Idea of Law in International Relations," *Proceedings of the American Society of International Law, 1939*, pp. 10 ff.).

keep an eye on the values of law in the abstract—continuity, good faith, order and justice—and also on the realities of law in the concrete—objectivity of sources, consistency of rules, regularity of observance, effectiveness of sanctions. It must remain in advance, but not too far in advance, of state conduct and must continually encourage social and institutional construction to raise the community to its level. The tendency of international law before World War II was toward reduction of the scope of domestic jurisdiction, especially in economic and military matters, limitation of the right of self-judgment, outlawry of war, and recognition of the individual as a subject of international law. Such developments, however, were not realized because of the inadequacy of procedures for preventing violence, for changing law, for adjudicating disputes, and for administering international services. Efforts to improve these procedures were hampered by the decline of general confidence in humanism and liberalism as social ends and of intelligence and tolerance as means for their achievement.

CHAPTER XIV

CONTRADICTIONS OF MODERN CIVILIZATION

A CIVILIZATION implies a certain consistency in the thoughts, sentiments, actions, and methods derived from the values which it supports. If the civilization is progressive, there will be some inconsistency and some conflict. If this inconsistency becomes too great, serious tensions will develop, causing frustrations and outbreaks of violence destructive of the civilization.[1]

Past civilizations have had a history of birth, rise, decline, and fall, the latter period being characterized by a declining population, lowered economic standards, pessimism, skepticism, and violence, both internal and external. These conditions may arise from widespread awareness of serious contradictions within the civilization. Different institutions may seem to work against each other. Progress in one field may be considered retrogression in another. The individual may feel that what he accomplishes on Sunday he destroys during the week. The accepted values of family life may seem to require acts or sentiments irreconcilable with those required by accepted political and economic values. The ideas supporting scientific thought may seem irreconcilable with those supporting religion. The standards supported by education may seem inapplicable in business and politics. Some such disharmonies are inevitable in a free country, where novel opinions are continually springing from many independent sources, but usually they are subordinated to a common belief in fundamentals.[2] As the development of extreme parties within a state threatens revolution, so the development of grave contradictions within a civilization, general awareness of these

[1] John Dollard, *Frustration and Aggression* (New Haven, 1934).

[2] A. Lawrence Lowell, *Public Opinion and Popular Government* (New York, 1914); *Public Opinion in War and Peace* (New York, 1922).

contradictions, and the polarization of conflicting programs for achieving consistency may account for the major periods of war.[3]

In recent times many writers have commented on such contradictions in the modern world. De Laisi has referred to the conflict of political myths and economic realities, Staley to the conflict of economic internationalism and political nationalism, and Mannheim to the conflict of reactionary ideologies and revolutionary utopias. Such contradictions lie behind the struggles of politics and business, of empire and nationality, of world-order and state sovereignty, of capitalism and socialism, of despotism and democracy.

It makes no difference whether awareness of such contradictions in a civilization results from the development of mutually defeating activities, ideas, evaluations, or procedures within the civilization or from improved analysis indicating the inconsistencies of activities, ideas, values, or procedures with which the civilization has been long familiar. The awareness of the contradictions is the important thing. When they are seen to be too great to be solved by suppressions, compromises, social reforms, or dialectics, when parties are so far apart that they can co-operate on no objectives, the civilization suffers from inhibitions and frustrations likely to lead to social disintegration or general war.

When such contradictions occur in the values or actions of geographically distinct groups, they may be measured by the concept of distance between the groups with respect to technology, intelligence, law, and politics.[4] When they occur in the premises or objectives of different institutions or associations functioning in the same area,[5] the concept of distance is difficult to apply. A qualitative description of the trends appears to be more enlightening. Viewing world-civilization as a whole, this procedure is the most feasible.

The major functions of civilized societies have been (a) the maintenance of order and justice, (b) the production and distribution of wealth, (c) the conditioning of individuals to social requirements,

[3] Edwin D. Dickinson, "The Law of Change in International Relations," *Proceedings of the Institute of World Affairs*, XI (1933), 175.

[4] The shrinking of "distances" with technological progress is discussed and illustrated with isochronic maps by E. Staley, *World Economy in Transition* (New York, 1939).

[5] F. H. Giddings called such associations "constituent" as distinguished from "component" societies (*Elements of Sociology* [New York, 1911], p. 7).

and (d) the justification of society in terms of individual desires.[6] Corresponding roughly to these functions, most advanced civilizations have differentiated the activities of politics, economics, education, and religion and the institutions maintly concerned with each— the state, the business enterprise, the school, and the church. Totalitarian states have attempted to coalesce these institutions, usually by subordination of all others to the state. Liberal states have encouraged the development of numerous voluntary associations for investigating facts and ideas, for influencing opinion, for exerting political pressure, for administering to the underprivileged, for advancing the arts and sciences, for facilitating friendship among the members, and for numerous other purposes. These associations have often co-operated with similar associations in other countries. As a consequence numerous unofficial international associations have developed. While these associations have engaged in some of the activities mentioned, they have seldom rivaled, in contemporary importance, the four major institutions, though they have provided the initiative for changes in opinion and eventually in these great institutions themselves. They have been the dynamic element in the democracies, a function monopolized by the leader and his clique in the despotisms. In the world-community voluntary international associations and national leaders have competed for dynamic leadership.

In chapter viii the general but not uniform trend of modern history was traced, with the suggestion that it had been toward a world-order based on the consent of autonomous nationalities supporting humanism, liberalism, pragmatism, and relativism. The trend in the four major social activities will now be examined with the object of ascertaining the inconsistencies and contradictions which may account for the conflicts of the twentieth century.

I. POLITICAL TRENDS

Medieval politics were characterized by the theoretical unity of Christendom under pope and emperor and, in its later development,

---

[6] Compare with longer list by Clark Wissler, *Man and Culture* (New York, 1923), p. 263. B. Malinowski states that all human cultures can be compared with respect to the functions of politics, law, and custom; economies and technology; education and traditional knowledge; religion, morals, recreation, and art ("Culture as a Determinant of Behavior," *Factors Determining Human Behavior* ["Harvard Tercentenary Publications" (Cambridge, Mass., 1937)], p. 138).

the actual anarchy of numerous feudal jurisdictions under princes and barons. Since the breakdown of this system in the fifteenth century, European politics has been dominated by four conceptions, successively recognized in the treaties terminating the great wars: (a) territorial sovereignty, (b) balance of power, (c) concert of power, and (d) nationality.[7]

a) *Territorial sovereignty.*—The Treaty of Westphalia, ending the Thirty Years' War (1618–48), recognized the sovereignty of the prince to determine the law and religion of the people within his domain. The doctrine of territorial sovereignty had been long developing in the British, French, and Spanish kingdoms, had been rationalized by Bodin, and had been reduced to an international system by Grotius. The territorial divisions established at Westphalia, with the amendments in subsequent treaties, became and still are recognized as the "public law of Europe," disregard for which permits if it does not require vigorous action by the "great powers" who have considered themselves guardians of that law.[8]

The idea of the prince's territorial sovereignty began as a royal and national revolt against the uneconomic character of the anarchy of minute feudal jurisdictions after trade had transcended the limits of town markets, as well as against the universal claims of pope and emperor resting on religious and historic dogmas which were not believed by the rising bourgeois. General acceptance of the idea of royal sovereignty changed Europe from a chaos of thousands of overlapping lordships to a score of states, each sufficiently large to be self-sustaining under the still dominantly agricultural condition of the seventeenth and eighteenth centuries. A number of the small feudal principalities existed in Germany and Italy until the latter part of the nineteenth century, and it was not until that century that the national groups in the Balkans began to acquire independence from the quasi-religious Ottoman Empire. While the process of rounding out national frontiers involved hostilities, territorial sovereignty was capable of providing the basis for a relatively stable European order

[7] This division of modern history at the years 1648, 1713, 1815, and 1920 differs from that utilized in chap. x mainly by separation of the period of political absolutism into two periods by the War of the Spanish Succession.

[8] H. J. Tobin, *The Termination of Multipartite Treaties* (New York, 1933), pp. 218 ff.; Henry Wheaton, *Histoire des progrès du droit des gens* (4th ed.; Leipzig, 1865), I, 116.

under the conditions of economy and military technology of this period.

b) Balance of power.—Stability was also sustained by conscious application of the doctrine of balance of power. While coalitions of the weak against the powerful aggressor have been practiced in all civilizations composed of a number of sovereign states in contact with one another, the practice became a doctrine in British policy of the later seventeenth century and was formally recognized as the basis of the Peace of Utrecht (1714), ending the second great war period of modern Europe (1688–1714).[9]

Acceptance of the balance of power as a doctrine implied a certain solidarity of the powers in support of European public law and preserved considerable stability in eighteenth-century Europe, particularly in view of the opportunities for an expanding economic life in the extra-European colonial areas now open for exploitation, and to the dominant position of Great Britain, which from its insular invulnerability could "hold the balance of power." Wars were mainly concerned with a division of the new lands overseas, but the rising power of Russia and Prussia gradually modified the relative power of the European states. The first partition of Poland, at a time (1772) when France, Poland's natural ally, was weak and in an area where British influence was at a minimum, manifested the breakdown of the balance of power, soon to be followed by modern Europe's third great war period (1789–1815).

c) Concert of power.—The Treaty of Vienna (1815), while recognizing the public law of Europe and the balance of power, introduced a third principle, the concert of Europe which had been receiving theoretic exposition since the Grand Design reputed to Henry IV two centuries earlier. Under this principle the great powers were to

---

[9] Among the pursuers and expounders of balance-of-power policy in the late seventeenth century were the British minister Sir William Temple, William of Orange, Lisola, and Fénelon. See Sir William Temple, *Letters* (London, 1700), pp. 153 ff.; P. Grimblot, *Letters of William III and Louis XIV* (London, 1848), esp. I, 296, 345; F. P. de Lisola, *The Buckler of State and Justice, 1667* (2d ed.; London, 1673), pp. 276 ff.; Fénelon, *Œuvres* (Paris, 1870), III, 347. See also D. J. Hill, *A History of Diplomacy in the International Development of Europe* (New York, 1905–7), III, 127–28; J. W. Gerard, *The Peace of Utrecht* (New York, 1885), pp. 118, 133; and materials on the balance of power collected by A. F. Kovacs for the Causes of War Project (manuscript, University of Chicago Library).

consult before any changes in the public law of Europe could become valid, and it was hoped such consultations might prevent hostilities.[10]

These principles were generally accepted but were most actively supported by Great Britain, whose navy and financial power were capable of controlling extra-European events and of localizing European wars.[11] Under them Europe enjoyed the most stable and least warlike century since the age of the Antonine Caesars.[12] Energy was devoted to the industrial revolution, the increase in population, and the extension of European civilization to the world.

d) Nationality.—The principal threat to this stability was the idea of nationalism which, though discernible in medieval France and England and stimulated by the French Revolution, was prevented from becoming a force in European politics during the first half of the nineteenth century because of general exhaustion from the Napoleonic Wars and the astuteness of Metternich. But the increase in communication, in literacy, and in prosperity and the activity of nationalist propagandists rapidly augmented the influence of nationalism after the middle of the century. Its influence in Italy, Germany, and the Balkans threatened the stability of Europe particularly when socialistic and imperialistic ideas had been added to it, pressing the nation-state to governmentalize more activities within and to acquire colonial areas without.[13]

As a result, the fourth great war period[14] began in 1914. After the first stage of hostilities, the treaties of Versailles, St. Germain, Tria-

[10] Tobin, *op. cit.*, pp. 211, 227; W. Alison Phillips, *The Confederation of Europe* (London, 1920); Thomas E. Holland, *The European Concert in the Eastern Question* (Oxford, 1885).

[11] Great Britain reduced its responsibility for European order after Castlereagh (1821) but continued to support the concert in matters concerning the Low Countries, the Near East, the Far East, and Africa (Sir Alfred Zimmern, *The League of Nations and the Rule of Law* [London, 1936], chaps. vi and vii).

[12] The *pax Romana* (A.D. 96–180), the *pax ecclesia* (1189–1270), and the *pax Britannica* (1815–1914) relied, respectively, on a world-state, a world-church, and a balance of power, but all had a certain measure of success.

[13] Staley, *op. cit.;* Walter Lippmann, *The Good Society* (New York, 1937).

[14] It may become known as the second Thirty Years' War (see Thomas Lamont, "American Business in War and Peace," *Academy of Political Science*, November, 1939, p. 3).

non, Neuilly, and Sèvres were drawn up upon the principle of national self-determination. Old boundaries were obliterated in favor of national lines, minorities were protected, and even colonial areas were placed under mandate with the expectation of eventual self-determination. A dozen plebiscites were arranged as the practical means for defining the geographical limits of nationalities, but in fact doubtful cases were usually decided in favor of victors. The public law of Europe, while resting on a matrix of territorial sovereignty, was, according to these treaties, to consist primarily of the Covenant of the League of Nations establishing a more perfect concert not of Europe but of the world. Its procedures to suppress violence, to administer justice between states, and to promote peaceful change were to supersede the balance of power. The latter had proved increasingly difficult to administer when the democratic control of foreign policy, with it sudden shifts in party control, had made it hard for foreign offices to maintain the traditions of continuity of foreign policy, of the priority of foreign over domestic policies, and of the privacy of diplomatic bargaining.[15]

After the immediate disturbances of World War I had been finally liquidated by the treaties of Lausanne and Locarno in 1924 and 1925, the League system worked for five years in spite of the injury to its prestige, the sense of betrayal in France, the doubt of economic sanctions in Britain, and the encouragement of a spirit of revenge in Germany—all directly or indirectly traceable to the American withdrawal. These conditions were in a measure responsible for the failure of the League to assure moderate freedom of trade and moderate equality of armaments and to modify the more onerous provisions of the Treaty, especially those dealing with reparations. The failure to re-establish a secure world-economy and to restore the self-respect of the defeated states in time led first to economic collapse, then to aggressions, accompanied by military, economic, and moral rearmament among all countries. The war again became active in the Far East in 1931 and soon spread to Ethiopia, Spain, Austria, Czechoslovakia, Poland, and Finland, by which time the great powers of Europe and Asia—Germany, France, Great Britain, Russia, and

[15] Carl J. Friedrich, *Foreign Policy in the Making* (New York, 1938).

Japan—were all actively engaged.[16] The war then spread to Scandinavia, the Low Countries, the Balkans, and Africa.

It is clear that conditions have arisen under which these four principles involve serious contradictions with one another. Territorial sovereignty, initiated by Renaissance monarchs, combined with nationalism, initiated by nineteenth-century private associations, was developed by recent despots into totalitarianism. The sovereign authority was extended not only to the maintenance of law and order but also to the people's economy, religion, and opinion, thus rendering all international relations governmental. At a time when technological inventions were creating numerous interests—political, economic, and cultural—across national boundaries, such governments found their territorial limits too small. Furthermore, sovereignties resting on an intense nationalism inflamed by continuous propaganda have proved unamenable to law, unreliable collaborators in international institutions, and disposed to regulate economy in the interests of military power rather than of popular welfare.[17] The balance of power, initiated by seventeenth-century autocrats, was able to preserve moderate stability when diplomats, uninhibited by popular sentiments and democratic institutions, could juggle alliances with rapidity and secrecy.[18] It, however, degenerated into dangerous rivalry in the creation of mechanized armaments, econom-

[16] E. H. Carr, *International Relations since the Peace Treaties* (London, 1937); Bernadotte E. Schmitt, *From Versailles to Munich, 1918–1938* ("Public Policy Pamphlet," No. 28 [Chicago, 1938]); Raymond L. Buell, *Isolated America* (New York, 1940); J. W. Wheeler-Bennett, "From Brest-Litovsk to Brest-Litovsk," *Foreign Affairs*, January, 1940, pp. 196 ff.; W. H. C. Laves and F. O. Wilcox, *The Middle West Looks at the War* ("Public Policy Pamphlet," No. 32 [Chicago, 1940]). Russia made peace with Finland in March, 1940.

[17] Sir Alfred Zimmern, "The Problem of Collective Security," in *Neutrality and Collective Security*, ed. Q. Wright (Chicago, 1936), pp. 58 ff.; W. E. Rappard, *The Crisis of Democracy* (Chicago, 1938), pp. 117 ff.; Charles E. Merriam, *The New Democracy and the New Despotism* (New York, 1939), pp. 191 ff.; Eduard Beneš, *International Security* (Chicago, 1939).

[18] The need for concentration of authority in handling foreign affairs was insisted on by Locke, Montesquieu, Blackstone, Hamilton, Washington, De Tocqueville, and many more recent writers (see Q. Wright, *Control of American Foreign Relations* [New York, 1922], pp. 363 ff.). Even the moderate democratic control of the post-Napoleonic British Parliament presented some difficulties to balance-of-power diplomacy (see C. K. Webster, *The Foreign Policy of Castlereagh, 1815–1822* [London, 1925], pp. 157 ff.; Zimmern, *The League of Nations and the Rule of Law*, p. 70).

ic invulnerability, and fanatical loyalty when foreign policy came under the influence of nationalism. All states, by desire or by necessity, moved toward totalitarian organization, and wars became extraordinarily violent and destructive.

Internationalism had developed under the influence of private associations organized to deal with problems arising from new means of rapid world-communication, from growing economic interdependence, from the destructiveness of new methods of war, and from the growth of humanitarian and democratic sentiment—all fruits of the political and economic revolutions which began in the late eighteenth century. Internationalism and the concert of Europe provided the basis for widespread official international organization, especially after 1870. Diplomatic conferences, general conventions, arbitrations, international, judicial, and administrative agencies, established rules and practices purporting to qualify the exercise of national sovereignty in many fields. The functioning of this intricate system clearly required a more certain foundation than a balance of power inadequately implemented by *ad hoc* conferences of the great powers. Consequently, at the Hague conferences of 1899 and 1907, at the Paris conference of 1919, and in the League of Nations repeated efforts were made toward limitation of armament, compulsory adjudication of international disputes, military or economic sanctions against violence, or even international legislation tending to limit not merely the exercise of sovereignty but sovereignty itself.[19]

Throughout the modern period the world-constitution has found it difficult to reconcile the basic concepts of state sovereignty and a world-community,[20] but the development of sovereignty into totali-

[19] Felix Morley, *The Society of Nations* (Washington, 1932), chap. xvi; Sir Arthur Salter, *The United States of Europe* (New York, 1933); T. P. Conwell-Evans, *The League Council in Action* (Oxford, 1929); H. R. G. Greaves, *The League Committees and World Order* (Oxford, 1931); Zimmern, *The League of Nations and the Rule of Law*, Part III.

[20] The problem is dealt with by all the classical writers on international law but frequently with indifferent success. Vattel attempts a solution by distinguishing between the "voluntary" or positive and "natural" law of nations. He rejects Wolff's *civitas maxima* of which "all the nations of the world are members" as the basis of "voluntary" law because "each independent state claims to be and actually is independent of all the others" (Preface [Carnegie ed.], p. 9a). He, however, acknowledges that the "universal society of the human race is an institution of nature itself" and the source of the "natural" law of nations (Introd., sec. 11, p. 5). See also H. Bonfils, *Manuel de droit international public* (6th ed. [Fauchille]; Paris, 1912), sec. 24, p. 10; James Lorimer, *Institutes of the Law of Nations* (London, 1883), I, 11; above, chap. xiii, sec. 3.

tarianism and of the world-community into an effective international organization has changed the difficulty into a contradiction. This can be nowhere better illustrated than in the confusion over the concept of neutrality. International law has been faced by an increasing gap between the professions and the practices of its subjects. The law of neutrality for a century successfully compromised the conflict between the sovereign right of war and the general interest of the family of nations in continued peaceful intercourse, but since 1914 it has been unable to do so. For some, neutrality has come to mean policies of political and economic isolationism to avoid war,[21] for others, policies of political and economic collaboration to prevent war,[22] while others proclaim the end of neutrality,[23] and still others wish to go back to the traditional rules of the nineteenth century.[24] Advocates of outlawing war have questioned old rules for determining the validity of territorial titles, of treaties, and of international status,[25] while advocates of national sovereignty have questioned established titles on pleas of equity or necessity as expediency suggested or have even repudiated the principles of international law altogether.[26] As a result, international law has been considerably shaken.[27] The conflicting movements toward more absolute sover-

[21] George Soule, chairman, "Report of Committee on Maintenance of American Neutrality," *Plan Age*, November–December, 1937.

[22] Georg Cohn, *Neo-neutrality* (New York, 1939).

[23] H. Lauterpacht, "Neutrality and Collective Security," *Politica*, II (November, 1936), 149 ff.; Clyde Eagleton, *Analysis of the Problem of War* (New York, 1937), chap. viii; Luigi Carnovale, *Only by the Abolition of Neutrality Can War Be Quickly and Forever Prevented* (Chicago, 1922), p. 13 (1st ed., 1917).

[24] Edwin Borchard and W. P. Lage, *Neutrality for the United States* (New Haven, 1937).

[25] Q. Wright, "The Stimson Note of January 7, 1932," *American Journal of International Law*, April, 1932, pp. 342 ff.; "The Meaning of the Pact of Paris," *ibid.*, January, 1933, pp. 39 ff.

[26] John H. Herz, "The National Socialist Doctrine of International Law," *Political Science Quarterly*, December, 1939, pp. 536 ff. "The Influence of Totalitarianism upon International Law" is discussed by W. Friedman, *British Year Book of International Law, 1938*, pp. 118 ff., and by William T. R. Fox, "Some Effects upon International Law of the Governmentalization of Private Enterprise" (manuscript thesis, University of Chicago, 1940).

[27] W. Friedman, "The Disintegration of European Civilization and the Future of International Law," *Modern Law Review*, December, 1938, pp. 194 ff.; Q. Wright, "The Munich Settlement and International Law," *American Journal of International Law*, January, 1939, pp. 12 ff.

eignty and toward a more united world-community both continue. Obviously, civilization cannot be stable until these ideas are reinterpreted into a greater consistency.[28]

2. ECONOMIC TRENDS

The economy of the modern world has been transformed by applied science. The time of travel, transport, and communication has been tremendously reduced, thus increasing the speed with which persons, goods, processes, and ideas diffuse throughout the world. The rate of invention has also tended to increase, though somewhat irregularly, producing changes not only technological and economic but, after a certain lag, political and social. The rise of labor-saving devices, industrialization of production, geographical and functional division of labor, and large-scale economic organization dependent upon widely distributed markets and sources of raw materials have had the effect of increasing both population and the average standard of living. These changes have resulted in more complicated interactions of regions and classes, experts and entrepreneurs, producers and consumers, and agriculture and industry.[29]

This developing economic interdependence of human groups throughout the world, coupled with the equivocal political situation described, has generated new contradictions. To some the broadening of international trade, evidence of interdependence, means economic vulnerability to be combatted by every variety of artificial barrier—tariffs, quotas, embargoes, exchange controls, etc.—while to others such trade means an economic division of labor, the essential basis for maintaining and increasing the welfare of every people. The economic condition of the world becomes a source of war or of prosperity according as one envisages it through the glasses of totalitarian sovereignty or of an international order. Since it has been actually envisaged as both, little progress has been made toward solving the contradiction.[30]

[28] R. M. MacIver, M. J. Bonn, and R. B. Perry, *The Roots of Totalitarianism* (Philadelphia: American Academy of Political and Social Science, 1940).

[29] Staley, *op. cit.*

[30] See *Report of Commission of Inquiry on National Policy in International Economic Relations*, R. M. Hutchins, chairman (Minneapolis, 1934), pp. 101 ff., 281 ff.

3. INTELLECTUAL TRENDS

The philosophy of the modern world has tended to move toward humanism, liberalism, tolerance, and scientific method. The latter has been given a technological interpretation under which welfare, personality, truth, and justice have been conceived not as approaches to an ideal but as necessary consequences of adequate procedures.[31] Thought has tended to move from cause to effect rather than from end to means, as it did in the Middle Ages.[32] Instead of justifying means, methods, and procedures by the ends achieved, ends, purposes, and objectives have been justified by the means employed to achieve them. If the best scientific instruments and forms of analysis are employed, the result is considered true. If an honest jury has been impaneled and the judge applies the law, the result is considered justice. If policies are approved by democratic processes, they are considered wise.[33] If the most progressive educational methods have been employed, the personality which the child develops must be good. Truth, justice, wisdom, and goodness thus defined have not, however, always proved harmonious, particularly when the methods and procedures upon which they depend have been colored by varying national and class idiosyncrasies. Values growing from local processes cease to be either universal or permanent. Life tends to become a whirl of activity without meaning. Civilization ceases to have any unity. Its activities go on, each for its own sake but without harmony. Science, pragmatism, and instrumentalism in

---

[31] "The safety of science depends on there being men who care more for the justice of their methods than for any results obtained by their use" (Morris Cohen, *An Introduction to Logic and Scientific Method* [New York, 1934], p. 402). Cohen, however, is talking of "the safety of science," not of society; thus his interpretation of "instrumentalism" does not justify the popular "technologism" which holds that whatever is done "with the use of perfected scientific means is good" (Ralph Barton Perry in MacIver, Bonn, and Perry, *op. cit.*, p. 29).

[32] "In all things which are ordered toward some end, wherein this or that course may be adopted; some directive principle is needed through which the due end may be reached by the most direct route" (Thomas Aquinas, *On the Governance of Rulers* [1267] [London, 1938], p. 33).

[33] Considering war the best method of action, Nietzsche, in the same spirit, said that "a good war justifies any cause."

the hands of philosophers do not support this technologism, but they do suggest it to the laity and they do make for a pluralist universe which, while it assures change, may harbor such contradictions as to promote disintegration.[34]

4. RELIGIOUS TRENDS

The religions of the modern world have tended to co-ordinate thought and action about particular symbols. In the sixteenth and seventeenth centuries the symbols of traditional Christianity dominated in Europe, but, as contacts with other religions were developed, common elements were emphasized, differences were obliterated, and human welfare, individual personality, truth, and toleration became accepted ends in all religions.[35] To the religious mind, however, these ideas were not hypotheses to be proved by the application of sound methods but ideals to be established by the individual's introspection and to be realized by his activity, guided by familiarity with the life and personality of the great religious leaders.

While this liberal religion, stimulated by world-conferences of all religions, has progressed among the most literate élite throughout the world, it has come to be combatted by the new religion of nationalism, subordinating all other ideals to the glorification of the national symbols, heroes, and cultures.[36] Marxist doctrine has sought to give a similar religious color to class symbols. More recently fusions of national, race, and class symbols, either with or in opposition to symbols of traditional religion, have produced new religions of communism, fascism, and Naziism.

These new religions, in opposition to the philosophy of liberalism, have linked themselves to the cult of efficiency. While in all religions the ideal end, the *summum bonum*, has justified the means in the sense that it has been an important element in evaluating acts and events, these new religions, like the Spanish Inquisition, have justified

---

[34] See above, chap. viii, sec. 2c.

[35] Walter Lippmann, *A Preface to Morals* (New York, 1929).

[36] Hans Kohn, "The Nature of Nationalism," *American Political Science Review*, XXXIII (December, 1939), 1001 ff.

all temporal means, including violence and fraud, on the sole ground that they promoted the particular national, racial, or class ideal avowed by the cult. Because of the multiplicity of gods in this new pantheon, the cult of efficiency has made wars more certain and more formidable. Not only do the new religions contradict one another, but they all contradict the universal religion of humanism and the traditional religions from which humanism developed.[37]

5. TREND OF WAR

The political, economic, philosophic, and religious trends of the modern world have in increasing degree led to contradictions which have bred violent conflict and war. And war itself has tended to become more severe. Military inventions have increased the vulnerability of populations and of wealth to attack. Propaganda inventions have increased fanaticism and hatred. Political inventions have increased the size and discipline of armies. Economic inventions have increased the industrialization of armies, the proportion of the national wealth involved in war, and the number of men behind the lines necessary to support the soldiers at the front.[38] War has contradicted the ideals of universal religion, the assumptions of modern philosophy, the aims of international economics, and the objectives of world-politics. It has even contradicted the aims of *national* policy, economy, religion, and philosophy. The more powerful becomes the war machine, the more certain has it been that war will bring losses far in excess of gains to all concerned. The devotion of all the national energy to augmenting the power of the state not only has rendered the state less efficient to do anything but fight but, as all states augment their military power equally, it has made fighting a less efficient instrument for accomplishing national objectives.

If the institutions and activities of a civilization do not reciprocally support each other but instead destroy each other, the civilization is in peril. The signs of disintegration in modern civilization are mani-

---

[37] Charles Hartshorne, *Beyond Humanism* (Chicago, 1937).

[38] Hans Speier, "Class Structure and 'Total War,'" *American Sociological Review*, June, 1939, pp. 370 ff.; Hans Speier and Alfred Kähler (eds.), *War in Our Time* (New York, 1939); above, chap. xii, sec. 2.

est. The grave contradictions must be resolved in a higher dialectic f more frequent and more destructive wars are to be avoided. Can his vast and multiplex civilization be grasped as a whole in the minds of men so that those values can be perceived and accepted which both contribute to the civilization and result from the application of the best procedures which the civilization has yet developed? Can the spontaneous desires and behaviors of men, deriving from he past, be adjusted to the technologies and needs of society of the present and future?

CHAPTER XV

CHANGES IN WAR THROUGH HISTORY

THE preceding chapters have tried to make it clear that the frequency, intensity, and character of war have varied greatly in times and places. This chapter will set forth (1) a summary of the changes in warfare during the four great periods considered, (2) certain generalizations from this history, (3) a general theory of historic change, and (4) an application of this theory to contemporary civilization.

1. CHANGES IN WAR

a) Animal warfare.—Serious animal warfare seldom occurs between members of the same species. The war of the lion on the lamb resembles human operations in the slaughter-house rather than on the battlefield. Situations involving rivalry for possession of an object, jealousy, frustration of activity, and intrusion of a stranger in a group often lead to fighting among apes, monkeys, and other animals as they do among children and adult human beings. Birds, fishes, and certain mammals commonly defend definite nesting territories from other pairs of the same species. The male of gregarious animals fights for a mate and defends his harem from intrusion by other males. A specific dominance drive has been found behind most fighting of monkeys and apes. These types of territorial, sexual, and social hostilities within the species are usually found among animals which are not heavily armed. Such combats are not ordinarily lethal and serve a racial function in the process of reproduction and in the distribution of the species.[1]

The social insects defend the nest or the hive from others of the same or related species often by the use of a specialized soldier caste.

[1] H. E. Howard, *Territory in Bird Life* (London, 1920); F. Alverdes, *Social Life in the Animal World* (New York, 1927); S. Zuckerman, *The Social Life of Monkeys and Apes* (London, 1932); E. F. M. Durbin and J. Bowlby, *Personal Aggressiveness and War* (New York, 1939); see above, chap. v, and below, Appen. VII.

Certain ants even engage in aggressive hostilities against closely related species mainly for the purpose of taking slaves. It is only
among the social insects, especially the ants, that fighting is organized
and resembles human warfare. War as a behavior pattern more
specialized than individual violence or fighting is a function of animal societies rather than of animal nature, although the two are related. Societies are a consequence of conditioned drives of individuals. Ants, like men, are social animals.[2]

  b) Primitive warfare.—Human warfare probably began a million
years ago, when primitive human types began to talk at first by manual gesture and then by verbal articulation and to form hordes,
clans, and other groups.[3] There is a school of thought which denies
this and believes that war originated in the Near East after a dominant class had imposed its authority upon the workers and that it
then spread like other cultural patterns along definite routes of contact.[4] This may be true of organized war for economic and political
conquest, but among all primitive peoples, not wholly isolated, war of
some sort is occasionally resorted to—war for expiation, for revenge,
for sport, for sexual prestige, for territorial defense, and particularly
for manifesting and preserving the solidarity of the group. The
latter function is served by the displacement upon an external enemy
of aggressive impulses which might disrupt the group. Such impulses exist in varying degree in most individuals as a consequence
of the suppression by family or group authority of those desires incompatible with group life.[5] The importance of this function of
primitive war is indicated by the fact that in many of the Pacific
islands the population of only a few hundred is divided into two

[2] W. M. Wheeler, *Social Life among the Insects* (New York, 1923).

[3] R. M. Yerkes and A. W. Yerkes, *The Great Apes* (New Haven, 1929); S. Zucker-
man, *Functional Affiliations of Men, Monkeys and Apes* (New York, 1933); M. R. Davie,
The Evolution of War (New Haven, 1929); W. G. Sumner, *War and Other Essays* (New
Haven, 1911).

[4] W. J. Perry, *An Ethnological Study of Warfare* ("Memoirs of Manchester Literary
and Philosophical Society," Vol. LXI, No. 6 [1917]); *The Growth of Civilization* (New
York, 1923).

[5] L. T. Hobhouse, G. C. Wheeler, and M. Ginsburg, *The Material Culture and Social
Institutions of the Simpler Peoples* (London, 1915); Durbin and Bowlby, *op. cit.;* see
above, chap. vi.

tribes habitually at war with each other. Each needs an enemy in order to preserve its internal solidarity. The same need is manifested by the grouping of clans into two actually or ceremonially hostile groups among the North Pacific Indians, the Incas, and the Iroquois.[6] The dualism of government in ancient Egypt, of church and state in medieval Europe, of military and civil government in feudal and modern Japan, of age groups among certain African tribes, may have served a similar function.[7] Anthropologists have generalized such observations by considering that "the constant function of war is to strengthen the bonds of union between the individuals of the fighting community and make them increasingly conscious that they are members of a single unit."[8]

c) *Historic warfare.*—Civilization was invented something over five thousand years ago in the Near East, perhaps independently in China and Mexico. A written language permitting of the storage of ideas and of communication at a distance was its essence. From these the possibility of an organization larger than the primary group developed. War, however, was certainly a major instrument in the formation of these larger communities. It served to impose governors upon the reluctant governed, to expand the area and population under the governors, to defend the community from attacks by others, and to maintain a sense of unity in the community. These basic functions of war were, however, continuous and did not account for the outbreaks of war at particular times. War was actually resorted to when an improvement in technique—invention of a new weapon, military formation, or means of military transportation—or the rise of a strategic genius induced a particular military group to believe with conviction that conquest would be practicable and when the current ideology with respect to the justice and expediency of war made this enterprise fit into popular thinking sufficiently to assure the necessary support. In the early stages of a civilization, however,

---

[6] W. C. McLeod, *The Origin and History of Politics* (New York, 1931), pp. 112, 218–19, 225, 290.

[7] *Ibid.*, pp. 40, 185, 195.

[8] Camilla H. Wedgewood, "Some Aspects of Warfare in Melanesia," *Oceania*, I (April, 1930), 6–9; see also McLeod, *op. cit.*, p. 81. Perry (*op. cit.*) interprets the frequency of this dualism as evidence of diffusion from Egypt.

the masses of the population were politically unimportant. Reasons and rationalizations for war were needed to persuade only the limited governing class.[9]

As civilization progressed, war tended to play an increasing role in society. Its function as a population regulator probably tended to increase, although until recent times it has never been as important in this connection as pestilence, famine, and practices of religious celibacy and postponed marriage.[10]

War was persistently recognized among the historic peoples as an institution with specialized personnel, traditions, and ideology, but its effectiveness as an instrument of defense or of policy, its ideology and the popular attitude toward it, varied in great oscillations dependent upon the changes in its technique, favoring now the defensive and now the offensive. These oscillations were especially noticeable in the successive invasions by nomadic tribes on the periphery of the great centers of civilization.[11] The cumulative effect of the tendency of the great civilizations to expand and of the periodic barbarian invasions was to create a realization of the dependence of each community upon a larger world, continually urging a political organization, either by conquest or by federation, capable of maintaining order and permitting peaceful intercourse throughout this wider area. A civilization, however, after expanding externally and becoming more integrated internally for several centuries, usually achieved a certain stability and then began to disintegrate under the influence of the destructiveness of war, the exhaustion of resources, widespread epidemics, or other conditions. During the life of a civilization war tended to rise and then to decline in magnitude with accompanying changes in its characteristics and objectives.

These great oscillations make it difficult to detect persistent trends in the character of war during the historic period. It seems probable that there was a tendency for the destructiveness of war to increase

---

[9] See above, chap. vii.

[10] A. M. Carr-Saunders, *The Population Problem* (London, 1922).

[11] See Martin Sprengling, "Moslem North Africa," *Open Court*, XLVI (December, 1933), 505 ff.; Owen Lattimore, *China and the Barbarians, Empire in the East*, ed. Joseph Barnes (New York, 1934), pp. 3–39; A. J. Toynbee, *A Study of History* (3 vols.; Oxford, 1934), Vol. III; F. J. Teggart, *Rome and China* (Berkeley, 1939).

and for the periods between wars to become longer in equivalent stages of successive civilizations.[12]

d) Modern warfare.—The age of discovery less than five centuries ago marked the beginnings of a new epoch in human history. The possibility existed to organize the human race as a single unit. Previous civilizations had had unknown men on their peripheries. Rome had been surrounded by barbarians. After the relatively isolated Western, far eastern, and American civilizations were brought into continuous contact by the labors of Columbus, Da Gama, Magellan, Cortez, and Pizarro, a family of nations with no periphery began to develop. For the first time a universal league of nations became possible.[13]

The epoch since the age of discovery, the first of genuine world-history, was initiated by the invention of printing in the West and has witnessed the discovery, exploration, and mapping of all parts of the world by Europeans; the rise of humanism, liberalism, tolerance, and experimental science; the development of world-trade and geographical division of labor; the invention of steam and electric communication, transportation, and power devices, and their utilization by peoples in all parts of the world. These changes developed continuous contact between all branches of the human race and increasing economic, political, and cultural interdependence of widely separated human groups. The human personality and human societies during this period tended toward greater uniformity and greater unification. Improvements in technology, sanitation, and industrial organization, the opening of new areas, and the development of humanitarian ideologies made it possible to raise the plane of living in spite of the increases in population and reduced the importance of religious celibacy, postponed marriage, pestilence, and famine as methods of population regulation. At the beginning of the nineteenth century, however, Mathus and others perceived that there was a limit to the continuous increase of population although tremendous expansion of population still proved possible. In the nine-

---

[12] G. F. Nicolai, *The Biology of War* (New York, 1918); H. C. Engelbrecht and F. C. Hannighan, *Merchants of Death* (New York, 1934); see above, chap. vii, sec. 3*a*. But see Pitirim Sorokin, *Social and Cultural Dynamics* (New York, 1937), III, 297, 361.

[13] See above, chap. viii, sec. 1.

teenth century the new check of birth control gradually spread and promised to become the main equilibrating device. It has already produced population stability in many areas.[14]

War continued to occupy a dominant role as a means of preserving the ruling class, the consciousness of national unity, and the balance of power. It was also an important means of expanding the influence of the principal centers of modern civilization over the more backward areas. These functions of war have been continuous. They differ little from the functions of war among earlier civilizations. The significant change has been in the techniques and ideologies of war.[15]

The invention of guns and explosives, the improvement of ships and the effectiveness of blockades and embargoes as populations became dependent upon overseas trade, the application of steam, electric, and gasoline power in military and naval movements, the invention of submarine and aerial transportation, and the increased vulnerability of maritime commerce and civilian centers to military attack—these changes taken together made war a more effective instrument of policy when utilized by the industrialized against the nonindustrialized states. They, however, made war a less effective instrument of policy between equally industrialized states. The new methods made it more likely that a war among such states would end by mutual attrition, after protracted stalemate and losses to both belligerents beyond any possibility of gain to either. For this very reason, however, the threat of war became a more potent, even if more hazardous, weapon in the hands of reckless despots.[16]

War had been an instrument of political power in all civilizations. In modern civilization as war became more capitalized and as the professional class permanently devoted to it increased, war and military supply offered business opportunities to many. Powerful opposition to the reduction of war was therefore assured. The changes in the techniques of war tended to make wars progressively more destructive, absolutely and relatively to the population, in military and civil life, and in economic disorganization.[17]

---

[14] See above, chap. viii.

[15] See above, chap. x.

[16] See above, chap. xii, sec. 3.

[17] See above, chaps. ix and xi.

These changes in the material character of war were accompanied by changes in its moral character. Individual philosophers, satirists, poets, and mystics like Euripides, Aristophanes, Isaiah, Moti, and Jesus spoke against war in all civilizations, but even the utopians could not picture in detail a terrestrial society without it. After the seventeenth century, however, the idea of a warless world commanded increasing attention. Law and organization to realize such a world developed, and war was conceived as an abnormal if not wicked mode of behavior; yet wars recurred of increasing destructiveness, thus manifesting the most serious contradiction in modern civilization.[18]

To recapitulate, among animals war was an element in the balance of nature and contributed to static equilibrium among species and societies in the biological community. Among men, as measured by destructiveness of life, by its cataclysmic effect upon social organization, war tended since its beginning in primitive human history to increase in importance, but the increase was slow and gradual during the first epoch when war was a continuous and normal custom of primitive social life. With the development of pastoral and agricultural economies, changes in military technique became more rapid and tended to maintain society in dynamic equilibrium.

During the historic period the importance of war oscillated in fluctuations marking the rise and fall of civilizations, but successive fluctuations tended to increase in amplitude and to decrease in length. In the modern period of world-civilization fluctuations of war and peace have tended to become stabilized at about fifty years, although the severity of each war period has tended to increase. The technique of war and the justifications for its use have tended to be more consciously adapted to changing conditions, but such adaptations have progressively tended to increase the destructiveness of war and to decrease the influence of customary limitations. War has had a more and more catastrophic effect upon human existence.

While the destructiveness of war has had an upward tendency, other periodic visitations which formerly upset human society, such as pestilence and famine, have tended to be controlled. Thus war has stood out more and more as a recurrent catastrophe in civilized hu-

[18] See above, chaps. xiii and xiv and Appen. III.

man existence, and, while the increasing regularity of its fluctuations *appears* to make prediction of the approximate time of general wars more practicable, this appearance is probably illusory. Predictions of the effect of war upon the population of areas or upon the human race as a whole are probably less accurate than ever before because of the increasing size and decreasing number of states, the more intensive contact among them, the incalculability of new inventions, and the development of international political controls. These same factors which have qualified the statistical basis for prediction have augmented both the need and the practicability of controlling war.

Treating the history of life on the planet as a unit, war began as an inevitable condition, the temporal effect of which might have been predicted from an application of statistical averages to the known tendencies of the organic drives of a multitude of individuals. It has become a partially controlled institution, the temporal consequences of which cannot be predicted from a study of any persistent factors, but which might be more completely controlled through the application of known political and mechanical techniques.[19]

[19] War was originally a function of the internal structure of each fighting unit, and, as there were very many of these units, the probability of any unit of a class being at war in a given time might have been calculated from statistical averages. Change has been in the direction of reducing the number of fighting units so that there is less statistical basis for such calculations. Change has also been in the direction of integrating this smaller number of units into a single unit so that war has tended to become a function not of the fighting unit but of the entire human community of which all fighting units are parts. Thus the problem of war has shifted from that of classifying fighting units to that of analyzing the organization of human society as a whole. Accepting Mead's conclusion, "the more the process of nature can be described in terms of laws, the greater is man's freedom" (George H. Mead, *Movements of Thought in the Nineteenth Century*, ed. Merritt H. Moore [Chicago, 1936], p. xxii), the trend has been to reduce the freedom of the individual fighting unit to escape war through intelligence and to increase the freedom of the human race as a whole to escape war, provided the laws governing its present organization can be discovered. Prediction, from being based upon the analysis and measurement of numerous independent agencies insusceptible of central control, has come to be based upon the analysis of a few personalities exercising central control. The moral and subjective factors have tended to become more important than the material and objective factors. War can less and less be treated from a deterministic point of view. More and more it must be treated from a constructive point of view. The individual can less profitably be interested in studying the historical causes of war in order to decide a policy for himself or his group. He can more profitably be interested in the engineering of peace for the human race as a whole.

2. WAR AND HISTORIC CHANGES

The history of war suggests certain general relationships of war to economic, political, military, and cultural change.

a) Economic and social change.—When independent groups, utilizing markedly different military techniques, have come into close economic and social contact, continuous war has been usual until the group with the less efficient technique has been exterminated or conquered or has adopted a more efficient technique. Among animals the balance between carnivorous and herbivorous species in the same area has been maintained by the more rapid breeding of the latter, compensating for the predations of the former. A similar balance has often prevailed for long periods between aggressive nomads and peaceful agriculturalists. Where such an equilibrium exists, hostilities have been continuous and of unvarying intensity. Among primitive peoples the development of new external contacts has broken such a balance and increased the amount of warfare sometimes resulting in important political and social changes. The development of intercivilization contacts have similarly stimulated imperial war by civilized states.[20] Such contacts arose, for example, from the exploratory, missionary, and commercial expansion of European states into the hitherto unknown areas of America, Asia, and Africa after 1500. In these cases long periods of war eventuated in conquest and forms of imperial organization in which the group with superior military technique dominated, permanently or until the subject people had acquired enough of that technique successfully to revolt.

When independent groups, utilizing similar military techniques, have rapidly come into closer economic or social contact with each other, periodic wars of serious proportions separated by relatively long intervals of peace have usually occurred. The rapid expansion of international communication, travel, and trade has tended to increase the amount of war. Intergroup political organization, though often attempted in such circumstances, has seldom proceeded with sufficient rapidity to adjust the problems arising from such contacts peacefully. Among the Greek city-states and the medieval feudal principalities the development of international political organization, attempted in the Amphyctionic Council and the Holy Roman Em-

---

[20] See above, chap. v, sec. 4; chap. vi, sec. 2; chap. vii, sec. 3b.

pire, lagged so far behind the development of economic and cultural contacts that increasingly severe wars destroyed the civilizations. Among the Hellenistic states the lag was less. Rome developed a superior military technique, absorbed all these states in an empire, and maintained political stability for several centuries. The destructive wars, before this universal political organization was achieved, may, however, have sowed the seeds of later decay. In the modern period the British Empire developed a superior naval technique and maintained a precarious peace during much of the eighteenth and nineteenth centuries, but in the twentieth century that political organization proved inadequate to adjust the problems arising from the closer economic and social interdependence of nations stimulated by modern inventions.[21]

While increasing economic and social contacts tend toward wars of union, decreasing contacts tend toward wars of separation. When politically associated groups, utilizing similar military techniques, have diminished their economic and social contacts, because of the development of technological, ideological, or other barriers, they have become involved in wars of revolt, unless political decentralization has kept pace with the growth of economic and cultural autonomy. The failure of the Roman Empire to decentralize politically with sufficient rapidity may have contributed to the revolts in Armenia, Mesopotamia, Palestine, Mauretania, Palmyra, Egypt, Britain, and elsewhere after the end of the first century. The failure of the British Empire to decentralize led to the American Revolution, an experience which has been avoided with respect to the other British colonies of European population by application of the decentralizing dominion-status policy. The wars of independence of Spanish and Turkish dependencies and of the Confederate States of America in the nineteenth century and the violent breakup of the Hapsburg and Romanoff empires in the twentieth century illustrate the same principle. The revolts of Japan, Italy, and Germany from the public law of the world in 1931 may be in part attributed to overrapid centralization under the League of Nations. These propositions may be otherwise stated: that sporadic war is likely whenever, among groups

---

[21] "Economic change has tended to run ahead of political readjustment" (Eugene Staley, *War and the Private Investor* [New York, 1935], p. 458).

using similar military techniques, the forces of social and economic change outstrip the capacity of recognized peaceful procedures to effect an adjustment between the standards implied by such changes and those established by existing law. Procedures for continually keeping international and constitutional organization in accord with social and economic changes are as necessary as procedures for better enforcing existing law.[22]

The maintenance of a rate of political and legal centralization or decentralization in exact proportion to the rate of economic and social integration or disintegration has hitherto been the price of peace. This co-ordination may, of course, be maintained not only through the adjustment of law and organization to social and economic change but also through the control of opinion and economy by political and legal authority.[23]

b) Political change.—Balance-of-power policies, practiced by groups of states utilizing similar military techniques, have tended toward polarization of all states about the two most powerful of the group, leading to serious wars involving all of them. Such a polarization has usually resulted when alliances, counteralliances, and armament races have been utilized to maintain the balance of power. These practices have tended not only to group all the states by alliance in one or the other of two groups but also to create a conviction of the inevitability of war between these groups. This trend is illustrated in the history of the ancient Greek city-states, the Hellenistic states, the medieval Italian city-states, and the modern European states.[24]

Related to the tendency of a balance-of-power system to generate periodic general wars has been its tendency to make each civilization the cockpit of the next. The balance of power having reached a state of polarization within a given civilization, each faction tries to draw in states from the outside. As a result, when economic and social contacts have sufficiently progressed, a larger balance of power, dominated by states of a different civilization, has developed

---

[22] See John Foster Dulles, *War, Peace and Change* (New York, 1939).

[23] See above, chap. xiii, sec. 3.

[24] See above, chap. ix, sec. 2*d*; chap. xii, sec. 4*c*.

around the original area. The states of the original area, even though utilizing more advanced military techniques, remain divided by historic animosities and are unable to defend their civilization as a unit. Consequently, the civilization is overwhelmed. The ancient civilizations of Syria and Palestine became the cockpit of the surrounding monarchies of Egypt, Mesopotamia, Anatolia, and Persia. The ancient Greek civilizations of the Aegean, Greece, and Sicily became the cockpit for wars among the Hellenistic states of Macedonia, Rome, and Carthage. The area of the ancient Roman Empire after its decadence and division became the cockpit for crusading wars of Islam and Christendom in the Middle Ages. The area covered by the highly developed Italian city-states of the late Middle Ages became the cockpit for wars between France, Spain, Austria, and Great Britain in the sixteenth century. The disintegrating Holy Roman Empire was the cockpit for wars of all Europe in the seventeenth century. Europe, still intent upon its balance of power, has been and promises to continue to be the cockpit for wars involving the United States, Japan, Russia, and the British Empire. With a world balance of power established among these states, this process can no longer continue without interplanetary wars.[25]

c) Military change.—Wars among a group of states which have utilized a common military technique without radical change over a long period of time have tended to end in stalemate or mutual attrition. Without change in rules, weapons, or tactics the strategic defensive has tended to gain over the strategic offensive, and wars have tended to end only by mutual attrition. They have become rarer and worse. As a corollary to this tendency, among such states the gravity of war has tended to be inversely related to its frequency. As a civilization has advanced, its wars have tended to become absolutely and relatively more destructive and less frequent. At its height there may be a period of comparative tranquillity. As a civilization has declined, it has sometimes had more frequent but less destructive wars initiated by groups revolting from within or attacking from without but utilizing inferior military techniques. Under such circumstances, however, the attackers have gradually acquired the

[25] This idea was suggested to the author by A. J. Toynbee.

improved techniques, and the tendency toward attrition has developed again, usually wrecking the civilization.[26]

Closely related to this tendency of the severity of war to rise and fall in long waves during the life of a civilization has been the tendency for very severe war periods to be followed by movements for peace. A strong pacifistic sentiment arose in Greece during and after the Peloponnesian wars, but the movements for federation were inadequate.[27] The desire for peace after the severe imperial and civil wars at the end of the Roman republic created the conditions for the successful organization of the empire.[28] In the Middle Ages the destructiveness of the raids of nomads from the steppes and the Vikings from the sea created a strong desire for peace, utilized by the church in such organizations as the truce of God and the peace of God.[29] In the late Middle Ages the hardships of the Crusades and the wars of dynastic rivalry led to the pacifism of humanists and of reformist sects and to many proposals for world-organization in the sixteenth and seventeenth centuries.[30] The devastating Napoleonic Wars led to the Holy Alliance and to numerous peace organizations after 1815. The mid-nineteenth-century wars of nationalism led to a powerful movement for arbitration and the codification of international law after 1870. World War I led to the League of Nations and worldwide peace movements in the 1920's.[31]

This natural reaction toward pacifism after very severe wars has tended to widen the gap between wars of that type, as also has the necessity for a measure of economic recovery before further hostilities are practicable, especially in the modern period of highly capitalized war. Anthropologists have pointed out that even primitive peo-

[26] Above, chap. vii, sec. 3c; chap. xii, sec. 3b. To similar effect see Sorokin, *op. cit.*, III, 364. See also Figs. 24, 25, 26, Appen. XVI; Table 61, Appen. XXIV.

[27] See Euripides, *Trojan Women;* Aristophanes, *Lysistrata.*

[28] For early Christian and Stoic pacifism see C. J. Cadoux, *Early Christian Attitude toward War* (New York, 1919).

[29] A. C. Kray, "The International State of the Middle Ages, Some Reasons for Its Failure," *American Historical Review*, XIX (October, 1922), 3 ff.

[30] See Wolsey's peace plan, 1518 (Garrett Mattingly, "An Early Non-aggression Pact," *Journal of Modern History*, X [1938], 1 ff.), and attitude of Erasmus, the Quakers, the Mennonites, etc. See above, chap. vii, n. 203; below, Appen. III.

[31] See below, Appen. III.

ples, whose military equipment is very simple, may fight wars of steadily increasing gravity until there is a "war to end war" which, because of its extensive destructiveness of life, is followed by a considerable period of peace.[32]

d) *Cultural change.*—With the progress of a civilization the justification for resort to war has tended to become more abstract and more objective. As the civilization has become economically and culturally integrated, the subjective desire of a small group has appeared to constitute a less and less adequate reason for resort to violence. More and more the interest of the civilization as a whole, objectively manifested in principles of law, has been invoked. From being justified as a protection of "natural rights" interpreted by the fighting group itself, war has progressively been justified as a "duel" or "trial by battle" to vindicate honor or to establish rights in pursuance of the general interest that disputes and feuds be definitively settled; as an instrument of policy authorized by legitimate authority to improve the welfare of the community; and finally as a sanction for enforcing peace and justice within the civilization as a whole.[33]

But whatever the theory or rationalization, in practice, war has been resorted to in response to the subjective interpretation of their interests by the entities actually possessing political power. Usually the earlier stages in the development of a civilization have been marked by the integration of smaller into larger units. Political power has tended to expand, so the evolution of legal justifications for war has been parallel to the realities of politics. War has in fact and in law been initiated in the interest of expanding communities. But in the later stages of a civilization disintegration has taken place. Effective political units have become smaller, though the theoretical political unit has become as large as the civilization itself. The trends

[32] See W. Lloyd Warner, "Murngin Warfare," *Oceania*, I (1931), 473; above, chap. ix, sec. 2d.

[33] See chap. vii, secs. 7b, d; Table 61, Appen. XXIV. Luigi Sturzo illustrates these changes from medieval and modern history (*The International Community and the Right of War* [New York, 1930]). See also William Stubbs, "On the Characteristic Differences between Medieval and Modern History (1880)," in *Lectures and Addresses* (3d ed.; Oxford, 1900), pp. 238 ff.

of legal pretexts and of political objectives have thus been in opposite directions.

This tendency of the *pretexts* of war to depart farther and farther
from the *reasons* for war, as a civilization declines from its maximum,
is paralleled by the usual inability of a civilization to develop a political organization in pace with the integration of its economy and culture. Both of these tendencies, illustrated in the later Middle Ages
and the Renaissance, contributed to the perpetuation of war and the
destruction of the civilization. During that period wars undertaken
in the name of Christian solidarity or for the promotion of justice
were usually really intended solely for princely aggrandizement or
plunder.[34]

These tendencies, together with that resulting from the development of a given military technique (see sec. *c*), have given a normal
sequence to the character of war during the life of a civilization. Civilizations have usually begun with a period of imperial and balance-of-
power wars thus characterized both in law and in fact. These wars
have tended to become increasingly destructive, after which there
has sometimes been a period of tranquillity followed by wars of internal revolt and defense from external invasion. Both sides have
usually tried to justify resort to such wars in the name of the political
and legal authority of the civilization. Actually, however, political
authorities interested neither in the internal police nor in the external
defense of that civilization have initiated such wars. Such authorities have in fact been initiating a new civilization, though often asserting loyalty to the principles of the one they are destroying.[35]
These wars also have increased in gravity, ending with the complete
disintegration of the civilization.

If organic evolution as a whole is envisaged, the initiating causes
of war have tended better to accord with its theoretical justification.

[34] See C. Von Vollenhoven, *Three Stages in the Evolution of the Law of Nations* (The
Hague, 1919), chap. i; *The Law of Peace* (London, 1936). Disgust with the hypocrisy
implied by continued formal assertion of the medieval doctrine of just war led to the
"realism" of Machiavelli. The League and the Pact may similarly have contributed to
the "realism" of Mussolini and Hitler. See Table 61, Appen. XXIV.

[35] The barbarians of the fifth and sixth centuries usually warred in the name of
Rome, and the princes of the fifteenth and sixteenth centuries or even later in the name
of Christianity and the Holy Roman Empire.

Animal warfare, instituted in response to the hereditary drives of the individual animal, has functioned primarily in the interests of that animal, but, because of natural selection, it has tended to serve also the species of which the individual animal is a member, although the service is unperceived by the initiating animal. Primitive warfare, undertaken at the dictates of the group mores, has served at first the primary fighting group—the clan or the village—but, with the integration of a tribe or even a tribal federation or kingdom as the fighting group, war has served that larger unit. Historic warfare, undertaken in response to the group's conception of its interest, has served at first the military chief. With political integration, however, it has served the kingdom, the empire, or even the civilization as a whole until the latter has disintegrated. Modern war, which has been undertaken in response to the authority of national law, has served at first the ambitious prince or faction, later the national state or the alliance. The idea of making it serve primarily the world-community has been developed in theory but not yet in practice. War has not yet become the police activity of the world-community.

The failures to achieve co-ordination between the motives of war and the needs of the continually expanding social group have resulted in the eventual extermination of most animal species, most primitive peoples, and most civilizations, but the process of evolution has approached nearer to achieving such a co-ordination with each successive attempt. If contemporary efforts to reduce war to the position of a servant of the world-community fail, there will probably be further such efforts in the future.[36]

3. THEORY OF HISTORICAL CHANGE

Changes can be classified as movements toward (*a*) static stability or as movements involved in (*b*) dynamic, (*c*) oscillating, or (*d*) adaptive stability.

a) *Static stability* is a condition in which there is no change at all or in which there are regular and predictable cycles. The movement of a bag of marbles dropped on the floor to positions of rest, or the movements of heavenly bodies, after a celestial collision, into regular orbits would be changes toward this type of stability. The second

[36] See Table 60, Appen. XXIV.

law of thermodynamics asserts that all isolated physical systems tend toward a condition of static stability in which entropy is maximized. It seems probable that this tendency exists in any entity in proportion as it is isolated. If time enough is allowed in which no external influence occurs, the elements of any entity, whether it is a physical system, an organic population, a community, or an ideology, will eventually, whether through chance combination or through the exhaustion of internal springs of action, achieve a condition more stable than any other condition, after which no change can occur until the whole is affected by some external influence.

Static stability, however, depending upon an adjustment to an unchanging external environment, and having within itself no elements of adjustment, is likely to result in catastrophe if any change in external conditions should occur. Such a situation is illustrated by a solar system approaching too near a star, a prisoner for fifty years set at liberty, a tribal community confronted by explorers from overseas, or a religious ideology propagandized in a wholly different culture.[37]

b) *Dynamic stability* is a condition in which the whole suffers no radical or sudden change in configuration or constituents but continually undergoes gradual change in response to external conditions or circumstances. Dynamic stability is not manifested by the mere unrolling of tendencies inherent in the whole. Development or evolution according to the preformationist theory illustrates static, not dynamic, stability. Dynamic stability is manifested only by change in response to unanticipated external influences—changes of the kind assumed by the epigenetic explanation of development and evolution.[38]

Dynamic stability may be manifested by a persistent trend as in organic and social evolution, although this trend normally proceeds

[37] R. L. Buell describes the curious transformations of Christianity among the native Africans (*The Native Problem in Africa* [New York, 1928], I, 120, 747; II, 601 ff.). There were similar transformations of Christianity among the pioneers in the American West creating new religions such as Mormonism. A. J. Toynbee points out that "arrested societies," such as colonial insects, human nomads and utopias, have achieved such static stability that they cannot adapt themselves to changing conditions (*op. cit.*, II, 88 ff.).

[38] See J. H. Woodger, *Biological Principles* (New York, 1929).

through oscillations or sympodial branchings if examined carefully. Thus among organic races the immortal germ cells undergo gradual change, but the animals, within which these cells are carried at any moment, pass through a life-history. The evolving organic population of the earth similarly undergoes oscillations as one dominant type of animals—invertebrates, fishes, reptiles, mammals—successively gives way to another by a sympodial process through geologic time. The same is true of lesser biological communities. Human society may have progressed through steady cumulation of traditions and knowledge, but there have been many oscillations as each civilization in which these traditions are carried has risen and declined, giving way to another.[39] In this case, however, the tradition has sometimes been in large measure lost with the fall of the civilization; consequently, the condition should be considered one of oscillating rather than of dynamic stability.

Dynamic stability can only characterize wholes which are continuously subject to external influences of not too varied or too drastic a sort and which have within themselves some capacity for adaptation. This capacity seems to result from a very delicate balance of the tendency to persist in an existing state (inertia) and the tendency to yield completely in response to an external influence (gravitation).[40] This delicate balance seems to be manifested most perfectly in the immortal genes which carry heredity and provide the basis for organic, social, and ideological evolution. They have "the essential property of duplicating themselves with most extraordinary precision quite regardless of the characteristics of the organism in whose

[39] Mendel and De Vries in biology (mutation theory), Lester Ward and Sorokin in sociology (sympodial theory), and Planck and Bohr in physics (quantum theory) have indicated limitations to the doctrine of continuity or gradualness in nature (*natura non fecit saltum*). See chap. iii, n. 11.

[40] Freud assumes a similar psychological balance between aggression (instinct toward isolation and dissolution) and libido (instinct toward ever closer union) ("Psychoanalysis: Freudian School," *Encyclopaedia Britannica* [14th ed.], XVIII, 673). A. J. Toynbee utilizes the similar conception of Confucianism, Yin and Yang (the passive and active principles whose interaction creates heaven and earth) to account for historic growth. The creative minority successively withdraws to comprehend the permanent and essential (Yin) and returns to modify the ephemeral and nonessential (Yang), thus facilitating successful response by the society to the challenges presented by new conditions (*op. cit.*, III, 374–76).

cells they are carried." Consequently, "certain highly improbable states of organization are hereby multiplied instead of being dissipated as in ordinary thermodynamic systems."[41] The dynamic stability displayed by some social entities results from a delicate balance between the opposing tendencies toward liberty and unity, but the balance is seldom so perfect as to avoid occasional catastrophes and oscillations.[42]

Conditions of dynamic stability have the capacity to persist for very long epochs and amid most extraordinary diversities of conditions as indicated by Percival Lowell in his discussion of the possibility of an organic population upon the planet Mars,[43] but this is only true if changes are never too radical or sudden. Time is the essence of the matter. The delicate balance on which these equilibriums depend will be destroyed by shocks. Consequently, if the environment threatens such shocks, the entity must either eliminate them or anticipate and avoid them in order to save itself.

c) *Oscillating stability* is a condition where even radical or sudden changes in the configuration or constituents of a whole set up reactions in the opposite direction so that over a period of time the whole appears to recover its identity. Such stability, although manifested by the capacity of certain animals to repair themselves from serious injury, such as the loss of limbs, are most characteristic of communities. They may survive radical revolution, prolonged civil war, or even complete subversion of institutions for protracted periods. The supreme court of Poland held in 1922 that the post-war Poland was

[41] Sewall Wright, "Statistical Theory of Evolution," *American Statistical Journal, Supplement*, March, 1932, p. 202. Ethnologists often treat "culture" as a form of dynamic stability (R. H. Lowie, *Culture and Ethnology* [New York, 1917]), and sociologists discuss the equilibrium of societies (N. S. Timasheff, *An Introduction to the Study of the Sociology of Law* [Cambridge, Mass., 1939], p. 141).

[42] See sec. *c*, below. Gierke thus describes the equilibriums in human associations: "But this development from apparently unconquerable variety to unity presents only one side of social progress. All spiritual life, all human endeavours would perforce perish if the idea of unity were alone and exclusively triumphant. With equal force and equal necessity, the opposing idea breaks its way: the idea of persistent multiplicity in every realized unity, of individuality still persisting in the generality, the idea of the rights and independence of all the narrower unities converging in the higher unity, even those of single individuals—the idea of *liberty*" (quoted by John D. Lewis, *The "Genossenschaft" Theory of Otto von Gierke* [Madison, Wis., 1935]).

[43] *Mars as the Abode of Life* (New York, 1908).

the same entity as that which existed before the partitions of over a century earlier, declaring:

> The tradition of Polish statehood has been in existence for at least ten centuries, and the outward expression of the will of the nation to maintain its statehood were the self-sacrifices of hundreds of thousands of Poles who died for their country, and the constantly repeated revolutionary attempt to throw off the laws and institutions imposed by the three conquering powers.[44]

This type of change, most characteristic of the history of human communities, is less calculable than the others. Certain changes may be repeated, thus manifesting a cyclical tendency. Such cycles, however, are usually confused by the influence of longer or shorter fluctuations of different origin, by general evolutionary trends, and by fortuitous external events entirely lacking in cyclical character.

While communities can survive far graver catastrophes than can organisms, there is clearly a limit; consequently, the maintenance of even oscillating stability depends upon control or avoidance of the gravest catastrophes by alert anticipation, possible only if contact with the sources of danger is more or less continuous.

d) *Adaptive stability.*—Changes which may be characterized as adaptive stability do not include all changes in direct conformity to new conditions or circumstances. A whole which responds immediately and completely to changed conditions is so dependent upon its environment that it can hardly be distinguished as a whole at all. A cloud shifting rapidly through many forms, a person who shifts his opinions with his company, a crowd which dissolves at a word, and a logical system which alters its premises at every attack lacks individuality. The gradual change of the form or substance of an entity in response to actual or anticipated conditions or circumstances will not, however, destroy the individuality of the entity, if deliberation is sufficient and, particularly, if the change contributes to a modification of external conditions in the interest of the persistence of the entity. If the lag in mutual adjustment of an entity and its environment is too great, catastrophe will probably result for the entity. If too short, the entity will be indistinguishable from the conditions which alter it.

---

[44] J. F. Williams and H. Lauterpacht, *Annual Digest of Public International Law, 1919–1922* (London, 1932), p. 36.

Stability of this type is most characteristic of ideologies. A science is ready to change its most treasured generalizations in response to an experiment or observation, but it does not do so without sufficient deliberation to make sure of the conflict and of the impossibility of reconciling the observation with established generalizations. A religion, if it is to have stability, must have a living church to reinter- pret doctrine in the light of changing conditions, but in words which facilitate belief in the continuity of doctrine. A supreme court may alter the basic law and a treaty may surrender aspects of sovereignty without destroying a constitution, if these changes are accomplished with due deliberation and with a proper form of words.[45]

Devices for timing the lags in legal or ideological change are as delicate and important for social stability as are devices in organ- isms for maintaining the balance between persistence and adapta- tion. Change of this type may be in a continuous direction, cyclical, or sporadic. Changes of law in respect to currency, for example, may be in response to periodic changes in population and monetary de- mand, in response to seasonal demands, or in response to a depres- sion or disaster. Major social changes, however, usually result from the synthesis of opposing proposals for adaptive change. Since the formulation of the opposing proposals and the solution eventually accepted are affected by an infinite variety of circumstances, such changes cannot be predicted. History has in it elements of choice, contingency, and indeterminism.

[45] "In cases involving the Federal Constitution, where correction through legislative action is practically impossible, this court has often overruled its earlier decisions" (Brandeis, J., dissenting in *Burnet* v. *Coronado Oil and Gas Co.*, 285 U.S. 393, 406 [1932]; M. P. Sharp, "Movement in Supreme Court Adjudication: A Study of Modified and Overruled Decisions," *Harvard Law Review*, XLVI [1933], 361, 593, 795). In 1938 and 1939 the Supreme Court overruled, or "distinguished" with difficulty, its earlier deci- sions in some twenty-five instances, yet the constitutional system continued to exist, though some conservatives registered doubts (R. E. Cushman, "Constitutional Law in 1938–1939," *American Political Science Review*, XXXIV [April, 1940], 249 ff.). "The Court declines to see in the conclusion of any treaty by which a state undertakes to per- form or refrain from performing a particular act an abandonment of its sovereignty. No doubt any convention creating an obligation of this kind places a restriction upon the exercise of the sovereign rights of the State, in the sense that it requires them to be exercised in a certain way. But the right of entering into international engagements is an attribute of state sovereignty" (Permanent Court of International Justice, *Publica- tions* [Ser. A, No. 1], p. 25). See also H. Lauterpacht, *The Development of International Law by the Permanent Court of International Justice* (London, 1934), p. 90.

e) Prediction and change.—The accuracy of prediction depends on the type of change involved. Movements of an entity toward static stability can be predicted in a closed system, the laws of which are known; movements of an entity in dynamic stability can be predicted when the elements of the equilibrium situation, both internal and external, have been analyzed and measured; movements of an entity in oscillating stability cannot be predicted, unless the oscillations have repeated a sufficient number of times to be susceptible of equilibrium analysis, as in the case of a dynamic equilibrium. Otherwise, descriptive knowledge of past reactions of the entity to past environmental changes may provide some basis for judging the probabilities of a not too distant future. Movements manifesting adaptive stability are even more difficult to predict. A variety of adaptive devices may be used and estimates of the probability, the character, and the time of external changes cannot be precise. A doctor may well hesitate to predict what a healthy patient will do when next sick, the nature or incidence of the sickness being still a matter of speculation. A historian can scarcely predict from a study of past conflict situations what the character or the consequences of the next political or ideological conflict will be.

Four processes may be distinguished to account for social change and for the transition from one type of stability to another. (1) *Catastrophe*—the sudden pressure of events, wholly external to the entity under consideration—has been of first importance in producing change in animal and primitive societies. The influence upon history of seasonal or cyclical changes in temperature or climate, floods and droughts, the multiplication of parasites and other natural phenomena producing epidemics, famines, and migrations, has declined with the advance of civilization. (2) *Conquest*—compulsion, penetration, or deprivation arising from conflict or competition with distinct but similar entities—has been an important instrument of change in all stages of culture. Because of the reciprocity inherent in social relations, the victim is seldom entirely lacking in responsibility for such occurrences as military occupation, invasions of alien labor or business, or loss of essential external markets or resources leading to its change or extinction. (3) *Corruption*—gradual internal economic, political, cultural, and social change—has been especially significant in the rise and decay of the historic civilizations. Minor annual changes in the birth and death rates, in the accumulation and distribution of wealth, in the position of classes, in the observance of customs, in the use of technologies and social procedures, in the prestige of institutions, have often cumulated, until the conditions on which social stability has depended are destroyed. (4) *Conversion*—religious and ideological changes flowing from internally or externally initiated propagandas and educational movements—has sometimes so modified public opinion in a short time that the basis of the existing social equilibrium has been destroyed. The importance of this factor in producing change has increased with advancing civilization and means of communication.

Catastrophe, conquest, corruption, and conversion may, singly or in combination, operate to destroy a social equilibrium and to terminate a civilization.[46] These processes lie in the realm of contingency rather than determinism. They resist prediction.

f) Stability and war.—These conceptions of stability and change may explain the history of warfare. Animal warfare, while contributing to the dynamic stability of life during geologic periods, has tended to maintain a condition of static equilibrium during the life of particular biological species, communities, and societies. Fundamental changes in the equilibriums of organic groups and periods of rapid evolution have usually arisen from catastrophes such as mountain formations separating races, widespread glaciations, land elevations or submergencies leading to large-scale migrations, and exterminations.[47] It has been suggested that the last European glaciation was

[46] These four processes are important in accounting, respectively, for physical, biological, sociological, and ideological change. It is, therefore, not surprising that philosophers of history have emphasized one or the other according to the discipline from which they approached the subject. Geographers and meteorologists like Ratzel, Ellsworth Huntington, and Griffith Taylor have emphasized the influence of climate and other features of the physical environment on history. Pseudo-biologists and military men like Gumplowitz, Ratzenhofer, and Colonel Fuller, have emphasized the role of struggle and conflict. Anthropologists, sociologists, economists, and social historians like Karl Marx, Flinders-Petrie, Pitirim Sorokin, and Clark Wissler have emphasized changes in population, institutions, and technologies. Humanists, philosophers, and cultural historians like Hegel, Spengler, and A. J. Toynbee have emphasized the influence of ideas, personalities, and responses to challenges (see above, chap. vii, sec. 2*b*).

[47] See above, chap. iv, sec. 1. Ellsworth Huntington, *World Power and Evolution* (New Haven, 1919), chap. ix.

primarily responsible for the emergence of modern human types from the earlier ape men and for the transition from animal to primitive warfare.[48]

Primitive warfare has assisted in preserving a condition of dynamic stability among primitive peoples. The great traditions and inventions—the use of language, ideas, tools, fire, agriculture, loyalty to customs, social subordination—slowly cumulated and diffused through the stimulation and contacts of war. The total human population increased and distributed itself over the entire earth. While catastrophes such as flooding of the Nile or Mesopotamian valleys may have stimulated the survivors in the area, contributing to social evolution and the emergence of civilizations, it seems more probable that inventions in the field of writing, agriculture, government, and military technique and the wars accompanying these changes were the immediate cause of the transition from primitive culture to historic civilizations. These inventions not only intensified intergroup contacts but also increased the value of land to be attacked or defended, the size and co-ordination of political groups, and the efficiency of instruments of conquest. War for conquest and political unification initiated civilization and spread it.[49]

Historic warfare has contributed toward the oscillating stability which has characterized the course of civilization during the last five or six thousand years. Civilizations have risen and fallen, and in their fall the human race has often lost traditions and inventions of great value; sometimes permanently, sometimes not beyond hope of recovery centuries or millenniums later. Yet the reaction of humanity has always been adequate to invent or rediscover the instruments, institutions, and ideas necessary to build a new civilization. Catastrophes—desiccations, epidemics, famines—have sometimes contributed to the downward sweep of these great cycles. Wars have also contributed. Military conquests and migrations have expanded civilizations. Wars of attrition have destroyed civilizations. But probably more important than either catastrophe or conquest in

[48] Huntington, *op. cit.*, chap. viii; Alfred S. Romer, *Man and the Vertebrates* (Chicago, 1933); Julian Huxley, "Climate and Human History," *Atlantic Monthly*, April, 1930, pp. 512 ff.

[49] Above, chap. iv, secs. 2, 3; Appen. VI.

causing the disintegration of historic civilizations has been the cumulative and corrupting effect of gradual internal population and institutional changes. Population has outgrown the food supply; differential birth rates and excessive race mixtures or excessive inbreeding has deteriorated the stock; wealth and influence differentials have developed, leading to conflict and revolution; and institutions under the influence of tradition have grown inflexible and incapable of making the necessary adjustments.[50]

In the more recent changes of civilization, conversion through conscious propaganda has perhaps been more important than catastrophe, conquest, or corruption. People with a philosophy or religion have consciously sought to modify public opinion, to change institutions, and to reshape society in the direction of an ideal.[51] The early Christians, as pointed out by Gibbon, may have contributed to the fall of Rome, along with the epidemics of the second century, the exhaustion of Italian soil, the barbarian invasions, the decay of Roman institutions, and the decline of population.[52] Certainly the most recent great transition, that from the medieval to the modern world-civilization, while due in part to the epidemics of the fourteenth and fifteenth centuries, to the attrition of later medieval wars, to the discoveries and military conquests in the sixteenth century, and to the decay of medieval secular and ecclesiastical institutions, was due in part to the conscious propaganda of the philosophy of science and liberalism by societies and writers assisted by the art of printing.[53] In recent times general literacy, the press, the radio, and the cinema have greatly increased the importance of education, propaganda, and conversion as agencies of change.

During the last four centuries of world-contact all of these influences toward change have been operative, but on the whole the influence of natural catastrophe has diminished with the progress of medicine and technology, while the influence of war and conquest

---

[50] Above, chap. vii, sec. 2b.   [51] Above, chap. viii, sec. 2c.

[52] A. J. Toynbee (op. cit.) compares the influence of the internal and the external proletariat upon the fall of civilizations.

[53] Above, chap. viii, sec. 1; Appen. XVII. See Harcourt Brown, Scientific Societies in Seventeenth Century France, 1620–1680 (Baltimore, 1933); Andrew D. White, A History of the Warfare of Science and Theology in Christendom (New York, 1896); Martha Ornstein, The Role of Scientific Societies in the Seventeenth Century) Chicago, 1928).

has increased. War has been an important instrument in building world-interdependence and world-civilization, but changes in its techniques, coupled with the very intimacy of world economic and cultural interdependence, threatens to make it an agency to destroy what it has built. Though the absolute influence of war has increased, its relative influence has probably declined. Change has proceeded more rapidly than ever before, and its most important agencies have probably been the corruption of old and the construction of new institutions, the abandonment of old and conversion to new faiths.[54] Has this historic analysis provided any basis for judging the trend of the epoch in which we now are? Can modern civilization be indefinitely maintained in adaptive equilibrium?

4. STABILITY IN CONTEMPORARY CIVILIZATION

A human community cannot suddenly emancipate itself from its history; nevertheless, it has a measure of control over its own future. According to the degree of its isolation, a community has ordinarily pursued policies designed to maintain itself in static, dynamic, oscillating, or adaptive stability. These policies require a community to devote attention respectively to the degree of its isolation from external events, to its general defensive position with reference to external attacks, to the strategical position of its most probable enemy, and to the degree of its dependence upon the community of which it is a part. These directions of attention are likely to lead to policies, respectively, of isolation, preparedness, balance of power, and collective security.

a) Isolation.—If the community is very completely isolated and if it is not already in a condition of static stability, the nature of the static stability toward which its internal forces tend may be estimated. Normally, fission or disintegration of the community is to be anticipated. As a closed physical system tends, according to the second law of thermodynamics, toward a homogeneous distribution of its matter and energy, so a completely isolated community tends toward an equal and anarchic distribution of authority. Organized communities have seldom wished to disintegrate; consequently, they

---

[54] See above, chap. viii, sec. 3; chap. x, secs. 2, 3. For general trends of forms of stability and agencies of change in history see Table 60, Appen. XXIV.

have usually avoided policies of complete isolation. Such a community has realized that a personalized enemy, actual or potential, has been an important stimulus to social integration; consequently, isolation and aggressiveness have often been associated. Public policy based on the assumption of relative isolation, whether the natural result of geography or the artificial result of commercial barriers and political aggressiveness, has tended to produce inflexibility to external changes and to result in disaster in case such changes actually occur on a large scale.

b) Preparedness.—A community which is only moderately isolated has usually pursued policies designed to preserve its identity in dynamic stability and has naturally paid first attention to its defensive position vis-à-vis all probable external influences. Such influences have come to communities in the form of famine, pestilence, or other natural disaster or in the form of military, economic, or propaganda attacks from other states. Such a community may analyze its position in terms of the protection offered against such attack by distance, natural barriers, a satisfied population, an efficient health administration, and reserves of food and raw materials; in terms of the striking power against such attacks by armies and military equipment and by medical and technical experts; in terms of the capacity of the members of the community to transport themselves and supplies, to mobilize at a given point, and to observe instructions; in terms of the morale of the population in pursuing a policy and enduring privations.

Public policy based on the assumption of a strong defensive position has tended to emphasize the most favorable aspects of that position whether in armor, striking power, mobility, or tenacity. The community has tended, as have organic forms affected by orthogenetic evolution, to differentiate from its neighbors in that aspect of its position. When attention has been directed to defensive position, the natural interest of human beings in conflict rather than in harmony has tended to emphasize material agencies of defense and attack, sometimes stimulating policies of aggressiveness on the theory that an offensive is the best defense. Specialization in a certain type of material defense, such as walls or fortifications, has sometimes reduced the community's capacity easily to adapt itself to other methods and eventually, when conditions have arisen for which the type of specialization is not suitable, like the Jurassic dinosaurs, the community has succumbed. Organic evolution has proceeded through extinction of the main lines of evolution in each geologic period. Less specialized forms have dominated in the next period, themselves to become overspecialized in time. Social evolution, relying on defensive specialization, has followed the same course. A dynamic equilibrium, though it may progress gradually for a long time, eventually produces great oscillations.[55]

c) Balance of power.—A community with numerous contacts and anxious to maintain its identity has usually anticipated oscillation in its history. Unable to defend itself by its own resources from all the external threats to its existence, it has concentrated on its most dangerous enemies and by alliance and occasional war has hoped to maintain a precarious independence. When the attention of a community has been devoted less to its own strength than to the changing policy and strength of probable enemies, overspecialization on a particular form of defense has been unlikely. A readiness to adapt in any direction has been preserved. The community has made use of the anticipatory advantage which, as a community, it enjoys over biological organisms. Such a policy has led to rapid or gradual change in the community contingent upon particular external circumstances. The disadvantage of this policy lies in the difficulty of anticipating and appraising sources of danger in an anarchic and dynamic world. As probable enemies have become more numerous, the game of juggling the balance of power has become more difficult. The tendency toward polarization of the equilibrium and toward expansion of the system has sometimes resulted in termination of the independence of the community and sometimes in the extinction of the civilization in which it figured.

d) Collective security.—When a community's contacts with and dependence upon external conditions has become very great, it may envisage that external environment as a whole and direct its policy

---

[55] G. Elliot Smith (*Human History* [London, 1930]) regards the slight morphological specialization of man as compared to most other animals as an important asset. Herbert Spencer notes the inevitability of evolution eventuating in dissolution (*First Principles*, chap. xxiv)

toward gradually modifying the environment if it can and adapting itself to the environment if it must. A community so completely integrated with its milieu by communication and transportation that its parts naturally adapt themselves immediately in response to external changes has been able to preserve its identity only in so far as it could exercise a reasonable influence in the regulation of this environment. Thus when the public policy of a community has recognized its high degree of dependence on the larger group, it has attempted to organize that group into a dependable community, whose behavior it can in a measure predict and whose policy it can in some measure influence. Such a task of building a federation and of adapting itself to membership therein has presented problems so difficult that the policy has often failed and the civilization has collapsed.[56]

e) *National policies and stability.*—In the changing conditions of the modern world no particular state has persistently followed any one of these policies. Since World War I, the United States, while at times moving toward isolationism and at other times toward collective security, has in general pursued the policy of concentrating on its own defense, by disarmament agreements if possible and by armament-building if necessary. Germany, Italy, and Japan, while exponents of collective security after Locarno, abandoned that policy because they considered the existing procedures of peaceful change inadequate and after 1931 oscillated between policies of balance of power and of artificial isolation by autarchy and aggression. The Soviet Union after some experiments with balance-of-power policies accepted collective security until 1936, when it began to ape the United States in a purely defensive policy. In 1939 it began to follow Germany in aggressiveness. For fifteen years after World War I, Great Britain and France championed collective security adulterated, however, by the balance of power. After formation of the

[56] These four policies of isolation, defensive specialization, balance of power, and collective security have a relation to the four policies which the technical changes in war have suggested (see chap. xii, sec. 4). An important English group in 1935 discussed "armed isolation, balance of power and alliances, and collective security" as alternative policies which had been suggested for preventing war with the conclusion that only the latter offered "a prospect of real security for the British Commonwealth and the world's peaceful development" (*The Next Five Years: An Essay in Political Agreement* [London, 1935], pp. 221–26).

Rome-Berlin axis, there followed half-hearted balance-of-power policies. Britain, like the United States and the Soviet Union, at times manifested a disposition to retire to defensive specialization. The smaller powers, after failure of sanctions in the Manchurian and Ethiopian wars, attempted to improve their military defenses, to gain the protection of balance-of-power alliances, or to withdraw into the isolation of neutrality—sometimes to do all three at once.

The circumstances of states in recent times has not precisely conformed to the conditions which have in the past often led to the adoption of one or the other of these policies. The natural isolation of all states has decreased. All the world has, under the influence of communication, trade, and technology, become a single community.[57]

Reliance upon natural isolation for security has resulted in disaster. Reliance upon an artificial isolation by declarations of neutrality or by a truculent policy has proved even more dangerous.

Reliance by a state upon its own defensive resources alone has become increasingly dangerous as military inventions (the submarine and airplane), propaganda inventions (the radio and "fifth column"), and economic inventions (currency and commercial controls) have increased the difficulties of immediate defense and the probability of an eventually destructive stalemate. Specialization on armament, on economic self-sufficiency, or on domestic-opinion control may court the fate of the dinosaurs. Military, moral, and economic disarmament by agreement has proved difficult to achieve and to enforce and, when not co-ordinated with procedures of peaceful change, has proved too inflexible for a dynamic world.

For a state to estimate the strategic position of probable enemies in order to preserve the balance of power has become increasingly difficult. A larger number of states enter into the balance than former-

---

[57] "Three major concepts—that large overseas outlets for population no longer exist, that through state intervention in economic life the world has a new international pattern, and that internal policies adopted by nations may yield profound international complications—were brought out in the Thirteenth Institute [under the Norman Wait Harris Memorial Foundation]" (*Geographic Aspects of International Relations*, ed. C. C. Colby [Chicago, 1938], Editor's Foreword). This is one of numerous illustrations of the degree in which careful observers perceive that the fact of increasing integration of the world-community in its material aspects impinges upon the freedom of national policies. See above, chap. xiii, sec. 2d; chap. xiv, sec. 2.

ly, contacts are more numerous, the factors in the equilibrium are more difficult to calculate, and governments, bound to consider the opinion of their own publics, cannot act with sufficient rapidity. Despotisms have proved better adapted to balance-of-power policies than democracies.

f) Modernism and stability.—Each of the historic civilizations eventually reached a point at which some of its members recognized that they were dependent on the whole. Attempts were often made to organize the entire civilization into a federal community within which each could preserve its identity. These attempts failed to produce adequate institutions usually because of influences external to the whole civilization or because of inadequate internal communications. After World War I, for the first time in human history, with means of instantaneous communication available throughout most of the world, the attempt was made to organize the whole world politically.

The dependence of nations upon the world-community was obscured during the nineteenth century because the rapid development of applied science gave national communities a sense of mastery over the food supply and because the liberal influence of British sea power assured moderate national security and freedom of trade. More recently, through the development of propaganda and policies of national self-sufficiency, governments have acquired a mastery over internal public opinion. This has again given them an exaggerated sense of independence. These subjective attitudes, however, have not emancipated communities from ever greater dependence on the world-community if their present population and planes of living are to be preserved. This thought was expressed by a special committee of the League of Nations on the development of international co-operation in economic and social affairs on the eve of World War II.

There has never been a time when international action for the promotion of economic and social welfare was more vitally necessary than it is at the present moment. The work of the League in these fields has developed and changed its nature in recent years, and the changes that have taken place necessitate, as we see it, a careful consideration of the means by which the mechanism of international collaboration can be rendered at once more efficient and more available to all.

There are two tendencies in the world today which render the need for Government co-operation in economic and social questions more urgent than heretofore, and at the same time give greater opportunities for the success of such co-operation.

The world, for all its political severance, is growing daily closer knit; its means of communication daily more rapid; its instruments for the spread of knowledge daily more efficient. At the same time the constituent parts of the world, for all their diversity of political outlook, are growing in many respects more similar; agricultural States are becoming rapidly industrialized, industrial States are stimulating their agriculture. Nothing is more striking in this connection, or more characteristic, than the swift industrial development of the great Asiatic countries.

These changes inevitably give rise to new problems that can only be solved by joint effort. Thus trade and personal contacts are facilitated, but simultaneously economic depression becomes more widespread; and, were there any relaxation of control, human and animal disease would spread more widely and more rapidly. Neither the economic nor the physical contagion—nor, indeed, the moral—can be checked by national action alone, except by recourse to almost complete isolation.

Indeed, to attempt such isolation is one of the first natural reactions to the more frequent and intenser impact of these world forces. But it reflects rather a blind instinct to ward off these impacts than a desire of the constituent parts of a changing world to adapt themselves to what in the long run must prove the irresistible dynamism of these changes; and there can be no development without adaptation.[58]

This statement suggests that the historic cause of war has been the "blind instinct" of a group to preserve its identity by isolation from the "irresistible dynamism" of increasingly frequent and intense contacts. The blind instinct of civilized communities has been the faith, handed down from the communities past, constituting its unity and establishing the values by which its members guide their lives. The functioning of faiths has in the past depended upon general belief in their eternal validity; consequently, whatever has appeared to impair the integrity of the faith has been resisted by the community.

The inevitable dynamism of increasing world-contacts has been the consequence of the development and diffusion of science and technology which have continuously modified the human signifi-

---

[58] *League of Nations Monthly Summary, Special Supplement*, August, 1939, p. 7.

cance of time, space, and matter, have continuously elevated the horizon of men, and have continuously disclosed new ways of living unknown to the historic faiths. The cumulative growth of science and invention has offered men the opportunity to rise above the limitations of earlier faiths. On the other hand, the political, social, and religious traditions, the continued existence of the community, itself, has persistently demanded that they keep within those limits.

Expanding contacts have therefore been the cause both of progress and of war—of progress because human contacts are the condition of science, invention, and change; of war because change has always been resisted by human institutions, customs, and faiths.[59] Among primitive people war became serious when borrowing or invention broke the control of custom.[60] Among civilizations the slow advance of science, though suggesting new policies, could not at first modify those sanctioned by traditional beliefs and supported by powerful institutions. Thus in each civilization the disparity between policies based on what has been and those based on what might be grew, until the gap was closed by long periods of violence in which the civilization often collapsed.[61]

In modern civilization the cumulative and accelerating growth in the achievements and prestige of science has made the obsolescence of traditional beliefs more rapid than ever before, while the power behind the advocates of both the future and the past have become greater. Science, seeking to eliminate human catastrophes and ready to be converted to new ideas, has been in conflict with faith, seeking to prevent the corruption of ancient formulations and institutions but prepared to conquer a wider area in which they might flourish.[62] Modernism has sought to develop a higher frame of reference in which both science and faith might be subsumed.[63] It has envisaged

---

[59] See sec. 2a, above.   [60] See chap. vi, sec. 2.   [61] See chap. vii, sec. 3b.

[62] J. W. Draper, *History of the Conflict between Religion and Science* (1874); White, *op. cit.*

[63] Charles Hartshorne (*Beyond Humanism: Essays in a New Philosophy of Nature* [Chicago, 1937]), inspired by Whitehead and Peirce, seeks to combine quantum physics with modern theology and modern philosophy into what may be called "theistic naturalism" or "naturalistic theism."

society as a process by which institutions and beliefs are continuously adjusted to the most accurate forecasts which science can offer
of the future. Modernism has hoped to eliminate human catastrophes and conquests by social and scientific procedures for continuously testing the present value of ideas and beliefs. It has, however,
recognized that such procedures can be effective only if humanity
becomes less reluctant to accept the new and to abandon the old
than it has been in the past.[64]

[64] Chap. viii, n. 13.

APPENDIXES

APPENDIX I

THE CAUSES OF WAR PROJECT AT THE UNIVERSITY OF CHICAGO

These volumes bring to an end a study of war begun at the University of Chicago in 1926. In the spring of that year, on the initiative of Professor Charles E. Merriam, several members of the departments of political science, economics, history, sociology, anthropology, geography, psychology, and philosophy met together and discussed topics for research on the causes of war. There was no general theory of the subject to begin with, but the present writer prepared a twelve-page memorandum which grouped the suggestions developed by the discussion into eighteen major projects, subdivided into a total of some seventy-five studies. The major projects were grouped under three general heads: (a) antecedents of war, (b) attitude of political groups, and (c) international maladjustments. This arrangement was justified by the following statement:

The situation normally leading to war may be provisionally defined as follows: certain unusual events occur which cause a sensitive political group to react with external violence in the direction of existing international tensions. The following outline is based on the assumption that the initiating events, the reaction patterns of the group, and the conditions causing international tension are sufficiently independent so that each can be studied under the assumption that the others remain constant.

In the autumn of 1927 a document selecting twenty-nine of these studies for prior consideration was submitted to the Social Science Research Committee of the University of Chicago. This document elaborated the statement quoted from the earlier document.

There appear to be three general points of view from which this investigation may be approached. Every war is preceded by certain incidents or events which account for its having occurred at just the time it did. It is also true that wars occur between nations, but that nations differ in the frequency and circumstances under which they fight. Finally, at all periods of history and in all parts of the world there are varieties of international contacts which create varying probabilities of war. Thus, three general lines of study are suggested. The first takes a *war* as a center and attempts to determine its causes. A second takes the *nation* as the center and attempts to determine the internal conditions which predispose it to fight. The third takes *international relations* as the center and attempts to discover the tensions of the modern world which occasion wars.

1. *Antecedents of war.*—The first line of study may be hoped to yield information as to the relative importance of the various factors which have caused modern war and as to the dependence of these factors upon permanent or temporary conditions. Thus, for instance, data might be collected which would furnish some basis for judging the relative importance of the search for markets and raw materials, of nationality movements, of the feeling of insecurity, of propaganda from interested sources, etc., in the causation

of modern war. Information also might be found as to which of these factors are peculiar to the modern industrial age and which of them were important in the causation of wars in earlier periods of history and in different civilizations.

2. *Attitude of political groups.*—A superficial examination shows that the war histories of nations differ very greatly. Some are fighting very frequently, some very rarely; some are fighting wars of one type and some of another. Thus a series of studies designed to define these national differences, and in so far as possible trace their causes, would seem pertinent.

3. *International maladjustments.*—The subject matter as well as the methods of international relations has differed considerably geographically, historically, and functionally. Thus, studies designed to show the consequences of various forms of international contact, financial, territorial, migrational, cultural, etc., may be devised with a view to forecasting the seriousness of different forms of international contact under varying circumstances.

The studies are all designed with the scientific object of discovering the actual causes of war and with little reference to the problem of control. It is to be hoped, however, that the conditions which can and cannot be affected by human effort may be disclosed and the lines of effort suggested. Thus the studies may not be without practical value.

The Social Science Research Committee approved certain of these investigations and during the next seven years made grants to its subcommittee on the Causes of War of which the present writer was chairman. Twenty-five research assistants, mostly of graduate student level, were employed for periods of one or more years each. These assistants worked under the supervision of members of the faculty in the social science departments of the University. While the initial organization of the study was to some extent preserved, there was no effort to prevent modifications as lines of investigation proved profitable or the reverse. In addition to the studies carried on by research assistants, several others which fitted into the project were undertaken by students working for advanced degrees or by members of the faculty, with the result that sixty-six manuscripts have been completed. These roughly fall into the following seven groups, of which Groups 1 and 2 deal in general with the antecedents of war; Groups 3, 4, and 5 with the attitude of political groups; and Groups 6 and 7 with international maladjustments. While this organization of the subject, which figured in the original outline, has had some influence upon the arrangement of Part IV of the present study, which deals with the control of war, it has seemed advisable to precede this by a broad historical background (Part II) and by an analysis distinguishing the technological, ideological, sociological, and psychological aspects of war (Part III).

1. War and Battle Statistics
   *Mary J. Brumley, "Minor Wars in the British Empire since 1900" (1928)
   †Lula Caine, "Minor Wars and Interventions of the United States" (1929)
   William T. R. Fox, "A Classification of Military Campaigns in the World since
      1900" (1937)
   *Ruby Garrick (Mrs. Clifton Utley), "Campaigns in the Pacific since 1900" (1930)
   James C. King, "European Battle Statistics since 1620" (1934)

*John F. Melby, "Wars, Revolutions, and Interventions in Latin America" (1936)

Clifton Utley, "European Wars since 1700" (1929)

*Edna Wallace (Mrs. F. Lowell Curtis), "French Wars in North Africa" (1930)

*Wilbur W. White, "Wars in Arabia since 1900" (1929)

2. Military Policy and Armaments

*Lois Anthes, "The German Demand for Armament Equality" (1934)

†Marion Boggs, *Attempts To Define and Limit "Aggressive" Armament in Diplomacy and Strategy* ("University of Missouri Studies," Vol. XVI, No. 1 [1941]).

*Charles Gray Bream, "American Munitions Makers in Latin America" (1939)

†Bernard Brodie, "Major Naval Inventions and Their Consequences in International Politics, 1814–1918" (published as *Sea Power in the Machine Age,* by the Princeton University Press, 1941)

Alice M. Christenson, "British Naval Policy, 1876–1900" (1928)

*Ralph Kinsley, "The Control of the Arms Trade" (1929)

†A. F. Kovacs, "Military Legislation of Germany and France" (1934) (thesis deals only with Prussian and German military history)

*William Mackenson, "An Analysis of Admiral Mahan's Sea-Power Theory" (1936)

Nathan Reich, "Military and Naval Expenditures of the Great Powers since 1870" (1929)

Max Swearingen, "The French Parliament and Armaments since 1870" (1930)

3. Politics and Diplomacy

*Edward H. Buehrig, "Why We Annexed the Philippines" (1934)

†Royden Dangerfield, "The Treaty-making Power in the United States" (published as *In Defense of the Senate,* by the University of Oklahoma Press, 1933)

†James C. King, "Some Elements of National Solidarity" (1933)

A. F. Kovacs, "The Development of the Principle of the Balance of Power" (1932)

†James Q. Reber, "War and Diplomacy in the German Reich" (1939)

†Walter H. Ritsher, *Criteria of Capacity for Independence* (Jerusalem: Syrian Orphanage Press, 1934)

Fred Schuman, *War and Diplomacy in the French Republic* (New York: McGraw-Hill Book Co., 1931)

*Janice Simpson, "The Effect of Changes in the Technique of International Communications on Diplomacy" (1932)

†Tatsuji Takeuchi, *War and Diplomacy in the Japanese Empire* (New York: Doubleday, Doran & Co., 1935)

†Wilbur W. White, *The Process of Change in the Ottoman Empire* (Chicago: University of Chicago Press, 1937)

4. Propaganda and Public Opinion

*Hazel Benjamin, "Official Propaganda of the French Press during the Franco-Prussian War" (published in part in *Journal of Modern History,* June, 1932)

†Philip Davidson, *Propaganda in the American Revolution* (Chapel Hill: University of North Carolina Press, 1941)

†Schuyler Foster, "Studies of American News of the World War" (published in part in *American Journal of Sociology,* January, 1934)

Luella Gettys (Mrs. V. O. Key), "Propaganda in the Wars of the United States" (1930)

*Charles Hauck, "Religion and the Peace Movement in the United States since 1920" (1936)

*Mary Frances Hedges, "Education for Internationalism in the Elementary Schools of the United States" (1938)

†Frank Klingberg, "Studies in the Measurement of Relations among Sovereign States" (1939)

Egon Lentner, "Italian Irredenta Propaganda in the Tyrol" (1930)

Carl J. Nelson, "Attitudes in the United States toward China and Japan, 1937–38" (published in substance with Quincy Wright, in *Public Opinion Quarterly*, January, 1939)

*Margaret Otis, "Measurement of National Attitudes during a War Crisis" (1940)

James T. Russell, "National Attitudes in the Far Eastern Controversy" (published in substance with Quincy Wright, in *American Political Science Review*, August, 1933)

5. Anthropology and Psychology

Walter Dyk, "The Effect of Changes of Technique on Warfare among Primitive and Barbarous People" (1931)

*Harry Hoijer, "Primitive Warfare" (1929)

Harold Lasswell, *World Politics and Personal Insecurity* (New York: McGraw-Hill Book Co., 1935)

Charles K. A. Wang, "Attitudes on War and Peace" (1932)

6. Economics and Finance

Brent D. Allinson, "Population Pressure as a Cause of War" (1930)

†W. B. Harvey, "Tariff Policy and European Wars, 1870–1917" (1938)

H. P. Jenkins, "Economic Dependence of States in Relation to War, 1870–1914" (1931)

Eugene Staley, *War and the Private Investor* (New York: (Doubleday, Doran & Co., 1935)

Jacob Viner, "World Politics and Public Finance" (published in the *Journal of Business of the University of Chicago*, April and July, 1928, and *Southwestern Political and Social Science Quarterly*, March, 1929)

7. Law and Organization

†William B. Ballis, *The Legal Position of War: Changes in Its Practice and Theory from Plato to Vattel* (The Hague: Martinus Nijhoff, 1937)

*Margaret Chandler, "The Intension and Effect of Article 16 of the League of Nations Covenant" (1936)

Rogers Churchill, "Transfers of European Territory since 1815" (1928)

†William T. R. Fox, "Some Effects upon International Law of the Governmentalization of Private Enterprise" (1940)

†W. N. Hogan, "The Problem of Nonbelligerency since the World War" (1939)

†Lawrence V. Howard, "Settlements of International Disputes to Which the United States Was a Party" (1931)

*Sydney Hyman, "Responsibility of States in Respect to Hostile Utterances of Officials" (1938)

*Raymond Ickes, "Impartiality and Neutrality in International Law" (1936)

†Majid Khadduri, *The Law of War and Peace in Islam* (London: Luzac & Co., 1938)

*Harry Malm, "A Comparison of the Method of Settling Disputes between States of the United States and between Sovereign States" (1934)

†Helen M. Moats, "The League of Nations Secretariat" (1936)

†Janice Simpson, "The Position in International Law of Measures of Economic Coercion Carried on within a State's Territory" (1935)

†John E. Stoner, "The Origin of the Outlawry of War" (1937)

†Vernon Van Dyke, "The Responsibility of States in Connection with International Propaganda" (published in part in *American Journal of International Law*, January, 1940)

*Henry Wei, "The Sino-Japanese Hostilities and International Law" (1939)

*Max White, "Pacific Settlement Engagements among Pacific Countries" (published in part in J. B. Condliffe [ed.], *Problems of the Pacific, 1929*, pp. 602–20)

Quincy Wright, Studies on the Legal Position of War in Contemporary International Law (*American Journal of International Law*, October, 1924; January, 1925; April, 1932; January, 1933; July, 1935; December, 1935; January, 1936; July, 1938; January, 1939; July, 1940; October, 1940; April, 1941)

Of these sixty-six studies, forty-five were accepted as theses for Master's (indicated by *) or Doctor's (indicated by †) degrees in the University of Chicago, and the manuscripts are in the University of Chicago Library. Ten of the studies have subsequently been published in full as books (indicated by italics), and seven have been published in substance as journal articles. The remaining studies are in manuscript form in the custody of the Causes of War Committee at the University of Chicago.

While it was felt that the project would justify itself if it stimulated research and publication in the field, it was hoped that it might also provide the basis for a more complete analysis of the causes of war than had heretofore appeared, perhaps pointing the way toward practical steps for the prediction and the control of war. When the mass of manuscripts had been completed, it fell to the present writer to attempt to digest them, as well as such portions of the vast literature of the field as he could examine, into a logical and useful system.

A preliminary attempt in this direction was made in a series of ten lectures given by the present writer at the University of Chicago in the spring of 1933 and in part repeated in five lectures given at the Graduate Institute of International Studies at Geneva in the autumn of 1934. The latter course of lectures was published under the title *The Causes of War and the Conditions of Peace* (London: Longmans, Green & Co., 1935). A briefer summary was presented to the American Sociological Society at its annual meeting in December, 1937, and subsequently published in the *American Sociological Review* for August, 1938. The present volumes further elaborate the general design of these lectures.

APPENDIX II

CO-OPERATIVE RESEARCH ON WAR

The history of this project contained in Appendix I and in the Preface indicates that the project was a co-operative one, in that the topics of the initial investigations emerged from the discussion of a group of scholars, in that there was much discussion and comment among the collaborators as the investigation continued, and in that the results in the published studies and the present résumé were criticized when completed by members of the group. Each of the manuscripts and publications, however, is the work of an individual scholar who alone is responsible for its data, methods, and conclusions. There has been no effort to arrive at a collective interpretation, much less to impose the views of the director of the project, or of anyone else, upon any collaborator. Topics which fitted into the initial outline were in many cases suggested to the research assistants, but some of the most valuable studies were initiated by the assistants themselves, and, as the project progressed, the original outline suffered considerable modification.

1. NATURE OF CO-OPERATIVE RESEARCH

The experience of working with this project for fifteen years has convinced the writer that co-operative research is valuable in proportion as it is flexible. The participants should be free to initiate and develop their projects with a minimum of group control and a maximum of group encouragement. Effective research is a work of individual scholarship free to modify conceptions and to reinterpret data as the subject develops.

It is true that certain routine tasks of assembling materials from well-known sources and analyzing them according to well-established techniques can be accomplished by individuals acting under detailed direction. In the social and other sciences a competent research worker can often accomplish much more in a given time by using assistants to perform these routines. But in such a case the assistants are not engaged in research much more than are stenographers or adding machines that are similarly used for routine work. Valuable integration of ideas with materials is seldom accomplished except by the person who has, through his own thought, made the ideas part of his personality and devised the means for establishing them by the assembly and organization of concrete data.

Co-operative research thus consists in the attraction of the interest of a group of research workers to a subject, the encouragement and mutual assistance which flows from a free discussion of the problem, and the self-criticism which may be stimulated by comment upon and criticism of results by others working on the problem from a different point of view.[1]

Proposals for co-operative study of war prior to the present project had been made by governments, by international institutions, and by national associations.

2. NATIONAL GOVERNMENTS

The larger governments have available important materials for studying the problem of war and peace. It might be supposed that they would have the interest to maintain continuous investigations in this field. They spend a large proportion of their revenues and energies on preparation for war, and on war itself, and it would appear that the most authoritative information bearing upon the probability of the state becoming involved in war in general or with a particular country and upon the factors affecting this probability would make possible a more efficient direction of defensive and preventive measures.

With this in mind the writer in 1930 addressed letters to high officers of the United States Army and Navy and the Department of State, asking whether any such studies had ever been made. Courteous replies were received indicating that the planning division of the general staff of the army makes, on the one hand, *general plans* for improvement of the defense of the most vulnerable points of attack upon the United States without specific reference to any particular foreign state and, on the other hand, *specific plans* "for operations against a particular state if and when it appears that war with that state had entered the field of reasonable possibility. The greater the probability of war with that state, the further will such plans be carried toward completion." While the general staff has not evolved "any formula for determining the degree of probability of war with a particular state that is better than the reasoned judgment of any other equally well informed person or group," it does make occasional "estimates of the situation" which seek "to analyze and give due weight to the political, economic, social, racial and any other factors" that bear upon that probability. Such estimates are, of course, so interwoven with plans of defense that they are confidential. The general board of the navy continually makes similar plans and estimates of the situation.

The Department of State has a division of research and publication, a division of cultural relations, two advisers on political relations, and an economic adviser, but none of these agencies are specifically charged with studying the causes of war. Bills have been debated in congress for establishing a division for that purpose.[2] The Department of State official addressed in 1930 commented

[1] See Louis Wirth (ed.), *Eleven Twenty-six: A Decade of Social Science Research* (Chicago, 1940), especially comments by Robert T. Crane (p. 122), Mark A. May (p. 131), James C. Bonbright (p. 134), W. F. Ogburn (p. 138), Beardsley Ruml (p. 139), Meno Lovenstein (p. 140), Franz Neumann (p. 142), L. J. Henderson (p. 144), Rensis Likert (p. 145), and A. R. Hatton (p. 146).

[2] See H. J. Res. 304, *To Establish a Peace Division in the Department of State*, introduced by Representative Dirksen of Illinois (73d Cong., 2d sess. [Washington, 1935]).

on the "difficulty and delicacy of attempting to analyze the sources of the mass emotions which produce the symptoms of 'war fever,'" and inclosed the following suggestive summary of "a few of the elements which might be considered."

1. Unsettled political problems, especially those relating to recent transfers of territory, treatment of minorities, border incidents, recent invasions or interventions.

2. Political propaganda conducted by official or private agencies in the interest of irredentism, territorial expansion, economic salesmanship on a basis of hatred for the products of a certain country, and social or subversive agitation.

3. Economic discriminations levied against the trade of one or more countries, or measures designed to perpetuate a state of national economic inferiority for a politically weak nation, tariff wars, etc.

4. Armaments, competitive in character or disproportionate to the military strength of a neighbor, preparations for war made with undisguised reference to the power or policy of another country.

5. Economic and social unrest, unemployment, business depression, tending to make domestic difficulties appear the result of foreign political developments, or to make war appear as the most practical substitute for radical domestic unheaval.

6. Individual boredom, weariness of pulling levers and punching timeclocks, failure to dramatize peacetime activities or to sublimate belligerent tendencies through sport, motion pictures, literature, etc.

7. Journalism. The fact that controversy has a greater news interest than agreement, that catastrophe is more interesting than order, that war is more exciting to write or read about than is peace, and that prejudice against the foreigner is a universal trait among all peoples.

While the writer has no direct information concerning the activities of other national governments in the field, it is probable that all the defense and foreign offices consider the subject but that comprehensive co-operative studies of the problem have been rare and, if made, are highly confidential.

Legislative bodies, legislative committees, and courts have occasionally considered the causes of particular wars or of war in general. Assumptions with respect to these causes have frequently underlain the action of such bodies in declaring war or policy, in approving treaties and territorial transfers, in legislating on neutrality or military preparation, or in interpreting and applying international law and national legislation affecting international relations. The testimony and discussion adduced by such bodies often contain valuable materials bearing upon the subject. The official acts, reports, and opinions of such bodies, however, have seldom stated explicit conclusions on the subject, and, on the rare occasions when they have, the conclusions have been based on undisclosed or unargued assumptions or on evidence relevant to a particular situation and have contributed little to scientific understanding of the problem.[3]

[3] The numerous and often voluminous hearings by the United States congressional committees on disarmament, neutrality, defense, annexations, and treaties have occasionally elucidated theories on the causes of war but have seldom resulted in reports dealing explicitly with the subject. The hearings on the Treaty of Versailles and the League of Nations Covenant (66th Cong., 1st sess., Sen. Doc. 105) contained very little

3. THE LEAGUE OF NATIONS

In April, 1929, the Economic Committee of the League of Nations undertook a study of "Economic Tendencies Affecting the Peace of the World." Memorandums prepared by Professors André Siegfried and J. Bonn suggested certain topics for inquiry in the fields of population, raw material, loans, transportation, and commercial policy. This activity arose from the resolution of the Economic Conference of 1927 which "recognized that the maintenance of world peace depends largely on the principles on which the economic policies of nations are framed and executed," and recommended that "the governments and peoples of the countries here represented should together give continued attention to this aspect of the economic problem, and look forward to the establishment of recognized principles designed to eliminate those economic difficulties which cause friction and misunderstanding in a world which had everything to gain from peaceful and harmonious progress." In spite of the insistence by certain mem-

---

testimony concerning the theory of war and peace upon which the Covenant was based, but the majority report of the Senate Foreign Relations Committee stated categorically that the treaty would "breed wars" (66th Cong., 1st sess., Sen. Rep. 176, September 10, 1919, p. 7), while the minority report stated with brief argument that "it would save the world from war and preparations for wars" (*ibid.*, Part II, p. 5). The War Policies Commission of 1931, on the other hand, in its hearing adduced numerous theories concerning the causation and prevention of war (72d Cong., 1st sess., H. Doc. 163, December 10, 1931, pp. 612 ff.), but, while considering itself authorized by the preamble of Resolution 98 on which it acted to study means "to promote peace," reported only on "practical" questions of policy in case of war (*ibid.*, p. ix, and 72d Cong., 1st sess., H. Doc. 271, p. 1). The Nye Committee investigating the munitions industry in 1934 on the basis of Resolution 206 (73d Cong., 2d Sess.), which assumed that "the influence of the commercial motive is one of the inevitable factors often believed to stimulate and sustain war" (*Hearings*, I, 1, and address by Senator Nye including article from *Fortune Magazine* [*Congressional Record*, March 6 and 12, 1934]), reported that private shipbuilding, munition, and newspaper interests working for profits may ignite "the powder keg of international relations" (*Munitions Industry: Preliminary Report of the Special Committee on Investigation of the Munitions Industry Pursuant to S. Res. 206, 74th Cong., 1st Sess., Sen. Rep. 944* [Washington, 1935], pp. 2 and 6). (More than five thousand pages of hearings were recorded from September, 1934, to February, 1935.) Courts have assumed that negligence in protecting acknowledged rights of foreign governments may lead to war (see *Emperor of Austria* v. *Day and Kossuth*, 2 Gifford 628 [1861]; *Schooner Exchange* v. *McFaddon*, 7 Cranch 116 [1812]); have sometimes determined the origin and character of wars and other types of hostilities (*The Prize Cases*, 2 Black 635 [1863]; *Talbot* v. *Seemans*, 1 Cranch 1 [1801]; *Durand* v. *Hollins*, 4 Blatch. 451 [1860]); and have more rarely attributed responsibility for the initiation of war or hostile acts (*The Lusitania*, 251 Fed. 715 [1918]; *The Prize Cases*, 2 Black 635 [1863]). They have, however, commonly regarded such questions as political and have sought and followed the opinions of the political organs of government. Consequently, they have contributed little to the theory of the causation of war (Q. Wright, *The Control of American Foreign Relations* [New York, 1922], pp. 83 ff., 172 ff.).

418 A STUDY OF WAR

bers of the Economic Consultative Committee of the League that this "ought
to be treated as something more than a pious resolution," the Economic Committee thought "the subject as a whole is not at the present state suitable for the
treatment pursued in other cases, namely, an expert inquiry leading immediately
to international conferences and conventions"; consequently, "unofficial discussion and a wider basis of public interest and education are desirable," and "it
would be of great help if the interests of economists and others could be stimulated." The committee hoped that the memorandums of Professors Bonn and
Siegfried might provide such stimuli.[4] While the League made many investigations on concrete projects for improvement of the economic and other relations
of states,[5] this discussion indicates that its methods of work were not adapted to
producing a broad analysis of the causes of war.

The Committee on Intellectual Cooperation of the League of Nations through
its executive organ, the International Institute of Intellectual Cooperation, and
through the Permanent International Studies Conference established in 1928,
has made definite and continuous efforts to stimulate research on the subject of
war and peace. The collections of correspondence published by this Institute
and the voluminous data-papers presented to the sessions of the Studies Conference by scholars of many nationalities provide a mine of materials for investi-
gators of the field, but they have not developed a unified conception of the causes
of war.[6]

4. THE INSTITUTE OF PACIFIC RELATIONS

A similar stimulus has been given to studies on problems of peace and war
among the countries with territories bordering the Pacific Ocean by the Institute
of Pacific Relations. This organization has held conferences every two or three
years since 1925 attended by groups of scholars selected by unofficial national
councils in each of the Pacific countries.[7] A mass of data-papers has been pre-

[4] League of Nations, *Economic Tendencies Affecting the Peace of the World* (Geneva),
April 9, 1929); *ibid.*, May 21, 1929, reprinting extracts from *Transactions of the Economic
Committee* (27th and 28th sess.), from the Economic Consultative Committee (1st and
2d sess.), and from the *Proceedings of the World Economic Conference* (1927).

[5] See Herbert Feis, *Research Activities of the League of Nations* (Old Lyme, Conn.:
Margaret Peabody Fund, 1929); Secretariat of the League of Nations, *The Aims, Meth-
ods and Activity of the League of Nations* (Geneva, 1935). The Bruce Report (League of
Nations, *The Development of International Cooperation in Economic and Social Affairs*
[Geneva, August, 1939]), published by a special committee of the council on the eve
of World War II, contained a brief analysis of the causes of international tension.

[6] International Institute of Intellectual Cooperation, *Why War?* ("Correspondence"
[Paris, 1933]); *L'Esprit, l'éthique, et la guerre* (Paris, 1934). See also International Studies
Conference, *The State and Economic Life*, Vol. I (Paris, 1932), Vol. II (Paris, 1934);
Collective Security, ed. Maurice Bourquin (Paris, 1936); *Peaceful Change* (Paris, 1938);
The Reconstruction of World Trade, ed. J. B. Condliffe (New York, 1940).

[7] *Institute of Pacific Relations* (Honolulu, 1925); *Problems of the Pacific* (Honolulu,
1927; Chicago, 1929, 1931, 1933, 1936; New York, 1939).

sented to each conference by the national groups and by the international secretariat. An inquiry into the problems arising from the conflict in the Far East was published in 1940.[8]

5. THE CARNEGIE ENDOWMENT FOR INTERNATIONAL PEACE

Professor John Bates Clark of Columbia University initiated the work of the Division of Economics and History of the Carnegie Endowment for International Peace by a conference at Bern, Switzerland, among European scholars in the summer of 1911. The object of this conference was "to plan scientific investigations as to the causes and effects of war." During the conference three commissions were appointed which suggested investigations, respectively, of (1) "The Economic and Historical Causes and Effects of War" (16 projects), (2) "Armaments in Time of Peace" (12 projects), and (3) "The Unifying Influences on International Life" (9 projects). A number of studies of the human and military costs of war and armaments and of national economic policies were completed, but no general analysis of the subject was produced.[9]

When the United States entered the World War in 1917, this division of the Carnegie Endowment diverted its attention to the social and economic effects of the World War, and under the editorship, first, of Dean David Kinley and, later, of Professor James T. Shotwell over a hundred volumes were produced by scholars of many countries on this topic.[10] These studies did not lead to a general elaboration of the causes of war, though they indicated the extraordinary pervasiveness of modern war in all phases of the economy and culture as well as the government of both belligerent and nonbelligerent communities.[11]

6. NATIONAL VOLUNTARY INSTITUTES AND ASSOCIATIONS

Since World War I, universities, institutes, and associations in many countries have devoted attention to the problems of peace and war, with various objectives of research, education, and practical action.[12]

[8] International Secretariat, Institute of Pacific Relations, *Monographs in the I.P.R. Inquiry on the Far Eastern Conflict* (24 vols.; New York, 1940, 1941). See also *Post-War Worlds*, ed. Percy E. Corbett (New York, 1941).

[9] Carnegie Endowment for International Peace, *Report of the Director of the Division of Economics and History* (Washington, 1911, 1912, 1914, 1918).

[10] For titles of these volumes see Carnegie Endowment for International Peace, *Year Book, 1940* (Washington, 1940), pp. 158–96.

[11] See *ibid.*, p. 123; J. T. Shotwell, *War as an Instrument of National Policy* (New York, 1929), chap. iv; *What Germany Forgot* (New York, 1940).

[12] International Institute of Intellectual Cooperation, International Studies Conference, *University Teaching of International Relations*, ed. Sir Alfred Zimmern (Paris, 1939); S. H. Bailey, *International Studies in Modern Education* (London, 1938); Ruth Savord, *Directory of American Agencies Concerned with the Study of International Affairs* (New York, 1931); Edith E. Ware, *The Study of International Relations in the United States* (New York, 1938).

Collective researches on certain problems related to war and peace have been conducted by the Royal Institute of International Affairs (London),[13] the Council on Foreign Relations (New York),[14] the Twentieth Century Fund (New York),[15] Committee on International Relations of the Social Science Research Council (New York),[16] the Society for the Psychological Study of Social Issues (New York),[17] the International Consultative Group (Geneva),[18] and others.[19] Most of these studies have been oriented toward the solution of international problems of the moment.

Symposiums and monograph series dealing with war and peace have been organized and published by the American Sociological Society (Chicago),[20] the

[13] *International Sanctions: Report by a Study Group of Members of the Royal Institute of International Affairs* (London, 1936); *The Colonial Problem* (London, 1937); *World Order Papers* (London, 1941).

[14] Philip C. Jessup, *International Security* (New York, 1935); Frederick S. Dunn, *Peaceful Change: A Study of International Procedure* (New York, 1937); Eugene Staley, *Raw Materials in Peace and War* (New York, 1937).

[15] Evans Clark (ed.), *Boycotts and Peace: A Report by the Committee on Economic Sanctions* (New York, 1932).

[16] Studies on the contributions of the various social sciences to the study of international relations (manuscript, unless otherwise noted, 1929): Carl Alsberg, "Technological Changes"; L. L. and Jessie Bernard, "Sociology"; Isaiah Bowman, "Geography"; Joseph P. Chamberlain, "International Unions"; Herbert Feis, *League of Nations* (Old Lyme, Conn.: Margaret Peabody Fund, 1929); Carlton J. H. Hayes, "Nationality"; Charles P. Howland, "Diplomatic History"; Jesse L. Kandel, "Education"; Lewis L. Lorwin, "World-Economics"; Dexter Perkins, "History"; Jacob Viner, "Economics"; Quincy Wright, *Research in International Law since the War* (Washington: Carnegie Endowment for International Peace, 1930).

[17] Ross Stagner, "Psychology of Peace and War" (manuscript, 1940).

[18] "Surveys and Reports" (mimeographed, Geneva), especially second series, No. 1: "Reflections on the Political Causes of the Peace Failure, 1919–39" (November, 1939); No. 2: "Economics of the Peace Failure, 1919–39" (December, 1939); No. 3: "Spiritual Factors in the Peace Failure, 1919–39" (May, 1940).

[19] Mention may be made of the Brookings Institution (Washington); Bureau of International Research, Harvard University and Radcliffe College (Cambridge, Mass.); Institute for Advanced Study (Princeton); Institute of International Studies of Yale University (New Haven); Social Science Research Committee of the University of Chicago; Columbia University Council for Research in the Social Sciences (New York).

[20] Scott E. W. Bedford (ed.), *War and Militarism in Their Sociological Aspects* ("Publications of the American Sociological Society," Vol. X [Chicago, 1915]); symposium on "The Sociology of War," American Sociological Society, 1937, papers published in *American Sociological Review*, III (August, 1938), 461–86; *American Journal of Sociology*, XLIV (March, 1939), 620–48. See also symposium on war in *American Journal of Sociology*, XLVI (January, 1941), 431–590.

Academy of Political Science (New York),[21] the American Academy of Political and Social Science (Philadelphia),[22] the American Society of International Law (Washington),[23] the Foreign Policy Association (New York),[24] the Norman Wait Harris Memorial Foundation (Chicago),[25] the Graduate Faculty of Political and Social Science of the New School for Social Research (New York),[26] the New Commonwealth Institute (London),[27] the Geneva Research Center (Geneva),[28] the Geneva Institute of International Relations (Geneva),[29] the Graduate Institute for International Studies (Geneva),[30] the Netherlands Medical Association (Amsterdam),[31] and many others.[32] These are in most cases collections of individual studies rather than co-operative enterprises, although in some cases discussions of the principal contributions are included.

[21] "National Conference on War Economy," *Proceedings*, Vol. VIII, No. 1 (July, 1918); "The Preservation of Peace," *ibid.*, Vol. XIII, No. 2 (January, 1929); "The Stabilization of Peace," *ibid.*, Vol. XVI, No. 2 (January, 1935).

[22] "American Policy and International Security," *Annals*, July, 1925; "Present-Day Causes of International Friction and Their Elimination," *ibid.*, July, 1929; "The Shadow of War," *ibid.*, September, 1934; "The Attainment and Maintenance of World Peace," *ibid.*, May, 1936; *European Plans for World Order*, ed. W. P. Maddox ("James-Patten-Rowe Pamphlet Series," No. 8 [March, 1940]); "When War Ends," *Annals*, July, 1940.

[23] "Addresses on War, Neutrality, and International Organization," *Proceedings*, April, 1917.

[24] *Are Sanctions Necessary to International Organization* (Pamphlet No. 82, June, 1932); *What Causes War?* (Pamphlet No. 87, January, 1933).

[25] Q. Wright (ed.), *Public Opinion and World Politics* (1933); *Neutrality and Collective Security* (1936); *An American Foreign Policy toward International Stability* ("Public Policy Pamphlet," No. 14 [1934]); Walter H. C. Laves (ed.), *International Security* (1939); *The Foundations of a More Stable World Order* (1941); Walter H. C. Laves and Francis O. Wilcox, *The Middle West Looks at the War* ("Public Policy Pamphlet," No. 32 [1940]).

[26] Hans Speier and Alfred Kähler, *War in Our Time* (New York, 1939).

[27] "Monograph Series" (London, 1934———).

[28] "Studies Series" (Geneva, 1939———).

[29] "Problems of Peace Series" (Geneva, 1926———).

[30] *The World Crisis* (London, 1938); *Publications* (London, 1930———).

[31] *Medical Opinions on War* (Amsterdam, 1938).

[32] Mention may be made of the publications of the Institute of Politics (Williamstown); the Institute of International Relations (University of Southern California, Los Angeles); the World Peace Foundation (Boston); the Grotius Society (London); the Arnold Foundation (Dallas, Tex.); the United States Naval Institute (Annapolis); the American Military Institute (Washington). See also H. J. Stenning (ed.), *The Causes of War* (London, 1935); Willard Waller (ed.), *War in the Twentieth Century* (New York, 1940).

A STUDY OF WAR

Unofficial groups interested in promoting national or international policies have often stated or implied theories concerning the causes of war in their meetings and publications and have had an influence in stimulating research on the problem of war. Such bodies include the Conference on the Cause and Cure of War (Washington),[33] the World Conference for International Peace through Religion (London),[34] the Next Five Years Group (London),[35] the Commission of Inquiry into National Policy in International Economic Relations (New York),[36] the Commission To Study the Organization of Peace (New York),[37] the National Policy Committee (Washington),[38] the *Fortune* Round Table (New York),[39] and others.[40] Such bodies, instituted with the object of influencing affairs rather than of advancing science, have not lent themselves to broad scientific investigation of the causes of war.

[33] *Proceedings* (1925————).

[34] Arthur Porritt (ed.), *The Causes of War* (London, 1932).

[35] *The Next Five Years: An Essay in Political Agreement* (London, 1935).

[36] *International Economic Relations* (Minneapolis, 1934).

[37] *Preliminary Report* (New York, 1940).

[38] *The Purpose of the Armed Forces* (Washington, 1939); *Toward a Durable Peace* (Washington, 1940).

[39] "America's Stake in the Present War and the Future of World Order," *Fortune Magazine*, January, 1940; "Peace Aims," *ibid.*, April, 1941.

[40] Mention may be made of the League To Enforce Peace, *Enforced Peace* (New York, 1916); *Win the War for Permanent Peace* (New York, 1918); American Association for International Conciliation, *Towards an Enduring Peace* (New York, 1916); American Committee for the Outlawry of War, *Outlawry of War* (67th Cong., 2d sess., Sen. Doc. 115 [Washington, 1922]); "America and World Peace" *Christian Century*, December 23, 1926; Chatham House Conference, *Steps To Be Taken To Restore Confidence* (London: Carnegie Endowment for International Peace, March, 1935); National Peace Conference, *World Economic Cooperation* (Washington, 1938); National League of Women Voters, *Publications* (Washington); American Council on Public Affairs (Washington); World Citizens Association, *Publications* (Chicago, 1939————); *The City of Man* (New York, 1940); Political and Economic Planning, *European Order and World Order* (London, 1940); Federal Union, Inc., *Bulletins*, ed. Clarence K. Streit (New York, 1940————); World Government, *Bulletins*, ed. W. B. Lloyd, Jr. (Chicago, 1940————). See also W. Evans Darby, *International Tribunals: A Collection of the Various Schemes Which Have Been Propounded and of Instances in the Nineteenth Century* (4th ed.; London, 1904); Theodore Marburg, *Development of the League of Nations Idea, Documents and Correspondence* (2 vols.; New York, 1932). Annotated bibliographies of proposals for dealing with the problems of war have been prepared by the Carnegie Endowment for International Peace Library, M. Alice Matthews (ed.), *Peace Projects* (Washington, 1936), *The Peace Movement* (Washington, 1940), *The New World Order* (Washington, 1940), and by the American Committee for International Studies, Fawn M. Brodie (ed.), *Peace Aims and Post-war Reconstruction* (Princeton, 1941).

APPENDIX III

APPROACHES TO THE STUDY OF WAR

There have been many popular approaches to the consideration of war—moralistic, literary, historical, and political. There have also been many learned approaches—legalistic, technological, sociological, psychological, biological. The fourfold classification here adopted does not distinguish popular from learned writings but classifies writings of both types according as interest centers upon (1) the human personalities involved in war as initiators, actors, or victims; (2) the weapons, movements, plans, or other technical aspects of warmaking; (3) the concepts, assumptions, justifications, or rules of war; and (4) the process, significance, or value of war under varying cultural and historic conditions.

The psychological approach is exemplified not only in the writings of professional psychologists and propagandists but also in most literary and poetic works on war and in the conversation of the man in the street who regards war as a plague or an adventure. Abstractly it conceives war as a dominant state of mind within the group exhibiting great animosity toward a concrete enemy.

The technological approach is usually exemplified by the attitude of professional military men and diplomats, in writings on strategy and diplomacy, and in the conversation of the man in the street who regards war as a mistake or as a useful instrument. Abstractly it conceives war as the use of regulated violence for political ends.

The ideological approach is found in the opinions of courts and the debates of legislative bodies, in the writings on international law and organization, and in the attitudes of the man in the street who regards war as a normal procedure or a criminal aggression. Abstractly, it conceives war as a condition involving violence which the law recognizes with approval or disapproval.

The sociological approach is exemplified in the writings of sociologists and anthropologists and in the attitude of the average citizen who considers war as a historical anachronism or a condition of affairs which may be expected to recur. Abstractly it conceives war as an institutionalized intergroup conflict involving violence.

Each of these points of view could be illustrated from the early literature of most civilizations, though there has been a tendency for the technological and psychological approaches, exhibited, for example, in the historical books of the Bible, in Homer, Confucius, Lord Shang, Sun and Wu, Kautilya, and Beowulf to appear earlier in the history of a civilization than the more abstract ideological and sociological approaches illustrated in the prophetic books of the Bible, in Plato and Aristotle, in Mencius, in the Mahabharata, and in Gratian and

Aquinas.[1] Contemporary civilization, at least in its international aspects, dates from the Renaissance and Reformation. Four books from that period have been selected to illustrate the assumptions and methods characteristic of these respective approaches—the *Anti-polemus* of Erasmus (1510), the *Il Principi* of Machiavelli (1511), the *De jure belli ac pacis* of Grotius (1625), and the *Nouveau Cynee* of Crucé (1625). In discussing each, the historical development of the point of view it exemplifies will be indicated.

I. THE PSYCHOLOGICAL APPROACH

The Reformation shifted the emphasis of religion from the city of God to the individual human soul, and the practical bourgeois mind interested itself in the amelioration of the material surroundings of that soul in this world.[2] A host of humanitarian movements to abolish slavery, sickness, slums, and suffering generally grew up as increasing knowledge made such amelioration possible. Even before Luther, Erasmus had applied the technique of humanitarian thought, which starts with sympathy for the concrete, subjective experiences of human beings, to the problem of war and peace.

If there is in the affairs of mortal men any one thing which it is proper uniformly to explode; which it is incumbent on every man, by every lawful means, to avoid, to deprecate, to oppose, that one thing is doubtless war. There is nothing more unnaturally Wicked, more productive of misery, more extensively destructive, more obstinate in mischief, more unworthy of man as formed by nature, much more of man professing Christianity. . . . . Laying aside all *vulgar prejudices*, and accurately examining the *real nature of things*, we contemplate with the eyes of philosophy, the portrait of man on one side, and on the other, the picture of war! If anyone considers a moment the organization and external figure of the body, will he not instantly perceive that nature, or rather the god of nature, created the *human animal* not for war, but for love and friendship, not for mutual destruction, but for mutual service and safety; not to commit injuries, but for acts of reciprocal beneficence. . . . . Why need I dwell on the evil which morals sustain by war, when everyone knows, that from war proceeds at once every kind of evil which disturbs and destroys the happiness of human life?[3]

Erasmus studied war as it affects and is affected by the human organism and personality. The point of view emphasized in the most recent pacifist writing is the same. It assumes that "those who devote themselves to the art of life have

[1] See Frank M. Russell, *Theories of International Relations* (New York, 1936), pp. 19 ff., 38 ff., 51 ff., 93 ff.; William Ballis, *The Legal Position of War: Changes in the Practice and Theory from Plato to Vattel* (The Hague, 1937), pp. 17 ff., 45 ff.; Sun and Wu, *The Book of War* ("Military Classic of the Far East," trans. E. F. Calthorp [London, 1908]).

[2] B. Groethuysen, *Origines de l'esprit bourgeois en France* (3d ed.; Paris, 1927); Stefan Zweig, *Erasmus* (London, 1934); Preserved Smith, *The Age of Erasmus* (New York, 1920).

[3] *Anti-polemus, or the Plea of Reason, Religion, and Humanity against War* (1st ed.; about 1510; London, 1794), pp. 1, 3, 10.

no place left for the art of death"; that "the recognition of the value of personality is one of the points at which the pacifist begins"; and that "the pacifist believes that the means and the end are so intimately related that it is impossible to get a coordinated and cooperative world by destructive methods that violate personality and increase antagonism and distrust."[4]

This psychological approach to the problem of war and peace is to be found in the words of Gautama, Confucius, Mo-ti, Isaiah, Epictetus, Jesus, Tertullian, St. Francis, and Las Casas, in the comedies of Aristophanes, in the oratory of Charles Sumner, in the novels of Tolstoy, von Suttner, and Barbusse, and in the pamphlets of hundreds of peace societies.[5] This literature has not all expressed the evils of war and the blessings of peace. Homer, Virgil, and Shakespeare have written in praise of war. Alexander, Caesar, Napoleon, and Mussolini have by their oratory stirred men to welcome it. Nietzsche has taught that "a good war hallows every cause."[6]

This approach to war through consideration of the drives and motives involved in it has produced in the main literary, practical, or inspirational works, although in recent times it has produced histories[7] and analyses.[8] In the nine-

[4] Devere Allen, *Pacifism in the Modern World* (New York, 1929), pp. xviii, 5, 11.

[5] See Chieh Meng, "The Ideals of the Chinese Republic," in *New Orient*, ed. Berthold Laufer (Chicago, 1933), II, 282 ff.; Russell, *op. cit.*, pp. 25 ff., 59 ff., 92 ff.; C. J. Cadoux, *Early Christian Attitude toward War* (London, 1919); Charles Sumner, *Addresses on War* (Boston, 1911); A. C. F. Beales, *The History of Peace* (London, 1931); M. E. Hirst, *The Quakers in Peace and War* (London, 1923); Merle Curti, *The American Peace Crusade, 1815–1860* (Durham, N.C., 1929); E. H. Wilkins (ed.), *Report of the Commission on the Coordination of Efforts for Peace* (Oberlin, 1933).

[6] Nietzsche's thought went through several changes during his life. It was during the last two periods after 1883 that he glorified war and the dangerous life in *Thus Spake Zarathustra* and *The Will to Power*. The quotation is from the chapter "Of Wars and Warriors" in the former (see Charles Andler, "Nietzsche," *Encyclopaedia of the Social Sciences*, and O. Levy, "Nietzsche," *Encyclopaedia Britannica*). The views of Proudhon and Sorel on violence were similar (see Georges Sorel, *Reflections on Violence* [New York, 1912]; Sydney Hook, "Violence," *Encyclopaedia of the Social Sciences*).

[7] Cadoux, *op. cit.;* Christian Lange, *Histoire de l'internationalisme jusqu'a la paix de Westphalie, 1648* (Christiania, 1919); *Histoire de la doctrine pacifique* ("L'Academie de droit international, recueil des cours," Vol. XIII [The Hague, 1926]); Beales, *op. cit.;* Curti, *op. cit.; Peace or War: The American Struggle, 1637–1936* (New York, 1936).

[8] Thomas Hobbes, *Leviathan* ("Everyman's Library" [London, 1651]); Sigmund Freud and Albert Einstein, in International Institute of Intellectual Cooperation, *Why War? An International Series of Open Letters* (Paris, 1933); Bertrand Russell, *Why Men Fight* (New York, 1930); Caroline E. Playne, *The Neuroses of Nations* (New York, 1925); George M. Stratton, *Social Psychology of International Conduct* (New York, 1929); George W. Crile, *A Mechanistic View of War and Peace* (Cambridge, Mass., 1927); Robert Waelder, "Lettre sur l'étiologie et l'évolution des psychoses collectives," in Institut international de cooperation intellectuelle, *Correspondance sur l'esprit, l'éthique et la guerre* (Paris, 1934); Karl Mannheim, "The Psychological Aspect," in C. A. L. Man-

teenth century the theory of motives developed by Bentham and adopted by the
utilitarians was applied to the problem of war and produced a considerable literature on the relations of economics and war.[9] In the twentieth century more
complicated theories of personality and motives developed by Freud and others
have suggested the treatment of war and revolution as consequences of the interaction of the personality of the leaders and of the led under specific conditions of
communication, propaganda, and social disorganization.[10]

2. THE TECHNOLOGICAL APPROACH

Scientific method, stimulated after the Renaissance by the writings of Leonardo, Copernicus, Bacon, Galileo, and Descartes, carried the critical attitude of
the humanists into fields other than classical and biblical texts. Anticipated in
the field of politics by Machiavelli (1469–1527), this approach starts with the
concrete and objective evidence of the senses and attempts to create from this
evidence logical structures capable of predicting events in the future and practical techniques capable of controlling them.[11]

The application of this type of thought to the problem of peace and war was
illustrated by Machiavelli, who wrote at about the same time as Erasmus.

---

ning (ed.), *Peaceful Change in International Relations* (London, 1937); Harold D. Lasswell, *Propaganda Technique in the World War* (New York, 1927); *World Politics and
Personal Insecurity* (New York, 1935).

[9] Richard Cobden, *Three Panics*, in *Political Writings* (London, 1867), II, pp. 209 ff.;
F. W. Hirst, *The Political Economy of War* (London, 1915); Norman Angell, *The Great
Illusion* (New York, 1910); J. H. Jones, *The Economics of War and Conquest* (London,
1915); A. C. Pigou, *The Political Economy of War* (London, 1921); J. M. Clark, Walton
Hamilton, and H. G. Moulton, *Readings in the Economics of War* (Chicago, 1918);
Thorstien Veblen, *An Inquiry into the Nature of Peace* (New York, 1917); R. G. Hawtrey,
Economic Aspects of Sovereignty (London, 1930); Warren S. Thompson, *Danger Spots in
World Population* (New York, 1930); Jacob Viner, "Political Aspects of International
Finance," *Journal of Business of the University of Chicago*, April and July, 1928, and
Southwestern Political Science Quarterly, March, 1929; Eugene Staley, *War and the
Private Investor* (New York, 1935); Leo Hausleiter, *The Machine Unchained* (New York,
1933); Lionel Robbins, *The Economic Causes of War* (London, 1939).

[10] See G. Mosca, *The Ruling Class* (New York, 1939); Robert Waelder, *Psychological
Aspects of War and Peace* ("Geneva Studies," Vol. X, No. 2 [Geneva, 1939]); Peter F.
Drucker, *The End of Economic Man* (New York, 1939); Q. Wright (ed.), *Public Opinion
and World Politics* (Chicago, 1933), and Freud, Mannheim, and Lasswell, above, n. 8.

[11] *Nature non facit saltum* or "continuity" is the underlying assumption of science.
Alfred Marshall put the motto on the title-page of his *Principles of Economics* and explained it in his Preface. "There is not in real life a clear line of division between things
that are and are not Capital, or that are and are not Necessaries, or again between labor
that is and is not Productive" (2d ed., p. xiii). B. Ginzberg ("Science," *Encyclopaedia
of the Social Sciences*, XIII, 591) defines science as "a far flung system of knowledge
couched in terms which allow it to serve as a theoretical basis for practical technique."
See also chap. viii, sec. 4*b*, above.

A prince ought to have no other aim or thought nor select anything else for his study, than war and its rules and discipline; for this is the sole art that belongs to him who rules, and it is of such force that it not only upholds those who are born princes, but often enables men to rise from a private station to that rank. And, on the contrary, it is seen that when princes have thought more of peace than of arms, they have lost their states. . . . . For among other evils which being unarmed brings you, it causes you to be despised, and this is one of those ignominies against which a prince ought to guard himself, as is shown later on. Because there is nothing proportionate between the armed and the unarmed; and it is not reasonable that he who is armed should yield obedience willingly to him who is unarmed, or that the unarmed man should be secure among armed servants. . . . . But to exercise the intellect the prince should read histories, and study there the actions of illustrious men, see how they have borne themselves in war, to examine the causes of their victories and defeats, so as to avoid the latter and imitate the former. . . . . A wise prince ought to observe some such rule and never in peaceful times stand idle but increase his resources with industry in such a way that they may be available to him in adversity, so that if fortune changes it may find him prepared to resist her blows.[12]

If Erasmus was inspired by the approach to the problem exemplified in early Christian history and Stoic philosophy,[13] Machiavelli was inspired by the historical realism disclosed in the classical histories of Thucydides, Polybius, and Livy and in the military handbooks of Caesar, Frontinus, and Vegetius.[14] Erasmus saw the problem as that of realization by all human beings, or at least by the élite in every land, of an ideal personality, while Machiavelli envisaged it as the application of historical experience to political ends.

From the Machiavellian point of view a huge literature has developed of books on strategy and power politics such as those by Clausewitz, Jomini, Mahan, and Van der Goltz. Whether analytical, technical, or historical, this literature has conceived the problem of war and peace as the practical understanding of the interaction of the material forces at the disposal of statesmen. It has sought to relate tactics to strategy and to policy. The art of war, thus

[12] *The Prince* ("Everyman's" ed. [1st ed., 1511]), pp. 115–16; see also *The Art of War; Florentine History.*

[13] See Robert P. Adams, "The Pacifist or Anti-military Idealism of the Oxford Humanist Reformers, John Colet, Erasmus, Sir Thomas More, Vives and Their Circle, 1497–1535" (manuscript, University of Chicago Library, 1936).

[14] F. L. Taylor, *The Art of War in Italy, 1494–1529* (Cambridge, 1921), chap. viii, distinguishes among military writers of the Renaissance: "The writer of the military text book expounds the facts of war as he finds them, ... the scientific inquirer seeks from a minute study of the practice of the present to devise improvements for use in the future, the political philosopher, taking human society as his theme and all time as his province, attempts to establish general rules for the universal guidance of military effort" (pp. 157–58). Machiavelli, though of the last type, learned from all, relying especially on Vegetius for his art of war. He may also have been familiar with the *Roser des guerre* written by Louis XI and Pierre Choisinet shortly before his time (see D. B. Wyndham Lewis, *King Spider* [New York, 1929], pp. 494 ff.).

developed, instructs the general how to break the equilibrium of military forces and to obtain victory with a minimum of cost under varying conditions and it instructs the statesman in the uses of war as an instrument of policy.[15] It has, however, influenced both general staffs and governments to contemplate war as continuous with peace, as tending toward absolute destruction, and as inevitable with the result that they have increasingly devoted attention to preparedness, to mobilization plans, and in general to subordinating all policy to the requirements of war. Instead of war being considered an instrument of policy, policy has been considered an instrument of war.[16]

This technical point of view has had a considerable influence upon related fields. International lawyers have gained from strategical writers the concept of military necessity and of its importance in a realistic law of war.[17] Pacifists have gone to military writers for information as to trends of military techniques and their probable effects upon the future of the world-society.[18] Writers with a point of view primarily political or economic have also been affected. Hume recognized that maintenance of the balance of power would require occasional wars but recommended that they be fought with a prudent regard to the national exchequer and the propensity of an ally to relax his efforts when aid is tendered.[19] Karl Marx considered war a necessary consequence of the growth of capital in a class society.[20] Ivan Bloch thought the evolution of military technique might lead to a stalemate, thus rendering war an ineffective instrument.[21]

[15] Among more recent books with this point of view are: Major-General Sir George Aston (ed.), *The Study of War for Statesmen and Citizens* (London, 1927); Friederich Bernhardi, *On War of Today* (London, 1911); Commandant J. Colin, *France and the Next War* (London, 1914); Marshal Ferdinand Foch, *The Principles of War* (London, 1918); Colonel J. F. C. Fuller, *The Reformation of War* (New York, 1923); Captain B. H. Liddell-Hart, *The Remaking of Modern Armies* (London, 1927); Hoffman Nickerson, *Can We Limit War?* (Bristol, 1933); R. E. Dupuy and G. F. Elliott, *If War Comes* (New York, 1937).

[16] This trend is emphasized by Nickerson, *op. cit.*, and Guglielmo Ferrero, "Forms of War and International Anarchy," in *The World Crises* ("Graduate Institute of International Studies" [London, 1938]), pp. 85 ff.

[17] John Westlake, *Chapters on the Principles of International Law* (Cambridge, 1894), pp. 238 ff.

[18] Ivan Bloch, *The Future of War* (1st ed.; 7 vols.; St. Petersburg, 1898; Boston, 1914); Interparliamentary Union, *What Would Be the Character of a New War?* (London, 1931).

[19] David Hume, *Of the Balance of Power* (1751), in *Philosophical Works* (Boston, 1854), III, 364–73. Fuller and Nickerson give a similar emphasis.

[20] Robbins, *op. cit.*

[21] *Op. cit.* See also Hans Speier and Alfred Kähler, *War in Our Time* (New York, 1939).

Norman Angell believed that economic relations had developed so as to assure more loss than gain from war, thus rendering war an economically useless instrument.[22] Lord Davies believed that military sanctions might be so developed that the military aggressor would be defeated, thus rendering war a politically inexpedient instrument.[23] After creation of the League of Nations, the literature of disarmament and sanctions was greatly augmented. It was suggested that the force of military aggression might be neutralized by minimizing the power of the offense and maximizing that of the defense, or by opposing to aggression effective political, economic, or military sanctions.[24]

3. THE IDEOLOGICAL APPROACH

Starting from the abstract conception of objective law, Grotius sought to deal with the problem of war by logical analysis. His treatise *On the Law of War and Peace* begins with a demonstration that "there is a common law among nations which is valid alike for war and in war."[25] The demonstration consisted in logical deductions from the assumption that man is intelligent. The application of intelligence shows that law is essential to social order and that social order is essential to satisfactory existence of an intelligent being.

This maintenance of the social order, which we have roughly sketched, and which is consonant with human intelligence, is the source of law properly so called,[26] [and] if no

[22] *The Great Illusion* (New York, 1913); Jones, *op. cit.*

[23] *The Problem of the Twentieth Century* (London, 1930). See also publications of the New Commonwealth Institute, London.

[24] Victor Lefebure, *Scientific Disarmament* (New York, 1931); Salvador Madariaga, *Disarmament* (New York, 1929); Evans Clark, *Boycotts and Peace* (New York, 1932); Sir Arthur Salter, *The United States of Europe* (New York, 1933); Sir Alfred Zimmern, *The League of Nations and the Rule of Law* (London, 1936); Marion Boggs, "The Distinction between Aggressive and Defensive Armaments in Diplomacy and Strategy" (manuscript thesis, University of Chicago Library, 1940). See also Royal Institute of International Affairs, *Sanctions* ("Information Department Papers," No. 17 [New York, 1935]); *The Future of the League of Nations* (New York, 1936).

[25] *De jure belli ac pacis* (1st ed., 1625), trans. Kelsey (Carnegie Endowment ed.), Prolegomena, sec. 28.

[26] *Ibid.*, sec. 8. Dante's method in *De monarchia* (1311) was the same, though, instead of assuming, he sought to demonstrate the intelligence of man. He assumed that things exist to manifest their distinctive functions and since "the differentiating characteristic of humanity is a distinctive capacity or power of intellect . . . . humanity as a whole was ordained" to manifest this function which it alone can manifest. But it can only be manifested in peace and peace can only exist with justice which in turn requires universal monarchy (trans. Aurelia Henry [Boston, 1904], pp. 10, 13, 19, 29, 40). He therefore differed from Grotius in concluding that the essential ingredient of justice was its sanction, "monarchy," rather than its source, "law," although Grotius also saw the need of sanctions.

association of men can be maintained without law, as Aristotle showed by his remark-able illustration drawn from brigands, surely also that association which binds together the human race, or binds many nations together, has need of law.[27]

Grotius defines war as "the condition of those contending by force." Thus he does not exclude private war, and he recognizes that contentions by force may grow out of contentions by words. All controversies are therefore within the scope of his study.

Controversies among those who are not held together by a common bond of munici-pal law are related either to times of war or to times of peace. Such controversies may arise among those who have not yet united to form a nation, and those who belong to different nations, both private persons and kings; also those who have the same body of rights that kings have, whether members of a ruling aristocracy, or free peoples. War, however, is undertaken in order to secure peace, and there is no controversy which may not give rise to war. In undertaking to treat the law of war, therefore, it will be in order to treat such controversies, of any and every kind, as are likely to arise. War itself will finally conduct us to peace as its ultimate goal.[28]

Law, thus broadly treated, would be sufficient to explain and perhaps to abolish war, if Grotius' basic assumption, that human behavior is in the main intelli-gent, were true.

Although this treatment of the subject did not produce continuous peace, it inspired a voluminous literature of international law. This literature gave form to practices and declarations by statesmen, judges, soldiers, and sailors. The whole came to be conceived as the law which regulated the modern family of na-tions in war and peace.

The roots of Grotius' treatment are to be found in the discussions of just war and proper war among the ancients, Plato, Aristotle, and Cicero; the theologians Augustine, Isadore of Seville, and Thomas Aquinas; the medieval jurists and philosophers, Bartolus, Hostiensis, and Legnano; the founders of modern inter-national law, Victoria, Gentili, Suarez, Belli, and Ayala. Grotius' ideas were elaborated in the volumes by Puffendorf, Zouche, Bynkershoek, Wolff, Vattel, and the increasing number of commentators upon international law from every land in the nineteenth and twentieth centuries.[29]

4. THE SOCIOLOGICAL APPROACH

While Grotius was writing his treatise, building a skeleton of international law which might regulate war, Emeric Crucé was attempting to create the flesh and blood of a world-community which might eliminate war. Starting from an

---

[27] *De jure belli ac pacis*, sec. 23.   [28] *Ibid.*, Book I, chap. i, sec. 1.

[29] Ballis, *op. cit.* See also T. E. Holland, "The Early Literature of the Law of War," in *Studies in International Law* (Oxford, 1898), pp. 40 ff.; Luigi Sturzo, *The Interna-tional Community and the Right of War* (New York, 1930); Alfred Vanderpol, *La Doc-trine scolastique du droit de guerre* (Paris, 1919); Robert Regout, *La Doctrine de la guerre juste* (Paris, 1935); John Eppstein, *The Catholic Tradition of the Law of Nations* (Wash-ington, 1935); T. A. Walker, *The History of the Law of Nations* (Cambridge, 1899), pp 30 ff.; Q. Wright, *Research in International Law since the War* (Washington, 1930).

abstract and subjective faith in the existence of that community, he attempted to deal with the problem of war and peace by the methods of political and social analysis and construction. "Human society," he wrote, "is a body all of whose members have a common sympathy, so that it is impossible that the sickness of one shall not be communicated to the other."[30] The realization of this nascent community was to be achieved through the acceptance by all princes of the policy of peace; through the diversion of national activity from war to the "most useful occupations" such as promoting commerce, developing communication, safeguarding the seas, developing practical arts and the exact sciences; and through the establishment of a perpetual assembly, representing all sovereigns, for dissolving differences which might arise.

If Grotius was inspired by the technique of scholastic rationalism, Crucé utilized the methods of constructive faith equally dominant in medieval thought. Grotius saw the problem of war and peace as that of applying the conceptions of law familiarized by Thomas Aquinas, while Crucé saw it as the realization on earth of Augustine's city of God. "True peace shall be there, where no one shall suffer opposition either from himself or any other."[31]

Although less voluminous, the literature of international organization has as long a history as that of international law. In his *De monarchia*, written about 1311, Dante had expounded the need of a unified world under the Holy Roman Emperor, successor of the Caesars.[32] Shortly before (1302), Pope Boniface VIII, in his bull *Unam sanctam*, had expressed his faith in a unified world-community under the pope, thus marking the apogee of an idea which had been stimulated two centuries earlier by the energy of Hildebrand, Pope Gregory VII.[33] But while Ghibelline and Guelf, writers, were urging world-unity under a single personality, whether emperor or pope, Pierre Dubois conceived a world-unity through a federation of sovereign princes. The project had the primary object of recovering the Holy Land and may also have intended the hegemony of the French monarch, Philip le Bel, but the maintenance of peace among Christian monarchs was to be the means for these achievements.[34]

---

[30] *Le nouveau Cynee* (1st ed., 1623), trans. T. W. Balch (Philadelphia, 1899), pp. 9–10. I have used the translation in W. E. Darby, *International Tribunals* (London, 1904), p. 24. Crucé has been credited with originating not only the modern idea of international organization but also the economics of free trade and the politics of monarchical liberalism and social legislation (Pierre Louis-Lucas, *Un plan de paix générale* [Paris, 1919], pp. 79 ff.).

[31] *The City of God*, Book xxii ("Post-Nicene Latin Father, Early Christian Literature Primers," ed. G. P. Fisher, p. 130).

[32] The *De monarchia* of Dante Alighieri, above, n. 24. Bryce notes that Dante's book was "an epitaph instead of a prophecy" (*Holy Roman Empire* [London, 1873], p. 264).

[33] August C. Krey, "The International State of the Middle Ages: Some Reasons for Its Failure," *American Historical Review*, XXVIII (October, 1922), 1 ff.

[34] Pierre Dubois, *De recuperatione terre sancte* (1306), trans. Ruth Hardy (Berkeley, Calif., 1920); Eileen E. Power in *Social and Political Ideas of Some Great Medieval*

Dubois's conception, and the somewhat inadequate information about the Greek Amphictyonic Council,[35] inspired others than Crucé to apply their pens to peace plans during the warlike seventeenth century. Sully described the "Grand Design" for European federation of his master, King Henry IV of France; the Landgraff Hesse-Rheinfels had a plan; as did William Penn, the Quaker. It appears, however, that while Sully may have discussed with Henry extensive plans of alliance, the notion of world-federation may have sprung from his reading of Crucé long after the death of the king. Subsequent plans inspired by the "Grand Design" sprang, therefore, indirectly from Crucé. In the eighteenth century Abbé St. Pierre, Rousseau, Bentham, and Kant[36] contributed to the idea, which, during the Napoleonic period, inspired Czar Alexander I to propose the Holy Alliance.[37] The nineteenth and twentieth centuries witnessed an expansion of this literature in works by William Ladd, Bluntschli, David Dudley Field, Leonard Woolf, and others as well as the practical efforts of Czar Nicholas II, resulting in the Hague conferences,[38] and of Woodrow Wilson, resulting in the League of Nations.[39] The outbreak of World War II stimulated the production of many new plans.[40]

Thinkers, ed. F. J. C. Hearnshaw (London, 1923); W. J. Brandt and Pierre Dubois, "Modern or Medieval?" *American Historical Review*, XXX (1929), 507 ff.; F. M. Russell, *op. cit.*, pp. 106 ff.

[35] E. A. Freeman, *History of Federal Government in Greece and Italy* (2d ed.; London, 1893), chap. iii; Darby, *op. cit.*, pp. 1 ff.

[36] These plans are set forth in Darby, *op. cit.;* F. M. Russell, *op. cit.;* see also Elizabeth York, *Leagues of Nations, Ancient, Medieval and Modern* (London, 1919); Lord Phillimore, *Schemes for Maintaining General Peace* ("Peace Handbooks," Vol. XXV, No. 160 [prepared under the direction of the Historical Section of the Foreign Office, London, 1920]); Lange, *Histoire de l'internationalisme;* Jacob ter Meulen, *Der Gedanke der internationalen Organisation in seiner Entwicklung (1300–1889)* (2 vols.; The Hague, 1917 and 1929); J. A. R. Marriott, *Commonwealth or Anarchy?* (New York, 1939). Sully's plan differed from Crucé's and St. Pierre's in excluding Moslem states. Kant's plan was designed to be truly universal. See S. Cybichowski, "National Sovereignty and International Cooperation," *Annals*, July, 1936, pp. 110 ff.

[37] W. Alison Phillips, *The Confederation of Europe* (2d ed.; London, 1920).

[38] Walther Schucking, *The International Union of the Hague Conferences*, trans. C. G. Fenwick (New York, 1918); J. B. Scott, *The Hague Peace Conferences of 1899 and 1907* (2 vols.; New York, 1909).

[39] Theodore Marburg, "Documents and Correspondence," *Development of the League of Nations Idea* (2 vols.; New York, 1932); David Hunter Miller, *The Drafting of the Covenant* (2 vols.; New York, 1928); Sir Alfred Zimmern, *op. cit.;* Georg Schwarzenberger, *The League of Nations and World Order* (London, 1936).

[40] Clarence Streit, *Union Now* (New York, 1939); William P. Maddox, *European Plans for World Order* ("Annals of the American Academy of Political and Social Science" [Philadelphia, 1940]).

As practical experience with international conferences increased, the difficulties of the problem had become more obvious.[41] Rousseau's faith in the potential existence of the world-community was less thoroughgoing than had been that of Crucé. In his commentary upon St. Pierre's elaboration of the grand design, Rousseau recognized:

That, with the exception of Turkey, there prevails among all the peoples of Europe a social connection, imperfect but more compact than the general and loose ties of humanity; that the imperfection of this society makes the condition of those who compose it worse than would be the deprivation of all society amongst them [and] that these primary bonds which render the society harmful, make it at the same time easily capable of improvement, so that all its members may derive their happiness from that which actually constitutes their misery, and change the state of war which prevails among them into an abiding Peace.

The methods for doing this he outlines in detail and concludes "if in spite of all that, this project remains unexecuted, it is not because it is at all chimerical; it is that men are insane and that it is a kind of folly to be wise in the midst of fools."[42]

Kant was more optimistic. He believed that even unintelligent statesmen by trial and error would eventually achieve a stable world-commonwealth. Conflict, itself, he considered an element in this achievement.

Nature has accordingly again used the unsociableness of men, and even of great societies and political bodies, her creatures of this kind, as a means to work out through their mutural antagonism a condition of rest and security. . . . . All wars are, accordingly, so many attempts—not, indeed, in the intention of man, but yet according to the purpose of nature—to bring about new relations between the nations; and by destruction, or at least dismemberment, of them all to form new political corporations. These new organizations, again, are not capable of being preserved either in themselves or beside one another, and they must therefore pass in turn through similar new revolutions, so at last, partly by the best possible arrangement of the civil constitution within, and partly by common convention and legislation without, a condition will be attained, which, in the likeness of a civil commonwealth and after the manner of an automaton, will be able to preserve itself. . . . . Universal violence and the necessity arising there-

[41] On the difficulties of organizing the congresses of Westphalia (1642–48), Utrecht (1711–13), Vienna (1814–15), etc., see K. Colegrove, "Diplomatic Procedure Preliminary to the Congress of Westphalia," *American Journal of International Law*, XIII (July, 1919), 450 ff.; Sir Ernest Satow, *A Guide to Diplomatic Practice* (London, 1917), Vol. II, chaps. xxv and xxvi; *International Congresses* ("Peace Handbooks," Vol. XXIII, No. 151 [London, 1920]); C. K. Webster, *The Congress of Vienna* ("Peace Handbook," Vol. XXIV, No. 153).

[42] J. J. Rousseau, *Extrait du projet de paix perpetuelle de M. L'Abbé de Saint Pierre*, trans. Darby, *op. cit.*, pp. 104–16. A project of *Universal and Perpetual Peace* written by Pierre-Andre Gargaz, a former galley slave, printed by Benjamin Franklin at Passy in 1782, was reprinted with translation by George S. Eddy (New York, 1922).

from must finally bring a people to the determination to subject themselves to national law and to set up a political constitution, a necessity which is the very method that reason itself prescribes. And, in like manner, the evils arising from constant wars by which the states seek to reduce or subdue each other will bring them at last, even against their will, also to enter into a universal, or cosmopolitical, constitution. Or, should such a condition of universal peace—as has often been the case in overgrown States—be even more dangerous to liberty on another side than war, by introducing the most terrible despotism, then the evils from which deliverance is sought will compel the introduction of a condition among the nations which does not assume the form of a universal commonwealth or empire under one sovereign but of a federation regulated by law, according to the law of nations as concerted in common.[43]

During the eighteenth century political scientists and social philosophers had thought in terms of internal checks and balances and external balances of power. In the nineteenth century these mechanical analogies were modified by biological analogies suggesting war as an inevitable struggle for existence among societies in a world without living room for all.[44] More recently sociologists have eschewed all analogies and have treated social and political phenomena as the product of the total social milieu in which they occur. The specific character of wars, writes Hans Speier, "is dependent upon the specific organization of society in times of peace."[45] Thus they have assumed, as did Crucé, that the character of the world-community as a whole must be analyzed and understood before war can be dealt with effectively. In such analyses some have treated war as a specific culture trait functioning to manifest the unity and to preserve the distinctiveness of the group.[46] Others have analyzed the roles of violence [47] and of conflict[48] in all levels of social relationship and have studied the conditions under which these behaviors assume the specific form of war.

[43] Eternal Peace (1st ed., 1795; Boston, 1914), pp. 14, 15, 62, 63.

[44] L. Gumplowitz, Der Rassenkampf (1883); G. Ratzenhoffer, Wesen und Zweck der Politik (1893); F. Ratzel, Politische Geographie (1897).

[45] "Class Structure and 'Total War,'" American Sociological Review, IV (June, 1939), 370.

[46] Camilla H. Wedgewood, "Warfare in Melanesia," Oceania, I (1931), 32 ff.; W. Lloyd Warner, "Murngin Warfare," Oceania, I (1931), 457 ff.; A. M. Carr-Saunders, The Population Problem (Oxford, 1922), pp. 305 ff.

[47] P. J. Proudhon, La Guerre et la paix (1861) (Paris, 1927); Sorel, op. cit.; Hymen E. Cohen, "Theories of Violence (manuscript, University of Chicago, 1936).

[48] J. Novicow, War and Its Alleged Benefits (1893) (New York, 1911); Charles Letourneau, La Guerre dans les diverses races humaines (Paris, 1895); Havelock Ellis, The Philosophy of Conflict (New York, 1919); S. R. Steinmetz, Soziologie des Krieges (1907) (Leipzig, 1929); Georg Simmel, "The Sociology of Conflict," American Journal of Sociology, IX (1904), 490–525, 627–89, 798–811; Jean La Gorgette, Le Rôle de la guerre (Paris, 1906); G. F. Nicolai, The Biology of War (New York, 1918); Speier and Kähler op. cit.

5. THE SYNTHETIC APPROACH

Of these four approaches to the problem of war,[49] the ideological and sociological, typified by the works of Grotius and Crucé, attempt to deduce concrete rules and procedures from abstract principles, while the psychological and technological, typified by the works of Erasmus and Machiavelli, attempt to develop general rules and procedures from immediate experience. Grotius and Machiavelli, however, sought to support the principles or experiences from which they started by recorded history, while Crucé and Erasmus sought to support them rather by invoking the introspection of the reader. It is perhaps significant that of the writers taken as typical, those starting from objective evidence tended to favor or to tolerate war,[50] while those starting from subjective sentiment tended toward pacifism. War apparently appeared more inevitable to those who studied history and observed practices than to those given to introspection and armchair philosophy. This difference, however, was not inherent in the method.[51] The legal and military approaches have produced pacifists like Ralston, Levin-

[49] These four points of view seem to be based on the assimilation of the fighting group, respectively, to an ideology, an organization, an organism, and a mechanism; or in the terminology of transcendental essences they are seeking, respectively, the *verum*, *bonum*, *unam*, and *quiddity* of war.

[50] Grotius certainly did not favor war but he did tolerate it and criticized Erasmus for being too pacifistic (*op. cit.*, Prolegomena, sec. 29). Subsequent international lawyers in general followed his moderate attitude, though some, like Bynkershoek, were ready to give more scope to war and some, like Wolff, less. The latter came nearer than others of the classical writers to "outlawing war." "It is not allowable by the law of nature to desire to decide a disputed case by force of arms, or that war is by nature illegal which is undertaken for the purpose of deciding a disputed right. . . . . If nations wish to settle a disputed case by force of arms, or undertake a war for the purpose of deciding a disputed right, the war is the same as a duel. Therefore, since a duel is by nature illegal, the war also is by nature illegal, which is undertaken for the purpose of deciding a disputed right . . . ." (*Jus gentium methoda scientifica pertractatum*, sec. 632). This conclusion is, however, virtually nullified by the explanation that nations do not ordinarily fight to determine the right as in a duel but each, being judge in his own case, assumes that the right belongs to him and denies it to the other, thus each fights to enforce the right (but see sec. 572).

[51] This analysis of approaches to the study of war and of the attitudes of typical writers toward war may be indicated as follows:

	Objective		Subjective	
	Not Pacifistic	Pacifistic	Not Pacifistic	Pacifistic
Abstract	Ideological		Sociological	
	Grotius	Ralston	Proudhon	Crucé
Concrete	Technological		Psychological	
	Machiavelli	Bloch	Nietzsche	Erasmus

son, and Bloch,[52] although those utilizing these points of view have usually regarded war as rational or necessary. On the other hand, the sociological and psychological approaches, though generally leading to the conclusion, favorable to peace, that war is merely customary or capricious, have produced believers in violence such as Proudhon and Nietzsche.[53]

New books are continually being written on war which attempt to synthesize several points of view. Legal analysis is seen to be ineffective without social and political organization; political construction must await the evolution of public opinion; humanitarianism without clear concepts has no goal; and scientific method is difficult to apply to entities which resist precise measurement. There is thus a disposition to look upon a generalization derived from any point of view as only relatively true and in need of supplementation by generalizations derived from other points of view.[54]

Even in the biological and physical sciences the idea of relativity has penetrated. It is possible that such thinkers as Einstein, Morgan, Wheeler, Ehrenfels, Freud, and Smuts, with ideas attributing explanatory or creative power to "relation," "emergence," "configuration," "complex," and "whole," may eventually provide intellectual foundations for methods capable of analyzing and synthesizing the numerous points of view possible in human problems.[55] His-

[52] Jackson H. Ralston, *Democracy's International Law* (Washington, 1922); J. E. Stoner, "Salmon O. Levinson and the Peace Pact" (manuscript, University of Chicago Library, 1937); Bloch, *op. cit.*

[53] Proudhon, *op. cit.*, Friedrich Nietzsche, above, n. 6.

[54] See chap. x on pragmatism and relativity in modern civilization.

[55] See A. Einstein, *Relativity* (New York, 1920); Lloyd Morgan, *Emergent Evolution* (New York, 1923); W. M. Wheeler, *Emergent Evolution* (New York, 1928); K. Koffka, "Gestalt," *Encyclopaedia of the Social Sciences;* A. N. Whitehead, *Science and the Modern World* (New York, 1926); Jan C. Smuts, *Holism and Evolution* (New York, 1926) and "Holism," *Encyclopaedia Britannica* (14th ed.). From the point of view of analysis these words may add little to Berr and Febvre's suggestion that "contingency" may be elevated to a rank equal to necessity and logic in explaining historical causation, or to Alfred Marshall's suggestion that time be treated as a residual factor in all economic problems. "Economic problems are imperfectly presented when they are treated as problems of statical equilibrium, and not of organic growth. For though the former treatment alone can give us definiteness and precision of thought, and is therefore a necessary introduction to a more philosophic treatment of society as an organism, it is yet only an introduction. But not all this imperfection lies in the nature of the case; part of it results from the imperfection of our analytical methods, and may conceivably be much diminished in a later age by the gradual improvement of our scientific machinery. We should have made a great advance if we could represent roughly, as a function of time itself, the chief of the changes in those elements which we are not specially considering; that is, in the particular case of demand and supply schedules, if we could represent the normal demand price and supply price as functions both of the amount normally produced and of the time at which that amount became normal" (*op. cit.*, p. 496). From the point of view of synthesis Bertrand Russell's experience is, perhaps, as good an ex-

toriography in the past has generally been purely literary, purely factual, or purely convenient as in encyclopedias and chronologies.[56] War should be studied by a method which, while not ignoring the analyses provided by studies, each based upon a clear and consistent point of view, will be able to integrate the results from many such analyses for the purpose of understanding or of intervening in the process by which wars arise. The entities involved in the problem of war are complex and in continuous change, not only because they respond consistently to changing conditions but also because they plan for anticipated contingencies. Certain social scientists have worked toward such a method in dealing with the history of war[57] and others in discussing its control,[58] but such studies are still in the pioneering stage.

---

planation as any of the power of wholes: "In writing a book, my own experience—which I know is fairly common, though by no means universal—is that for a time I fumble and hesitate, and then suddenly I see the book as a whole, and have only to write it down as if I were copying a completed manuscript" (*Philosophy* [1927], quoted in Koffka, *op. cit.*).

[56] For suggestive studies of historical method see Lord Acton, *The Study of History* (London, 1905); Viscount Haldane, *The Meaning of Truth in History* (London, 1914); G. M. Trevelyan, "History and Literature," *History* (N.S.), Vol. IX (1924); F. A. Woods, *The Influence of Monarchs* (New York, 1913), chap. ii; F. J. Teggert, *Theory of History* (New Haven, 1925), *Rome and China* (Berkeley, Calif., 1939); James Harvey Robinson, *The New History* (New York, 1912); J. T. Shotwell, *An Introduction to the History of History* (New York, 1922); Henri Berr and Lucien Febvre, "History," *Encyclopaedia of the Social Sciences*; A. J. Toynbee, *A Study of History* (Oxford, 1934).

[57] Bloch, *op. cit.*; La Gorgette, *op. cit.*; M. R. Davie, *The Evolution of War* (New Haven, 1929); J. T. Shotwell (ed.), *Economic and Social History of the World War* (134 vols.; New Haven, 1921–34).

[58] Veblen, *op. cit.*; F. W. Hirst, *The Political Economy of War*; Nicolai, *op. cit.*; Salter, *op. cit.*; Speier and Kähler, *op. cit.*

APPENDIX IV

THE NATURE OF HISTORY

Is history a science or an art? While it has elements in common with each, it is different from both.[1]

1. HISTORY AND SCIENCE

It differs from science in that its data are distinctive and unique events, while the data of science are normal and recurrent events. Science attempts to produce from its data propositions of predictive or control value, while the object of history is the delineation of a natural unity in time and space, the narration of the development of such a unity from its origin to its termination, and the description of the characteristics which differentiate it from all others.[2]

A historical generalization is always limited to the past time and the limited

[1] "Truth is the criteria of historical study, but its impelling motive is poetic. Its poetry consists in its being true. There we find the synthesis of the scientific and literary views of history" (G. M. Trevelyan, "History and Literature," *History* [N.S.], IX [1924], 91).

[2] "The subject matter of history consists of occurrences which are unusual and out of the common, of events which for one reason or another compel the attention of men, and which are held worthy of being kept in remembrance. . . . . Natural science systematizes and classifies, history individualizes and narrates" (F. J. Teggert, *Theory of History* [New Haven, 1925], pp. 11, 51). Aristotle considered science the knowledge of the universal, history of the particular, and the same idea was expressed by Bacon, Hobbes, and Windelband (*ibid.*, p. 51; R. E. Park and E. W. Burgess, *An Introduction to the Science of Sociology* [Chicago, 1921], p. 8). J. R. Seeley emphasizes the nongeneralizing character of history when he defines history as "the residuum which has been left when one group of facts after another has been taken possession of by social science" (*Introduction to Political Science* [London, 1896], p. 13). Henri Pirenne emphasizes the subjective character of history when he writes: "The sociologist uses facts only with a view to the elaboration of a theory; the historian considers them as the episodes of a great adventure about which he must tell" (Stuart Rice [ed.], *Methods in Social Science* [Chicago, 1931], p. 436). Most historians conceive of their subject as dealing with the unique or unusual, the particular or time-space limited, the subjective or emotionally interesting, while they think of science as dealing with the general or common, the universal or abstract, and the objective. This refers to the product of historiography, the completed history, not to historical research, which insists on the objectivity of its facts and the employment of scientific method in their verification. Furthermore, history may, as Lord Haldane has said, seek "to make the idea of the whole shine forth in the particulars in which it is imminent" (*The Meaning of Truth in History* [London, 1914], p. 22). But the "wholes" in which it is interested, though they may cover large spaces and long times, always imply some limitation of time and space and include everything within these limits by implication if not by specification. They therefore lack the character of scientific "universals" or "abstractions."

space about which the history is written. If generalization is assumed to apply to other times—for instance, to the future—or to other places, it ceases to be a historical generalization. History may, however, contribute to scientific generalization. The historian may provide data which do not prove to be entirely distinctive, and the scientist may discover that certain historical generalizations have an application wider than the period and area concerning which they were made. Furthermore, the historian often gives warning, through emphasizing circumstances which actually are unique, that contingencies may occasionally disappoint expectations based upon even the best verified scientific generalizations.[3]

[3] While the usual conception of history emphasizes the unrepeatability of its subject matter (see n. 2, above), there have always been historians who believed that history can provide practical guidance. Thucydides thought that history could be a "guide to the future" (*Peloponnesian War* ["Everyman's" ed.] i. 22); Polybius thought "the knowledge of history the truest education and gymnastic for public affairs" (*Histories* i. 1); and Bolinbroke described history as "philosophy teaching by example" (*On the Study and Use of History*, Letter 2). The advocates of "comparative history" like E. A. Freeman (*Historical Essays*) and Prothero (*National Review*, December, 1894) and advocates of the "new history" like James Harvey Robinson (*The New History* [New York, 1912], p. 20) and Harry Elmer Barnes (*The New History and the Social Studies* [New York, 1925], p. 16) take the same view, but they apparently believe the practical value lies in the subjective understanding rather than in the objective knowledge which history can give. F. J. Teggert, refining the comparative method employed by Seeley, Freeman, and Toynbee, has attempted to make history a handmaid of science. "The study of the past can become effective only when it is fully realized that all peoples have histories, that these histories run concurrently and in the same world, and that the act of comparing is the beginning of knowledge. Only by facing an undertaking of new scope and of significant difficulty can history fulfill its obligation of making inquiry, not merely into what has happened, but into the way things actually work in the affairs of men" (*Rome and China: A Study of Correlations in Historial Events* [Berkeley, 1939], p. 245). The latter task is that of social science, as distinct from history, but Teggert illustrates how history, in the proper sense, can contribute to social science. His method proceeds by four steps: (1) Investigation of the correlation between apparently separated series of historic events, as, e.g., military disturbances on the frontiers of China and barbarian incursions on the Rhine and Danube in the period from 58 B.C. to A.D. 107. This is pure history, novel only in that it deals with a whole—the Eurasian continent—larger than that which has ordinarily concerned historians of the period (pp. vii ff., 235 ff.). (2) Investigation of the reason for any correlation which may be discovered. In this instance the high correlation was explained by the influence in closing one end of a trade route upon people at the other end. This is a proper historical generalization when confined to the time and area investigated (pp. ix ff., 240 ff.). (3) The suggestion that this explanation of migrations and disturbances may be of more universal validity than other theories such as those of population pressure, climatic change, a spirit of adventure, etc. This suggestion converts a historical generalization into a scientific hypothesis which clearly needs additional verification before it can be considered a scientific law (pp. 225 ff., 242 ff.). (4) The warning that the consequences of such cutting-off of trade routes may be different in modern times because of different circumstances. This is a proper warning for the historian to give the social scientist (p. 244).

The distinctive and abnormal differ only in degree from the normal. Given sufficiently large numbers, even the occurrence usually considered rare may be many times repeated. The autumn withering is unique in the life of the leaf but normal in the life of the tree. Death is abnormal in the life of the individual but normal in the life of the population. War is abnormal in the life of an administration but normal in the life of most civilizations.[4] Thus, by covering a long enough time and a broad enough area, historical data of many types have proved susceptible of generalization.

Wars have in modern civilization been regarded as abnormal and catastrophic. Perhaps for that reason history has been particularly interested in them. But, if a sufficiently extended time and space are taken as a unit of history, wars may manifest regularity in character or in recurrence. The history presented in this study attempts to discover such regularity and thus departs from the normal characteristics of history.

A history attempts to delineate the characteristics of a natural, a social, or a political unity, but in fact every such unity is a part of a larger whole, and reciprocally every part may be treated as a whole with parts of its own. Because of this, the historian has ample opportunity for creative imagination.[5] Having discovered, or created, the entity about which his history is to be written, the historian seeks to explain it in terms of the relation of its parts in successive spatial configurations. Each of these configurations is conceived to be determined by its immediate predecessor and to determine its immediate successor throughout the birth, development, maturity, decline, and death of the whole. At the same time the parts are interpreted by the function they play in the life of the whole. Each successive configuration and the completed whole thus has an influence upon the characteristics and behavior of every part at every moment. The historian is, therefore, most at home when dealing with a whole which is dead. When he attempts to interpret a living whole, he is confronted by the problem of prediction or of control. Who can say what the whole will become, what it is, or even whether it is a whole at all, until its history is completed?

If the historian assumes the role of prophet, he ceases to be a historian. He is not describing relations within a particular whole, but he is utilizing historical materials to support a science or a philosophy. It makes no difference whether his theory, in accord with analytic science, attributes unchangeable characteristics to the ultimate parts and assumes that their arrangement determines the

4 Biologists recognize that events which are "pathic," i.e., beyond the range of easy tolerance of an entity, at one level of organization may be healthy and normal at another level (George K. K. Link, "The Role of Genetics in Etiological Pathology," *Quarterly Review of Biology*, VII [June, 1932], 136 ff.).

5 See quotation from Lord Haldane, above, n. 2. Pitirim Sorokin (*Social and Cultural Dynamics* [New York, 1937], I, 10 ff.) discusses the ways and degrees in which cultures may have unity (see above, chap. vii, n. 16).

whole,[6] or, in accord with rational philosophy, attributes an unchangeable character or idea to the whole and assumes that the parts are logical deductions from this idea.[7] In either case he is not writing history but applying a scientific or a logical method. The historian as such is not concerned with customary relations or with logical relations but only with actual relations in a particular time-space. He does not deal with universals except as they operate in particular conjunctions or configurations or contingencies.

Causality is woven from very diverse elements which, however, may be divided into three categories: contingency, necessity and logic. There are in history contingent phenomena, and it is on this point that the *historiens historisants* have especially insisted. Chance is the phenomenon which is the effect neither of a law nor of a will, but of a coincidence of a series of independent phenomena and which thus is not and cannot be foreseen by the human mind. Individuality (or wholeness) is the sum of all the phenomena resulting from chance and relative to a human being, a collectivity, an epoch, a group or a crowd.[8]

2. HISTORY AND ART

History resembles art in that it justifies itself by its intrinsic interest.[9] It, however, differs from art because it insists on the actual occurrence of the events

[6] Henry Harrisse (*The Discovery of North America* [London, 1892], pp. v ff.) illustrates the confidence of one generation of historians in scientifically ascertained facts. "This process consists in determining with documentary proofs, and by minute investigation duly set forth, the literal, precise, and positive inferences to be drawn at the present day from every authentic statement, without regard to commonly received statement, without regard to commonly received notions, to sweeping generalities, or to possible consequences." Teggert thus explains the disappointments of this method. "The critical study of documents is one thing, the statement of the results of such inquiry another. Preoccupation with original documents brings with it a sense of security, a conviction that work based upon primary materials must necessarily be sound and enduring. Hence the academic historian holds to the belief that, having discovered the facts, all that remains to be done is to state what he has found without prejudice or bias. It is not to be wondered at that having adopted this view he should be nonplussed and eventually irritated when it is pointed out that the end of all this effort is the composition of a narrative marked by partisanship and emotion" (*Theory of History*, p. 25).

[7] Teggert appears to identify history with "idealistic philosophy." "At bottom the difference between idealistic philosophy and history on the one hand and science on the other is the difference between aesthetic appreciation and knowledge, between emotional realization of a scene or situation and painstaking investigation" (*Theory of History*, p. 54).

[8] Henri Berr and Lucien Febvre, "History and Historiography," *Encyclopaedia of the Social Sciences*, VII, 361.

[9] Herodotus amply appreciated the dramatic in history. He wrote in order that "the story of the past might not be obliterated by lapse of time and that the great and marvellous deeds performed by Greeks and Barbarians might not lose their fame." See also quotations from Pirenne (above, n. 2) and Balfour (below, n. 10).

with which it deals in the past time and space assigned to them, while art insists only on the possibility of the events it portrays. Furthermore, in art, techniques and data are subordinate to the effect of the whole upon the audience or, if it is a practical art, to the utility of the whole to the beneficiaries. A history, on the other hand, must subordinate the total effect to the data and to the techniques by which they have been established. The creative imagination of the historian has an opportunity, but his imagination is more hampered by his materials than is that of the artist.[10] Historians have often warped fact to improve the dramatic quality of their product or have utilized historical materials to persuade readers that the epoch recorded had a desired meaning.[11] If the historian is writing about an existing entity and his rhetoric is sufficient, his interpretation may influence opinion and so justify itself by subsequent, even if not by antecedent, events. His procedure, however, will not have been history but art or propaganda.

In the dialectical method of Hegel and Marx, the attempt was made to integrate methods of prediction and of control with history. These writers assumed that the data of history were continually analyzed into predictive propositions on the basis of which a feasible purpose or idea of the whole might be developed and a course of action planned. Whether the character of this idea was more influenced by the material conditions of the society's life or by the human minds which utilized these conditions was thus insoluble.[12] Society would not exist if

[10] "What has, in the main, caused history to be written, and when written to be eagerly read, is neither its scientific value nor its practical utility, but its aesthetic interest. Men love to contemplate the performances of their fellows, and whatever enables them to do so, whether we belittle it as gossip or exalt it as history, will find admirers in abundance. . . . . Directly it appears [however] that the governing preoccupation of an historian is to be picturesque, his narrative becomes intolerable. This is because the interest—I mean the aesthetic interest—of history largely depends upon its accuracy, or (more strictly) upon its supposed accuracy. . . . . Fact has an interest, because it is fact; because it actually happened. . . . . On this interest the charm of history eventually depends" (A. J. Balfour, *Theism and Humanism* [London, 1915]). See also above, n. 1.

[11] Livy frankly wrote history for edification: "The things to which I would have everyone for himself bend his keen attention are these: What Roman life and character have been; through what men and by what arts, at home or in the field, the empire was won and extended; then let him follow with attention how, as discipline gradually relaxed, character first as it were, declined, then lapsed more and more, then began to go headlong until we can endure neither our vices nor their remedies." Lord Acton considered history essentially a method of moral guidance: "The record of truths revealed by experience is eminently practical, as an instrument of action, and a power that goes to the making of the future. . . . . Unlike the dreaming prehistoric world, ours knows the need and the duty to make itself master of the earlier times, and to forfeit nothing of their wisdom or their warnings" (*A Lecture on the Study of History* [London, 1905], pp. 3, 11).

[12] Hegel gave the human mind priority, and in his general emphasis Marx gave priority to the material environment, especially to the system of production, but in his

either were lacking. The members of a society support and propagandize its idea by investigation of historic materials (thesis), but this investigation discloses discordances between the idea and changing conditions. This precipitates demands for reform which in time attack the idea itself (antithesis). The controversy between defenders and attackers of the traditional ideology eventually leads to a new idea of the society as a whole (synthesis). This reinterpretation, buttressed by the data of advancing history, modifies earlier predictions, stimulates new controls, and the dialectic process goes on, both making and being made by history.[13] The dialectic method is, however, not a historical method

---

exposition of his dialectic method he recognized the interaction of the two as essential. "The materialistic doctrine that men are products of their environment and education, different men products of different environment and education, forgets that the environment itself has been changed by man and the educator himself must be educated. That is why it separates society into two parts of which one is elevated over the whole. The simultaneity of change in the environment and human activity or self change can only be grasped and rationally understood as *revolutionary* practice." Quoted from Marx by Sidney Hook ("The Marxian Dialectic," *New Republic*, LXXIV [1933], 151), who thus explains the final cryptic sentence: "Refusing to dissociate social experience into something which is only cause, the external world, and something which is only effect, consciousness, Marx tries to show how social change arises from the interacting process of nature, society and human intelligence. From objective conditions, social and natural (thesis), there arise human needs and purposes which, in recognizing the objective possibilities in the given situation (antithesis), set up a course of action (synthesis) designed to actualize these possibilities. . . . . The process of creative development continues forever. At a critical point in the complex interaction of (1) social institutions from which we start, (2) the felt needs which their immanent development produces and (3) the will to action which flows from knowledge of the relation between institutions and human needs, new laws of social organization and behavior arise." It is the change at this critical point which Marx denominates "revolutionary practice." See also Karl Mannheim, *Ideology and Utopia* (New York, 1936), pp. 112 ff. Hegel also recognized the continual reaction of thought on conditions in history, but his assumption of a spiritual absolute in the background, of which history is a mere unrolling, gave consciousness, in contact with this absolute, a priority. The perpetual "becoming," which is the reality of history and philosophy, is for religion but a disclosure of the higher reality of the eternal "being." "The philosophy of Hegel is idealism, but it is an idealism in which every idealistic unification has its other face in the multiplicity of existence. It is realism as well as idealism and never quits its hold on facts. . . . . The universe is a process or development, to the eye of philosophy. . . . . In the background of all, the absolute is eternally present; the rhythmic movement of thought is the self-unfolding of the absolute" (William Wallace and J. B. Baillie, "Hegelian Philosophy," *Encyclopaedia Britannica* [14th ed.], XI, 382).

[13] Sidney Hook ("Materialism," *Encyclopaedia of the Social Sciences*, X, 213 ff.) writes: "Marx's theory of history is a method of making history" (p. 216). H. D. Lasswell emphasizes the union of the subjective and the objective in the making both of histories and of history: "One of the most potent reenforcing appeals of Marxism lies in its 'objectivity.' The words which allude to the past and future are not handled as tenta-

but a theory of the relation between history in the sense of an exposition of the life of an entity and history in the sense of the life of the entity itself. The theory, however, suggests one reason why the writing of history is always influenced by the history of the time and place in which the historian lives.

3. SUBJECTIVE AND OBJECTIVE

History has as its object the realization of the character of past wholes; consequently, it is especially interested in wholes and parts that obviously have a subjective as well as an objective aspect. It is possible to write the history of a mountain or of a geometry, but history actually has been written mainly about personalities and societies. Realization is the process whereby a subject and an object become identified with each other. From the manipulative point of view, the process consists in the creation or concretization of the object from ideas and plans of the subject. The architect's plan is *realized* when it stands in brick and mortar. From the contemplative point of view the process consists in the understanding or conceptualization of the object by the subject. The reader of Gibbon *realizes* the Roman Empire. The historian may be a manipulator in fact, but qua historian he is a contemplator. He is not interested, as is the engineer and the statesman, in the future realization of present ideas but, like the pure scientist, in the present realization of past events. The pure scientist's audience is small because it is difficult to induce in a reader ideas and feelings identical with the contours of molecules and geologic ages. The historian of human events can more readily invoke in his reader states of mind identical with those of past men and societies, however remote they may appear superficially.

Since the historian can assume his reader's interest in the subjective aspects of the entities he writes about,[14] his task is to relate the objective to the subjective aspect of those entities.[15] Sometimes he interprets phenomena as evidences of the human spirit at a particular stage of development[16] and sometimes he in-

---

tive conjectures but as overwhelming compulsions of the world historical process. The primacy of the material environment in the control of ideas reduces the individual to an episode in the triumphant evolution of reality. Dialectical materialism is the reading of private preferences into universal history, the elevating of personal aspirations into cosmic necessities, the remolding of the universe in the pattern of desire, the completion of the crippled self by the incorporation of the symbol of the whole. No competing symbolism rose to such heights of compulsive formulation" (*World Politics and Personal Insecurity* [New York, 1933], p. 135). See also Mannheim, *op. cit.*, pp. 97 ff.

[14] See n. 10, above.

[15] The pure scientist has the same task, but the subjective aspect of his material must be mainly provided from the abstract categories of his own mind, as developed by past study. This is because his materials themselves do not express sentiments or ideas. His interpretations, therefore, interest the nonspecialized reader less than those of the historian.

[16] As by Hegel and also by Spengler (above, n. 12).

terprets ideals and aspirations as consequences of the material phenomena of the time.[17]

Wholes must actually have both an objective and a subjective aspect, however obscure one or the other may be. A whole exists only because some consciousness, whether within or without, has distinguished it from its surroundings and from its parts. Individuality or wholeness consists in the organization of objective events into a unit by the intuitive feeling, the purposive action, or the observant intelligence of consciousness. Matter might exist without consciousness, but not wholes or individuals. The latter must have both form and substance, both belief and evidence, to be realized.[18]

The relative importance of the subjective and of the objective aspect of a thing may, however, differ in degree. A whole, which can be isolated from its surroundings only by a consideration of the spirit, ideas, or sentiments of its elements—as can a civilization, a historical epoch, or a nation—is highly subjective; whereas a whole, whose individuality is apparent from the organization of its material elements—as a planet, a picture, or an elephant—is highly objective. As the criteria for identifying the former type of entity are vague, the personality and preferences of the historian who writes about them play an important part in the history he writes. Consequently, the history of most epochs has been often re-written. So long as the milieu of the historians change, so long will history change.[19]

[17] As by Buckle and Marx. The latter considered the means of production utilized by a society as the most important condition of its culture. Thus his "historical materialism" is to be distinguished both from the "economic determinism" which regards economic self-interest as the most important human motive, and from "physical determinism" (Buckle, Huntington) which regards climate, geography, or other nonsocial material phenomena as the major controls of human culture. (Hook, "Materialism," *op. cit.*, pp. 216 ff.).

[18] Jan Smuts (*Holism and Evolution* [1926]; "Holism," *Encyclopaedia Britannica* [14th ed.]), Otto von Gierke (*Die deutsche Genossenschaftsrecht* [1873]), J. D. Lewis (*The Genossenschafts Theory of Otto von Gierke* [Madison, 1935], chap. iv), and C. M. Child (*Individuality in Organisms* [Chicago, 1915]) discuss the problem of identifying real individuals or wholes, respectively, from the philosophic, legal, and biological points of view.

[19] Although the natural scientist can identify and isolate the objects of his study more easily than can the historian, he can find less in the material itself for its own interpretation. The reader is even more at the mercy of the scientist's categories and logics than he is at the mercy of the historian's selections (see n. 13, above). The reader can be sure the scientist knows what he is talking about but less sure that he is saying anything important about it. On the other hand, he is sure the historian is saying a great many important things but doubtful about what he is saying them. The scientist, in William James's phrase, gives more "knowledge about" his subject, the historian more "knowledge of acquaintance."

4. ABSTRACT AND CONCRETE

History is formulated in terms of concrete events, but events may occupy time-spaces of varying magnitude. A rifle shot, a battle, a war, a nation, or a civilization may be treated as events, although the latter may cover a continent and last a millennium. Propositions true throughout a whole composed of such large events obviously have a relatively abstract character. The philosopher treats an abstraction as an assumption or definition stimulating him to logical deduction or experimental testing; the engineer treats it as a rule or instruction to guide his work of physical, social, or spiritual construction. The historian, however, notes that the abstraction was formulated by definite persons at definite times and places, that it was known or believed and influenced human behavior within definite time-spaces, or that it accurately expresses relations that existed within definite times and places. Certain abstractions may be true of the whole of time and space, but most of them are more limited.

The historian's task, therefore, is to break up the whole with which he deals into subwholes about each of which more can be said than about the whole; and these in turn into parts. The parts, however, in a true history constitute complete time-spaces rather than analytical subdivisions. A history of science, for instance, is half-history and half-analysis, for at every step the analytic question must be answered, "What is science?" The only proper boundaries for a history are time and space boundaries. Analytic distinctions enter in only to formulate propositions which are true of the whole of a given time-space.

5. PHILOSOPHY OF HISTORY

Studies of comparative history[20] and of theories of history[21] are not history but sciences or philosophies of history.[22] If the histories of two or more distinct periods, nations, or civilizations are compared and resemblances or differences are used to support generalizations supposedly applicable to all histories, the result is a science. If logical deductions from assumptions about the nature of man or society are used to explain the histories of distinct societies, the result is a philosophy. Sciences and philosophies of history may mutually support each other. The modern social sciences have resulted from both methods.

Many attempts have been made to formulate sciences and philosophies of history.[23] The most general formulations have interpreted each particular history as a process of development like the growth of a tree, of construction like

---

[20] Freeman, *op. cit.*; A. J. Toynbee, *A Study of History* (3 vols.; Oxford 1934), III, 192, 375; Henry Adams, "A Letter to History Teachers" in *The Degradation of Democratic Dogma* (New York, 1919); Teggert, *Rome and China*.

[21] See above, nn. 12 and 13.

[22] See above, nn. 6 and 7. The comparison of different parts of the same whole in order to better characterize the whole is properly history (see above, chap. iii, n. 3).

[23] Above, chap. 3, sec. 3.

the building of a house, or of interaction like the conduct of a conversation.[24] If history is a process of development, every particular history has been determined by the complex of conditions from which it started, in the same way as the character and biography of a plant or animal, according to the preformationists, has been determined by the fertilized cell from which it originated.[25] If history is a construction, every particular history has been the consequence of persistent efforts of individuals and groups to realize the faith or complex of ideas which has identified the group as the proper subject of a history.[26]

The interpretations of history as processes either of development or of construction have a deterministic character. They respectively assume that the essentials of a society at any point in its existence have been determined by its origin or by its destiny, by its first cause or by its final cause. The more common interpretation of history, however, has recognized the role of creativeness and contingency in social change,[27] as have the epigenecists in explaining the character and biography of an organism.[28] A particular history, according to this view, has been the consequence of continuous interaction between external conditions, pressures, and influences and internal organizations, beliefs, and activities; between traditions of the past and aspirations of the future; between the inertia of tendencies and the persuasiveness of plans; between challenges and responses; between opposing ideals and activities and organizations.[29]

Although it reduces the role of determinism, the interpretation of history as a process of interaction, like the other interpretations, has usually resulted in a theory attributing to the history of a given class of entities a normal succession of stages or periods. Different theories, however, have varied greatly in the amount of deviation from the normal which they have anticipated.[30] Among such theories have been those which interpret a history as a continuous response and adaptation to changes in the material environment;[31] as a life-cycle of birth, growth, decline, and death;[32] as a series of oscillations in which withdrawal and planning is followed by return and accomplishment;[33] or as a succession of periods respectively dominated by artistic, religious, political, and economic interests.[34]

[24] These correspond respectively to the evolutionary, functional, and diffusionist interpretations of the customs of primitive peoples (see below, Appen. V, nn. 10–12).

[25] See above, n. 17.   [26] See above, n. 16.   [27] See above, n. 8.

[28] J. H. Woodger, *Principles of Biology* (New York, 1929).

[29] Toynbee (*op. cit.*) emphasizes the interactions of challenge and response. A. L Lowell illustrates the interaction of constructive effort and social tendencies ("An Example from the Evidence of History," in *Factors Determining Human Behavior* ["Harvard Tercentenary Publications" (Cambridge, Mass., 1937)], pp. 119–32). See also above, nn. 12 and 13.

[30] See above, chap. iii, sec. 3.   [32] See above, chap. vii, sec. 2b, n. 41.

[31] See above, chap. iii, n. 6.   [33] See above, chap. xv, sec. 3c, n. 40.

[34] See above, chap. viii, sec. 3, and views of Plato and Aristotle, chap. vii, sec. 2b, n. 42. Alfred Marshall points out that man's character has been molded by economic, re-

As the entity about which a history is written approaches universality and eternity, the history approaches a philosophy of history. The history of war at-

---

ligious, military, and artistic influences; their relative importance, he thinks, writing in an economic age, being in the order named. Though he admits that at times one or the other influence has been predominant, he does not suggest any definite sequence (*Principles of Economics* [2d ed.; London, 1891], p. 1). Leonard Bloomfield writes: "An individual may base himself upon a purely practical, an artistic, a religious, or a scientific acceptance of the universe, and that aspect which he takes as basic will transcend and include the others. The choice, at the present state of our knowledge, can be made only by an act of faith" (*Linguistic Aspects of Science* [Chicago, 1939], p. 13). Sir Arthur Salter finds that in modern history "the four main causes of war—the dynastic, the religious, the political, and the economic—have each in turn, and in the order named, assumed the leading place" ("War Risks in Economic Conflicts," *Yale Review*, XIV [July, 1925], 683 ff.). Brooks Adams suggests a succession from an interest in art and love to an interest in religion, then war, and finally economics (*Law of Civilization and Decay*, chap. xii). W. F. Ogburn points out that in American history the family and the church have declined in social significance while the governmental and economic organizations have gained (*Recent Social Changes* [New York, 1933], I, xii). W. M. Flinders-Petrie (*The Revolutions of Civilization* [New York, 1911]) has suggested a succession from the spatial arts (architecture, sculpture, and painting) through the temporal arts (literature, music, and the dance) to the practical arts (science, politics, and business). F. Delaisi suggests that a myth passes through four stages during its life, presided over, respectively, by religious mystics, realistic statesmen, corrupting manipulators, and literary satirists (*Political Myths and Economic Realities* [New York, 1927], pp. 54–57). Pareto assumes that at first each period is dominated by an élite of "lions" who act forcibly upon the "residue of persistent aggregates," i.e., upon an unquestioning belief in the existing symbolic structure. Later the "lions" give way to an élite of "foxes" who act by ruse rather than violence upon the "residue of the instinct of combination," i.e., upon a disposition to break up existing symbolic structures and recombine their elements to achieve immediate and practical ends. This distinction resembles that between Platonists, who assume the reality of ideas, and Aristotelians, who assume the reality of observations. Each of the successive periods might thus be divided, the artistic into moities dominated, respectively, by classicists and romanticists; the religious into moities dominated, respectively, by preachers of the faith and skeptical interpreters. The halves of the political period would be dominated, respectively, by lawyers and politicians, the economic by *rentiers* and speculators. Pareto recognizes only three aspects of the cycle—political, economic, and ideological. Thus he combines the artistic and religious periods into one (Vilfredo Pareto, *The Mind and Society*, IV [New York, 1935], 1515 ff., and "Pareto," *Encyclopaedia of the Social Sciences*. P. Sorokin argues convincingly that all rational writing and discussion assumes some recurrence in history, though the form and degree of recurrence may vary. All phenomena thus exhibit a unique or particular and a recurrent or universal aspect (*Social and Cultural Dynamics*, I, 161–91). He seeks to demonstrate in the arts, philosophies, and social relationships alternations of "ideational" and "sensate" periods with mixed and balanced ("idealistic") periods between. Although skeptical of the precise cycles of art forms asserted by Flinders-Petrie, Ligeti, and others (*ibid.*, pp. 198–221, especially table on p. 209), he presents objective evidence

tempted in this volume covers the struggles of life throughout the world from animals to contemporary world-civilization. It therefore approaches a philosophy of history.

---

of pulsations in the dominance of visual and ideational elements in art with mixed and balanced (idealistic) periods between (I, 404); of pulsations in the dominance of empirical and rational philosophies with mixed periods between often exhibiting skepticism, mysticism, criticism, and fideism (II, 32, 629, 630); of pulsations in the dominance of "familistic" and "contractual" social relationships with "compulsive" and mixed systems of relationships between (III, 123 ff.). Sorokin properly thinks of social change as a fugue or polyphony which builds harmony in "horizontal" melodic threads instead of in "vertical" chordal lumps, but his periods of "ideational" and "sensate" domination may correspond to periods of predominantly religious and economic interest, respectively, while the "mixed" and "idealistic" periods may be predominantly political or artistic. He also relates the alternations in forms of freedom to the political cycles discussed by Plato and Aristotle (III, 177).

APPENDIX V

THE RELATION OF HISTORY TO GEOGRAPHY

Historic and geographic discontinuities of social structure have been both a cause and a consequence of the opposing tendencies toward divergence and convergence in social evolution. War, while an expression of this opposition, has often been the bridge connecting these discontinuities. A history of war is therefore concerned with the geographic barriers and historic separations which have interfered with the orderly and continuous spread of races and of civilizations over the earth.

It is difficult to visualize the flow of history because its course has continually diverged from a common stream like the sap flowing from the trunk to the leaves of a tree, and at the same time its course has continually converged from numerous distinct sources into the main stream like the sap flowing from rootlets to the trunk of the tree or like the flow of water to a river from thousands of separated streamlets. Biologically the process by which phyla, orders, families, genera, species, and races have become isolated and differentiated has been the phenomenon most requiring explanation. Consequently, organic evolution has usually been represented as the branching of a tree, although actually somewhat differentiated races have continually come into contact and formed new types by hybridization. Sociologically, on the other hand, the processes of accommodation and assimilation by which families, villages, tribes, nations, empires, federations, and international unions have come into being is the phenomenon most requiring explanation. Consequently, social evolution has been represented as a river system, although actually migration to new lands and the influence of natural and artificial barriers have continually resulted in the isolation and differentiation of social units.[1]

[1] The distinction is illustrated by the title to the biologist Darwin's book, *The Origin of Species*, suggesting divergent evolution, contrasted to the title of the historian E. A. Freeman's lecture, "The Unity of History," suggesting convergence. Freeman, however, had reference to the continuity of historical streams and the repetitions to which the human spirit in different environments continually gives rise rather than to the trend of human history toward a co-ordination of all human groupings in a single group (*Comparative Politics* [2d ed.; London, 1896], pp. 192 ff.). Gierke expressed the latter conception as follows: "As the forward march of world history is inevitably realized, there appears in an unbroken ascending arch the noble structure of those organic associations which in ever greater and more comprehensive circles bring into tangible form and reality the interdependence of all human existence, unity in its multi-colored variations. From marriage, the highest of those associations which do not outlast their members, grow forth in abundant gradations, families, races, tribes and clans, *Gemeinde*, states and leagues of states, and for this development we can imagine no other limit

For hundreds of thousands of years the tree of preliterate human history occasionally branched, some of these branches becoming distinct human species— Trinil, Peking, Heidelberg, Piltdown, Rhodesian, Neanderthal men—each eventually breaking off or perhaps uniting with adjacent branches. Only the main branch survived the last glaciation some twenty-five thousand years ago. This event, while catastrophic to numerous species of mammals including earlier human species, may have been a main stimulus to mental evolution in *Homo sapiens*.[2] Since then the physical character of man has not changed greatly. Present races, although some may have branched earlier, are but variations of one species.[3]

Since recorded history began, some six thousand years ago, social factors have been more important than biological factors in human evolution.[4] With numerous isolated primitive groups at their sources, the various civilizations have, within the past few centuries, flowed into the great river of contemporary world-civilization.[5] From their formation until the age of discoveries only five hundred

---

than when some time in the distant future, all mankind shall be drawn together into a single organized community, which shall visibly demonstrate that all are but members of one great whole" (*Das deutsche Genossenschaftsrecht*, I, 1, trans. in John D. Lewis, *The Genossenschaftstheorie of Otto von Gierke* [Madison, Wis., 1935], p. 24).

[2] Cromagnon man, who may have flourished in Europe until 7000 B.C., was probably a race of *Homo sapiens* (see Ellsworth Huntington, *World Power and Evolution* [New Haven, 1919], pp. 115 ff.; Julian C. Huxley, "Climate and Human History," *Atlantic Monthly*, CXLV [April, 1930], 512 ff.). G. Elliot Smith (*Human History* [Oxford, 1924]) suggests that the Eolithic and Lower Paleolithic ages (including pre-Chellean, Chellean, Acheulian, and Mousterian cultures) be grouped as the Paleanthropic period when earlier human species flourished until exterminated during the last or "Wurm" glaciation, twenty-five to a hundred thousand years ago. He then groups the Upper Paleolithic or reindeer age (Aurignacian, Solutrean, and Magdalenian cultures), the Mesolithic (Azilian culture), Neolithic, and subsequent metal ages as the Neanthropic period because all human races seem to have then been of the present species, *Homo sapiens*. See Fig. 9.

[3] A. S. Romer, *Man and the Vertebrates* (Chicago, 1933); H. J. E. Peake and H. J. Fleure, *Apes and Men* (New Haven, 1927); H. F. Osborn, *Men of the Old Stone Age* (New York, 1915). See also above, chap. iv, n. 3.

[4] Walter Bagehot assumed that the more culture developed, the less the stress of natural selection fell on the body. The "race-making period" of human development gave way to the "nation-making period" (*Physics and Politics* [London, 1903], pp. 86, 108, 136). The idea is developed by Griffith Taylor (*Environment and Race* [Oxford, 1927]; *Environment and Nation* [Chicago, 1936]).

[5] See below, Fig. 12. A three-dimensional rather than a two-dimensional figure with a map at the top and irregular cones extending below it with their points all in contact at the point directly below the map where the human race started would more adequately represent the history of human groups. Any plane drawn through the whole parallel to the top would represent the map at a given time in history, and the area at which it cut each cone would indicate the area occupied by that group at that time. Diagrams of

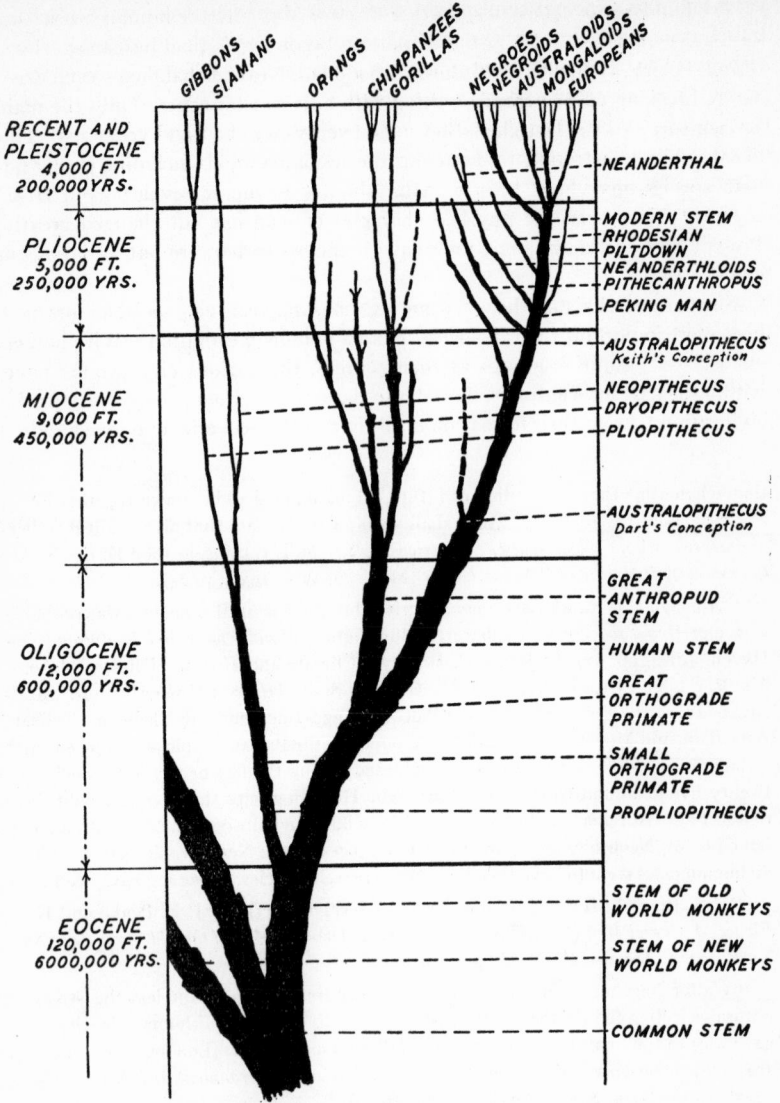

FIG. 9.—The relationship of human races. (From Sir Arthur Keith, *New Discoveries Relating to the Antiquity of Man* [London, 1931].)

years ago, the principal civilizations were so separated that contacts of trade, travel, communication, or war were unimportant, like the subterranean water seepages from one river system to another, or infrequent, like floods which occasionally join the streams of two rivers across a plain. At times the main streams of civilization meandered through deserts or were so augmented by waters from others that the stream below assumed a new character. The continuity of human history has been broken in time as well as in space.

The principal populations which have contributed to human history since the record began have been the American, the far eastern, and the Western, each divided into two or more subpopulations.[6] Each subpopulation has through most of its history been sufficiently unified by communication and sufficiently isolated from its neighbors by barriers to develop a body of distinctive beliefs and so to constitute a civilization.[7]

Evidence for locating the main barriers to population contact during the preliterate development of *Homo sapiens* can be found in maps showing the distribution of languages,[8] legal systems, myths, religions and rituals, artistic and architectural forms, social customs, dress, economic organizations, processes, and implements.[9] The historical conclusions to be drawn from the occasional

---

this kind might develop the habit of conceiving historical and geographical relationships simultaneously—a habit essential for understanding the processes of social change and conflict. Fortunately the most important geographical relationships, for this purpose, can, by processes of projection, be represented on a map in two dimensions; thus it is possible to add the time dimension without getting into the fourth dimension, which is impossible to represent graphically. Griffith Taylor has made some ingenious time-space diagrams in two and three dimensions (*Environment and Nation*, pp. 4, 126).

[6] These three populations divided into seven subpopulations alone acquired considerable densities and developed civilizations, but the minor population of the Australian-Melanesian area (which is most distinctive zoölogically) also developed a distinctive character as did that of Africa south of the Sahara. The latter population, however, has been less isolated and might even be considered a subpopulation of the Western population. A. J. Toynbee (*A Study of History* [London, 1934]) has detected twenty-one civilizations since history began. The people who carried these civilizations were related to the populations and subpopulations as indicated in Table 1, p. 461.

[7] The areas of these subpopulations were also characterized by an abundance of distinctive food plants, the domestication of which provided the material basis for the civilizations (see N. J. Vavilov, "Asia, Source of Species," *Asia*, February, 1937, p. 113, and below, Fig. 14).

[8] Linguistic map of pre-Columbian America (J. W. Powell, "Indian Linguistic Families," *Seventh Annual Report of Bureau of Ethnology, Smithsonian Institute* [Washington, 1886]), of Europe (H. E. Barnes, *The History of Western Civilization* [New York, 1935], II, 460).

[9] See, e.g., maps of arrow-release method in America and many other culture traits (C. Wissler, *The Relation of Nature and Man in Aboriginal America* [New York, 1926], pp. 39, 120, 229), of distribution of cannibalism, circumcision, human sacrifice (E. M.

appearance of a cultural trait throughout a given area are, however, uncertain. Such an appearance may be the result of independent invention and gradual convergent evolution of the culture trait within separate groups.[10] It may indicate a common origin of the trait in a group whose descendants subsequently scattered and diverged in other cultural characteristics.[11] It may indicate a diffusion of certain culture traits through a chance historic contact of separated

---

Loeb, *The Blood Sacrifice Complex* ["Memoirs of the American Anthropological Association," No. 30 (1923)], pp. 40 ff.), of distribution of couvade, megaliths, snake and sun cults, tatooing, the levirate, etc. (Griffith Taylor, "Race, Culture and Language," *Geographical Review*, XI [January, 1921], 79; and *Environment and Race*, Appen., Fig. 93).

[10] W. M. Wheeler (*Demons of the Dust* [New York, 1930]) and Henri Bergson (*Creative Evolution* [New York, 1911]) apply the concept of convergent evolution in organic evolution. Spinden (*Culture, the Diffusionist Controversy*, by G. E. Smith, B. Malinowski, H. J. Spinden, and A. Goldenweiser [New York, 1927]) explains its application in cultural evolution. The concept of convergence is also used by Franz Boas, Robert H. Lowie, and A. Goldenweiser. E. M. Loeb has pointed out that convergence may account for such a widely distributed custom as finger sacrifice where it is rationally related to a more complex custom such as blood sacrifice, one or more elements of which, such as cannibalism, human sacrifice, circumcision, are widely distributed (above, n. 9). See also Appen. VI, n. 16.

[11] Darwin explained the origin of organic species by the concept of gradual divergence from a common ancestor; Max Müller used the same concept to explain the variety of Indo-Germanic languages; and Spencer used it to explain the variety of societies. The "evolutionary school" of anthropology (E. B. Tylor, Lewis H. Morgan, Sir James Fraser), however, thinks of social change as analogous to the development of the organisms of a species (ontogeny) rather than to the differentiation of species (phylogeny). They combine the concepts of divergence and convergence and assume that however much societies may have diverged through different environmental influences, their common ancestry predisposes all human groups to converge their culture traits, although independently invented, to common patterns and stages of development. The "functional school" of anthropology (B. Malinowski, A. R. Radcliffe-Brown, G. H. L. F. Pitt-Rivers), though disclaiming an interest in cultural origins, seems to make similar assumptions. To explain the meaning of each single custom they show its relationship to the other customs, to the general system of ideas and sentiments of the group (Radcliffe-Brown, *The Andaman Islands* [Cambridge, 1922], p. 230), but these "relationships" turn out to depend upon the existence of a common stock of human values and behavior patterns (ends and means) shared by all cultures, including that of the investigating anthropologist. The custom has "meaning" when it is seen that its form has diverged from a common human pattern for representing a sentiment or accomplishing an end, and that its substance or function has converged to serve a need of all human groups (B. Malinowski, "Culture as a Determinant of Behavior," in *Factors Determining Human Behavior* ["Harvard Tercentenary Publications" (Cambridge, Mass., 1937)], pp. 135 ff.). For comparison of the various schools of anthropology see Pitt-Rivers, *The Clash of Culture and Contact of Races* (London, 1927), chap. i. See also Appen. VI, n. 17.

groups.[12] Only if it indicates continuous contact among the groups throughout the area does it suggest that barriers within the area have never been formidable. Only where complexes of many cultural traits exist throughout the area can the latter situation be assumed.[13]

Evidence for locating the main barriers to population contact during even more remote periods of human evolution can be found in maps showing the distribution of racial traits such as head form, nose shape, hair character, skin color, blood groups, and eye shape.[14] But here also it is often uncertain whether the occasional appearance of a racial trait throughout an area is the result of independent variation toward a common type in different parts of the area,[15] of common origin and persistence of certain characters in spite of subsequent separation of the groups,[16] of infiltration of a dominant gene from sporadic contact with a separated group,[17] or of continuous interbreeding throughout the area over a

[12] G. Elliot Smith (*Culture, the Diffusion Controversy*) expounds the theory of the "diffusionist" or "historical" school of anthropologists (W. H. R. Rivers, W. J. Perry, W. C. MacLeod). If we assume that diffusion proceeds regularly from the periphery of the area occupied at a given time and that divergence in form is also gradual, it follows that the degree of both diffusion and divergence will be proportionate to the time during which they have been going on. Consequently, the age of a culture, race, or species can be estimated from the size of the area connecting its most distant occurrences and to the number and importance of the variations which it exhibits. The original home will be near the center of the area and the original form will be the average of the varieties. Willis has applied this "age-area" theory to plants, Mathews to animals, Griffith Taylor to human races, and Clark Wissler to cultures (see Taylor, "Racial Migration Zones and Their Significance," *Human Biology*, II [February, 1930], 34 ff.). The possibilities of wide, rapid, and sporadic diffusion of culture traits emphasized by the "diffusionists" or even of genes (n. 17, below), especially with improved means of transportation, suggest caution in the application of this theory.

[13] See H. J. Spinden, *Culture, the Diffusionist Controversy;* Loeb, *op. cit.*, pp. 4–5.

[14] See Roland B. Dixon, *The Racial History of Man* (New York, 1923), pp. 184, 248, 344, 400, 448; Griffith Taylor, *Environment and Race*, Frontispiece; Ellsworth Huntington, *The Character of Races* (New York, 1924), p. 77; W. C. MacLeod, *Origin and History of Politics* (New York, 1931), p. 83; A. C. Haddon, *The Wanderings of Peoples* (Cambridge, 1919), pp. 125 ff.

[15] Wheeler, Bergson, above, n. 10. L. H. D. Buxton (*The Peoples of Asia* [New York, 1925], pp. 21 ff.) notes the extent to which most of these indices may be directly affected by the environment. A dark skin, fuzzy hair, and flat nose perhaps tend to develop in any race exposed for sufficient generations to a very hot climate.

[16] The traits used for purposes of genetic classification by taxonomists have this character (see W. B. Scott, *A History of Land Mammals of the Western Hemisphere* [New York, 1913]). Taylor, Dixon, and Huntington (above, n. 14) assume that groups as widely separated as South America, Melanesia, and Africa are of the same race if they have certain selected racial characteristics in common (see above, n. 11).

[17] The distribution of blood groups throughout the human population has probably resulted from such sporadic contacts.

long period. The greater the number of common genetic traits, the more probable is the latter.[18]

Evidence for locating the main barriers to prehuman population movements may be found in maps showing the distribution of the main species, genera, and families of animals.[19]

After giving due weight to the influence of convergence, divergence, diffusion, and association, these types of maps suggest that there have been variations in the formidableness of geographical barriers at different times, that human groups did not reach the Americas until after the last glaciation, and that they did not reach the islands of the Pacific until after the beginning of the Christian Era.[20] They suggest, however, that man was widely distributed in Asia, Europe, and Africa before he received his present specific character and that the most important geographic barriers have not changed greatly since before the advent of man.[21]

[18] M. Wagner, *Die Entstehung der Artendurf räumliche Sonderung* (Berlin, 1889). The relative weight to be given to selection of mutations, random variation of genetic traits, cross-breeding, and inbreeding in accounting for organic evolution has been studied by Sewall Wright ("Evolution in Mendelian Populations," *Genetics*, XVI [March, 1931], 97 ff.; *Proceedings of the Sixth International Congress of Genetics*, I [1932], 356 ff.). Two points of view may be distinguished with respect to the influence of geography and history on both cultural and physical traits. Certain writers have tended to measure and to study the occurrence throughout the human race of a few traits selected because they are easy to identify and to deal with. Concentrating upon these traits, the writers have come to regard them as persistent and determining factors in whatever time or place they might appear and to provide data for the interpretation of the racial or cultural history of human populations. Elliot Smith, Rivers, and Perry of the diffusionist school have done this for culture traits while Taylor, Dixon, and Huntington have done it for physical traits. Other writers have tended to study either the physical or the cultural characteristics of a limited population as a whole, assuming that nothing less would provide a basis for interpreting the meaning of a particular trait and for preparing a classification of cultures or races which could throw certain light on historic relations. Malinowski and Radcliffe-Brown of the functional school have done this for certain cultures, while Haddon and Buxton have attempted it for physical anthropology. The desideratum would doubtless be a method which would combine the precision and comparability of the first method with the comprehensiveness of the second. That is difficult to achieve, but perhaps Karl Pearson's complicated mathematical formulas for reducing variable frequencies of numerous physical characteristics to a single number points the way (see Buxton, *op. cit.*, pp. 7 ff.). The adaptation of such a method to a study of culture would be even more difficult.

[19] See Fig. 10. W. L. and P. L. Sclater, *The Geography of Mammals* (London, 1899); D. M. S. Watson, "Zoological Regions," *Encyclopaedia Britannica* (14th ed.). From the standpoint of civilization the distribution of plant species is even more important than that of animal species (see Fig. 14, p. 465).

[20] Spinden, *Culture, the Diffusionist Controversy.*

[21] The barrier of the Mediterranean between Europe and Africa may have been less at times.

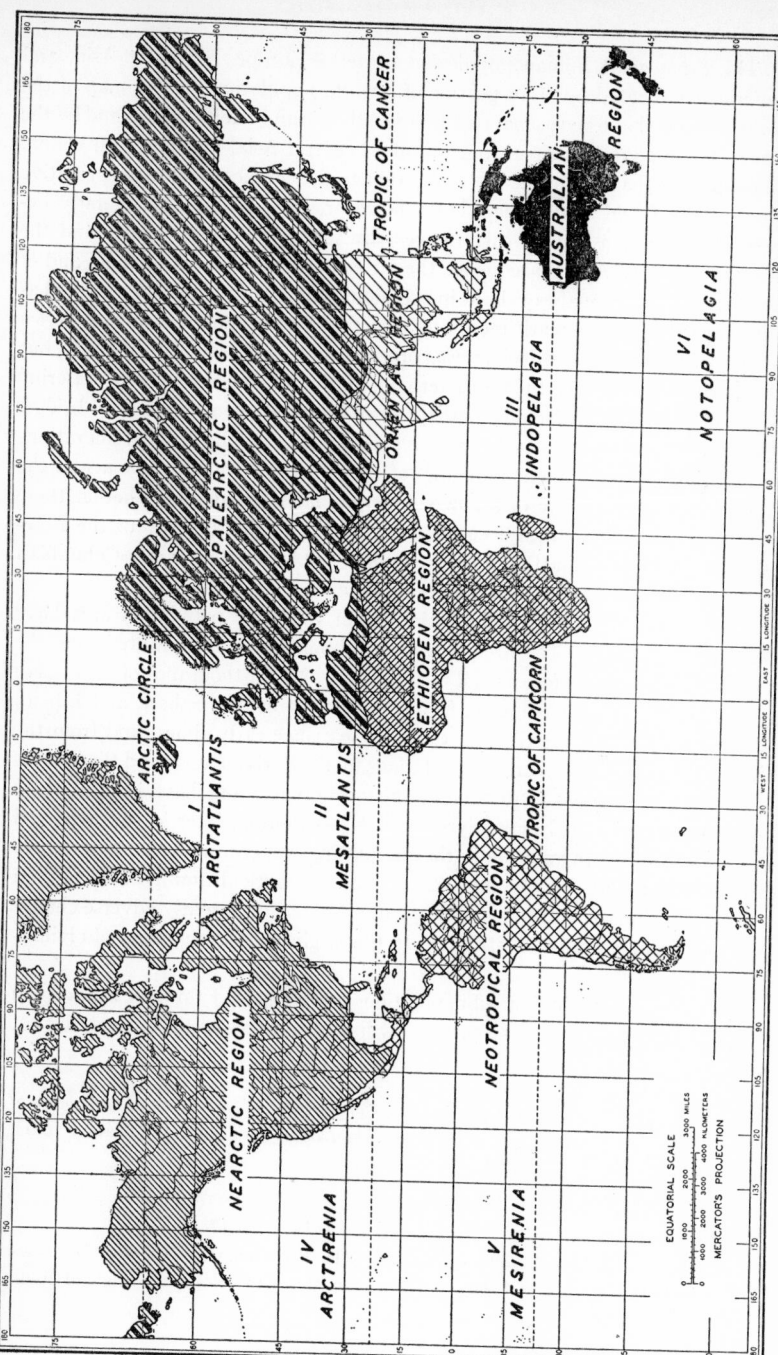

Fig. 10.—Main areas of distribution of animal forms. (From W. L. and P. L. Sclater, *The Geography of Mammals* [London, 1899], pp. 16, 216.)

The three great human population centers—Europe, southeast Asia, and America—indicated by an inspection of a world-population density map of the present time,[22] have been separated by the Atlantic and Pacific oceans and by the desert and mountain strip through Arabia, central Asia, and northern China. These barriers have been the most deterrent to the contact of animals, primitive man, and civilized man. There have, however, been bridges, particularly between the Western and far eastern areas by way of the Indus Valley and the Siberian steppes. As a consequence the far eastern populations of India and of northern China have always been in occasional contact with the West as well as with each other. The maritime route from the Western population to America by way of Greenland and Iceland was probably not used until historic times, but the maritime route from the far eastern population to America by way of Bering Strait or the Aleutian Islands, perhaps once forming a continuous land bridge, was probably used much earlier as the main avenue for the original migrations to America. Whether some ancestors of the American Indian came across the Atlantic perhaps by way of a now submerged land bridge, and whether there were pre-Columbian cultural contacts across the Pacific by way of the Polynesian Islands, is a matter of controversy.[23] The isolation of pre-Columbian America was, in any case, relatively complete.

The barriers separating subpopulations of the same population area have been less formidable. The Mediterranean subpopulation is separated from the northern European by forests and mountains, which for thousands of years have presented but a slight obstacle; from the African by the Sahara and Libyan deserts, bridged by the Nile and the Red Sea since early times; and from the Mesopotamian and Persian subpopulations by the Syrian Desert and the Taurus Mountains. The great centers of the historic civilizations have been at these bridge points, first in Egypt, Syria, and Mesopotamia, later in southern and western Europe.[24] In addition to the stimulating influence of the close contact of diverse cultures at these points, factors such as agricultural possibilities,[25] a stimulating climate,[26] and the challenge of a sudden, apparently adverse change in the environment have contributed to the origin and development of civilizations.[27]

The Chinese and Indian subpopulations are connected through Indo-China as well as through Tibet. The earliest civilizations in this area, however, did not

[22] See Fig. 11.

[23] See Spinden, *Culture, the Diffusionist Controversy;* W. J. Perry, *The Growth of Civilization* (New York, 1923); John Fiske, *The Discovery of America* (Boston, 1901), Vol. I, chaps. i and ii; n. 6, above.

[24] See Figs. 12 and 13 and Table 2.

[25] See Fig. 14. [26] Cf. Figs. 16, 17, and 18.

[27] See A. J. Toynbee, *A Study of History,* J. H. Breasted, *The Dawn of Conscience* (New York, 1933), chap. i, and above chap. vii, sec. 2b, for theories of the origin of civilization.

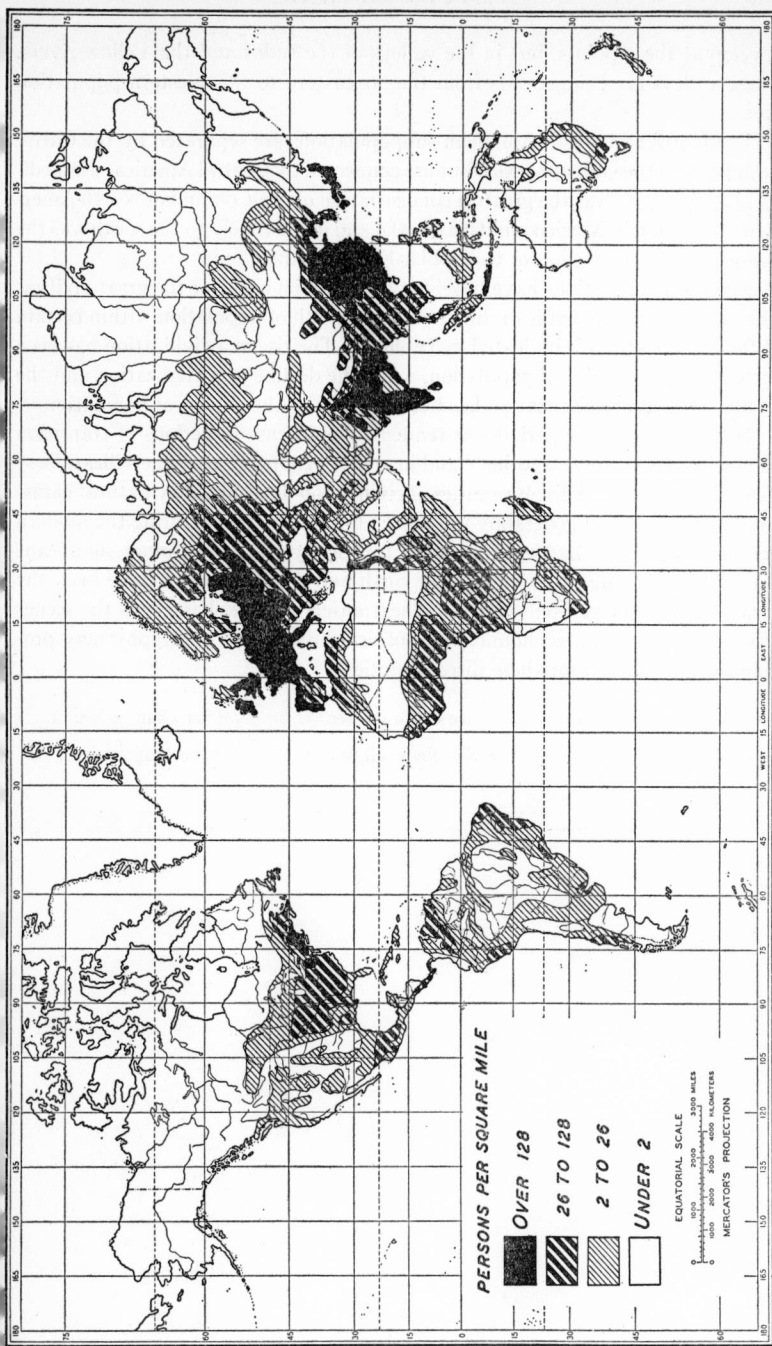

PERSONS PER SQUARE MILE

OVER 128

26 TO 128

2 TO 26

UNDER 2

EQUATORIAL SCALE

MERCATOR'S PROJECTION

Fig. 11.—Population density of the world. (From A. J. Toynbee, *The World after the Peace Conference* [London, 1925], p. 92)

develop at these points, but in the valleys of the Indus and the Yellow rivers. These valleys are bridgeheads from the far eastern to the Western population areas.

The North and South American subpopulations are separated by the Caribbean Sea and the Gulf of Mexico but are connected by Central America. Immediately to the north was the greatest concentration of pre-Columbian North American population in Mexico and Guatemala, and immediately to the south was the dense Andean population of Colombia, Ecuador, and Peru.

These subpopulations have provided the material basis for the great civilizations as indicated in Tables 1 and 2.[28] The growth of population within certain of these civilizations is indicated in Table 3.[29] The rise of a civilization has been accompanied by a rise of population, while the decline of a civilization and the transition to a new civilization has been marked by the decline of population.

During the historic period war tended to be intense in periods of transition from one civilization to another[30] and in areas of contact between civilizations.[31] Temporal and spatial discontinuities of civilization determined by natural catastrophes and physical geography were often bridged by war. During the modern period changes and barriers instituted by society have been more significant than those instituted by nature. The birth and death of states have been the occasion for the most intense wars.[32] The frontiers of states have been the scenes of such war.[33] Social, economic, and political history and geography may provide the explanation for these discontinuities.

[28] See Figs. 12 and 13.

[29] See Fig. 15.

[30] See chap. vii, sec. 3c.

[31] See chap. vii, sec. 1.

[32] See chap. x, sec. 2.

[33] See chap. ix, sec. 1b.

TABLE 1*

RELATION OF POPULATIONS, SUBPOPULATIONS, AND CIVILIZATIONS

POPULATIONS (ZOÖLOGICAL REGIONS)	SUBPOPULATIONS	CIVILIZATIONS	
		Extinct	Living
Far Eastern (Oriental)	Far Eastern	Sinic	Chinese Japanese
	Indian	Indic	Hindic
Western (Palaearctic)	Oriental	Mesopotamian Babylonic Syriac Tartar	Iranic Arabic
	Mediterranean	Hittite Egyptic	
		Minoan Classic	Orthodox
	European	Nestorian Germanic Scandinavian Irish	Russian Western
American (Nearctic)	North American	Mayan Yucatec Mexican	
(Neotropical)	South American	Andean	
South and Central African (Ethiopian)			
Australian-Melanesian (Australasian)			

* From A. J. Toynbee's *A Study of History*, with some modifications. Those civilizations marked "living" have been to some extent absorbed in modern world-civilization, and remnants of some of the "extinct" civilizations have not been wholly absorbed.

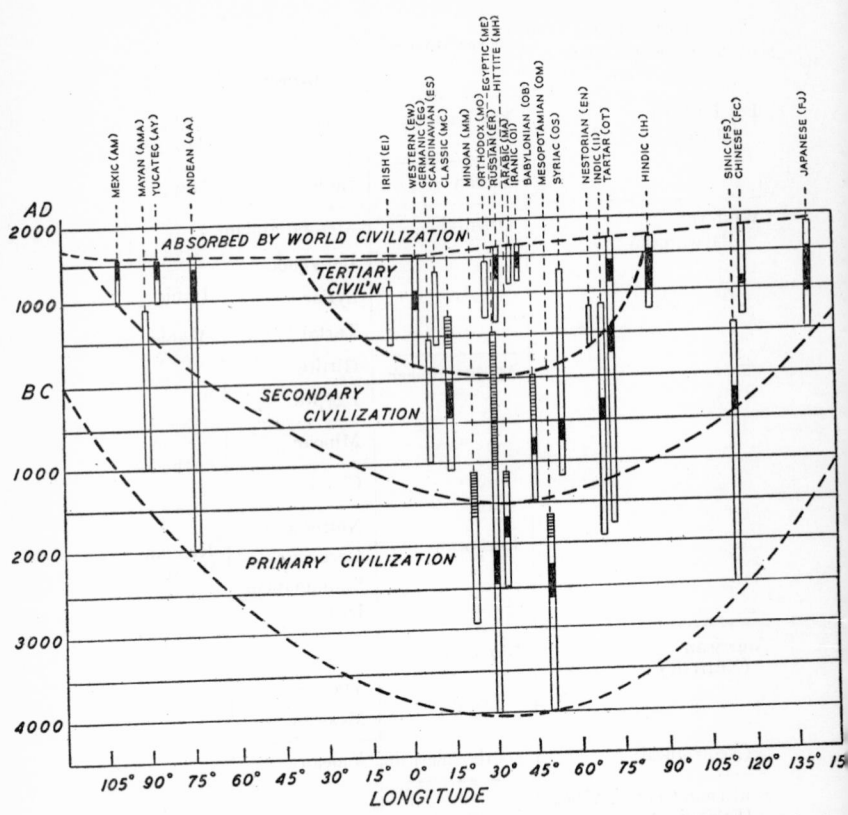

FIG. 12.—Duration, propinquity, and stages of civilizations. (Data from A. J. Toynbee, *A Study of History* [Oxford, 1934].)

ORIGIN, STAGES, AND TERMINATION OF THE HISTORIC CIVILIZATIONS

Civilization	Heroic Age (Youth)	Time of Troubles (Adolescence)	Universal State (Maturity)	Disintegration (Senescence)	Total Duration in Years	Average Duration
Primary Civilizations						
Egyptic (ME)	4000 B.C.	2424–2060 B.C.	{2060–1788 B.C.; 1540–1250 B.C.}	500 A.D.	4,500	
Mesopotamian (OM)	4000 B.C.	2650–2298 B.C.	2298–1905 B.C.	1700 B.C.	2,300	
Minoan (MM)	3000 B.C.	....	2000–1700 B.C.	1425–1125 B.C.	1,875	
Hittite (MH)	2500 B.C.	1900–1750 B.C.	1480–1200 B.C.	1200–1125 B.C.	1,375	
Sinic (FS)	2500 B.C.	479–221 B.C.	221 B.C.–170 A.D.	170–600 A.D.	3,100	
Andean (AA)	2000 B.C.	1000–1430 A.D.	1430–1530 A.D.	1530 A.D.	3,530	
Indic (II)	1900 B.C.	500–323 B.C.	{323–184 B.C.; 375–475 A.D.}	475–775 A.D.	2,675	2,751
Tartar (OT)	1750 B.C.	{300–600 A.D.; 1150–1400 A.D.}	....	1750 A.D.	3,500	
Mayan (AMa)	1000 B.C.	....	300–600 A.D.	600–800 A.D.	1,800	
Secondary Civilizations						
Babylonic (OB)	1500 B.C.	900–750 B.C.	750–538 B.C.	500–0 B.C.	1,500	
Syriac (OS)	1200 B.C.	750–500 B.C.	{500 B.C.–375 A.D.; 675–975 A.D.}	975–1275 A.D.	2,475	
Classic (MC)	1125 B.C.	430–31 B.C.	31 B.C.–250 A.D.	375–675 A.D.	1,800	
Germanic (EG)	1000 B.C.	....	....	400 A.D.	1,400	
Japanese (FJ)	500 A.D.	1050–1598 A.D.	1598–1854 A.D.	1854 A.D.	1,354	1,317
Chinese (FC)	600 A.D.	1100–1380 A.D.	1380–1830 A.D.	1830 A.D.	1,230	
Hindic (IH)	800 A.D.	1000–1525 A.D.	1525–1707 A.D.	1707–1804 A.D.	1,004	
Mexican (AM)	975 A.D.	1375–1520 A.D.	....	1520 A.D.	545	
Yucatec (AY)	975 A.D.	1375–1520 A.D.	....	1520 A.D.	545	
Tertiary Civilizations						
Western (EW)	400 A.D.	850–1020 A.D.	1020–1350 A.D.	1450–1550 A.D.	1,150	
Nestorian (EN)	400 A.D.	....	....	737 A.D.	337	
Irish (EI)	432 A.D.	....	....	1090 A.D.	658	
Scandinavian (ES)	450 A.D.	....	....	1300 A.D.	950	
Arabic (MA)	717 A.D.	1237–1462 A.D.	....	1454 A.D.	737	795
Orthodox (MO)	812 A.D.	....	1470–1605 A.D.	1667 A.D.	855	
Russian (ER)	622 A.D.	1192–1350 A.D.	....	1517 A.D.	895	
Iranic (OI)	1071 A.D.	1350–1519 A.D.	1453–1572 A.D.	1854 A.D.	783	

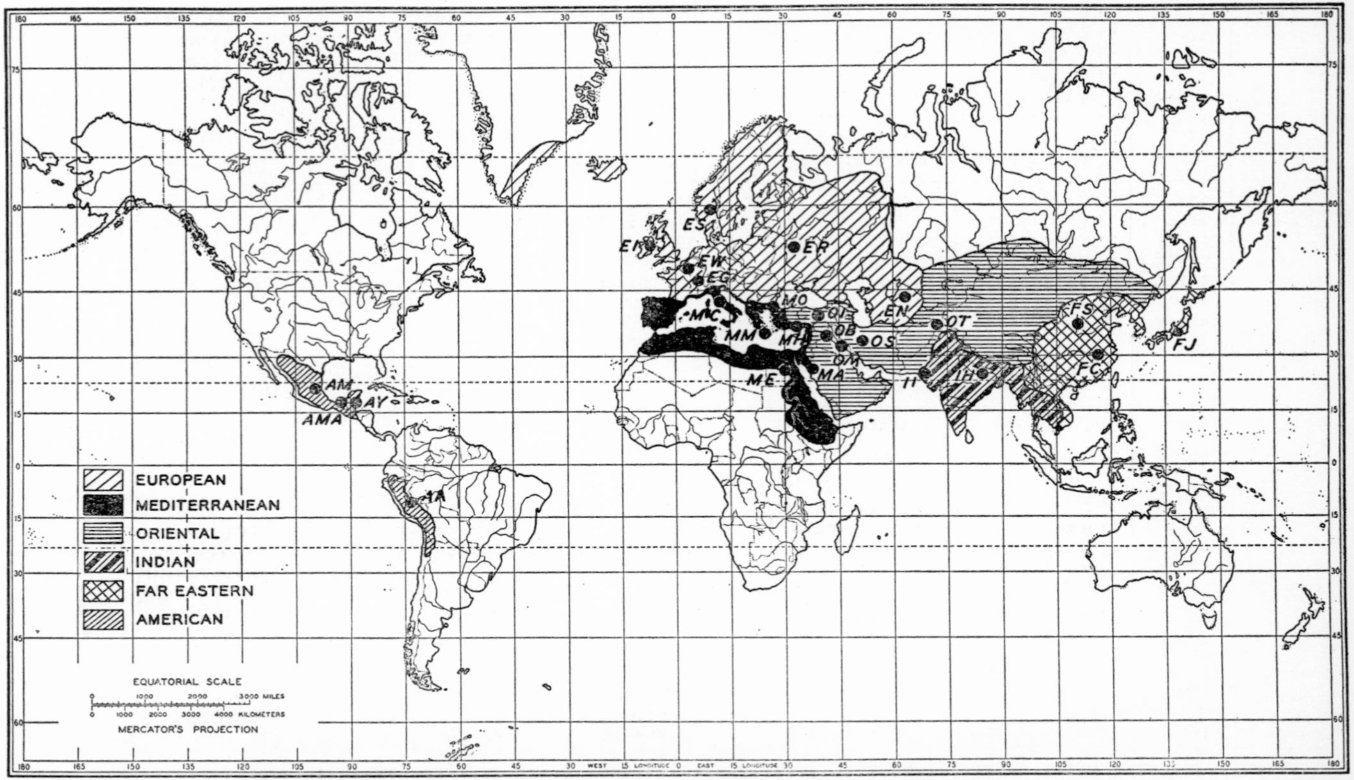

Fig. 12 — Centers and extension of the various civilizations. For interpretation of the letters see Fig. 12 and Table 2.

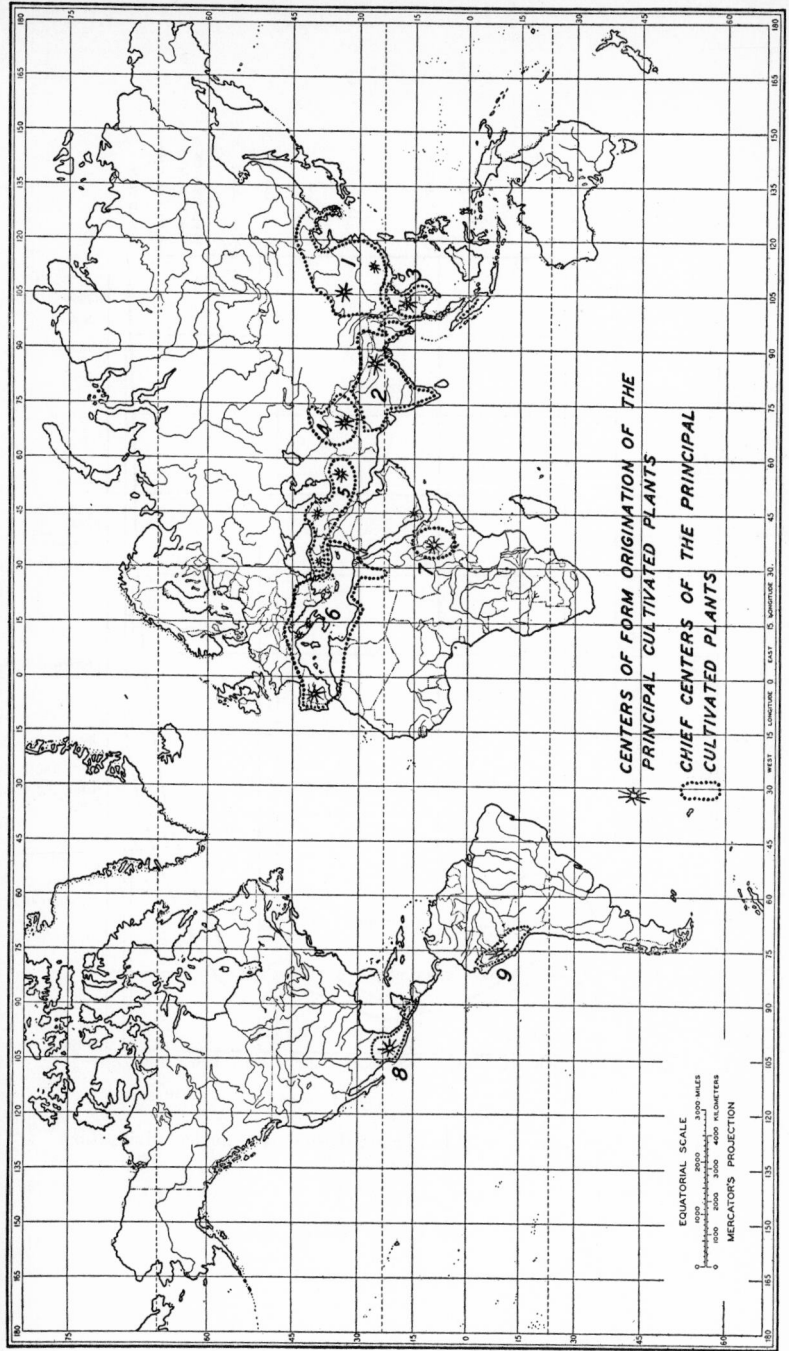

FIG. 14.—Centers and origin of cultivated plants. (From N. I. Vavilov, *Asia*, February, 1937, p. 112)

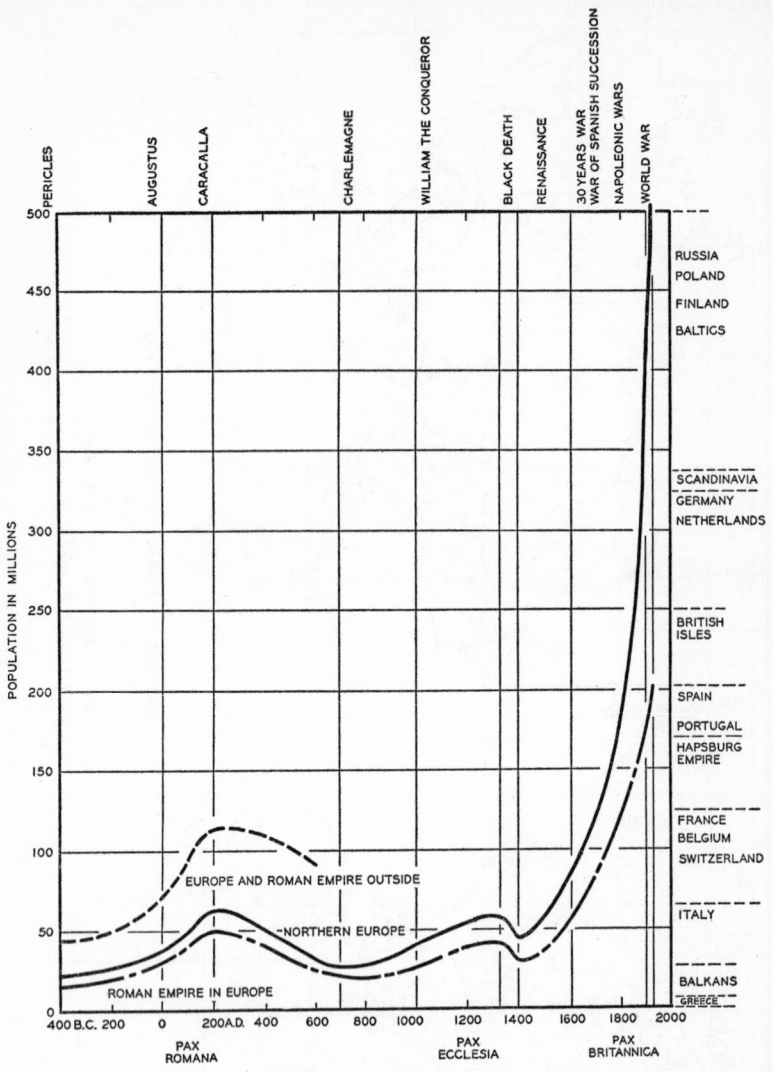

FIG. 15.—Population changes in Classic, Western, and modern civilization

466

TABLE 3

POPULATION CHANGES IN CLASSIC, WESTERN, AND MODERN CIVILIZATIONS

(000,000 omitted)

	400 B.C.*	0*	A.D. 200*	700†	1000†	1328†	1400†	1600‡	1900§	1930§
North Africa.....	5	10	20	.....	.....	.....	.....	.....	.....	.....
Egypt...........	6	7.5	8	.....	.....	.....	.....	.....	.....	.....
Roman Asia.....	10	16	22	.....	.....	.....	.....	.....	.....	.....
Total Roman Empire outside Europe	21	33.5	50	.....	.....	.....	.....	.....	.....	.....
Russia‖.........	1	1	1	1	2	3	2.5	10	113	167
Scandinavia¶....	2	2	3	1	1	2	1.5	2	10	13
Germany**......	3	3	7	3	9	9	7	12	61	74
British Isles......	1	1	2	1	2	4	3	6.5	41	49
Total northern Europe.	7	7	13	6	14	18	14.0	30.5	225	303
Spain††.........	2	6	12	4	5	6	4	10	24	30
Danube Basin‡‡..	1	3	5	3	4	6	4	9	46	50
France§§........	3	6.5	14	6	8	14	10	17	53	54
Italy...........	4	6	7	4	6	11	8	13	33	42
Southeast Europe‖‖........	1	3.5	6	1	0.5	1	1	3.5	17	20
Greece.........	4	5	6	3	3	3	3	4	4	6
Total Roman Empire in Europe....	15	30	50	21	26.5	41	30	56.5	177	202
Total Europe.	22	37	63	27	40.5	59	44	87	402	505
Total Roman Empire.....	36	63.5	100	.....	.....	.....	.....	.....	.....	.....

* From estimates by Jules Beloch, "Die Bevölkerung im Altertum," *Zeitschrift für Socialwissenschaft*, II (1899), 505 ff.

† Beloch, "Die Bevölkerung Europas im Mittelalter," *ibid.*, III (1900), 405 ff.

‡ Beloch, "Die Bevölkerung Europas zur Zeit der Renaissance," *ibid.*, III (1900), 765 ff.

§ R. R. Kuczynski, "Population," *Encyclopaedia of the Social Sciences*, XII, 244. See also Appen. XVII, Table 18.

‖ Russia in Europe before World War I.

¶ Sweden, Norway, and Denmark.

** Including Netherlands.

†† Including Portugal.

‡‡ Hapsburg Empire before World War I.

§§ Including Belgium and Switzerland.

‖‖ Balkans before World War I.

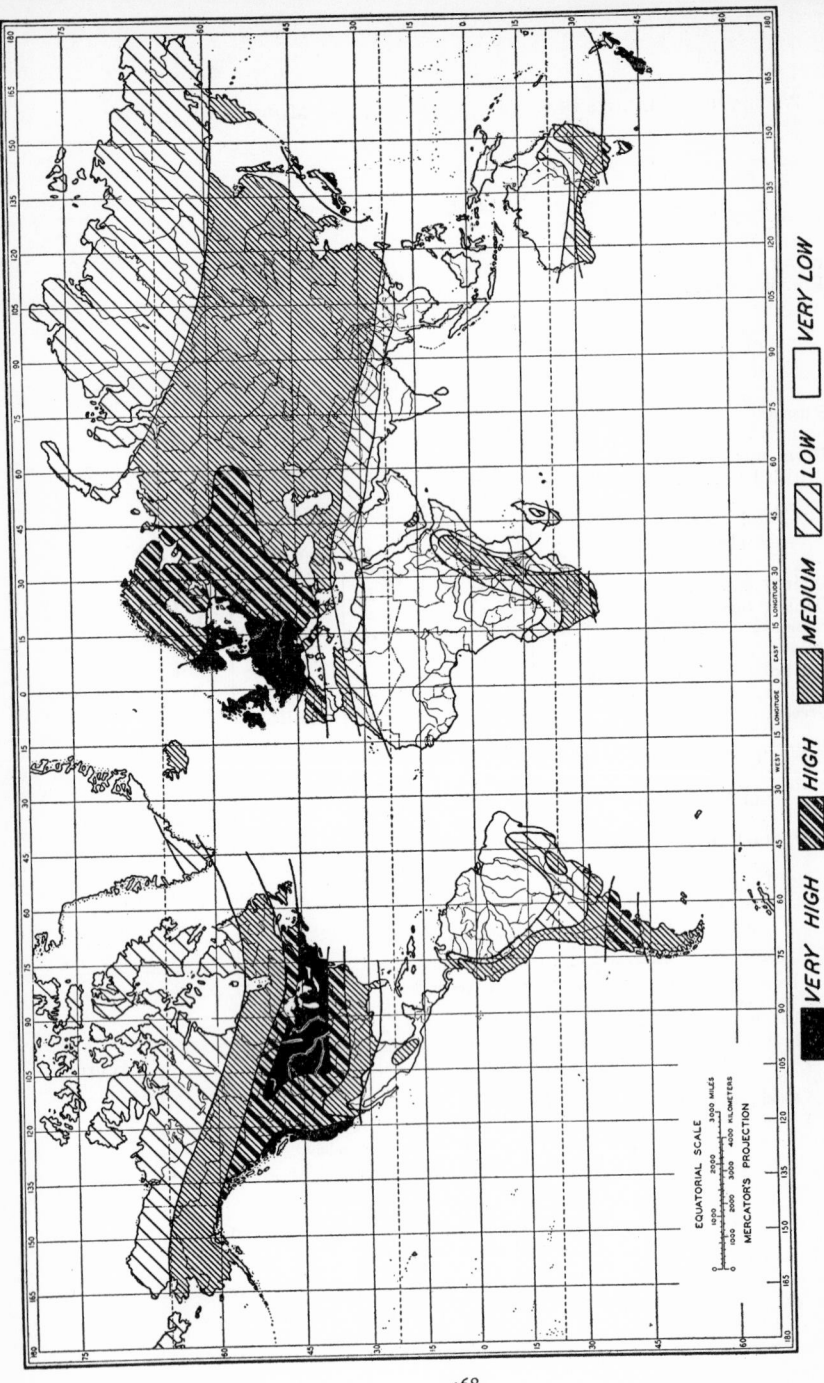

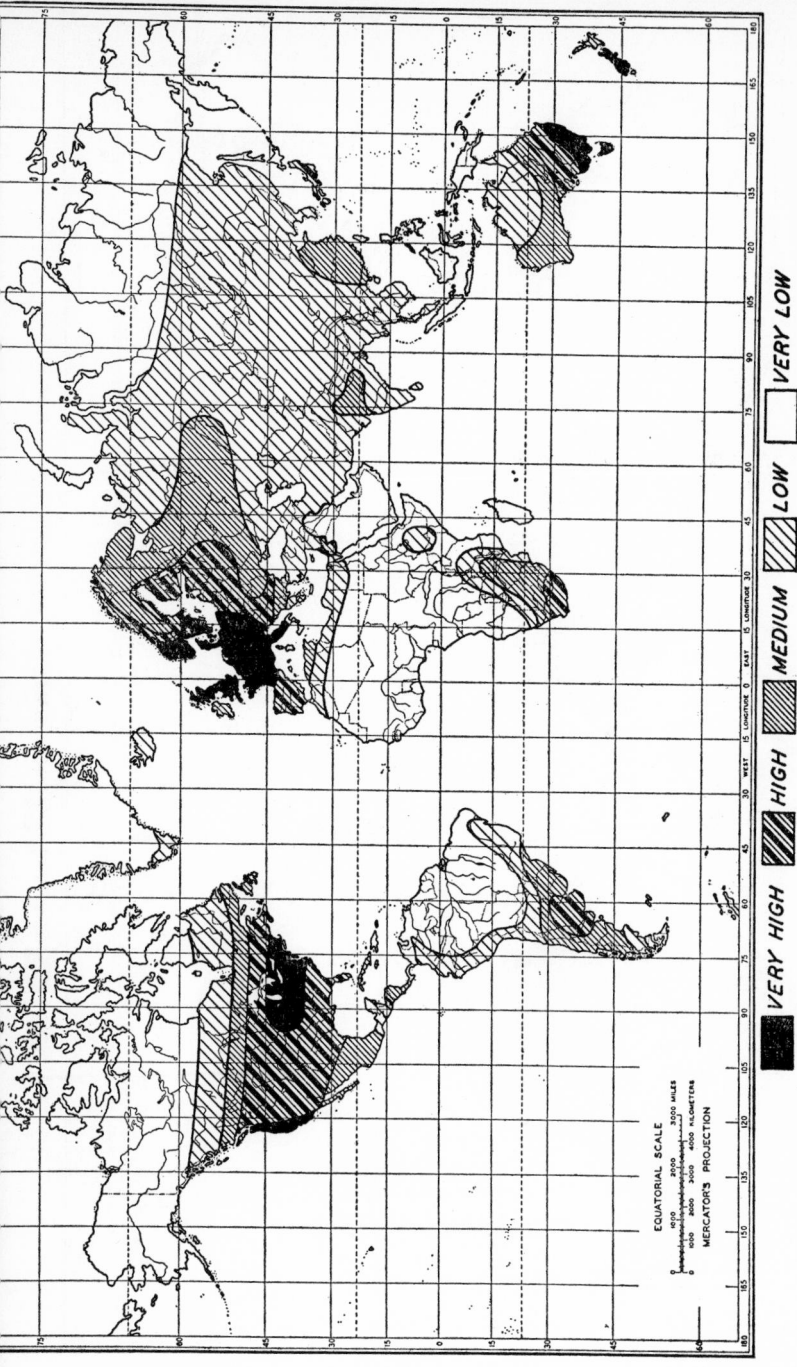

VERY HIGH   HIGH   MEDIUM   LOW   VERY LOW

FIG. 17.—Heights of civilization in the contemporary world. (From Huntington and Cushing, *op. cit.*, p. 294)

EQUATORIAL SCALE

MERCATOR'S PROJECTION

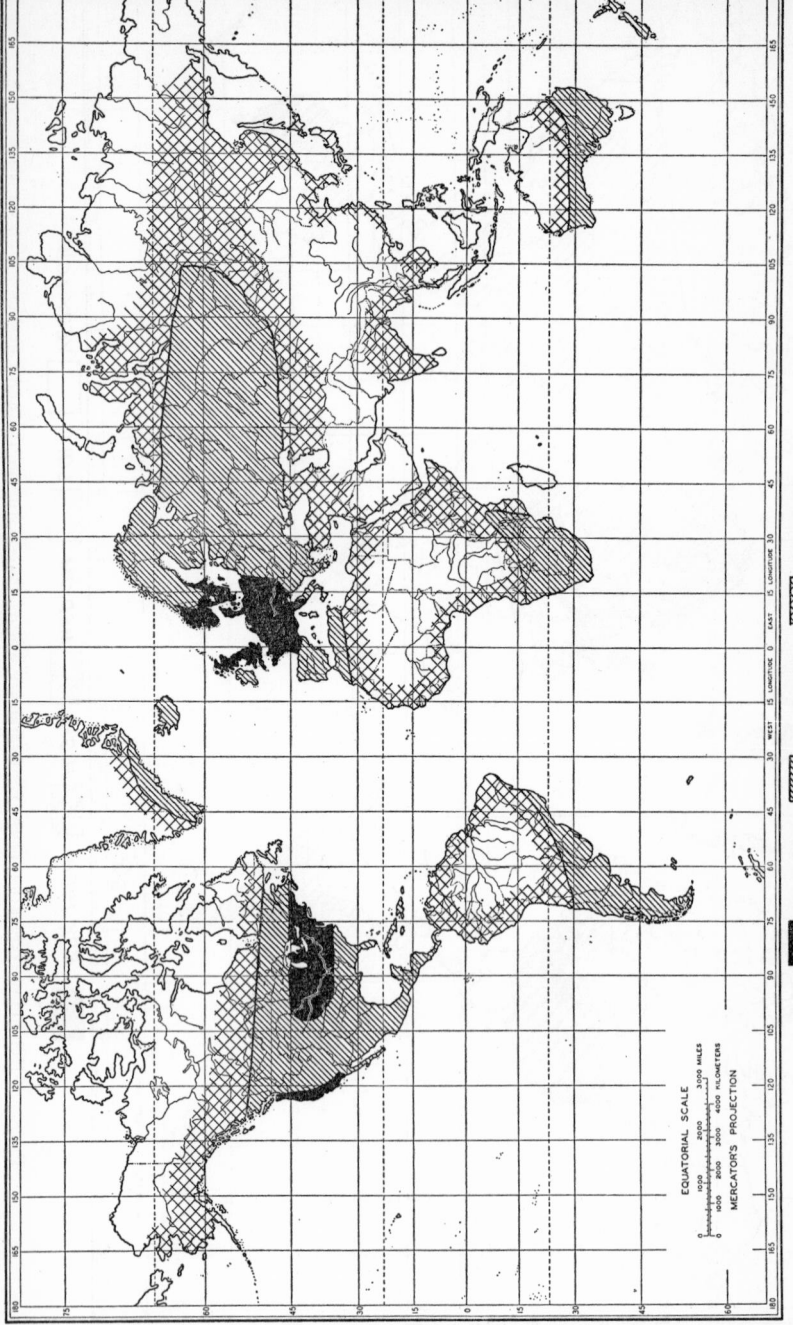

EQUATORIAL SCALE

MERCATOR'S PROJECTION

CENTRAL   MARGINAL   INTRUSIVE

APPENDIX VI

THEORY OF THE UNIQUE ORIGIN OF WAR

The theory that warfare is an invention which diffused from one or a small number of centers in which the invention was made has been supported by W. H. R. Rivers,[1] G. Elliot Smith,[2] and W. C. MacLeod.[3] Bronislaw Malinowski and other functionalists consider that war defined "as the use of organized force between two politically independent units in the pursuit of tribal policy . . . . entered fairly late into the development of human societies."[4] The most elaborate and extreme exposition of the diffusionist theory has been that by W. J. Perry, who contends that war was invented in predynastic Egypt and has gradually diffused throughout the world from that country.[5]

Agriculture, according to Perry, was for the first time invented by the predynastic Egyptians. The process of irrigation required a calendar and central management, and the inventors of the calendar became a ruling class, thus establishing for the first time a class state. The sun's importance for agriculture associated it with the kings who came to be considered "Children of the Sun." When the king became old and feeble, he was unable to rule properly and he must be killed so that agriculture could flourish under the control of a more energetic successor. Presently the king found a substitute to save himself, and the practice of human sacrifice began—a practice subsequently associated with agriculture everywhere. To obtain victims for sacrifice and slaves to engage in cultivation and to maintain the ruling class in power, more violence was necessary. Thus after man had existed as a peaceful food-gatherer in a Garden of Eden for over half a million years, agriculture, civilization, and war were invented in the valley of the Nile.

The "Children of the Sun," the nobles of this civilization, according to this theory, traveled far and wide in a search for gold, pearls, tin, cedar, resins, and other substances necessary for their crafts, as well as "life-giving substances,"

[1] *History and Ethnology* (London, 1922).

[2] *The Evolution of Man* (Oxford, 1924); *Culture, the Diffusion Controversy* (New York, 1927); *Human History* (New York, 1930).

[3] *The Origin and History of Politics* (New York, 1931), pp. 47 ff., 70 ff.

[4] B. Malinowski, "Culture as a Determinant of Behavior," in *Factors Determining Human Behavior* ("Harvard Tercentenary Publications" [Cambridge, Mass., 1937]), p. 141; see also Margaret Mead, "Warfare Is Only an Invention—Not a Biological Necessity," *Asia*, August, 1940, pp. 402–5; above, chap. vi, n. 18.

[5] *Memoirs of Manchester Literary and Philosophical Society*, Vol. LXI, No. 6 (1917); *Hibbert Journal*, October, 1917; *The Children of the Sun* (London, 1923); *The Growth of Civilization* (New York, 1923); above, chap. iv, n. 16.

cowrie shells, dyes, etc., necessary for their cult of an afterlife. These travels took place especially during the pyramid-building age of Egypt in the third millennium B.C. and extended to Syria, Mesopotamia, India, and China; to Greece, Italy, France, and England; and later to Indonesia, the islands of the Pacific, and eventually to Peru and Mexico. Some of these places were reached by travelers direct from Egypt in seagoing ships, others were reached only by travelers from these colonies, but everywhere the "Children of the Sun" left a trail of mines, dolmens, polished stone instruments, and the traditions of their cult. Thus was the "archaic civilization" of agriculture, class society, sun worship, and human sacrifice established over a great area,[6] with three well-marked centers in the Mediterranean Basin, China, and Middle America.

From these centers, the theory continues, the archaic culture spread to the surrounding food-gatherers and soon degenerated—in fact, the degeneration of civilization, according to this school of thought, has been more characteristic and more normal than its upbuilding. At certain points on the borders of the "archaic civilization" the barbarians maintained enough contact with the centers of that civilization to learn its art of war which steadily developed as a necessity to keep the lower classes down. The barbarians with appetite whetted by the riches to be plundered in the centers of civilization took to a nomadic existence and invaded these centers, sometimes conquering them and always requiring them to militarize even more. The warrior barbarians—the Kassites, Hyksos, Semites, Dorians, Achaeans, Etruscans, Celts, Teutons, Bantus, Taishans, Mongols, Turks, Tartars, Aztecs, Polynesians, and Vikings—developed war on a large scale in their attacks upon the agricultural civilizations from the deserts, the steppes, and the sea. As war was originated by the extension of the food-producing "Children of the Sun" among the primitive food-gatherers, so, according to this theory, it was developed by the attack upon the centers of agricultural civilization by the nomadic and piratical warriors whose leaders themselves claimed to be of the noble class.

The original ruling class has, according to this theory, been proliferated and still constitutes the divine-right rulers of many military states. War has been, and is, their instrument for maintaining rule at the expense of their subjects, and expanding it at the expense of their neighbors.

It is impossible to examine in detail the voluminous evidence adduced to support this theory. The assumption that the food-gatherers were peaceful is supported by observation of certain food-gathering people who remain, such as the Eskimos, the Veddahs of Ceylon, and certain California Indians, who are said to indulge in neither individual nor group hostilities; by a study of the cave drawings and stone implements of Paleolithic food-gatherers of Europe which are said to give no indication of war; and by the common tradition of a golden age of peace. Thus does Perry support the Rousseauan concept of primitive man in an idyllic state of nature, against the Hobbesian concept of the state of nature as a state of war of all against all.

[6] See Fig. 19.

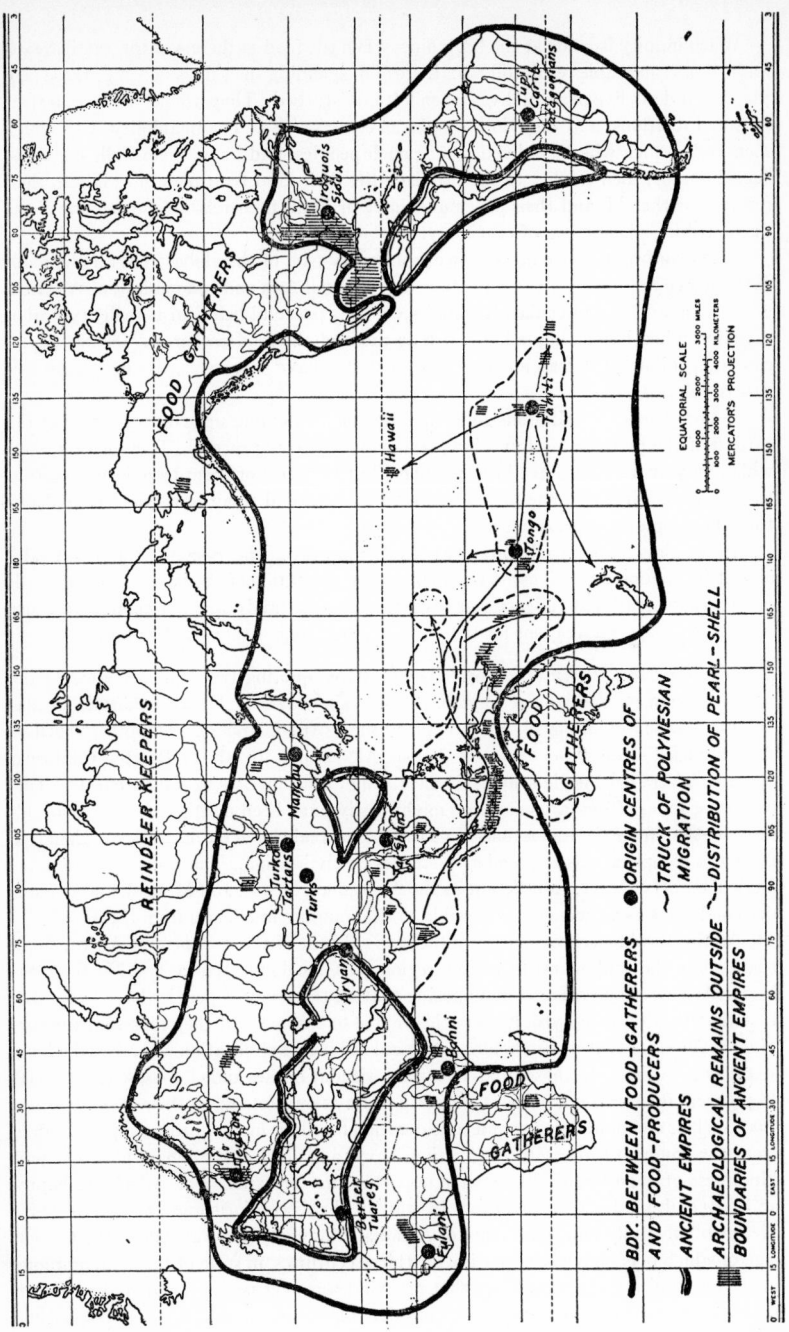

FIG. 19.—Spread of "archaic culture." (From W. J. Perry, *The Growth of Civilization* [New York, 1923], p. 76)

When inquiry is made at the beginning, when the food-gatherers of the earth are ex-amined, a remarkable result follows. Instead of spending their days fighting, these peo-ple, one and all, live peaceful lives when left undisturbed. They use no violence in their personal relations, and they do not fight as communities. The unanimity with which men and women who have lived among such peoples, and know them well, testify to their honesty, their fidelity to the marriage tie, their kind treatment of children, their respect for the old, and their peaceful behaviour in all their relationships, is one of the most striking phenomena of ethnology.

When confronted with facts drawn from every part of the globe, from all the food-gathering communities already mentioned (9 tribes of Asia and Indonesia, 5 of America, 2 of Africa, and 2 of Oceania), it would seem that peaceful behavior is really typical of mankind when living simple lives such as those of the food-gatherers. If that be ac-cepted, it follows that man must somehow or other have become warlike as human cul-ture developed. . . . .

Not only does the Old Stone Age fail to reveal any definite signs of weapons, but the earliest of the predynastic Egyptians also evidently were peaceful. They made maces, which may or may not have been weapons, but very few of them have been found in their graves. Similarly, the first settlements at Susa and Anau have yielded evidence that the people were peaceful.

Are we thus to look back into a Golden Age of peace, when violence was practically absent from human relations? I see no other interpretation of the facts. It may be ad-mitted that occasional violence was present, but it certainly was not enough to cause men to make special weapons for the purpose of fighting as they did later on.[7]

[7] *The Growth of Civilization*, pp. 194–96. After quoting travelers' accounts of the African Pygmies, Veddahs of Ceylon, Semang and Sakai of Malay Peninsula, Anda-manese, Kubus of Sumatra, Punans of Borneo, Aru Islanders, Philippine Negritos, Australians, Eskimos, Dene Indians, Salish, Algonquins, Beothuks, Paiutes, California Indians, Tierra del Fuegans, and Siberians, Elliot Smith writes to similar effect: "This extensive series of quotations, which might easily have been multiplied a hundredfold, represent an impartial and unbiased picture of the real character of mankind when free from the complications and embarrassments of civilization. The Food Gatherers in-clude members of races as different as the Australian, Negro, and Mongol, and live un-der conditions as varied as it is possible to be—ranging in climate from the Tropics to the Arctic, and in environment from the tropical heat of the continent of Africa, small islands like the Andamans, to the icy regions of Greenland, Alaska, and Northern Si-beria. As there is no reason for supposing that all these varied peoples have lost a cul-ture that they once enjoyed, it seems justifiable to assume that they represent the sur-vival of the state that was common to all mankind before civilization was created, about sixty centuries ago. In those times men were without houses and clothes, without social or political organization, without property or any restraints upon their freedom other than such as common decency and consideration for other human beings imposed. Free from the common causes of exasperation, envy, and malice, the innate goodness and kindliness of Man found unhampered opportunities for expression. Men were happy and peaceful, kind and considerate. In spite of the discomforts and anxieties of daily life, men cheerfully enjoyed a state of Arcadian simplicity. It was indeed the Golden Age of which poets have been writing for thirty centuries, in spite of the contemptuous denials of cynics and philosophers that mankind was ever peaceful and contented. In the next section of this book we shall consider the circumstances that were responsible

The opponents of this theory have marshaled a no less formidable body of evidence.[8] The chronology of this expansion of Egyptian culture is rather confused. Although the culture said to have been diffused throughout the "archaic civilization" is assumed to be that of the Egyptian pyramid-building age (2600 B.C.), the diffusionists place the inauguration of Mexican civilization at the time of Christ; thus for twenty-six hundred years this culture, although greatly changed in Egypt, was preserved somewhere en route to be deposited in Mexico. The diffusionists have to accept this late date for the transmission of culture across the Polynesian Islands because there is no evidence of any human habitation of these islands earlier, but even the time of Christ is not late enough. Students of the Polynesian Islands are unwilling to admit any human habitation until at least the fourth or fifth century A.D. This would clearly be too late for the origin of Mexican culture. Most Americanists, in fact, believe that Mexicans and Peruvians must have been developing agriculture, pottery, and astronomy in situs for over two thousand years before their historical record begins in the fifth or sixth century A.D. Evidences of some of these cultures are, in fact, found in burials beneath the pedregal, a volcanic deposit near Mexico City dated by some geologists earlier than 1000 B.C. Alleged cultural similarities relied upon by the diffusionists, sculptured elephants in Mexico (said by Spinden to be Macaws), human sacrifices, serpent symbols, types of textile weaving, artistic designs, burials and stone construction, often appear fanciful on close inspection.

While certain contemporary food-gatherers do not understand formal war, others do, and few of them enjoy genuine peace free of occasional fighting.[9]

---

for the introduction of the serpent of discord into the Garden of Eden" (*Human History*, p. 252). Charles Letourneau finds that among the most primitive men "warlike conflicts have generally been retaliatory; they have assumed a juridical character and have been rare and not bloody. From this point of view, there was a golden age of the human race" (*La Guerre dans les diverses races humaines* [Paris, 1895], p. 104). H. C. Engelbrecht (*Revolt against War* [New York, 1937], p. 42) cites evidence to similar effect from Sir Henry Maine (*Early History of Institutions*); William C. MacLeod (*The American Indian Frontier*); Mabel Powers (*The Indian as Peace Maker*); B. Malinowski (*op. cit.*); and especially studies of the Zuni Indians (Ruth Benedict, *Patterns of Culture*) and of the Arapesh of New Guinea (Margaret Mead, *Sex Differences*).

[8] Most of it is summarized by H. J. Spinden in *Culture, the Diffusionist Controversy* (New York, 1927).

[9] See M. Ginsburg, "A Symposium on the Psychology of Peace and War," *British Journal of Medical Psychology*, Vol. XIV; E. F. M. Durbin and John Bowlby, *Personal Aggressiveness and War* (New York, 1939), pp. 106 ff.; L. T. Hobhouse, G. C. Wheeler, and M. Ginsburg, *The Material Culture and Social Institutions of the Simpler Peoples* (London, 1915), pp. 228 ff. Elliot Smith admits fighting among several of the food-gatherers he describes but "we must not overlook the consideration that the violence was provoked by other people intruding into their domains and was inspired by the idea of safeguarding their means of livelihood which, rightly or wrongly, they believed was being threatened" (*Human History*, pp. 201, 259). These circumstances would account for a good share of the violence among more advanced peoples.

Some anthropologists hold that man first differentiated in the temperate grass-lands and resembled the warlike pastoral nomads rather than the peaceful food-gatherers of tropical forest or arctic sea.[10] Certain Paleolithic implements might have been used for fighting other men as well as animals, and some cave draw-ings of the Magdalenian and Capsian periods may represent hostilities between men.[11] Certain anthropologists, impressed by the rarity of primitive tribes which do not fight, support the Hobbesian conception of the natural man.[12]

There was no Arcadian peace and simplicity in the elder ages. Men always quar-reled, if they did not fight it was because they were too broken, cowed-down, or coward-ly. It was only as time went on that peace was found to be a more expedient policy. Peace was a benefit to be striven for; it did not come as a natural boon. The more back-ward the savage is, the less he knows about methods other than the nearest ones for the attainment of self-preservation; and there is no recourse closer than force, and no suspi-cion of others more vivid than the misgivings that they are preparing to use force. Fa-miliarity with violence is common to all animal life. Under civilization the individual gets away from it, but it cannot be said that societies have yet done so. Hostility and war are what we are moving away from, and also what we fall back upon whenever the supporting structure of civilization breaks down. It is the primordial thing, like poverty. Generalization as to the warlike or unwarlike disposition of the savage must take ac-count of many varying types; but it is fair to infer that mutual suspicion and fear were the rule among the scattered groups of early man, competing as they were for precarious sustenance.

[10] See chap. vi, n. 33.

[11] "But hunting is not the whole story of these [Capsian] pictures. Now and then you get quite unmistakable sketches of fighting—the very first battle-pictures that were ever drawn in the world; and I suppose that we can only believe that these were drawn to secure victory in battle, as the hunting ones to secure success in the hunt. There is one picture of a combat of archers, where they are in such deadly earnest that you won-der if anyone will be left alive when the fight is over, and another one in which a plumed bowman, his bow slung across him, is slinking off the field, crouching low, covering the ground with great strides, and taking three arrows with him, one in his thigh, one in his knee, and another right through the calf of the other leg. No doubt there was war in the world many centuries before this; but this is the first absolute representation of it that exists in the world so far as is known" (James Baikie, *Peeps at Men of the Old Stone Age* [London, 1928]). See reproduction of a Magdalenian drawing which may represent war, although it may represent a hunt, in Paul Schmitthenner, *Krieg und Kriegfuhrung im Wandel der Weltgeschichte* (Leipzig, 1930), p. 10. See also Jean La Gorgette, *Le Rôle de la guerre* (Paris, 1906), p. 35, and H. W. Van Loon, *The Arts* (New York, 1937), p. 24. These drawings may, however, have been subsequent to the origin of civilization in Egypt.

[12] W. G. Sumner and A. G. Keller, *The Science of Society* (New Haven, 1927), I, 18–19 and 368 ff.; M. R. Davie, *The Evolution of War* (New Haven, 1929); William McDougal, *An Introduction to Social Psychology* (9th ed.; London, 1915); F. Müller-Lyer, *The History of Social Development* (New York, 1921); La Gorgette, *op. cit.*, pp. 32–35.

The extreme diffusionists, or, as they call themselves, the "historical school," insist that anthropologists should abandon the idea of spontaneous generation of culture traits, as biologists abandoned the spontaneous generation of life, and consequently should, in the absence of clear evidence to the contrary, assume that each social institution, practice, or technique diffused from a single source.[13]

The biologist, it is true, assumes that life always comes from life, but he does not assume that the resemblances in either the form or the behavior of living things always show a common ancestry of these traits. The wing of the bird and of the bat, the fin of the whale and of the fish, the eye of the octopus and of the vertebrate, the trapping behavior of the ant lion and of the worm lion, the colonial habits of the ant and of the termite, are believed by zoölogists to have been independent developments. Such resemblances indicate convergent evolution, that is, the tendency for structures or traits of different origin to become similar in adaptation to similar situations of the organisms.[14]

Certain resemblances of animals are used by taxonomists as evidence of close genetic relationship, but resemblances of a nonfunctional nature are particularly important in this regard, as, for instance, resemblance in the details of teeth, vertebra, and toes. Such resemblances give evidence of divergent evolution, that is, the tendency for structures or traits with a common origin to develop different functions in adaptation to different situations of the organisms.[15]

Instances of both convergent and divergent evolution of culture traits can be historically authenticated. Leibnitz and Newton independently invented the calculus. Darwin and Wallace independently stated the theory of organic evolution. Numerous patents have been granted which on litigation proved to be duplicates of inventions previously made.[16] There are equally well-authenticated instances of borrowing. The Irish potato was not developed in Ireland but borrowed from Spain, to which it had been brought from Peru. The Indo-Germanic languages probably originated at a common center after which they diverged. The present dominant cultures of the United States, of Australia, and of South Africa undoubtedly came from Europe.[17]

It would appear that both convergent and divergent evolution occur in respect to culture traits, and without clear historical evidence it cannot be assumed that similar culture traits found in different regions had a common origin. The evidence in each case must be weighed in the light of the possibilities of independent invention as well as of diffusion. If the resemblance lies only in a func-

---

[13] W. J. Perry, *The Growth of Civilization*, p. 1.

[14] Above, Appen. V, n. 10.

[15] Above, Appen. V, n. 11.

[16] Holding that invention is response to a new need of a society, S. C. Gilfillen regards duplicate invention as a normal expectation (*The Sociology of Invention* [Chicago, 1935], pp. 10, 76).

[17] See Appen. V, n. 12.

tional adaptation (as the wing of the bird and of the bat) rather than in a non-functional similarity (as the cloven hoof of the hippopotamus and the giraffe), caution should be observed in assuming a common ancestry. If two groups have not only one but a great number of traits in common, whether these traits are physiological or cultural, the probability that these traits had a common ancestry is greater.[18]

[18] W. B. Scott, *A History of Land Mammals of the Western Hemisphere* (New York, 1913); Spinden, in *Culture, the Diffusionist Controversy*. See Appen. V, n. 13.

APPENDIX VII

ANIMAL WARFARE

Among human beings the term "warfare" is usually applied only to violent conflicts in which both sides are organized human groups. Employing the same conception, animal warfare should be confined to violent conflicts between organisms of the same species, thus excluding the most lethal form of violence—that in which food is the object—except in the relatively rare cases of cannibalism.[1] It seems best to adopt a wider definition and to admit as warfare violent conflicts in which the opponents belong to species which are not far distant from one another. It also seems well to include in the conception of animal warfare conflicts between individual animals as well as conflicts between groups. Some writers on human warfare have included in the subject individual duels and private war as well as public war.[2]

Attention will be given successively to the (1) drives, (2) functions, (3) techniques, and (4) theories of animal warfare.

1. DRIVES OF ANIMAL WARFARE

Violent behavior by one animal against another can usually be interpreted as a consequence of the psychic organization of at least one of the fighting animals, urging it (a) to obtain food, (b) to satisfy sex, (c) to secure a home territory, (d) to be active, (e) to preserve its own body and life, (f) to preserve the society of which it is a member, (g) to dominate over others, (h) to free itself from control.[3] Sometimes one, sometimes several, of these urges will be involved in a particular fight.

---

[1] Many writers have insisted that because of this there is no analogy between animal and human "war" (see Mitchell Chalmers, *Evolution and War* [London, 1915]; A. M. Carr-Saunders, *The Population Problem* [London, 1922], p. 304, and "Biology and War," *Foreign Affairs*, VII [1929], 431). J. Sageret finds no real animal war except among the dogs of oriental cities and among insects (*Philosophie de la guerre et de la paix* [Paris, 1919], chap. iii).

[2] See, e.g., J. Legnano, *Tractatus de bello, de reprisalis, et de duello* (1360) (Carnegie ed., Washington, 1917).

[3] C. Letourneau, considering drives from the standpoint of animal warfare, emphasizes food, sex, territory, and society (*La Guerre dans les diverses races humaines* [Paris, 1895], pp. 7, 11 ff.). W. T. Hornaday considers food and sex the commonest cause of quarrels among animals "in a state of nature" (*The Minds and Manners of Wild Animals* [New York, 1922], p. 272). From a study of monkeys A. H. Maslow emphasizes dominance, activity, sociability, and sex ("Dominance-Feeling, Behavior and Status," *Psychological Review*, XLIV [July, 1937], 420 ff.; "The Dominance Drive as a Determiner of Some Behavior in Infrahuman Primates," *Psychological Bulletin*, XXII [1935],

These behavior patterns have been called "drives" to avoid commitment on the relation of heredity and environment in their origin[4] or on the relation of impulse and deliberation in the psychic process.[5] They may be defined as relatively stable modes of action which all the adult individuals of the species manifest in some degree in response to concrete situations. Though characteristic of the species, or even of a large class, a particular drive may vary in intensity among different individuals. Thus each animal has an individuality or personality because of the great variety of possible combinations of degrees of intensity of each of the drives characteristic of the species. Among most animals the characteristics of each drive may be modified by individual experience or training, at least if such environmental pressures are begun when the animal is young

---

714 ff.; "The Role of Dominance in the Social and Sexual Behavior of Infrahuman Primates," *Journal of Genetic Psychology*, XLVIII [1936], 261 ff.). See also Alfred J. Lotka, *Elements of Physical Biology* (Baltimore, 1925), p. 396, and below, Appen. VIII, for an analysis of psychological drives.

[4] Some sociologists disparage the search for innate behavior patterns in the individual and insist that innate ideas, sensations, wishes, and drives "must be defined in terms of the social process, not the process in terms of them" (Ellsworth Faris, "Of Psychological Elements," *American Journal of Sociology*, XLII [September, 1936], 176). But this leaves unexplained the differences between individuals reared in the same milieu and between the different social potentialities of, say, a man, a chimpanzee, and an earthworm. As the relative influence of heredity and environment in any particular behavior pattern of an individual can be determined by mathematical methods (Sewall Wright, "Statistical Methods in Biology," *American Statistical Journal*, March supplement, 1932), so the relative influence of the individual's behavior patterns and the society's pressures can, at least theoretically, be distinguished for any segment of history. This does not deny that the human "dispositions" of social significance are complex, socially conditioned combinations of original capacities (see Graham Wallas, *The Great Society* [New York, 1917], chap. ii, and L. L. Bernard, "Instinct," *Encyclopaedia of the Social Sciences*, VIII, 82).

[5] Psychologists have distinguished "reflexes," "instincts," and "inborn capacities" among the unlearned behavior patterns of human beings. Each successive word implies a lesser degree of precision in the stimulating situation and the behavior response and of inevitability in their connection (E. L. Thorndike, *The Original Nature of Man* [New York, 1913], pp. 12 ff.). If the beginning, progress, and end of the sensory motor circuit is not entirely definite, there may be an intervention of psychic processes involving choice, deliberation, reflection, or reason. The same distinction applies to learned patterns for which the words "impulse," "habit," and "skill" may serve. The words "drive" and "disposition" refer to general classes of behavior pattern with the exception of the purely "biological" reflexes and tropisms, on the one hand, and the rationally controlled skills and intentions on the other. The word "drive" implies less variability in stimulus and response than does the word "disposition" and is therefore more suitable in dealing with animals, though it by no means excludes some influence of the experience and choice of the particular animal in the particular situation (see below, Appen. VIII).

enough; consequently, the expression of a drive in the adult may be due to experience as well as to heredity.[6]

The influence of experience becomes increasingly important as the animal scale is ascended toward man. Situations involving rivalry for possession of some material object, involving jealousy or possessiveness toward an individual, usually of the opposite sex, involving intrusion of a stranger in the group, or involving interference with or frustration of an activity in progress, have been reported by observers to be at the root of most fighting among monkeys, apes, and children. These situations usually stimulate several drives of the participating individuals. Complicated by such psychic mechanisms as displacement, projection, animism, rationalization, and symbolism, these same situations have been found by some anthropologists and psychologists to be at the root of much of adult fighting and war among both primitive and civilized peoples. Throughout most of the animal kingdom, however, fighting can be explained more simply. A fight can usually be explained as the response expected from the stimulation of one or a few of these drives with little reference to the history of the particular individual or to its interpretation of the total situation.[7]

a) *Fights for food.*—Violent behavior for food *within the same species* is rare, though instances of cannibalism or eating of the same species can be cited in most of the orders of animal life. Alverdes, in fact, says it is "a frequent occurrence" and cites cases of insects, crayfish, reptiles, birds of prey, shrew mice, and predatory mammals. The aged and weak are sometimes killed and devoured by various species, especially preceding a migration or other activity in which their presence might be detrimental to the group. The most common type of cannibalism, however, is the eating of the male by the female after the sexual function is performed, a procedure which Fabre dramatically describes in the case of the mantis. It also occurs among certain spiders, the golden gardener beetle, and the scorpion of Languedoc. "It is probable," he says, "that this deadly aversion of the female for the male at the end of the mating season is fairly common, especially among carnivorous insects." Cannibalism, thus limited, would obviously have no adverse effect upon the race. The killing of surplus queens and of drones who have performed their function and the occasional eating of eggs, larvae, and pupae by the workers, all of which occur among the social insects, may have a value as a means of keeping the population within bounds and may have a resem-

[6] J. Boulenger points out that animals can be trained to fight under a variety of stimuli (*Animal Mysteries* [New York, 1927], pp. 110 ff.). W. C. Allee (*Animal Aggregations* [Chicago, 1931]) has shown that the disposition of ants of different species or even of the same species and different colonies to fight on meeting can be eliminated if the young are introduced into an alien colony and brought into physical contact with all members of the colony for a series of days. A harmonious social unit composed of ants of different species or even genera can thus be artificially built up. Such composite colonies also occur in nature (see below, nn. 13, 14, and Appen. VIII).

[7] E. F. M. Durbin and John Bowlby, *Personal Aggressiveness and War* (New York, 1939); above, chap. v, sec. 1.

blance to the practices among certain primitive peoples of killing the aged and of infanticide.[8]

The territorial war presently to be considered is indirectly motivated by considerations of the food supply, although other factors play a part. Among gregarious animals gathered about a source of food, minor quarrels frequently arise among members of the same species, but these are seldom serious.[9] The social insects, however, sometimes make war on a large scale for food, not only on very different animals as do the driver ants, or on closely related species as do certain robber ants and bees which prey on the stores and larvae of other insects,[10] but even on other societies of the same species.[11]

b) *Fights arising from sex.*—Violence with an immediate sexual object can occur only within the same species. It is common between males of gregarious herbivores, kangaroos, monkeys, and to a limited extent carnivores. The importance of the sex motive in the intraspecific fighting of many species is indicated by the fact that horns, tusks, mane, and other offensive and defensive weapons are often a secondary sexual characteristic. They are possessed only by the males and may be attributed to the influence of "sexual selection." Those males who are better equipped with these weapons overcome their rivals, father the next generation, and pass the advantage on to their sons. Although sometimes used for defense against enemies of other species, these weapons are frequently

[8] F. Alverdes, *Social Life in the Aminal World* (New York, 1927), pp. 138 ff., 146; J. H. Fabre, *Social Life in the Insect World* (New York, n.d.), pp. 80–84, 114–19; W. M. Wheeler, *Foibles of Insects and Men* (New York, 1929), pp. 213 ff.; Allee, *op. cit.*, pp. 138–39. Professor Allee informs me that among certain species the disposition to fight increases with hunger, but this is not true of all species. The *Chicago Tribune* for March 16, 1936, printed an Associated Press photograph of two male elephant beetles caught by the camera as they fought in North Queensland, Australia. See also n. 56 below.

[9] Alverdes, *op. cit.*, p. 134. Zuckerman points out that among primates only the dominant member of the group will attack the inferior to steal food (*The Social Life of Monkeys and Apes* [London, 1932], p. 234). Females who have stolen food often escape the dominant male's wrath by presenting themselves sexually. This may be submissive behavior induced by recognition of the dominance of the leader rather than prostitution (*ibid.*, p. 242, and Maslow, "Dominance Feeling, Behavior and Status," *op. cit.*, p. 428). "The fact that no serious battles occurred over the possession of food is of importance, especially when . . . . this is also found to be true of many primitive human societies. Of course it is not known for certain what happens in wild communities of baboons. The fact that there were no serious fights over food in the London Zoo may only be a tribute to the diet provided in captivity. It is possible that in harder circumstances rivalry for food might constitute as serious a cause of fighting as rivalry over females. Nevertheless what evidence is available points to sexual rivalry as the sole cause of serious fighting among baboons" (Durbin and Bowlby, *op. cit.*, p. 58). Maslow ("Dominance Feeling, Behavior and Status," *op. cit.*) would add dominance feeling as another cause of serious fighting. See n. 3 above.

[10] See below, n. 21. Letourneau, *op. cit.*, pp. 17 ff.

[11] Below, nn. 32, 60.

useless for this purpose, and, if they had arisen through "natural selection," the females would have been similarly equipped.

The sexual motivation for fighting is sometimes associated with the desire of the male to obtain leadership of the herd. Among monkeys in captivity the decline of the leader's powers may lead to protracted quarrels over the females, who are frequently killed, until a new order of dominance is established. These fights for females may also be motivated by a desire for activity or adventure. It is said that a stag will leave his harem, on hearing the distant bellowing of a rival, in order to engage in a fight when there appears to be no immediate danger of intrusion. These fights are not ordinarily deadly, although male stags sometimes kill each other. Male birds often fight in the presence of a female, but more often they fight when the female is not present, the immediate drive being apparently the maintenance of territory. This, however, is associated with the desire to monopolize a female within that territory and also with the assurance of a sufficient food supply for both the parents and the young.[12]

c) *Fights for territory.*—Violence to acquire and maintain a territory is characteristic of all life. Plants crowd other plants out of a suitable area no less than do animals; in fact, territorial occupation is more characteristic of plant species than of animals. The latter more easily establish symbiotic relations or commensalism among members of different or the same species within an area. Fighting to monopolize an area for a group within the species is, however, a common animal characteristic.

[12] Alverdes, *op. cit.*, pp. 144 ff.; Zuckerman, *op. cit.*, pp. 252 ff.; P. Kropotkin, *Mutual Aid, a Factor of Evolution* (London, 1910), p. 24; H. E. Howard, *Territory in Bird Life* (London, 1920), pp. 74 ff. R. A. Fisher supports Darwin's thesis as to the evolutionary influence of both male sexual combat and female sexual preference (*The Genetical Theory of Natural Selection* [Oxford, 1930], pp. 131, 139), suggesting that in some cases the bright colors of the male may have survived because of their war propaganda value against other males rather than because of their attractiveness to females. For numerous illustrations of male specialization for combat see Charles Darwin, *The Descent of Man* (London, 1881) and *Selection in Relation to Sex* (London, 1871), and A. R. Wallace, *Darwinism* (London, 1889). Huxley points out that, because of the oestrous cycle among most mammals, female preference and hence habits of courtship and secondary sexual adornments are not as developed as among birds; instead, "the winning of females by battle will secure them as mates, and consequently size and strength, as of the elephant seal, offensive weapons like stags' antlers or stallions' canines, and defensive weapons like the lion's mane or the baboon's 'cape' of long hair are the chief secondary male characters" ("Courtship of Animals," *Encyclopaedia Britannica* [14th ed.], VI, 610). See also W. P. Pycroft, *The Courtship of Animals* (New York, 1914), pp. 13, 41, 51. Victor E. Shelford (*Animal Communities in Temperate America* [Chicago, 1913], pp. 31 ff.) points out that in general breeding behavior is most important in determining the range and ecological relationships of animals. This is a commentary on the economic interpretation of history which puts food-getting behavior first, but the two are related because the procuring of food for the young is an important element in breeding behavior. See above, n. 9, and below, sec. 1g.

Ants of different nests, even if of the same species, are hostile to one another, except in the relatively rare cases of parasitism where neighboring intercommunicating or even common nests have developed.[13] This hostility is manifested by vigorous defense of the nest, and even of a surrounding territory monopolized for feeding purposes. Ants of a different nest are apparently known by the smell. Strange ants once ensconced in a nest, if not immediately killed, gradually acquire the odor of the nest and may be adopted. Termites, although genetically widely separated from the ants, are similar in their behavior and defend the termitary with their specialized soldier cast.[14]

Land birds usually fly in flocks until a phase of the breeding cycle is reached, when the males often migrate for long or short distances in search of a suitable habitat. When found, an area is bounded by the initial flight of the bird around it from bush to bush. This area is then defended by vigorous attacks upon any male invader. Continuous observation is maintained from a particular tree or bush selected as headquarters by the master of the area. In a week or so the females come through the area, one chooses to stay with the male occupant, and the pair then unite in defending the area from either males or females of the species, sometimes even from related species. They build a nest and rear young, the area ordinarily being adequate to supply food for the family. Any foraging for food outside would involve risk of attack from the master of that area.

In the case of birds whose food supply is abundant, but who lack suitable nesting areas, as is often true among sea birds, which require a peculiar beach formation for nesting but can fish for food anywhere in the sea, the size of the area defended may be only a few square inches of a ledge sufficient to lay an egg or two upon. Certain birds, such as rooks whose nests and young are subject to attack by birds of prey, defend as a group an area adequate for food and nest together in a single tree.

The behavior of birds which defend an area in single families is markedly different when in the area than when in migration or when in neutral ground which sometimes exists in the vicinity of the apportioned areas. Among such species warfare is confined to definite times and spaces related, respectively, to the breeding cycle and to the location of the nest.[15]

Similar territorial warfare is found among fishes, seals, and some terrestrial mammals. Gorillas and chimpanzees mate in permanent families to which the young remain attached for several years. Four or five of these families form a horde which lives in a defined area and defends it from other hordes of the

[13] Below, n. 14. Kropotkin, however, quotes Forel and MacCook to the effect that ant colonies with hundreds of nests may maintain friendly internal relations (*op. cit.*, p. 18).

[14] Wheeler, *Social Life among the Insects* (New York, 1923), p. 200; Alverdes, *op. cit.*, pp. 94, 162. See above, nn. 32, 60.

[15] Howard, *op. cit.*, and *An Introduction to the Study of Bird Behavior* (Cambridge, 1929).

species.[16] It seems possible that the custom of defending an area is related to the mobility of the species and the absence of dangerous offensive weapons. Among such mobile and inoffensive animals as birds, territorial war does not often results in destruction of the defeated, who can usually escape by flight, and, on the other hand, it is a device well calculated to distribute the species over the maximum suitable area. Those defeated in the home area can fly great distances and breed in new areas.[17] Among the more heavily armed land animals, however, efforts to apportion territory might result in many being killed, and those not killed would find it difficult to migrate far enough to find an unoccupied area. They would therefore return to the attack, and the incessant war would certainly be destructive to the species. Thus such animals often graze, browse, or hunt in areas which they do not monopolize, tolerating one another, and only pushing out from the frontiers into new areas because of inadequacy of the food supply, not because of hostility of others of the species. Where, however, predacious animals of a species are not very numerous, as is true of the Indian tiger, they tend to monopolize a definite area.

d) Fights from a desire for activity.—Animals play and also fight perhaps in order to exercise their faculties, perhaps to see how things work, perhaps to have new experiences, and perhaps from mere restlessness. Activity, including the use of skills for their own sake, for curiosity, and for mobility may be a primitive drive which under certain circumstances may lead to violent behavior. The instinct of pugnacity described by some psychologists may be the same drive. Puppies spat each other in play, a cat plays with a mouse to test her skill, and stags, monkeys, and game cocks often fight for the love of fighting.[18] A spirit of adventure or restlessness may motivate random or directed movements to new territories, which when collective are called migrations.[19]

Migration has been defined as a persistent, self-directed movement of groups usually belonging to the same species but sometimes to several species, ending away from the scene of daily movement before the migration began. The space traversed may be a few feet or thousands of miles. The population involved may be a dozen or a billion. The movement may occur periodically in the life of the individual, periodically in the history of the race, with intervals of several generations between, or sporadically. The movement may or may not involve re-

---

[16] Alverdes, *op. cit.*, pp. 38 ff., 160 ff.; Allee, *op. cit.*, p. 345; Letourneau, *op. cit.*, p. 11.

[17] Howard, *Territory in Bird Life*, pp. 171 ff. The lack of this behavior in the passenger pigeon led to extreme crowding of the species in a few enormous flocks, which were rapidly exterminated by men with firearms. The same was true of the American bison.

[18] Above, nn. 46, 57, 58. See also Lieut.-Gen. A. Lane-Fox Pitt-Rivers, *The Evolution of Culture and Other Essays* (Oxford, 1906), pp. 57–58, who refers to induced fighting between various animals as evidence of a universal instinct of combativeness.

[19] Hornaday, *op. cit.*, pp. 235 ff.; R. M. and A. W. Yerkes, *The Great Apes* (New Haven, 1929), p. 254.

turn to the place of origin.[20] The motive is sometimes sex, food, overcrowding, escape from enemies, or unhealthy environmental conditions, but sometimes no motivation except perhaps boredom and the search for adventure is apparent.

Bees swarm and ant queens often lead off portions of the ant colony when the community gets too large. There seems to be no objection to such migration by the community and no attempt to hold the migrants to any form of allegiance. The march of driver ants is definitely predatory. They move continuously like an army, devouring everything in their path, often large animals. The emigration of the lemmings, a small rodent of the subarctic region, takes place every three and one-half years, probably as the result of overpopulation. It produces cycles in the animal population which preys on this key food supply of the area, and the line of march is marked by intensive eating of the vegetation by the emigrants, and by eating of the emigrants by pursuing predators, but no resistance to the movement by other lemmings occurs. The advantage belongs to those who remain behind. The emigrants usually die by the perils of travel or even throw themselves into the sea when it obstructs their line of march. The migration of certain species may be caused by the migration of others; foxes and birds of prey follow the flight of the lemming, and the predatory animals, left in the area depopulated by this movement, lacking food, may move south, causing other displacements in the balance of nature.[21]

The migration of butterflies is known only obscurely. The monarch butterfly travels from Canada to the Gulf Coast in the late summer and autumn, and sometimes the same individuals return in the spring. Other butterflies emigrate sporadically, sometimes with billions in a group, over fronts of hundreds of miles, for distances of thousands of miles, with no apparent intention of returning. Often these movements, like those of the lemmings, lead to barren regions where most of the emigrants perish.[22]

The migration of birds is the most regular of all migrations. Many species migrate annually in relation to the breeding cycle, the spring movements north being in search of a nesting site. Migrants travel together in flocks, often of several species, sometimes of one, sometimes of both, sexes, though the males tend to go in advance. On reaching the nesting region, these flocks usually divide. Each male occupies an area which he defends. The migration is the prelude to the territorial wars characteristic of birds. The same is probably true when mi-

[20] See C. B. Williams, *The Migration of Butterflies* (Edinburgh, 1930), pp. 10, 352; Howard, *Territory in Bird Life*, chap. vii; Boulenger, *op. cit.*, pp. 186 ff.; J. A. Thomson, *Problems of Bird Migration* (London, 1926), and "Migration of Animals," *Encyclopaedia Britannica* (14th ed.). W. Heape (*Emigration, Migration and Nomadism* [Cambridge, 1931]) confines "migration" to cases where the migrant returns, "emigration" to directed movements from an area well occupied by the species to a new area, and "nomadism" to vague wanderings. Yerkes and Yerkes note the "nomadism" of apes (*op. cit.*, p. 256).

[21] Allee, *Animal Life and Social Growth* (Baltimore, 1932), pp. 80 ff.

[22] Williams, *op. cit.*, pp. 327 ff.

grations occur among fish, mammals, or other animals which habitually establish and maintain territorial monopoly during the nesting season.[23]

Migratory bird or mammal aggregations have been reported on rare occasions to engage in sanguinary wars when meeting another aggregation of the same or a different species. Letourneau refers to a war between magpies and jays in the fifteenth century in France, and a war between two huge flocks of starlings is said to have occurred in England in the eighteenth century.[24] The red squirrels are said to have engaged in a sanguinary conflict, utilizing the method of emasculation to drive the gray squirrles out of New England in 1935.[25]

Migration may thus be a cause of violence because of the need of spacial apportionment within the species, because of the upset of the balance of nature among dependent species in the area either of origin or of destination, or because of chance meeting of migrating hordes. Resistance to such movements is not, however, common. One other type of violence, sometimes associated with migration, is the destruction by the aggregation prepared to migrate of the old or disabled members of their own group. Such behavior has been observed preceding migration and also preceding hibernation, which has sometimes been considered a substitute for migration, in the case of marmots, beavers, and storks.[26]

e) Fights in self-defense.—Defense is often spoken of as a drive of animal as well as human warfare when the thing defended is the family, territory, or society to which the individual engaged in hostility belongs. As a drive of animal warfare it seems better to confine the term to defense of the individual's own life, body, or bodily freedom—to self-defense in the strict sense. In this sense defense is not a primary war drive. Fights for defense can only occur after an aggressor, activated by some other drive, has made or is about to make an attack.

[23] Howard, *Territory in Bird Life*, chap. vii.

[24] Letourneau (*op. cit.*, p. 12) refers to Rabelais's satiric account of this battle (*La Gargantua et la pantagruel*, Book IV).

[25] Ralph C. Jackson, "Migration of Gray Squirrels," *Science*, LXXXII (December, 1935), 549. Donald C. Peattie writes that in the Great Lakes forest belt the fox squirrels are gradually driving out the flying squirrels but are giving way to the gray squirrels, who have begun to be pressed from the East by the red squirrels (*Today*, February 22, 1936). A correspondent in the *London Times* of August 25, 1937, however, reports seeing a gray squirrel jumping down a tree at Bracknel with a young red squirrel dead in its mouth, in 1934, and that the gray squirrels have chased the red out of her garden and now help themselves to all the walnuts. Ordinarily the gradual supersession of one species by another in a large area results from the superior adaptation of one for breeding and food-getting in that environment and not from anything resembling war. It was thus that the dingo superseded the Tasmanian wolf in Australia and that the brown rat has been generally superseding the black. This process resembles economic competition between individuals rather than war (see Carr-Saunders, "Biology and War," *op. cit.*, pp. 428 ff.).

[26] Alverdes, *op. cit.*, p. 138.

Animals which are the habitual victims of predation in the balance of nature defend themselves more often by flight, burrowing, retreat to prepared sanctuaries, mimicry, or reliance upon size or invulnerability of armor than by giving battle. When the latter is resorted to, collective action and mutual aid are common. Predatory species usually prey upon animals of unrelated species over whom they have a great advantage in a fight.[27] Such a case as the mongoose, which eats formidable serpents, is exceptional. Lions and tigers usually prey upon herbivorous animals whom they can easily overcome if they can attack them alone. Only if other game is lacking will a lion attack a buffalo or other animal so formidable that he may be the victor. Consequently, the evolution of species which are victims of the predators has been toward specialization in the arts of retreat, camouflage, fortification, and mutual aid. In predatory fights the aggressor betrays himself by his offensive armament. The problem which has troubled international lawyers so much in human war—who is the aggressor— is easily solved.

This, however, is not true in animal fights arising from sex, territory, or society. In such fights the combatants are usually of the same or closely related species, the result of the conflict may be long in doubt, and it is difficult to designate one or the other as clearly acting in defense. Both may be aggressors.[28]

In animal warfare, therefore, it is possible to speak unequivocally of fighting in defense only if the drive responsible for the conflict is predation upon the individual engaged in defense. If a male buck attacks an intruding male about to cover a female of the herd, if a pair of finches joins in attacking a male of the species entering their territory, if soldier ants go forth to hold back an advancing enemy, defense may appear to be a primary drive; but in such cases the individual did not begin his hostile activity to defend himself but to defend his family, territory, society, or something else external to himself. The drive responsible for his belligerent behavior should be described as sex, territory, or society rather than as self-defense.

f) Fights for society.—An individual animal, not urged by hunger or sex, not moved by a territorial invasion or a threat to its life or even by a love of adventure, may behave in a belligerent manner in response to the needs or policy of the group of which it is a member. Belligerency from such a motive may be called societal war. This war drive may arise from natural selection of animal groups enjoying the advantage of mutual aid, collective action, and division of labor. Social behavior has manifest advantages for food-getting, sexual functioning, and care of the young as well as for common defense. Sociability may be an original drive supporting such behavior. The belligerent behaviors and specializations within some animal societies seem to be related to this drive. Hunting

[27] See below, n. 60; T. Roosevelt, *African Game Trails*, p. 169, quoted by Shelford, *op. cit.*, p. 7.

[28] Within the species weaker animals defend themselves from attack by the leader through prostitution or flight (above, n. 9).

bands are known among certain carnivores, and they may sometimes defend a territory from other predacious animals as Mowgli's wolf pack fought off the red dogs.[29] Certain insects are organized for predation, robbery, or slave-taking. Social organization, however, is both more intensive and more common among animals which live on a vegetarian diet, are not parasitic, and accept a system of social subordination and division of labor without violence.

Many instances of aggregation and social behavior for common defense can be cited. Rhinoceroses, chimpanzees, elephants, and many other animals will at once come to the aid of a member of the herd on hearing his cry of distress, and some herds of herbivores are said "to maintain a system of outposts and sentries."[30] Migrating birds, shoals of fish, and flights of insects can defend themselves better from temperature changes, storms, and predatory animals when close together. Most animals seem to have more courage when in groups than when alone. Allee has demonstrated the value of optimal crowding for animals at all points of the evolutionary scale, from paramecia to primates. Great aggregations, sometimes of the same and sometimes of different species, primarily for protective purposes are as universal a phenomenon in the animal world as are societies based upon sex and reproduction.[31]

Among the social insects, collective defense has developed the soldier caste ready to defend the hive, the nest, or the termitary from every enemy with the utmost loyalty. Huber's observation of a great war originating in predation between two nests of ants of the same species some hundred steps distant from each other is thus recounted by Letourneau:

On the field of battle, some thousands of the ants struggled two by two, holding each other with their mandibles; others were searching for each other, attacking each other, forcing each other to come as prisoners into their city where they awaited an end most cruel. The combatants deluged each other with venom and rolled interlaced in the dust. On the other hand the fellow citizens of each side gave each other mutual assistance. Did it happen that in the melee some compatriots were attacked in error? Immediately they recognized each other and the blows were followed by caresses. While the two armies thus displayed prodigies of carnage and of valor, the civil population of the two cities, not required for the work of destruction, continued to travel on the paths of the forest, carrying on their useful and peaceful work. Only on the side where the battle was being waged was there a going and coming of warriors; unceasingly the ants de-

[29] But see n. 57 below.

[30] Durbin and Bowlby, *op. cit.*, p. 5; Alverdes, *op. cit.*, pp. 133 ff. Zuckerman (*op. cit.*, pp. 296 ff.) believes that among primates this response is an individual reflex rather than a socially conditioned response. He finds no evidence that monkeys have a concept of the group whose members are to be defended but respond instinctively on hearing a cry of distress from a member of the species. See also chap. v, nn. 21, 22 above.

[31] Allee, *Animal Aggregations;* S. J. Holmes, *The Evolution of Animal Intelligence* (New York, 1911), p. 207. T. Roosevelt commented on the close companionship often observed between wholly different species of game in Africa, *African Game Trails*, p. 24. See also below, n. 85.

parted for the war; unceasingly the combatants in charge of prisoners re-entered their native city. In these curious wars the tactics of the ants is always free and courageous. Without doubt they sometimes resort to ambushes but only in skirmishing. In the great wars, they attack with open force and without recourse to ruse. They struggle, moreover, with extraordinary tenacity and it is more easy to tear them to pieces than to make them prisoners. Indeed when a combatant ant has been sectioned in the middle of the body, the anterior part, the head and thorax separated from the abdomen, still carry in their protection the menaced nymph. Often in the heat of action, one sees the severed head of an ant still suspended from the legs or antennae of the victorious adversary; sometimes it is a dead body which is thus dragged and which does not cease to move its legs convulsively. Thus in the ant world, devotion to the public is complete and without reserve; among the workers, much more even than among the primitive clans of human society, altruism has completely conquered egoism; the instinct of conservation, so powerful among the most civilized men, is directed among the ants only to the social community, to the republic. The famous word of Horace, "Dulce et decorum est pro patria more" is only an exact expression of the truth if one applies it to the ants.[32]

Such specialization for collective defense, however, easily leads to an offensive as the best defense and thus to predatory expeditions. It is probably out of this specialization for defense that ants of certain species develop the habit of slave-taking and other forms of intraspecific parasitism. The preparation of a technique for collective defense leads to exaggerated subordination of the individual to the society and may be a major cause of aggression. Ant parasitism probably originated from predatory aggressions rather than from the extension of the custom, common in certain species, of the virgin queen's return to the parental nest after the nuptial flight. It had been suggested that by accident such queens might occasionally return to the nest of an alien species, out of which parasitism might arise. It, however, seems more probable that the practice began with predatory expeditions to take slaves, the queen's entry to the servile nest developing later.[33]

Whatever its origin, belligerent behavior in response to social needs and customs is characteristic of animals which live in societies. The occasions which

[32] Op. cit., pp. 23–24, citing P. Huber, Recherches sur les moeurs des fourmis indigenes (Paris, 1861), pp. 133–56. The warfare of termites against ants has been thus described: "When their enemies, the ants, succeed in breaking into the nest, soldiers [termites] appear at the opening and take up the fight. The body of the soldier consists chiefly of a terrific jaw which opens and closes automatically. Other soldiers have glands which they use as machine guns; they spurt out a fluid which is destructive to the enemy. During the battle the laborers in the rear of their own soldiers build a new wall. Thus the soldiers are sentenced to death. Their function is to fight and keep back the enemy until the laborers have had time to build up the fort" (Franz Alexander, "A Note on Falstaff," Psychoanalytic Quarterly, II [1933], 604). Carr-Saunders is skeptical of such interpretations ("Biology and War," op. cit., pp. 430 ff.).

[33] Wheeler, Social Life among the Insects, p. 218.

will stimulate such behavior vary greatly according to the characteristics of the society. The consequences of this societal drive involves, therefore, a study taking the society rather than the individual animal as the unit. Some societies are predatory, some parasitic, some agricultural, but on the whole societies, exploiting the vegetable world and confining collective belligerency to defense of the group and its territory from invasion, have been most successful in the evolutionary struggle.[34]

g) Fights for dominance.—Dominance is both a cause and an effect of social organization among animals. On the one hand, "dominance feeling," which may exist in varying degrees of intensity among individuals of the same species, is a drive, tending toward "dominant behavior" (strutting, bullying, initiative in feeding and other activity) in some, and toward "subordinate behavior" (cringing, prostration, passivity or flight in case of aggression) in others of a group.[35] On the other hand, "dominance status" results from a given state of social organization and is not always precisely correlated with dominance feeling, though it also results in "subordinate behavior" of the rank and file toward those enjoying that status. The compulsion to manifest this behavior may, however, be resented, and the behavior is frequently abandoned by those with a high dominance drive.[36]

The existence of this drive appears to have been demonstrated, at least in the case of certain monkeys, by A. H. Maslow:

[34] Above, n. 65.

[35] Maslow defines "the *dominant* animal as one whose behavior patterns (sexual, feeding, aggressive and social) are carried out without deference to the behavior patterns of his associates. The *subordinate* animal is one whose behavior patterns are suggested, modified, limited, or inhibited by the behavior patterns of its more dominant associates." He prefers these terms to the terms "ascendance" and "submission," used by Allport, Zuckerman, Harlow, and others because "the less dominant animal sometimes does not occupy his secondary position with any evidence of willingness or submission, but is forced to assume the attitude by the violence of his superiors. The dominance drive of the less dominant monkey is not lost but is merely submerged or overshadowed or expresses itself through other channels and will continue to assert itself whenever the opportunity arises. In other words the drive for dominance is continuous and the mere fact that the more dominant animal attains permanent or temporary superiority does not imply submission by the less dominant animal." Greater size, fighting capacity, and confidence augment the dominance drive and assist in the establishment of dominant status. Maslow suggests that "dominance is determined or actually is a composite of social attitudes, attitudes of aggressiveness, confidence or cockiness that are at times challenged, and which must then, of course, be backed up by physical prowess. A very apparent sizing up process goes on during the first moments of meeting, and it is during these moments and during this process that dominance seems to be established" ("The Role of Dominance in the Social and Sexual Behavior of Infrahuman Primates," *op. cit.*, pp. 263, 305).

[36] Maslow, "Dominance Feeling, Behavior, and Status," *op. cit.*, pp. 404 ff.

The remarkably high correlation that the author has demonstrated between many kinds of social behavior in the catarrahine monkey are best understood as manifestations of a dominance drive in the individual animals. This drive furnishes a link between individual and group behavior, since it is an *individual* mechanism leading to *social* behavior. This drive is probably characteristic of all birds and mammals.[37] . . . . If our theory that dominance is a determiner of social behavior is correct, we should expect to find differences in social behavior and social organization correlated with differences of dominance in these groups. Such behavior differences are found.[38]

The howler monkeys with little family organization, no male ownership of females, little fighting, bullying, or jealousy, and a weak social hierarchy seem to manifest a low dominance drive compared with the baboons which live in family groups, the males maintaining a considerable harem, with much fighting and a marked social hierarchy. Chimpanzees manifest a mid-range of dominance with real friendship, mutual aid, and few of the rough and brutal manifestations of dominance but with some social hierarchy.

The concept of dominance is pushed even further by C. M. Child, who writes: "Leadership, dominance, the pacemaker, play eventually the same role in social and physiological integration." He points out that automatically imposed dominance is found in the more primitive forms of organisms and societies and is a less effective means of integration than democratic systems resting "upon dynamic correlations of an excitatory-transmissive character."[39] A similarly broad concept of dominance is implied by Seilliere's use of the word "imperialism."[40] He finds this a universal phenomenon of nature, referring to tree imperialism as the ability of certain trees to crowd out other vegetation in the area, or to animal imperialism as the custom of predatory, territorial, or social mastery. In this sense parasitism is a form of dominance.[41]

As a specific drive, however, the intensity of dominance varies greatly among different species, as does its tendency to induce fighting. Among lower animal forms such as the starfish and sea anemone, leadership is so lacking in the organism that the legs may attempt to walk off in different directions at the same time, thus rending the animal to pieces. Leaders of herds of gregarious animals some-

[37] Maslow refers to studies by Schjelderup-Ebbe and Murchison on birds, Davis on rats, and Zuckerman, Yerkes, Harlow, and Maslow on primates.

[38] "The Dominance Drive as a Determiner of Social Behavior in Infrahuman Primates," *Psychological Bulletin*, XXXII (1935), 714-15.

[39] *Physiological Foundations of Behavior* (New York, 1924), pp. 280, 287, 288 ff.

[40] Ernest Seilliere, *Introduction à la philosophie de l'imperialisme* (Paris, 1911); Michel Pavlovitch, *The Foundations of Imperialist Policy* (London, 1922), pp. 16 ff. Kropotkin uses the words "competition and struggle" in this broad sense but thinks their importance in evolution has been greatly overrated (*op. cit.*, p. 70). Carr-Saunders insists that biological crowding-out has no resemblance to war ("Biology and War," *op. cit.*, p. 428). Below, sec. 4c.

[41] Wheeler, "Insect Parasitism and Its Peculiarities," *Foibles of Men and Insects* (New York, 1928), pp. 49 ff.; *Social Life among the Insects*, pp. 200 ff. Below, n. 62.

times secure and maintain their leadership by violence, but this is often associated with the sex drive. Kangaroos live in large herds dominated by an old male. Hens gain leadership by establishing a peck order through fighting.[42] Cattle sometimes fight for herd leadership, as do monkeys.[43] Leadership by seniority is also found among cows and is perhaps more common. The female sometimes assumes leadership of a harem, even when the male is present, among certain deer, other herbivorous animals, and monkeys.[44] Leadership in a flock of migrating birds seems to result from greater speed, not from military prowess. The leader of a flock of geese is sometimes abandoned by the flock, which, ignoring his leadership, turns aside. When the leader observes his solitary condition, he catches up with the flock and again takes the leading position. Leadership may result from ability to follow in front rather than from ability to lead.[45]

The importance of dominance as an independent cause of fighting depends upon the intensity of the drive in the species and upon the form of social organization. If social organization is very rigid, it may induce insubordination, and, if very loose, it may induce continual rivalry for leadership. If the species also has a strong activity drive or disposition toward fighting for its own sake, the frequency of fighting will be greatly augmented. Maslow's studies clearly indicate the greater frequency of fighting when both of these drives are intense, especially if they are intense in both members of a pair of monkeys.[46] The association of the dominance and the sexual drive may also be a common source of animal fighting.[47]

[42] T. Schjelderup-Ebbe, "Social Behavior of Birds," in *A Handbook of Social Psychology*, ed. Carl Murchison (Worcester, 1935), pp. 947 ff.

[43] Maslow notes that a new animal in a group will often take a position of dominance or subordination without display of force ("The Role of Dominance . . . ," *op. cit.*, p. 272).

[44] Alverdes, *op. cit.*, pp. 36, 45; Maslow, "The Role of Dominance . . . ," *op. cit.*, p. 270. Among birds the males dominate if larger, as among cocks and hens. The female Australian shell parakeet dominates over the male except in the breeding season.

[45] Alverdes, *op. cit.*, pp. 33 ff., 161 ff.; Zuckerman, *op. cit.*, pp. 234 ff., 253 ff.; Allee, *Animal Aggregations*, pp. 344, 348; *Animal Life and Social Growth*, pp. 152 ff.

[46] Maslow's careful recording of the behavior of pairs of monkeys indicated an early establishment of relations of dominance and subordination which persisted with varying amounts of fighting. If the strength of the dominance drive of the two was very different or if the activity drive of each was weak, there would be little fighting. If, on the other hand, the dominance drive was more nearly equal in each and one or both had a strong activity drive, there would be frequent fights usually initiated by the dominant monkey. When larger numbers were put together, behavior might be very unexpected. In a group of three, two, which had each been subordinate to the third, when individually paired with him might band together and subordinate him, the initiative being taken by a monkey with a strong activity drive ("The Role of Dominance . . . ," *op. cit.*, XLIX 1936], 196 ff.).

[47] Zuckerman (*op. cit.*, p. 224) emphasizes this relationship too much in Maslow's opinion ("The Role of Dominance . . . , " *op. cit.*, XLVIII, 261 ff.).

The caste organization of insects usually results without violence from th
genetic constitution of the eggs or from early feeding practices. The collection c
aphids by ants is a mutually beneficial nonviolent procedure.[48] These practice
are neither established nor maintained by war or violence. To this, howevei
there is an exception, in the behavior of ant and bee queens in sometimes killin
their rivals. Wars in the interest of the society may solidify its existing interna
organization.

Certain ants make slave raids and maintain other ant species in servitude
Wheeler describes five varieties of social parasitism among ants that live in com
pound or adjoining nests (brigandage, thieving, neighborliness, tutelage, an
hospitality) and three varieties in mixed colonies (slavery, temporary, and pei
manent social parasitism). In mixed colonies the relationship is usually betwee
closely related species, while in the compound colonies it is commonly betwee
species of different genera.[49]

The procedure of slave-taking ants resembles human warfare for dominance
although it is seldom intraspecific. A species known as Amazons have mandible
good for fighting but useless for digging, so they are dependent upon workers c
other species. Wheeler writes:

Like *Sanguinea*, the *Amazons* [*polyergus*] make periodical forays which for some ur
known reason are always carried out in the afternoons, but their armies show a mor
perfected tactical organization and the subjugation and plundering of the *fusta* colonie
are affected with much greater dispatch and precision—one might say with the mos
consummate éclat. At the approach of the Amazons the *fusta* workers usually flee in dis
may, but if they offer any resistance, the Amazons pierce their heads with the sickle
shaped mandibles. The young on emerging from the kidnapped pupae excavate th
nest, feed the *polyergus*, and bring up their brood but do not accompany the armies o
their raids. The initial stages in founding the colony have been studied by Emery, wh
found that the young *polyergus* queen secures adoption in some small weak *fusta* colony
after killing its queen by piercing her head. She then produces her brood, which wi
later make the slave raids on the *fusta* colonies. Since this raiding proclivity neve
lapses even in old colonies, *polyergus* is to be regarded as a chronic or obligatory slave
maker.[50]

Such parasitic species, however, are relatively rare or local. Parasitism has nev
er, according to Wheeler, been a successful expedient for the parasite. The hos
species suffers less.

A dominance drive is probably a widespread characteristic of higher animal
but fighting for dominance is less characteristic of animals in general than of hu
man beings. Among the higher animals, dominance status in social organizatio
is more rapidly adjusted to the intensity of the dominance drives of the membei

[48] Wheeler, *Social Life among the Insects*, pp. 160–61, 174 ff., 199.

[49] *Ibid.*, pp. 199 ff.; Letourneau, *op. cit.*, pp. 19 ff.; above, n. 60.

[50] *Social Life among the Insects*, pp. 210 ff.; see also Letourneau, *op. cit.*, pp. 19 ff
and above, n. 32.

of the group than in the more rigid human societies; thus resentment of the subordinate is less common. On the other hand, the very looseness of the organization induces rivalries, especially when the capacity of the leader wanes. Simian organization in this respect resembles that of the family of nations more than the group organization of either primitive or civilized man. Its stability depends upon a very delicate balance of power. From his observation of "Monkey Hill" in the London Zoo, Zuckerman concludes:

> The number of fatal fights that have followed deaths on the Hill is too great to be without significance, and the meaning of the correlation is obvious. The equilibrium of a social group is dependent upon the mutual reactions of all its members. The death of any single individual upsets the state of balance, and fighting commonly breaks out before a new equilibrium is reached.[51]

Leadership is, of course, necessary for the organization of cells into an organism or of organisms into a community, but it characteristically develops among animals, not by violence and struggle, but by gradual differentiation of function, recognition of mutual interdependence and acceptance of some simple expedient such as age, speed, or physiological specialization (as in the colonial insects) as the test of leadership. There is no evidence outside of Aesop's fables that the head feels either superior or inferior to the stomach, or that the worker bee feels either superior or inferior to the queen or to the soldier. Among many higher animals, however, expecially the primates, such feelings do exist, and the leader often uses violence to establish and maintain his position.

h) *Fights for independence.*—The belligerent reaction arising in any organism from interference with, or frustration of, an activity in progress is perhaps at the root of the drives for freedom and independence characteristic of men and of human societies. Wars of independence imply continuous resentment at relationships of dominance and subjection. Such hostilities occur very rarely among animals. Slave ants may resent their position, but they do not revolt, and the hosts in other forms of parasitism submit permanently when conquered. The fights among monkeys and apes when the leader's powers wane result immediately from a sexual urge to appropriate his wives and from a dominance urge to

---

[51] Zuckerman, *op. cit.*, p. 225; Durbin and Bowlby, *op. cit.*, p. 56; above, n. 46. In reading a detailed account of primate behavior, one is impressed by its resemblance to that of sovereign states. Monkeys are more nearly in the "state of nature" than are primitive men. The intricate social organization of the latter is remote from the "natural society" posited by either Hobbes or Locke, but the monkeys manifest dominance and pugnacity with considerable individuality; the dominant ones strut, bully, and demand deference by prostrations resembling the kowtow; the society is in unstable equilibrium according to the fluctuations of power as determined by size, fighting capacity, and confidence; disturbances to the equilibrium result from the entry of newcomers into the group, often precipitating violent conflict, and the balance of power is operated by the alliance of the weak against the strong. Conflicts over food and sex occur, but they appear to be subordinate to the drives of dominance and activity in determining the organization of the group and its principal hostilities.

become the new leader, though continuing resentment at a subordinate position seems to often increase the tension. Wars of independence imply imagination of a future relationship different from the present, which seems not to figure in the consciousness of animals below the primates.

Migration might be regarded as a move for independence, originating in a sense of dissatisfaction with habitual surroundings when more obvious urges of sex, overpopulation, insufficient food supply, increase of enemies, or environmental changes are not present.[52] This phenomenon, however, may proceed from the pull of adventure or curiosity rather than from the push of oppression or hardship and so has been considered as a fight for adventure. Furthermore, where migration proceeds from a parent society, as in swarming bees and ants, that society makes no effort to restrain the departing citizens. Independence, if that is the motive, can be achieved without struggle.

Wars for independence have played an important role in human history, but they seem to require a collective memory of social oppression and a collective vision of future possibilities not often found in animal societies.

2. FUNCTIONS OF ANIMAL WARFARE

According to the Darwinian hypothesis, behavior patterns among animals no less than bodily structure exist because in the struggle for existence they have assisted the species to survive. Whatever may have been the *origin* of a particular type of behavior or structure, according to this hypothesis, the behavior or structure has *persisted* because it *functioned* in the survival of the *species*.

Recent investigation, however, has made it clear that most of the differences distinguishing species and subspecies are not adaptive—that "the principal evolutionary mechanism in the origin of species must thus be an essentially non adaptive one."[53] It cannot therefore be assumed that all violent behavior serves a function for the species except indeed as an element in a trial-and-error process which may eventually maximize organic adaptation to the environment. It must be assumed, however, that such behavior, and indeed all behaviors and structures, have not been greatly to the disadvantage of the species during its history. If they had been, the species would have perished; indeed, species are continually perishing because changing conditions render characteristics once advantageous or innocuous positively disadvantageous. Disadvantageous characteristics may, however, last for a considerable time before they or the species are eliminated.

Types of violent behavior are in the animal world generally related to particular species, not to particular individuals, societies, areas, or environments. There is a relationship between these entities. A genetic variety is composed of similar individuals usually confined to a characteristic environment in a particular terri-

[52] Kropotkin classes migration with hibernation and mutual aid as means for avoiding competition (*op. cit.*, p. 74).

[53] S. Wright, "The Roles of Mutation, In-breeding, Cross-breeding, and Selection in Evolution," *Proceedings Sixth International Congress of Genetics, 1932*, I, 363–64.

tory. The geographic range may be quite extensive, and within it the organic and inorganic environment may vary considerably. In spite of this, the violent behavior of all animals of the species is usually found to be similar in all parts of the range. While individuals and local races within the species vary much more in regard to behavior than in regard to structure,[54] and among certain colonial insects fighting castes exist, in general animal behavior like structure is correlated more closely with genetic relationship than with experience, environment, or status.[55] Animal warfare, so far as it has a function at all, is functionally related to the race. It is functionally related to the individual, society, or biological community only in so far as the preservation of such entity is of value to the race.

It is doubtless due to this fact that violent behavior between animals of the same species is seldom lethal. There are rare instances as in encounters between male stags, where one is killed, and in the social insects the queen often kills her rival. Cannibalism also occurs, but usually at the expense of individuals who have ceased to be sexually valuable.[56] In general, war within the same species has the function of distributing the species evenly over the available environment and does not result in killing. This type of violence has been especially developed among animals which are not armed so heavily as to make encounters deadly, especially birds, fish, and herbivorous animals. If such heavily armed animals as lions and tigers were accustomed to fight each other, they would kill each other off and the species would suffer.[57] Finches and warblers, however, can

[54] Hunters and cockfighters often comment on the individual differences in fighting behavior of animals of the same breed (see T. Roosevelt, *African Game Trails*, in *Works* [New York, 1926], 55; "Cockfighting," *Fortune*, March, 1934, p. 91). Hornaday (*op. cit.*, pp. 14 ff.) emphasizes the temperamental differences of individuals and species.

[55] The behavior of human beings is probably more rapidly adaptable to environmental changes than is that of other animals (see Lotka, *op. cit.*, p. 428). The extensive literature upon the relative importance of heredity and environment in determining human behavior, especially studies of identical twins separated at birth and of foster-children, have not shown that environment has a greater influence than heredity (see S. Wright, "Statistical Method in Biology," *op. cit.*; H. H. Newman, "Mental and Physical Traits of Identical Twins Reared Apart," *Journal of Heredity*, XXIII [January, 1932], 17). See also below, n. 66.

[56] See above, n. 8. Kropotkin emphasizes the rareness of struggle within the species (*op. cit.*, p. 61; above, n. 40). Letourneau believes that, while close relationship decreases direct violence for food, it increases economic war or rivalry for a common food supply (*op. cit.*, p. 8). See also Hornaday, *op. cit.*, pp. 225 ff.

[57] Even distinct carnivorous species seldom fight each other. Such battles as that which Kipling recounts between the wolves and red dog in India (*The Jungle Book*) appear to be apocryphal. See H. F. Blanford, *The Fauna of British India, Mammilia* (London, 1888–91), pp. 144–46, cited by Sageret, *op. cit.*, p. 18. The *Chicago Tribune* for February 11, 1934, however, printed pictures said to have been taken by an American motion picture company in an expedition to the Indian, Siamese, Indo-Chinese, and Malayan jungles of fights between a Malayan bear and a hyena, a lion and a tiger,

and do fight each other but with no result other than driving the weaker from the area chosen for his nest by the stronger, who thereby gains a better chance of rearing young successfully.[58]

In a general way it can be said that the deadliness of animal violence declines with the closeness of genetic relationship of the combatants. In this respect it differs greatly from human war, which is always within the same species and is often most destructive when between peoples of the same race.[59] Among animals the really deadly violence on a large scale occurs in the utilization of one species as food by another, but the species are usually widely separated genetically.[60]

---

a leopard and a Malayan bear, a crocodile and a black panther, a leopard and a python. Pitt-Rivers (*op. cit.*, p. 58) mentions artificially induced fights between crickets, fish, game cocks, quail, partridges, geese, bulls, elephants, rhinoceroses, hogs, rams, and buffalo against tiger. None is carnivorous except the tiger, which is matched against a noncarnivore, and most of these species are not equipped with powerful offensive weapons. Grotius (*De jure belli ac pacis*, Proleg. 7) quotes from Juvenal (*Sat.* xv. 163. 159), "Tigress with ravening tigress keeps the peace; the wild beast spares its spotted kin," and others to prove a natural law of restraint in intraspecific relations.

[58] Below, nn. 15, 16. This belligerence of birds may be exaggerated by breeding, and their weapons may be artificially improved as is done with game cocks, bred from the Indian jungle fowl in a remote antiquity and equipped with steel spurs for combat. They provided sport in ancient India, China, and Persia. Themistocles, on the way to Salamis (480 B.C.), inspired his army by calling attention to a cockfight, which they passed, with the words: "These animals fight not for the gods of their country, nor for the monuments of their ancestors, nor for glory, nor for freedom nor for their progeny but for the sake of victory and that one may not yield to the other." These characteristics are verified by modern observers. Game cocks fight for the love of fighting. They attack each other at sight and will not be diverted by food or sex, fighting always to the death with a "blind, stubborn, uncompromising courage." But this characteristic is maintained only by continuous careful breeding. A bird with a bit of ordinary chicken blood is worthless for the cockpit (see *Fortune*, March, 1934, pp. 90 ff., and "Cock-fighting," *Encyclopaedia Britannica*).

[59] The Australian whites for a time hunted the blacks like wild beasts (C. M. Curr, *The Australian Race* [Melbourne, 1888], I, 100 ff.), and similar deadly hostilities occurred during the early stages of white migration to America, parts of Africa, and the Pacific Islands; but, in general, human war has been between closely related peoples (see James Bryce, *The Relation of the Advanced and Backward Races of Mankind* [Oxford, 1903]).

[60] A diagram of food relationships in an area illustrates this point (see Allee, *Animal Life and Social Growth*, p. 63). Professor Allee informs me that the disposition of ants to fight each other increases as the relationship becomes more distant. Ants of different species fight more bitterly than those of different nests of the same species, but even ants of different species if taken young and touched to each other at least once a day can be formed into a peaceful colony. See also Lotka, *op. cit.* chaps. xiii and xiv, on interspecies equilibria; Howard, *Territory in Bird Life*, chap. vi; and Carr-Saunders, "Biology and War," *op. cit.*, p. 431.

Although violence, properly speaking, this is no more war than is man's operations upon cattle and swine in the slaughter-house or upon other animals and birds in hunting. Even such predatory activities of one species upon another would cease to have survival value for the aggressor if pushed too far. He would destroy his own food supply. Usually the balance is maintained through the fertility of the preyed-upon. Antelopes multiply rapidly. Consequently, lions can safely catch and eat many of them. Predatory animals seldom kill more than they need to eat. To that extent they conserve the food supply of the species.

In some cases conservation is pushed further, as when ants preserve aphids or ant cows as a perpetual source of nourishment, and bacteria often reach an accommodation with the host so as to feed parasitically upon it a long time without killing it. It has been suggested that human diseases only arise from microbes which are in the early stages of accommodating themselves to the use of a human host as food. After a sufficiently long time the typhoid, diphtheria, pneumonia, and other parasitic bacteria, the malaria, sleeping sickness, dysentary, and other parasitic protozoa may evolve to a condition where they can live in the human host without killing him. Microbes that did this would have a survival advantage over those that exterminated their food supply. For this reason we may expect new diseases continually to arise, perhaps causing devastating epidemics, but gradually to subside as the microbe responsible for them evolves an accommodation more satisfactory both to itself and to its host.[61]

Using parasitism in the broad sense of any nonreciprocal use of one organism by another in its food-getting activity,[62] these considerations suggest the important distinction between individual, racial, and social parasitism.[63] In the first the parasite is so dependent upon the particular host that the death of the latter results in the death of the parasite. For such a parasite to kill his host is suicide, and thus bad for the parasite's race.

A racial parasite is dependent on a host species, but it can afford to kill individuals of that species provided enough survive to continue the food supply. Pathogenic bacteria are of this type. They have a means of escape from the

[61] Carr-Saunders, *Population Problem*, pp. 155 ff.; Arthur I. Kendall, *Civilization and the Microbes* (New York, 1923), pp. 173, 209. The normal rhythm of an epidemic is, of course, a much shorter cycle arising from the death of the most vulnerable part of the host population and the development of immunities by the survivors (see Lotka, *op. cit.*, pp. 79 ff.).

[62] See G. K. Link, "Etiological Phytopathology," *Phytopathology*, XXIII (November, 1933), 855.

[63] These distinctions, which have in view the consequences of the relationship upon the parasite, should not be confused with the common distinctions between an episite which kills the host outright, a parasite which lives upon the host without killing it immediately, a saphrophite which lives on a dead body, and a symbiont which gives in return for what it gets, all of which have in view the consequence of the relationship upon the host (see Lotka, *op. cit.*, p. 77; C. S. Elton, "Ecology," *Encyclopaedia Britannica* [14th ed.], VII, 921).

host but must be careful not to kill him so soon as to shut off escape. The animal world as a whole can be considered a parasite upon the vegetable world which alone can synthesize chemicals into animal food. If an animal community browzes away the entire vegetation of its habitat, it destroys itself. Carnivorous animals might also be called racial parasites although predation or epistism, in which feeding upon the host necessarily kills it immediately, is usually distinguished from parasitism. Most carnivorous animals are not dependent upon a given species of animals. They may eat up one race and yet survive on another, but there are distinct limits to their adaptability. The plains Indian was in this sense parasitic upon the bison and had to leave when the herds were exterminated. Civilized man might almost be considered a parasite on cattle, hogs, and sheep, but since he maintains their numbers artificially and can get along on many substitutes, the term "parasite" is hardly applicable.

Social parasitism exists when the parasite is dependent upon the maintenance of the social functioning of the host who may be of the same species. Commensalism, in which one species uses food collected by another, is a form of social parasitism. It must, however, be distinguished from symbiosis or mutualism, in which both share equally in the advantages of the relationship. Thus the queen ant or termite is not really a parasite upon the workers as she contributes to their existence and welfare. The same is perhaps true of the relations of parent and child, although the contribution of each may be made at different stages in a time series. Unalloyed cases of social parasitism are not common because the parasite usually has some interest in the survival of the host. If parasite and host are of the same species, obviously the relationship, if destructive to the host, would be bad for the species. There are, however, cases of slavery, brigandage, and thievery among related types of ants.[64] Both ant and human societies, according to Wheeler, have gone through hunting, pastoral, and agricultural stages. The latter, in which the species has reduced its dependence upon the destruction of other animals, has proved to have the greatest survival value.[65]

[64] Wheeler, *Social Life among the Insects*, pp. 200 ff.

[65] Kendall (*op. cit.*, p. 209) writes: "If the question were asked, which of two nations would be more enduring, one very arrogant and aggressive, the other more patient and persevering, the instinctive answer would be in favor of the first. If the same question were asked with reference to two microbes, one very virulent and capable of rapidly overwhelming its host, the other less virulent and capable of overpowering its host slowly, the same instinctive response would in all probability be made. The history of man and of microbes alike indicates the reverse is true. Many nations and many microbes have failed to act in obedience to nature's great law of balance among living things. Some nations, and some microbes even have defied repeatedly the consequences of the great natural law of biologic balance. The end is inevitably the same. For certain periods they have seemed to overstrain the trite saying that 'history repeats itself, historians repeat each other,' but each and every aggressively militant nation and each and every exceptionally virulent microbe which may have leaped into hideous notoriety, has sooner or later burned itself out, even as a shooting star blazes in the firmament, fades

3. TECHNIQUE OF ANIMAL WARFARE

The technique of war is the art of preparing military instruments for mastering, with the least cost, all possible enemies and of utilizing available military instruments in the most efficient combination against an actual enemy.

From the standpoint of preparation, technique is a problem of weapon type, material, and organization. From the standpoint of utilization it is a problem of mobilization, strategy, and tactics. In considering war by individual animals, preparation lies in the realm of morphology, while utilization lies in the realm of behavior. The latter is undoubtedly more malleable than the former.[66] Animal behavior may be to a considerable extent instinctive, but modification in the

---

and is gone." Wheeler (*Social Life among the Insects*, p. 198) writes: "Biology has only one great categorial imperative to offer and that is: Be neither a parasite nor a host." See also *ibid.*, pp. 177 ff., 219. In an earlier article, "Insect Parasitism and Its Peculiarities," *Popular Science Monthly* (1911), reprinted in *Foibles of Men and Insects*, pp. 49 ff., Wheeler gives a useful definition and many instances of parasitism but is less emphatic in respect to its disgenic tendency. H. Reinheimer (*Symbiosis: A Socio-physiological Study of Evolution* [London, 1920], pp. ix ff. and Part I, chap. iii) finds that there is a biologic morality, enforced by natural penalties, which decrees that co-operation and symbiosis are good and predatoriness and parasitism bad. See also Hornaday (*op. cit.*, pp. 195 ff.), who notes that while cobras kill 17,000 people in India annually, this leads to government bounties, as a result of which 117,000 cobras are killed annually. The conception of symbiosis has served as the foundation for the state, at least since Aristotle, though the term appears to have first been used and the conception developed in this connection by Johannes Althusius in 1603 (*Politica methodica digesta*, ed. Carl J. Friedrich [Cambridge, Mass., 1932], pp. lxvii ff.). Kropotkin (*op. cit.*, p. 75) extolled "mutual aid" and considered struggle "injurious to the species." Bagehot writes, "The compact tribes win and the compact tribes are the tamest" (*Physics and Politics* [London, 1903], p. 52). It cannot be denied that animal species and societies have, under certain conditions, gained by specializing in violence for food. Man was originally differentiated from other apes, which are frugiferous, by his hunting habits. It may be even that his tool-using capacity developed from this habit. The Australian kea, an originally vegetarian parrot, became carniverous on the introduction of sheep to Australia. It multiplied rapidly on a diet of sheep's kidneys. It appears, however, that races and societies have more often gained by avoiding dependence upon predation and parasitism. Civilized men, domestic cats and dogs, bears, and ants have tended to become vegetarian. In animal communities, niches suitable for large carnivores support small numbers of individuals (Elton, *op. cit.*). Among the higher animals, both the articulates and the vertebrates, those partially or wholly emancipated from carnivorousness have been the most numerous. See above, n. 34; below, nn. 81, 99.

[66] Shelford (*op. cit.*, pp. 25, 32) points out that for this reason behavior rather than structure should be the center of ecological research. Animals do not develop structural adaptations to an environment but behave so as to survive in the environment where they happen to be and with the structure which they happen to have. Of course, from a longer time point of view environment indirectly influences the morphology of the race by selection (see above, n. 55).

light of special circumstances, or learning by the individual, seems to be a characteristic of all organisms. The sharp distinction which earlier writers sought to make between intelligent and instinctive behavior tends to fade in the more recent investigations of the subject.[67]

On the other hand, the structure of an animal is little, if any, under individual control. It is a function of the genes, not of experience. A tiger cannot enlarge his claws or jaws, toughen his hide, or increase his weight, strength, or speed to any very great extent by individual effort. When, however, we consider a group as the unit making war, the distinction between preparation and utilization is less clear. While an individual ant cannot strengthen his shell, increase his mobility, or enlarge his mandibles, the size and organization of an ant army and the defensive structure of the nest is a problem of ant behavior, capable of change even within a generation. It is, therefore, very important to distinguish whether the unit making war is an organism or a group of organisms. If the defense unit is the individual animal, intraspecific hostilities are rare with the exception of birds, and in their relatively innocuous battles for territorial defense the pair often act together. If the defense unit is a family or social group, on the other hand, intraspecific war is common both within the group for sex and to a less extent for leadership or exploitation and outside the group for predation or defense. Except among gregarious or social animals, the species is the only distinguishable group beyond the family; consequently, if an animal is to recognize any exemptions from its aggressions beyond its immediate family, it necessarily exempts all its species. As intraspecific hostilities, if lethal, would usually be disadvantageous to the species, evolution has tended to develop such an exemption.

In the definition proposed for the technique of war the concept of a military instrument is important. Some writers have suggested that the technique of war is equivalent to the technique of survival, that it is the art of preparing for all contingencies endangering the unit, whether individual, social group, or species, and for utilizing them in emergencies. But instruments facilitating flight, concealment, mutual aid, fertility, though means of preserving individuals, groups, and species, would not usually be regarded as military instruments. If war is to be distinguished from other activities of organisms and groups, the concept of military instruments must be limited. In animal life the instruments and behaviors

<hr>

[67] Howard, *An Introduction to the Study of Bird Behavior*. Wheeler (*Social Life among the Insects*, p. 15) writes: "Human and insect societies are so similar that it is difficult to detect really fundamental biological differences between them," but see my comments below, sec. 4d. See also Holmes, *op. cit.;* Wallas, *op. cit.*, pp. 36 ff. "Give the apes just one thing—speech—and the bridge [to man] is closed" (Hornaday, *op. cit.*, p. 314). Yerkes and Yerkes find that apes lack speech and culture but have the physical bases for both (*op. cit.*, pp. 255, 302), and Zuckerman agrees, though he finds little evidence for considering apes superior to monkeys. Man's superiority results from his use of "cultural instruments" (speech, fire, tools) and perhaps from certain social habits (omnivorous diet and monogamous marriage) rather than from any physical differentiation (*Functional Affiliations of Man, Monkey and Ape* [New York, 1933], pp. 656 ff.).

ontributing to survival of the individual, society, or species are so interrelated
hat sharp analysis is exceptionally difficult.

A military instrument may be defined as a means used by an animal, or group
f animals, to destroy or to control by violence a similar animal or group of ani-
1als or to ward off such destruction or control.

The concept is confined to relations between animals. Relations between
•lants or between plants and animals, or between an animal and a geographic
rea, are excluded. A horse's teeth in so far as used to eat grass are not military
nstruments, and the fertility of jack rabbits, used gradually to occupy Australia,
; not a military instrument.

Destruction or control by violence means suddenly and against the will of the
rganisms controlled. The antennae of ants used to stroke aphids so as to induce
hem to yield nectar are not military instruments, and the same is true of all in-
truments employed in giving mutual aid between animals.

There must be some similarity between the enemies. Human beings do not
onsider the instruments used in butchering cattle military instruments. Only
1struments used to destroy or control other human beings in combat are con-
idered military. The military instruments of animals are regarded more broad-
y. From the standpoint of technique, animals of the same genus or even of the
ame order or phylum or perhaps even of similar size, however widely separated,
hould be regarded as sufficiently similar. The leucocytes, employed by animals
or destroying internal parasitic bacteria, would not, however, be military instru-
1ents, nor would the bear's tongue used for eating ants be such an instrument.
'he closer are the animals engaged in mutual violence to each other in the genet-
: scale and in general appearance, the more appropriate it is to classify the in-
truments used against one another as military. The illustration of the bacteria
1ggests that importance is attached to similarity rather than to equality in the
ght. Even though it is nip and tuck whether the man or the bacteria will win,
till the leucocyte would not be regarded as a military instrument.

Weapons of both defense and offense are included in the definition. This is
he usual practice in considering human war, although among animals it is more
ommon to exclude defensive instruments, such as the turtle's shell, from the
oncept.

The efficiency of a military instrument results from the total situation, the na-
ıre of the enemy, the area, and the combination of offensive and defensive ele-
ıents. An analysis of the elements composing a military instrument is neces-
arily arbitrary, but any useful comparison requires such an analysis. Striking
ower, mobility, protection, and holding power seem to be the essential elements
f a military instrument. The first three of these have been recognized by tech-
ical writers on human war.[68] They will be considered successively for individ-
al animals and for animal societies.

[68] Col. J. F. C. Fuller, *The Reformation of War* (New York, 1923), pp. 25 ff. Lotka
p. cit., pp. 358–61) analyzes the offensive power of an animal species by considering

WAR TECHNIQUE OF INDIVIDUAL ANIMALS

a) Striking power.—Striking power is the ability to paralyze, wound, or kill an enemy in spite of distance and defensive armor. While in human warfare the power may exist, when the enemy is at a distance, through the use of long-range guns, among animals the striking power lies in the use of jaws, claws, teeth, poison fangs, quills, stench, leap, charge, or hug when at close quarters.[69]

If striking power is highly developed in the individual, as in carnivorous animals, poisonous reptiles, wasps, bees, skunks, etc., violent behavior is normally practiced only on weaker animals of very different species or in self-defense from different species. Intraspecific hostilities with such weapons are rare.

b) Mobility.—Mobility is the power to move rapidly through space, irrespective of obstacles. It is most remarkable where the aerial space can be used as in birds and insects, next where the aquatic spaces can be used as in fish, whales, porpoises, seals, and least where only terrestrial areas can be moved in. Among terrestrial animals, however, there are great differences. Those adapted to the plains, such as antelopes and giraffes, and those adapted to arboreal life, such as apes and monkeys, have greater mobility than the inhabitants of the forest floor or mountains.

Great mobility is associated with frequent resort to intraspecific hostilities among animals, especially if such mobility is accompanied by comparatively little striking power. Such a combination robs war of its lethal character, and the mobility of the species renders it a good means of species dispersion. Thus

---

the field of influence (striking power), velocity (mobility), per cent of captures within the field of influence (tenacity), and defensibility (protection) of the individual animal and of the individual of the species preyed upon, with the conclusion that, if the total mass of the predatory species is constant, its offensive power will increase and its defensive power diminish with increase in number and diminution of the size of the individual animals—a conclusion scarcely consistent with the strategic principle of concentration (see R. E. Dupuy and G. F. Eliot, *If War Comes* [New York, 1937], pp. 28 ff.)

[69] Boulenger (*op. cit.*, pp. 92, 159, 197, 212) describes various offensive devices, and Emerson mentions a "specialized gas defense" of certain termites ("Social Coordination and Superorganism," *American Midland Naturalist*, XXI [1939], 184). Monkeys occasionally throw stones in combat (Letourneau, *op. cit.*, p. 15). Yerkes and Yerkes think apes are above monkeys in intelligence because of their tool-using habits, but Zuckerman (*Functional Affiliations of Man, Monkey and Ape*, pp. 124 ff.) doubts this. Pitt-Rivers, though recognizing that the use of missiles or other tools by animals is very rare, cites the cuttlefish, archer fish, llama, porcupine, polar bear, and monkey as possible exceptions (*op. cit.*, pp. 82 ff.). Instruments used in terrorizing propaganda or in destroying food, water, or other sources of existence might be regarded as instruments of striking power, and it has been suggested that the bright colors of some male animals may in this sense be an offensive weapon useful for scaring enemies away (Fisher, *op. cit.*, p. 139). But it seems better to confine the term "military technique" to methods and instruments for coercing an enemy by direct violence, thus excluding propaganda and economic techniques, however useful the latter may be in war.

under these conditions, hostilities, especially for territory, may be of value for race preservation.[70]

c) Protection.—Protective armor is the ability to withstand striking power and is found in the shell of the mollusks, the carapace of the tortoise, armadillo, or lobster, and the thick skin of the elephant, rhinoceros, and crocodile. Such equipment, being heavy, usually interferes with mobility, although it may be accompanied by considerable striking power and for short distances by considerable speed. Intraspecific hostilities among the heavily protected animals are rare. Orthogenic evolution in the direction of protective armor tends to an increase in size of the animal. This doubtless accounts for the usual tendency of all evolutionary lines to increase in size. The horse is much larger than Eohippus and the elephant is much larger than Moeritherium. The increase in size has meant that the animals' strength, which varies as the square of the muscle diameter, becomes less capable of managing its own bulk, which varies with the cube of the muscle diameter, and the animal becomes more clumsy. At the same time his food consumption increases and his habits become less flexible. The possibilities of an arboreal or subterranean existence or a change of diet decline. Consequently, as he becomes larger, he becomes more dependent on a particular environment and less capable of moving long distances to find a similar environment if his traditional habitat changes in character. Thus the advantages of heavy armor have not compensated for the losses through increasing size and declining mobility, with the result that many genetic lines specializing in this direction, such as the dinosaurs, the titantotheres, and the mastodons, have become extinct.[71] The disadvantages of bulk are less in an aquatic environment

[70] See above, n. 17.

[71] See an article on "The Size of Living Things" by Julian S. Huxley, *Atlantic Monthly*, CXLIV (September, 1929), 289, 301, which states: "Land vertebrates are limited by their skeletons which for mechanical reasons must increase in bulk more rapidly than the animals total bulk until it becomes unmanageable and water animals are presumably limited by their food getting capacities." See also Lotka (*op. cit.*, p. 297), who writes: "Unable to gather in a day's run sufficient food to fill their monstrous paunch, they became the victims of their colossal ambition." He also quotes J. B. S. Haldane to the effect that the vicious circle leading the dinosaurs to suicidal size may have been due to the steady increase of the pituitary gland. The secretions of this gland create size, size results in high blood pressure and capillary leakage, which is stopped by pituitrin. Thus those with a larger pituitrin secretion survived because capillary leakage was stopped, but with larger pituitary glands they became even bulkier, and so the orthogenetic pocess went on until they perished of hyperpituitarism. The rhinoceros is one of the most heavily protected of existing animals, and it seems likely that it will be among the first to become extinct because, relying on this protection, it approaches hunters from curiosity who, fearing that it intends to charge, kill it in self-defense. Its stupidity is in marked contrast to the intelligence of the elephant, which also is heavily protected (see Roosevelt, *African Game Trails*, pp. 102, 200). While defensive power increases with size, offensive power increases with numbers; thus, if total mass is limited, small size of units benefits the offensive (above, n. 68).

than on the land and greatest in the air. Thus, in general, aerial forms have specialized least in armor and in size. Aquatic forms, although often very large, are perhaps less likely to be heavily armored than terrestrial forms.

Protective devices other than armor, such as defensive camouflage or mimicry of the inorganic environment, plants, or other animals, found in many butterflies, other insects, rodents, and deer, and burrowing or flight to a prepared sanctuary, if successful, avoid hostilities altogether.[72] Exceptional mobility, especially into an element in which the pursuer cannot follow, is also a protective device. Thus, birds, bats, flying insects, seals, amphibians, and reptiles which live in two elements have a protective advantage as do terrestrial animals that can take to the trees or underground. These devices, however, should perhaps be excluded from military protection as propaganda should be excluded from military striking power.

d) Holding power.—Holding power is the ability to hold through time a desired object or territory or, conversely, ability to capture, destroy, or drive away all enemies threatening such possession. It is seen in the mongoose, who will hang onto a cobra's neck, in the bulldog, and in the boa constrictor. Among such animals intraspecific war is particularly uncommon. It would probably result in death by attrition of both, to the great detriment of the species. This is not the result, it is true, of fights utilizing territorial tenacity within species of birds and certain other animals, but the fact that such combats result in dispersion rather than in suicide of the species may be attributed rather to the mobility and innocuousness of the combatants than to their holding power. Furthermore, in such encounters it is only the original occupant, not the invader, which displays much holding power.

Thus among individual animals specialization in mobility, making for a war of maneuver, is particularly favorable to intraspecific war, while holding power, making for a war of attrition, is particularly unfavorable. Specialization in striking power, making for a war of pounce, and in protective armor, making for a war of shock, is moderately unfavorable.

The advantage which an animal will have in battle depends, of course, upon the particular combination of all these factors. An organism combining maximum mobility, maximum striking power, maximum holding power, and maximum protective armor would create a perfect fighting instrument, but these qualities in fact are more or less incompatible with one another, and selection has usually tended toward specialization in one. On the whole, it appears that genetic lines specializing in mobility and holding power have prospered most,

[72] See E. B. Poulton, *The Colours of Animals* (New York, 1890). Mimicry and other devices here considered are difficult to attribute to natural selection operating upon slight variations because enemies are not sufficiently discriminating and intermediate stages are usually lacking but rather to the natural selection of the complete forms arising because of the limited number of possible patterns which gene combinations can produce (R. C. Punnett, *Mimicry in Butterflies* [Cambridge, 1915], pp. 146 ff.; but see Fisher, *op. cit.*, p. 169).

although the first has maximized and the second minimized intraspecific hostility. Lines specializing in protective armor have prospered among certain invertebrates but not among large land animals. Species specializing in striking power have not greatly increased in number. Clumsiness and predatoriness have not characterized the most numerous species among the higher animals.

But better than any of these military instruments for preservation of the species has been the specialization in fertility and mutual aid. These two devices are to some extent incompatible. Mutual aid proceeds best when, as among insects and man, population is artificially limited, but fertility also has its advantages, and it perhaps remains a question whether the bacteria and the protozoa, specializing in unrestrained fertility or ants, and men, specializing in society, will eventually inherit the earth. The answer may depend upon the ability of the latter to comprehend the source of its strength and to eliminate the elements of superfertility, predatoriness, and parasitism whose persistence interferes with the full development of societies. The apparent dependence of social development upon the continuance of intersociety hostility renders the problem difficult.

WAR TECHNIQUE OF ANIMAL SOCIETIES

Where military techniques apply to a group, always more disposed than an individual to intraspecific hostilities, the effects of specialization in one or the other of the elements of military technique are less easy to see.

a) Collective striking power is illustrated by the march of driver ants, the armies of Amazon ants, the rush of the buffalo herd, and the maneuver of wolf packs. Violent behavior may occur between such groups of the same or closely related species usually for predacious or territory-maintaining purposes.

b) Collective mobility is not really found among animals. Each animal must move by its own power, but mass movement takes place and the effect is to create a greater striking power as in the instances cited. Writers have noted the greater momentum and persistence of migrating masses of animals. The mass seems to augment the mobility of each of its units. But, as has been noted, specialization toward such collective mobility is only incidentally related to hostile behavior.

c) Collective protective armor has the characteristics of a fort and is illustrated by the termitary with its walls of almost concrete hardness, often rising to a height of ten or fifteen feet, like a skyscraper. Nests and hives of other social insects are less formidable but nevertheless provide collective protection. The same is true of the beaver house, although among higher animals collectively made structures are not common.

Intraspecific hostilities may occur in groups relying on such defenses, either within the group or between groups, but on the whole they are not common. The use of collective armor prevents collective mobility and may have some of the disadvantages connected with the development of protective armor for the individual animal. Termites, relying upon the strength of the termitary, have on the whole been less successful than the ants, depending rather on mobility and adaptiveness. While ants are the most widely distributed animals, termites flourish in a more restricted zone.

d) Collective holding power may be associated with collective armor like the hard walls of a termitary. The inhabitants cannot easily be dislodged from the fortified territory. It may also be associated with mass mobility over a wide front. Such a movement effectively occupies a territory. Animals in the path of the driver ants find it difficult to escape. Collective ability to hold a territory and to utilize all of it may also arise from great fertility and wide dietary as among the locust and rabbits which will occupy an area to the exclusion of everything else, but the best illustration of collective tenacity is to be found in the loyalty of members of the society to the society. The termitary and the anthill persist through generations of workers because each labors for the whole. This tenacious loyalty to the group has been a major factor inducing intraspecific warfare. Members of the group within a nest or hive have a smell which can be distinguished from other members of the species. Thus the collective determination to keep the group as a unit has induced warfare within the species, although reducing it to a minimum within the society.

4. THE THEORY OF ANIMAL WARFARE

By the theory of war is meant the system of general propositions explaining the occurrence and methods of war. From the point of view of the participant the theory may make it possible to exercise some control over war and from the point of view of the observer it may make it possible to predict some of the phenomena of war.

There is no theory of animal warfare from the point of view of the participating animals. Professor W. M. Wheeler in his letter from Wee Wee, forty-third neotenic king of the 8,429th dynasty of the bellicose termites,[73] Rudyard Kipling, Ernest Thompson Seton, and others have attempted to elaborate such a theory by imaginative personification of animals.[74]

The theory of animal warfare from the point of view of the observer has been abundantly documented. This theory in its most general terms is the theory of evolution. At its root is the proposition that the fittest will survive in the struggle for existence or, more accurately, that the unfit will not survive.[75] Any bio-

[73] Wheeler, *Foibles of Insects and Men*, pp. 213 ff.

[74] Theodore Roosevelt's warning against "nature fakers" is well to have in mind in judging some of this material.

[75] See above, n. 53. The astronomer can best appreciate the relativity of the conceptions "fit" and "unfit." Suggesting that we "try to evaluate this mixture of biological and physical conflicts in the light of the stars—in the light of those points of the universe which best exemplify stability and endurance," Harlow Shapley ("Man and His Young World," *Nation* [New York], May 7, 1924) notes that from apelike ancestors to the editorial board of the *Nation* is at most a few million years, though some cynics think it much less. At any rate, compared to the 200,000,000 years of cockroaches, man's his-

logical entity, whether an individual animal, a species, a biological community, or a society, which fails to get sufficient food and to escape enemies and accidents, i.e., which fails to solve its economic and its political problems as they arise, will not survive. Any of these entities tends to engage in hostilities or to avoid hostilities when and if an opposite behavior would contribute to its extinction. This is merely a tendency or normative law, not an invariable law. Many have failed to observe it but at the price of eventual extinction. Some animals and societies now existing frequently violate the law, and the consequence may not be manifested immediately. There is no reason to infer that the actors in the drama of animal warfare consciously guide their conduct by this law. Human observers of the drama have, however, produced a voluminous literature on the causes of the survival of biological forms and of their evolution toward more perfect adaptation to their environments. In recent years such writers as Alfred J. Lotka, R. A. Fisher, and Sewall Wright have attempted to express some of the principles supported by these materials in mathematical form.[76]

In order to analyze the factors affecting the survival of a biological entity, it is necessary to have clearly in mind the types of biological entities under discussion. These include (a) individual animals, (b) species, (c) biological communities or biocoenoses, and (d) societies. Other types of biological entities, such as aggregations or close groups of animals not organized, as is a society, and not including all of the life in an area, as does a biocoenosis, closely resemble, from the present point of view, one or another of the four types considered. The word "aggregation" may be used as a comprehensive term to cover all of these four types if an individual animal is considered merely an aggregation of cells.[77]

These four types of entities are interrelated, but it by no means follows that the survival of one type will promote the survival of another. A biological community is made up of all the animals and plants of various species occupying a definite time-space. Consequently, its duration or the persistence of its character depends on the relative survival of these organisms, species, and societies. The survival of a particular animal, a particular species, or a particular society may

---

tory is short. There is a drift in the universe "the reward of which is survival of the individual, of the species, of the protoplasm." The human individual's survival is in any case too brief to be worth troubling about, and even the species by utmost co-operation with the drift has no chance in competition with the stars. In competition with other organisms "there is a fair chance, an optimistic scientist would say, if it were not that man's worst enemy is man."

[76] See Lotka, *op. cit.*; Fisher, *op. cit.*; S. Wright, "The Genetical Theory of Natural Selection," *Journal of Heredity*, XXI (August, 1930), 349–56; "Evolution in Mandelian Populations," *Genetics*, XVI (March, 1931), 97–159; "Statistical Theory of Evolution," *op. cit.*; "The Roles of Mutation, In-breeding, Cross-breeding and Selection in Evolution," *op. cit.*, pp. 356–66.

[77] See Allee, *Animal Aggregations*, for discussion of these terms. Emerson (*op. cit.*, pp. 182 ff.) points out the similarity of all in exhibiting dynamic equilibrium.

be of little importance to it. In fact, its stability depends upon the maintenance of equilibrium and is as much a function of the adequate elimination as of the adequate survival of its components. The same is true of species and of societies in relation to the individual animals which collectively compose them. Consequently, a pathic event or an antesurvival mode of behavior for one of these types of entities may be a beneficent event or a survival mode of behavior for another.[78] Before the survival value of behavior can be discussed, it is necessary to decide whose survival is being discussed. The same is true of the relation of man and the state; the survival of a particular individual may militate against the survival of the state and vice versa.

a) The survival of animals.—An individual animal, such as an elephant or a gnat, will survive in proportion as it is able to find food, to escape enemies and accidents, and to retain sufficient flexibility to adapt itself to climatic and other changes in its environment. The inherent conditions of its internal organization which determine that eventually it will die of old age are not here considered. So far as its survival is concerned, it may make little difference whether it leaves progeny, moves out or stays in a particular area, does or does not assist other animals. Its behavior in these respects may indirectly affect its own survival, but directly its survival, through a normal life-span, depends on its efficiency in solving its economic, political, and educational problems. Education refers to behaviors which adapt the animal to its existing environment and also to behaviors which maintain flexibility and adaptability. The latter aspect is of importance only if the animal's life-span is so long that significant environmental changes are likely to take place within it.

Individual animals promote their survival primarily through superior efficiency in the specializations, characteristic of the race, for food-getting and defense. The strongest lion, heaviest shelled tortoise, fleetest antelope, and most tenacious mongoose will tend to survive, although a point may be reached where such efficiency becomes suicidal because it renders the animal inflexible to environmental contingencies. A tortoise with a shell so heavy that it cannot move, a pathogenic bacteria so efficient that it kills its host before it can escape, a dinosaur so large that it cannot get food enough in a day to live, have each pushed specialization to the point of suicide.

The role of war with respect to the survival of individual animals appears, therefore, to be indeterminate. For predacious animals efficiency in preying is a desideratum and for herbivorous animals efficiency in fleeing combat is a desideratum, provided a certain flexibility of behavior is retained. Specialization of the race having reached a certain point, the individual cannot turn back. Consequently, evolution tends to move in orthogenetic lines.[79]

[78] G. K. K. Link, "The Role of Genetics in Etiological Pathology," *Quarterly Review of Biology*, VIII (June, 1932), 134, 136.

[79] There are, of course, exceptions. Hereditary change often results from random variations or occasional crossings of races which have diverged when divided by geographical barriers (see S. Wright, "The Roles of Mutation, In-breeding, Cross-breeding and Selection in Evolution," *op. cit.*).

b) The survival of species.—A species is a group of animals with continuity of interbreeding and with a certain similarity of organic structure. A species is often confined to a limited area, but some species such as man are distributed over the whole earth. As has been noted, both structural and behavioristic specialization for combat are, among animals, related primarily to species. A species to survive must solve not only the food, defense, and educational problems of its members but also their sexual problems. If the individuals of the species do not reproduce adequately, the species will die. A species, because of its long life, must expect many major changes in its environment, so retention of flexibility is more important for it than for the individual. Furthermore, a species must meet the problems of occupying the maximum of suitable habitats, of developing mutual aid relations within societies or aggregations of the species, and even of developing such relations among more distant biological entities in this area. Species survival involves not only economic, political, and educational problems but racial, territorial, and social problems as well.

Some species have survived with little change since earliest geological times, but most species have evolved to new specific forms. There appears to be a tendency toward sympodial[80] evolution, that is, the most rapidly changing lines become extinct and new lines are developed from a more primitive type. This tendency is due to the orthogenetic tendency of evolutionary specialization which usually results eventually in a suicidal degree of specialization.

If by preservation of a species is meant the preservation of a type of mature individual, adaptation to a type of environment likely to be persistent through geologic ages is the important element. If, on the other hand, by preservation of a species is meant preservation of a genetic line, moderation in the rate of change and maintenance of flexibility is the desideratum. Orthogenetic tendencies toward extreme specialization must be kept in check.

Vegetable food is more abundant than animal food, large aggregations provide shelter for reproductive activities and for care of the young, and co-operation facilitates the maintenance of large aggregations. Because of these circumstances, among large animals, species with a vegetarian diet and a social behavior have tended to outlive and outrange species relying upon predacious and parasitic specialization. Aggregations and societies tend to fix the significant environment of the individual. Consequently, orthogenetic tendencies of species utilizing these devices are kept in check and the species type is more persistent. The meek species, which confine their violent behavior to attacks upon vegetation and defense against other animals, never themselves resorting to aggression, tend to inherit the earth. While fighting has played a role in the survival of many species, belligerency has not been an element in the survival of the most numerous and most stable species.[81]

---

[80] This term was applied to evolution by Lester F. Ward by analogy to a form of growth in plants where the branch grows not from the terminal bud but from an axial bud.

[81] See above, n. 65.

c) The survival of biological communities.—A biological community or bio-coenosis such as a forest, a prairie, a pond, with its entire organic content, must solve not only its food, defense, and adaptation problems but also, like a species, territorial, social, and racial problems. It is rooted in the territory, its motion being confined to expansion along its edges. Consequently, it must correlate all its behavior to the potentialities of a particular area. It outlives the individuals and societies and sometimes even the species which compose it. So the racial problem of reproduction is important. Its character is usually determined by the dominant organic form within the area. The perpetuation of the biological community as a whole can, therefore, be regarded as the perpetuation of that dominance. The social problems of division of labor and of dominance are, therefore, important. Furthermore, the long life of the biocoenosis makes the preservation of its flexibility in the presence of radical climatic and geological change of great importance.

Observations of organic communities indicate that they often, on being started in a barren area, undergo rapid changes in the characteristics and relative numbers of constituent species and that, even when a point of stability is reached, slight environmental changes may set in motion changes in the characteristics of the biocoenosis often of an oscillating character. Allee, for instance, cites the cycle of changes occurring in the biological life of a tank of hay tea, exposed to the atmosphere, and of the aspen belt between the prairies of western Canada and the United States.[82]

The survival of a biocoenosis with fairly persistent characteristics depends primarily on its ability to exploit to the utmost the inorganic resources of the territory, to create an environment defended from any but the most radical cosmic changes, and to attract a wide variety of organic species with their populations in self-regulating equilibrium.

The most extensive types of terrestrial biocoenoses have been those dominated, respectively, by grasses, by trees, and by man. Apart from human intervention the forest appears to be more persistent than the prairie. The amount of rainfall is the main determining factor. The trees reach deeper into the soil with their roots, thus making available a larger supply of inorganic materials. The forest leaf cover more efficiently photosynthesizes the sunlight falling on the area, and the forest floor more efficiently conserves the water supply. The greatest variety of plants and animal species develop in such an area, especially at the forest margin which provides an abundance of stable environments of different characters at different levels. This abundance of species provides superior opportunities for gradual development of the relative significance of existing forms in order to adapt the biocoenosis to changing cosmic conditions. The resistance of trees to wind and the protection they offer to the inhabitants of the area from any but the most radical changes of climate is also an element important for

---

[82] See Allee, *Animal Life and Social Growth.*

preservation of the whole. The forests normally tend to encroach upon prairies under natural conditions. They succumb only to man.

The biocoenosis dominated by civilized man is able to control the forests as well as the prairies. Savage man was merely a member of a prairie or a forest biocoenosis, and even agricultural human societies have struggled against the forest, as witness Kipling's story of "Letting in the Jungle." Civilized man, however, has dominated both. He is the first animal that has dominated any terrestrial organic community with the possible exception of limited areas dominated by sea birds, by ants, or by very prolific herbivorous animals, such as the American bison, capable of controlling the growth of vegetation.

Because of the fact that most biocoenoses have been dominated by plants which can hardly be said to fight, the direct role of war in the survival of the biocoenosis is confined to that latest type dominated by man. The preservation or extension of a particular type of terrestrial organic community has been an important factor in human war.[83]

Even in more primitive biocoenoses, however, combat plays a secondary role in maintaining equilibrium among the animal species, facilitating their distribution throughout the biocoenosis and expanding it around the edges. If most species were not the natural food of others, the great variety of animal life, valuable for the survival of a biocoenosis, could not continue. A few species would soon crowd all the others out. Thus, while herbivorous species are at an advantage in the competition among species, from the standpoint of a biocoenosis the existence of predacious species is also important.

d) The survival of animal societies.—A society is an organized group of animals of the same species, although animals of other species sometimes perform essential services for the dominant species.[84] It resembles an individual animal in the orderly division of labor among its parts, a species in the similarity of its organic constituents, and a biological community in its close attachment to a definite territory, although animal societies whether insect or human are usually capable of movement.

The peculiarity of a society lies in the fact that its members subordinate their individual activities to co-operative activities for preserving the society as a whole, but without complete absorption of the individual animals. The problems of division of labor, sometimes involving dominance and subordination, and of reproduction are of outstanding importance because upon them depends the maintenance of the balance between the individual and the society.

[83] The invasion of parts of the Americas, Africa, and Oceania by western Europeans, of parts of Manchuria, Mongolia, and Malaya by Chinese, of parts of Palestine by Jews, and of parts of Siberia by Russians has greatly altered the animal and vegetable life in these areas. The process of change is discussed in I. Bowman, *The Pioneer Fringe* (New York, 1931) and *Limits of Land Settlement* (New York, 1937).

[84] See Wheeler, *Social Life among the Insects*, pp. 198 ff.

War has probably played a more important role in the preservation of societies than it has in the preservation of either individuals or biological communities. It has been an agency for promoting internal solidarity and also for maintaining external defense and sources of food.[85] Nevertheless, societies, both insect and human, have varied greatly in their dependence upon this device, and on the whole it appears that societies have survived the longest that have succeeded in substituting other devices for both of these purposes. Wheeler finds that predacious and parasitic ant societies have been relatively unsuccessful, the hunting and pastoral modes of ant subsistence giving way, under the stern law of survival, to the agricultural. The same evolution is to be observed in human societies.[86] In other respects, however, the two types of society indicate important differences. Ant societies are in general more highly organized and less given to intraspecific hostilities than human societies. Is it likely that human societies, which are relatively much more recent in the history of the world, will develop in a similar direction?

A major difference between the two types of society lies in the fact that ants communicate only over short distances, especially by the senses of smell and feeling, while human beings communicate at a distance by the senses of sight and hearing, aided by various methods of writing, electrocommunication, and power locomotion.[87] This has given human societies the capacity to expand over larger areas beyond the range of direct contact and at the same time to multiply opportunities for conflict between such societies. Ants cannot organize beyond the nest, while the human organization may extend to the world. Each anthill in its restricted area generally has little contact with the other hills.

Another difference lies in the fact that an ant society has usually developed from a single queen. The society's life has, therefore, been limited to the fertile life of that queen or in rare cases to the lives of one or two of her successors. Its members, however, have necessarily been genetically homogeneous, and the social instincts have tended to evolve continuously. Human societies, on the other hand, have developed from individual matings. This favors variety among the members of the society and permits genetic selection within the society; continuous adaptation of the society to new conditions and immortality are therefore possible.[88] This possibility, however, has not been realized in civilized societies. Superior fertility, which has determined the genetic evolution of the soci-

---

[85] "External danger is the force which compels animals to become collective; they are enabled to overcome the danger by means of mutual help and division of labor" (Franz Alexander, paraphrasing Sigmund Freud, "A Note on Falstaff," *Psychoanalytic Quarterly*, II [1933], 605). See also Letourneau, *op. cit.*, p. 16, and above, n. 31.

[86] Wheeler, above, n. 65.

[87] Wheeler, *Social Life among the Insects;* Lotka, *op. cit.*, pp. 363, 365, 378, and table opposite p. 410, illustrating artificial elaboration of man's "receptors," "effectors," and "communicators."

[88] See Fisher, *op. cit.*, pp. 180 ff.; Lotka, *op. cit.*, pp. 414 ff.

ety, has not usually been associated with traits making the individual of superior social value. Individuals with high intelligence and broad social outlook have often had the fewest offspring. Sometimes social institutions, such as religious celibacy, have encouraged this condition. Furthermore, social complexity has usually tended to routines of social procedure tending to suppress originality. There seems to be a tendency for the very growth of a society to favor the belligerent and the unimaginative in respect both to relative numbers and to relative influence. As social complexity has increased with the widening area of the society, both the hereditary and the acquired characteristics of the population have become less capable of adapting the society to changes incident upon this increasing complexity, and the society has eventually collapsed.[89]

A third difference related to that just mentioned lies in the fact that division of labor has among the ants been pushed to the structural differentiation of castes through heredity and infant feeding,[90] while in human societies division of labor is neither genetic nor structural. It has been a product of social stratification and education which has seldom obliterated the individual's awareness of his varied functional potentialities, even though most of them remain unrealized.

Ant societies with their social reproductive system have not been troubled with internal dissension, but, on the other hand, they have seldom endured through more than one or two generations of queens and have rarely if ever produced geniuses to invent new modes of social behavior. Ant societies today seem closely to resemble those of fifty million years ago, a fact which may be taken as evidence of the extreme conservatism and inflexibility of ant society. There are however more ants in the world today than there are individuals of any other multicellular animal. This success of the ants in the struggle for existence with little organic or social change may be taken as evidence of the extraordinary perfection which ant society had achieved at a remote age. Human societies with their individual reproductive system are beset by frequent civil dissensions arising from divergent tastes and aims of their members. In spite of this, they have often endured for scores of generations. This may be attributed to the wide opportunity for genetic selection, to the considerable variation in the character of successive generations, to the frequent production of genius, and to the conscious adaptation of education and institutions to changing conditions made possible by an individualistic reproductive system.[91]

[89] Fisher, *op. cit.*, chaps. x and xi; Corrado Gini, "The Cyclical Rise and Fall of Population," in *Population* ("Harris Foundation Lectures" [Chicago, 1930]); Walter Lippmann, *The Good Society* (New York, 1937), pp. 60–63; below, n. 95.

[90] There is some doubt whether the castes of social insects are genetically different (Emerson, *op. cit.*, p. 186).

[91] Wheeler (*Social Life among the Insects*) indicates high admiration for ant and termite societies, but Alexander (*op. cit.*) considers the state of the termites as "a horrible nightmare." In explaining the universal human urge for preserving the antisocial in-

An ant society is like an individual organism in that its unity is dependent upon conditions which confine it to a limited time and space which assure it a uniform genetic character, and which provide it with an adequate functional differentiation of parts. Personal contact, harmonious internal relations, and a period of development followed by senescence and death are as inherent in the structure of the ant society as in that of multicellular organisms, which can in fact be considered a society of protoplasmic cells. A human society, on the other hand, resembles a biological community in that it owes its unity to continuous modification of its organization. Such modifications are necessary to reconcile the divergent individual and social tendencies of the society's components and to preserve its distinctive character in the face of continuous interpenetration of and interdependence with other communities. A human society is *sui generis*, however, in that intelligence is added to natural selection as a major equilibrating device. If a human society is to persist, it must continually produce inventors to modify its institutions in response to new conditions. Human society has been less stable than that of the ants, but, on the other hand, it has a potential extension as broad as the world and a potential duration as long as geological and meteorological conditions are suitable for human life on the planet.[92]

The evolution of societies like that of species has tended to move in orthogenetic lines, molding the form and behavior of their members to the type of

---

dividualism of primitive human nature illustrated by the character of Falstaff, Alexander compares termite and human societies as follows: "The termites are perhaps one of the weakest biological beings. Even the ants, who have an armored hard body, can destroy these soft helpless beings. The external danger is the force which compels animals to become collective; they are enabled to overcome the danger by means of mutual help and division of labor. Why should man, who considers himself the crown of creation, who has no serious enemy among living beings except his fellow man, submit to a similar renunciation of his individuality? He is composed of cells which already have renounced entirely their individual independence for the sake of the whole. This new higher unity, the composite human cell-state, seems to be such a successful experiment of nature that there is hope that it will be able to safeguard, at least to a certain degree, man's independence and permit him to escape the fate of the termites" (p. 606). Lotka gives a more objective evaluation of the two types of social adjustment—the ant based on adequate inheritance of social instincts and the human based on intelligent pursuit of self-interest (*op. cit.*, pp. 414 ff.). See also Fisher, *op. cit.*, pp. 180 ff.

[92] Julian Huxley points out that, while ants and men have both adapted themselves to all parts of the world, "in man each new mode of life requires only a new habit and tradition flowering out of the old germ plasm while in the insect it demands a new species with change of germ plasm." Thus while there is now only one human species, and in all times have been less than half a dozen, there are probably ten thousand species of ants. "The social insects thus exploit the world as a group of separate species in uncombinable biological units, man as a single biological unit, the separateness of whose various groups is in the main transitory and preventable" ("Are Ants like Men?" *Discovery* [London], XI [March, 1930], 72).

specialization which has become established. It is probable that ants and men, rather than converging to a common type of society, will persist in the direction of the peculiarities of social organizations which each has developed. Ant societies will tend to rely even more on the intense and inflexible social solidarity which has served them well for so many years. Human societies, on the other hand, will tend to rely even more on the development of intelligence and the power of conscious adjustment of society to new conditions, sacrificing to that end the efficiency of intense social specialization and solidarity. Human beings will continue to stress instinct less and intelligence more than do the ants.[93]

Biological advocates of both socialism and individualism for human society have not been wanting. Doubtless here, as in most cases, a *via media* can be found. Human societies need not choose between the extreme socialism of the ant, admired by Wheeler, and the extreme individualism of nineteenth-century laissez faire, admired by Herbert Spencer and given some support by R. A. Fisher.[94] Individualism is necessary to give an opportunity for the continuous evolution of intelligence, but intelligence, like most other lines of specialization, may be pushed too far. If pushed to the extent of accepting no values without demonstration intelligence might result in group suicide.[95] The most intelligent persons in human civilizations have sometimes failed to perpetuate themselves, thus leaving the burden of continuing the society upon genetically decadent generations, incapable of preserving the civilization bequeathed them even if they wished.[96] With the foresight of intelligence they have hesitated to take risks even when the preservation of the society calls for courage and sacrifice.[97] The substitution of intelligence and reason for instinct and faith may, if too thoroughgoing, terminate the society, the civilization, or even the race. Social institutions capable of maintaining a sense of the community's essential values and of maintaining the interest of the socially competent in reproduction may be essential for the continuity of human societies.[98] Reason and faith, intelligent

[93] Both Lotka and Fisher (above, n. 91) seem to believe that man, having begun to build his society on intelligent self-interest, must continue to do so.

[94] See above, n. 91. For classic statement of individualism see Herbert Spencer, *Social Statics* (1st ed., 1850). A more qualified statement has been made by Lippmann, *op. cit.*

[95] P. W. Bridgeman, "The Struggle for Intellectual Integrity," *Harper's Magazine*, December, 1933, pp. 18 ff.; Lotka, *op. cit.*, pp. 431, and quotation from Veblen, *ibid.*, p. 395; Wallas, *op. cit.*, pp. 37 ff.; J. W. Krutch, *The Modern Temper*, quoted in *New Republic*, October 11, 1939, p. 264.

[96] Above, n. 89.

[97] Pacifism to a degree suicidal to the state has been urged by leading philosophers (see Bertrand Russell, *Which Way to Peace?* [London, 1936], p. 144; see also above, chap. x, n. 43).

[98] Fisher, *op. cit.*, chap. xii; Graham Wallas (*op. cit.*) suggested on the eve of World War I, which he anticipated, remedies for the situation resulting from the fact that in

self-interest and emotional social conscience, must continually react on each other.

Though human society has diverged from that of the insects, it can maintain balance by studying the sources of their stability. In one respect it may converge toward them. The experience of both suggests that survival is promoted by minimizing predation, parasitism, and other forms of violent behavior.[99]

---

the Great Society to which man is imperfectly adapted "the human material of our social machinery will continue to disintegrate just at the points where strength is most urgently required. Men whom we are compelled to trust will continue to prefer the smaller to the larger good" (p. 13).

[99] See above, n. 65.

APPENDIX VIII

ANALYSIS OF PSYCHOLOGICAL DRIVES
AND MOTIVES

A drive is a characteristic of the adult members of a class of organisms manifested in the similarity and relative stability of their responses to similar concrete situations. Drives result from the similar conditioning of common inherited tendencies throughout a population. A particular drive, therefore, will characterize the members of a population only in so far as they have a similar heredity and environment. As the responses of no two individuals is ever precisely the same, the identification of drives results from classification of the behaviors of the members of such a population. Those behaviors which are considered sufficiently similar to be grouped for the purpose in hand constitute a drive.

The effort to identify the drives, sentiments, motives, faculties, instincts, or other elements which together constitute "human nature" is as old as human thought. These words have different connotations and may imply different philosophies, but under them all lies the thought of an analysis of human nature which will explain both the similarities and the differences of personality which men must have observed since they began to live in groups.

According to modern terminology, an appropriate conditioning of inherited human tendencies creates the normal drives behind social institutions and organizations; education is the process by which such conditioning is effected, and abnormalities in the drives or in their relationships account for much psychopathic and antisocial behavior. Improved knowledge of drives may, therefore, assist in developing social institutions, in improving education, in conducting propagandas, in explaining the differences of societies and groups, in determining vocational aptitudes, and in remedying abnormalities of individual behavior. The most useful definition of the drives may prove to be different according as attention is directed toward the uniformity or toward the variety of personality.[1]

Knowledge of human nature was at first gathered from introspection or from observation of the working of familiar social institutions. More recently controlled studies have been made of animals, of children, and of primitive peoples. The mental patterns of adults in civilized communities have been studied through careful recording of prolonged interviews or through utilization of objective tests and questionnaires. This body of material has provided a broad basis for comparison and analysis with a view to distinguishing the organic, human, cultural, and individual elements of personality and the drives characteristic of a given group.

[1] See John Dewey, "Human Nature," *Encyclopaedia of the Social Sciences.*

Aristotle assumed essential differences in the nature of persons, of different sex, class, or group; the Stoics and Christians assumed essential equality among human beings; and recent biologists and psychologists have found that men have many traits in common with other animals. It has, however, been recognized that traits may vary in intensity and combination by heredity and may be subjected to a great variety of modifications through environmental conditioning. Human personalities differ at birth, and further differences result from experience. Classifications of personality types are, therefore, possible and are indicative of the traits regarded as important by the classifier.[2]

Because of the variety of purposes and methods in studying drives, the influence of popular language and traditional categories, and the inherent difficulties of analyzing so intangible a phenomenon as personality, it cannot be said that any list of drives has been generally accepted. It cannot even be said that the drives (together with wants, attitudes, motives, and interests) which collectively account for the individual's response to his environment have been distinguished from other personality traits such as the capacity for sensation, perception, memory, imagination, conception, feeling, attention, judgment.[3] Different writers have discriminated all the way from one to fifty drives, and the various lists often show little relation to one another.[4]

Biologists have tended to relate the primary drives to the processes of *nutrition, reproduction,* and *protection* (Wheeler).[5] Social philosophers have often based their systems on one or two complex drives or dispositions such as *reason*

---

[2] Among such classifications are those by Kretschmer, based on physical characteristics (cyclothymic associated with pycnic build and schizothymic associated with asthenic and athletic builds); by Alfred Adler, based on attitudes toward one's own physical characteristics (over- and undercompensated inferiority complexes); two by Carl Jung, based, respectively, on sources of values (introverts and extroverts) and on dominant psychic process (thinking and feeling or "rational" types; sensory and intuitive or "irrational" types); and by A. H. Maslow (high, middle, and low dominants), based on "dominance feeling" which is distinguished from "cultural dominance status," "dominance behavior" which may result from compensations, and "desire for dominance" (see Edward Sapir, "Personality," *Encyclopaedia of the Social Sciences;* Horace Kallen, "Psychoanalysis," *Encyclopaedia of the Social Sciences;* A. H. Maslow, "Dominance-Feeling, Behavior, and Status," *Psychological Review,* XLIV [July, 1937], 404 ff.).

[3] It has been doubted whether these "states of consciousness" assumed by "structural psychologists" can be abstracted from the "stream of behavior" studied by the "functionalists" and "behaviorists." See E. B. Holt, *The Freudian Wish and Its Place in Ethics* (New York, 1915), pp. 3–56; J. B. Watson, "The Psychology of Wish Fulfillment," *Scientific Monthly,* III [1916], 479–86, reprinted in part in R. E. Park and E. W. Burgess, *Introduction to the Science of Sociology* (Chicago, 1921), pp. 478 and 482; Edward L. Thorndike, *The Psychology of Wants, Interests and Attitudes* (New York, 1935), p. 3; Appen. VII, nn. 4 and 5.

[4] See L. L. Bernard, "Instincts," *Encyclopaedia of the Social Sciences.*

[5] See above, chap. v, n. 1.

(Grotius), *fear* and *greed* (Hobbes), *sympathy* and *utility* (Adam Smith), *pleasure* and *pain* (Bentham), *habit* (Maine), *love* (Comte), *altruism* (Kropotkin), *will-to-power* (Nietzsche), *imitativeness* (Tarde), *suggestibility* (LeBon), *gregariousness* (Trotter), *constructiveness* and the *instinct of workmanship* (Woodworth, Veblen), and *acquisitiveness* (Tawney).[6]

Psychologists such as James, Kilpatrick, and MacDougal made long lists of instincts or the inherited element of drives. The latter mentioned *flight, repulsion, curiosity, pugnacity, self-abasement, self-assertion,* the *parental instinct, reproduction,* the *gregarious instinct, acquisitiveness,* and *constructiveness.* E. L. Thorndike discusses these and other lists, producing an even longer one of his own but emphasizing the malleability through education of most of the original traits of human nature.[7] Freud emphasized *hunger, sex,* and the *social* instincts as the principal constituents of the id or original personality, but analyzed the various manifestations of these empirically into the *ego instincts,* which are directed toward self-preservation, and the *object instincts,* which are concerned with relations to external objects (discussed by Ruml as the *egoic* and *nostalgic* sentiments, respectively). "Theoretical speculation," writes Freud, "leads to the suspicion that there are two fundamental instincts which lie concealed behind the manifest ego-instincts and object-instincts; namely, (*a*) *Eros,* the instinct which strives for ever closer union, and (*b*) the instinct for destruction, which leads toward the dissolution of what is living" (*death*).[8]

Recently psychologists have attempted by factor-analysis methods to ascertain the least number of independent drives which will account for the major types of personality.[9] A. H. Maslow, applying such a method to the results of empirical studies of monkeys and human beings, finds that *dominance, activity, sociability,* and perhaps *sex* are factors which vary independently in intensity and that combinations of the appropriate intensity of each can account for the principal personality types.[10] These factors may be compared to the analyses

[6] Graham Wallas, *The Great Society* (New York, 1917), chap. v.

[7] *The Original Nature of Man* (New York, 1913), pp. 16 ff. He classifies these drives, each of which is described as a relatively precise connection between a definite stimulus and a definite behavior, under these heads: (1) sensitivity; (2) attention; (3) gross bodily control; (4) food-getting and habitation; (5) fear, fighting, anger; (6) human intercourse; (7) satisfaction and discomfort; (8) minor bodily movments and cerebration; (9) emotions and their expression; and (10) consciousness, learning, remembering (pp. 43 ff.). To illustrate the type of analysis under each head, he finds that the "fighting" response (5) results from (1) restraint of activity; (2) interference by moving object; (3) being seized, slapped, or chased; (4) suffering pain; (5) awareness of a rival; (6) jealousy of male during courtship; and (7) continuous thwarting of purposes (pp. 68 ff.).

[8] Sigmund Freud, "Psychoanalysis," *Encyclopaedia Britannica* (14th ed.); Kallen, *op. cit.;* Beardsley Ruml, "The Nostalgic and Egoic Sentiments," paper read to American Psychological Association, September 7, 1933.

[9] See L. L. Thurstone, *The Vectors of Mind* (Chicago, 1935).   [10] *Op. cit.*

of personality by social psychologists. W. I. Thomas distinguished four fundamental wishes, *recognition, new experience, security,* and *response.*[11] The drives of
dominance, activity, self-preservation, and *sex* are respectively similar. Independence, food, territory, and society are related to self-preservation, though territory and society also have a close relationship to sex, and independence to
activity and dominance.

These drives have been distinguished mainly in terms of the need felt by the
organism in a given situation driving it to action. A drive, however, consists of a
flow of behavior from awareness (physiological or psychological) of one situation, known as the stimulus, through various internal changes of the organism,
to the response affecting the external environment and satisfying the wish.[12] The
stimulating situation may be analyzed into two elements: (1) awareness through
the senses (sight, hearing, smell, taste, touch, pain) of some external circumstance, as the proximity of food or of a dangerous enemy, and (2) awareness
through the feelings (glandular or hormonic activity) of a need such as hunger or
a need of food, fear or need to be alert to danger. The response may also be analyzed into two elements: (3) the want, or internal response through attention,
and preparation to act; as the desire for food or for bodily security, and (4) the
overt response as the acts of searching for, seizing, and eating food or of flight
from or resistance to attack.

These aspects of the drive flow into each other imperceptibly. A feeling or
need is a stimulus. Attention to this feeling constitutes a want and is the begin-

[11] "The Persistence of Primary Group Norms in Present Day Society," in Jennings,
Watson, Meyer, and Thomas, *Suggestions in Modern Science concerning Education*
(New York, 1917), restated in Park and Burgess, *op. cit.,* pp. 488 ff. "Apparently these
four classes comprehend all the positive wishes. Such attitudes as anger, fear, hate, and
prejudice are attitudes toward those objects which may frustrate a wish. Our hopes,
fears, inspirations, joys, sorrows, are bound up with these wishes and issue from them.
There is, of course, a kaleidoscopic mingling of wishes throughout life, and a single given
act may contain a plurality of them. Thus when a peasant emigrates to America he may
expect to have a good time and learn many things (new experience), to make a fortune
(greater security), to have a higher social standing on his return (recognition), and to
induce a certain person to marry him (response). The 'character' of the individual is
determined by the nature of the organization of his wishes. The dominance of any one
of the four types of wishes is the basis of our ordinary judgment of his character" (*ibid.,*
p. 490). H. G. Lasswell reduces the classes of wishes to three—safety, income, and
deference (*World Politics and Personal Insecurity* [New York, 1935], p. 3).

[12] "Behaviorism proposed the S-R (stimulus-response) formula as the simple pattern of all behavior and assumed that this formal statement was adequate. It ignored
the vital factor of the organism, which decisively, and in each type of organism dis-
tinctively, determines which of all the physical and generally environmental forces shall
act as stimulus (S), and what the manner (including the absence) of response shall be.
The true formula is S-O-R, stimulus-organism-response. The 'Gestaltist' recognized
that the integration pattern—which is the Gestalt—is present from the outset" (Joseph
Jastrow, "Psychology," *Encyclopaedia of the Social Sciences,* XII, 595).

ning of response. Need and want usually seem to be identical if viewed introspectively, because one becomes aware of his needs only after he has focused attention upon them. They have then become wants. For the observer, however, needs and wants may be very different. A physician may know that the patient needs something which he does not want. Introspectively one is aware of wants, but behavioristically one observes needs.

TABLE 4
RELATION OF DRIVES AND RESPONSES

DRIVES		WISHES	
Stimulus	Need	Want	Response
Sight of food	Hunger	Desire for food	Seizing and eating food
Sensing proximity of member of opposite sex	Sexuality	Desire for sexual activity	Approach to and mating with member of opposite sex
Observation of intrusion upon home	Territoriality	Desire for security of home	Attack upon intruder
Sensing proximity of friend, rival, or enemy	Activity	Desire for movement, play, fighting, or adventure	Acts of restlessness, playing, or fighting
Sensing of immanent danger	Fear	Desire for bodily security	Flight from or resistance to attack
Sensing threat to society	Gregariousness	Desire for social security	Resistance to attack on or disruption of society
Observation of insubordination	Dominance	Desire for submission of associates	Strutting, bullying, or attack upon subordinate
Suffering from oppression	Freedom	Desire for independence	Sulking, resentment, migration, or attack upon superior

The terms "stimulus" and "response" are used in a narrow sense to denote, respectively, the sensory awareness and the external response which can be described by external observation of the organism. The terms "need" and "want" are used to denote, respectively, the affective awareness and internal response of the organism which can only be described by introspection or physiological examination, and which together may be called its "affectivity." Table 4 analyzes these aspects of each of the eight drives.

The terms "drive" and "wish," while each is used in a broad sense to denote the psychological pattern responsible for the entire process from stimulus to completed response, are used in narrower senses to refer, respectively, to the organism's "receptivity" and "adaptivity" patterns.[13] Drives, in this sense, are the patterns resulting from a conditioning of the organism by heredity and experience promptly to receive situations presented with relative frequency by the environment. Wishes, in the narrow sense, are the patterns resulting from a conditioning of the organism promptly to adapt its behavior successfully to deal with such situations. Since wishes can be best studied by introspection or interviews, the term, and others related to it, are in the main confined to human psychology. Drives, on the other hand, can be studied by observation, and so the term is commonly used in comparative psychology dealing with animals as well as with man.

Drives and wishes are related to other terms frequently employed in functional psychology. Each of these terms has numerous connotations, but the relationship of several of them to the terms "drives" and "wishes" may be indicated by emphasizing the generality, stability, and origin of the patterns they denote.[14]

Dispositions and *motives* refer to general patterns of the personality applicable in a variety of situations, while *interests* and *attitudes* refer to patterns applicable to more concrete situations, symbols, or objects. The term "disposition" suggests considerable intervention of the characteristics of the particular organism between stimulus and response. Consequently, it is often considered more suitable when dealing with human behavior than the more general term "drive."[15]

Motives like wishes are characteristics of the personality which account for its adaptive reactions. Wishes, however, as used by psychoanalysts, manifest

[13] See R. M. Yerkes, "Comparative Psychology," *Encyclopaedia of the Social Sciences*.

[14] It cannot be expected that this or any other simple classification will exhibit all the relationships between these terms.

	BEHAVIOR PATTERNS CLASSIFIED ACCORDING TO:					
	Generality		Stability		Origin	
	General	Concrete	Permanent	Changeable	Hereditary	Acquired
Drives	Dispositions	Interests	Beliefs	Impressions	Instincts	Habits Reasons
Wishes	Motives	Attitudes	Purposes	Opinions	Emotions	Sentiments Intentions

[15] Wallas (*op. cit.*, pp. 21, 22) uses the term "disposition" to refer to "facts of the human type" which together constitute "human nature." He, however, excludes "acquired elements" from the conception. "At no period of his life does a man's 'nature' actually exist. . . . . The man at any given moment is the result of the action of his experience on his nature." Wallas' conception of "complex dispositions," of dispositions adapted to new situations, and of dispositions developed by "acquired powers," suggests, however, a wider usage of the term (p. 52).

the unity of the personality in adapting to different situations. The wishes are persistent, however much they may be repressed or sublimated.[16] Motives, on the other hand, emphasize the disunity of the personality. The term has been associated with introspective analysis and suggests the struggle of opposing tendencies within the personality as a result of which one motive eventually triumphs and controls action in a given situation.

The analysis of dispositions and motives tends to become stabilized in a given culture and to acquire ethical implications. This analysis changes as the culture changes, but there may be considerable lag in the rejection of an old and acceptance of a new analysis by persons within the culture. In periods of rapid cultural change a variety of analyses of motives may be prevalent. Today the traditional distinction between good and bad motives, the utilitarian distinction between rational and irrational motives, and the Freudian distinction between reasonable and rationalizing motives are all current and result in considerable confusion. Everyone tends to judge his own behavior by the system of analysis on which he was brought up and the behavior of others by the most recent system of which he has read. Thus any social judgment of motives becomes paralyzed.[17]

Interests differ from dispositions in that they refer to concrete external situations rather than to general patterns of the organism or personality. The term "interest" may be used subjectively to refer to an object, symbol, or situation which a given person considers himself interested in, or objectively to refer to something which a given culture assumes that persons are interested in. In the latter sense the classification of interests and motives tends to become the same. Culturally approved motives tend to be reflected in culturally protected interests. The acquisitive motive is reflected in the protection of concrete property interests. The sexual and parental motives are reflected in the protection of concrete marital and family interests.

Classifications of both motives and interests change in a dynamic and self-conscious society; consequently, an individual's interpretation of his interests in a given situation may differ from that which society assumes. Furthermore, both the individual and the society may interpret motives according to a classification different from that applied to interests. A person may, because of the system of motives impressed upon him by early training, act contrary to what he now considers his interests.

Attitudes, like interests, are concrete; but, like motives, they refer to the organism or personality rather than to the situation. An individual's attitude to-

[16] J. B. Watson, "The Freudian Wish," in Park and Burgess, *op. cit.*, pp. 452 ff. Social psychologists consider that wishes may frequently conflict; consequently, they make little distinction between wishes and motives (see quotations from William James and W. I. Thomas, *ibid.*, pp. 486, 490).

[17] See Kenneth Burke, *Permanence and Change: An Anatomy of Purposes* (New York, 1936), chap. ii.

ward the numerous objects, persons, symbols, and ideas within his experience may be characterized as favorable, unfavorable, or indifferent in varying degrees of intensity and persistence.[18] Like motives and interests, attitudes tend to become socially conditioned and stabilized.[19] The attitudes of the members of a group toward symbols, ideas, and persons may be thought of collectively as the attitude of the group. When formulated, this constitutes its public opinion.[20]

The terms "motive," "interest," and "attitude" lend themselves to more refined analysis than do the terms "drive" and "wish" because they imply distinctions discoverable only by introspection. Consequently, in proportion as the self-consciousness of the group develops and the speed of social change increases, there is an advantage in using these terms—an advantage gained, however, at the expense of objectivity.

Beliefs and *purposes* are relatively stable patterns of the personality persistent over a considerable period of time, while *impressions* and *opinions* are more likely to change in short periods. Opinions are usually intended to influence others. Consequently, the term implies an overt, usually a verbal, expression. This expression may or may not correctly represent the attitude of the person who formulates it. A person's opinions may, however, constitute the only available evidence of his attitudes.

Instincts and *emotions* are inborn, inherited, innate, or original patterns of the organism or personality little affected by experience, while *habits*, *reasons*, *sentiments*, and *intentions* are patterns developed through experience.

The terms "belief" and "reason" refer to patterns consciously relating behavior to a situation. They are often used by historians. The terms "purpose" and "intention" refer to patterns consciously relating means to ends preceding actual or potential action. They are often used by lawyers to place responsibility for an act. Examination of the beliefs, reasons, purposes, and intentions of a person cannot, however, yield a complete analysis of the causes of behavior. They neglect the unconscious and irrational aspects of personality.

[18] L. L. Thurstone, "Attitudes Can Be Measured," *American Journal of Sociology,* XXXIII (1928), 532 ff.; "The Measurement of Social Attitudes," *Journal of Abnormal and Social Psychology,* XXVI (1931), 249 ff.; S. A. Rice, *Methods in the Social Sciences* (Chicago, 1931), pp. 460, 586, 726.

[19] See L. L. Bernard, "Attitudes, Social," *Encyclopaedia of the Social Sciences.*

[20] J. T. Russell and Q. Wright, "National Attitudes in the Far Eastern Controversy," *American Political Science Review,* XXVII (August, 1933), 555 ff.

APPENDIX IX

RELATION BETWEEN WARLIKENESS AND OTHER CHARACTERISTICS OF PRIMITIVE PEOPLES

Over six hundred and fifty distinctive primitive peoples* have been arranged alphabetically by continents and described with respect to warlikeness and other characteristics in Table 5. This is followed by tabulations indicating the relation between warlikeness and continental location (Table 6), temperature (Table 7), natural habitat (Table 8), climatic energy (Table 9), race (Table 10), culture (Table 11), political organization (Table 12), social organization (Table 13), and intercultural contacts (Table 14). The meaning of these characteristics is indicated in the notes to Table 5. The concepts "warlikeness" and "race" are further examined in Appendixes X and XI. The significance of the relationships here exhibited is discussed in chapter vi.

* *Primitive people.*—The concept "primitive people" is described in chap. vi. In practice the list of peoples given by Hobhouse, Wheeler, and Ginsburg (*The Material Culture and Social Institutions of the Simpler Peoples* [London, 1915]) has been here adopted. For the facts concerning these groups the writer has, where possible, utilized that book. In addition, much material on cultural, racial, and sociological characteristics has been conveniently collected in Deniker (*The Races of Man* [London, 1901]); Haddon (*The Races of Man and Their Distribution* [New York, 1925]); Keane (*Man, Past and Present* [Cambridge, 1900] and *Ethnology* [Cambridge, 1916]); Max Schmidt, (*The Primitive Races of Mankind* [London, 1926]); W. Schmidt and W. Koppers (*Volker und Kulturen*, Vol. I: *Gesellschaft und Wirtschaft der Volker* [Regensburg, 1924]); and the *Encyclopaedia Britannica* (14th ed.). Further material on racial characteristics has been utilized from Dixon (*The Racial History of Man* [New York, 1923]); Hooton (*Up from the Ape* [New York, 1932]); Huntington (*The Character of Races* [New York, 1924]); Taylor (*Environment and Race* [Oxford, 1927]); and on military characteristics from Marett (*Psychology and Folklore* [London, 1920]); Davie (*The Evolution of War* [New Haven, 1929]); Dyk ("A Study of the Effect of Change of Technique on the Warfare of Primitive Peoples" [unpublished, 1931]); Hoijer ("The Causes of Primitive Warfare" [unpublished, University of Chicago Library, 1929]); Spencer (*The Principles of Sociology* [3d ed.; New York, 1896]); Sumner and Keller (*The Science of Society* [4 vols.; New Haven, 1927]). These general ethnological books have been supplemented by books and articles dealing with the ethnology of more restricted areas of which the more useful have been: *Asia*—Buxton (*The Peoples of Asia* [New York, 1925]); Cole (*The Tinguian* ["Field Museum Anthropological Series," Vol. XIV, No. 2]); Crooke (*Natives of Northern India* [London, 1907]); Hose and McDougal (*The Pagan Tribes of Borneo* [London, 1912]); Hutton (*The Angami Nagas* [London, 1921]); Kroeber (*Peoples of the Philippines* [New York, 1928]); Mills (*The Ao Nagas* [London, 1926] and *The Lhota Nagas* [London, 1922]); Philippine Islands, *Census* (Manila, 1921]); Radcliffe-Brown (*The Andaman Islanders* [Cambridge, 1922]); Risley (*The Peoples of India* [London, 1915]); Skeat and Blagdon (*Pagan Races of the Malay Peninsula* [London, 1906]); Thurston (*Castes and Tribes of Southern India* [7 vols.; Madras, 1909]): *Australia*—Curr (*The Australian Race* [4 vols.; Melbourne, 1886]); Howitt (*The Native Tribes of South-east Australia* [London, 1904]); Radcliffe-Brown ("The Social Organization of Australian Tribes," *Oceania*, Vol. I); Spencer and Gillen (*The Native Tribes of Central Australia* [London, 1899] and *The Northern Tribes of Central Australia* [London, 1904]); Warner ("Murngin Warfare," *Oceania*, I [1931], 457 ff.): *Oceania*—Malinowski ("War and Weapons among the Natives of the Trobriand Islands," *Man*, January, 1920, pp. 10–12); Seligman (*The Melanesians of British New Guinea* [Cambridge, 1910]); Wedgwood ("Some Aspects of Warfare in Melanesia," *Oceania*, I [1930], 5 ff.): *Africa*—Keane (*Africa* [London, 1895]); Hunter (*Reaction to Conquest: Effects of Contact with Europeans on the Pondo of South Africa* [London, 1936]); Roscoe (*The Bagesu and Other Tribes of the Uganda Protectorate* [Cambridge, 1924]); Torday (*African Races*, descriptive sociology or groups of sociological facts classified and arranged by Herbert Spencer [London, 1930]): *North America*—Kroeber (*Handbook of the Indians of California* [Smithsonian Institute, Bureau of American Ethnology, Bull. 78 (Washington, 1925)]); Powell ("Indian Linguistic Families," *Seventh Annual Report of the Bureau of Ethnology* [Washington, 1885–86]); Swanton (*Indian Tribes of the Lower Mississippi* [Bureau of American Ethnology, Bull. 43 (Washington, 1911)]); Hodge (*Handbook of the Indians North of Mexico* [Bureau of American Ethnology, Bull. 30]); *South America*—Church (*Aborigines of South America* [London, 1912]); Metraux (*La Civilisation materielle des tribus Tupi-Guarani* [Paris, 1928]); Thurn (*Among the Indians of Guiana* [London, 1883]). In some cases there was considerable difficulty in identifying the same group in different books because of differences in spelling or different naming. The spelling of Hobhouse, Wheeler, and Ginsburg is used primarily. Other names and spellings are sometimes cross-referenced. Where the same group appears twice, it is because branches of it seemed to have different cultural or other characteristics; thus, in reality, it constituted more than one 'people' under a common name.

TABLE 5

CHARACTERISTICS OF PRIMITIVE PEOPLES

ASIA AND INDONESIA	Region†	Character of War‡	ENVIRONMENT			RACE		CULTURE		ORGANIZATION		
			Climate§	Habitat‖	Climatic Energy¶	Race**	Subrace††	Culture‡‡	Subculture§§	Political‖‖	Social¶¶	Intercultural Relation***
Abakan Tartars	3	E	C	G	M	Y	N	P	L	....	C	M
Abkhases	4	S	T	M	M	W	A	A	L	....	C	M
Abors (see Padam Abors)												
Adighe	4	E	T	G	M	W	A	A	H	V	C	C
Aeneze	5	E	T	D	L	W	M	P	L	T	C	I
Aeta (see Negritos of Negros and Alabat)												
Agusan (see Manobos of Agusan)												
Ainu	2	S	T	G	M	B	A	A	L	T	P	I
Alabat (see Negritos of)												
Albay (see Negritos of)												
Alfures	13	S	H	F	L	Y	S	A	H	T	....	I
Altaian Kalmucks	3	E	T	M	M	Y	N	P	H	T	....	M
Andamanese	11	S	H	F	L	P	N	H	L	C	S	I
Angama Nagas	10	S	T	M	L	Y	S	A	H	V	....	M
Angat (see Negritos of)												
Ao Nagas	10	S	T	M	L	Y	S	A	M	V	C	M
Arunese	....	....	....	....	....	....	....	A	L	T	C	....
Arunese	....	....	....	....	....	....	....	A	M	T	C	....
Atkwar	....	S	H	....	L	....	S	H	D	V	P	C
Badjus	16	....	H	S	....	Y	S	A	M	....	....	....
Badoga	7	S	H	M	L	H	D	A	H	T	....	M
Bagobos	16	S	H	F	L	Y	S	A	H	....	C	M
Balinese	13	S	H	F	L	Y	S	A	H	T	C	I
Baluchis (see Biloch)												
Bataks (see Karo Bataks)												
Bataks of Palawan	11	S	H	F	L	A	P	H	D	T	P	C
Bataks of Sumatra	12	E	H	F	L	Y	S	A	H	T	C	M
Bengal Tharu (see Tharu of)												
Benya	....	S	H	....	L	....	....	H	D	V	P	C
Bhills	8	E	H	G	L	A	P	A	L	V	P	I
Bhuiyar	....	S	H	....	L	....	....	H	D	T	P	C
Biloch	6	E	H	G	L	B	I	P	L	V	C	M
Birhor	9	S	H	F	L	H	D	A	L	....	....	M
Boksas	....	....	....	....	....	....	....	A	M	....	....	....
Bonthuks	7	D	H	M	L	H	D	H	D	V	P	C
Bontoc	16	E	H	M	L	A	P	A	M	T	....	M
Bugis	15	E	H	S	L	Y	S	A	H	T	C	M
Bukit (see Orang Bukit)												
Bungians	....	....	....	....	....	....	....	A	H	....	C	....
Buriats	3	E	T	G	M	Y	N	P	L	....	C	M
Bygas	8	S	....	....	....	....	....	A	L	....	....	....
Calingas	7	S	H	....	L	H	D	A	M	V	....	C
Camarines (see Negritos of)												

TABLE 5—*Continued*

ASIA AND INDONESIA —*Continued*	Region†	Character of War‡	ENVIRONMENT Climate§	Habitat‖	Climatic Energy¶	RACE Race**	Subrace††	CULTURE Culture‡‡	Subculture§§	ORGANIZATION Political‖‖	Social¶¶	Intercultural Relation***
Candios								A	L	V		
Catalanganes	16							A	M			
Central Sakai	11	D	H	F	L	A	P	A	L	T	S	M
Chakma	10	S	T	M	M	Y	N	A	M	T		M
Chenchu	7	E	H	M	M	Y	D	H	D	T	P	C
Chewssures	3	E	T	D	M	Y	N	P	L	V	C	M
Chukchi (*see* Tuski)												
Chuvanzi (*see* Shahsewenses)												
Circassians (*see* Adighe)												
Daians								A	H		C	
Dhimals	10	S	T	M	M	Y	S	A	M	T		M
Dodonga								A	M			
Dophla								A	M		C	
Dumagat (*see* Negritos of)												
Dusun	14	S	H	F	L	Y	S	A	H			M
Dyaks (*see* Sea and Land Dyaks)												
Engano	16	S	H	S	L	Y	S	A	M	T	C	I
Erivan (*see* Kurds of)												
Flores	13	S	H	S	L	N	P	A	M	T	C	I
Garontalo (*see* Java, Garontalo)												
Garos	10	E	H	M	L	Y	S	A	H	V	C	M
Ghiliaks	2	D	T	G	M	B	S	A	H	V	C	I
Gold	2	S	T	F	M	B	A	H	H	C	S	M
Gonds	8	P	H	M	L	A	P	A	M		S	M
Guinane	16		H		L			A	M			
Iban (*see* Sea Dyaks)												
Igorots	16	E	H	M	L	B	I	A	H	T	C	M
Irulas	7	S	H	M	L	A	P	H	D		P	C
Irulas	7	S	H	M	L	A	P	A	M			M
Italmen	2	S	C	F	L	B	A	H	H	T	C	I
Italones								A	M			
Itelmi (*see* Italmen)												
Jakun	11	D	H	F	L	Y	S	A	L	T	S	M
Java, Garontalo	13	E	H	F	L	Y	S	A	H	T	C	M
Juang	7	S	H	M	L	A	P	A	L	L		M
Kabards	3	E	T	D	M	B	A	P	L		C	I
Kachari	10	S	T	M	M	Y	S	A	M		C	M
Kafirs	6	E	T	M	M	B	I	A	H	T	C	C
Kalmucks (*see* Altaian Kalmucks)												
Kalyo Nagas	10	S	T	M	L	Y	S	A	M	V	C	M
Kami	4	E	T	G	M	Y	N	A	M	T	C	M
Kandhs	8	S	H	M	L	A	Y	A	M	T	C	M
Kara Kirghiz	3	E	T	M	G	Y	P	P	H	T	C	C
Kardar		E	H		L		N	H	D		P	C

TABLE 5—*Continued*

ASIA AND INDONESIA —*Continued*	Region†	Character of War‡	Climate§	Habitat‖	Climatic Energy¶	Race**	Subrace††	Culture‡‡	Subculture§§	Political‖‖	Social¶¶	Intercultural Relation***
Karens (*see* Red Karens)												
Karo Bataks	12	E	H	F	L	Y	S	A	H	....	C	M
Kasias	10	S	T	M	M	Y	S	A	H	S	C	M
Katodi	..	S	H	...	L	....	....	H	D	....	P	C
Kaupui Nagas	10	S	T	M	L	Y	S	A	M	V	C	M
Kayans	14	S	H	F	L	Y	S	A	H	T	C	M
Kayans of Mahakam	14	S	H	F	L	Y	S	A	H	T	C	M
Kayans of Mindalam	14	S	H	F	L	Y	S	A	H	T	C	M
Kazak Kirghiz	3	E	T	G	M	Y	N	P	H	T	C	C
Keddah Semang	11	D	H	F	L	P	N	H	H	T	S	I
Keddah Semang	11	D	H	F	L	P	N	A	L	T	S	I
Kei	15	S	H	S	L	N	P	A	M	T	C	L
Kenyah	14	S	H	F	L	B	I	A	H	T	C	M
Kharrias	9	S	H	M	L	A	P	A	H	....	....	M
Kharwar	9	S	H	G	L	A	P	A	M	T	....	M
Khiva	3	P	T	D	M	W	A	A	H	S	C	M
Khonds	8	S	H	M	L	A	P	A	M	T	V	M
Kiangans	..	..	..	..	..	..	..	A	M	V	C	...
Kirghiz (*see* Kara and Kazak Kirghiz)												
Klementan (*see* Land Dyaks)												
Kocch (*see* Pani Kocch)												
Kolarians (*see* Kols)												
Kols (*see also* Munda Kols)	18	E	H	M	L	A	P	A	M	T	....	M
Kols, Northwest	8	E	H	M	L	A	P	A	M	....	....	M
Korantes	9	S	H	G	L	A	P	A	M	....	....	M
Koras (*see* Korantes)												
Korumba	7	E	H	M	L	A	P	H	D	V	P	C
Korwa	10	S	H	....	L	A	P	H	D	T	P	C
Kuala Kurnam Sakai	11	D	H	F	L	A	P	A	L	C	S	M
Kubu	12	D	H	F	L	A	P	H	L	C	S	I
Kubu	12	D	H	F	L	A	P	A	L	V	S	M
Kuki	10	S	T	M	M	Y	S	A	L	T	P	M
Kurds of Erivan	4	E	T	G	M	W	A	P	L	T	C	C
Lahupa Nagas	10	S	T	M	L	A	S	A	M	V	C	M
Land Dyaks	14	S	H	F	L	B	I	A	M	T	C	M
Larbas	..	..	..	..	..	..	..	P	H	....	....	...
Lepcha	10	S	T	M	M	Y	S	A	M	....	....	M
Lhota Nagas	10	S	T	M	L	Y	S	A	M	V	C	M
Limbus	10	S	T	M	M	Y	N	A	M	....	....	M
Maghs	9	E	T	M	M	Y	S	A	M	....	....	M
Maguindanaos	16	P	H	F	L	Y	S	A	H	S	C	M
Mahakam Kayans (*see* Kayans of)												
Majhwar	..	..	..	..	..	..	..	A	M	T	....	M
Malays	12	E	H	F	L	Y	S	A	H	T	C	M
Mangkassares	15	E	H	S	L	Y	S	A	H	T	C	M

TABLE 5—*Continued*

ASIA AND INDONESIA —*Continued*	Region†	Character of War‡	Climate§	Habitat‖	Climatic Energy¶	Race**	Subrace††	Culture‡‡	Subculture§§	Political‖‖	Social¶¶	Intercultural Relation***
			ENVIRONMENT			RACE		CULTURE		ORGANIZATION		
Manobos of Agusan....	16	S	....	F	L	Y	....	A	L	V	C	....
Manobos of Rio Bay...	16	S	H	F	L	Y	S	H	H	V	C	I
Mantra...............	11	D	H	F	L	Y	S	A	L	T	C	M
Marea................								A	L	....	....	....
Mentawez............	12	E	H	S	L	B	I	A	M	V	S	I
Midhi................								P	H	V	C	....
Milanos..............	14	S	H	F	L	B	I	A	M	....	C	M
Mindalam Kayans (*see* Kayans)												
Miris of the Hills......	10	S	T	M	M	Y	S	A	H	....	....	M
Miris of the Plains.....	10	S	T	G	M	Y	S	A	H	....	....	M
Mishmis..............	10	S	T	M	M	Y	S	P	H	T	....	M
Munda Kols..........	8	S	H	G	L	A	P	A	H	T	....	M
Muruts...............	12	S	H	F	L	Y	S	A	M	....	....	L
Nagas (*see* Angami, Ao, Kalyo, Kaupui, Lahopa, Lhota, Sema)												
Negritos of Alabat.....	16	S	H	F	L	P	N	H	L	V	S	I
Negritos of Albay......	16	S	H	F	L	P	N	H	L	C	S	I
Negritos of Angat......	16	S	H	F	L	P	N	H	L	C	S	I
Negritos of Camarines..	16	S	H	F	L	P	N	H	L	C	S	I
Negritos of Dumagat...	16	S	H	F	L	P	N	H	L	V	S	I
Negritos of Negros.....	16	S	H	F	L	P	N	H	L	C	S	I
Negritos of Zambales...	16	S	H	F	L	P	N	A	L	C	S	N
Negros (*see* Negritos of)												
Niadi.................		S	H	....	L	....	....	H	D	....	P	C
Nias.................	12	S	H	S	L	Y	S	A	H	T	C	I
Nicobarese...........	11	S	H	S	L	Y	S	H	H	C	S	I
Nicobarese...........	11	S	H	S	L	Y	S	A	M	C	S	I
Nundail..............		S	H	....	L	....	....	H	D	V	P	C
Orang Bukit..........	11	D	H	F	L	Y	S	A	L	V	C	M
Orang Bukit..........	11	D	H	F	L	Y	S	A	M	....	....	I
Oraons...............	9	S	H	G	L	A	P	A	M	....	C	M
Osettes..............	4	E	T	G	M	Y	N	A	H	T	C	C
Ostyak...............	1	S	C	G	L	B	A	P	L	....	S	I
Padang Malays (*see* Malays)												
Padem Abors..........	10	S	T	M	M	Y	S	A	H	T	C	M
Paharia..............	9	S	H	M	L	A	P	A	M	....	....	M
Palawan Bataks (*see* Bataks of Palawan)												
Pani Kocch...........	10	S	T	M	M	Y	S	A	M	T	C	M
Paniyans.............	7	S	H	F	L	A	P	A	L	T	....	M
Passumahians.........						Y		A	H	T		
Pathans..............	6	E	H	G	M	B	I	A	A	V		C
Perak Sakai..........	11	D	H	F	L	A	A	H	H	T	S	I
Perak Sakai..........	11	D	H	F	L	A	A	H	L	T	S	M
Punan...............	14	D	H	M	L	B	I	H	L	C	S	I
Red Karens...........	9	S	T	F	L	Y	N	A	M	....	C	M

TABLE 5—*Continued*

ASIA AND INDONESIA —*Continued*	Region†	Character of War‡	Environment			Race		Culture		Organization		
			Climate§	Habitat‖	Climatic Energy¶	Race**	Subrace††	Culture‡‡	Subculture§§	Political‖‖	Social¶¶	Intercultural Relation***
Rio Bay (*see* Manobos of)												
Sakai (*see also* Perak, Central and Kuala Kurnam Sakai)......	11	D	H	F	L	A	P	H	L	C	S	M
Samales..............	16	S	H	S	L	Y	S	A	M		C	M
Samoyedes...........	1	S	C	D	L	B	A	P	L		C	I
Santals.............	9	E	H	G	L	A	P	A	L	T		C
Santals.............	9	E	H	G	L	A	P	A	M	T		C
Sea Dyaks...........	14	E	H	S	L	Y	S	A	M	T	C	M
Sema Nagas..........	10	S	T	M	L	Y	S	A	M	V	C	M
Semang (*see also* Keddah Semang)...........	11	D	H	F	L	P	N	H	L	C	S	I
Shahsewenses.........	3	S	C	G	L	B	A	P	L	T	C	I
Singkel.............	12	P	H	F	L	Y	S	A	H	S	C	C
Singphos............	10	S	T	G	M	Y	N	A	H	V	C	M
Soligas.............								A	L			
Sonthals............	9	E	H	G	L	A	P	A	H	V		C
Suanes.............								A	H	T	C	
Subanos............								A	M		T	
Sumatra (*see* Battas)												
Tagals..............	14	S		F	L	Y	S	A	M		C	M
Tartars (*see* Abakan Tartars)												
Teleuts.............	3	E	C	G	M	Y	N	A	M			C
Tharu of Bengal.......	8	S	T	G	L	H	D	A	M			M
Tharu of Northwest....	8	S	T	G	M	H	D	A	M			M
Timorese............	13	S	H	F	L	Y	S	A	H	V	C	I
Tinguians	16	S	H	M	L	Y	S	A	H			M
Tinos (*see* Zambales)												
Tipperah............	9	S	T	M	M	Y	S	A	H			M
Tjumba.............		D						A	H			
Toda...............	7	S	H	G	L	B	I	P	L		C	M
Toungtha............			H			Y	S	A	M		C	
Turkomans...........	3	P	T	G	M	Y	N	P	H	V	C	C
Tuski..............	2	S	C	G	L	B	A	H	H	C	C	I
Uzbegs.............	3	E	T	G	M	Y	N	P	H	T	C	C
Veddah.............	7	S	H	F	L	A	P	A	L	C		I
Vilee..............		S						H	D			C
Waralis.............								A	M			
Yakuts.............	2	E	C	D	L	Y	N	P	H	V	C	M
Yanadi.............	7	E	H	G	L	H	D	P	D	T	P	C
Yourouks............	1	S	C	G	L	B	A	P	L			C
Zambales, Tinos (*see also* Negritos of).........	16	E	H	F	L	Y	S	A	L		C	M

TABLE 5—*Continued*

AUSTRALIA	Region†	Character of War‡	ENVIRONMENT			RACE		CULTURE		ORGANIZATION		
			Climate§	Habitat‖	Climatic Energy¶	Race**	Subrace††	Culture‡‡	Subculture§§	Political‖‖	Social¶¶	Intercultural Relation***
Ballardong		S				A	A	H	L		S	I
Bangerang	4	S	T	F	H	A	A	A	H	L		S	I
Bantamura		S				A	A	H	L	C	S	I
Belyanda River	8	S	H	F	L	A	A	H	L		S	I
Bunalong	4	S	T	H	F	A	A	H	L	T	S	I
Bungyarlee		S				A	A	H	L		S	I
Central Australia	2	S	H	D	L	A	A	H	L		S	I
Chepara	7	S	T	F	M	A	A	H	L		S	I
Darling River	6	S	T	F	M	A	A	H	L		S	I
Darwin (*see* Port Darwin)												
Dieri	3	S	T	G	L	A	A	H	L	T	S	I
East Victoria (*see* Victoria)												
Encounter Bay	3	S	T	F	M	A	A	H	L		S	I
Etecup	1	S	T	F	M	A	A	H	L		S	I
Euahlayi	1	S	T	D	L	A	A	H	L		S	I
Geawegel	6	S	T	F	M	A	A	H	L	T	S	I
Goulborn	6	S	T	F	M	A	A	H	L	V	S	I
Gournditchmara	4	S	T	F	H	A	A	H	L		S	I
Gringai	6	S	T	F	M	A	A	H	L	T	S	I
Herbert River	8	S	T	F	L	A	A	H	L	C	S	I
Jackson (*see* Port Jackson)												
Jupagalk	4	S	T	F	H	A	A	H	L		S	I
Kabi		S				A	A	H	L	C	S	I
Kamilaroi	6	S	T	F	M	A	A	H	L	C	S	I
Karabara	7	S	T	F	M	A	A	H	L	V	S	I
King George's Sound	1	S	T	F	M	A	A	H	L	C	S	I
Koynup	1	S	T	F	M	A	A	H	L		S	I
Kurnai	4	S	T	F	H	A	A	H	L	C	S	I
Lincoln (*see* Port Lincoln)												
Maryborough	7	S	T	F	L	A	A	H	L		S	I
Milya Uppa		S				A	A	H	L		S	I
Mukjarawint	4	S	T	F	H	A	A	H	L		S	I
Murngin	2	S	H	G	L	A	A	H	L	C	S	I
Mycoolon		S				A	A	H	L	T	S	I
Narrangi	3	S	T	F	M	A	A	H	L		S	I
Narrinjerri	3	S	T	F	M	A	A	H	L	V	S	I
New Castle	6	S	T	F	M	A	A	H	L		S	I
New South Wales	6	S	T	F	M	A	A	H	L	V	S	I
New South Wales	6	S	T	F	H	A	A	H	L	V	S	I
Ngumba		S				A	A	H	L		S	I
Ngurla		S				A	A	H	L		S	I
North Queensland (*see* Queensland)												

TABLE 5—*Continued*

AUSTRALIA—*Continued*	Region†	Character of War‡	Climate§	Habitat‖	Climatic Energy¶	Race**	Subrace††	Culture‡‡	Subculture§§	Political‖‖	Social¶¶	Intercultural Relation***
			Environment			Race		Culture		Organization		
Northern Australia	2	S	H	D	L	A	A	H	L	T	S	I
Northwest Central Queensland (*see* Queensland)												
Perth	1	S	T	F	M	A	A	H	L	C	S	I
Port Darwin	2	S	H	G	L	A	A	H	L	....	S	I
Port Jackson	6	S	T	F	M	A	A	H	L	....	S	I
Port Lincoln	3	S	T	D	M	A	A	H	L	C	S	I
Powell's Creek	7	S	H	G	L	A	A	H	L	T	S	I
Queensland	8	S	H	F	L	A	A	H	L	....	S	I
Queensland, North	8	S	H	F	L	A	A	H	L	T	S	I
Queensland, Northwest Central	8	S	T	G	L	A	A	H	L	V	S	I
Queensland, South	7	S	T	G	L	A	A	H	L	....	S	I
Riverina	....	S	....	....	....	A	A	H	L	V	S	I
South Queensland (*see* Queensland)												
Swan River	1	S	T	F	M	A	A	H	L	C	S	I
Tasmania	5	S	T	F	H	P	N	H	L	C	S	
Tatuthi	6	....	T	F	M	A	A	H	L	....	S	I
Theddora	4	S	T	F	H	A	A	H	L	....	S	I
Tongaranka	6	S	T	D	L	A	A	H	L	C	S	I
Turbal	7	S	T	F	M	A	A	H	L	C	S	I
Turra	....	S	....	....	....	A	A	H	L	....	S	I
Victoria, East	4	S	T	F	H	A	A	H	L	....	S	I
Victoria, West	4	S	T	F	M	A	A	H	L	V	S	I
Waaka	....	S	....	....	....	A	A	H	L	C	S	I
Waimbaio	4	S	T	F	H	A	A	H	L	....	S	I
Wakelbura	8	S	H	F	L	A	A	H	L	C	S	I
Walgal	6	S	T	F	H	A	A	H	L	....	S	I
Wallaroi	3	S	T	D	L	A	A	H	L	....	S	I
Warburton River	7	S	H	D	L	A	A	H	L	....	S	I
Watchandee	....	S	....	....	....	A	A	H	L	V	S	I
Wayook	....	S	....	....	....	A	A	H	L	....	S	I
West Victoria (*see* Victoria)												
Western Australia	....	S	T	F	M	A	A	H	L	C	S	I
Wide Bay	7	S	T	F	L	A	A	H	L	....	S	I
Wiradjuri	6	S	T	F	M	A	A	H	L	....	S	I
Wotjobaluk	4	S	T	F	H	A	A	H	L	V	S	I
Wudthaurung	4	S	T	F	H	A	A	H	L	....	S	I
Wurunjerri	4	S	T	F	H	A	A	H	L	....	S	I
Yantrawanta	3	S	T	D	L	A	A	H	L	T	S	I
Yara Yara	....	S	....	....	....	A	A	H	L	....	S	I
Yerkla Mining	3	S	T	F	M	A	A	H	L	V	S	I
Yerwaka	....	S	H	D	L	A	A	H	L	T	S	I
Yuin	6	S	T	F	H	A	A	H	L	T	S	I

TABLE 5—*Continued*

OCEANIA	Region†	Character of War‡	Environment			Race		Culture		Organization		
			Climate§	Habitat‖	Climatic Energy¶	Race**	Subrace††	Culture‡‡	Subculture§§	Political‖‖	Social¶¶	Intercultural Relation***
aining	2	S	H	F	L	N	P	A	L	C	C	I
artle Bay	1	S	H	S	L	N	P	A	M	V	C	I
ogadjim	1	S	H	F	L	N	P	A	M	C		I
ugotu			H	S	L			A	M			I
ijians	2	P	H	S	L	N	P	A	M	S	C	M
lorida	2	S	H	S	L	N	P	A	M	T		I
azelle Peninsula	2	S	H	S	L	N	P	A	M	C		I
ilbert Islands	4	S	H	S	L	B	P	A	M	T	C	I
awaiians	4	P	H	S	L	B	P	A	M	S	C	M
bim	1	S	H	F	L	N	P	A	M	V		I
auralaig	1	S	H	S	L	N	P	H	H	V	C	I
oita	1	S	H	F	L	N	P	A	M	T		I
ouisiades	2	S	H	S	L	N	P	A	M			I
acklay Coast	1		H	S	L			A	M			I
lafulu	1	S	H	M	L	N	P	A	M	C		I
lalo	1	S	H	S	L	N	P	A	M		C	I
aoris	3	P	H	S	L	B	P	A	M	T	C	M
arquesas	4	E	H	S	L	B	P	A	M	V	C	I
arshall Bennett	2	S	H	S	L	N	P	A	M	T		I
arshall Islands	5	S	H	S	L	Y	S	A	M	V	C	I
ekeo	1	S	H	F	L	N	P	A	M			I
elanesians, Southern	2	S	H	S	L	N	P	A	M			I
oanu			H	S	L			A	M	V	C	I
otu	1	S	H	F	L	N	P	A	M	V		I
owat			H	S	L			A	M	T		I
urray Islands	2	S	H	S	L	N	P	A	M			I
aaiabui			H	S	L			A	M			
eu Pommern	2	S	H	S	L	N	P	A	M			I
euforesen	2	S	H	S	L	N	P	A	H	V	C	I
ew Caledonians	2	S	H	S	L	N	P	A	M	T	C	I
ew Hebrides	2	S	H	S	L	N	P	A	M			I
ew Mecklenberg, North	2	S	H	S	L	N	P	A	M			I
ew Mecklenberg, South	2	S	H	S	L	N	P	A	M			I
ew Zealand (*see* Maoris)												
eleu Islands	5	S	H	S	L	N	P	A	M			I
arotongans	4	S	H	S	L	B	P	A	M	T	C	I
oro	1	S	H	F	L	N	P	A	M	T		I
otumians	4	S	H	S	L	B	P	A	M	T		I
aa			H	S	L			A	M			I
t. Christóbal	2	E	H	S	L	H	P	A	M			I
amoa	4	E	H	S	L	B	P	A	M	S		M
avage Islands	4	E	H	S	L	B	P	A	M	C		I
olomon Islands, Southeast	2	S	H	S	L	N	P	A	M		C	I
ulka	2	S	H	S	L	N	P	A	M	V		I
ahitians	4	P	H	S	L	B	P	A	M	S	C	I

TABLE 5—*Continued*

OCEANIA—*Continued*	Region†	Character of War‡	Environment			Race		Culture		Organization		
			Climate§	Habitat‖	Climatic Energy¶	Race**	Subrace††	Culture‡‡	Subculture§§	Political‖‖	Social¶¶	Intercultural Relation***
Tongans.............	4	S	H	M	S	B	P	A	M	S	C	M
Torres Group.........	2	S	H	S	L	N	P	A	M	T	....	I
Torres Straits (*see* Kauralaig, West Torres Straits)												
Trobriand Islands......	2	S	H	S	L	N	P	A	M	V	....	I
Tubi Tubi............	2	S	H	S	L	N	P	A	M	....	....	I
Waga Waga...........	1	S	H	S	L	N	P	A	M	C	....	I
West Torres Straits....	1	S	H	S	L	N	P	A	L	V	C	I
Woodlark Islands......	2	S	H	S	L	N	P	A	M	....	....	I
AFRICA												
Ababua..............	3	E	H	F	L	N	N	A	H	T	C	C
Abandia.............	3	E	H	G	L	N	N	A	M	....	....	C
Adio................	3	E	H	G	L	N	N	A	M	T	....	C
Akamba.............	5	E	H	G	M	N	N	A	H	T	C	M
Akikuyu (*see* Wakikuyu)												
Alur................	3	E	H	G	L	H	H	A	H	T	P	C
Ama Xosa...........	6	P	T	G	M	N	N	P	H	T	C	M
Ama Zulu...........	6	P	T	G	M	N	N	P	H	S	C	M
Amahlubi...........	6	P	T	G	M	H	H	A	H	T	P	M
Angoni.............	5	E	H	G	M	N	N	A	M	T	C	M
Anyanza............	5	S	H	G	M	N	N	A	H	T	C	M
Azambo.............	6	....	H	G	L	N	N	A	M	T	C	....
Azande.............	3	E	H	G	L	N	N	A	H	T	C	C
Bafiote.............	2	S	H	S	L	N	N	A	H	T	C	M
Baganda (*see* Buganda)												
Bageshu.............	3	S	H	M	L	N	N	A	M	T	....	I
Bahima.............	5	S	H	G	L	H	H	P	H	T	C	M
Bahuana............	3	S	H	F	L	N	N	A	M	T	C	M
Bakongo............	3	S	H	G	L	N	N	A	M	T	C	M
Bakundu............	2	S	H	F	L	N	N	A	M	....	C	M
Bali................	2	S	H	F	L	N	N	A	M	T	C	M
Baluba.............	6	E	H	G	L	N	N	A	M	T	C	M
Bambala............	3	E	H	F	L	N	N	A	H	T	C	M
Bambara............	1	P	H	G	L	N	N	A	H	S	C	C
Bambugu (*see* Wambugu)												
Bambuk (*see* Wambugwe)												
Bamsalala...........	....	P	H	....	....	N	N	A	H	T	C	....
Banaka.............	1	P	H	G	L	N	N	A	M	T	C	C
Banduku (*see* Bapuku)												
Bangala.............	3	S	H	F	L	N	N	A	M	T	C	M
Banyai.............	6	E	H	G	M	N	N	A	M	....	C	M
Banyoro............	5	E	H	G	L	N	N	A	H	S	C	M
Bapuku.............	1	P	H	G	L	N	N	A	M	T	C	C

TABLE 5—*Continued*

AFRICA—*Continued*	Region†	Character of War‡	Environment			Race		Culture		Organization		
			Climate§	Habitat‖	Climatic Energy¶	Race**	Subrace††	Culture‡‡	Subculture§§	Political‖‖	Social¶¶	Intercultural Relation***
Baquerewe............	5	E	H	G	M	N	N	P	H	T	C	M
Baquiri..............	5	E	H	G	M	N	N	A	M	T	....	M
Barea...............	5	E	H	G	L	H	H	A	M	V	C	C
Baronga.............	6	P	T	G	L	N	N	A	H	T	C	M
Barotse (*see* Marutse)												
Basoga Batamba.......	5	E	H	G	M	N	N	A	H	T	P	M
Basonge Meno.........	3	S	H	F	L	N	N	A	H	T	C	C
Basutos..............	6	P	T	G	M	N	N	A	H	S	P	M
Batamba (*see* Basoga Batamba)												
Batauana.............	6	E	T	G	M	N	N	P	L	T	C	M
Bateke...............	3	E	H	F	L	N	N	A	M	....	C	C
Batom................	....	....	H	....	....	N	N	A	M	....	C	....
Batua................	3	D	H	F	L	P	B	H	L	C	S	I
Bawendi..............	....	....	....	....	....	N	N	A	H	T	....	....
Bayaka...............	6	S	H	G	L	N	N	A	H	T	C	M
Bayanzi..............	3	S	H	F	L	N	N	A	M	T	C	M
Bayong...............	....	....	H	....	L	N	N	A	M	....	C	....
Bechuana.............	6	E	T	G	M	N	N	P	H	T	C	M
Beduan...............	4	E	H	D	L	W	M	P	H	T	C	C
Beni Amer............	4	E	H	D	L	H	H	P	L	T	C	C
Benin Natives........	2	P	H	F	L	N	N	A	H	S	P	C
Bihendos.............	3	S	H	F	L	N	N	A	H	T	C	....
Bogos................	4	E	H	G	L	H	H	P	H	T	C	M
Bondei...............	5	E	H	G	M	N	N	A	M	....	C	M
Bongos...............	4	E	H	G	L	N	N	A	H	....	....	C
Bosaga...............	5	E	H	G	M	N	N	A	M	....	....	M
Buganda..............	5	P	H	G	M	N	N	A	H	S	C	M
Bukoba Natives.......	5	E	H	G	M	N	N	A	H	T	....	M
Bushmen..............	6	S	T	G	L	P	B	H	L	C	S	I
Bushonga.............	3	E	H	F	L	N	N	A	H	T	C	M
Calabar..............	2	P	H	F	L	N	N	A	H	T	C	C
Casembe..............	3	P	H	G	M	N	N	A	H	S	C	C
Chevas...............	....	....	H	....	....	N	N	A	H	....	....	....
Colonial Hottentots (*see* Hottentots)												
Danakil..............	4	E	H	G	L	H	H	P	H	T	C	C
Diakite Saracolays.....	2	P	H	G	L	H	H	A	H	T	C	C
Dinka................	4	E	H	G	L	N	N	P	L	T	C	C
Duallas..............	2	S	H	F	L	N	N	A	H	T	C	M
Ewe..................	2	P	H	F	L	N	N	A	H	T	C	C
Fang.................	2	E	H	F	L	N	N	A	M	T	P	C
Fanti................	2	P	H	F	L	N	N	A	H	T	C	C
Foola Jalon..........	2	S	H	G	L	H	H	A	H	T	C	C
Foola Torra..........	2	S	H	G	L	H	H	A	H	T	C	C
Fula (*see* Foola)												
Gallas...............	4	E	H	G	M	H	H	P	H	T	C	C
Gallinas.............	....	....	H	S	....	N	N	A	M	T	C	....
Geges................	....	....	H	....	L	N	N	A	H	T	C	....

TABLE 5—*Continued*

AFRICA—*Continued*	Region†	Character of War‡	Environment			Race		Culture		Organization		
			Climate§	Habitat‖	Climatic Energy¶	Race**	Subrace††	Culture‡‡	Subculture§§	Political‖‖	Social¶¶	Intercultural Relation***
Herero (*see* Ovaherero)												
Hottentots, Colonial....	6	S	T	D	L	P	B	P	L	T	C	M
Indikki.................			H	....	L	N	N	A	H	T	C	....
Jalon (*see* Foola Jalon)												
Jekris.................			H		....	N	N	A	H	T	C	....
Joloff (*see* Woloff)												
Khoi-Khoin...........	6	S	T	D	L	P	B	P	L	T	C	M
Kilwa................	5	E	H	S	L	N	N	A	H	T	S	C
Kimbunda............	6	S	H	G	L	N	N	A	H	T	C	M
Kioko................	3	E	H	G	L	N	N	A	H	T	C	M
Kongo (*see* Bakongo)												
Korana...............	6	S	T	G	M	P	B	P	L	T	....	M
Kuku.................		E	H		L	N	N	A	H	T	C	C
Kunama..............	3	E	H	G	L	H	H	A	M	V	C	C
Latika...............	5	E	H	G	M	N	N	A	M	T	....	C
Lendu...............	6	S	H	F	L	N	N	A	M	T	....	M
Lunda...............	6	E	H	G	L	N	N	A	H	S	C	M
Mabode..............	3	E	H	F	L	N	N	A	H			C
Mabum..............	2	P	H	G	L	H	H	A	M	....	C	C
Makololo............	6	P	H	G	M	N	N	P	H	S	P	M
Mandja..............	3	S	H	F	L	N	N	A	M	T	....	I
Mangbetu...........	3	E	H	F	L	N	N	A	M	T	C	C
Maravis.............	6	E	H	G	M	N	N	A	M	T	C	M
Marutse.............	6	P	T	G	M	N	N	A	H	S	C	M
Masca...............	4	P	H	G	L	H	H	A	H	T	C	C
Massai..............	5	E	H	G	M	H	H	P	L	T	C	C
Mayombe...........	3	S	H	F	L	N	N	A	H	T	C	M
Mbengas............	2	....	H	S	L	N	N	A	H	T	C	....
Monbutu............	3	E	H	G	L	N	N	A	M	S	C	C
Mpongwe............	2	S	H	S	L	N	N	A	M	....	C	M
Mucassequeres........	6	S	H	G	L	P	B	H	L	....	C	M
Mundombe...........	6	....	H	G	L	N	N	P	L			
Mundombe...........	6	....	H	G	L	N	N	A	M			
Nagos...............	2	S	H	F	L	N	N	A	H	T	C	M
Nandi..............	5	E	H	G	M	H	H	A	H	T	....	C
Niam Niam..........	3	E	H	F	L	N	N	A	M	S	C	C
Nosse be............	7	E	H	S	L	Y	S	A	H	T	C	C
Ondonga............	6	P	H	D	L	N	N	A	H	T	C	M
Oupoti..............		....	H		....	N	N	A	M	....	C	....
Ovaherero...........	6	E	T	D	L	N	N	P	L	T	C	M
Quissama............		....	H	....	M	N	N	A	M	V		
Saracolays (*see* Diakite Saracolays)												
Segoo...............	1	P	H	G	L	N	N	A	H	S	C	C
Sereres.............	1	P	H	G	L	N	N	A	H	T	C	C
Sese Islanders........	5	E	H	S	L	N	N	A	H			M
Somali..............	4	E	H	G	L	H	H	P	H	T	C	C
Suaheli.............	5	E	H	S	L	N	N	A	H	S	C	C
Takue..............	1	P	H	D	L	H	H	A	H	V	C	C

TABLE 5—*Continued*

AFRICA—*Continued*	Region†	Character of War‡	Climate§	Habitat‖	Climatic Energy¶	Race**	Subrace††	Culture‡‡	Subculture§§	Political‖‖	Social¶¶	Intercultural Relation***
				ENVIRONMENT		RACE		CULTURE		ORGANIZATION		
Tekrur (*see* Takue)												
Torra (*see* Foola Torra)												
Tshi...................	2	P	H	F	L	N	N	A	H	T	C	C
Tuchilange............	....	....	H	....	L	N	N	A	M	T	....	....
Uganda (*see* Buganda)												
Urundi (*see* Warundi)												
Wachagga.............	5	E	H	G	L	N	N	A	H	T	C	M
Wadigo...............	5	E	N	G	L	N	N	A	H	....	....	M
Wadoe................	5	E	H	G	L	N	N	A	M	T	C	M
Wafiomi..............	5	....	H	F	L	N	N	A	M	V	....	....
Wafipa...............	....	....	H	....	....	N	N	A	H	T	....	....
Waganda (*see* Buganda)												
Wagenia..............	3	S	H	F	L	N	N	H	H	....	S	I
Wagogo...............	5	E	H	G	L	H	H	A	H	T	C	M
Waheisi..............	5	P	H	G	M	N	N	A	M	T	....	M
Wajiji...............	....	....	H	....	L	N	N	A	M	....	C	....
Wakikuyu.............	5	E	H	F	M	N	N	A	H	T	C	M
Wambugu.............	1	E	H	G	L	N	N	P	L	T	....	....
Wambugwe...........	1	P	H	G	L	N	N	A	M	T	S	C
Wanyakyusa.........	5	E	H	G	M	N	N	A	H	....	....	M
Wanyamwesi.........	5	E	H	G	M	N	N	A	H	T	C	M
Wanyaturu...........	5	E	H	G	L	N	N	A	M	C	....	M
Wanyiki (*see* Wanyatu-ru)												
Wanyuki (*see* Wataturu)												
Wapare...............	5	E	H	G	M	N	N	A	H	T	C	M
Wapokomo............	4	E	H	G	L	N	N	A	H	V	C	M
Warangi..............	....	....	H	....	L	N	N	A	H	V	....	....
Warege...............	3	S	H	F	L	N	N	A	M	T	S	M
Warundi..............	5	E	H	G	M	N	N	A	H	S	P	M
Washambala..........	5	E	H	G	M	N	N	A	H	T	C	M
Wasibe...............	....	....	H	....	L	N	N	A	H	T	C	....
Wasinja..............	3	E	H	G	M	N	N	A	H	T	C	M
Wasuaheli (*see* Suaheli)												
Wataturu.............	5	E	H	G	M	N	N	P	H	T	C	M
Woloff...............	1	P	H	G	L	N	N	A	H	S	C	C
Xosa (*see* Ama Xosa)												
Yao..................	5	E	H	G	M	N	N	A	H	T	C	M
Yaunde...............	2	E	H	F	L	N	N	A	M	C	C	C
Yomba...............	2	P	H	G	L	N	N	A	H	T	C	C
Zulu (*see* Ama Zulu)												
NORTH AMERICA												
Abnaqui..............	7	....	T	F	H	R	A	A	L	T	S	M
Aleuts (*see* Unalaska, Athka)												
Algonquins, Quebec....	4	F	T	F	H	R	N	A	L	V	S	M

TABLE 5—*Continued*

NORTH AMERICA—*Continued*	Region†	Character of War†	Climate§	Habitat‖	Climatic Energy¶	Race**	Subrace††	Culture‡‡	Subculture§§	Political‖‖	Social¶¶	Intercultural Relation***
			Environment			Race		Culture		Organization		
Apache	6	E	T	D	M	R	A	H	H	V	C	C
Apalachites	8	E	T	F	M	R	A	A	H	T	C	M
Assiniboins	3	E	C	G	M	R	N	A	H	V	S	C
Athka Aleuts	1	S	T	S	M	R	E	H	H	V	C	I
Behring Eskimos (*see* Eskimos)												
Bellacoola	2	S	T	S	H	R	A	H	H	T	C	I
Blackfeet	3	E	C	G	M	R	N	H	H	S	C	M
Californians (*see* Lower Californians, Southern Californians)												
Caribs	12	E	H	S	L	R	N	A	M	V	S	C
Caribs, Continental	11	E	H	F	L	R	N	A	M	V	S	C
Carriers	2	S	C	F	H	R	N	H	H	C	C	I
Chepewayans	3	D	C	F	M	R	N	H	H	C	C	I
Chilcotin	2	S	C	F	H	R	N	H	H	C	C	I
Chippewa (*see* Ojibways)												
Coast Salish	5	E	T	S	H	R	A	H	H	T	C	I
Cochimis	9	E	T	D	L	R	A	H	L	S	S	I
Comanche	6	E	H	G	M	R	A	H	H	V	S	C
Creeks	8	E	T	F	M	R	A	A	M	S	C	M
Crees	4	S	C	F	M	R	N	H	H	T	S	C
Dakota	6	E	T	G	M	R	N	A	L	S	S	M
Delaware	7	E	T	F	H	R	N	A	L	S	S	M
Eskimo, Behring	1	S	C	S	L	R	E	H	H	V	S	M
Eskimo, Central	1	D	C	S	L	R	E	H	H	C	S	I
Eskimo, Greenland	1	D	C	S	L	R	E	H	H	C	S	M
Eskimo, Labrador	1	D	C	S	L	R	E	H	H	C	S	S
Eskimo, Point Barrow	1	D	C	S	L	R	E	H	H	V	S	I
Eskimo, Western	1	S	C	S	L	R	E	H	H	C	S	I
Etechemins	4	S	T	F	H	R	A	H	H	V	S	
Galino Mero						R	A	H	H	T		
Greenland Eskimo (*see* Eskimo)												
Gualala	5	S	T	F	H	R	A	H	H	V	S	I
Guatemala	11	P	H	F	L	R	A	A	H	S	C	C
Guaymi	11	S	H	M	L	R	A	A	L	V	S	M
Haida	2	E	T	S	H	R	A	H	H	T	C	I
Halkamelen	2	S	T	S	H	R	A	H	H	T	C	I
Heiltsuk	3	E	C	S	H	R	A	H	H	T	C	C
Hidatsa	6	E	T	G	H	R	A	A	L	V	S	M
Hopi	6	S	T	D	M	R	A	A	H	V	C	C
Huicols	9	S	T	M	M	R	A	A	M	T	C	C
Hurons	7	E	T	F	H	R	N	A	L	S	S	M
Illinois	7	E	T	G	H	R	A	A	M	S	C	M
Iowa	6	E	T	G	H	R	A	A	L	V	S	M
Iroquois	7	P	T	F	H	R	N	A	L	S	S	M
Isthmians	11	S	H	F	L	R	A	A	L	V	S	M
Jupa	5	S	T	F	H	R	A	H	H	C	S	I

TABLE 5—*Continued*

NORTH AMERICA—*Continued*	Region†	Character of War‡	Climate§	Habitat‖	Climatic Energy¶	Race**	Subrace††	Culture‡‡	Subculture§§	Political‖‖	Social¶¶	Intercultural Relation***
			ENVIRONMENT			RACE		CULTURE		ORGANIZATION		
Kariaks	1	D	C	S	L	R	N	H	H	C	S	I
Kark	5	S	T	F	H	R	A	H	H	C	S	I
Kelta	5	S	T	S	H	R	A	H	H	C	S	I
Kenai	1	S	T	S	M	R	A	H	H	V	S	I
Kiowa	6	E	T	G	H	R	A	H	H	T	S	M
Kiskakong	7	S	T	F	H	R	A	H	H	T	S	M
Kitchin	3	S	C	F	M	R	N	H	H	V	C	I
Klamaths, Oregon	5	E	T	F	H	R	A	H	H	V	S	M
Kombo	5	S	T	F	H	R	A	H	H	V	S	I
Koniagas	1	S	T	S	M	R	N	H	H	V	S	I
Kootenay	3	S	T	F	H	R	N	H	H	T	C	I
Kowitchen	2	S	T	F	H	R	A	H	H	V	C	I
Kwakiutl	2	E	T	S	H	R	A	H	H	T	C	I
Labrador Eskimo (*see* Eskimo)												
Lassiks	5	S	T	F	H	R	A	H	H	V	S	I
Lilooet	2	S	C	F	H	R	A	H	H	T	C	I
Lkungen	2	S	T	S	H	R	A	H	H	T	C	I
Loucheux	3	S	C	M	M	R	N	H	H	V	C	I
Lower Californians	9	S	H	D	L	R	A	H	L	C	S	I
Luisenos	5	S	T	F	H	R	A	H	H	C	C	I
Mach-el-chel						R	A	H	H			
Malecutes (*see* Etechemins)												
Malemutes	1	S	C	S	M	R	N	H	H	C	S	I
Mandan	6	E	T	G	H	R	A	A	L	V	S	M
Mayas	10	P	H	F	L	R	A	A	H	S	C	C
Mexicans, Northern (*see also* New Mexicans)	9	E	H	D	L	R	A	H	H	V	S	C
Micmacs	4	E	T	F	H	R	A	H	H	T	S	I
Miwok	5	S	T	M	H	R	A	H	L	T	C	I
Modocs	5	E	T	M	H	R	A	H	H	V	C	M
Mohare	5	E	T	D	M	R	A	A	L	T	C	M
Montagnais	4	S	T	M	M	R	N	H	H	T	S	I
Moqui	6	S	T	D	M	R	A	A	H	T	C	C
Nahane, East	3	S	C	F	H	R	N	H	H	V	S	I
Nahane, West	3	S	C	F	H	R	N	H	H	V	S	I
Natchez	8	E	T	F	M	R	A	A	M	T	S	M
Navahoes	6	E	T	D	M	R	A	P	L	C	S	M
New Mexicans (*see* Pueblos)												
Nez Perces	6	S	T	M	M	R	A	H	H	V	S	I
Nishinan	5	S	T	F	H	R	A	H	H	C	S	I
Niska	2	E	T	S	H	R	A	H	H	T	T	I
Nootka	2	E	T	S	H	R	A	H	H	T	C	I
Ojibways	7	E	T	F	H	R	A	A	L	T	C	M
Omaha	6	E	T	G	M	R	A	H	H	V	S	M
Oregon Klamaths (*see* Klamaths)												

TABLE 5—*Continued*

			ENVIRONMENT			RACE		CULTURE		ORGANIZATION		
NORTH AMERICA— *Continued*	REGION†	CHARACTER OF WAR‡	Climate§	Habitat‖	Climatic Energy¶	Race**	Subrace††	Culture‡‡	Subculture§§	Political‖‖	Social¶¶	Intercultural Relation***
Ottawa	4	S	T	F	H	R	A	H	H	T	S	M
Papago	9	S	T	D	L	R	A	A	H	V	C	C
Patwin	5	S	T	F	H	R	A	H	L	V	S	I
Pawnees	6	E	T	G	M	R	A	A	M	S	C	M
Pericui	9	S	T	D	L	R	N	H	L	C	S	I
Petaweet	5	S	T	D	M	R	A	H	H	V	S	I
Petengawats (*see* Petaweet)												
Pima	9	E	T	D	M	R	N	A	H	T	C	C
Pit River	5	S	T	F	H	R	A	H	H	V	S	I
Point Barrow Eskimo (*see* Eskimo)												
Pomo	5	S	T	F	H	R	A	H	H	V	S	I
Porto Rico	12	E	H	S	L	R	A	A	M	T	C	M
Pueblos, New Mexico	6	S	T	D	L	R	A	A	H	T	C	C
Sakahl (*see* Tsitsaut)												
Salish (*see* Coast Salish)												
Sarcees	3	S	C	G	H	R	A	H	H	V	S	I
Seminoles	8	E	T	F	M	R	A	A	M	T	C	M
Seri	9	S	T	D	L	R	A	H	H	T	S	I
Shastika	5	S	T	F	H	R	A	H	H	V	S	I
Shoshones	6	E	T	F	H	R	N	H	L	T	S	M
Shushwap, Eastern	2	S	C	F	M	R	A	H	H	V	C	I
Shushwap, Western	2	S	C	F	M	R	A	H	H	V	C	I
Sia	6	S	T	D	M	R	A	A	H	T	C	C
Similkameen	2	S	C	F	H	R	A	H	H	T	C	I
Souriquois (*see* Micmacs)												
Southern Californians	5	S	T	D	L	R	A	H	H	V	S	I
Tao	6	S	T	D	M	R	A	A	H	T	C	C
Tarahumare	9	S	T	D	L	R	A	A	M	T	C	C
Tepehaunes	9	E	T	D	L	R	A	A	M	T	C	C
Thlinkeet	2	E	T	S	H	R	A	H	H	V	C	I
Thompson River	2	S	C	F	M	R	A	H	H	C	C	I
Tlelding (*see* Kelta)												
Tolowa	5	S	T	S	H	R	A	H	H	C	S	I
Towka						R	A	A	M			I
Tsekhene	3	S	C	M	M	R	A	H	H	C	S	I
Tsimshian	2	E	T	S	H	R	A	H	H	T	C	I
Tsitsaut	2	S	C	F	H	R	A	H	H	V	S	I
Tskaus (*see* Tsitsaut)												
Unalaska Aleuts	1	S	T	S	M	R	E	H	H	T	C	I
Walpi (*see* Moqui)												
Wappo	5	S	T	M	H	R	A	H	H	V	S	I
Winnebagos	7	S	T	F	H	R	A	A	L	V	S	M
Wintun	5	S	T	F	H	R	A	H	L	V	S	I
Woolwa						R	A	A	M			
Wyandot	7	E	T	F	H	R	N	A	M	T	S	M
Yakuts	5	S	T	F	H	R	A	H	H	T	S	I
Yuki	5	S	T	M	H	R	N	H	H	V	S	I
Yurok	5	D	T	F	H	R	A	H	H	C	S	I
Zapotecs	10	P	T	F	L	R	A	A	H	T	C	C
Zuni	6	S	T	D	M	R	A	A	H	T	C	C

TABLE 5—*Continued*

SOUTH AMERICA	REGION†	CHARACTER OF WAR‡	ENVIRONMENT			RACE		CULTURE		ORGANIZATION		
			Climate§	Habitat‖	Climatic Energy¶	Race**	Subrace††	Culture‡‡	Subculture§§	Political‖‖	Social¶¶	Intercultural Relation***
Abipones	6	E	T	G	L	R	A	H	H	V	C	M
Akkek						R	A	H	H			
Antioquia	1	T	F	M	R	A	A	L	C	S	M	....
Apiaco	2	S	T	F	H	R	A	A	M	....	S	I
Araucanians	3	E	T	M	H	R	A	A	H	S	C	C
Arawak	1	S	H	F	L	R	N	A	L	V	C	M
Arecuna	1	S	H	G	L	R	A	A	L	V	S	M
Auca	3	....	T	M	H	R	A	H	H	T	C	I
Boni	...	S				R	A	A	M	T		I
Bororo	2	E	H	F	L	R	A	A	M	T	S	I
Botocudos	5	S	H	F	L	R	N	H	L	C	S	I
British Guiana	1	S	H	F	L	R	A	A	L	V	S	M
Campos	3	S	T	M	M	R	A	A	M	C	S	C
Canea	5	S	H	F	L	R	A	A	L	C	S	I
Chaco, North	4	E	H	G	L	R	A	H	H	V	S	M
Chambioza						R	A	A	M			
Charentes	5	S	H	G	L	R	N	A	L	C	S	I
Charrua	1	E	H	G	L	R	A	H	H	C	S	M
Chiquito	2	S	H	G	L	R	A	A	M	V	C	M
Chirigirano	2	S	H	G	L	R	A	A	M	T	C	M
Churruges (*see* Charrua)												
Coroades	5	S	H	F	M	R	A	H	H		S	I
Coropo	2	S	H	F	M	R	A	A	L	C	S	I
Cureto	2	D	H	F	L	R	A	A	M	C	S	I
Fuegians	7	S	T	S	M	R	N	H	L	C	S	I
Gagua	1	S	T	M	L	R	A	A	M			
Ges	5	S	H	G	L	R	A	A	M	C	S	I
Goyanaz	1	E	H	F	L	R	A	H	H	....	C	I
Goyatacoz												
Guana	4	S	H	G	L	R	A	A	L	C	C	C
Guarayo	2	E	H	G	L	R	A	A	M	....	S	M
Guato	4	S	H	F	L	R	A	A	M	C	S	I
Guaycuru	4	E	T	F	L	R	A	H	H	C	S	M
Guiana (*see* British Guiana, Goyanez)												
Icanna	2	S	H	F	L	R	A	A	M			
Ipurina	2	S	H	F	L	R	A	A	L	V	S	I
Ite	2	S	H	F	L	R	A	A	L	C	S	I
Itene (*see* Ite)												
Jivaro	3	S	T	M	H	R	A	A	M	....	S	C
Jumana						R	A	A	M			
Karayaki	5	S	H	F	L	R	A	A	L	V	S	I
Lengua	4	S	H	G	L	R	A	A	L	T	S	M
Macovi	6	E	T	G	L	R	A	H	H	....	S	M
Macusi	2	S	H	G	L	R	A	A	L	V	S	M
Manctaneris	2	S	H	F	L	R	A	A	M	....	S	C
Manoa	2	S	H	F	L	R	A	A	L	S	C	I
Maraua	2	S	H	F	L	R	A	A	L	L	S	I
Matacco	4	S	T	G	L	R	A	A	L	V	S	M

TABLE 5—*Continued*

SOUTH AMERICA—*Continued*	Region†	Character of War‡	Climate§	Habitat‖	Climatic Energy¶	Race**	Subrace††	Culture‡‡	Subculture§§	Political‖‖	Social¶¶	Intercultural Relation***
Mataguayos	4	S	Y	G	L	R	A	A	L	C	S	M
Mauhes	2	S	H	F	L	R	A	A	L	....	S	I
Mbaya (*see* Mbevaera)												
Mbevaera	4	E	H	F	L	R	A	A	L	....	C	C
Minuares	....	..	..	..	..	R	A	H	H	....	..	....
Miranha	2	S	H	F	L	R	A	A	L	V	C	I
Miranha	2	S	H	F	L	R	A	A	M	V	C	I
Mosetenes	2	S	T	F	M	R	A	A	M	C	S	C
Moxo	2	S	H	F	L	R	A	A	M	V	C	M
Mundrucu	2	E	H	F	L	R	A	A	M	....	C	I
Mura	2	E	H	F	L	R	A	H	H	....	S	I
Paravilhana	5	S	H	F	L	R	A	A	L	T	S	I
Paressi	2	S	H	F	L	R	N	A	M	T	S	I
Paumaris	2	D	H	F	L	R	A	H	H	....	C	I
Paumaris	2	D	H	F	L	R	A	A	L	....	S	I
Payagu	4	E	T	G	L	R	A	H	H	C	S	M
Pitagoa	5	E	H	F	L	R	A	H	H	....	S	I
Puelches	6	S	T	G	H	R	A	H	H	T	C	M
Puri	5	S	H	F	M	R	A	H	H	....	S	I
Roucoyennes	2	S	H	F	L	R	A	A	L	C	C	I
Sambioa	....	..	..	..	..	R	A	A	M	V	..	....
Senci	....	..	..	..	..	R	A	A	M	....	C	....
Shingu	....	..	..	..	..	R	A	A	L	....	S	....
Tapui	5	S	H	F	L	R	N	A	M	C	S	I
Tapuya	5	S	H	G	L	R	N	A	M	C	S	I
Tehuelches	6	E	T	G	H	R	A	H	H	T	S	M
Tobas	4	E	T	G	L	R	A	P	L	C	C	M
Topanez	....	..	..	..	..	R	A	H	H	V	S	....
Tupian (*see* Tapui)												
Uanambua	....	..	..	..	..	R	A	A	M	....	C	....
Uaupe	2	S	H	F	L	R	A	A	M	V	C	I
Ucayali	2	S	H	F	L	R	A	A	L	....	S	I
Vilela	4	S	T	F	L	R	A	H	H	....	S	I
Yonca	3	S	T	D	M	R	A	A	M	S	C	I
Yunga (*see* Yonca)												
Yuracares	2	S	H	G	L	R	A	A	L	C	S	I
Zaparo	2	S	H	F	L	R	A	H	H	C	S	I

† *Region.*—The numbers refer to regions as indicated in Fig. 20. The regions are those occupied by the people in question when they first entered the historical records of European civilization since the age of discoveries in the latter part of the fifteenth century. The continuous and direct contact with civilization which often followed such recording frequently changed not only the culture and organization of a primitive people and, through cross-breeding, their race but also their location and physical environment. Such changes have been, as far as possible, ignored in this tabulation. It is, of course, true that most primitive people have always been subjected to some contact with people of different culture, direct or indirect, and that, partly as a result of this and partly by internal development, race, culture, organization, environment,

[Notes to Table 5 continued on p. 546]

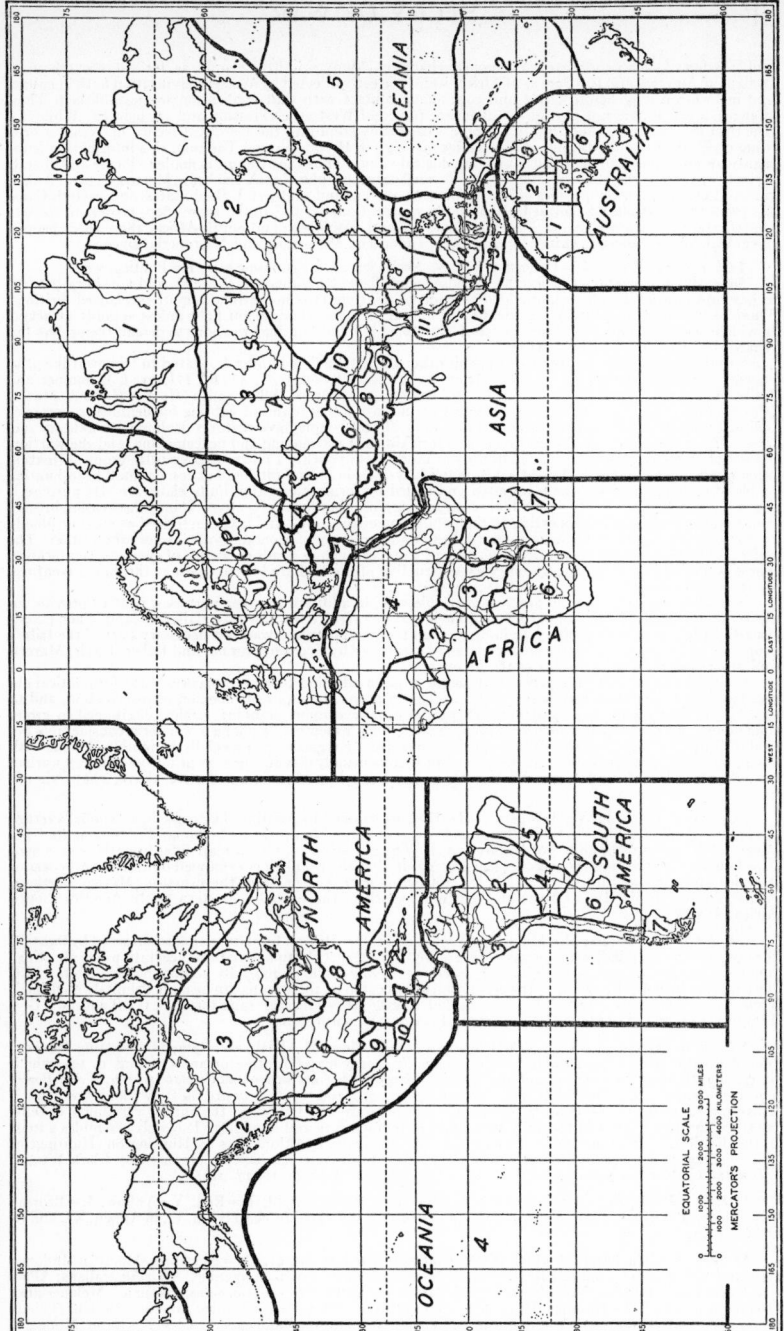

FIG. 20.—Regional classification of primitive peoples

and location of such people are continuously changing. Many primitive people, as, for instance, the plains Indians of America and the Bantus of Africa, were indirectly affected by Western civilization both in culture and in location long before direct and continuous contact with that civilization was established. These changes, however, are not part of the historical record of Western civilization and are ignored. While it is true that information about primitive people occasionally crept into the historical record of Western or of other civilizations before the age of discoveries (as, e.g., in Herodotus and Tacitus), this information is too scanty and unreliable to be of much anthropological value. Thus the attempt is made to locate and characterize the people as they were at roughly the following dates: peoples of the Caribbean, Mexico, Central America, and Peru, 1500–1600; peoples of South America, eastern and southern United States, and eastern Canada, 1600–1700; peoples of central United States, central Canada, and India, 1700–1800; peoples of western United States, western Canada, Australia, New Zealand, Polynesia, and South Africa, 1800–1870; peoples of central Africa, Siberia, central Asia, Malaya, Indonesia, Melanesia, and Micronesia, since 1870.

‡ *Character of War.*—D = Defensive war; S = Social war; E = Economic war; P = Political war.
Defensive war refers to the practice of those people listed by Hobhouse, Wheeler, and Ginsburg (p. 229) as having no war in their mores, provided no evidence was found to the contrary in more specialized writings. These people have no military organization or military weapons and do not fight unless actually attacked, in which case they make spontaneous use of available tools and huntings weapons to defend themselves but regard this necessity as a misfortune.
Social war refers to the practice of people other than those listed under D, stated to be unwarlike or to engage only in mild warfare by such writers as Spencer (*Sociology,* I, 564 ff., III, 615 ff.), Sumner and Keller (IV, 115 ff.), Davie (pp. 244 ff.), Perry (*Manchester Memoirs*), Elliot Smith (*Human History*), Marett (*Psychology and Folklore,* pp. 32 ff.), provided no indication was found of fighting for definite economic or political purposes in the more specialized literature. These people have customs dealing with military tactics, military weapons, the circumstances and formalities of warmaking and peacemaking, and the warriors consist of all men of the tribe trained in the war mores from youth. Tactics involve little group formation or co-operation but consist of night raids, individual duels in formal pitched battles, or small head-hunting or blood-revenge parties. War is initiated and ended by formalities, often quite elaborate. Its purpose is blood revenge, religious duty, individual prestige, sport, or other social objective. It may on occasion involve considerable casualties in proportion to the population of the group and is characterized as cruel or bloody by some writers because prisoners are not taken. Land or booty of economic value is not taken either. The object is slaughter of the enemy or acquisition of trophies, such as heads or scalps, of symbolic significance. These wars are, however, usually not very destructive of life and are looked upon as thrilling adventures by the participants.
Economic war refers to the practice of people who, in addition to other purposes, fight to provide for the economic needs of the group, such as women, slaves, cattle, tools, raw materials, and land. Such people usually have a system of military training in mass tactics and regard war as a necessary part of the tribe's economic activities. The people characterized as "warlike" by Spencer, Sumner and Keller, Davie, Marett, and others usually belong in this or the following class.
Political war refers to the practice of people who, in addition to other purposes, fight for political objectives, i.e., to maintain a ruling dynasty or class in power, to suppress rebellion or insurrection, and to expand political territory or control. Such people usually support standing armies, disciplined in group maneuvers and utilizing specialized weapons and methods which may prolong a war for a considerable period of time. Among them the military profession is usually regarded as especially honorable. People with such practices are on the verge of civilization, but writers usually classify them as primitive but very warlike (see Spencer, I, 558 ff.; III, 578 ff.; Marett, p. 33; Davie, pp. 251 ff., 255 ff.; see above, chap. vi, nn. 24, 25.

§ *Climate.*—C = Cold; T = Temperate; H = Hot, ascertained by locating the people in an annual average isothermal map. See Fig. 21. "Cold" means an average annual temperature below 30° F.; "temperate," between 30° F. and 70° F.; and "hot," above 70° F. The isotherms on such a map differ from those on a map based on winter and summer averages (see Fig. 22) in that the cold belt is expanded down the west coast of America and narrowed in Siberia, while the hot belt is narrowed north of the Equator (Mexico, northern Africa, Arabia, India, Indo-China) and expanded south of the Equator (western South America, South Africa, Australia).

‖ *Habitat.*—F = Forest; M = Mountain; S = Seashore; D = Desert; G = Grassland, ascertained by locating the peoples on a map indicating physical geography and the distribution of natural vegetation (see Huntington and Cushing, p. 307; Griffith Taylor, *Environment and Race,* p. 209). By combining the habitat with the climate symbols, the nature of the vegetation as indicated on these maps can be more definitely identified. Thus CF = Coniferous forest, TF = Broadleafed forest, HF = Tropical rain forest, CG = Tundra, TG = Temperate grassland or steppe, HG = Tropical savanna or shrub forest.

¶ *Climatic energy.*—L = Low climatic energy; M = Medium; H = High, ascertained by plotting the location of the people on Ellsworth Huntington's climatic energy map (Huntington and Cushing, p. 294, which differs slightly from Huntington's earlier climatic energy map, *Civilization and Climate,* p. 228; *World Power and Evolution,* p. 230). The "high" and "very high" are grouped together as are the "low" and "very low." This map takes into consideration the average temperature and humidity, the annual variability of temperature and humidity, and the daily variability of temperature and humidity. It closely resembles a map of the distribution of civilization prepared from the answers to questionnaires by Huntington (Huntington and Cushing, p. 294) and also a map of the spread of Euro-American culture prepared by Clark Wissler (*Man and Culture* [New York, 1923], p. 346; above, Appen. V, Figs. 16, 17, 18).

** *Race.*—P = Pygmy; A = Australoid; N = Negroid; H = Hamitoid; R = Red; Y = Yellow; B = Brown; W = White. The reasons for this classification are further indicated in chap. vi, n. 34, in Appen. XI, and in the following footnote on subraces.

†† *Subrace.*—The letters of which the first refers to the race mean: PN = Negritoes, Malayan, Indonesian, and Melanesian pygmies; PB = Bushmen, Negrilloes, Batwa, African pygmies; AA = Australians; AP = Pre-Dravidians of India; NN = Negroes and Bantus of Africa; NP = Papuasians, Papuans, Melanesians, Oceanic Negroes; HH = Hamites; HD = Dravidians of India; RN = Narrowheaded American Indians (Paleo-amerinds); RE = Eskimos; RA = American Indians, broad- and mediumheaded; YN = Northern Mongols;

YC = Chinese; YS = Southern Mongols, Oceanic Mongols, and True Malays; BA = Arctics of Asia; BI = Indonesians; BP = Polynesians; WN = Nordics; WA = Alpines; WM = Mediterraneans. See Fig. 23.

The classification follows in general that of Haddon (*The Races of Man and Their Distribution* [New York, 1925], pp. 15 ff.), giving primary significance to the more obvious and consequently socially significant physical characteristics, skin color, hair type, nose type, stature, and secondary consideration to the less obvious physical characteristics such as head form. Geographical separation also is important in distinguishing the subraces.

The eight races fall into two groups, the first four tending to be very dark and sometimes grouped as the "black" races, the remainder being lighter. Each of these falls into two natural groups: the dark peoples into the frizzy-haired pygmies and Negroids and the curly-haired Australoids and Hamitoids; and the lighter peoples into the straight-haired red and yellow races and the wavy-haired brown and white races.

The interrelations of these races and subraces is, of course, much more intricate, as the "black" Hamitoids and "white" Mediterraneans closely resemble the "brown" Indonesians with whom they are sometimes grouped as the "brown race." So also the Arctics and the Eskimos have a good deal in common as do the Alpines, Mongols, and some Polynesians. Interesting efforts to represent graphically these interrelationships have been made by Haddon (p. 169) and by Hooton (p. 582). The more important distinguishing characteristics of the races and subraces are indicated in Table 15, Appen. XI.

‡‡ *Culture.*—H = Hunters; P = Pastorals; A = Agriculturalists. The classification follows Hobhouse, Wheeler, and Ginsburg, who in turn follow Nieboer and many others in making the methods of getting food the basic cultural distinction. This method determines whether the mode of life shall be nomadic or sedentary and emphasizes the important distinction between collection of natural products and foresighted production. Furthermore, the method of food-getting is relatively easy to determine. The reason for this classification is further indicated in the following note on subculture.

§§ *Subculture.*—The letters of which the first refers to the culture mean: HL = Lower hunters; HH = Higher hunters; HD = Dependent hunters; PL = Lower pastorals; PH = Higher pastorals; AL = Lower agriculturalists; AM = Medium agriculturalists; AH = Higher agriculturalists, as these terms are defined and applied by Hobhouse, Wheeler, and Ginsburg. This book contains further information concerning the characteristics of these subcultures and the difficulties in applying the classification to the actual data because of (1) inadequacy of the published observations, (2) difficulty of determining the unit to which a given observation applies, (3) the complicating influence of cultural diffusion in comparing observations made at different times, and (4) inconsistent nomenclature of primitive peoples.

Lower hunters live on fruits, nuts, shellfish, reptiles, insects, and worms which they collect. They have no permanent dwelling but live in caves or under palm-leaf windbreaks. They do not spin, make pottery, or use metals. They sometimes have poor canoes but no domestic animals except the dog.

Higher hunters live on animals which they hunt. They have constructed houses or tents. They spin, weave, make pottery, have good canoes, and sometimes have horses or other domestic animals, although these are not their main food reliance.

Dependent hunters refer to certain peoples in India who supplement their hunting activity by trade with surrounding agricultural villages.

Lower pastorals live mainly on domestic animals, have no agriculture, and little development of the arts.

Higher pastorals live mainly by domestic animals but partly by agriculture practiced by serfs or tributary people. Their social organization centers around the pasturage needs of their herds.

Lower agriculturalists get most of their substance from collecting and hunting natural products, but this is regularly supplemented by a crude agriculture which is an exclusively women's occupation. There are no domestic animals but the dog. The arts, textiles, and pottery are nonexistent or very rudimentary, and there is no trade at all or only a very primitive barter.

Medium agriculturalists live mainly from agriculture, although this is supplemented by hunting and fishing. They spin, weave, and make pottery but have no specialized industry or trade and few domestic animals.

Higher agriculturalists practice plowing, irrigation, manuring, and may even understand crop rotation. They have domestic animals both for food and for draft purposes and specialized industries in woodwork, metal, textiles, and pottery, and usually engage in regular trade.

These cultures differ in kind and cannot be regarded as a continuous sequence from lower to higher. Rather, the higher hunters, pastorals, and advanced agriculturalists are parallel developments from the lower hunters and lower agriculturalists.

‖ ‖ *Political organization.*—C = Clan; V = Village; T = Tribe; S = State, with reference to the nature of the unit which appears to be sovereign in the sense of constituting the normal unit under whose authority criminal justice is administered internally and war is conducted externally. As primitive societies nearly always exhibit an intricate relationship of blood, territorial, and cultural groups, a considerable element of judgment is necessary in applying these distinctions. The classification here used compares with Herbert Spencer's distinction (*Sociology*, I, 551 ff.) between simple societies without a head or with only occasional headship (clan); simple societies with a head (village); compound societies (tribe); double compound societies (state). To place the groups in this classification, materials set forth by Hobhouse, Wheeler, and Ginsburg were utilized as follows:

Clan—Peoples listed as without government (p. 51) or without public administration of justice (p. 121, col. 1).

Village—Peoples organized in primary groups with public administration of justice (p. 121, col. 2; p. 125; p. 127, col. 2) or with only retaliation in the tribe (p. 127, col. 1) and not listed under clan.

Tribe—Peoples with government in the secondary group (p. 83) or with administration of justice in the secondary group (p. 127, col. 2 [3], and col. 3) and not listed under village or state.

State—Peoples listed by Spencer as doubly compound (p. 534) or indicated in other authorities to have that characteristic.

¶ ¶ *Social organization.*—S = Sex and age; P = Professional; C = Caste.

Sex and age refer to peoples among which no evidence was found of any social distinctions or economic division of labor based on factors other than sex or age.

[Notes to Table 5 continued on p. 551]

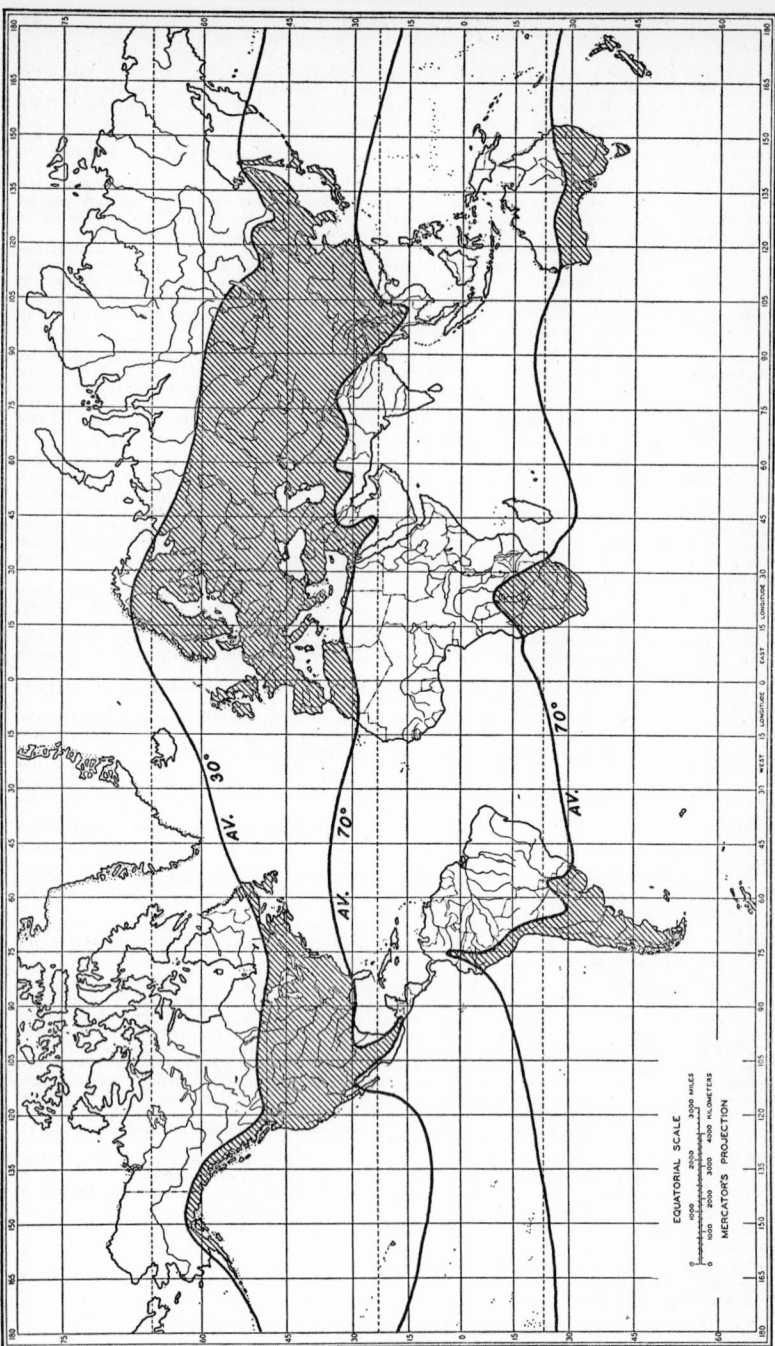

FIG 21.— Average annual temperature. (From Griffith Taylor, *Environment and Race* [London, 1936], p. 30.)

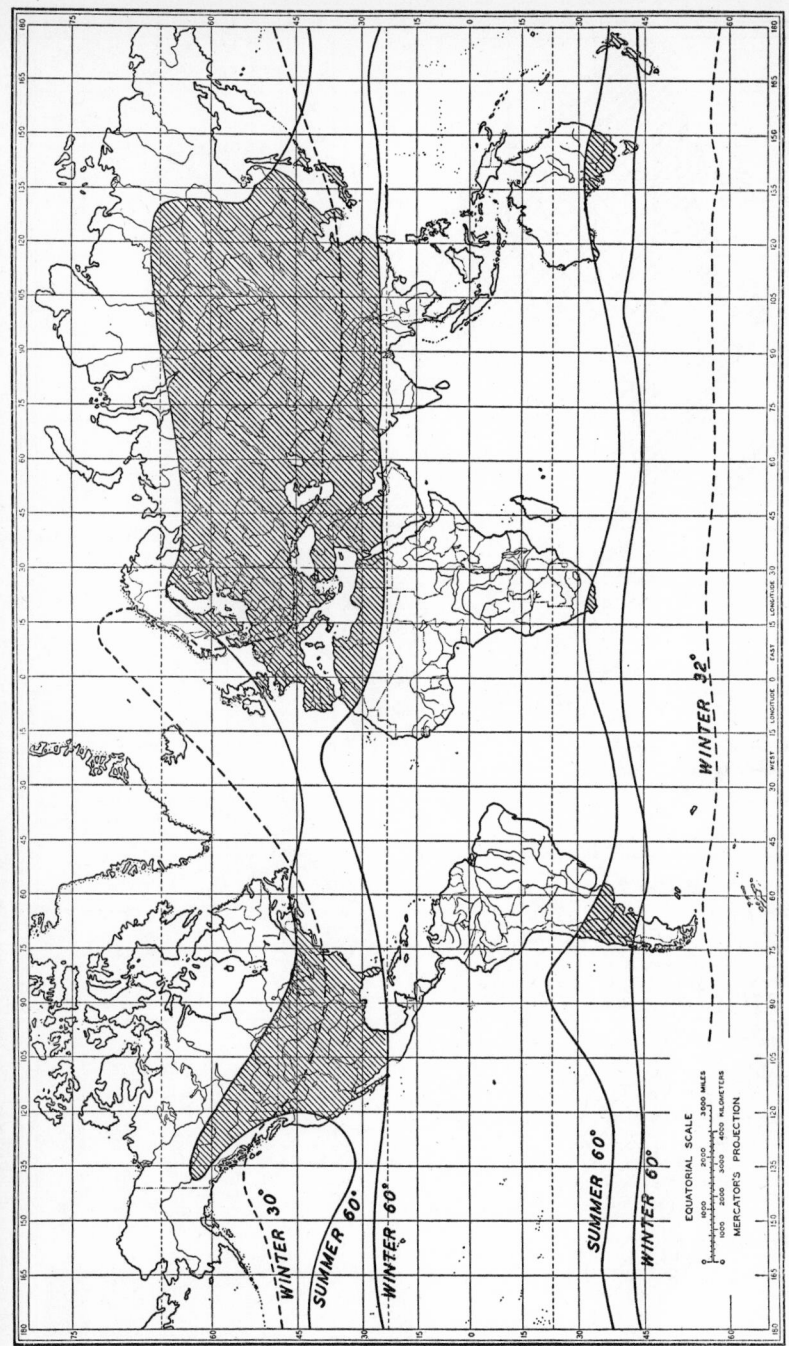

FIG. 22.—Winter and summer average temperature. (From Huntington and Cushing, *op. cit.*, p. 256)

TABLE 6

RELATION BETWEEN CONTINENTS AND WARLIKENESS

Continent	1. Defensive War	2. Social War	3. Economic War	4. Political War	Total	Mean Average Warlikeness*
	No. of Primitive Peoples in Each Continent Practicing Each Type of Warfare					
Asia and Indonesia.......	18	91	42	4	155	2.21
North America...........	7	67	44	4	122	2.37
South America...........	4	48	17	0	69	2.19
Africa..................	1	28	67	28	124	2.99
Australia...............	0	75	0	0	75	2.00
Oceania................	0	37	4	4	45	2.27
Total..............	30	346	174	40	590	2.38
	Percentage of Primitive Peoples in Each Continent Practicing Each Type of Warfare					
Asia and Indonesia.......	12	59	27	2	100	2.21
North America...........	6	55	36	3	100	2.37
South America...........	6	69	25	0	100	2.19
Africa..................	1	23	54	22	100	2.99
Australia...............	0	100	0	0	100	2.00
Oceania................	0	82	9	9	100	2.27
All peoples...........	5	59	29	7	100	2.38

* This figure was obtained by multiplying each figure by the number at the head of the column, adding the products in the row, and dividing this sum by the totals at the end of the row.

[Notes to Table 5 continued from p. 547]

Professional refers to peoples among whom certain artisan, religious, or other groups were specialized but without evidence that such specialization was compulsory by reason of birth or legal status.

Caste refers to people among whom exist compulsory distinctions between social, political, racial, or occupational classes through such institutions as slavery, serfdom, caste, hereditary nobility, or tributary peoples.

*** *Intercultural relations.*—I = Isolated; M = Moderate contact; C = Close contact. Contact with peoples of the same cultural level and type, and direct contact with European civilization, since the age of discoveries at the end of the fifteenth century are ignored (see n. †).

"Isolated" refers to people who before discovery by modern European civilization had for a long time had no, or very infrequent, direct contact with any people of higher culture.

"Moderate contact" refers to people who before discovery by modern European civilization had had indirect contact with civilization (including therein not only Western civilization but also the civilizations of the ancient East, India, China, Mexico, and Peru) or frequent contact with a primitive people of higher or very different culture.

"Close contact" refers to people who, apart from contacts with modern European civilization, had been for a long time in direct contact with some civilization.

In making these judgments, the region occupied by the people when first discovered by modern European civilization was considered with reference to its accessibility and its propinquity to higher cultures or civilizations as well as to actual references to contact and borrowings in the ethnological descriptions.

TABLE 7

RELATION BETWEEN ANNUAL AVERAGE TEMPERATURE AND WARLIKENESS

Average Temperature	1. Defensive War	2. Social War	3. Economic War	4. Political War	Total	Mean Average Warlikeness*
	No. of Primitive Peoples in Each Temperature Belt Practicing Each Type of Warfare					
H Hot (above 70° F.)....	20	161	106	30	317	2.46
T Temperate (30°–70° F.).............	2	137	58	10	207	2.37
C Cold (below 30° F.)....	6	25	6	0	37	2.00
Total..............	28	323	170	40	561	2.39
	Percentage of Primitive Peoples in Each Temperature Belt Practicing Each Type of Warfare					
H Hot.................	6	51	33	10	100	2.46
T Temperate..........	1	66	28	5	100	2.37
C Cold...............	16	68	16	0	100	2.00
All peoples..........	5	58	30	7	100	2.39

* See note to Table 6.

TABLE 8

RELATION BETWEEN NATURAL HABITAT AND WARLIKENESS

Habitat	No. of Primitive Peoples in Each Type of Habitat Practicing Each Type of Warfare					Percentage of Primitive Peoples in Each Type of Habitat Practicing Each Type of Warfare						Rank Order of Habitats
	1. Defensive War	2. Social War	3. Economic War	4. Political War	Total	1. Defensive War	2. Social War	3. Economic War	4. Political War	Total	Mean Average Warlikeness*	
HM Hot mountainous...	2	12	7	1	22	9	54	32	5	100	2.33	
TM Temperate mountainous.........	0	29	5	0	34	0	85	15	0	100	2.15	
CM Cold mountainous..	0	2	0	0	2	0	100	0	0	100	2.00	
M Total mountainous..........	2	43	12	1	58	3	74	21	2	100	2.22	2
HD Hot desert........	0	5	3	2	10	0	50	30	20	100	2.70	
TD Temperate desert...	0	20	10	1	31	0	65	32	3	100	2.38	
CD Cold desert........	0	1	1	0	2	0	50	50	0	100	2.50	
D Total desert.....	0	26	14	3	43	0	60	33	7	100	2.47	4
HG Savanna...........	0	25	60	15	100	0	25	60	15	100	2.90	
TG Steppe...........	1	12	21	7	41	3	29	51	17	100	2.82	
CG Tundra...........	0	5	4	0	14	0	56	44	0	100	2.44	
G Total grassland...	1	42	85	22	150	1	28	56	15	100	2.85	5
HF Tropical rain forest.	17	81	22	9	129	13	63	17	7	100	2.48	
TF Broadleaf forest....	1	66	15	2	84	1	79	18	2	100	2.21	
CF Coniferous forest...	1	13	0	0	14	7	93	0	0	100	1.93	
F Total forest......	19	160	37	11	227	8	71	17	4	100	2.17	1
HS Hot seashore.......	1	38	14	4	57	2	66	25	7	100	2.37	
TS Temperate seashore.	0	10	7	0	17	0	59	41	0	100	2.41	
CS Cold seashore......	5	4	1	0	10	50	40	10	0	100	1.60	
S Total seashore....	6	52	22	4	84	7	62	26	5	100	2.29	3
Grand total.......	28	323	170	40	561	5	58	30	7	100	2.39	......

* See note to Table 6.

TABLE 9

RELATION BETWEEN CLIMATIC ENERGY AND WARLIKENESS

Climatic Energy	1. Defensive War	2. Social War	3. Economic War	4. Political War	Total	Mean Average Warlikeness*
	No. of Primitive Peoples in Each Climatic Energy Zone Practicing Each Type of Warfare					
H High..............	1	54	25	1	81	2.32
M Medium............	2	73	54	11	140	2.53
L Low	26	202	90	29	347	2.34
Total..............	29	329	169	41	568	2.39
	Percentage of Primitive Peoples in Each Climatic Energy Zone Practicing Each Type of Warfare					
H High..............	1	67	31	1	100	2.32
M Medium............	2	52	38	8	100	2.53
L Low	8	59	25	8	100	2.34
All peoples..........	5	58	30	7	100	2.39

* See note to Table 6.

TABLE 10

RELATION BETWEEN RACE AND WARLIKENESS

RACE		No. of Peoples of Each Race and Subrace Practicing Each Type of Warfare					Percentage of Peoples of Each Race and Subrace Practicing Each Type of Warfare						Rank Order of Races
		1. Defensive	2. Social	3. Economic	4. Political	Total	1. Defensive	2. Social	3. Economic	4. Political	Total	Mean Average Warlikeness*	
PN	Negritoes	3	9	0	0	12	25	75	0	0	100	1.75	
PB	Bushmen, etc.	1	5	0	0	6	17	83	0	0	100	1.83	
P	All pygmies......	4	14	0	0	18	22	78	0	0	100	1.78	1
AA	Australians........	0	74	0	0	74	0	100	0	0	100	2.00	
AP	Pre-Dravidians....	7	15	8	1	31	23	48	26	3	100	2.09	
A	All Australoids...	7	89	8	1	105	7	84	8	1	100	2.03	2
NN	Negroes, etc........	0	21	55	23	99	0	21	56	23	100	3.02	
NP	Papuasians........	0	35	1	1	37	0	94	3	3	100	2.09	,
N	All Negroids.....	0	56	56	24	136	0	41	41	18	100	2.77	7
HH	Hamites...........	0	3	9	4	16	0	18	56	25	100	3.04	
HD	Dravidians........	1	5	2	0	8	12	63	25	0	100	2.13	
H	All Hamitoids...	1	8	11	4	24	4	33	46	17	100	2.76	6
BA	Arctics...........	1	8	1	0	10	10	80	10	0	100	2.00	
BI	Indonesians.......	1	4	5	0	10	10	40	50	0	100	2.40	
BP	Polynesians.......	0	4	3	3	10	0	40	30	30	100	2.90	
B	All brown race...	2	16	9	3	30	6	54	30	10	100	2.44	5
RN	Paleoamerinds.....	2	21	11	1	35	6	60	31	3	100	2.31	
RA	Amerinds.........	4	96	42	3	145	3	66	29	2	100	2.30	
RE	Eskimos..........	4	4	0	0	8	50	50	0	0	100	1.50	
R	All red race......	10	121	53	4	188	6	64	28	2	100	2.26	3
YN	Northern Mongols .	0	4	11	1	16	0	25	69	6	100	2.81	
YC	Chinese...........	0	0	0	0	0	0	0	0	0	......	......	
YS	Southern Mongols .	5	35	11	2	53	9	66	21	4	100	2.20	
Y	All yellow race...	5	39	22	3	69	7	57	32	4	100	2.33	4
WA	Alpines...........	0	1	2	1	4	0	25	50	25	100	3.00	
WM	Mediterraneans	0	0	3	0	3	0	0	100	0	100	3.00	
WN	Nordics	0	0	0	0	0	0	0	0	0	......	......	
W	All white race...	0	1	5	1	7	0	14	72	14	100	3.00	8
	Total.............	29	344	169	40	577	5	59	29	7	100	2.38	......

* See note to Table 6.

TABLE 11

RELATION BETWEEN CULTURE AND WARLIKENESS

Culture		1 Defensive War	2. Social War	3. Economic War	4. Political War	Total	Mean Average Warlikeness*
		No. of Primitive Peoples in Each Cultural Class Practicing Each Type of Warfare					
HL	Lower hunters...........	5	91	2	0	98	1.97
HH	Higher hunters...........	12	62	29	0	103	2.20
HD	Dependent hunters.......	1	10	4	0	15	2.20
H	All hunters...........	18	163	35	0	216	2.09
AL	Lower agriculturalists.....	9	37	14	1	61	2.10
AM	Medium agriculturalists...	2	98	51	10	161	2.43
AH	Higher agriculturalists ...	1	38	46	25	110	2.85
A	All agriculturalists......	12	173	111	36	332	2.51
PL	Lower pastorals..........	0	8	15	0	23	2.65
PH	Higher pastorals.........	0	2	13	4	19	3.10
P	All pastorals..........	0	10	28	4	42	2.85
	All peoples.............	30	346	174	40	590	2.38
		Percentage of Primitive Peoples in Each Cultural Class Practicing Each Type of Warfare					
HL	Lower hunters..........	5	93	2	0	100	1.97
HH	Higher hunters..........	12	60	28	0	100	2.20
HD	Dependent hunters	7	66	27	0	100	2.20
H	All hunters...........	8	75	17	0	100	2.09
AL	Lower agriculturalists ...	15	61	23	1	100	2.10
AM	Medium agriculturalists..	1	61	32	6	100	2.43
AH	Higher agriculturalists ...	1	35	42	22	100	2.85
A	All agriculturalists......	4	52	33	11	100	2.51
PL	Lower pastorals	0	35	65	0	100	2.65
PH	Higher pastorals.........	0	11	68	21	100	3.10
P	All pastorals..........	0	24	67	9	100	2.85
	All peoples.............	5	59	29	7	100	2.38

* See note to Table 6.

TABLE 12

RELATION BETWEEN POLITICAL ORGANIZATION AND WARLIKENESS

Political Organization	1. Defensive War	2. Social War	3. Economic War	4. Political War	Total	Mean Average Warlikeness*
	No. of Primitive Peoples in Each Type of Political Organization Practicing Each Type of Warfare					
C Clan sovereignty......	12	66	7	0	85	1.94
V Village sovereignty....	4	77	31	2	114	2.27
T Tribal sovereignty.....	7	97	91	18	213	2.56
S State sovereignty	0	3	13	20	36	3.46
All peoples..........	23	243	142	40	448	2.45
	Percentage of Primitive Peoples in Each Type of Political Organization Practicing Each Type of Warfare					
C Clan sovereignty......	14	78	8	0	100	1.94
V Village sovereignty....	3	68	27	2	100	2.27
T Tribal sovereignty.....	3	46	43	8	100	2.56
S State sovereignty	0	9	37	54	100	3.46
All peoples..........	5	54	32	9	100	2.45

* See note to Table 6.

TABLE 13

RELATION BETWEEN SOCIAL ORGANIZATION AND WARLIKENESS

Social Organization	1. Defensive War	2. Social War	3. Economic War	4. Political War	Total	Mean Average Warlikeness*
	No. of Primitive Peoples in Each Type of Social Organization Practicing Each Type of Warfare					
S Sex-age...............	21	165	35	2	223	2.08
P Professional-occupational.................	1	11	9	4	25	2.64
C Caste................	4	106	104	33	247	2.66
All peoples...........	26	282	148	39	495	2.41
	Percentage of Primitive Peoples in Each Type of Social Organization Practicing Each Type of Warfare					
S Sex-age...............	9	74	16	1	100	2.08
P Professional-occupational.................	4	44	36	16	100	2.64
C Caste................	2	43	42	13	100	2.66
All peoples...........	5	57	30	8	100	2.41

* See note to Table 6.

TABLE 14

RELATION BETWEEN INTERCULTURAL CONTACTS AND WARLIKENESS

Intercultural Contacts	1. Defensive War	2. Social War	3 Economic War	4 Political War	Total	Mean Average Warlikeness*
	No. of Primitive Peoples with Each Type of Intercultural Relations Practicing Each Type of Warfare					
I Isolated peoples	17	219	22	1	259	2.03
M Moderate	9	86	93	17	205	2.59
C Close	1	31	56	23	111	2.91
All peoples	27	336	171	41	575	2.39
	Percentage of Primitive Peoples with Each Type of Intercultural Relations Practicing Each Type of Warfare					
I Isolated peoples	7	84	9	0	100	2.03
M Moderate	4	42	46	8	100	2.59
C Close	1	28	50	21	100	2.91
All peoples	5	58	30	7	100	2.39

* See note to Table 6.

APPENDIX X

THE WARLIKENESS OF PRIMITIVE PEOPLES

The problem of determining the warlikeness of primitive groups proved very difficult. (1) The terms "warlike" and "unwarlike" are used in very different senses by different writers. Some refer to the frequency of war, some to the functional importance of war in the culture, some to the cruelties of war methods as judged by civilized standards, some to the proportion of casualties in battle, and some to the degree of divergence of war objectives from those of civilized people. (2) The writers frequently do not adequately identify the groups which they characterize as warlike or unwarlike. (3) Descriptions of war practices are frequently omitted or inadequate in materials dealing with a particular people. (4) Changes in war practices occur within the same group especially after it comes into contact with a more civilized people, and it is not always easy to determine the time to which an author refers in considering the war practices of a primitive people.

A little investigation indicated that data were inadequate to measure warlikeness among many tribes directly by the frequency of war or by the proportion of losses in battle and that judgments as to the cruelty of war practices or the justice of war causes were too subjective to be of any value. It appeared, however, that material existed to determine for a considerable number of tribes the objects of war, the nature of military organization, the types of strategy and tactics employed, and the attitude of the group toward war; that these four variables were closely correlated with one another; and that the series thus provided did have a close relation to at least some conceptions of warlikeness.

If war is never embarked upon except for immediate defense of the group against attack, military organization is usually nonexistent, tactics consist in the spontaneous use of methods and weapons employed in the hunt, and war is generally regarded as a calamity when it occurs. Groups with these characteristics are almost universally characterized as unwarlike. Even more does this characterization apply to the few tribes who do not even defend themselves from attack.[1]

If war is never embarked upon for economic or political purposes, but is regularly utilized to slaughter extra-group individuals or groups for purposes of revenge, religious expiation, sport, or personal prestige, there is seldom a specialized military class, though all boys are likely to have military training; tactics follow established methods of raid, ambush, and pitched battle, utilizing special-

---

[1] See Margaret Mead, "Warfare Is Only an Invention," *Asia*, August, 1940, p. 402; see also above, chap. vi, n. 24.

ized military weapons; and portions of the tribe, at least, are inclined eagerly to embark upon war as a laudable and sporting adventure. While some writers characterize groups with this practice as warlike, and undoubtedly they are more warlike than groups of the first type, it seems appropriate to regard them as less warlike than those who utilize war for providing economic necessities.

If war, in addition to utilization for defensive and social purposes, is an important method for acquiring slaves, women, cattle, pastures, agricultural lands, or other economic assets essential to the life of the group, there are usually age groups specializing in warfare, trained in techniques of mass attack and mutual support, directed toward the most efficient achievement of the intended economic objects, and the group usually regards war as a necessary routine in its economic activities. As the objects of such war usually include the taking of women or slaves, enemies are, if possible, made prisoners instead of being slaughtered. Consequently, this type of war may seem more humane, and groups using it are by some considered less warlike than those in the second group. It appears, however, that the casualties of this kind of war are usually greater in proportion to the population than in purely social war. When defending his possessions, the enemy is more formidable than when his sole object is to save his skin or his head, for which purpose flight is adequate. Furthermore, groups which use war for economic purposes usually also employ it for social purposes, such as the provision of victims for human sacrifice or for blood revenge, frequently on a larger scale than do people in the second group.

Finally, if war is fought not only for defensive, social, and economic purposes but also to maintain a ruling class in power and to expand the area of empire or political control, there is usually a specialized standing army, trained in mass maneuver, obedience to command, and the construction of artificial defenses. War is conducted by complicated operations often involving the co-operation of specialized military services, and war is regarded as particularly honorable and praiseworthy. It seems appropriate to regard people employing this type of war as the most warlike of all, not only because of their peculiarly favorable attitude toward war but also because they receive and inflict the greatest losses of population from war of any primitive people. The high morale which armies developed by people of this type customarily display enables them to endure more mutual slaughter than can the less-disciplined warriors involved in other types of primitive warfare. Furthermore, the tactics and weapons used by people of this class are more efficient for purposes of slaughter.[2]

[2] For further details see Appen. IX, Table 5, n. ‡.

APPENDIX XI

THE CLASSIFICATION OF RACES

Most writers are clear that race refers to a biological rather than to a cultural classification of human beings and that it is to be determined by the common possession of certain characteristics by the members of the group (Table 15).[1] Beyond this, however, there is little agreement as to either the meaning or the criteria of race. Three points of view may be distinguished.

1. After the time of Darwin biological relations were assumed to mean genealogical relations; that is, the more ancestors in common, the closer the racial relationship. Physical anthropologists have often assumed that two individuals were of the same "race" because they had nearer ancestors in common than either of them had with any individual of another "race." An illustration will show the danger of making such an assumption on the basis of any physical criteria. An American octoroon who is almost indistinguishable from a white man probably has nearer ancestors in common with any Guinea coast Negro than does a Papuan from New Guinea, who, however, very closely resembles the Guinea Negro in almost all physical characteristics. With this conception of race, clearly any conclusions drawn from a comparison of physiological characteristics should be carefully checked by consideration of geographic separation, history of actual migrations, and appreciation of the possibilities of rapid change of physical characteristics because of hybridization or the direct or indirect influence of changing environment, customs, and standards.

2. Modern geneticists are tending to modify the conception of biological relationship. According to their conception every living organism is in essence a combination of genes which, apart from infrequent mutation, are unchangeable and immortal, handed on from generation to generation. Among all organisms there are perhaps one thousand gene types, of which each may appear in perhaps ten alternative forms or allelomorphs. This would make, utilizing all possible combinations, 10^{1000} possible organic individuals. That this is a large number can be realized when it is pointed out that the total number of electrons and protons in the whole visible universe is much less than 10^{100}. Although this mathematically possible field of gene combinations cannot be realized, yet enough of it can so that "there is no reasonable chance that any two individuals will have exactly the same genetic constitution in a species of millions of millions of individuals persisting over millions of generations."[2] With this conception, bio-

[1] See, e.g., A. C. Hadden, *The Races of Man and Their Distribution* (New York, 1925), p. 1. This classification is followed in the main in Table 15.

[2] Sewall Wright, "The Roles of Mutation, Inbreeding, Cross-breeding and Selection in Evolution," *Proceedings of the Sixth International Congress of Genetics*, I (1932), 356

Race and Subrace	Color	Hair	Hirsuteness	Head	Face	Nose	Eye	Stature	Habitat
Pygmy:									
PN Negrito	Black	Frizzy	Smooth	Broad	Broad	Flat	Wide	Short	Indonesia
PB Bushman	Yellow	Frizzy	Smooth	Medium	Medium	Flat	Wide	Short	Africa
Negroid:									
NN Negro	Black	Frizzy	Smooth	Narrow	Narrow	Flat	Wide	Variable	Africa
NP Papuan	Black	Frizzy	Smooth	Narrow	Narrow	Flat	Wide	Variable	{Indonesia / Melanesia
Australoid:									
AA Australian	Dark brown	Wavy	Hairy	Narrow	Narrow	Flat	Wide	Medium	Australia
AP Pre-Dravidian	Black	Wavy	Hairy	Narrow	Narrow	Flat	Wide	Medium	Asia
Hamitoid:									
HH Hamite	Dark brown	Curly	Smooth	Narrow	Narrow	Straight	Wide	Medium	Africa
HD Dravidian	Dark brown	Curly	Smooth	Narrow	Narrow	Straight	Wide	Medium	Asia
Red:									
RN Narrow Head	Reddish brown	Straight	Smooth	Narrow	Narrow	Straight	Narrow	Medium	America
RE Eskimo	Reddish yellow	Straight	Smooth	Narrow	Broad	Straight	Narrow	Short	America
RA Amerind	Reddish brown	Straight	Smooth	Broad	Broad	Straight	Narrow	Tall	America
Yellow:									
YN Northern Mongolian	Tawny	Straight	Smooth	Broad	Broad	Medium	Mongolian	Tall	Asia
YC Chinese	Yellow	Straight	Smooth	Medium	Medium	Medium	Mongolian	Medium	Asia
YS Southern Mongolian	Yellow brown	Straight	Smooth	Medium	Medium	Medium	Mongolian	Medium	Indonesia
Brown:									
BA Arctic	Light brown	Wavy	Medium	Narrow	Narrow	Straight	Narrow	Medium	Asia
BD Indonesian	Light brown	Wavy	Medium	Narrow	Narrow	Straight	Narrow	Medium	Indonesia
BP Polynesian	Light brown	Wavy	Medium	Medium	Medium	Straight	Narrow	Medium	Oceania
White:									
WN Nordic	White	Wavy	Hairy	Medium	Medium	Straight	Wide	Tall	Europe
WA Alpine	White	Wavy	Hairy	Broad	Broad	Straight	Wide	Tall	Europe
WN Mediterranean	Brunette	Wavy	Hairy	Narrow	Narrow	Straight	Medium	Medium	Mediterranean

logical relationship refers to the number of gene forms which two individuals have in common. Two individuals would thus be of the same race when they have in common a certain minimum of gene forms greater than the number which is shared with any individual of another race. Natural dividing-lines between races might be determined by observed discontinuities in the total series of possible gene combinations. As every change in gene form presumably produces changes in the adult individual, there is some relationship between physical characteristics and gene constitution, but it is not a one-to-one relation. A change in one gene may produce changes in many somatic characteristics, and, conversely, to produce a particular somatic change, a change in several genes may be necessary. Thus to distinguish races, those physiological characteristics should be compared which would indicate a maximum genetic difference. Such characteristics are not necessarily those which are most obvious. From this point of view geographic or historic factors would be less significant than physiological measurements. Writers like Griffith Taylor, Roland Dixon, Ellsworth Huntington, and W. C. MacLeod, who have emphasized physical measurements and largely ignored geographical separations in distinguishing races, may have presented evidence bearing upon this conception of race, although they have sought to bring it into relationship with the genealogical theory. They have accounted for the wide distribution of many of these "races" by assuming that new races have originated in Asia in successive waves, each wave pushing the earlier races out toward the periphery of the land mass.

3. Biological relationship might also refer to the amount of interbreeding which is actually going on in a group. Thus Flinders-Petrie has defined a "race" as "a group of human beings, whose type has become unified by their rate of assimilation exceeding the rate of change produced by foreign elements."[3] An organic species has recently been defined as "a group of individuals fully fertile, *inter se*, but barred from interbreeding with other similar groups by its physiological properties (producing either incompatibility of parents, or sterility of the hybrids, or both)."[4] Most taxonomists have, in fact, given weight in distinguishing species to geographical isolation which actually prevents interbreeding even when physiologically possible. All contemporary human races have been regarded as of the same species because there are no physiological bars to interbreeding. There have been, however, at all times, if we assume a multiple origin for the human race, or at all times since the first division of the primitive human group by migration, actual barriers to interbreeding among different groups either because of geographic distance, geographic barriers, or psychological barriers.

[3] Address to the British Association, Ipswich, 1895, quoted by A. H. Keane, *Man, Past and Present* (Cambridge, 1900), p. 37.

[4] T. Dobzhansky, "A Critique of the Species Concept in Biology," *Philosophy of Science*, II (July, 1935), 353.

Most anthropologists have, in classifying races, actually paid attention to such barriers.[5]

Groups which are geographically separated have usually been regarded as distinct races, or at least subraces, even though they closely resemble one another, as, for instance, the Negroes and Papuans, or the Polynesians and Alpines, or the Australians and pre-Dravidians of India.

Furthermore, the most obvious physiological features are usually selected as criteria of race. Such features as skin color, hair character, and nose shape are not only easiest for the anthropologist to observe but also most likely to enter into subjective standards of beauty of the peoples concerned. Differences in such features, therefore, usually influence sexual attractiveness and so present psychological barriers to interbreeding even among groups occupying the same or adjacent areas.

It is to be observed that sociological characteristics—language, dress, religion, legal status—may equally constitute a bar to interbreeding. This conception of race is not, therefore, wholly unrelated to the conceptions of culture and nationality. Two physiologically similar groups in close contact may, because of divergent cultures or nationalities, actually refrain from interbreeding. If this continued for a long time, they would in the sense now under consideration be distinct races. Such long isolation, however, would probably cause the two groups to diverge physiologically and thus to become distinct races in the other two senses.

A race will, therefore, be defined as a group of human beings which for a long period of time (thousands of years) have been barred from interbreeding with other similar groups because of geographic or psychological barriers. It is clear that the progress of travel and communication during the last five hundred years has greatly reduced the influence of geographic barriers, but numerous psychological barriers to race amalgamation still exist. Probably those based on culture are tending to be of more importance than those based on physiological characters. Consequently, if human differences are viewed dynamically, racial differences which in earlier times tended to bring about cultural differences may in the future be determined by cultural differences. Cultural and national differences may lead to psychological barriers to interbreeding and consequently in time to racial differences. Democratic and humanistic theories tend to minimize such a tendency, while aristocratic and "racial" theories tend to augment it.

---

[5] See, e.g., classifications by Hadden, *op. cit.*, pp. 15 ff.; A. H. Keane, *Ethnology* (Cambridge, 1916), pp. 228 ff.; Max Schmidt, *The Primitive Races of Mankind: A Study in Ethnology*, trans. A. K. Dallas (London, 1926), pp. 203 ff. See Fig. 23, Appen. IX.

APPENDIX XII

POPULATION CONTROLS AMONG
PRIMITIVE PEOPLES

It is possible to distinguish four theories which hold, respectively, that primitive peoples have (1) a low birth rate and a low death rate, (2) a high birth rate and a high death rate, (3) a variable birth rate and a variable death rate according to the biological character of the people, and (4) a variable birth rate and a variable death rate according to the sociological and environmental circumstances of the group.

The first theory holds that primitive women are less fecund than civilized women and that fertility is kept down by abstention during prolonged lactation periods and abortions, or surplus population is eliminated by infanticide or slaughter of the aged. Thus population seldom exceeds the optimum for the group's economic technique, and the death rate apart from these artificial eliminations is not high. Epidemic disease hardly exists, and famine and warfare take less toll than among civilized people.[1] This opinion is supported by the tendency of certain primitive populations, especially in Melanesia and Polynesia, to die out when subjected to new diseases and cultural contacts, indicating that the natural fecundity and fertility of these peoples is not sufficient to overcome increases in the death rate,[2] and by a few detailed studies of primitive groups. Among the Melanesians of New Ireland, for example, though abortion or effective contraception were not practiced, 455 women of three generations averaged only 2.6 children each (about the same as native white women in the United States in 1930), a rate which remained constant in spite of the decrease in the death rate in the first generation of white contacts, probably due to elimination of native warfare, and the increase in the death rate in the second generation of white contact, probably due to the importation of white man's diseases.[3]

The second theory holds that the fecundity of primitive women is ample, that the fertility is greater than among most civilized people, and that high death rates from infant mortality, disease, warfare, and occasional pestilence and famine keep the population down. This opinion is supported by observation of the numerous perils surrounding primitive people, and the consequent infrequency

[1] A. M. Carr-Saunders, *The Population Problem* (Oxford, 1922).

[2] W. H. R. Rivers, *Essays in the Depopulation of Melanesia* (1922); G. H. L. F. Pitt-Rivers, *The Clash of Culture and Contacts of Races* (London, 1927); S. H. Roberts, *Population Problems of the Pacific* (London, 1927).

[3] Hortense Powdermaker, "Vital Statistics in New Ireland," *Human Biology*, III (1931), 351 ff.

f "natural death" among them,[4] and by some observations of high fertility mong certain primitive women, especially American Indians. Boas found that 77 Indian women averaged 5.7 children each, and Hrdlicka found that Apache women averaged 6.7 children each, Pima women 7.03, and Pueblo women 9.4.[5] The fertility of African women seems to be less, but greater than the average of ative white women in the United States in 1930. French investigations in Togond indicated that each native woman on an average gave birth to 4.03 children uring her life, of which 3.02 lived after fifteen years.[6] Monica Hunter reported hat among the Pondos of South Africa each married woman averaged 3.91 children, of which 2.41 lived after maturity.[7]

The third theory refuses to characterize either primitive or civilized people as f either high or low fertility, high or low death rate, but compares the circulaion of the population to the metabolism rate of an organism which differs as etween organisms and in the same organism at different ages. According to his theory, young populations have high fecundity, high fertility, high birth ates, and high but lesser death rates, and so are increasing in size. Middle-aged opulations have less fecundity, less fertility, and lower birth rates, and lower eath rates, keeping at about stable size. Old populations have lower fecundity, ertility, and birth rates. Death rates, while lower, are sufficient gradually to iminish the size of the population until it dies out unless rejuvenated. This heory assumes that the immortal germ plasm passed on from generation to genration in a given population gradually diminishes in vigor, thus reducing fecundity, upon which fertility and the birth rate eventually depend, until it is ejuvenated by crossing with the germ plasm of a young population which has onquered or migrated into the senile group. The theory is supported by oberation of the wide variations of fecundity and fertility and birth rates of different opulations, both primitive and civilized, and of the rejuvenating influence of acial mixtures.[8] The believers in low fecundity among primitive peoples seem enerally to be most familiar with the peoples of the Pacific, while the believers high fertility are more often familiar with the American Indian, a fact sugestive of wide differentials among primitive peoples as assumed by this theory. he American Indian may be a relatively "young race," particularly as comared with Melanesian groups who have long interbred on small islands.

The fourth theory doubts whether fecundity varies very much among human roups and believes it is always ample to keep population increasing whenever

[4] A. B. Wolfe, "The Fecundity and Fertility of Early Man," *Human Biology*, V (933), 35.

[5] *Ibid.*

[6] R. L. Buell, *The Native Problem in Africa* (New York, 1928), II, 349.

[7] *Reaction to Conquest* (London, 1936), p. 147.

[8] Corrado Gini, "The Cyclical Rise and Fall of Population," in Gini *et al.*, *Population* 'Harris Foundation Lectures" [Chicago, 1930]); William Flinders-Petrie, *The Revoluons of Civilization* (3d ed.; London, 1922).

conditions permit, but attributes wide variations in fertility, birth rate, and
death rate to particular customs, circumstances, and vicissitudes of each group
Studies of population, which, as Pearl points out, have usually been most numer
ous after destructive wars,[9] have, since the Napoleonic period, started from th
Malthusian discussion of the tendency of population to increase more rapidl
than the food supply.[10] Some, however, suggest that adjustment results mainl
from external circumstances increasing the death rate, continuously or throug
occasional disasters, while others suggest the possibility of adjustment throug
group mores, limiting the birth rate, or through improvements in technology, in
creasing the food supply. Some of these studies follow Malthus in attempting
generalized mathematical treatment aimed at finding logistic or other curve
applicable to the different situations;[11] some carefully assemble statistics to sho
the actual components in the balance of births and deaths;[12] and some describ
the varying psychic, social, and material circumstances affecting the component
of population change.[13]

None of these methods has yielded results permitting a precise statement o
the relation between fertility and warlikeness among primitive peoples. Ther
seems to be some relationship between warlikeness and population increase
Such increase tends to cause migration and to disturb the equilibrium of inter
tribal relations.[14] It seems likely, however, that the rate of population increas
depends more upon social practices than upon natural fertility.[15]

[9] The Biology of Population Growth (New York, 1925), p. 2.

[10] T. R. Malthus, An Essay on the Principles of Population (1st ed., 1798).

[11] Pearl, op. cit.; J. Shirley Sweeney, The Natural Increase of Mankind (Baltimor
1926).

[12] Robert R. Kuczynski, The Balance of Births and Deaths (Washington, 1929); "Th
World's Future Population," in Gini et. al., op. cit., pp. 283 ff.; Sir G. H. Knibbs, Th
Shadow of the World's Future (London, 1928).

[13] James A. Fields, Essays in Population (Chicago, 1931); Warren F. Thompsor
Population Problems (New York, 1930); Danger Spots in World Population (New York
1930).

[14] Chap. vi, secs. 2 and 3, above.   [15] Chap. vi, n. 47, above.

APPENDIX XIII

EFFECT OF WAR UPON POPULATION
AMONG PRIMITIVE PEOPLES

Writers on population have expressed varied opinions upon the influence of war in keeping primitive populations down.[1] The small amount of statistical data available indicates that war has been a more important population eliminator among primitive than among civilized peoples.

Warner was able to learn of one hundred killed in seventy-two engagements during a period of twenty years in the Murngin population of about three thousand. He thought these figures should be doubled to account for the cases not heard of, thus making an average annual loss of ten a year, or 0.33 per cent of the population.[2]

Thurnwald estimates that in Buin of the Solomons, before white influence, with a population of seven thousand, an average of one man a week was killed by war or feud. This would mean the very large annual loss of 0.71 per cent of the population from these causes.[3]

Cole states that the Tinguians lost twenty-nine men in a memorably disastrous expedition in 1889.[4] The population waging this war was not over five thousand.[5] This loss would be comparable to a loss of 232,000 by France at the time of World War I, a figure considerably exceeded in the Battle of Verdun in 1916. This loss was very exceptional, and probably the average losses were not greater among the Tinguians than among the Murngins.

Radcliffe-Brown was able to learn of only six killed in eight attacks during a period of thirty years among the people of the South Andaman Islands numbering some twelve hundred, an annual average loss of less than 0.02 per cent of the population.[6]

Kroeber states that in their largest war, in 1830 or 1840, the Yurok, with a population of twenty-five hundred, collected an army of eighty-four, and half a

[1] Above, Appen. XII.

[2] W. Lloyd Warner, "Murngin Warfare," *Oceania*, I (January, 1931), 457 ff.

[3] "The Price of the White Man's Peace," *Pacific Affairs*, IX (September, 1936), 358.

[4] *The Tinguians* (Field Museum of Natural History Pub. 209, "Anthropological Series," Vol. XIV, No. 2).

[5] The Philippine census of 1918 gave a total Tinguian population of 7,034, of which about half were civilized. Cole, however, informs me that the total population was more nearly 20,000, of which about a quarter supported this war.

[6] *The Andaman Islanders* (Cambridge, 1922), p. 86. See also chap. vi, n. 24, above.

year later their enemy, the Hupa, retaliated with an army of a hundred. There seem to have been seldom over three to ten lost in such engagements, sometimes none at all.[7] Assuming an average loss of three in a raid, and an average of two raids a year, the percentage of casualties would be less than among the Murngins—0.24 per cent of the population. Kroeber also notes a deficiency of 27 males in the Yurok population of 1,052 counted in a census made in 1852. If his attribution of this deficiency to losses by war and feud is correct, it would mean a loss of 2.5 per cent in a generation from these causes, or, counting a generation about twenty-five years, 0.1 per cent a year. As some women and children were often killed in raids, the larger figure indicated above—0.24 per cent—is probably a more accurate estimate of the annual average Yurok losses from war and feud. Kroeber also refers to the important depopulating influence of the warlike habits of the Indians of eastern United States but gives no figures.[8]

It appears that during the nineteenth century France (probably the heaviest sufferer from war among modern nations), with an average population of about thirty-four million, lost from battle casualties about two and a half million men,[9] or an annual average of twenty-five thousand, amounting to 0.07 per cent of the population—less than the Murngin, Buin, or Yurok, but more than the Andaman.

To get a just impression of the influence of war losses, the proportion of these losses to the total annual deaths should be known. The average annual death rate of France during the nineteenth century was about 2.5 per cent of the population, of which the deaths from battle casualties amounted to about 3 per cent.[10] As pointed out in Appendix XII, some primitive people have a very high birth rate and a very high death rate, but others appear to have relatively low birth and death rates. The latter condition seems to have been common in Australia and the Pacific islands, while the former was more typical on the American continent. If we assume a death rate of 3 per cent among the Murngins, it would mean that war losses constituted some 11 per cent of all deaths. If we assume that the general death rate among the Yuroks was twice as great (6 per cent), the figures given would indicate that war losses constituted only 4 per cent of these deaths. Both of these figures are higher than the proportion of deaths caused by war in France during the nineteenth century.

[7] *Handbook of the Indians of California* (Smithsonian Institution, Bureau of Ethnology Bull. 78 [Washington, 1925]), p. 126.

[8] *American Anthropologist* (N.S.), XXXVI (January, 1934), 10.

[9] G. Bedart, *Losses of Life in Modern War* (Oxford, 1916), p. 156; see also below, Appen. XXI, Table 57.

[10] Bodart, *op. cit.*, p. 156.

CHARACTERISTICS OF THE HISTORIC CIVILIZATIONS

Certain characteristics of twenty-six civilizations are grouped in Table 16 according to geographical regions and in Table 17 according to degrees of warlikeness. The meaning of the terms characterizing the civilizations is indicated in notes referring to each column. Appendixes V (Figs. 12 and 15), XV, and XVI (Figs. 24, 25, 26, and 27) present the data utilized in these tables concerning duration, population, military characteristics, and battle frequency of certain of these civilizations.

TABLE 16
CHARACTERISTICS OF CIVILIZATIONS, REGIONALLY ARRANGED

Civilization	General Characteristics									Frequency of Battles				Military Techniques										Military Characteristics			
	0 Population	1 Period	2 Geography	3 Agriculture	4 Commerce	5 Intercivilization Contacts	6 Heterogeneity	7 Political Organization	8 Bloodthirstiness	9 Imperialistic	10 Interstate	11 Civil	12 Defensive	13 Morale and Discipline	14 Professionalization	15 Infantry	16 Cavalry and Chariotry	17 Navy	18 Archery	19 Hand Weapons	20 Body Armor	21 Fortification	22 Siegecraft	23 Attack Efficiency	24 Defense Efficiency	25 Superiority of Defense	26 Warlikeness
Mediterranean:																											
Egyptic (ME)	1	1	R	I	1	1	0	2		1	1	1	2	1	1	1	1	1	1	0	1	0		6	14	8	6 P
Minoan (MM)	0	1	M	D	2	2	0	2		1	0	1	1	1	1	0	1	2	1	1	0	2	0	7	15	8	5 P
Hittite (MH)	1	1	P	D	1	1	0	3	1	2	1	1	1	3	2	1	1	1	2	1	1	1	1	13	26	13	10 M
Classic (MC)	4	2	P	D	2	3	2	2	3	2	2	2	3	3	3	1	2	1	3	2	2	2	2	14	34	20	12 W
Orthodox (MO)	3	3	A	D	2	3	3	2	2	1	1	1	2	2	3	3	1	1	1	3	2	3	2	10	34	24	6 P
Arabic (MA)	1	3	S	G	1	2	1	2	2	3	1	1	1	2	1	2	3	1	3	1	1	0		12	20	8	10 M
Oriental:																											
Mesopotamian (OM)	1	1	R	G	2	1	1	1	1	1	1	1	2	1	1	1	1	2	1	1	1						9
Tartar (OT)	1	1	S	G	1	2	1	3	3	3	1	1	1	2	1	1	3	0	3	1	1	0	2	9	17	8	6 P
Babylonic (OB)	2	2	P	I	3	2	2	3	3	3	1	1	1	3	3	1	1	1	3	2	3	1	2	14	14	0	12 W
Syriac (OS)	3	2	P	D	2	3	2	3	2	3	1	2	2	2	3	3	2	1	2	2	3	1	2	10	38	28	13 W
Iranian (OI)	2	3	P	D	1	2	2	3	2	3	1	1	2	2	3	3	2	1	2	2	1	1	1	16	32	16	11 W
European:																											
Germanic (EG)	1	2	A	D	0	2	1	1	2	2	1	1	1	1	1	2	0	1	1	0	0	0	0	5	13	8	7 W
Western (EW)	3	3	A	D	2	3	3	1	1	2	2	2	2	2	3	3	2	2	3	3	3	2	2	10	38	28	8 M
Irish (EI)	0	3	A	D	1	2	1	1	1	1	1	1	1	1	1	1	1	0	1	1	1	1	1	5	13	8	8 P
Scandinavian (ES)	0	3	M	D	1	1	1	1	3	3	1	1	1	1	1	1	0	1	1	1	1	1	1	5	13	8	5 M
Russian (ER)	2	3	A	D	1	2	2	2	2	2	1	1	1	2	1	1	3	1	2	1	2	2	1	6	24	18	9 M
Nestorian (EN)	0	3	P	D	1	2	2	1	0	1	0	0	1	1	0	0	0	0	0	0	0	0	0	1	2	1	3 P
Indian:																											
Indic (II)	3	1	R	D	2	1	1	1	1	1	1	1	1	3	3	2	1	1	1	1	1	1	1	11	27	16	5 P
Hindu (IH)	4	2	A	D	1	2	2	1	1	1	1	1	1	3	3	2	1	1	1	1	1	1	1	11	27	16	5 P
Far Eastern:																											
Sinic (FS)	3	1	R	I	2	1	1	1	1	2	1	2	1	1	1	1	1	1	1	1	3	1		4	17	13	6 P
Japanese (FJ)	2	2	A	D	1	1	3	3	3	1	2	3	1	3	3	2	1	1	2	1	1	1	1	15	26	11	12 W
Chinese (FC)	4	2	A	D	2	2	1	2	0	2	1	2	2	1	1	1	1	1	1	1	3	1		4	17	13	6 P
American:																											
Andean (AA)	1	1	P	D	1	0	1	3	3	3	1	1	0	2	2	1	0	0	1	1	2	1		7	17	10	9 W
Mayan (AMa)	1	1	A	D	1	0	1	2	1	1	1	1	1	1	1	0	0	0	1	1	1	1	0	3	11	8	6 P
Mexican (AM)	1	2	P	D	1	1	2	3	3	3	1	1	1	1	1	0	0	0	1	1	1	1	0	2	14	12	11 W
Yucatec (AY)	1	2	A	D	1	1	2	3	2	2	1	1	1	1	1	0	0	0	1	1	1	1	0	2	14	12	8 M

TABLE 17

CHARACTERISTICS OF CIVILIZATIONS, ARRANGED ACCORDING TO DEGREES OF WARLIKENESS

Civilization	GENERAL CHARACTERISTICS									FREQUENCY OF BATTLES				MILITARY TECHNIQUES										MILITARY CHARACTERISTICS			
	0	1	2	3	4	5	6	7	8	9	10	11	12	13	14	15	16	17	18	19	20	21	22	23	24	25	26
	Population	Period	Geography	Agriculture	Commerce	Intercivilization Contacts	Heterogeneity	Political Organization	Bloodthirstiness	Imperialistic	Interstate	Civil	Defensive	Morale and Discipline	Professionalization	Infantry	Cavalry and Chariotry	Navy	Archery	Hand Weapons	Body Armor	Fortification	Siegecraft	Attack Efficiency	Defense Efficiency	Superiority of Defense	Warlikeness
Warlike:																											
Babylonic	2	2	P	D	3	2	2	3	3	3	1	1	1	3	3	3	1	1	1	3	2	3	1	10	38	28	13
Classic	4	2	A	D	2	3	2	2	2	3	2	2	2	3	3	3	1	2	1	3	2	2	2	14	34	20	12
Tartar	2	1	S	G	1	2	1	3	3	3	1	1	1	2	1	1	3	0	3	1	1	0	2	14	14	0	12
Japanese	2	2	A	D	1	1	3	3	3	3	1	2	3	1	3	3	2	1	1	2	1	1	1	15	26	11	12
Andean	1	1	P	D	1	0	1	3	3	3	1	1	0	2	2	1	0	0	1	1	1	2	1	7	17	10	12
Syriac	3	2	P	D	2	3	3	2	3	3	1	2	2	2	3	3	2	3	3	1	2	2	1	16	32	16	11
Iranian	2	3	P	D	1	2	2	3	2	3	1	1	2	2	3	3	2	1	2	2	1	1	1	13	29	16	11
Mexican	1	2	P	D	1	1	2	3	3	3	1	2	1	1	1	1	0	0	1	1	1	1	0	2	14	12	11
Moderately warlike:																											
Hittite	1	1	P	D	1	1	0	3	1	2	1	1	1	3	3	2	1	1	2	1	1	1	1	13	26	13	10
Arabic	1	2	S	G	1	2	1	2	2	3	1	1	1	2	1	2	3	1	3	1	1	0	1	12	20	8	10
Scandinavian	0	3	M	D	1	2	1	1	3	3	1	1	1	1	1	1	3	1	2	1	0	1	1	10	14	4	9
Western	3	3	A	D	2	3	3	1	1	2	2	2	2	2	2	3	3	2	2	3	3	2	1	10	38	28	8
Russian	2	3	A	D	1	2	2	2	2	1	1	1	1	1	2	2	1	1	2	2	2	1	1	6	24	18	8
Yucatec	1	2	A	D	1	1	2	2	2	2	1	1	1	1	1	1	0	0	1	1	1	1	0	2	14	12	8
Germanic	1	2	A	D	0	2	1	1	2	2	1	1	1	1	1	1	2	0	1	1	1	0	0	5	13	8	7
Peaceful:																											
Orthodox	3	3	A	D	2	3	3	2	1	1	0	1	2	2	3	3	1	1	1	3	2	3	3	10	32	24	6
Egyptic	1	1	R	I	1	1	0	2	1	1	1	1	2	1	1	1	1	1	1	1	0	1	0	6	14	8	6
Mesopotamian	1	1	R	I	2	1	1	1	1	1	1	1	2	1	1	1	2	1	1	1	1	1	1	9	17	8	6
Sinic	3	1	R	I	2	1	1	1	1	1	2	1	2	1	1	1	1	1	1	3	1	1	1	4	17	13	6
Chinese	4	2	A	D	2	2	1	2	0	2	1	2	2	1	1	1	1	1	1	3	1	1	1	4	17	13	6
Mayan	1	1	A	D	1	0	1	2	1	1	1	1	1	0	0	0	1	1	1	1	0	1	0	3	11	8	6
Minoan	0	1	M	D	2	2	0	2	0	1	1	1	1	1	1	0	2	1	1	0	2	0	0	7	15	8	5
Irish	0	3	A	D	2	1	1	1	1	1	1	1	1	0	1	1	1	1	1	1	1	1	1	5	13	8	5
Indic	3	1	R	D	2	1	1	1	1	1	1	1	1	3	3	2	1	1	1	1	1	1	1	11	27	16	5
Hindu	4	2	A	D	1	2	2	1	1	1	1	1	1	3	3	2	1	1	1	1	1	1	1	11	27	16	5
Nestorian	0	3	P	D	1	2	2	1	0	1	0	0	1	1	0	0	0	0	0	0	0	0	0	1	2	1	3

NOTES TO TABLES 16 AND 17

0. *Population.*—The figures (0, 1, 2, 3, 4) indicate the estimated population at the maximum for the civilization usually at the stage of the universal state. 0=Less than 10 million; 1=10–25; 2=25–50; 3=50–100; 4=100 million or over. It is probable that none of the civilizations reached much over 100 million or, with exception of the abortive Irish and Nestorian civilizations, fell much below 10 million at the maximum. The estimates for Classic and Western civilizations are from J. Beloch ("Die Bevölkerung im Altertum,""Die Bevölkerung Europas im Mittelalter,""Die Bevölkerung Europas zur zeit der Renaissance," *Zeitschrift für Socialwissenschaft* [Berlin, 1899], II, 505 ff., 600 ff.; III, 405 ff., 765 ff.). Those for the Andean, Mayan, Mexican, and Yucatec civilizations are from H. J. Spinden ("The Population of Ancient America," *Geographic Review*, XVIII [October, 1928], 641 ff.). Those for Chinese, Japanese, and Hindu civilizations are from W. F. Willcox ("International Migrations," *Publications of the National Bureau of Economic Research, 1929–1931,* II, No. 11, 49, 63). See also "Population," *Encyclopaedia of the Social Sciences,* XII, 241 ff. Estimates for the other civilizations are guesses based upon consideration of the occupied areas of the civilization at its maximum, the supportable density with prevalent types of economy, and accounts of the size of cities

1. *Period.*—The figures indicate whether the civilization is primary (originated among primitive people), secondary, or tertiary. (See Fig. 12, Appen. V, above.)

2. *Geography.*—R = River; S = Steppe; A = Arable; P = Plateau; M = Maritime, referring to the characteristic which exercised most control in the life of the civilization.

3. *Agriculture.*—G = Grazing; I = Irrigation; D = Dry farming, referring to the major source of food.

4. *Commerce.*—The figures (o, 1, 2, 3) indicate the relative importance of commerce as compared with agriculture in the economy of the civilization. o means no commerce at all, and 3 means that commerce was very important.

5. *Intercivilization contacts.*—The figures (o, 1, 2, 3) indicate the estimated importance of intercivilization contacts whether from commerce, war, missionary enterprise, travel, or migration.

6. *Heterogeneity.*—The figures (o, 1, 2, 3) indicate the estimated average degree of variation in social behavior patterns among groups within the civilization, whether such groups are defined by race, locality, caste, class, or nationality during the mature stage of the civilization before decline has begun. Consideration is given to the rate of cultural assimilation or differentiation and the rate of migration and intermarriage.

7. *Political organization.*—The figures (o, 1, 2, 3) indicate the average degree of absolutism in the typical state during the mature stage of the civilization. If the civilization developed a universal state, it would refer to the characteristics of that state.

8. *Bloodthirstiness.*—The figures (o, 1, 2, 3) indicate the degree in which the average individual of the civilization was habituated to human bloodshed, whether in religious sacrifices, sports and spectacles, executions, feuds, and private wars during its mature stage. The frequency and bloodiness of public war is not considered here.

9. *Imperialistic wars.*—The figures (o, 1, 2, 3) indicate the frequency of battles by a state or group of states of the civilization within the domain of another civilization. Where statistical data were available, as with Classic and Western civilizations, the standard was: o = Less, on the average, than 1 recorded battle a century during the mature stage of the civilization; 1 = Average between 1 and 5 such battles a century; 2 = Average of between 5 and 15 a century; 3 = Over 15 a century. In most cases no statistical data were available, and the estimate was based on general accounts of the civilization.

10. *Interstate wars.*—The figures (o, 1, 2, 3) indicate the frequency of battles between states of the civilization estimated as stated under 9.

11. *Civil wars.*—The figures (o, 1, 2, 3) indicate the frequency of battles between factions or parties within a state of the civilization, estimated as stated under 9.

12. *Defensive war.*—The figures (o, 1, 2, 3) indicate the frequency of battles by groups within the civilization engaged in fighting invading groups from other civilizations, estimated as stated under 9.

13. *Morale.*—The figures (o, 1, 2, 3) indicate the degree of discipline and enthusiasm of the population participating in war, during the stage of maximum military development, usually the end of the time of troubles and the beginning of the universal state. (This last statement applies to the indices in cols. 13–22.)

14. *Professionalization.*—The figures (o, 1, 2, 3) indicate the length of service and amount of military training of the average soldier. The meaning is roughly: o = Wholly untrained militia levy for war; 1 = Small cadre with some training about which a slightly trained militia might be organized in war; 2 = Short-service volunteer or conscript standing army, based on feudal or national obligation, using militia only as reserves; 3 = Long-service professional or mercenary army. Period as stated under 13.

15. *Infantry.*—The figures (o, 1, 2, 3) indicate the importance of the infantry in the army as evidenced by the number of infantry soldiers in the standing or immediately summonable army. The figures mean: o = Less than 100 thousand; 1 = 100–200; 2 = 200–300; 3 = Over 300 thousand, adding all the states of the civilization. Period as stated under 13.

16. *Cavalry and chariotry.*—The figures (o, 1, 2, 3) indicate the relative importance of these branches of the service compared with infantry. Period as stated under 13.

17. *Navy.*—The figures (o, 1, 2, 3) indicate the relative importance of the navy and naval operations in the warfare of the civilization. Period as stated under 13.

18. *Archery.*—The figures (o, 1, 2, 3) indicate the degree of perfection of archery and its relative importance in the military operations of the civilization. Period as stated under 13.

19. *Hand weapons.*—The figures (o, 1, 2, 3) indicate the degree of perfection of swords, spears, pikes, and other weapons used for cutting or thrusting as well as the relative importance of such weapons. Period as stated under 13.

20. *Body armor.*—The figures (o, 1, 2, 3) indicate the degree of perfection of shield, helmet, and body armor. Period as stated under 13.

21. *Fortification.*—The figures (o, 1, 2, 3) indicate the skill displayed in the art of fortification, both permanent and field, and the relative importance of permanent walls and forts in the military operations of the civilization. Period as stated under 13.

22. *Siegecraft.*—The figures (o, 1, 2, 3) indicate the degree in which rams, catapults, and other siege engines were devised and the skill with which they were actually used by the civilization. Period as stated under 13.

23. *Attack efficiency.*—It is assumed that any military organization or instrument has one or more of the qualities of mobility (M), striking power (S), protection (P), or holding power (H) (see J. F. C. Fuller, *The Reformation of War* [New York, 1923], pp. 25 ff., and above, Appen. VII, sec. 3). *Mobility* is measured by the rapidity of movement in space, allowing for the average impediments of the medium through which the instrument passes in war. *Striking power* is measured by the rate, penetrability, and range of destructive impulses discharged from the instrument. *Protection* is measured by the durability of the instrument under attack. *Holding power* is measured by the duration, extensiveness, and completeness with which the instrument can hold territory under attack. Assuming that the enemy has the same military instruments and uses them with the same efficiency as the military force under consideration, it would seem that attack efficiency would increase with the first three of these qualities but would diminish with holding power be-

cause, as the holding power of each side increases, the engagement tends toward stalemate; consequently, attack efficiency can be represented by the expression $M + S + P - H$. With the same assumption it appears that the mobility of a military instrument or force or organization would be assisted by high morale (m), professionalization (p), efficient cavalry (c), navy (n), archery (a), and hand weapons (h)—all of which would assist movement in hostile territory—and by efficient siegecraft (s), which would rapidly reduce such obstacles to progress as walls and fortresses. On the other hand, mobility would be reduced by large infantry forces (i) which travel slowly and present difficult commissariat problems, by heavy body armor (b) which impedes motion, and by great attention to fortification (f) which takes time and emphasizes fixed positions. Thus

$$M = m + p + c + n + a + h + s - i - b - f.$$

With the same assumption it would appear that striking power would be aided by high development of all the factors except fortification and body armor. The height of towers gives added force to archery, javelins, and other missiles, and the walls provide a shelter from which sallies may be made; but, on the other hand, reliance upon fortifications makes it easier for the enemy to keep out of range. The influence of fortification may, therefore, be regarded as neutral. The influence of heavy body armor, reducing the play of muscle, seems to be adverse to striking power in spite of the fact that the weight of an armored knight adds to his momentum and the force of the blow of the lance. Thus

$$S = m + p + i + c + n + a + h + s - b.$$

Protection seems to be unaffected by the relative importance of infantry, cavalry, archery, navy, or hand arms, always bearing in mind the assumption that the enemy has these advantages in the same degree. Protection would be adversely affected by the perfection of siegecraft which would render fortresses less safe. Thus

$$P = m + p + b + f - s.$$

Holding power would seem to be favorably affected by all these factors except siegecraft, which would have an adverse influence. Consequently,

$$H = m + p + i + c + n + a + h + b + f - s.$$

Combining these formulas, attack efficiency (A) becomes

$$A = M + S + P - H = 2m + 2p - i + c + n + a + h - 2b - f + 2s.$$

The figures in col. 23 were found by applying this formula to the figures in cols. 13–22. It is, of course, recognized that attack efficiency is affected by factors such as type of organization, commissariat, etc.; type of tactical formation and maneuver; leadership and strategic ideas, which are not directly considered, although they enter into such factors as morale and professionalization. It is also recognized that the factors considered may not in reality be of the same importance. The estimate is of necessity a crude one, based on averaging of those factors which could even roughly be compared among all the civilizations.

24. *Defense efficiency.*—It appears that, with the same assumptions and definitions as in 23, striking power, protection, and holding power would aid defense, but that mobility, which reduces the efficiency of fixed fortifications, would hinder it. The principle that the offensive may be the best defensive applies equally to both sides. Consequently, the offensive advantage of mobility is neutralized from the defensive point of view. Defense considered by itself can be more efficient if limited to a fixed area, but mobility tends to a continuous widening of the area of operations. Defense efficiency (D) was therefore ascertained from the formula

$$D = S + P + H - M = 2m + 2p + 3i + c + n + a + h + 2b + 3f - 2s.$$

25. *Superiority of defense.*—These figures were found by subtracting those in col. 23 from those in col. 24. They are not related to warlikeness but are roughly related to the primary or derivative character of the civilization. There was a tendency for defensive efficiency to be greatest both absolutely and in relation to offensive efficiency in the tertiary civilizations and lowest in the primary civilizations. Tertiary civilizations which did not develop considerable defensive efficiency were short lived (see chap. vii, n. 56, above).

26. *Warlikeness.*—This figure is intended to indicate both the attitudes and the behavior of the people of the civilization with respect to war. It is assumed that a people habituated to bloodshed, with a high morale and an autocratic government, are warlike, especially when they have frequently engaged in aggressive war. Thus the figure is the sum of those in cols. 7, 8, 9, 10, and 13. Economic and military technology and the relative efficiency of attack and defense influence warlikeness only indirectly as they influence these five factors. If the index is 6 or less, the civilization is designated peaceful (P); where 7 to 10, it is designated moderately warlike (M); and where 11 or over, it is designated warlike (W).

APPENDIX XV

MILITARY CHARACTERISTICS OF THE
HISTORIC CIVILIZATIONS

An army is an institution of a state and, except during the stage of the universal state, not of a whole civilization. The fluctuations in the military techniques of a state are affected by borrowing among the states in contact with one another—a process which tends to produce uniformity in military methods throughout a civilization, where, by definition, the contacts between the states are rather continuous. These fluctuations are, it is true, affected also by inventions and experience in the use of a particular invention—processes which tend toward a differentiation of techniques among the states. But as these processes are not likely to operate rapidly unless there is intense military competition, and as such competition would assure a relatively rapid distribution of any new military invention, military methods are likely to change synchronously in all the states within a civilization. Certain of the characteristics of military organization and activity in the civilization and where possible in each of the four periods of each civilization will be indicated. The Heroic Age, Time of Troubles, Period of Stability, and Period of Decline will be indicated by the numerals I, II, III, and IV. The dates of these stages are given in Table 2, Appendix V.

I. PRIMARY CIVILIZATIONS

EGYPTIC CIVILIZATION[1]

I. There is little evidence of organized military activity before 2500 B.C. beyond that of the champion and his followers characteristic of the higher primitive peoples.

II. In the sixth dynasty, which began about 2500 B.C., an invasion was met by a great army of militia summoned from each province organized into companies of archers and light and heavy infantry.

III. The middle empire, which began about 2000 B.C., developed the art of fortification but conducted few military operations until this stable period was broken by the invasion of the warlike Hyksos about 1750 B.C. They brought with them the horse, and, when they were expelled from Egypt about 1500 B.C.,

---

[1] See O. L. Spaulding, H. Nickerson, and J. W. Wright, *Warfare: A Study of Military Methods from the Earliest Times* (London, 1924), pp. 7–17; G. H. Perris, *A Short History of War and Peace* (New York, 1911), p. 37; G. T. Wrench, *The Causes of War and Peace* (London, 1926), pp. 7, 13; J. H. Breasted, *A History of Egypt* (New York, 1905), pp. 17, 168, 233, 234; C. H. Ashdown, *British and Foreign Arms and Armour* (London, 1909), pp. 22–24; "Egypt," *Encyclopaedia Britannica* (14th ed.), VIII, 55, 61.

they were succeeded by a new Egyptian empire which was centralized, warlike, and imperialistic, utilizing mercenaries extensively. Breasted writes: "It was under the Hyksos that the conservatism of millennia was broken up in the Nile valley. The Egyptians learned aggressive war for the first time, and introduced a well organized military system, including chariotry, which the importation of the horse by the Hyksos now enabled them to do. Egypt was transformed into a military empire."[2]

IV. After recovery from the Assyrian conquest in the seventh century B.C., Egypt relied even more upon mercenaries, and its military spirit degenerated. After the Persian conquest in the sixth century, Egypt did not regain independence, although the civilization retained its main characteristics under foreign rulers until the sixth century A.D.

MESOPOTAMIAN CIVILIZATION[3]

I. Little is known of the military organization in the first stage of Sumerian and Akkadian civilization in Mesopotamia.

II. Before the time of Sargon, however, about 2550 B.C., bas-reliefs show heavy infantry with spears apparently in close-order formation.[4]

III. The succeeding period, in which Hammurabi codified the laws, about 2100 B.C., appears to have been one in which blood feuds were suppressed, relative stability prevailed, and business flourished.

IV. This universal empire degenerated from internal revolt and external war with the Hittites and was shattered by the invasion about 1780 B.C., of the warlike Kassites, who conquered the country and destroyed the civilization.

MINOAN CIVILIZATION[5]

The Minoans in Crete apparently had a highly centralized government and engaged in maritime commerce and the policing of the seas against piracy, but they were unwarlike with no special military class and no body armor. They used large shields, spears, and rapiers. In the later period they surrounded some of their cities with powerful fortifications and acquired a considerable empire by trade and maritime controls. Through most of their civilization they appear to have relied on their insular position and upon ships for defense.

[2] Breasted, op. cit., p. 17.

[3] Spaulding, op. cit., pp. 19 ff.; Perris, op. cit., pp. 23 ff.; A. T. Olmstead, "The Babylonian Empire," American Journal of Semitic Languages and Literature, XXV (January, 1919), 65–100; "Babylonia and Assyria," Encyclopaedia Britannica, II, 843–48.

[4] A. J. Toynbee (A Study of History [3 vols.; Oxford, 1934], I, 428) credits the Sumerians with inventing phalanx infantry-fighting about 3000 B.C.

[5] J. D. S. Pendlebury, The Archaeology of Crete (London, 1939), pp. 271 ff.; Wrench, op. cit., pp. 6–8; Stanley Casson, "The Palace of Minos," Atlantic Monthly, August, 1936, p. 239; "Crete," Encyclopaedia Britannica, VI, 684 ff.

HITTITE CIVILIZATION[6]

I. Little is known of the Hittite military organization before the second millennium B.C., though there is evidence of wars with the Akkadians.

II. There appear to have been many wars in the eighteenth century B.C., including imperial expeditions into Syria and Mesopotamia. This was followed by a period of civil war.

III. The new empire of the fourteenth century B.C. had a strict military and political organization regulated in the smallest details. It engaged in several wars with Egypt and Syria.

IV. The empire declined in the twelfth century and was overrun by Babylonians, by "sea peoples," and by Indo-European Thracians, Phrygians, and Armenians.

SINIC CIVILIZATION[7]

I. In the most ancient times the Chinese seem to have been peacefully inclined, although they had a moderate military organization consisting of foot soldiers, mounted infantry, and chariots. The soldiers wore leather armor and used the bow and arrow as the principal weapon. Wars seem to have had somewhat the character of sporting events with few casualties.

II. Copper and bronze swords were used in the late Chow dynasty (722–225 B.C.), a period when numerous states in northern and central China evolved an elaborate system of diplomacy, balance of power, and war. Iron weapons were used in the Han dynasty (206 B.C.–A.D. 25) as well as scale and plate armor. There was also a great improvement in military organization and fortification, especially the improvement of the great wall by the "first emperor," Ch'in Shih Huang-ti, who unified the empire about 225 B.C.

III. Laufer asks, "What great movement in military tactics caused the radical transformation of armor experienced by the people of China, Central Asia and Siberia around the first century of our era?" and answers that probably the Persian cavalry tactics depending upon the organized charge of horsemen equipped with sword, shield, and armor (instead of bow or cast javelin) was transmitted to China by the Turks of the steppes.

IV. After the Han dynasty this method fell into disuse during the "three kingdoms" period of revolutionary violence in which the old civilization of China collapsed.

[6] Perris, *op. cit.*, p. 20; "Hittite," *Encyclopaedia Britannica*, XI, 599, 604–5.

[7] Berthold Laufer, *Prolegomena on the History of Defensive Armour* ("Field Museum Anthropological Series," Vol. XIII, No. 2 [Chicago, 1914]), pp. 180 ff.; R. S. Britton, "Chinese International Intercourse before 700 B.C.," *American Journal of International Law*, XXIX (October, 1935), 616, 619; C. C. Shih, "International Law in the Ch'un Ch'iu Period, 722–481 B.C." (manuscript, University of Chicago, 1941).

ANDEAN CIVILIZATION[8]

The Andean civilization of Peru developed from the contact of coast and highland Indians for a thousand years or more before the Christian Era to a period of imperial conquest from the seventh to the ninth century A. D. This was followed by a period of disintegration and decline, which in turn was succeeded by the rise of the Inca empire in the fifteenth and sixteenth century. It was cut off at its height by Pizarro's conquest in 1540.

Both before and after the "Dark Age," from A.D. 800 to 1100, there was a highly centralized government, rigorous military discipline, and extensive construction of fortifications.

Vase pictures indicate a Chimu warrior of the early period with helmet, spearthrower, javelin, club, and a small shield in the left hand and an ax hanging from the belt. Battle pictures indicate a specialization of troops, some more and some less armed.

In the Inca period armies of four to eight thousand existed, and there were elaborate fortifications around the capital at Cuzco. There was a definite order of battle and advance under command with music and yells. Clubs and maces were used by the infantry fighters, supported by slingers, archers, and javelin-throwers in the rear.

INDIC CIVILIZATION[9]

I. Vedic literature indicates that the invading Aryans were warlike, though after their conquest of India they sought to rule through religion and caste prestige with a small military caste and isolation of the masses from war.

II. Invasions occurred from the north and west during the fifth and fourth centuries B.C. Janism and Buddhism were initiated as a response to this time of troubles.

III. The Maurya empire developed a centralized government and a powerful military force in the fourth century B.C., which lasted for over two centuries. After an interregnum of invasion of over four centuries the Gupta dynasty (A.D. 300–450) re-established stability and a powerful army.

IV. After the disintegration of the Gupta dynasty disorder followed, leading to the collapse of the civilization.

TARTAR CIVILIZATION[10]

The word "Tartar" is intended to apply to the Scythian, Turkish, and Mongolian nomads of the Russian, central Asian, Siberian, and Mongolian steppes. They were always warlike but appear to have initiated their periodic invasions

[8] P. A. Means, *Ancient Civilizations of the Andes* (New York, 1931), pp. 47, 74–75, 104, 243–61; "South American Archaeology," *Encyclopaedia Britannica*, II, 72.

[9] "India," *Encyclopaedia Britannica*, XII, 183–87.

[10] Wrench, *op. cit.*, pp. 99 ff.; Toynbee, *op. cit.*, III, 12 ff., 395 ff.; Owen Lattimore, "China and the Barbarians," in Joseph Barnes (ed.), *Empire in the East* (New York, 1934), pp. 3–38, and his penetrating review of several books on Mongolia in *Pacific Af-*

to the east, west, and south because of deteriorating pasturage due to climatic change or because of a weakening of the defenses of neighboring agricultural civilizations. They utilized archery and great mobility of light horse without much change from the earliest times. Variations in the success of using this technique depended upon the discipline and organization, the morale and the strategic ideas, which the particular leader was able to develop. Genghis Khan was a military genius. He was able to mobilize, discipline, and maintain a vast host continually moving. He utilized ruses of retreat and strategies of outflanking at will. He also had powerful siege rams and catapults constructed, and he utilized fire effectively in attacking fortified places. The Mongols were ruthless in war. They are said to have delighted in slaughtering the inhabitants after a successful siege.

MAYAN CIVILIZATION[11]

The Mayas lived under urban conditions in the humid lands of Central America as early as 613 B.C., and their population rapidly increased to perhaps eight million by A.D. 600. Soon afterward (A.D. 630) there was a sudden collapse and migration from all of these cities because of epidemic disease or diminution of soil fertility in the surrounding territory.

The Mayas did not have human sacrifice, and "warfare does not seem to have been highly developed, for none of the early Mayan cities were fortified."[12]

2. SECONDARY CIVILIZATIONS

BABYLONIC CIVILIZATION[13]

I. The Assyrians who originated the "Babylonic civilization" were warlike lion hunters who had considerably expanded their empire by 1100 B.C. through utilizing chariots and horsemen.

II. The army became more disciplined and professional during the wars with Egypt and Palestine in the eighth century.

III. After Sargon II a regular army of 50,000–150,000 men was maintained, using infantry in open-order formation assisted by mounted archers, all disciplined and skilled in fortification and siege operations.

---

fairs, X (December, 1937), 462–79; Sir Henry Howorth, *History of the Mongols from the Ninth to the Nineteenth Century* (London, 1876–1927); Harold Lamb, *Genghis Khan* (New York, 1927); *Tamerlane* (New York, 1928); E. H. Parker, *1000 Years of the Tartars* (New York, 1924); Walter Dyk, "A Study of the Effect of Changes of Technique on the Warfare of Barbarian People" (manuscript, Causes of War Study, University of Chicago, 1931).

[11] H. J. Spinden, "The Population of Ancient America," *Geographical Review*, XVIII (October, 1928), 641 ff.; "Central American Archaeology," *Encyclopaedia Britannica*, V, 130–32.

[12] Spinden, *op. cit.*, p. 649.

[13] Spaulding *et al.*, *op. cit.*, pp. 18–26; Ashdown, *op. cit.*, pp. 20–22; "Babylonia and Assyria," *Encyclopaedia Britannica*, II, 848–52.

IV. After the flareup of the Chaldean empire at Babylon there was a decline in military morale before the Persian conquest in the sixth century B.C.

SYRIAC CIVILIZATION[14]

The Syriac civilization as defined by Toynbee included the people under the Persian empires of the Achmenidae and the Sassanids as well as the Abbaside caliphs.

I. The Persians, like most civilized people in their early stages, followed the method of Homeric warfare in which each chief led his own men very much as he pleased.

II. The Median king Cyaxares "first divided the troops of Asia according to arms, and organized them into separate companies, spearmen and archers and horsemen; until then they had been mixed together."[15] The mounted archers with short swords and great mobility were the principal arm.

III. In the sixth century Cyrus improved the discipline of the standing army, recruited local levies to create vast expeditionary forces, and greatly extended the Persian empire. Delbrück, like other modern commentators, declines to accept the enormous figures for the Persian armies offered by Herodotus.[16] The cavalry armor was increased in weight by Darius, who also frequently substituted the javelin for the bow. There were interregnums in portions of the Syriac civilization between the time of the Achmenidae and the Sassanids when much of the territory was Hellenized by the conquest of Alexander. There were also interregnums between the Sassanids and the Abbasides when the Arabs overran much of the area. But the military methods did not greatly alter.

IV. The discipline of the Abbaside caliphs' army declined after the tenth century A.D., and the civilization collapsed before Arabs and Turks in the thirteenth century. The attacks upon Syriac civilization by the mobile nomads of desert and steppe may be compared to the attacks upon Western Christian civilization by the mobile vikings of Scandinavia.

CLASSIC CIVILIZATION

The stages in the military development of the Greek and Roman branches of Classic civilization were not wholly synchronous, so in this case each will be treated separately.

GREECE[17]

I. There are indications in the Homeric epic of considerable bodies of troops organized in phalanxes in addition to the heroes to whom most attention is giv-

---

[14] Spaulding et al., op. cit., pp. 26–34; Herodotus i. 103 ff.; René Grousset, "The Role of Iran in the History of Asia," in B. Laufer (ed.), The New Orient (Chicago, 1933), II, 44–52.

[15] Herodotus i. 103–4; Spaulding et al., op. cit., p. 26.

[16] Herodotus vii. 186; Hans Delbrück, Geschichte der Kriegskunst (6 vols.; Berlin, 1900–1929), I, 10; Spaulding et al., op. cit., p. 33; see above, chap. vii, n. 3.

[17] Spaulding et al., op. cit., pp. 37–97; Ashdown, op. cit., pp. 24–33; Perris, op. cit., pp. 45–54; Toynbee, op. cit., III, 165 ff.

en. Thucydides, in fact, estimates, from these passages of Homer, 100,000 in the Greek army before Troy.[18] Probably, however, the individual hero in chariot or on foot played an important part, the lesser troops having the character of personal retainers.

II. Before the Persian wars, however, the characteristic Greek organization based on heavy infantry—the hoplite or armored pikeman in close-ordered phalanx relying upon shock—was the mainstay of the army, supported by archers and in some cases by a navy. The Macedonian army of Phillip, based on Greek mercenaries, utilized Greek organization and tactics and increased its flexibility by making the phalanx deeper, the lances longer, and combining cavalry corps on the flanks. Alexander further increased the flexibility of the army by creating supplementary light-armed infantry capable of freer maneuver. He also developed siegecraft and various types of auxiliaries. This division of the army into specialized segments, coupled with Alexander's mastery of strategy and the inculcation of morale, made possible its adaptation to a wide range of conditions. Alexander's successors retained his system, but gradually, with overrefinement and professionalization, it lost morale for field operations, took to heavier armor, to elephants, and to fortifications, with the result of disintegration and conquest by Rome.

ROME[19]

F. J. Haverfield writes:

In the long life of the ancient Roman army, the most effective and long-lived military institution known to history, we may distinguish four principal stages. (1) In the earliest age of Rome the army was a national or citizen levy such as we find in the beginning of all states. (2) This grew into the Republican army of conquest, which gradually subdued Italy and the Mediterranean world. A citizen army and infantry, varying in size with the needs of each year, it eventually developed into a mercenary force with long service and professional organization. This became (3) the Imperial army of defence, which developed from a strictly citizen army into one which represented the provinces as well as Italy, and was a garrison rather than a field army. Lastly, (4) the assaults of the Barbarian horsemen compelled both the creation of a field force distinct from the frontier garrisons and the inclusion of a large mounted element, which soon counted for much more than the infantry. The Roman army had been one of foot soldiers; in its latest phase it was marked by that predominance of the horseman which characterized the earlier centuries of the middle ages.[20]

I. During the first stage the army progressed from the type of Horatius at the bridge with relatively undisciplined retainers to the general militia organization of Servius Tullius with a certain specialization into heavy and light infantry and cavalry with emphasis on the foot organized into a phalanx but enrolled only in time of war for the fighting season.

---

[18] *Iliad*, Book ii; Thucydides i. 10–11.

[19] Spaulding *et al.*, *op. cit.*, pp. 101–265; H. P. Judson, *Caesar's Army* (Boston, 1888); Wrench, *op. cit.*, pp. 145 ff.; "Roman Army," *Encyclopaedia Britannica*, XIX, 393 ff.

[20] "Roman Army," *Encyclopaedia Britannica*, XIX, 393–94.

II. During the fourth century B.C., Camillus, or someone else, introduced longer service, still based, however, on the duty of allegiance, improved weapons and armor and discipline, and loosened the phalanx to the more open-order maniple organized into legions with 4,500–6,000 men (3,000 heavy infantry, 1,200 light infantry, 300 horse). It is said that during the Second Punic War, with a population of three-quarters of a million, Rome maintained an army of 65,000 in the field and 55,000 reserves.

III. The growing wealth and division of labor in the late Republic tended toward a wholly professional army and a lengthening of service for distant campaigns. Marius (102 B.C.) incorporated these changes in his reform and also increased the size of the legion and of the maniple. He "at once democratized the army and attached it more closely to its leader for the time being. He swept away the last traces of civil distinctions of rank or wealth within the legion, admitted to its rank all classes, and substituted voluntary enlistment under a popular general for the old-fashioned compulsory levy. The efficiency of the legion was increased at the cost of complete severance of the ties which bound it to the civil community and to the civil authorities."[21] Augustus divided the army into two grades—the legion of Roman citizens and the auxiliaries recruited from subjects of the empire, organized into cohorts. He also created the Pretorian guard. Service became wholly mercenary, and the legion with the auxiliaries (a total of some 400,000, at first about equally divided, though later the auxiliaries greatly outnumbered the legionaries) were distributed at widely separated points, their function being wholly frontier defense.

IV. In the third century the Romans became less inclined to military service, and auxiliaries and cavalry became more important in the army. The growing power of barbarian cavalry outside the empire made adoption of a similar method by the Roman army expedient. Constantine increased the proportion of Germanic mercenary cavalry stationed at strategic interior points capable of rapidly moving to reinforce the line of fortresses at the frontier.

The general trend of this thousand years of development is thus stated by Brooks Adams:

In early ages every Roman had been a landowner, and every landowner had been a soldier, serving without pay. To fight had been as essential a part of life as to plough. But by the fourth century military service had become commercial; the legions were as purely an expression of money as the bureaucracy itself.

From the time of the Servian constitution downward, the change in the army had kept pace with the acceleration of movement which caused the economic competition that centralized the state. Rome owed her triumphs over Hannibal and Pyrrhus to the valor of her infantry, rather than to the genius of her generals; but from Marius the census ceased to be the basis of recruitment and the rich refused to serve in the ranks. This was equivalent in itself to a social revolution; for, from the moment when the wealthy succeeded in withdrawing themselves from service, and the poor saw in it a

[21] "Rome," Encyclopaedia Britannica, XIX, 491.

trade, the citizen ceased to be a soldier, and the soldier became a mercenary. From that time the army could be used for "all purposes, provided that they could count on their pay and their booty."[22]

The administration of Augustus organized the permanent police, which replaced the mercenaries of the civil wars and this machine was the greatest triumph and the crowning glory of capitalism. Dio Cassius has described how the last vestige of an Italian army passed away. Up to the time of Severus it had been customary to recruit the Praetorians either from Italy itself, from Spain, Macedonia, or other neighboring countries, whose population had some affinity with that of Latium. Severus, after the treachery of the guard to Pertinax, disbanded it and reorganized a corps selected from the bravest soldiers of the legions. These men were a horde of barbarians, repulsive to Italians in their habits, and terrible to look upon.[23] Thus a body of wage earners, drawn from the ends of the earth, was made cohesive by money. For more than four hundred years this corps of hirelings crushed revolt within the Empire, and regulated the injection of fresh blood from without, with perfect promptitude and precision; nor did it fail in its functions while the money which vitalized it lasted.

But a time came when the suction of the usurers so wasted the life of the community that the stream of bullion ceased to flow from the capital to the frontiers; then, as the sustaining force failed, the line of troops along the Danube and the Rhine was drawn out until it broke, and the barbarians poured in unchecked.[24]

GERMANIC CIVILIZATION[25]

The Nordic and Alpine migrants to northern and central Europe in the first and second millenniums B.C., who formed the Hallstatt and La Tène cultures, were warlike, used chariots and iron weapons, but did not perfect military organization beyond that of individual combat by war chiefs and retainers until they had been for a considerable time in contact with the Mediterranean civilizations. In Caesar's time they fought with a close-order phalanx, protected by overlapping shields both in front and overhead.

The barbarians were alert in borrowing ideas of organization, tactics, and strategy. With superior mobility through the use of the horse and superior numbers, they at times were victorious over the Roman legions, as Arminius over Varus and the Goths over Valens.

JAPANESE CIVILIZATION[26]

I. The Japanese are traditionally a nation of soldiers, a characteristic attributed to the successive invasions of people from the north, from Korea, and from Malaya which contributed to the present Japanese stock. The early fight-

[22] Joachim Marquardt, *L'Organisation militaire chez les Romains* (Paris, 1891), p. 143.

[23] *Dio Cassius* lxxiv. 2.

[24] *The Law of Civilization and Decay* (New York, 1896), pp. 45–46.

[25] "La Tène," *Encyclopaedia Britannica*, XIII, 737–39; "Hallstatt," *ibid.*, XI, 103; Tacitus *Germania*; Caesar *De bello Gallico*; Judson, *op. cit.*, pp. 104–8.

[26] Wrench, *op. cit.*, pp. 35–54; "Japan," *Encyclopaedia Britannica*, XII, 916–20.

ing was doubtless similar to that in the heroic age of most countries between leaders, followed by relatively unorganized retainers. The Fujiwara, who introduced Chinese culture, including Buddhism, ruled by religion and intelligence, but they created a trained warrior caste which gradually grew until it included from one-fourth to one-third of the able-bodied males. It was organized into divisions of six hundred horse and four hundred foot, recruited for a definite service period and armed at expense of the state. The control of this force became the monopoly of the Taira clan in the south and the Minamota clan in the north. In the tenth century, under clan influence, military service became hereditary and the samurai, or soldiers, following the code of Bushida, acquired a position of prestige, rigorous rules of discipline, and the remarkable privilege of hara-kiri—a form of suicide to expiate for crimes or as a protest.

II. The long and bloody civil wars between the Taira and the Minamota during the twelfth century developed the characteristic Japanese military courtesies; the use of the bow and arrow, sword and spear, and the curious body armor but little organized tactics, in spite of the frequent reference to the Chinese military classics. Mass tactics were learned from the Mongol invasion of 1274 and developed with modification during the tyrannous Ashikaga period, which Hearn called the darkest of Japanese history.[27] Archers and musketeers were in the front line, spearmen and swordsmen in the second line, and cavalry in the third line.

III. More completely organized armies based on feudal service were developed by Hideyoshi in the sixteenth century and utilized during the relatively peaceful Tokagawa shogunate, when Japan defended itself by a policy of isolation. There were continual small hostilities between the Daimyos during this period.

IV. The system of feudal war with its characteristics of courtesy, fortified castles, inconclusive action, and decentralization rapidly broke down after international contacts were renewed by Japan in 1854. Following the restoration of the emperor in 1867, Japan became, from the military point of view, a member of the world-community with a reorganized modern army.

CHINESE CIVILIZATION[28]

The Chinese civilization which arose after the period of civil war, invasion, and disintegration from A.D. 220 to 600 was in many respects different from the older Sinic civilization, particularly in the general adoption of Buddhism brought in by Mongol invaders.

I. This disturbed period, while marking the collapse of one civilization, was the heroic age of the next, and the art of war developed an aggressive spirit leading to imperial expeditions after union was achieved by the Sui and Tang dynas-

[27] Lafcadio Hearn, *Japan: An Attempt at Interpretation* (New York, 1904), p. 299.

[28] Laufer, *op. cit.*

ties. Tactics emphasized cavalry, and chain and ring-mail body armor was developed.

II. The later Sung dynasty was characterized by civil war and invasion. Plate armor was adopted, and more thoroughly organized tactics were developed. In the Mongol period mass tactics were further emphasized.

III. The Ming and early Manchu dynasties were comparatively tranquil. Military operations were, in the main, defense from northern barbarians. The Manchus divided their army into the Manchu banner and the Chinese army. The latter soon degenerated because the Manchus, not having confidence in it, did not support it, and the profession of arms sank into general contempt.

IV. The development of contacts with Europe resulted in the collapse of the military system after the numerous military defeats suffered by China after 1839. It was not until after the inauguration of the republic in 1911 that the beginnings were made toward organizing an army on the Western model.

HINDU CIVILIZATION[29]

The Hindu civilization, which developed after the Hun invasion and civil wars which occupied three centuries following the Gupta age, differed from the earlier Indian civilization in its abandonment of Buddhism. The caste systems of Hinduism and the limitation of military affairs to a small section of the population continued.

I. There were many wars between the many states into which India was divided from the seventh to the eleventh century with relatively small armies.

II. The Mohammedan invasions from the eleventh to the fifteenth century, including Timur's invasion of 1398, resulted in larger and better-disciplined armies.

III. After establishment of the Mogul empire by Babur in 1526, the Moguls gradually extended their sway to all of India, particularly during the reign of Akbar (1556–1605). The Mogul armies used artillery for the first time in India, greatly improved discipline, and combined infantry, cavalry, and artillery in tactical operations.[30] They organized the country militarily in a sort of feudal system and built military roads. While there were insurrections and wars, during the Mogul period India was comparatively stable.

IV. After the death of Arungzeb the Mogul empire declined rapidly before internal insurrection, the Persian invasion, and European penetration. The latter had begun with the activities of the Portuguese in the sixteenth century, the British in the seventeenth century, and the French in the eighteenth century and ended in the establishment of the British raj in 1804, incorporating India with the world international system.

[29] "India," *Encyclopaedia Britannica*, XII, 187–90.

[30] Toynbee (*op. cit.*, I, 352) says Babur used the *Wagenburg* formation—a group of wagons with guns linked by chains—later used in Russia and Bohemia.

The Mexican civilization, formed among invaders from the north around Lake Tezcoco on the Mexican plateau, was borrowed from the Mayas but was more warlike. It developed a religion requiring 20,000 human sacrifices a year. To provide these wars were continually made. Warfare was of the primitive type until the Aztecs superseded the Toltecs as the dominant power in the fourteenth century. Under Itzcoatl after 1427, three cities about the lake formed a league and began, under Aztec leadership, to develop large armies with, however, slight discipline or organization and to create a loose empire of tribute-paying cities. This process was in progress when Cortez conquered the country in 1520.

The new Mayan empire, regarded by Toynbee as a distinct civilization with its centers at Chichen Itza and Uxmal in Yucatan, was formed by migrations from the old Mayan empire in Central America and by invasions by the Toltecs from the plateau in the twelfth century, when a maximum population seems to have been reached. This civilization appears to have been more warlike than the earlier Mayan civilization. Its culture was seriously impaired before the empire was conquered by Cortez in 1521.

3. TERTIARY CIVILIZATIONS

WESTERN EUROPEAN CIVILIZATION[33]

The armies of the Western European states were dominated by cavalry from the defeat of Valens in A.D. 278 to the destruction of British feudalism in the Wars of the Roses which ended in 1485—the period which Oman describes as medieval warfare. Changes in military organization and tactics can perhaps be best illustrated from England, although the developments were not wholly synchronous in other countries.

I. The Saxon army from the conquest of the fifth century to about A.D. 1000 consisted of the leader and companions supported by the fyrd based on a universal obligation of the citizens to military service. Armies were small in numbers and operations were not well organized.

II. In late Saxon times but especially after the Norman Conquest the feudal levy based on the military duty of feudal allegiance became the mainstay of the

---

[31] W. H. Prescott, *Conquest of Mexico* (New York, 1843); A. F. A. Bandelier, "On the Art of War and Mode of Warfare of the Ancient Mexicans," *Tenth Annual Report of the Peabody Museum* (Salem, Mass., 1877); "Aztec," *Encyclopaedia Britannica*, II, 831.

[32] Spinden, *op. cit.*, pp. 648–51; "Central America," *Encyclopaedia Britannica*, V, 130–31.

[33] Charles Oman, *A History of the Art of War in the Middle Ages* (London, 1924); *A History of the Art of War in the Sixteenth Century* (New York, 1937); D. J. Medley, *A Students' Manual of English Constitutional History* (Oxford, 1890), pp. 461–70; Ashdown, *op. cit.*, pp. 343 ff.; F. L. Taylor, *The Art of War in Italy, 1494–1529* (Cambridge, 1921).

army. Knights wore helmets and coats of mail and rode horses and provided retainers which they themselves paid for. The fyrd could still be summoned for
emergencies. This army was inadequately disciplined for mass action, and the
service period was extremely short; thus the army was practically useless except
for home defense. But for this, ample opportunity was offered by the frequent
local feuds and the repeated raids of the Norsemen.[34] The offensive spirit, however, was present, and the Crusades were fought to expand Christendom with
this inefficient military instrument.[35] Both in Europe and in the Holy Land the
building of castles steadily increased the power of the defensive and prevented a
centralization of authority.[36]

III. A change took place about 1300. Professional armies, mainly of foreigners, had been used by the Danes and Normans, but this practice was discon-
tinued after 1153 until the time of Edward I, who used professional longbowmen
in his Welsh and Scotch wars (1277-1328). The Hundred Years' War which followed was also fought mainly by mercenary armies. Greater maneuverability
was thus achieved. British longbowmen effectively stopped the charge of armored French knights at the Battle of Crecy in 1346, and British troops overran
much of France, but castles and steadily improving body armor of the knights—
plate had superseded chain mail—prevented permanent conquest of the territory.

IV. In the fifteenth century armor had become so heavy that it was customary for the knights to dismount and fight on foot supported by the archers.
Fortifications increased in strength, and the powers of defense were so augmented that war achieved a virtual stalemate, whether in the feudal siege operations
or in the relatively bloodless maneuvers in the field by heavily armed *condottiere*.
The efforts to break this deadlock, inherent in the prevailing type of technique,
did not begin in England until the Tudor period, when lighter-armed mercenaries
were resorted to, organized in companies of muskets and pikes. Much earlier on
the Continent, Swiss and Swabian pikemen in close-order formation had routed
armed knights until they themselves were dealt with by crossbowmen and pis-
toliers on horseback. The Hussites' *Wagenburg*[37]—a formation of mobile artillery—the Mongols light horse, the Turkish disciplined Janizary corps of the infantry, were new military ideas which looked forward to the modern period rather
than back to the Middle Ages and were serving to break the military deadlock.

[34] Paul Vinogradoff (*English Society in the Eleventh Century* [Oxford, 1908], pp. 30,
34) points out that in the tenth and eleventh centuries the democratic army, based on
a levy of freemen with one hide of land each, gave way to the aristocratic feudal army
of men with an average of five hides of land each, because horses and good armor were
necessary to fight Danes and Vikings and this equipment was too expensive for one-
hide men (see Toynbee, *op. cit.*, II, 200).

[35] The First Crusade is said to have cost 500,000 lives (Charles Bémont and G. Monod, *Medieval Europe from 395 to 1270* [New York, 1903], p. 355).

[36] Oman, *Art of War in the Middle Ages*, pp. 52 ff.   [37] See above, n. 30.

The medieval impetus, however, went on into the sixteenth century with ever heavier armor and stronger forts until the system collapsed with the development of firearms.

Gunpowder as a propellant is said to have been used during the Spanish wars by the Moors in the twelfth century, and its preparation is said to have been understood by Roger Bacon in the thirteenth century. Schwartz, a German Frank, perfected it in the fourteenth century, and Edward III used cannon in the Scotch wars in 1327. Froissart mentions cannon at Cambrai in 1339, and cannon were used at Crecy in 1346, but neither artillery nor musket became really effective in field or siege operations until the fifteenth century.[38]

IRISH AND NESTORIAN CIVILIZATION[39]

Toynbee distinguishes the far western or Irish and the far eastern or Nestorian Christian civilizations from the larger Western and Orthodox Christian civilizations. Both seem to have been remarkably peaceful and remarkably short lived. The Irish church extended missions over Western Europe from the monastery of St. Columba on the island of Iona in the sixth century, but the Irish were harassed by the Norsemen in the tenth century and conquered by the Anglo-Normans in the twelfth.

The Nestorian Christians established missions in central Asia, Mesopotamia, Persia, and India, but they were harassed by the Moslems and subdued by the Mongols in the eighth century.

SCANDINAVIAN CIVILIZATION[40]

Scandinavian civilization had its roots in Stone and Bronze Age peoples. Iron was used in Scandinavia during the Roman time, and peat-bog finds disclose a remarkable collection of fine swords, spears, axes, chain mail, helmets, and shields. Warfare appears to have been local, and life was agricultural and commercial until the Viking period. During this period naval expeditions were undertaken at first as raids for booty, later to establish settlements in England, France, Ireland, Russia, Iceland, Greenland, and America. Continuous fighting led to warlikeness and improvement of weapons, particularly the ax and the dragon boat.

ORTHODOX CHRISTIAN CIVILIZATION[41]

The Orthodox Byzantine Empire maintained its unity with a variety of peoples within and a troubled international environment by diplomacy rather than by war. Its policy was persistently to divide and rule.[42] It was in successive periods of its history at war with Persia (seventh century), with the Sara-

---

[38] See Ashdown, *op. cit.*, pp. 360 ff.; George Sarton, *Introduction to the History of Science*, I (Washington, 1927), 29.

[39] "Ireland," *Encyclopaedia Britannica*, XII, 598 ff.; "Nestorian," *ibid.*, XVI, 244.

[40] "Scandinavian Civilization," *ibid.*, XX, 48–49.

[41] "Roman Empire, Later," *ibid.*, XIX, 443–45.   [42] Wrench, *op. cit.*, p. 161.

cens (eleventh century), with the Seljuk Turks (eleventh and twelfth centuries), and with the Ottoman Turks (fourteenth and fifteenth centuries). Constantinople was several times attacked.[43]

The army tended to decline in size. In Constantine's time (third century) the army may have been 500,000 strong, stationed partly on the frontier and partly at interior points for use as reserves. In Justinian's time (fifth century) it was about 150,000 strong, and in the ninth century 100,000.

Like medieval Western armies, it consisted of cavalry with a few foot contingents. In the sixth and seventh centuries discipline was lax. The discipline, tactics, and strategy improved in the wars against the Saracens in the eighth and ninth centuries. In the tenth century Scandinavian mercenaries began to be employed, after Asia Minor had been lost to the Seljuk Turks. The army was always efficient compared to Western armies during the same period. Military textbooks were abundant, and strategy tended toward maneuver and Fabian tactics.

RUSSIAN CIVILIZATION[44]

I. Russian civilization originated from Scandinavian and Slavic elements inspired by Orthodox Christianity. The Varangians used horses and were organized in small groups of leaders and retainers. Christianity was introduced in A.D. 908.

II. The Mongol invasions resulted in the occupation of most of Russia in the fourteenth century and the burning of Moscow in 1383. Tamerlane raided Russia in 1395. Civil disorders continued until the middle of the fifteenth century. Under these tests military knowledge advanced. Firearms were introduced in 1475.

III. After 1462 the Mongol invaders were driven out and Russia became united.

IV. Peter the Great, at the beginning of the eighteenth century, gained a general recognition of Russia and brought it within the world family of nations.

IRANIC CIVILIZATION[45]

The most important army of the Iranic civilization has been the Ottoman or Turkish army, although the civilization also included Persia.

I. The Ottoman tribes were invited by the Byzantine emperor to assist him in the fourteenth century, but the invitation was declined. The Ottomans, like all nomadic people, were as a whole organized in a military way.

II. In the fifteenth century the Turks were defeated by Timur. They improved their military and political organization and expanded in both Europe and Asia during the next century. Armies of 100,000 were put in the field, notably at Mohacs (1526), composed of well-disciplined Janizary infantry using

---

[43] *Encyclopaedia Britannica*, XIX, 432.   [44] "Russia," *ibid.*, pp. 702, 714 ff.

[45] Wrench, *op. cit.*, pp. 174–80; Oman, *Art of War in the Sixteenth Century*, pp. 607 ff.; "Turkey," *Encyclopaedia Britannica*, XXII, 595, 598 ff.

archery and harquebus, supported by feudal troops, cavalry, and field artillery.[46] A considerable naval force was also developed.[47]

III. After the reign of Sulyman the Magnificent (1520–66) and the naval defeat at Lepanto (1572) there was a period of tranquillity in which efforts were made to rule by religion rather than by force.

IV. In the eighteenth and nineteenth centuries Turkey lost much territory, first to Russia and later to the Balkan and Arab states, and became more and more a ward of the powers, until the nationalist revolution under Mustapha Kemal Pasha in 1922. The Janizaries had been disbanded in 1826.[48]

ARABIC CIVILIZATION[49]

The Arabs, like all nomads, have been warlike in the sense that war has been part of the normal business life.[50] The religious enthusiasm of Mohammedanism further contributed to warlikeness.[51] The Arabs have fought on horseback with loose organization and great dependence upon the individual fighter, from the time of Mohammed to that of T. E. Lawrence.

I. The early caliphs divided the army into center, two wings, vanguard, and rear guard. The tribes, always the nuclei of Arab culture, preserved their identity in each. The cavalry in the wings used the lance while the infantry used bow and arrow and later shield and sword.

II. The Umayyad caliphs, borrowing from Greeks and Persians, professionalized and unified the army. The Abbasid caliphate may be regarded as a phase of Syriac rather than of Arabic civilization. It supported itself by mercenaries largely non-Arabic. Its army came to resemble the Roman pretorian guard and was defeated by Arabs and Turks in a prolonged period of disorder in the eleventh and twelfth centuries.

III. Saladin won victories by stimulating the morale of his armies rather than by organization, though his siege tactics, weapons (crossbow), and communication system (carrier pigeons) were superior to those of the Crusaders. His conquests gave political form to the declining Arabic civilization in the Ayyubite and early Mameluke empires which united Egypt and Syria in the thirteenth century.

IV. The later Mamelukes let the army decline and were conquered by the Turks in the early sixteenth century. In Spain the Arabs developed elaborate fortifications and siegecraft during the fourteenth century but lost the offensive spirit and were conquered by the Christians in the sixteenth century.

[46] Oman, *Art of War in the Sixteenth Century*, pp. 612, 657, 719.   [47] *Ibid.*, pp. 685 ff.

[48] See W. W. White, *The Process of Change in the Ottoman Empire* (Chicago, 1937).

[49] T. A. Walker, *A History of the Law of Nations* (Cambridge, 1899), pp. 73–79, 109–13; M. Sprengling, "Moslem North Africa," in Laufer (ed.), *The New Orient*, II, 375–82; Philip Hitti, *History of the Arabs* (London, 1940).

[50] Gibbon, *Decline and Fall of the Roman Empire* (V, 88), says there were seventeen hundred battles in the "time of ignorance" just before Mohammed.

[51] Majid Khadduri, *The Law of War and Peace in Islam* (London, 1940), p. 52.

APPENDIX XVI

THE FREQUENCY AND TYPES OF BATTLES IN CLASSIC, WESTERN, SINIC, AND CHINESE CIVILIZATIONS

There are obvious limitations upon the adequacy and comparability of the data here presented on the battles of Classic, Western, Sinic, and Chinese civilizations. The diagram for Classic civilization (Fig. 24), for which the data are probably most complete, exhibits a tendency for battles to be most frequent in the "time of troubles" and least frequent in the period of "the universal state." In the diagram for Western civilization (Fig. 25) the period of the universal state and the period of decline are probably exaggerated in Harbottle's list from which the data were taken because of the greater availability of historical sources in these periods and the principle of "historical proximity" which tends to emphasize events near the time and civilization of the writer. It is to be observed, however, that this diagram shows imperialistic and defensive battles at a maximum during the "time of trouble" and shows no civil and interstate battles at all during this period, though, from the most superficial historical knowledge, it is clear that there were a large number of battles of this type in Europe from A.D. 850 to 1025.[1]

The Chinese material (Fig. 26) assembled by J. S. Lee[2] includes only "internecine wars." Apparently this term covers only civil and interstate wars. Lee expressly excludes defensive and imperialistic wars such as those waged in the Han dynasty against barbarians in the north and southwest and in the late Sung and Mongol dynasties. Imperialistic wars in the latter period were very numerous and, if included, would have greatly augmented the relative number of battles in the Chinese "time of troubles."

It is not entirely clear upon what unit Lee bases his diagram. He describes this unit as "an open armed engagement," apparently meaning a battle rather than a campaign or a war. His original data were not available. Lee did not include the heroic age and time of troubles of the Sinic civilization but made the following statement with reference to the frequency of hostilities during those periods. "The Chow dynasty witnessed a period of peace in its first part some three to four hundred years. Then followed a period of disturbance with increasing intensity, the Ch'un Ch'iu and Chankuo periods."[3]

[1] See Sorokin's graph of internal disturbances in Europe, Fig. 27, below.

[2] J. S. Lee, "The Periodic Recurrence of Internecine Wars in China," *China Journal of Science and Arts*, XIV (1931), 111 ff., 159 ff.

[3] *Ibid.*, pp. 159–60.

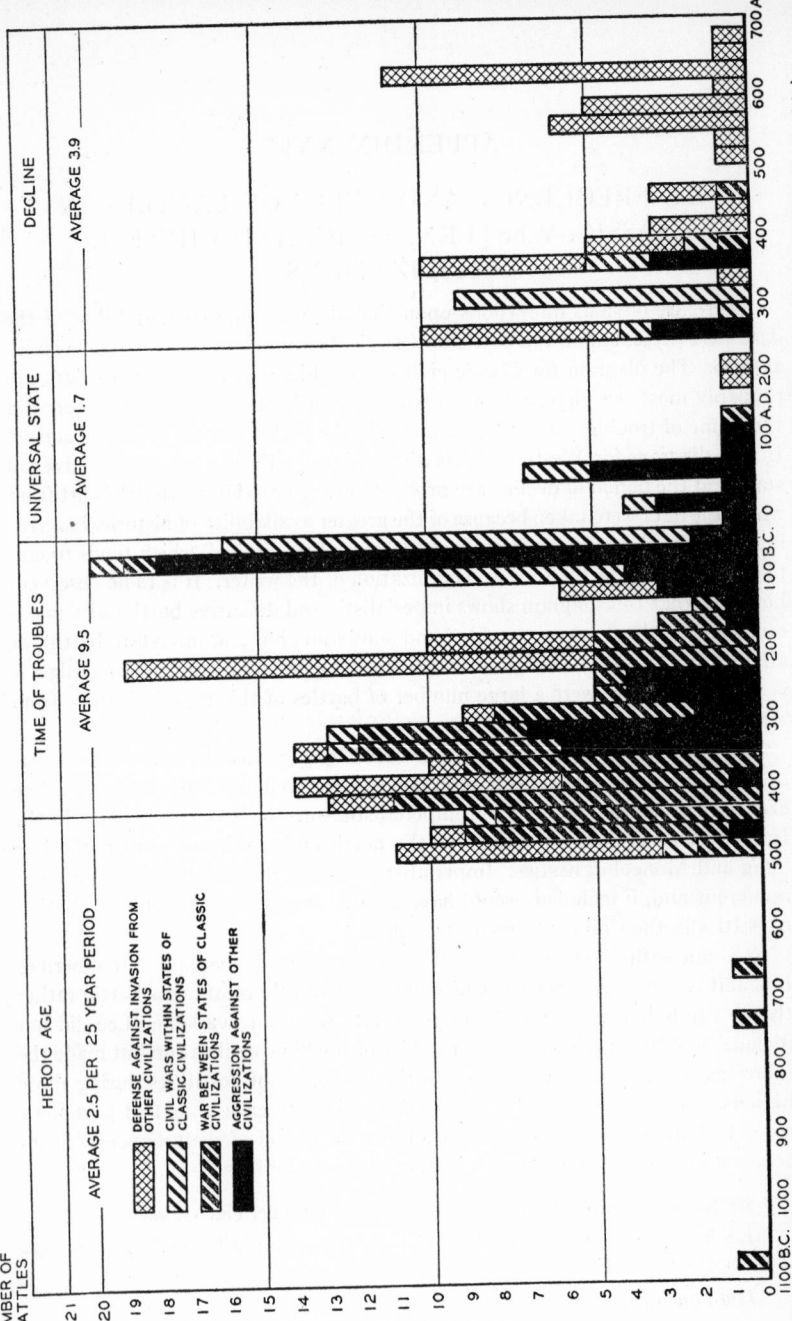

Military incidents of Classic civilization, by twenty-five-year periods. (Data from Harbottle, *op. cit.*)

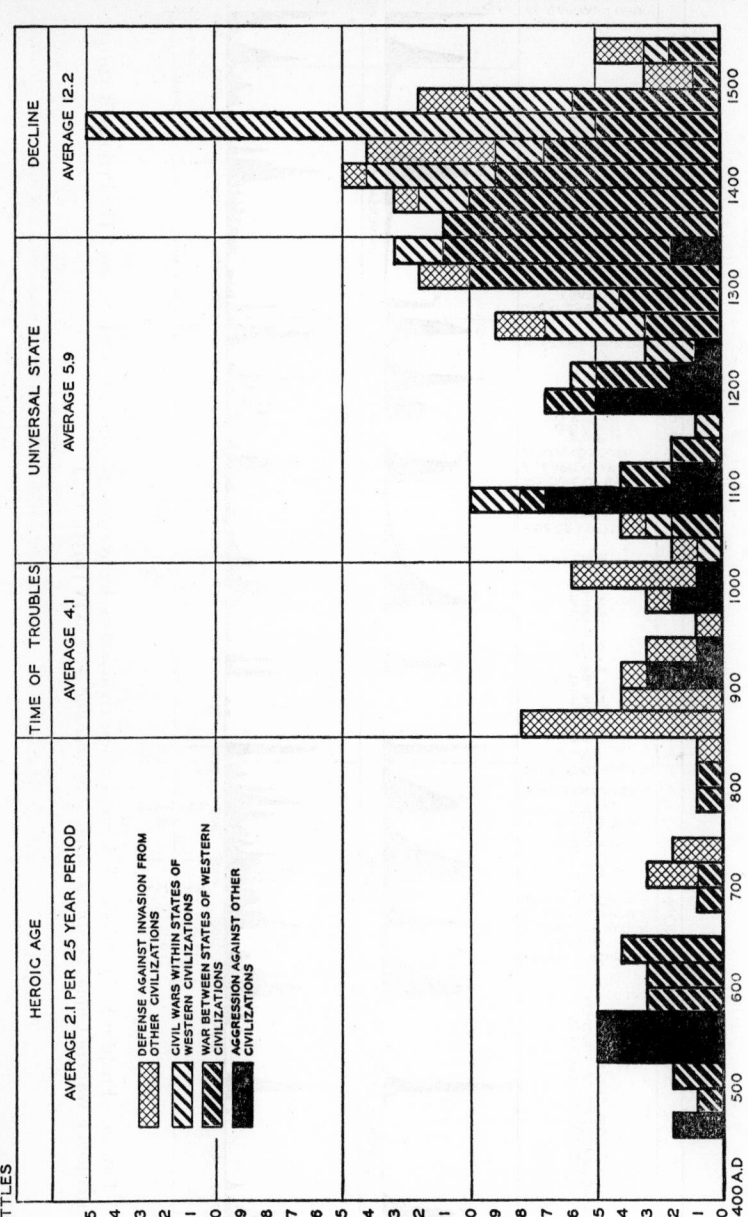

FIG. 25.—Frequency and types of battles in Western civilization. (Data from Harbottle, *op. cit.*)

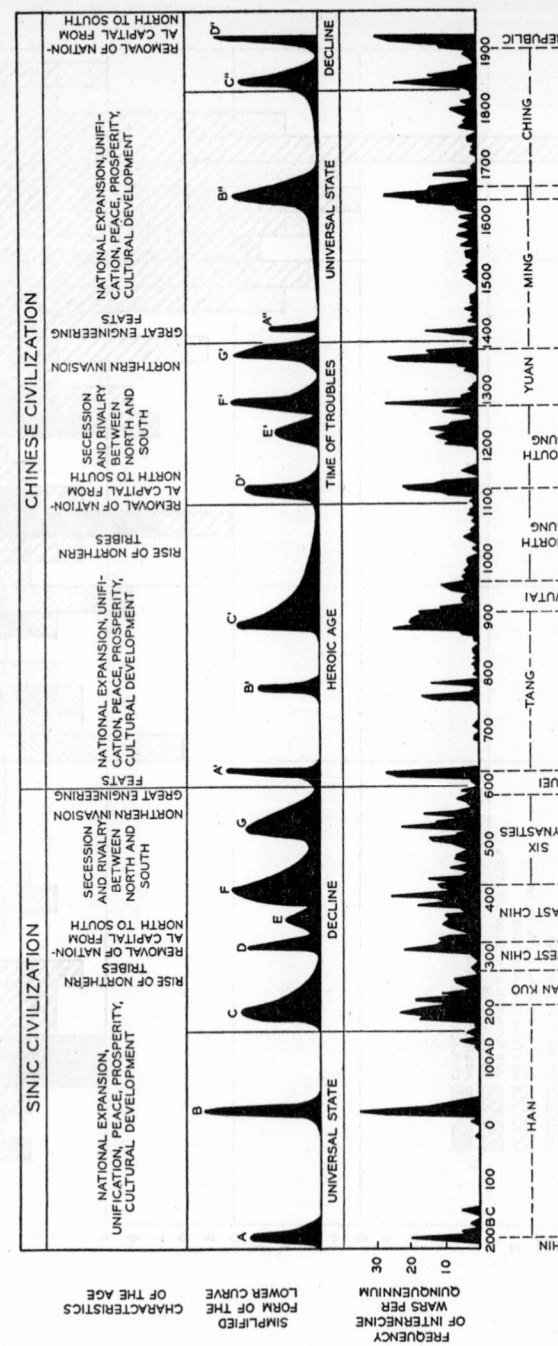

FIG. 26.—Frequency of battles in Sinic and Chinese civilizations, by five-year periods. (From J. S. Lee, "The Periodic Recurrence of Internecine Wars in China," *China Journal of Science and Arts*, XIV [1931], 114.)

594

The material for civil and interstate wars is much more complete in the Lee list than in the Harbottle list, from which the data for Classic and Western battles were taken.

The data for the heroic age of Classic civilization are obviously incomplete, but probably the remainder of the diagram comes nearest to presenting a typical picture of the relative frequency of wars during a civilization, because the sources are considerable, have been well studied by Western scholars, and the exaggeration of historical proximity is relatively small since the entire civilization is historically rather remote. This diagram indicates that the total number of battles and the number of imperialistic and civil battles were at a maximum during the time of trouble and that all types were at a minimum during the universal state period, the *pax Romana*. Defensive battles predominated during the period of decline.

Classic civilization was considered at an end in the West with the dethronement of Romulus Augustulus by Odoacer in A.D. 476 and in the East by the accession of Leo the Isaurian in A.D. 717, superseding the Heraclean dynasty. Leo was a Syrian, and by his time the Greek language had superseded Latin as the official language and the Eastern empire had lost its hold on southern Italy. The policy of importing Slavs to defend the frontiers was adopted, and the Greek Orthodox church had assumed its characteristic form, the long controversy over iconoclasm having just begun. The Orthodox civilization, politically organized in the Byzantine Empire, composed of Syrian, Greek, and Slavic elements, had definitely superseded the Classic civilization and the Roman Empire. Only battles of the Roman Empire, as thus defined in the West and the East, are included as battles of Classic civilization.

Battles listed by Harbottle and participated in by European barbarians after A.D. 400 are included as battles of Western civilization. Where such barbarians were attacking the Western empire before A.D. 476, the battles would appear in both diagrams—as imperialistic battles of Western civilization and as defensive battles of Classic civilization.

Western civilization was considered to end in Spain with the union of Castile and Aragon under Ferdinand and Isabella in A.D. 1479, an event followed by aggressive policies against the Moors and overseas: in England, with the feudal decimation of the Wars of the Roses and accession of the vigorous Tudor dynasty in 1485; in Italy with the advent of the secular pope, Alexander VI of the House of Borgia in 1492; in France, with the accession of the Orleanist dynasty under Louis XII in 1498—a dynasty which gave more definite expression to the nationalistic and secular statecraft initiated a generation earlier by Louis XI; in western Germany, with the death of Maximilian I, "the last of the Knights," in 1519, immediately followed by Luther's Reformation of 1520; in eastern Germany with the proclamation of Albert of Brandenburg as hereditary Duke of Prussia and a Protestant in 1525; and, in Austria, with the accession of the Protestantly inclined Maximilian II as emperor and king of Bohemia and Hungary in 1564. The reason for choosing these dates for the beginning of world-civilization and end of Western civilization in these areas is considered in chapter viii.[4] After these dates, battles by the respective states are regarded as battles of world-civilization.[5]

The diagrams from Sorokin (Fig. 27) indicate the number of internal disturbances and the gravity of external hostilities separately. Those for Greece and Rome are roughly similar to the diagram (Fig. 24) for Classic civilization, and those for Europe are roughly similar to the diagram (Fig. 25) for Western civilization, though Sorokin indicates far more civil disturbance in the twelfth and thirteenth centuries. These diagrams may also be compared with those indicating the number and casualties in battles of Classic and Western civilization presented in chapter vii.[6]

[4] Sec. 4d.

[5] Above, Fig. 8, chap. ix; below, Fig. 35, Appen. XIX.　　　　　[6] Figs. 1 and 2.

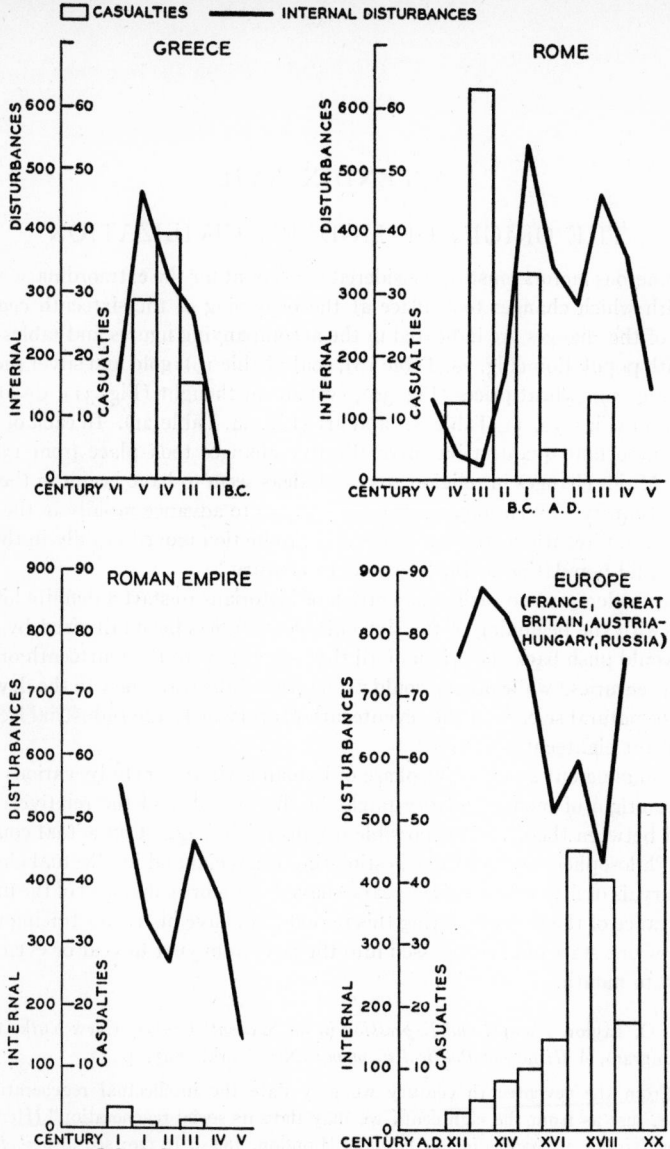

CASUALTIES ▭ INTERNAL DISTURBANCES ━━━

FIG. 27.—Relative war magnitudes by casualties and internal disturbances in ancient Greece and Rome and in Europe, 1100–1930. (From Pitirim Sorokin, *Social and Cultural Dynamics* [New York, 1937], III, 297.) Internal disturbances are measured by a figure which gives weight to the number, duration, and severity of these events (*ibid.*, p. 411). Casualties are measured by the total number during the century divided by the average population during that century (*ibid.*, p. 295).

APPENDIX XVII

THE ORIGIN OF MODERN CIVILIZATION

Numerous factors must be considered to account for the extraordinary rapidity with which changes took place at the beginning of the sixteenth century. Some of the changes are indicated in the accompanying figures and tables dealing with population (Fig. 28, Table 18), coal (Table 19), gold and silver production (Fig. 29), wheat prices (Fig. 30), systems of thought (Fig. 31), discovery, invention (Figs. 32, 33, Table 20) and art (Fig. 34, Table 21). In each of these fields important quantitative or qualitative changes took place from 1300 to 1700. Major changes in religion, art, and ideas seem to have begun in the thirteenth century. Invention and discovery began to advance rapidly in the fourteenth and fifteenth centuries. Prices and production moved rapidly in the sixteenth and population in the seventeenth century.

The tendency of an earlier generation of historians to start a definite historic epoch with the beginning of the sixteenth century has been criticized by some who would push back the origin of all that seems new to the fourteenth or thirteenth centuries,[1] while others would push forward the really new to the development of natural science in the seventeenth century or to the Industrial Revolution of the eighteenth century.[2]

By singling out a particular phase of human activity for study, various dates for the origin of modern history might be discovered, and the relatively long period between these various possible origins might suggest an actual continuity.[3] Philosophers and scientists, estimating the social and intellectual changes at intervals of fifty or a hundred years,[4] have been more convinced of the unique importance of the changes during this period than have historians tracing in detail how one state of affairs passed into the next from year to year or even from month to month.

[1] H. O. Taylor, *Thought and Expression in the Sixteenth Century* (New York, 1920); J. K. Ingram, *A History of Political Economy* (New York, 1893), p. 32.

[2] "From the seventeenth century we may date the intellectual regeneration of Europe; just as from the eighteenth we may date its social regeneration" (Henry T. Buckle, *History of Civilization in England* [London, 1869], I, 329; see also *ibid.*, pp. 339 ff.).

[3] See F. M. Powicke, "The Middle Ages," *Encyclopaedia Britannica* (14th ed.), XV, 449: "There has never been anywhere a complete breach with medieval institutions or modes of thought."

[4] See Martha Ornstein, *The Role of Scientific Societies in the Seventeenth Century* (Chicago, 1928).

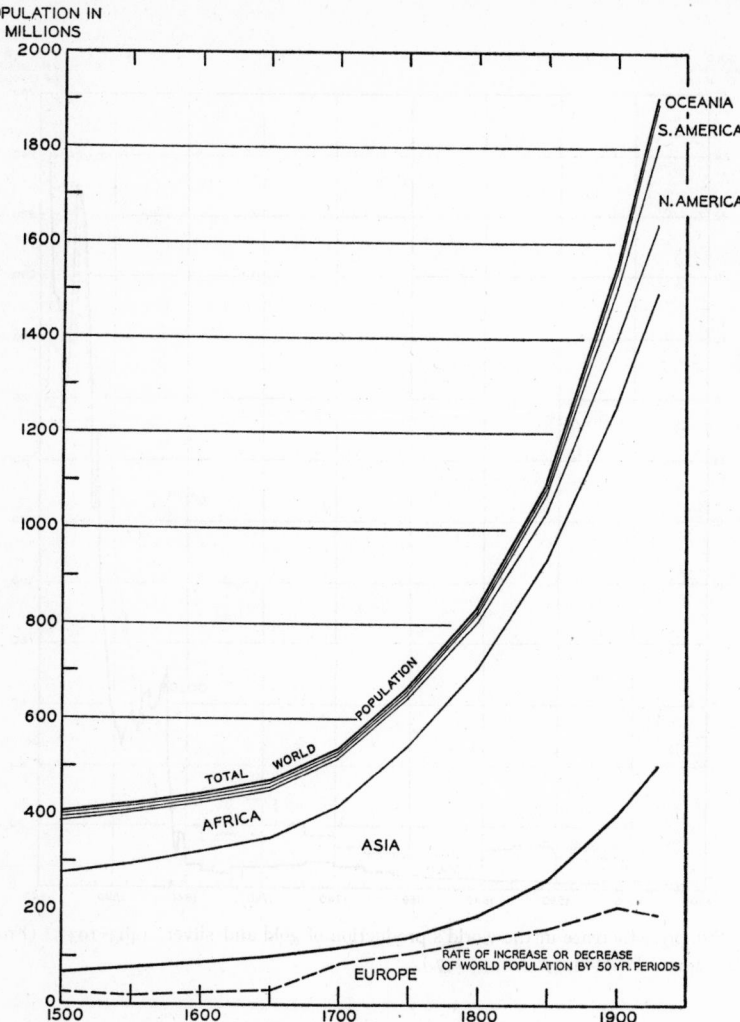

POPULATION IN
MILLIONS

OCEANIA
S. AMERICA
N. AMERICA

TOTAL WORLD POPULATION

AFRICA

ASIA

RATE OF INCREASE OR DECREASE
OF WORLD POPULATION BY 50 YR. PERIODS

EUROPE

FIG. 28.—Changes in world-population, 1500–1930 (see Table 18, p. 612)

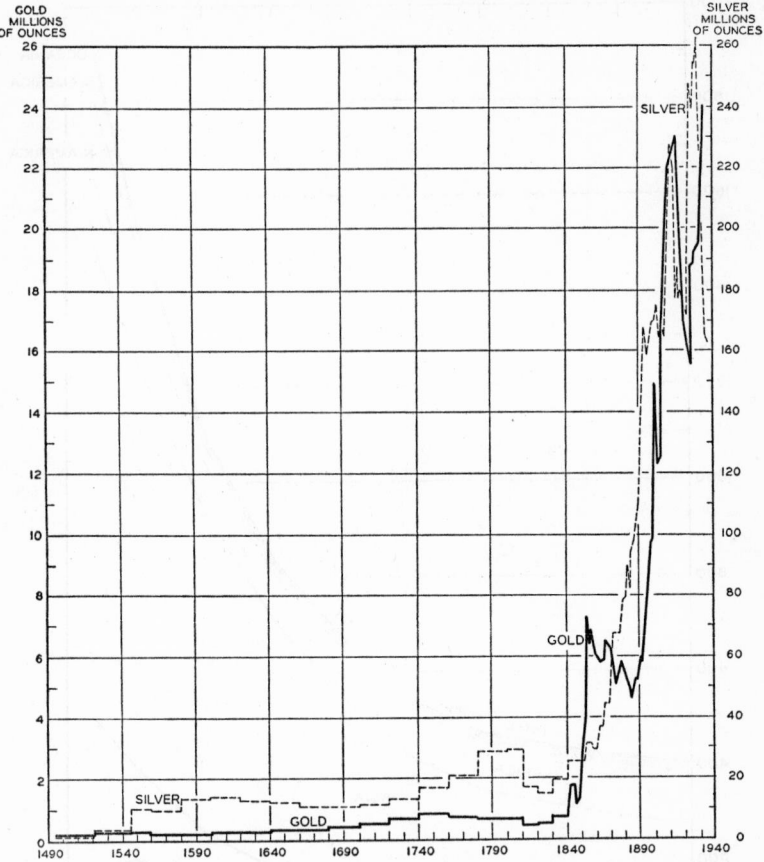

FIG. 29.—Increase in the world's production of gold and silver, 1493–1933. (From Warren and Pearson, *op. cit.*, p. 247.)

Bishop Creighton wrote:

After marshaling all the forces and ideas which were at work to produce [this change, the observer] still feels that there are behind all these an animating spirit which he can but most imperfectly catch, whose power blended all else together and gave a sudden cohesion to the force. This modern spirit formed itself with surprising rapidity, and we cannot fully explain the process.[5]

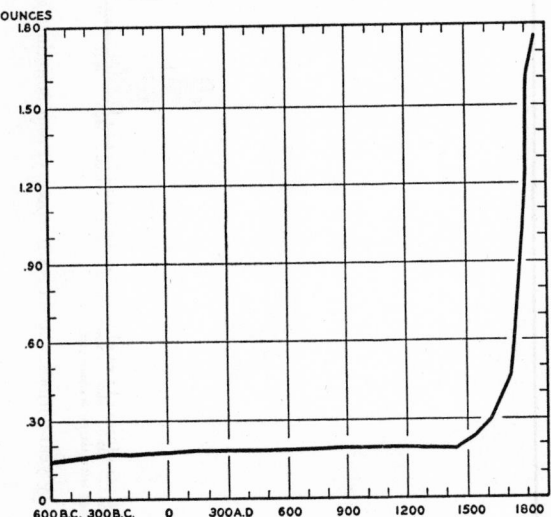

Fig. 30.—Changes in the prices of wheat (in silver), 600 B.C.–A.D. 1900. The price of wheat was comparatively stable until great quantities of silver came from America. Prices then rose, not because of the supply of wheat or the demand for it but because silver became abundant. (From Warren and Pearson, *op. cit.*, p. 436.)

It appears that no ordinary combination of tendencies could have wrought so profound a change but that the particular conjunction resulted in a sort of chemical union from which something wholly new emerged. Dampier-Whetham writes:

When a number of factors are at work, the total effect at the beginning is but the sum of the separate effects. But there comes a time when the effects overlap and intensify each other: cause and effect act and react. And so it is with all the material, moral and intellectual factors involved in the changes of the sixteenth century—somewhat suddenly they pass the critical stage. Growing wealth increased knowledge, and new knowledge in its turn increased wealth. The whole process became cumulative, and advanced with accelerating speed in the irresistible torrent of the Renaissance.[6]

[5] *Cambridge Modern History* (1902), I, 2.

[6] W. C. Dampier-Whetham, *A History of Science* (New York, 1930), p. 112.

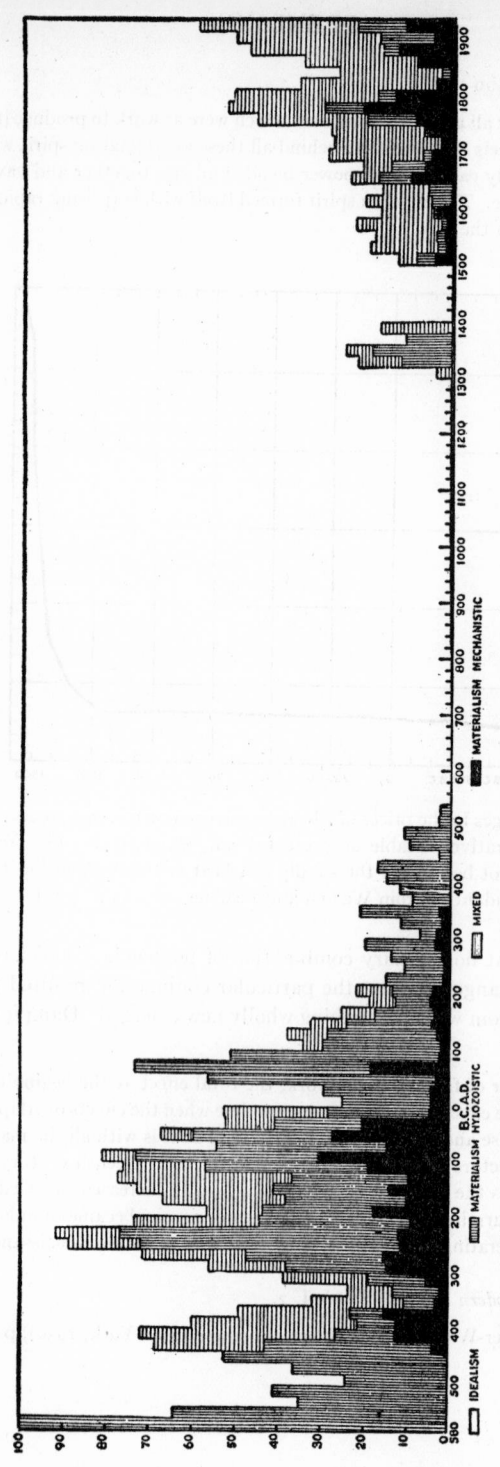

FIG. 31.—Fluctuation in the main systems of thought by twenty-year periods, 600 B.C.–A.D. 1900. (From Sorokin, *op. cit.*, II, 189)

The factors and events involved in this transition will be discussed under six heads: (1) the decline of medieval institutions; (2) inventions, discoveries, and learning; (3) pre-Renaissance changes; (4) intercivilization contacts; (5) Renaissance and Reformation; and (6) post-Renaissance institutions.

1. *Decline of medieval institutions.*—Confidence in the institutions of Western civilization began to decline in the fourteenth century. The Black Death of

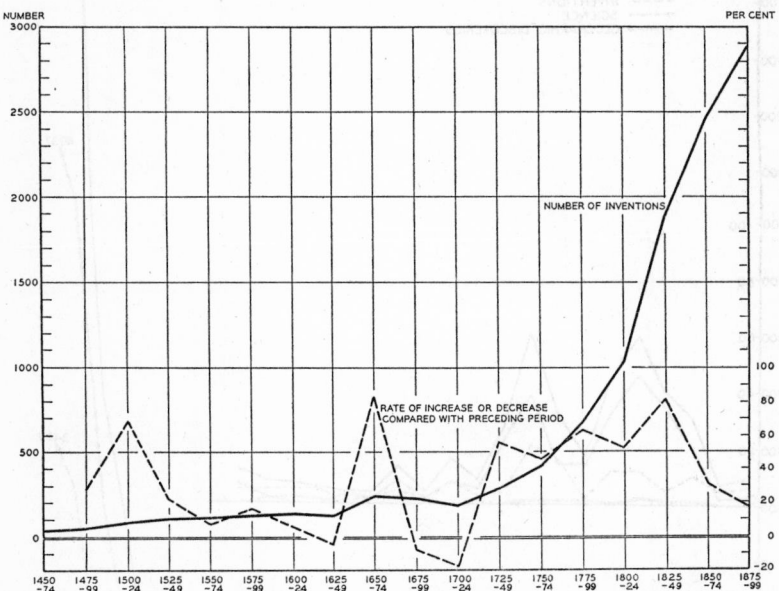

FIG. 32.—Increase and rate of increase in number of inventions, 1450–1900 (see Table 20, p. 613).

1348 had been followed by a century of epidemics and of diminishing population, creating a sense of insecurity and promoting social, economic, and political instability in Western Europe.[7] The deadlock of the existing military technique in the later campaigns of the Hundred Years' War, the Wars of the Roses, the later Crusades, and the mercenary hostilities in Italy and Germany had led to

[7] J. E. Thorold Rogers (*Six Centuries of Work and Wages* [abridged ed.; New York, 1890], pp. 63 ff.) thought the shortage of labor in England led to demands for improvement in the conditions of the peasantry, on the one hand, and to efforts to prevent a rise in wages by the statute of laborers, on the other, resulting in the peasants' revolt of 1381. This interpretation may be exaggerated, though the psychological effects of the epidemic, making important changes possible, is not denied (see "Black Death," *Encyclopaedia of the Social Sciences*, II, 57).

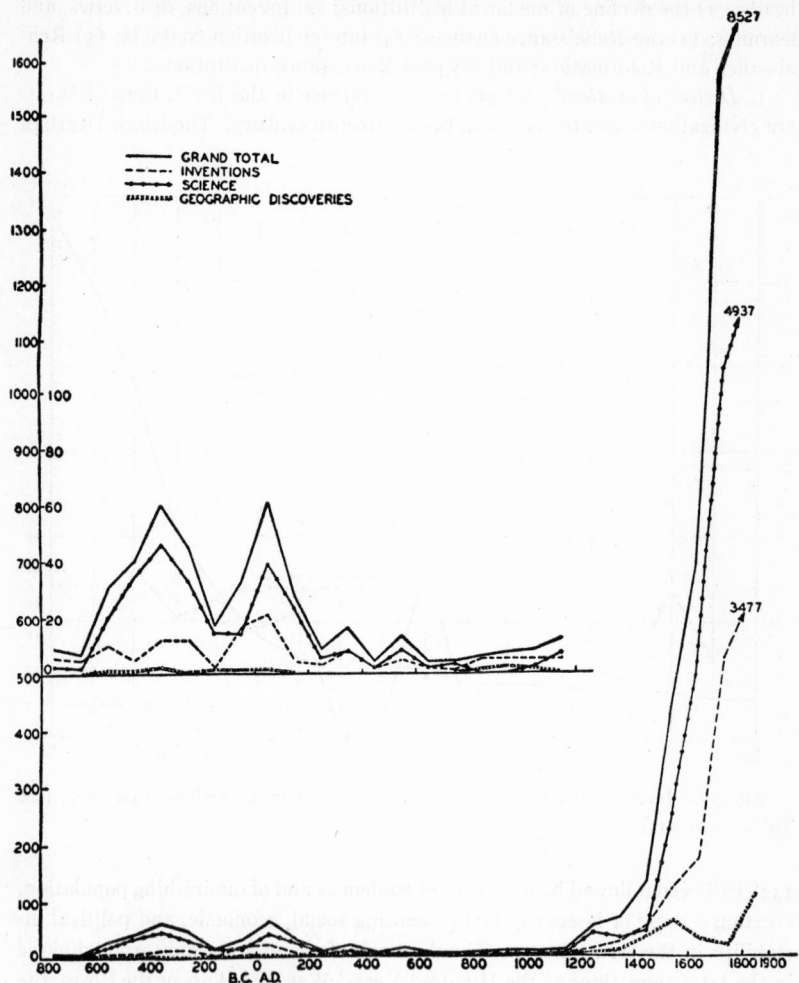

FIG. 33.—Changes in number of scientific discoveries and inventions, 800 B.C.–A.D. 1900 by centuries. (From Sorokin, *op. cit.*, II, 137.)

a decimation of the old feudal nobility and a general loss of their prestige.[8] The "Babylonian captivity" (1309–78), the struggles of popes with anti-popes and with emperors ending in the schism of 1378, the growing corruption and nepotism in the church, had steadily diminished the prestige of the papacy. The im-

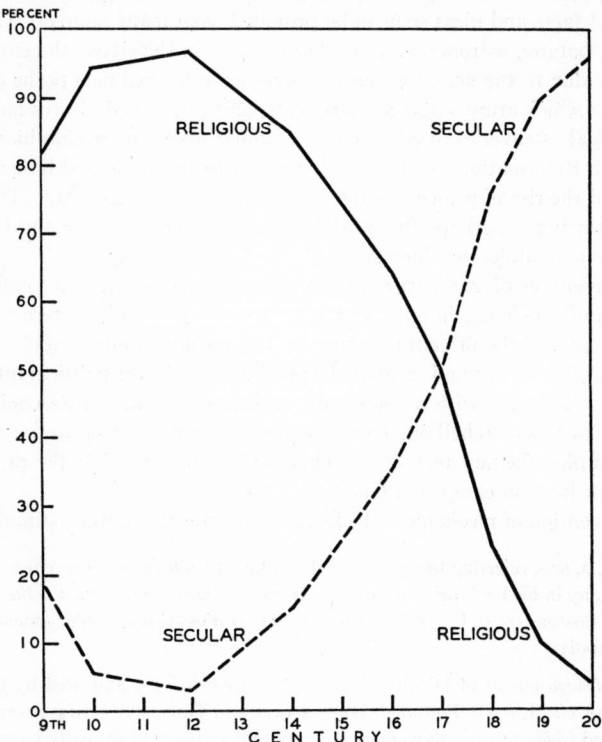

Fig. 34.—Rise of secular and decline of religious art in Europe, ninth to twentieth centuries (see Table 21, p. 614).

perial interregnum (1256–73) and the subsequent imperial wars in Italy resulted in a steady loss of authority by the Holy Roman emperors outside of Austria. There was a continuous decline in the quality of scholarly writing from 1300 to 1500.[9]

[8] Charles Oman, *History of the Art of War in the Middle Ages* (London, 1924), pp. 410, 428. E. P. Cheney notes the low spirits of the dying feudal class as manifested by the literature of the time of Henry VIII (*Social Changes in England in the Sixteenth Century as Reflected in Contemporary Literature* [Boston, 1895]).

[9] Lynn Thorndike, *A History of Magic and Experimental Science* (New York, 1929), IV, 614.

2. *Inventions, discoveries, and learning.*—New techniques resulting from inventions, discoveries, and learning were establishing new centers of power. Printing on paper from movable type, invented about 1438 in Germany, resulted in the wide circulation of the Bible, of classical writings, of empirical knowledge, and of contemporary propagandas, thus making possible the juxtaposition of facts and ideas soon to be provided from many sources. The rise of medicine, botany, astronomy, and other sciences in the sixteenth century may be largely due to the access which the press gave learned men to the empirical knowledge which army surgeons, herbalists, and others had always had.[10] The geographical discoveries owed much to a similar access to geographical knowledge;[11] the Reformation, to the broader access to the Bible and biblical literature;[12] and the rise of princes, to the ease of political propaganda.[13] The invention of printing is perhaps the most important single factor in the transition which we have under consideration.

The invention of gunpowder and artillery in the fourteenth century[14] resulted in radical change in military tactics after its possibilities were realized in the latter part of the fifteenth century.[15] These changes augmented the power of the offensive in war and created the possibility of larger political integration by force. Monarchs with a monopoly of military manufacture could batter down the castles of rebellious barons and conquer non-European peoples who did not employ the new technique. This in turn made possible the rapid diffusion of new ideas in conquered lands.

The invention of mechanical clocks in the fourteenth century stimulated the

---

[10] *Ibid.*, p. 600, referring to the use by the botanist Collenucius of recent writing and vulgar botany in his book printed in 1492. Henry Hallam (*Introduction to the Literature of Europe* [Boston, 1864], I, 251) refers to the "repertories of natural phenomena" among the incunabula.

[11] The *Imago mundi* of D'Ailly (1410) was printed in 1504 and used by Columbus (Hallam, *op. cit.*, I, 102). Fontana's book of 1420 and Toscanelli's of 1472 seem to have been printed (*ibid.*, p. 159), as were many maps and accounts of the early voyages, especially in Apian's *Cosmographicus* of 1524. Printing was introduced in Mexico as early as 1539 (see "Geography," *Encyclopaedia Britannica*, X, 146; Hallam, *op. cit.*, I, 200, 463).

[12] Erasmus and Luther used the press extensively. The Gutenburg Bible was printed in 1456. Hallam emphasizes the influence of printing on the Reformation in Germany (*op. cit.*, I, 258).

[13] The earliest publication of treaties was for purposes of propaganda (D. P. Myers, *Manual of Collections of Treaties* [Cambridge, 1922], pp. 586 ff.).

[14] Appen. XV, n. 38.

[15] O. L. Spaulding, H. Nickerson, and J. W. Wright, *Warfare* (London, 1924). Heavy canon were in regular use in the late fifteenth century as were heavy hand arms, but the latter acquired little efficiency until the seventeenth century (C. H. Ashdown, *British and Foreign Arms and Armour* [London, 1909], pp. 365 ff.; Oman, *op. cit.*, p. 431); chap. xii, sec. 1, above.

habit of time-counting which had been developed by monastic life. The perfection of the compass and the astrolabe in the latter part of the fifteenth century made extensive ocean navigation more practical and led to the improvement of sailing vessels.[16] The great extension in the use of water and windmills and the use of horseshoes and improved harness introduced new sources of power and of land transportation.[17] The introduction of double-entry accounting in Italy in the late fifteenth century stimulated large-scale business and the commercial spirit.[18] These inventions together originated the eo-technic period[19] and contributed to the transition from the Virgin to the dynamo as the prime mover of Western civilization.[20]

The critical examination of manuscripts and the collection of libraries, initiated by Petrarch in the fourteenth century, and developed by Scaliger, Erasmus, and others during the next century, made available the ideas of the classical, the biblical, and the early Christian writers as they were, in contrast to their scholastic interpretations.[21] This activity also stimulated the application of criticism to historical, literary, and artistic materials generally, not only from the point of view of authenticity and interpretation but also from that of aesthetic value, historical background, and social implications.[22]

The creation of a vernacular literature, which was at the same time popular and respectable, in Spain, France, Italy, Germany, and England in the thirteenth and fourteenth centuries[23]—a process similar to that going on in the twentieth century in China[24]—developed a spiritual union between the elite and the masses

[16] J. B. Scott, *The Spanish Origin of International Law* (Oxford, 1934), pp. 12 ff.

[17] Lewis Mumford, *Technics and Civilization* (New York, 1934).

[18] H. M. Robertson, *Aspects of the Rise of Economic Individualism* (Cambridge, 1933), p. 53, who quotes Sombart, *Die moderne Kapitalismus*, p. 118: "Capitalism without double entry bookkeeping is simply inconceivable. They hold together as form and matter." Hallam (*op. cit.*, I, 246) attributes the introduction of this method to Leonardo Fibonacci.

[19] Mumford, *op. cit.*, pp. 109 ff.

[20] Henry Adams, *Mont St. Michel and Chartres* (New York, 1913).

[21] G. E. B. Saintsbury, *A History of Criticism* (London, 1900–1904); J. A. Symonds, *The Renaissance in Italy* (London, 1875–88), Vol. II; S. R. Driver, *Introduction to the Literature of the Old Testament* (1891; 19th ed., 1913). Hallam (*op. cit.*, I, 187, 468) comments on the growth of libraries.

[22] See R. M. Lovett, "Criticism, Social," *Encyclopaedia of the Social Sciences*, IV, 600 ff.

[23] J. C. King ("Some Elements of National Solidarity" [manuscript, University of Chicago Library, 1933], chap. v) traces influence of vernacular literature on the rise of nationalism.

[24] Hu Shih, *The Chinese Renaissance* ("Chinese National Association for the Advancement of Education Publications," Vol. II, Bull. 6 [1923]), pp. 21 ff.; *The Chinese Renaissance* ("Haskell Lectures" [Chicago, 1934]).

in each of the nations, augmenting the spirit of nationalism at the expense of that of feudalism and of clericalism.[25]

3. *Pre-Renaissance changes.*—New economic, political, and cultural tendencies had been receiving institutional form during the later Middle Ages. Trade, industry, and finance had been developing since the twelfth century. The bourgeois had become organized in towns, guilds, and unions of trading cities with their own law and administration and steadily increasing wealth.[26] Dynastic monarchs claiming political sovereignty had been, since the eleventh century, interposing themselves, especially in France, England, and Spain, between the feudal barons, on the one hand, and the pope and emperor, on the other. This was contrary to the unitary theory of Western Christian civilization, but it provided the political framework within which nations could develop.[27] More naturalistic artistic standards had been developed, particularly in Italy since the time of Giotto in the late thirteenth and early fourteenth centuries. Religion had been undergoing new interpretations in the heresies of Wycliffe and Huss in the fifteenth century.

4. *Intercivilization contacts.*—More important than any of these factors as the immediate stimulus affecting the transition to modern civilization were a number of military and naval events bringing the élite of Western civilization into personal contact with the individuals of other civilizations. The reconquest of most of Moslem Spain by the Christian kingdoms in the twelfth and thirteenth centuries led to a close personal contact between their Arab and Jewish populations and the Christian rulers. Thus the basic ideas of Syriac and Arabic civilizations and of Classical civilization in the Arabic translation of Aristotle became known to Christian Europe. Syntheses such as that by Averroes were attempted. Even earlier, the Crusaders had brought Western civilization into contact with Syrian and Iranian civilizations, but the capture of Constantinople in 1453 by the Turks led to the dispersal through Europe of Jewish and orthodox Christian émigrés, carrying with them Greek and Latin manuscripts and the knowledge of Orthodox and Classic civilizations. The further advance of the Turks established permanent military contact of the Western civilization with this Iranian civilization.[28] By 1485 Russia under Ivan III as "the third Rome" came into territorial contact with the Catholic kingdom of Lithuania and established diplomatic relations with other Western countries. Marco Polo returned to Venice in 1295 intimately acquainted with Chinese civilization, which he described in his book of 1299. This stimulated both trading and papal missions to China. In the fourteenth and fifteenth centuries Portuguese navigators succes-

[25] Bernard Shaw illustrates this in his *Saint Joan.*

[26] Clive Day, *A History of Commerce* (New York, 1907), chaps. xii and xiv.

[27] Q. Wright, "National Sovereignty and Collective Security," *Annals of the American Academy of Social and Political Science*, CLXXXVI (July, 1936), 96–97.

[28] Dampier-Whetham, *op. cit.*, pp. 83, 107.

sively established intimate and continuous contact, through slave-traders, adventurers, merchants, and missionaries, with the primitive civilizations of the Guinea coast, with the Coptic Christian civilization of the kingdom of Prester John (Abyssinia), with India, the Moluccas, China, and Japan. After the voyage of Columbus in 1492, Spanish soldiers, adventurers, and missionaries established permanent contact with the primitive cultures of America and the civilizations of Mexico and Peru.[29] The invasion of Italy by French armies in 1495 opened the way for more intimate contact of the powerful monarchies of Western and Central Europe with the Italian cities and their direct tradition of Classical culture.[30]

Thus in the century between 1450 and 1550 Western civilization found itself in intimate and continuous contact by personal intercourse or literary remains with ten living and dead civilizations (Classic, Syriac, Orthodox, Russian, Iranian, Arabic, Hindu, Chinese, Mexican, Andean) as well as with many primitive cultures. It had lost the sense of being itself a universal civilization. It saw itself as but a small portion of a world of great variety. Its importance became relative, just as the importance of the world itself came to be relative after the astronomy of Copernicus, Bruno, and Galileo had superseded that of Ptolemy and Dante.[31]

This realization gave the *coup de grâce* to the basic postulate of Western civilization—its own universality in a geocentric universe with an ecclesiocentric religion, an imperiocentric polity, and a manoriocentric economy. The complete and rigid philosophy of Aquinas, expounded by ecclesiastically controlled universities, which had taught men how to adjust themselves to their closed world, perished before the vision of a great, varied, unexplored universe, presenting infinite opportunities.[32]

[29] Clive Day, *op. cit.*, chap. xv; L. A. Maverick, "Chinese Influences upon the Physiocrats," *Economic History*, III (February, 1938), 54–67.

[30] John Addington Symons and Luigi Villari say of Charles VIII's invasion: "He had convulsed Italy by this invasion, destroyed her equilibrium, exposed her military weakness and political disunion, and revealed her wealth to greedy and more powerful nations." A generation of invasion and intrigue in Italy by France, Spain, Germany, Switzerland, and England followed ("Italy," *Encyclopaedia Britannica*, XII, 797; see also Hume, *History of England*, Vol. III, chap. xxv, p. 47).

[31] "If the destruction of paganism was completed when all the gods were brought to Rome and confronted there, now, when by our wonderful facilities of locomotion strange nations and conflicting religions are brought into common presence—the Mohammedan, the Buddhist, the Brahman—modifications of them all must ensue" (J. W. Draper, *History of the Conflict between Religion and Science* [New York, 1875], p. 324).

[32] Dampier-Whetham, *op. cit.*, pp. 110 ff. "It is to the expansion of Europe, then, that we must look for a historical force sufficiently powerful and comprehensive to explain the origins of modern times" (Harry Elmer Barnes, *The History of Western Civilization* [New York, 1935], II, 6). "The history of the expansion of Europe . . . . includes colonization and vastly more. It may be regarded, in fact, as the record of the inter-

5. *Renaissance and Reformation.*—The immediate consequences of the change were (*a*) the Renaissance, radiating from Italy and substituting classic for Gothic art, classic philosophy for Christianity, *de facto* political power for delegated titles, and observational science for scholastic philosophy; (*b*) the Reformation, radiating from Germany and Switzerland and substituting the authority of the Bible for the authority of the church, salvation by faith for salvation by indulgence, Puritan morals for expectation of absolution, and rulership by divine right for rulership by delegated title; (*c*) the rise of ambitious monarchs utilizing Machiavellian methods and modernized armies to support demands for absolute sovereignty in matters temporal and religious over all the lands they could acquire; (*d*) the rise of science with new methods of observation, experiment, criticism, and mathematical formulation, placing the reports of the senses and of authentic documents above that of constituted authority and scholastic exegesis; (*e*) the rise of adventurous entrepreneurs with schemes to make money by the exploitation of mines and native labor, the control of capital, or the application of science to industry.

These movements were greatly stimulated by the activities of a few great minds—Leonardo, Machiavelli, Erasmus, Luther—in whom were joined many of the tendencies of the previous century but in whom these tendencies were synthesized into a new outlook. An intense interest in art, in religion, in politics, and in economics, normally following one another in succession, in this period of transition were often simultaneous in the same town such as Florence, or even in the same mind such as that of Leonardo. Such unusual conjunctions effected an extraordinary transition in a remarkably short time.[33]

6. *Post-Renaissance institutions.*—During the sixteenth and seventeenth centuries this new outlook became synthesized in new institutions—political, religious, educational, and commercial. The sovereign nation-state as expounded by Bodin, Althusius, Hobbes, and Locke, whether justified by force, divine right, contract, or utility, became the political center in a pluralistic universe. This universe, however, presently achieved a certain unity through the conception of a family of nations governed by international law which defined the limits of the domain, nationality, and jurisdiction of each sovereign and the procedures of diplomacy, war, and arbitration. This system was given prestige through its association with the Roman *jus naturale* and *jus gentiun* and was expounded in detail by Francis of Victoria, Albericis Gentili, Hugo Grotius, and others.[34] As time went on, the states tended to become democratic, con-

---

penetration of Europeans and non-Europeans the world over in all departments of human activity" (W. R. Shepherd, "The Expansion of Europe," *Political Science Quarterly*, March, 1919, p. 50).

[33] Charles Oman, *The Sixteenth Century* (London, 1936); Taylor, *op. cit.*

[34] Q. Wright, *Mandates under the League of Nations* (Chicago, 1930), pp. 274 ff; G. Butler and S. Maccoby, *The Development of International Law* (London, 1928), chap. viii, pp. 7–14; G. N. Clark, *The Seventeenth Century* (Oxford, 1929). C. Van Vollen-

stitutional, and national. The family of nations tended to become organized by permanent diplomatic and consular officials, international unions, general treaties, and leagues of nations.[35]

Churches became organized nationally under the doctrine of Erastianism and often became the tools of politics, although the papacy, with diminishing temporal authority and decreasing control within the states, maintained nominal unity. Churches undertook humanitarian reforms and missionary activities in distant lands, though, as non-Christian states became recognized members of the family of nations, this activity tended to become subject to the temporal sovereign.[36] As time went on, private associations devoted to humanitarian activities often superseded the churches as centers for the propaganda and application of ethical standards.[37]

Scientific societies and national academies of the type conceived by Bacon in "Salomon's House" superseded the ecclesiastically controlled universities as centers of scientific and critical thought. Eventually, however, as the universities adapted themselves to the secular character of the new age, new universities were established by cities and states to promote education and research in the spirit of science and criticism.[38]

International trading corporations utilizing scientific accounting methods and capable of accumulating a large capital, and of organizing production and transport on a large scale, came to be the dominant economic form. They engaged particularly in the development of new colonial areas and in providing the requirements of armies for the ambitious monarchs.[39] Their activities, however, developed the technology of production through the use of coal, which began to be mined in large quantities in England in the late sixteenth century. This development was stimulated by the exhaustion of forests, by the demands of expanding industries, and by the opportunity presented to private enterprise, through secularization of coal-bearing lands after the confiscations of church lands following the Reformation. Application of the new science also proved an industrial stimulus, until eventually commercial enterprises involved the world in a network of communication, transport, and trade.[40]

---

hoven (*The Law of Peace* [London, 1936], p. 82, quoting Ledeboer, *Appel au droit des gens avant 1667* [Amsterdam, 1932], pp. 72–73) writes: "Official reference to any law of nations recognized by the new states begins with the year 1570 or a little before that."

[35] Butler and Maccoby, *op. cit.*, chaps. xv, xviii.

[36] Layman's Foreign Mission Inquiry, *Rethinking Foreign Missions* (New York, 1932).

[37] Q. Wright, *Mandates under the League of Nations*, p. 9.

[38] Ornstein, *op. cit.*; Francis Bacon, *New Atlantis* (1st ed., 1629).

[39] Day, *op. cit.*, pp. 146–48.

[40] John U. Nef, *The Rise of the British Coal Industry* (London, 1932), I, 142 ff.

TABLE 18

INCREASE AND RATE OF INCREASE OF THE WORLD'S POPULATION
BY FIFTY-YEAR PERIODS, 1450–1940*

(000,000 omitted)

Continent	1450	1500	1550	1600	1650	1700	1750	1800	1850	1900	1940
Europe†	60	68	76	87	100	118	140	187	266	401	544
Asia‡	200	208	220	234	250	300	406	522	671	859	1081
Africa§	112	110	107	103	100	100	100	100	100	141	156
North America‖	8	7	6	6	7	6	6	15	39	106	190
South America‖	7	6	5	5	6	6	6	9	20	38	93
Oceania¶	2	2	2	2	2	2	2	2	2	6	11
Total	389	401	416	437	465	545	660	835	1,098	1,551	2,075

Percentage Rate of Increase or Decrease Each Fifty Years

	1450–1500	1500–1550	1550–1600	1600–1650	1650–1700	1700–1750	1750–1800	1800–1850	1850–1900	1900–1950**
Europe	13	12	14	15	18	19	34	42	51	41
Asia	4	6	6	7	20	35	29	29	28	33
Africa	− 2	− 3	− 4	− 3	0	0	0	0	14	19
North America	−13	−14	0	17	−14	0	150	160	170	86
South America	−14	−17	0	20	0	0	50	122	90	161
Oceania	0	0	0	0	0	0	0	0	200	100
World	5	4	5	6	17	21	27	32	41	40

* Estimates by R. Kuczynski, "Population," *Encyclopaedia of the Social Sciences*, XII, 241, using estimates by W. F. Willcox, *International Migrations* (New York: National Bureau of Economic Research, 1929–31), II, 78. See also *The Economic Almanac for 1940* (New York: National Industrial Conference Board, 1940), p. 169; *Statistical Year Book of the League of Nations* (Geneva, 1938), pp. 15–21.

† For sources of estimates before 1650 see Table 3, Appen. V.

‡ It is assumed that Asiatic population increased at an accelerating rate from 1450 to 1650, the time of the Ming empire in China, and of the rise of the Mogul empire in India and the Ottoman empire in the Near East. The figure for 1940 is based on Willcox's estimate which gave China 342,000,000 in 1930. The International Institute of Statistics and the International Institute of Agriculture, in 1929, and the League of Nations, in 1932, printed estimates of about 450,000,000. J. Lossing Buck (*Land Utilization in China* [Chicago, 1937], pp. 363 ff.) compared estimates based on the census of families (400,000,000) with those based on the average density in the areas which he had studied intensively (600,000,000) and concluded that the population was between 450,000,000 and 500,000,000. The figure given may, therefore, be more than 100,000,000 too small.

§ It is assumed that the African population declined from 1450 to 1600 as a result of slave-raiding and imported diseases.

‖ The various estimates of pre-Columbian American population are discussed by A. L. Kroeber, "Native American Population," *American Anthropologist* (N.S.), XXXVI (1934), 1–25, whose estimate of 8,400,000 for both continents in 1492 is far less than Sapper's estimate of 40,000,000–50,000,000 (*International Congress of Anthropology* [The Hague, 1924], XXI, 95–104), or than Spinden's estimate of 50,000,000–75,000,000 at the height of population in the thirteenth century (*Geographical Review*, XVIII [1928], 641–60). Kroeber notes that Sapper's estimate for America north of the Rio Grande is three times as great as the careful estimate by Mooney (Smithsonian Institution, Miscellaneous Collection, No. 7, 1928), which he adopts. If this correction were applied, Sapper's estimate for the continent would be 13,000,000–16,000,000. Willcox estimated the total population at 13,000,000 in 1650, though probably the losses of Indian population by white man's diseases, greatly emphasized by Spinden, had scarcely been compensated for by white immigration by that time. With these considerations in mind it seemed justifiable to increase Kroeber's estimate somewhat.

¶ It is assumed that Oceanic population was stable from 1450 to 1650.

** These figures are based on an extrapolation of the trend to 1950.

TABLE 19*

INCREASE AND RATE OF INCREASE OF COAL
PRODUCTION IN ENGLAND, 1500–1900

Date	Coal Production (Tons)	Increase Compared with Preceding Period (Tons)	Rate of Increase Compared with Preceding Period (Per Cent)
1551–60............	210,000	....	....
1681–90............	2,982,000	2,772,000	1,320
1781–90............	10,295,000	7,313,000	245
1901–10............	241,910,000	231,615,000	2,249

* Source: John U. Nef, *The Rise of the British Coal Industry* (London, 1932), p. 20.

TABLE 20*

INCREASE AND RATE OF INCREASE IN NUMBER OF
INVENTIONS, BY TWENTY-FIVE-YEAR
PERIODS, 1450–1900

Period	No. of Inventions	Increase or Decrease Compared with Preceding Period	Per Cent Increase or Decrease Compared with Preceding Period
1450–74......	39	....	....
1475–99......	50	11	28.0
1500–24......	84	34	68.0
1525–49......	102	18	21.5
1550–74......	109	7	7.0
1575–99......	127	18	16.5
1600–24......	135	8	6.0
1625–49......	129	− 6	− 4.5
1650–74......	237	108	84.0
1675–99......	218	− 19	− 8.0
1700–24......	180	− 38	−17.5
1725–49......	281	101	56.0
1750–74......	410	129	46.0
1775–99......	680	270	63.0
1800–24......	1,034	354	52.0
1825–49......	1,885	851	82.0
1850–74......	2,468	583	31.0
1875–99......	2,880	412	17.0

* Source: W. F. Ogburn (ed.), *Recent Social Trends* (New York, 1933), I, 126, citing L. Darmstaedter, *Handbuch zur Geschichte der Naturwissenschaften und der Technik* (Berlin, 1908).

TABLE 21*

RELATIVE PRODUCTION OF RELIGIOUS AND SECULAR ART IN EUROPE BY CENTURIES, 800–1930

Century	Per Cent Religious Art	Per Cent Secular Art
9th.........	81.9	8.1
10th.........	94.5	5.5
12th.........	97.0	3.0
14th.........	85.0	15.0
16th.........	64.7	35.3
17th.........	50.2	49.8
18th.........	24.1	75.9
19th.........	10.0	90.0
20th.........	3.9	96.1

* Source: Pitirim Sorokin, *Social and Cultural Dynamics* (New York, 1937), I, 382.

APPENDIX XVIII

THE EVALUATING IDEAS OF MODERN CIVILIZATION

Modern civilization has increasingly tended to regard *humanism* or equality, *liberalism* or freedom, *pragmatism* or reason enlightened by scientific method, and *relativism* or tolerance and a spirit of fraternity as expressions of fundamental values. Evidence in support of this proposition can be found in (1) statements by leading thinkers, (2) statistical and (3) philosophic analyses of ideas, (4) popular oratory, and (5) linguistic changes.

1. *Statements by thinkers.*—The ideas expressed by some or all of these words seem to be implied by the following efforts to characterize modern civilization. J. J. Rousseau[1] described the "humanitarianism, rationalism and tolerance" of the *philosophes* as "modernism"; the French Revolution expressed the idea in the slogan "liberty, equality, fraternity"; Jeremy Bentham emphasized the words "utility,"[2] "security, equality,"[3] and "fictions";[4] J. S. Mill emphasized "Utility, Liberty, Induction";[5] Alexis de Tocqueville saw an inevitable trend toward "Democracy and Equality";[6] Auguste Comte centered his philosophy about "positivism, religion of humanity, relativism";[7] Herbert Spencer emphasized the words "altruism,"[8] "individualism,"[9] "evolutionism,"[10] and "relativity";[11] W. E. H. Lecky wrote on *Democracy and Liberty;*[12] H. T. Buckle referred to the growth of "skepticism and toleration";[13] J. W. Draper characterized the post-Renaissance period by the development of "individualism and science";[14] J. Novicow discerned a trend toward "world solidarity, liberalism and intellec-

---

[1] Letter to M. D., January 15, 1769.

[2] *Theory of Legislation*, pp. 1 ff.   [3] *Ibid.*, p. 96.

[4] C. K. Ogden, *Bentham's Theory of Fictions* (New York, 1932).

[5] *Essays* (1844) and *A System of Logic* (1843).

[6] *The Republic of the United States of America* (New York, 1862), Introd.

[7] *A General View of Positivism*, pp. 365, 372; *Positive Philosophy* (1853), I, 28; II, 77, 92, discussed by L. M. Bristol, *Social Adaptation* (Cambridge, Mass., 1915), pp. 16, 20, 301.

[8] *Data of Ethics*, chap. xiii.

[9] *Social Statics*, chap. vi.   [10] *First Principles*, Part II, p. 417.

[11] *Ibid.*, Part I, chap. iv; *Data of Ethics*, chap. x.

[12] 2 vols.; London, 1899.

[13] *History of Civilization in England* (London, 1869), I, 350.

[14] *History of the Conflict between Religion and Science* (1875), pp. 324–25.

tual conflict";[15] Benjamin Kidd anticipated "equality of opportunity and social efficiency";[16] J. K. Ingram emphasized "individualism and criticism" as responsible for modern economic growth;[17] Simon Patten produced a classification of tendencies under the headings "social beliefs," "self-direction," "pragmatic thought," and "ideal philosophy";[18] Jane Addams wrote of *Democracy and Social Ethics*;[19] Graham Wallas linked the words "happiness, freedom, economy and intelligence";[20] A. J. Toynbee considered the contemporary world under the dominion of "the industrial system" (including the division of labor and the application of scientific thought), of "democracy" (responsible parliamentary representative government in a sovereign independent national state, tempered however by the sense of "being parts of some larger universe"), and of the "relativity of thought to the social environment";[21] Masaharu Anesaki used the words "progress," "freedom," "utility," and "activity" in "An Oriental View of Modern Civilization";[22] Bernard Fay regarded "humanity, democracy, and progress" as the gods of the nineteenth century with which some people are getting a bit weary;[23] Horace Kallen described "modernism" as "the endeavor to harmonize the relations between the older institutions of civilization and science";[24] Carlton J. H. Hayes has referred to "the rise of humanitarianism, of individualism, and latterly of the democratic spirit";[25] and E. P. Cheney formulated certain historical laws, including the trends toward "interdependence, democracy and freedom."[26]

The generally accepted criteria of progress perhaps constitute the fundamental values of any civilization. After examining numerous such criteria proposed by modern writers, A. J. Todd concludes that "an interest (more and more conscious and rationalized)in human well-being is the basic test of social progress."[27] George Catlin considers humanism, freedom, experiment, and tolerance as the leading values of "Anglo-Saxony";[28] and Ralph Barton Perry expresses the

[15] *Les Luttes entre les sociétés humaines* (1893), pp. 178, 426, 458, 572, 578, discussed in Bristol, *op. cit.*, pp. 260–82.

[16] *Social Evolution* (1895), p. 327.

[17] *A History of Political Economy* (New York, 1893), p. 33.

[18] "Reconstruction of Economic Theory," *Annals of the American Academy of Political and Social Science, Suppl.*, 1912, p. 92.

[19] New York, 1902, p. 11.

[20] *The Great Society* (New York, 1917), pp. 357 ff.

[21] *A Study of History* (Oxford, 1934), I, 1, 15.

[22] *The World Tomorrow*, October, 1928, p. 416.

[23] *Policy* (Chicago), January, 1930.

[24] "Modernism," *Encyclopaedia of the Social Sciences*, X, 565.

[25] "Nationalism," *Encyclopaedia of the Social Sciences*, XI, 241.

[26] *Law in History* (New York, 1927).

[27] *Theories of Social Progress* (New York, 1928), p. 147.

[28] *Anglo-Saxony and Its Tradition* (New York, 1939).

values of democracy by the words "universalism," "libertarianism," "intellectualism," and "moral purposiveness."[29] There has been opposition to the ideals of humanism and liberalism,[30] but until the rise of fascism that opposition was on the defensive.

2. *Statistical analysis of ideas.*—The existence of this trend can be supported by statistical evidence. Hornell Hart's study of trends of attitude in the United States, 1900–1932,[31] notes a sharp increase in scientific and a decline in religious interest, a decline in belief in traditional Christianity but a rise in religious humanism, a prominent position for "humanism, pragmatism and relativity" among topics of philosophical discussion, and "the long time shift in prevalent criteria of truth from traditional authority to open minded, objective investigation by means of experimentation, statistical surveys, scientific history, case studies and the like." Pitirim Sorokin's statistical examination of ideas similarly indicates an increasing importance of ideas related to liberalism, humanism, pragmatism, and relativism since the Renaissance, though he thinks a change in the trend may have begun in recent years.[32]

3. *Philosophical analysis of ideas.*—Merritt H. Moore in his Introduction to George H. Mead's *Movements of Thought in the Nineteenth Century*[33] suggests that the great post-Renaissance problems, in Mead's view, were those of society, the self, science, and the past. These were also the problems which most interested Mead himself, and the relation between his solutions of them has been thus expressed by his editor:

These may all be related in two directions: first, through his acceptance of the method of research science as underlying all significant developments in thinking; and second, through his basic assumption that the description of experience in every field is to be made in terms of processes rather than in terms of absolutes.

An examination of Mead's text suggests that his solutions of these four problems might be indicated, respectively, by the words "humanism," "liberalism," "pragmatism," and "relativism."

[1] For the positivist it is not the glory of God but the good of mankind that is the supreme value. . . . . Bentham and the Mills are, in a sense, companion figures to Comte. . . . . This is something all should see, and man's attitude toward it should be a religious attitude. This should be recognized as the supreme value that determines all others.

[2] We are solving problems, and those problems can appear only in the experience of the individual. It is that which gives the importance to the individual, gives him a value which cannot be stated. He has a certain preciousness which cannot be estimated.

[29] MacIver, Bonn, and Perry, *The Roots of Totalitarianism* (Philadelphia, 1940), p. 30.

[30] See chap. viii, n. 17, above.

[31] In W. F. Ogburn (ed.), *Recent Social Trends* (New York, 1933), I, 391, 395–96, 412–13.

[32] *Social and Cultural Dynamics* (New York, 1937); chap. viii, n. 92, above.

[33] (Chicago, 1936), pp. xxxvi, 349, 411, 412–17, 464.

[3] From a logical standpoint, the scientist is engaged in stating the past history of the world. . . . . And, of course, the process of stating the world, stating our past, is a process of getting control over that world, getting its meaning for future conduct. That is the importance of the pragmatic doctrine. It finds its test of the so-called "true" in hypotheses and in the working of these hypotheses. And when you ask what is meant by the "working of the hypotheses," we mean that a process which has been inhibited by a problem can, from this standpoint, start working again and going on.

[4] From the point of view of the most abstract of physical sciences, it has been recognized that the world, taken from the point of view of any particular physical particle or any particular physical structure, even such as that of an atom of iron, is shifting. . . . . That is the reality of the world: it is an organization of the perspectives of all individuals in it. . . . . The history which we study is not the history of a few years ago. We cannot say that events remain the same. We are continually reconstructing the world from our own standpoint. And that reconstruction holds just as really with the so-called "irrevocable" past as with reference to a future. The past is just as uncertain as the future is.

4. *Popular oratory* perhaps provides even better evidence of the values actually accepted in a society than the statistician's measurement of attitude trends or the philosopher's analysis of underlying assumptions. All four of these values are illustrated in an address by Senator Elbert D. Thomas of Utah to the Thirteenth Conference on the Cause and Cure of War, January 20, 1938:

May I suggest that in your magazine and newspaper reading you note the subtle attacks upon this institution [Congress] which does and will preserve our *liberties?* What do we mean by *liberty? Liberty* in an American constitutional sense is that freedom of individual initiative and action which is not curbed by law. Thus we have in our Constitution a recognition of the ideal that *liberty* shall be curbed only by governmental action and that government shall never destroy *liberty* and that democracy shall be preserved. . . . . Universal peace must rest upon democratic processes; and by universal peace I do not mean a state of bliss. I mean an active, energetic world where differences exist, where ambition and strivings still have a place, where differences of opinion may run rampant, where the cultures of the various nationalities shall contribute constructively to world progress instead of being used destructively for world chaos. States controlled by a single will cannot exist in a world of democracy and peaceful processes. . . . . Can we then take ourselves seriously enough, either as individuals or as a nation, to assume that we can plan for a better world and for a higher standard of living for men, women, and children in the world? To assume that we cannot is to become victims of a pessimism so dulling in its weight that life will become hardly worth while. To assume that we can, then, means the necessity of facing reality with an optimism, not necessarily the optimism of a Condorcet, but the optimism of a follower of Einstein, who understands that things are *relative* and that they can be made *relatively* better or *relatively* worse instead of being made perfect or desperate. . . . . An active, positive peace policy means the offering of cooperative interest and aid to every movement which will advance the standard of living throughout the earth and security for the people of the earth. I do not advocate such an idea as this on the basis of *humanitarianism*, although I do not belittle such an idea. I advocate it on a basis of downright selfishness. The fruits from such stability and an increase in the standard of living would not only solve our own problem but we ourselves would likely be the greatest secondary beneficiaries. America, darling of the gods in so many ways, becomes even more blessed if the world standards are increased.[34]

5. *Linguistic changes.*—Further evidence of the significance of these words in modern civilization can be found by examining their changing connotation in ordinary usage. Attention will be confined to the English words, though the parallel terms in other languages would, it is believed, exhibit parallel changes in connotation.[35]

The word "humanism" seems not to have been used until the nineteenth century, when it acquired four meanings, referring, respectively, to belief in the merely human character of Christ (1812); to devotion to the "humane studies" or "humanities" which included especially the classical poetry and literature to which the Renaissance "humanists" were devoted (1830); to interest in all things human (1836); and finally to a system of thought concerned with human interests as distinct from divine interests or interests of a special class or group —"the religion of humanity" (1860). This latter sense, here intended, is similar to that of the earlier term "humanitarianism." It has, however, a more favorable connotation. The tendency of this word and of cognate forms, "humanist" and "humanitarian," has been to expand from originally narrow meanings and to acquire an ethical tone and a more favorable connotation. Among the English-speaking people, at least, the "religion of humanity" has apparently grown in acceptance.[36]

Used philosophically, humanism may be regarded as an approach to the problem of values (axiology). It asserts that the source of values is not super-human (deism), or subhuman (naturalism), or "somehuman" (racialism, nationalism), or "superiorhuman" (fascism), but "allhuman." Values spring from the interests of all human beings.[37] Humanism seeks such a definition and order-

[34] *Congressional Record* (75th Cong., 3d sess.), LXXXIII, Part IX, 273–74. (Italics mine.)

[35] There may have been some differences. According to Fichte, "humanity, popularity, and liberty" (*humanitat, popularitat, libertat*) have no meaning to a German who has not studied other languages (*Address to the German Nation* [1808], quoted by Alfred Zimmern, *Modern Political Doctrines* [London, 1939], pp. 168 ff.).

[36] Murray, *Oxford Dictionary*.

[37] The spirit of humanism has extended to movements sympathetic to animals (anti-vivisection societies, societies for prevention of cruelty to animals, etc.). It is difficult to state any principle which would justify drawing a line of ethical consideration between man and other animals rather than between one race of men and another or between one phyla of animals such as the vertebrates and other animals. For an attempt to rationalize this distinction see Theodore de Laguna, *Introduction to the Science of Ethics* (New York, 1914), p. 27. Humanism, however, does draw that line. It treats the interests of nonhuman animals in a different category and as deserving ethical consideration only because and in so far as such consideration satisfies human interests. Thus Kidd writes: "If society is asked to permit vivisection, the only question it has to

ing of values as to maximize the enjoyment by human beings of their experience and to maximize the experiences which human beings enjoy.[38] Thus it recognizes that men are equal in spiritual value. Men are ends not means.

The word "liberalism" appears to have originated in the nineteenth century. The word "liberty" goes back to the Middle Ages, as does the word "liberal." The latter word had the rather narrow meaning, "devoted to general intellectual enlargement and refinement" as "the liberal arts" (1375), and "generosity in giving" (1387) and also the wider meaning but with unfavorable connotation— "free in speech and action, unrestrained, licentious" (1490). In the modern period, however, the word soon acquired a favorable connotation as "free from narrow prejudice, open-minded" (1781), and in the nineteenth century the political association of the word was emphasized "favorable to reform tending in the direction of freedom or democracy" (1801).[39] After Waterloo, the word was regarded in England as revolutionary and Continental, and applied scornfully by conservatives. But it soon acquired a favorable connotation as is amply indicated by its adoption as the title of one of the great political parties. The word "liberty" has also increased the favorableness of its connotation as the revolutions in England, the United States, and France, in which it served as a slogan, achieved success.[40]

Liberalism is said to be "a belief in the value of human personality, and a conviction that the source of all progress lies in the free exercise of individual energy; it produces an eagerness to emancipate all individuals or groups so that they may freely exercise their powers, so far as this can be done without injury

---

decide is, whether the benefits it may receive from the practice through the furtherance of medical science (even admitting them to be considerable), outweigh the injury it may receive through the weakening of the altruistic feelings which it tends to outrage" (*op. cit.*, p. 162, n. 1).

[38] The problem may be approached introspectively by attempting to ascertain the most generalized requirements of the developing human individual (Walter Lippmann, *Preface to Morals* [New York, 1929]), or it may be approached observationally by attempting to ascertain the interests people actually have (see Bentham's discussion of utility, *Principles of Legislation*, chap. i, and Benjamin Kidd's expansion of the theory in the light of evolution, *op. cit.*, pp. 290–91). The former, or religious, method might suggest certain cultural and educational goals which should be universal, whereas the latter, or ethical, method might suggest the expediency of great local and temporal variations in human institutions and customs. These two methods correspond, respectively, to the use of the *jus naturale* and the *jus gentium* to improve the *jus civile* in ancient Rome and to create modern international law in the sixteenth and seventeenth centuries (see Q. Wright, *Mandates under the League of Nations* [Chicago, 1930], pp. 346 ff.).

[39] Murray, *Oxford Dictionary*. Crabb (*English Synonymes* [New York, 1917]) notes that "liberal" has a more favorable connotation than "free."

[40] Ramsay Muir, "Liberal Party," *Encyclopaedia Britannica*, XIII, 1000.

to others."[41] Viewed philosophically, liberalism may be regarded as an approach to the basic problem of ethics and law. What are the sanctions of moral and legal rules? What is the justification for obedience? Liberalism asserts that the normal sanctions of human conduct should not be authority, superstition, custom, coercion, propaganda, influence, or any other external compulsion but deliberate free consent of the person bound by the rule. Liberalism differs from anarchism in recognizing that external sanctions are necessary to meet the case of antisocial individuals and that the need of adjusting law to social change requires legislative procedures eliminating the *liberum veto*, but it believes that such sanctions will not work in the long run unless the majority have been convinced of the wisdom of the rule, nearly all have consented to abide by it, and it is applied impartially to all. Liberalism assumes that human beings desire freedom and that obedience to law rests on the consent to any limitation of freedom by those subject to the limitation.[42]

[41] *Ibid.*

[42] See John Locke, *Two Treatises of Government*, Book II, sec. 131; J. Dickinson, "Social Order and Political Authority," *American Political Science Review*, XXIII (1920), 626–32; C. E. Merriam, *The Making of Citizens* (Chicago, 1931), p. 282; W. A. Rudlin, "Obedience, Political," *Encyclopaedia of the Social Sciences;* W. Lippmann, *The Good Society* (Boston, 1937).

The word "liberalism" seems to mean little different from individualism. The articles on the two words in the *Encyclopaedia of the Social Sciences* deal with almost the same doctrines. Liberalism is said to "posit a free individual conscious of his capacity for unfettered development and self expression" and individualism is said to contemplate a society "in which little respect is paid to tradition and authority"—where people "think for themselves" and are regarded as being "the best judges of their own interests."

Liberalism, however, has often been considered the opposite of conservatism, and individualism has been considered the opposite of socialism. Conservatism and socialism are not usually considered identical, although liberalism and individualism may both be contrasted with the primitive type of social organization in which "the overpowering dominance of tribal custom and tradition leaves little scope for individual initiative and concern and the members of the tribe are so absorbed in the group that it forms what anthropologists have called a tribal self" (*ibid.*, VII, 674–75). However, these antitheses are not really opposites. Liberalism and conservatism are said not to be "essentially antipathetic," as is evidenced by the fact that a "liberal party upon attaining power immediately dedicates itself to the conservation of the liberties already won" (*ibid.*, IX, 435), while "most of the differences between modern individualism, strictly so-called, and socialism are differences within these common assumptions" of encouragement of "individual moral judgment based on toleration and the maintenance of a system of rights" (*ibid.*, VII, 677).

Liberalism has also often been closely associated with "rationalism," and "individualism" with "egoism." Probably the difference between the four terms inheres in the aspect of human personality to which they respectively refer:

While liberalism seeks to justify itself as the best means to assure law observance and social order as well as to assure progress, it realizes the need of institutional protection to prevent its subversion through the power-seeking propensities of the élite. Consequently, liberalism favors diffusion rather than concentration of power. It prefers to see the social functions divided among separate institutions—the state, the church, the business corporation, the university—that can mutually check each other.[43]

It prefers to see governmental functions divided among independent agencies—the legislature, the executive, and the judiciary—in order that tyranny may be checked.[44] It prefers local home rule and federalism to political centralization.[45] It prefers that economic activity be controlled by competition in a free

(1) radicalism	liberalism	conservatism	reactionism
(2) anarchism	individualism	socialism	communism
(3) empiricism	rationalism	traditionalism	authoritarianism
(4) hedonism	egoism	altruism	fascism

The political significance of series (1) is discussed by A. L. Lowell (*Public Opinion in War and Peace* [1923], pp. 276 ff.), and good accounts of all the sixteen terms are contained in the *Encyclopaedia of Social Sciences* except reactionism (which is treated under "Anti-radicalism"), empiricism (which is treated under "Logic," IX, 601), and egoism (which is treated under "Altruism"). These groups of terms, which, from left to right, move from atomism to unification of society, refer, respectively, from (1) to (4), to the emotional, sensory, intellectual, and volitional aspects of personality. Liberalism connotes moderate freedom of sentiments and opinion, individualism connotes moderate freedom of experience and behavior, rationalism connotes moderate freedom of investigation and reasoning, and egoism connotes moderate freedom of action and motivation.

Liberalism is used here to include freedom in the satisfaction of all aspects of personality and thus includes all four terms. As freedom implies a high ratio between wishes and their satisfaction, it may be augmented by reducing wishes as well as by augmenting means of satisfying them. Sorokin distinguishes these two types of freedom and believes there may have been as much "ideational" freedom in the Middle Ages as there has been "sensate" freedom in the modern period (*op. cit.*, III, 161 ff.). Liberalism recognizes both roads to freedom—education to enjoy the obtainable as well as to obtain the enjoyable—but it has tended to emphasize the latter.

[43] H. J. Laski, *Studies in the Problem of Sovereignty* (New Haven, 1917), chap. i; Q. Wright, "Academic Freedom," *University of Chicago Magazine*, midsummer, 1935, pp. 334 ff.; and *Bulletin of the Association of University Professors*, Vol. XXVI (April, 1940), reviewing, E. P. Cheyney (ed.), *Freedom of Inquiry and Expression* (*Annals of the American Academy of Political and Social Science* [Philadelphia, 1938]).

[44] John Locke, *op. cit.*, sec. 143; Montesquieu, *L'Esprit des lois*, Book XI, chap. vi.

[45] See J. D. Lewis, *The Genossenschaft Theory of Otto von Gierke* (Madison, 1935), pp. 27, 77 ff.

market rather than by central planning and administration.[46] Furthermore, it regards general education as a necessary prophylactic against propaganda and superstition as well as a prerequisite to the voluntary acceptance of legislative innovations for adapting law to new conditions. Eternal vigilance has been recognized as always the price of liberty.[47]

The word "pragmatism" is defined in the philosophical sense as "the doctrine that the whole 'meaning' of a conception expresses itself in its practical consequences, either in the shape of conduct to be recommended, or of experiences to be expected, if the conception be true." In this sense, the word does not seem to have been used before 1898.[48] The specialized use in the phrase "the pragmatic sanction" and the unfavorable use as "officiousness, pedantry" were older. The *Oxford Dictionary* records a more favorable use in 1803 as a method of treating history practically and, in 1872, as a matter-of-fact treatment of anything. Evidently, the English-speaking world during the nineteenth century was becoming less supercilious with reference to "practical things" and "pragmatic knowledge."

Viewed philosophically, pragmatism has dealt primarily with the problem of knowledge (epistemology). It has rejected the assumptions that knowledge is a function of the knower (solipsism, Berkleian idealism), or of the thing known (materialism), or of universal ideas (idealism or Platonic realism), or of particular events (nominalism), but has asserted that it is a function of the practical procedures by which the knower, the known, the abstract, and the concrete have been related. As these procedures have steadily developed, so truth also has developed. Truth must be dated and located. Eternity or universality can never be guaranteed of any proposition.[49]

"Relativism" may have been implied by the intellectual activities of the last three centuries, but the bias of the human mind for a positive answer to the problem of reality is suggested by the unfavorable connotation of the word as late as 1885. Relativism is defined in the *Oxford Dictionary* as "the doctrine that knowledge is only of relations" illustrated by the quotation, "Hegel alone of all metaphysicians lifts us completely clear of Relativism."[50] There is probably still a bias against relativism, though in scientific circles it can hardly be doubted

---

[46] Henry C. Simons, *A Positive Program for Laissez Faire* ("Public Policy Pamphlet" No. 15 [Chicago, 1934]); Harry D. Gideonse, *Organized Scarcity and Public Policy* ("Public Policy Pamphlet" No. 30 [Chicago, 1939]).

[47] C. E. Merriam, "Civic Education in the United States," in *Report of the Commission on the Social Studies* (New York, 1934), Part VI, pp. x–xi, 183 ff.

[48] Murray, *Oxford Dictionary*, quoting William James.

[49] See above, chap. viii, nn. 54, 65.

[50] This statement seems dubious (above, chap. viii, n. 77).

that this term and the correlative one, "relativity," are mounting the ladder of general approval.[51]

Relativism deals with the problem of ultimate reality (ontology) by denying that there is any such reality, a conclusion anticipated by Kant, who admitted that the "thing-in-itself" was inaccessible to knowledge and had to be taken on faith, and by Hegel, who was unable to demonstrate any being but only a becoming. The absolute was a limit which might be approached but would never be reached.

Politically and socially relativism implies an attitude of tolerance and compromise, the acceptance of general opinion as a guide for practical action, and the evaluating of institutions as they serve to adjust law and society to changing conditions.[52]

[51] Jeans points out that "the scientific world in general" was troubled by the difficulties in the traditional theory presented by the Michelson-Morley experiment since 1887, and, consequently, Einstein's doctrine of relativity, stated in 1905, was "almost immediately accepted." He compares the significance of the theory for the advancement of science with the Copernican system of astronomy, the Newtonian law of gravitation, and the Darwinian principle of natural selection (*Encyclopaedia Britannica*, XIX, 89–90). Russell notes that nearly every philosopher interpreted the theory "as a great accession of strength to his own views" (*ibid.*, p. 99).

[52] T. V. Smith, *The Democratic Way of Life* (Chicago, 1926).

APPENDIX XIX

ANALYSIS OF THE BATTLES OF MODERN CIVILIZATION

The battles analyzed in the tables in this appendix include land and sea engagements and sieges and capitulations in which the total casualties were over a thousand in land engagements and over five hundred in sea engagements. In most of the tables the analysis is based on 2,659 battles during the period 1480–1940, though in some the analysis is confined to Bodart's list of 1,696 battles from 1618 to 1905.*

The tables indicate the participations by decades (Tables 22, Fig. 35) and by fifty-year periods (Table 23, Fig. 36), the types of engagements (Tables 24 and 25), the duration (Table 26) and seasonal distribution (Table 27) of battles, the battle honors awarded to British regiments (Table 28, Fig. 37), and the size of armies in successive fifty-year periods (Tables 29 and 30, Fig. 38).

* Sources: The battles from 1480 to 1618 were compiled from Harbottle, *Dictionary of Battles* (London, 1904), and Charles Oman, *A History of the Art of War in the Sixteenth |Century* (New York, 1937), p. 771.
The battles from 1618 to 1905 were compiled from G. Bodart, *Militar-historisches Kriegslexicon* (Leipzig, 1908), in which a tabulation for this period is presented on p. 618.
The battles from 1905 to 1924 were tabulated by Mr. J. C. King for this study. He provided the following comment on the sources used. The battles of the Italo-Turkish War, 1911–12, are reported in the *Encyclopaedia Britannica* (14th ed.), XII, 752, and in Sir T. Barclay, *The Turco-Italian War* (1912). An account of the campaigns of the Balkan Wars, 1912–13, may be found in W. H. Crawford Price, *The Balkan Cockpit* (London: T. Warner Laurie, Ltd., 1914). For World War I a fairly complete list of battles in chronological order may be found in the *History of the Great War: Principal Events, 1914–1918*, published by the British Committee of Imperial Defense (London: His Majesty's Stationery Office, 1922). More detailed though less conveniently compiled information is to be found in a number of publications dealing with the activities of the troups of a single country or with the operations on a given front. *Les Armées françaises dans la Grande Guerre*, published by the Service historique d'Etat-major de l'armée (Paris: Imprimerie nationale, 1922–24; 10 vols., each in several parts) gives a documentary history of French military operations. *Military Operations: France and Belgium*, by J. E. Edmonds, a part of the *History of the Great War* by the Committee of Imperial Defense (London: Macmillan & Co., Ltd., 1922–32), gives an account of the British operations on the Western Front. The Prussian General Staff has published a list of engagements in which German troops took part: *Die Schlachten und Gefechte des grossen Krieges* (Berlin: Verlag von Hermann Sack, 1919). An account of German operations is found in *Der Weltkrieg 1914 bis 1918* (Berlin: Verlegt bei E. S. Mittler und Sohn, 1925) compiled by the German Reichsarchiv. Nine volumes have appeared covering the period from the outbreak of the war to the end of 1915. *The Final Report of General John J. Pershing* (Washington: Government Printing Office, 1919) gives an account of the American operations on the Western Front. The naval operations are described in *History of the Great War: Naval Operations* (London: Longmans, Green & Co., 1920–31), by Sir J. S. Corbett, who prepared the first three volumes, and Henry Newbold, who prepared the last two. An account of the operations in Macedonia may be found in Captain Cyril Falls's *Military Operations: Macedonia* (London: His Majesty's Stationery Office, 1933) and in Luigi Villari's *The Macedonian Campaign* (London: T. Fisher Unwin, Ltd., 1922). The operations in Turkey, Egypt, and the Near East generally are covered by the following works: Brig.-Gen. C. F. Aspinall-Oglander, *Military Operations: Gallipoli* (London: Wm. Heinemann, Ltd., 1929); Edmund Dane, *British Campaigns in the Nearer East, 1914–18* (London: Hodder & Stoughton, Ltd., 1918); Sir George F. McMunn, *Military Operations: Egypt and Palestine* (London: His Majesty's Stationery Office, 1931), and Gen. Paul Emil Brig.-Gen. F. J. Moberly, *The Campaign in Mesopotamia* (London: His Majesty's Stationery Office, 1923–27). For the African campaigns the following were consulted: Brig.-Gen. J. H. V. Crowe, *General Smuts Campaign in East Africa* (London: John Murray, 1918); Brig.-Gen. F. J. Moberly, *Military Operations: Togoland and the Cameroons, 1914–16* (London: His Majesty's Stationery Office, 1931) von Lettow-Vorbeck, *Meine Erinnerungen aus Ost Africa* (Leipzig: Verlag von K. F. Koehler, 1921). On the activities in northern Russia there are a number of unofficial accounts of very unequal value. The following have been found useful in locating the sites of engagements: Ralph Albertson, *Fighting without a War* (New York: Harcourt, Brace & Howe, 1920); *Archangel: The American War with Russia*, by A Chronicler (Chicago: A. C. McClurg & Co., 1924); Sir Charles C. Maynard, *The Murmansk Venture* (London: Hodder & Stoughton, Ltd., 1928); J. R. Moore, *The History of the American Expedition Fighting the Bolsheviki* (Detroit: Polar Bear Publishing Co., 1920). No good account of the Russian revolutionary operations has been found. The following contain some useful information: Gen. A. Denikine, *The White Army* (London: Jonathan Cape, 1930); Phelps Hodges, *Britmis* (London: Jonathan Cape, 1931); and Morgan Philips Price, *War and Revolution in Asiatic Russia* (New York: Macmillan Co., 1918). On the Russo-Polish War there is Adam Przybylski's *La Pologne en lutte pour ses frontières* (Paris: Gebethner et Wolf, 1929). The story of the operations of the Greco-Turkish War of 1921–22 is to be found in Arnold J. Toynbee's *The Western Question in Greece and Turkey* (2d ed.; London: Constable & Co., Ltd., 1923).
The battles from 1924 to 1940 were compiled by Mr. Carl Christol from the *Annual Register*, supplemented by numerous special studies of particular wars.

TABLE 22

NUMBER OF BATTLES ENGAGED IN BY PRINCIPAL EUROPEAN POWERS, BY DECADES, 1480–1940† (see Fig. 35)

Decade	Great Britain	France	Spain	Austria	Prussia	Russia	Turkey	Netherlands	Denmark	Sweden	Participations by These States‡	Battles within Modern Civilization
1480–89.....	2	1	4	0	......	......	2	......	......	......	9	5
1490–99.....	1	2	2	2	......	......	1	......	......	......	8	4
Total...	3	3	6	2	......	......	3	......	......	......	17	9
1500–09.....	0	3	3	0	......	0	0	0	0	0	6	3
1510–19.....	4	4	0	0	......	1	3	0	0	0	12	8
1520–29.....	0	2	2	4	......	0	3	0	2	2	15	10
1530–39.....	0	1	5	0	......	0	1	0	0	0	7	8
1540–49.....	8	1	1	2	......	0	0	0	0	0	12	10
1550–59.....	3	3	1	1	......	0	1	0	0	0	9	7
1560–69.....	2	5	5	0	......	1	4	4	0	0	21	14
1570–79.....	1	1	13	0	......	0	1	12	0	0	28	16
1580–89.....	4	2	5	0	......	0	0	2	0	0	13	7
1590–99.....	1	1	1	1	......	0	1	2	0	1	8	4
Total...	23	23	36	8	......	2	14	20	2	3	131	87
1600–09.....	2	0	1	0	......	0	0	1	0	0	4	3
1610–19.....	0	0	0	0	......	1	0	0	3	4	8	4
1620–29.....	1	1	8	12	......	0	1	2	4	2	31	19
1630–39.....	0	18	16	27	......	0	0	1	0	22	84	39
1640–49.....	4	25	17	14	......	0	0	1	2	11	74	36
1650–59.....	10	5	4	1	......	1	8	10	2	4	45	27
1660–69.....	4	3	4	5	......	0	10	4	0	0	30	19
1670–79.....	5	27	13	9	......	0	2	16	4	4	80	35
1680–89.....	2	4	2	23	......	0	21	0	0	0	52	27
1690–99.....	10	20	10	11	......	1	10	13	0	0	75	30
Total...	38	103	75	102	......	3	52	48	15	47	483	239
1700–09.....	38	76	38	57	......	17	0	36	1	24	287	113
1710–19.....	10	18	15	34	......	5	10	15	4	7	118	49
1720–29.....	0	0	0	0	......	0	0	0	0	0	0	0
1730–39.....	0	10	7	28	......	7	18	0	0	0	70	35
1740–49.....	17	47	14	52	15	2	0	16	0	2	165	77
1750–59.....	29	32	0	31	38	4	0	0	0	2	136	71
1760–69.....	15	16	0	19	27	8	2	0	0	2	89	43
1770–79.....	11	3	0	2	2	14	14	0	0	0	46	27
1780–89.....	20	15	4	5	0	8	7	1	0	3	63	30
1790–99.....	46	284	24	179	32	36	11	42	0	5	659	336
Total...	186	501	102	407	114	101	62	110	5	45	1,633	781
1800–09.....	26	177	32	88	31	26	10	0	1	3	394	188
1810–19.....	35	178	42	34	64	93	11	2	0	3	462	189
1820–29.....	1	1	0	0	0	14	17	0	0	0	33	17
1830–39.....	0	0	0	0	0	6	5	0	0	0	11	12
1840–49.....	1	1	0	27	3	10	1	0	3	0	46	37
1850–59.....	6	12	0	5	0	12	10	0	3	0	48	17
1860–69.....	0	0	0	17	21	0	0	0	4	0	42	79
1870–79.....	0	53	0	0	53	26	26	0	0	0	158	92
1880–89.....	0	0	0	0	0	0	0	0	0	0	0	2
1890–99.....	10	0	4	0	0	0	1	0	0	0	15	18
Total...	79	422	78	171	172	187	81	2	11	6	1,209	651
1900–09.....	8	0	0	0	0	18	0	0	0	0	26	18
1910–19.....	218	81	7	117	310	213	137	0	0	0	1,083	662
1920–29.....	0	0	0	0	0	11	5	0	0	0	16	17
1930–40.....	3	3	100	0	20	2	0	1	0	0	129	195
Total...	229	84	107	117	330	244	142	1	0	0	1,254	892
Grand total	558	1,136	404	807	616	537	354	181	33	101	4,727	2,659

† Participation in battles by one of these states prior to its active relationship to the modern family of nations is not counted in this table.

‡ The figures in this column are usually greater than the corresponding ones in the last column because in most cases at least two of these powers participated in a single battle, although, in case of civil wars, only one participation by the state is counted. Where the figures in the last column are greater, it is because states in the modern family of nations other than the European states here listed were the participants in a considerable number of battles of the decade.

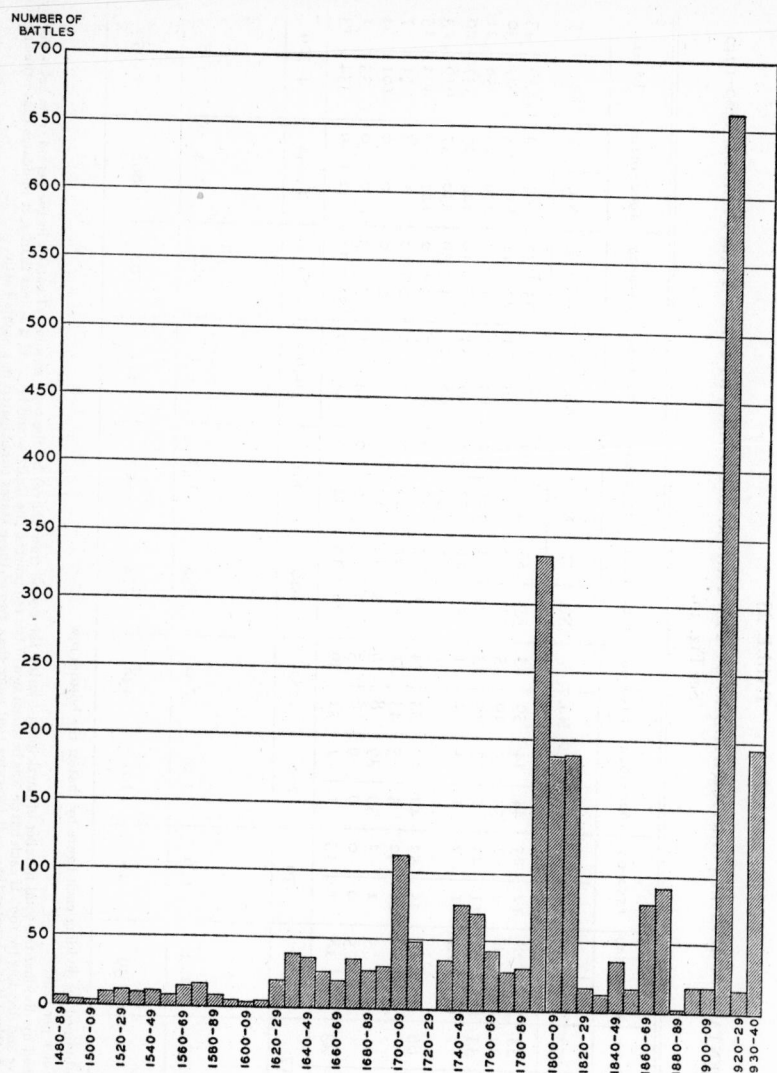

FIG. 35.—Number of important battles per decade in modern civilization, 1480–1940. (Data from Bodart, *op. cit.*, and other sources; see Table 22.)

TABLE 23

NUMBER AND PERCENTAGE OF BATTLES PARTICIPATED IN BY TEN PRINCIPAL POWERS, BY FIFTY-YEAR PERIODS, 1480-1940

(See Fig. 36)

POWER	1480-99		1500-1549		1550-99		1600-1649		1650-99		1700-1749		1750-99		1800-1849		1850-99		1900-1940		TOTAL	
	No.	%*	No.	%	No.	%	No.	%	No.	%	No.	%	No.	%	No.	%	No.	%	No.	%	No.	%
France	3	33	11	28	12	25	44	44	59	43	151	55	350	69	357	81	65	32	84	9	1,136	43
Austria	2	22	6	16	2	4	53	52	49	35	171	62	236	47	149	34	22	11	117	13	807	30
Great Britain	3	33	12	31	11	23	7	7	31	23	65	24	121	24	63	14	16	8	229	26	558	21
Russia			1	3	1	2	1	1	2	1	31	11	70	14	149	34	38	18	224	27	537	20
Prussia											15	5	99	19	98	22	74	36	330	37	616	23
Spain	6	66	11	28	25	52	42	42	33	24	74	27	28	6	74	17	4	2	107	12	404	15
Netherlands					20	42	5	5	43	31	67	25	43	8	2	†	0	0	1	†	181	7
Sweden			2	5	1	2	39	39	8	6	33	12	12	2	6	1	0	0	0	0	101	4
Denmark			2	5	0	0	9	9	6	5	5	2	0	0	4	1	7	3	0	0	33	1
Turkey	3	33	7	18	7	15	1	1	51	36	28	10	34	7	44	10	37	18	142	16	354	13
Total	17		52		79		201		282		640		993		946		263		1,254		4,729	
Average no. of these ten powers in each battle	1.9‡		1.3		1.6		2.0		2.0		2.3		1.3		2.1		1.2		1.4		1.8	
Total no. of battles	9		39		48		101		138		274		507		443		208		892		2,659	

628

* This percentage was obtained by dividing each figure by that of the bottom row.

† Less than five-tenths of 1 per cent.

‡ This figure was obtained by dividing the total number of participants during the period (row above) by the total number of battles in the period (row below) or by adding the percentages above and dividing by 100. If each battle was between two of the ten powers, the figure would be 2. If it is less than 2, it indicates that other states participated in some of the battles. If it is greater than 2 it indicates that more than two of these states participated in a single battle.

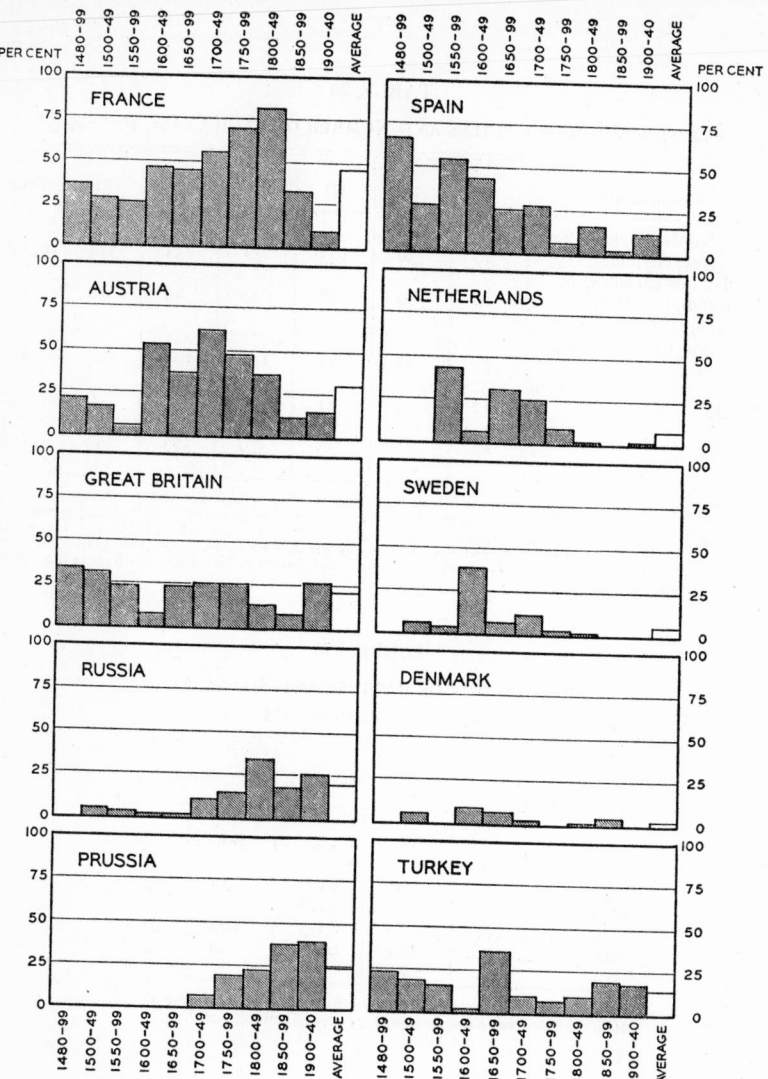

FIG. 36.—Percentage of battles participated in by principal European powers, by fifty-year periods, 1480–1940 (see Table 23).

TABLE 24

CLASSIFICATION OF BATTLES AND NUMBER OF EACH CLASS, 1618–1905*

Classification	I	II	III	IV	V	VI	Total
Land battles (*Schlachten, Treffen, Gefechte*)......	39	39	123	231	234	374	1,040
Sea battles (*Schlachten, Treffen, Gefechte*)......	10	20	28	20	25	19	122
Attacks, stormings, sieges, and capitulations of fortified places..........	21	25	71	121	108	144	490
Capitulations in the open field................	12	2	11	7	6	6	44
Total.............	82	86	233	379	373	543	1,696

* Bodart divides the engagements which he classifies into four qualitative and six quantitative categories. The quantitative categories are based on the total number lost in killed, wounded, and prisoners on both sides. For land battles these figures are as follows: category I, at least 30,000; II, 20,000; III, 10,000; IV, 5,000; V, 3,000; and VI, 1,000. For sea battles they are I, 10,000; II, 5,000; III, 3,000; IV, 2,000; V, 1,000; and VI, 500. The qualitative categories are self-explanatory in this table, which gives the number of engagements in each.

TABLE 25*

PERCENTAGE OF BATTLES AND SIEGES, BY CENTURIES, 1618–1905

CENTURY	BATTLES		SIEGES	
	No.	%	No.	%
17th.............	191	83.0	39	17.0
18th.............	565	74.8	190	25.2
19th.............	550	83.5	109	16.5
20th.............	601	98.4	10	1.6

* Source: Prepared by J. C. King from material in Gaston Bodart, *Militar-historisches Kriegslexicon, 1618–1905* (Leipzig, 1908).

TABLE 26*
DURATION OF BATTLES, BY CENTURIES, 1618–1905

DAYS	17TH		18TH		19TH		20TH	
	No.	%	No.	%	No.	%	No.	%
0.0–1.0	183	95.8	527	93.3	463	84.2	239	39.8
1.1–2.0	2	1.0	22	3.9	50	9.1	78	13.0
2.1–3.0	4	2.1	6	1.1	19	3.5	44	7.3
3.1–4.0	0	0.0	2	0.4	4	0.7	30	5.0
4.1–5.0	2	1.0	2	0.4	6	1.1	29	4.8
5.1–6.0	0	0.0	3	0.5	1	0.2	23	3.8
6.1 and more	0	0.0	3	0.5	7	1.3	158	26.3
Total	191	....	565	....	550	....	601	....

* Source: See Table 25.

TABLE 27*

SEASONAL DISTRIBUTION OF BATTLES, BY CENTURIES, 1618–1905

MONTH	17TH		18TH		19TH		20TH	
	No.	%	No.	%	No.	%	No.	%
January	7	3.1	17	2.4	33	5.3	15	3.4
February	7	3.1	17	2.4	41	6.5	15	3.4
March	10	4.4	37	5.1	37	5.9	24	5.4
April	10	4.4	51	7.1	55	8.8	30	6.7
May	28	12.3	71	9.9	62	9.9	30	6.7
June	39	17.1	79	11.0	64	10.2	22	4.9
July	37	16.2	92	12.8	60	9.6	42	9.4
August	37	16.2	88	12.2	59	9.4	72	16.2
September	21	9.2	104	14.5	52	8.3	60	13.5
October	17	7.5	82	11.4	60	9.6	65	14.6
November	11	4.8	50	7.0	58	9.2	45	10.1
December	4	1.8	31	4.3	47	7.5	25	5.6
Median month	6.3		6.9		6.4		7.6	
Middle range months (in which 50 per cent of battles were fought)	4.8–7.9		4.8–8.9		3.8–9.1		4.9–9.4	
Number months in middle range	3.1		4.1		5.3		4.5	

* Source: See Table 25.

TABLE 28*

Number of Battle Honors Awarded to British Regiments and Number of Battles for Which Such Honors Were Given by Decades, 1660–1900

(See Fig. 37)

Decade	Total No. Battles	Total No. Honors	Europe		Africa		Near East		India		Far East		Pacific		America	
			B†	H†	B	H	B	H	B	H	B	H	B	H	B	H
1660–69	1	5			1	5										
1670–79																
1680–89																
1690–99	1	14	1	14												
Total 17th century	2	19	1	14	1	5	0	0	0	0	0	0	0	0	0	0
1700–09	5	82	5	82												
1710–19																
1720–29																
1730–39																
1740–49	1	26	1	26												
1750–59	9	41	1	6					5	8					3	27
1760–69	10	65	3	14					4	24					3	27
1770–79	4	18	1	5					2	3					1	10
1780–89	4	22	1	3					2	18					1	1
1790–99	17	114	9	37					5	65					3	12
Total 18th century	50	368	21	173	0	0	0	0	18	118	0	0	0	0	11	77
1800–09	26	245	10	159	4	46	1	1	6	19					5	20
1810–19	34	423	18	356	1	1	1	1	6	37			3	9	5	19
1820–29	8	56			0	0	2	2	6	54						
1830–39	5	36			1	3	1	3	3	30						
1840–49	22	205			1	8			19	185	1	9	1	3		
1850–59	17	295	4	134	1	10	4	40	6	103	2	8				
1860–69	4	56			1	18					2	24	1	14		
1870–79	8	202			2	19			6	183						
1880–89	7	177			5	99			2	78						
1890–99	14	301			8	217			6	84						
Total 19th century	145	1,996	32	649	24	421	9	47	60	773	5	41	5	26	10	39
1900	9	107			7	83					2	24				
Total 20th century	9	107	0	0	7	83	0	0	0	0	2	24	0	0	0	0
Total	206	2,490	54	836	32	509	9	47	78	891	7	65	5	26	21	116

* Source: Compiled from C. B. Norman, *Battle Honors of the British Army* (London, 1911).
† B = Battles; H = Honors.

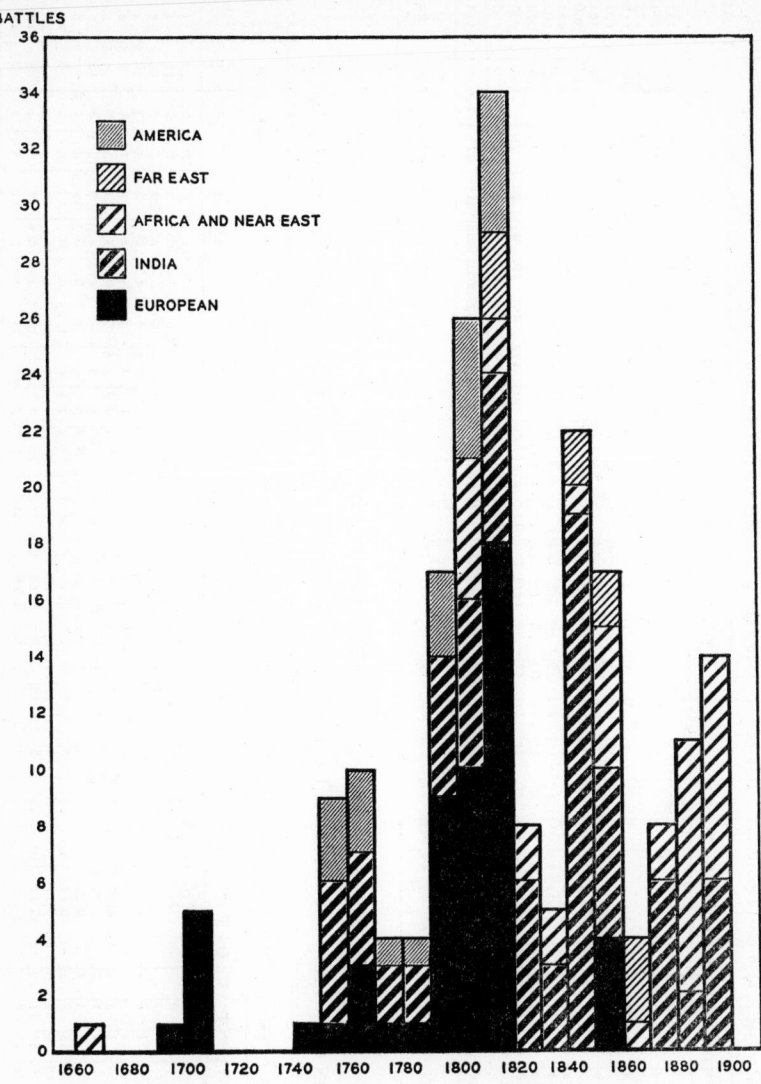

BATTLES

- AMERICA
- FAR EAST
- AFRICA AND NEAR EAST
- INDIA
- EUROPEAN

F<small>IG</small>. 37.—Number of battle honors given to British regiments, 1660–1900. (Data from C. B. Norman, *Battle Honors of the British Army* [London, 1911]. See Table 28.)

TABLE 29

NUMBER OF BATTLES FOR EACH SIZE OF ARMY, BY FIFTY-YEAR PERIODS, 1480–1940

SIZE OF ARMY	1480–1549 V*	D*	T*	1550–99 V	D	T	1600–1649 V	D	T	1650–99 V	D	T	1700–1749 V	D	T	1750–99 V	D	T	1800–1849 V	D	T	1850–99 V	D	T	1900–1940 V	D	T	TOTAL
Over 300,000																			1		1		1	1	125	125	250	252
200,000–300,000		2	2											1	1					1	1	6	2	8	115	115	230	244
150,000–200,000		3	3								1	1		1	1		2	2	5	1	6	1	7	8	140	120	260	275
100,000–150,000	2	1	3					1	1	3		3	3	5	14	4	5	9	10	6	16	13	7	20	60	50	110	156
75,000–100,000	2	3			1	2	1	1	2	6	4	9	9	5	28	4	5	9	10	9	22	25	20	45	30	20	50	122
50,000–75,000			2	1	1	2	5	17		11	10	4	23	5	48	34	18	52	13	30	46	25	10	20	50	30	80	294
40,000–50,000	1	3	6	1	5	6	21	17	38	23	17	32	33	15	48	25	19	44	29	38	83	25	10	52	85	148	233	306
30,000–40,000	3	6	9	1	5	9	38	13	58	48	17	32	69	48	117	48	35	83	45	57	125	25	27	79	68	64	132	444
20,000–30,000	1	21	21	5	4	6	37	37	69	47	35	82	84	58	117	84	45	129	45	88	213	37	24	52	53	54	107	592
10,000–20,000	12	9	36	3	4	9	32	19	47	8	31	47	69	58	112	142	125	267	125	88	173	37	42	45	60	59	119	974
5,000–10,000	8	12	20	19	14	33	6	19	18	13	13	26	36	58	93	100	112	212	49	93	155	16	26	44	74	75	149	930
1,000–5,000	22	14	36	22	20	42	6	12	18	8	13	13	36	116	152	44	120	164	49	106	155	16	28	44	51	51	102	734
Total	48	48	96	51	51	102	92	92	184	127	127	254	295	295	590	481	481	962	450	450	900	204	204	408	911	911	1,822	5,318
Average size army in thousands	15	25	20	9	17	13	19	18	18	27	25	26	27	15	21	22	18	20	27	23	25	42	40	41	135	129	132	60

TABLE 30

PROPORTION OF BATTLES FOUGHT WITH EACH SIZE OF ARMY, BY FIFTY-YEAR PERIODS, 1480–1940. (See Fig. 38)

SIZE OF ARMY	1480–1549 V*	D*	T*	1550–99 V	D	T	1600–1649 V	D	T	1650–99 V	D	T	1700–1749 V	D	T	1750–99 V	D	T	1800–1849 V	D	T	1850–99 V	D	T	1900–1940 V	D	T	TOTAL
Over 300,000																			0.5		0.5		0.5		6.5	6.5	13	5
200,000–300,000		2	2											0.5						0.5		1.5	1	2	6	6	12	4
150,000–200,000		3	3								1	1		1.5	2.5		0.5	0.5	1.5	0.5	1	2	3	4	7.5	7	14.5	5
100,000–150,000	2	1	3								2.5	2.5	1.5	2.5	5		1	1	3	1	2	4	4.5	6.5	3.5	3	6.5	3
75,000–100,000		3	3			2				4	3	3	3	2.5	5			1	3.5	3	7.5	3.5	2.5	5.5	1.5	1.5	3	2.5
50,000–75,000				2		2	2	8	4	5	18	14	4	7	5.5	3.5	3.5	5	3	3	6	4.6	4	7.5?	4.5	4.5	6.5	5.5
40,000–50,000	1	3		1		2	4	6	12	4	14	14	13	7	13.5	5.5	4.5	8.5	7	10	13.5	9	9	7.5	3.5	4.5	4.5	7.5
30,000–40,000	3	4	6	1	1	2	9	4	9	8	13	14	9	6.5	8.5	10	7.5	13	10	18	25	12.5	10	15	4.5	3.5	7.5	11
20,000–30,000	13	9	22	3	1	6	5	18	14	10	18	13	4	7	19	18	9.5	28	10	18	25	9	6.5	15	3.5	3.5	7.5	18
10,000–20,000	13	13	21	19	5	17	21	21	21	18	9	14	9	10	22	15	12	22	18	10	19	9	10	11	3	4	8	17
5,000–10,000	8	13	19	19	19	33	12	5	38	8	6	18	7	12	17	5	12	17	5	10	18	4.5	4.5	11	3	4	7	17
1,000–5,000	23	15	38	22	20	40	12	10	10	3	6	9	7	19	26	5	12	17	5	12	17	3	7	6	3	3	6	14
Total	50	50	100	50	50	100	50	50	100	50	50	100	50	50	100	50	50	100	50	50	100	50	50	100	50	50	100	100

*V = Victor; D = Defeated; T = Total.

634

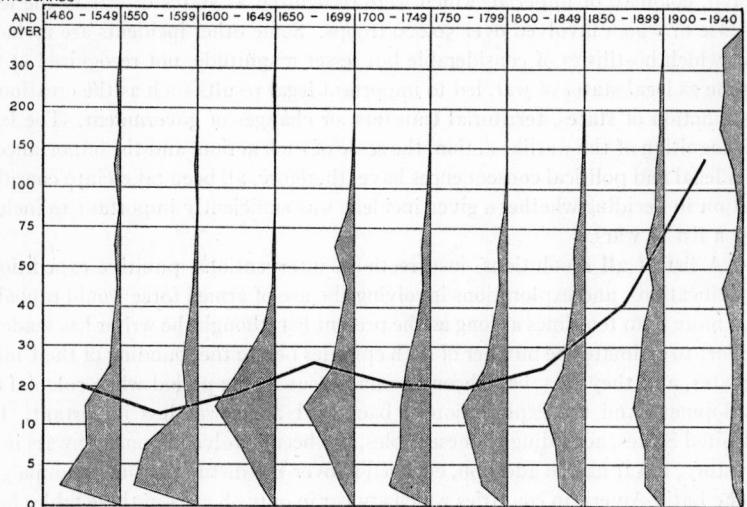

SIZE OF ARMY
IN THOUSANDS

AND OVER	1480 – 1549	1550 – 1599	1600 – 1649	1650 – 1699	1700 – 1749	1750 – 1799	1800 – 1849	1850 – 1899	1900 – 1940

300
200
150
100
75
50
40
30
20
10
5
0

FIG. 38.—Frequency of battles for each size of army by fifty-year periods, 1480–1940 (see Table 30).

635

APPENDIX XX

WARS OF MODERN CIVILIZATION

This list of wars from 1500 to 1940 (Tables 31–41) is intended to include all hostilities involving members of the family of nations, whether international, civil, colonial, or imperial, which were recognized as states of war in the legal sense or which involved over 50,000 troops. Some other incidents are included in which hostilities of considerable but lesser magnitude, not recognized at the time as legal states of war, led to important legal results such as the creation or extinction of states, territorial transfers, or changes of government. The legal recognition of the warlike action, the scale of such action, and the importance of its legal and political consequences have, therefore, all been taken into consideration in deciding whether a given incident was sufficiently important to include in a list of wars.

A list of all revolutions, insurrections, interventions, punitive expeditions, pacifications, and explorations involving the use of armed force would probably be more than ten times as long as the present list, though the writer has made no effort to estimate the number of such episodes before the founding of the United States, and they may have been less numerous in the period when colonial development and the exploitation of backward areas was less important. The United States, according to these tables, has been involved in only 12 wars in its history, but it has, in addition, engaged in over 170 distinct military campaigns. The Latin-American countries which appear in only 28 wars in these tables have resorted to military force in over 100 international and over 300 domestic events. Great Britain, which appears in only 6 wars in the twentieth century, participated in about 70 distinct military campaigns during that period, and all countries during the twentieth century participated in over 600 distinct military campaigns of which more than 500 were outside of the 24 wars here listed for that period.

In addition to the uncertainty in drawing the line between wars and other military events, there is the uncertainty of drawing a line around a single war. World War I, as indicated in Table 41, was a compound war which included 5 wars ended by independent treaties and 82 bilateral wars, most of them begun by independent declarations.[1] The Thirty Years' War, the War of the Spanish Succession, the Napoleonic Wars, and others were also compound wars. It has been thought better to group compound wars under a single name, as has usually been done by historians, though makers of lists of wars have often treated hostilities between each pair of states as a distinct war, a practice suggested by the

---

[1] See Table 42 and list of declarations in the United States Naval War College, *International Law Documents, 1917*, p. 15; *ibid., 1918*, p. 11.

procedure common before the nineteenth century of ending general wars not by a multipartite treaty but by a number of bipartite treaties.

A further difficulty in compiling this list lay in the scarcity of data. It was sometimes uncertain whether a given event was recognized as war or involved more than 50,000 troops. This difficulty was greatest in the earlier centuries when international law had not developed so clear a distinction between states of war and peace as it did in the nineteenth century. The most recent period is again witnessing the blurring of this distinction because of the doubt whether "aggression" can institute a "legal state of war."

There was also the difficulty of deciding what wars could be regarded as related to modern civilization. During the sixteenth, seventeenth, and eighteenth centuries there were many military events of considerable magnitude among native princes of America, Asia, and Africa, excluded from these tables because none of the participants were recognized members of the family of nations. Many of the events would appear in a list of wars of Hindu, Chinese, Iranian, or other civilizations, but they were not wars of the modern world-civilization which began in the fifteenth century as the Christian civilization of Europe. Wars of defense or conquest by recognized European states against Moslem or extra-European communities are, however, included. The United States and the Latin-American states were recognized as members of the family of nations in the late eighteenth and early nineteenth centuries; China, Japan, Turkey, Persia, Siam, Ethiopia, and other oriental states were recognized in the nineteenth and twentieth centuries. Thus an increasing number of American and oriental wars, involving no European state, or even no Christian state, are included in the later periods.

Having decided what wars should be included, there was the difficulty of deciding what entities were to be regarded as participants, and in this respect actual independence before or after the war rather than legal status under international law was the criterion used. Unrecognized princes like the Aztec and Inca rulers, semidependencies like the Barbary states, feudal principalities like the German and Italian states nominally subject to the Empire, and successful insurgents like the United States in 1775 have been listed as independent participants. Unsuccessful revolutionists, rebels, or insurgents which lacked even *de facto* status, except during the war itself, have not been so listed, and many of the small feudal principalities of the Holy Roman Empire have been ignored on the ground that, while enjoying some legal status though short of full independence under international law, their actual political importance was very slight.

The two sides in a war are distinguished by the use of italics or roman figures for the dates of entry. Italics are intended to indicate participation on the side which initiated the war, though this question is often controversial or indeterminate and sometimes a state changed sides during the course of a war. Civil wars are considered to have been initiated by the rebels and imperial wars by the expanding state.

Finally, no small difficulty was encountered in determining when a given war began and ended. Wars have seldom been separated from peace by a clearly marked line, as indicated by the detailed discussion of the origin of over a hundred "wars" from 1700 to 1870 by Brevet Lieutenant-Colonel J. F. Maurice.[2] The date of beginning is generally taken as the first important hostilities. Formal declarations of war have been rare and, when they have occurred, have often followed active hostilities. The date of ending is generally taken as the date of signature of a treaty of peace, or the date of its going into effect if that is different. In a good many cases, however, there was no formal treaty, and the date of armistice, capitulation, or actual ending of active hostilities is given.[3]

In view of the numerous occasions presented for exercising judgment, this list is not offered as definitive but as suggestive of the number, duration, and spread of wars in modern civilization.

The 278 wars listed (Tables 31-41) are followed by a special analysis of World War I (Table 42) and by a statement of the participation in the 15 general wars since 1600 (Table 43). The wars have been classified according as they were mainly fought in Europe or outside of Europe; according as European states did or did not participate; according as the war was between states of modern civilization, was within such a state, or was between a state of modern civilization and a state of a different civilization or culture. The latter class has been divided according as the modern state involved was defending modern civilization from encroachment or aggression by peoples of different civilization or was seeking to expand modern civilization at the expense of another culture. These four types of war may be called, respectively, balance-of-power, civil, defensive, and imperialistic wars. The results of the application of these classes in various ways is indicated in the summary tables (Tables 44 and 45). They suggest the following trends and relationships.

1. The number of European wars has declined from over 30 a half-century in the sixteenth and seventeenth centuries to less than half that number in the nineteenth and twentieth centuries. On the other hand, the number of extra-European wars has increased from only 3 or 4 a half-century to 20 or 30 in that period. This is the natural result of the expansion of the modern family of nations outside of Europe, since wars not involving modern civilization were not included in the tables.

2. The number of participants in a war has tended to increase from 2 or 3 in the sixteenth and seventeenth centuries to 3 or 4 in the nineteenth and twen-

[2] *Hostilities without Declaration of War* [London, 1883], p. 66.

[3] To ascertain these dates, reference has been made to numerous books. Maurice (*op. cit.*) and Phillipson (*Termination of War and Treaties of Peace* [London, 1916]) were especially useful. Among general reference books use was made of the *Annual Register* (London, 1777——); Ploetz, *Manual of Universal History* (Tillinghast trans. [Boston, 1915]); Putnam's *Handbook of Universal History* (New York, 1916); Haydn's *Dictionary of Dates*, ed. Vincent (New York, 1898); Keller, *The Dictionary of Dates* (New York, 1934), as well as numerous general and special histories.

tieth centuries, thus suggesting that wars spread more easily today than former-ly—a natural result of the development of means of transport and communications. There have been 15 general wars involving all or nearly all of the great powers since 1600, 4 in the seventeenth century, 7 in the eighteenth century, and 2 each in the nineteenth and twentieth centuries. While the average duration of wars has not varied greatly, tending if anything to decline from over to under four years, the average number of battles in a war has tended to increase greatly from one or two in the sixteenth century to ten times those figures at present. These phenomena are all evidence of the increasing intensity of war as modern civilization has progressed.

3. The seventeenth and twentieth centuries are remarkable for the long dura-tion of their wars and the twentieth century for the extraordinary intensity of its wars. The nineteenth century, on the other hand, is remarkable for the short duration of its wars and the small number of battles and participants, especially in the latter half. The Napoleonic Wars account for the larger figures in the first half. There were more wars in the nineteenth century than in any other century, taking the world as a whole, but this was due to the rapid expansion of the modern family of nations to other continents than Europe. The number of wars fought mainly in Europe was exceptionally small. The nineteenth century was outstandingly peaceful.

4. The number of balance-of-power wars and civil wars has been relatively stable, though both tended to drop in the eighteenth century; on the other hand, the number of wars in defense of modern civilization has tended to decline (a necessary consequence of the world-wide expansion of that civilization), and the number of imperial wars to expand that civilization tended to increase until the twentieth century, when most of the alien cultures had been absorbed.

Balance-of-power wars have constituted nearly half the total number of wars, and much more than that proportion of the military energy has gone into their prosecution. They have occurred wholly within the community of nations, and their effect has been to modify the structure of that community as a whole or locally. Sometimes the power of one or a group of states has been enlarged, en-abling them to order the whole by hegemony or domination. At other times lesser states have increased their capacity to resist such ordering and to secure their national independence. The struggle of the imperial against the national idea has been continuous in Europe. This type of war has increased among extra-European states in the nineteenth and twentieth centuries.

Second in importance have been civil wars by which states have sought to preserve internal order and unity or common standards of religion or nationality. These wars cannot be wholly separated from the balance-of-power wars because ideologies and religions spread across state lines, and civil wars have often led to intervention and changes in the balance of power. Civil wars have sometimes led states into crusades and sometimes to the need of defending themselves from intervention. This type of war was most numerous in the seventeenth century, though it again came to prominence in the nineteenth century. The respective importance of religion and of nationality in these two centuries probably accounts for this frequency of civil wars.

Wars for the defense of modern civilization were of great importance in the sixteenth and seventeenth centuries when Christian civilization was continuously attacked by the Moslems of the Ottoman Empire. Modern civilization began with the effort of Spain to drive out the Moors and continued with the series of Ottoman wars, until with the raising of the siege of Vienna in the late seventeenth century the Ottoman drive was ended and Turkey gradually became incorporated in Western civilization as an element in the balance of power. Gradually, thereafter, the family of nations lost its exclusively Christian character and became world-wide. Few alien cultures now remain outside from which it might have to defend itself. The problems of modern civilization have become internal. New doctrines and new cultural forms have continually developed within that civilization, especially in the twentieth century.

Finally, there are the imperial wars by which the states of modern civilization have expanded that civilization. Beginning after the age of discoveries with attacks by European states on America and Asia, this type of war increased until in the nineteenth century it absorbed as much, if not more, military energy than balance-of-power wars. In the twentieth century there have been fewer such wars because the opportunities for further expansion have become limited. It is significant that imperial expansion was less in the eighteenth century than in the centuries preceding or following.

LIST OF WARS, 1480–1550

WAR	DATE OF BEGINNING	DATE OF ENDING	NAME OF TREATY OF PEACE	WESTERN EUROPE						CENTRAL EUROPE											NORTHERN EUROPE				NEAR EAST, ASIA, AFRICA					AMERICA		NO. OF PARTICIPANTS AMONG 28 STATES	NO. OF IMPORTANT BATTLES*	TYPE OF WAR†
				England	France	Netherlands	Portugal	Scotland	Spain	Empire	Florence	Hungary	Lübeck	Malta	Milan	Naples	Papacy	Saxony	Switzerland	Venice	Denmark	Poland	Russia	Sweden	Algeria	India	Moldavia	Moors	Turkey	Aztecs	Incas			
War of Granada	-82	11- 1-92							82																			82				2	5	D
Italian Wars	-95	-04	Blois		95				00		95				95	95	95															6	4	B
Ottoman War	-92	-03															03			99									99			4		D
League of Cambrai	-08	-09			08				08	08							08			08												5	1	C
Moorish Insurrection	-09	-11							09																			09				2	1	B
Scottish War	-10	-11		10				10																								2	1	I
Conquest of Goa‡	2-15-10	-11					10																			10						8	3	B
War of Holy League	-11	-14	Orleans§	12	11				11	13					12		11			11												8	4	B
Russo-Polish War	-11	-26																				11	11									2		D
Ottoman War	-12	-19																												12			3	1	B
Franco-Swiss War	-12	11- 7-15	Geneva‖		15										15				15	15												2	1	B
Dano-Swedish War	-15	-25																			16			16								2	2	B
Conquest of Mexico‡	-16	-21																													20		3	2	I
1st War against Chas. V	-20	-26	Madrid		21				21	21		21																		21			4	2	B
Ottoman War	-21	-31												22																22			2	3	D
Scottish War	-21	-23		22				22																								2		B
Peasants' War	-24	-25								24								24														1	1	C
2d War against Chas. V	-26	-29	Cambrai		26				26	26						26	26 27															5	1	B
War of Kappel‡	-31	-31	Kappel																31													1	1	C
Conquest of Peru‡	-31	-31																													31	1		I
Ottoman War	-32	-34								32	32													32					32			2	4	D
Polish War	-32	-33																				32						32				3		B
Lübeck War	-33	-34											33							33	33			33								3	1	B
Russo-Polish War	-34	-37																				34	34									3		B
3d War against Chas. V	-36	6-18-38	Nice		36 36	36 36			36	36 37							36											36 37			6	1	B
Ottoman War	-37	-47								37																			37			3		D
Algerian Expedition‡	-41	-41							41																41							2	1	I
Scottish War	-42	-46		42				42																								3		B
4th War against Chas. V	-42	9-18-44	Crespy		42				42	42																						3	3	B
Siege of Boulogne	-44	6- 7-46		44 44	44																											3	1	B
Schmalkaldic War	-46	-47								46							46	46													2	2	D
Arundel's Rebellion	-49	-50		49	50			50																								3	3	C
Number wars participated in by each state				6	10	1	2	4	12	13	2	2	1	1	3	2	6	2	3	3	2	3	2	2	1	1	1	2	6	1	1	94	48	

* Battles included in Gaston Bodart, *Militär-historisches Kriegslexicon (1618–1905)* (Wien and Leipzig, 1908). Before that date battles included in Thomas B. Harbottle, *Dictionary of Battles from the Earliest Date to the Present Time* (London, 1904), and Charles Oman, *A History of the Art of War in the Sixteenth Century* (New York, 1937), p. 771. Since 1905 lists prepared from various sources.

† B = Balance-of-power war, in sense of a war among state members of the modern family of nations; C = Civil war, in sense of war within a state member of the modern family of nations; D = Defensive war, in sense of a war to defend modern civilization against an alien culture; I = Imperial war, in sense of a war to expand modern civilization at the expense of an alien culture.

‡ Wars fought mainly outside Europe.

§ France concluded peace with Spain and the Papacy in 1513 and with England and the Emperor in 1514.

‖ This treaty was made permanent in the Treaty of Fribourg, November 29, 1516.

TABLE 32

LIST OF WARS, 1550–1600

War	Date of Beginning	Date of Ending	Name of Treaty of Peace	England	France	Ireland	Netherlands	Portugal	Scotland	Spain	Brandenburg	Empire	Hungary	Papacy	Saxony	Switzerland	Venice	Denmark	Poland	Russia	Sweden	Turkey	No. of Participants among 19 States	No. of Important Battles*	Type of War†
				Western Europe							Central Europe							Northern Europe				Near East			
Ottoman War ... Chas. V	-51	-68	Adrianople									51	51									51	3	1	D
5th War against Chas. V	-52	4- 2-59	Cateau Cambresis‡	57	52					52		52			52								5	3	B
German Wars	-52	9-25-55	Augsburg								53	52			52								3	1	B
Russo-Swedish War	-54	-57	Moscow																	54	54		2		C
Wyatt's Rebellion	-54	-54		54																			1	1	B
Russo-Swedish War	-54	-61																		59	59		2		D
Ottoman War	-59	-64															60					59	2	1	B
Great Northern War	-61	-70	Stettin															61	63		61		3	1	C
1st Huguenot War	3-1-62	3-19-63	Amboise	62	62					59													4	2	D
Ottoman War	-65	-68	Andrianople									65										65	2	20	C
War of Dutch Independence	-66	-70					66			66													2	2	C
2d Huguenot War	-67	-68	Longjumeau		67																		1	2	C
Scotch Rebellion	-67	-68							67														1	2	C
3d Huguenot War	-69	-70	St-Germain		69																		1		B
Ottoman War	-69	-80	§							70				70			69					69	4	1	C
4th Huguenot War	-72	7- 8-73	Edict of Boulogne		72																		1		B
Russo-Swedish War	-72	-83																		72	72		2		B
Russo-Polish War	-72	-75																	72	72			2		C
Italian War	-75	-80			75											75	75						3	1	C
5th Huguenot War	-75	5- 6-76	Chastenoy		75																		1		C
6th Huguenot War	-76	9-17-77	Poitiers		76																		1		B
Spanish-Portuguese War	-79	-82						79		79													2	1	C
Irish Rebellion	-80	-80		80		80																	1		C
7th Huguenot War	-80	11-26-80	Fleix		80																		2		D
Ottoman War	-83	-90																	83			83	2	1	C
War of Three Henrys	-85	-90			85					85													2	3	B
War of the Armada	-85	5- 2-98	Vervins‖	85						85													2	3	B
Russo-Swedish War	-90	-95	Teusina																	90	90		2		C
Scotch Rebellion	-94	-94							94														1		B
Swedish-Polish War	-98	-99																	98		98		2	1	C
O'Neill's Rebellion	-98	-02		98		98																	2	2	C
Number wars participated in by each state				6	10	2	1	1	2	7	1	4	1	1	2	1	3	1	4	6	6	5	64	48	.....

* See Table 31.

† See Table 31.

‡ A truce between France and the Empire was signed at Vaucelles in 1556.

§ Venice concluded peace with Turkey on March 7, 1573.

‖ The Treaty ... ...

TABLE 33

LIST OF WARS, 1600–1650

War	Date of Beginning	Date of Ending	Name of Treaty of Peace	Western Europe						Central Europe																					Northern Europe				Asia			America	No. of Participants among 34 States	No. of Battles*	Type of War†
				England	France	Ireland	Netherlands	Portugal	Spain	Baden	Bavaria (Catholic League)	Bohemia	Brunswick	Germanic Empire	Hamburg	Hesse-Cassel	Hungary	Lorraine	Mantua	Mecklenburg	Modena	Naples	Palatinate (Protestant Union)	Prussia (Brandenburg)	Savoy	Saxe-Weimar	Saxony	Transylvania	Venice	Denmark	Poland	Russia	Sweden	Caucasus	Tatars	Turkey	Indian Tribes			
Dutch Independence	-00	-09					00		00																													2	1	C
Wars of Kalmar	-00	-29	Altmark																											00			00					2	3	B
Franco-Savoian War	-00	-01			00																			00													2		B
Polish-Swedish War	-00	-09																						00							00		00					2		B
Russo-Swedish War	-03	-17	Slatbourg																													13	13					2	1	B
Russian Civil War	-04	-10																													04						1		C
Daghestan Expedition‡	-05	-05																														05		05				2		I
Russo-Polish War	-09	-18																													09	09						2		B
Ottoman War	-10	-19																																		10		2		D
Hungarian Revolt	-11	-15														11											11										2		C
Austro-Venetian War	-15	-18	Madrid											15														15									2		B
Condé's Rebellion	-15	-15			15																																1		C
Spanish-Savoian War	-15	-17							15															15													2		B
Spanish-Venetian War	-17	-21							17																			17									2		B
Polish-Turkish War	-18	-21																												18				18		2	1	D
Spanish-Turkish War	-18	-19							18																										18		2		D
Thirty Years' War§	-18	10-24-48	Westphalia	27	27		21	41	20	20	20	18	25	18	30	35		30	31	27	30		18		26	30	32	20	18	25	21		26					25	86	B
Bohemian War	-18	-23	Nikolsburg‖									×		×									×				×	×												
Protestant Union War	-18	7- 3-20	Ulm								×			×									×																	
Palatinate War	-20	-23									×	×	×	×									×	×																
Dutch-Spanish War	-21	1-30-48	Münster				×		×					×																										
Danish War	-25	5-22-29	Lübeck	×										×																	×									
Spanish-English War	-25	11- -30		×					×																															
Swedish-Prussian War	-26	-29	Strohm																					×									×							
War of Mantua Succession	-27	4- 6-31	Cherasco¶	×	×				×										×						×															
Swedish-Imperial War	-30	10-24-48	Osnabruck**								×	×	×	×		×				×			×			×	×	×					×							
Saxon War	-30	5-30-35	Prague											×													×													
Danish-Hamburg War	-30	-43													×															×										
French-Imperial War	-35	10-24-48	Münster††		×						×	×		×		×		×					×			×	×	×					×							
Swedish-Danish War	-43	8-11-45	Bromsbro																											×			×							
Huguenot War	-21	-29	Paris	21	21																																	2		C
Russo-Polish War	-32	-34	Polisnovka																												32	32				32		3		B
Cossack Revolt	-34	-38																													34							2		I
Pequot War‡	-37	-37		37																																	37	2		I
Danish-Polish War	-38	-38																												38	38						2		B
Catalonian Revolt	-39	-59							39																													1		C
Spanish-Portuguese War	-40	2-13-68	Lisbon					40	40																													2	2	C
British Civil War	-40	-49		40																																		1	6	C
Irish Rebellion	-41	-43		41		41																																1		C
Andalusian Revolt	-41	-41							41																													1		C
Turkish-Venetian War	-44	-68																											44							44		2	10	D
Neapolitan Revolt	-46	-48							46													46																	2		C
Tatar Wars‡	-46	-49																															46		46		2		I
Cossack Rebellion	-48	-54																													48							1		C
La Fronde	-48	-52			48																																	1		C
Franco-Spanish War	-48	-59	Pyrenees	56	48				48									48							48														5	6	B
Irish Rebellion	-49	-52		49		49																																2		C
Number wars participated in by each state				7	6	2	2	2	11	1	1	1	3	1	1	2	1	1	1	1	1	1	1	1	4	1	1	1	3	3	7	7	4	1	1	5	1	87	116	

* See Table 31.

† See Table 31.

‡ Wars fought mainly outside Europe.

§ The Thirty Years' War consisted of 13 distinct but overlapping wars, involving over 50 bilateral wars and falling into 4 main periods between which there was very little fighting—the Bohemian (1618-23), Danish (1625-29), Swedish (1630-35), and French-Swedish (1635-48) periods.

‖ This treaty was confirmed at Vienna in 1623 and at Pressburg in 1672 after the wars by the Empire with Bethlen Gabor.

¶ The French and British signed a peace at St.-Germain in 1632.

** The treaty was signed by plenipotentiaries of the Emperor and the Queen of Sweden and by 38 plenipotentiaries in behalf of 67 electors, bishops, princes, and free cities of Germany. It declared that the pacification should extend to all the allies and adherents of the Emperor, including the King of Spain, the House of Austria, the electors of the Holy Roman Empire, the princes, including the Duke of Savoy and the other states, including the nobles "free and immediate of the Empire" and to all the allies and adherents of the Queen of Sweden, including the King of France, "the electors, princes and estates, including the nobles free and immediate of the Empire" and the Hanseatic cities; and also to the kings of England, Denmark, Norway, Poland, and Portugal, the Grand Duke of Muscovy, the Republic of Venice, the United Provinces of the Netherlands, the Swiss, the Grisons, and the Prince of Transylvania (Dumont, Corps diplomatique et universelle, VI, 469, 488).

†† This treaty was signed by plenipotentiaries of the Emperor and the King of France and by the same German plenipotentiaries as signed the Treaty of Osnabrück on the same day (Dumont, op. cit., p. 450). It did not end the wars between France and Spain, Savoy and Lorraine, which continued until the Peace of the Pyrenees in 1659, while the war between Spain and Portugal continued until the Peace of Lisbon in 1668 (see Koch, Abregé de l'histoire de traites de paix [1796], I, 111).

WAR	DATE OF BEGINNING	DATE OF ENDING	NAME OF TREATY OF PEACE	France	Netherlands	Portugal	Scotland	Spain	Bremen	Germanic Empire	Hamburg	Hungary	Prussia	Savoy	Venice	Denmark	Poland	Russia	Sweden	Barbary States	Central Asia	China	Turkey	Indian Tribes	No. of Participants among 22 States	No. of Battles*	Type of War†
Scottish War (Chas. II)	–50	–51		50			50																		2		C
Anglo-Dutch Naval War	–52	–55	Westminster	52	52																				2	1	B
Russo-Polish War	–54	–67	Andrusovo§														54	54							2		B
Great Northern War	–54	–60	Copenhagen‖		58								56			56	54	56	54						7	4	B
Dutch-Portuguese War	–57	–61			57	57																			2	8	D
Ottoman War	–57	–64	Temesvar	61						56		57											57		4	8	B
Sweden-Bremen	–65	–66	Habenhausen						66										66						2		B
Anglo-Dutch Naval War	–65	–67	Breda	65	65			65	65	66						66									5	4	B
Polish Civil War	–66	–66		66	66					66							66								1	1	C
Barbary States War‡	–66	–94		67	67			67	67											66					2		L
Franco-Spanish War‡	–67	5–2–68	Aix-la-Chapelle	67	67			67																	2		C
Cossack War	–68	–81																68							5		C
Hungarian Revolt	–70	–87								70		71													1		B
Anglo-Dutch Naval War	–72	–74	Westminster	72	72			72		74			72			75		73	75						3	4	B
1st Coalition against Louis XIV	–72	8–10–78	Nijmegen¶	72	72			72		74	76		72			76	76	73							8	28	D
Turkish-Polish War	–73	10–16–76	Zurawno		75																		73		3	2	B
King Philip's War‡	–75	–75																						75	1		I
Danish-Hamburg War‡	–76	–79									76					76									2		C
Covenanter Rising	–77	–79		77	77		77																		2		D
Russo-Turkish War	–77	–79																78					78		2		B
Bohemian Revolt	–78	–80								80															1		C
Revolt of Strelsi	–80	–81																82							1		C
Ottoman War	–82	1–26–99	Karlowitz							82		82		82	82		83	82					82		5	31	D
Franco-Spanish War	–83	–84	Ratisbon	83	83			83		83							83								3		B
Franco-Imperial War	–83	–84	Regensburg	83	83			83		83															3	2	B
English Civil War	–85	–86		85																					1		C
Danish-Hamburg War	–86	–88								86	86					86									2		B
2d Coalition against Louis XIV	–88	9–20–97	Ryswick**	88	88			88		88			88	88											7	25	B
Amour Expedition‡	–89	8–27–89	Nerchinsk															89				89			2		I
Azov Expedition‡	–95	–96																95			95				2		I
Number wars participated in by each state				10	8	8	2	6	1	8	2	3	3	1	1	5	5	8	4	1	1	1	4	1	85	119	

* See Table 31. † See Table 31. ‡ Wars fought mainly outside Europe.

§ An armistice was concluded at Vilna in 1656. Although the instrument signed at Andrusovo was called a "truce," it proved permanent. This war was known in Russian history as the Thirteen Years' War and is said to have exceeded the Thirty Years' War in brutality.

‖ Sweden concluded peace with Prussia at Königsberg, 1656; with Denmark at Roskilde, 1658; with Poland at Oliva, 1660; with Denmark at Copenhagen, 1660; and with Russia at Kardis, 1661.

¶ France concluded a truce with Prussia at Vossem, 1673, and concluded peace with Spain (September 17, 1678), and, in collaboration with Sweden, with the Emperor (February 6, 1679) at Nijmegen; with Prussia at St.-Germain, 1679; and with Denmark at Fontainebleau, September 2, 1679. Sweden concluded peace with Denmark at Lund, September 26, 1679, and with Netherlands at Nijmegen, September 2, 1679.

** France concluded peace with Savoy at Vigevano, 1696.

TABLE 35
LIST OF WARS, 1700–1750

Column groups: Western Europe = France, Great Britain, Netherlands, Portugal, Scotland, Spain. Central Europe = Austria, Bavaria, Germanic Empire, Hanover, Hungary, Prussia, Savoy (Sardinia), Saxony, Venice. Northern Europe = Denmark, Poland, Russia, Sweden. Near East = Turkey.

War	Date of Beginning	Date of Ending	Name of Treaty of Peace	France	Great Britain	Netherlands	Portugal	Scotland	Spain	Austria	Bavaria	Germanic Empire	Hanover	Hungary	Prussia	Savoy (Sardinia)	Saxony	Venice	Denmark	Poland	Russia	Sweden	Turkey	No. of Participants Among 20 States	No. of Battles*	Type of War†
Second Northern War	3-12-00	8-30-21	Nystadt‡		00	00									15		00		00	00	00	00		8	31	B
War of Spanish Succession	7-28-01	4-11-13	Utrecht§	01	01	01	01		01	01		01			01	01								9	105	B
Hungarian Insurrection	-03	-11	Nagy-Majteny							03				03										2	10	C
Catalonian Rebellion	-05	-15	......						05															1		C
Russo-Turkish War	-10	-12	Pruth																	10	10	12	10	4	2	B
British Civil War	-15	-16	......		15																			1		C
British-Swedish War	-15	11-20-19	Stockholm		15																	15		2		B
Ottoman War	-16	7-21-18	Passowitz							16								16					16	3	9	B
Seizure of Sardinia	8-	-17	......						17							17								2		B
War of Quadruple Alliance	8-11-18	12-17-20	London	18	18	19			18	18						18								6	6	B
Swedish-Hanoverian War	-19	-21	Nystadt										19								19	19		3		B
British-Spanish War	-26	11-9-29	Seville		26				26															2		B
War of Polish Succession	-33	11-18-38	Vienna	33					33	33					33	33				33	33			7	17	B
Russo-Austrian War	-35	-39	Belgrade							37											35		35	3	18	B
War of Austrian Succession	10-19-39	10-18-48	Aix-la-Chapelle‖	40	39	43			39	40	41				40	40	45				41			10	74	B
Russo-Swedish War	-40	-43	Abö																		40	41		2	2	B
Scotch Civil War	-45	-46	......		45			45																2	2	C
Orange Revolt (Netherlands)	-47	-47	......			47																		1		C
Number wars participated in by each state				4	8	5	1	1	7	7	1	1	1	1	4	5	2	1	1	3	7	5	3	68	276	

* See Table 31.

† See Table 31.

‡ Sweden concluded peace with Denmark at Travendahl, A... 1700; with Poland and Saxony at Altranstadt, 1706; with Denmark at Frederiksberg, 1720; with Prussia and Hanover at Stockholm, 1720; and with Russia and Pol... at Nystadt, 1721.

§ France concluded peace with Austria at Rastadt, April 11, 1714; with the Empire at Baden, 1714; and with Great Britain and Savoy at Utrecht, 1713.

‖ Austria ended the First Silesian War with Prussia by the Peace of Breslau, June 11, 1742; the Second Silesian War by the Peace of Dresden, 1745; and the war with France at Aix-la-Chapelle, 1748. Great Britain began the War of Jenkins' Ear with Spain in 1739 but did not make peace until 1748 at Aix-la-Chapelle.

TABLE 36

LIST OF WARS, 1750–1800

War	Date of Beginning	Date of Ending	Name of Treaty of Peace	Western Europe: France	Great Britain	Netherlands	Portugal	Spain	Central Europe: Austria	Bavaria	Brunswick	Genoa	Geneva	Germanic Empire	Hamburg	Hanover	Mecklenburg	Naples	Papal States	Prussia	Sardinia	Saxony	Switzerland	Venice	Northern Europe: Denmark	Poland	Russia	Sweden	Near East, Asia, Africa: Greece	India	Moscow	Persia	Turkey	America: U.S.A.	American Indians	No. of Participants among 32 States	No. of Battles*	Type of War†
Seven Years' War§	7–3–54	2–10–63	Paris‖	55	55		56	62	56		56			56	62	56				56	56	56			62		57	56		56					55	17	111	B
Sepoy Mutiny‡	–63	–65			63																									63						2	...	I
Russo-Turkish War	–68	7–12–74	Kutchuk Kainarji																								68						68			2	16	B
Seizure of Corsica	–68	6–16–69		68								68																								2	...	B
Confederation of Bar	–68	–72																								68	68									2	...	B
Falkland Islands‡	–70	–70			70			70																												2	...	B
Greek Revolt	–70	–70																											70				70			2	...	C
Russian Revolt	–73	–74																									73									1	...	C
Spanish-Moroccan War‡	–75	–75						75																							75					2	...	I
American Revolution‡	4–19–75	9–3–83	Paris¶	78	75	80		79																										75		5	13	C
Mahratta War‡	–78	–82	Salbai		78																									78						2	...	I
War of Bavarian Succession	12–30–77	5– –79	Teschen						78	78							78			78		78														5	2	B
Seizure of the Crimea	–83	–84																									83						83			2	...	B
Brabant Revolt	–87	–90							87																											1	...	C
Austro-Turkish War**	12–20–87	–92	Sistova††						87																		87						87			3	13	B
Russo-Swedish War	–88	–90	Verelii																						88		88	88								3	8	B
French Revolution	7–14–89	–02	Amiens	89	93	93	93	93	92				98	98		92		98	96	92	92	92	92	96	01		99	01					98	98		21	334	B
First Coalition	4–20–92	10–17–97	Campo Formio‡‡	×	×	×	×	×	×							×				×	×	×	×	×														
Vendee	3– –93	–96		×																																		
Franco-American War	5–28–98	9–30–00	Paris	×																														×				
Egyptian Expedition	7–1–98	–01		×	×																												×					
Second Coalition	4– –99	3–27–02	Amiens§§	×	×	×	×	×	×				×	×				×		×		×			×		×	×										
Polish Insurrection	–92	–95																		92						92	92									3	12	C
Tippu Sahib‖‖	–92	–99			92																									92						2	...	I
Russo-Persian War‡	–95	–96																									95					95				2	...	I
Number wars participated in by each state				4	7	2	2	5	5	1	1	1	1	2	1	2	1	1	1	4	2	3	1	1	3	2	10	3	1	4	1	1	5	2	1	81	509	..

* See Table 31.

† See Table 31.

‡ Wars fought mainly outside Europe.

§ This war began in America in 1754, did not begin in Europe until April 10, 1756, and was formally declared by England against France May 17, 1756. Prussia entered the war in August, 1756.

‖ France concluded peace with Spain and Portugal at Fontainebleau, 1762, and with Great Britain at Paris, 1763. Prussia concluded peace with Russia at St. Petersburg, May 5, 1762; with Sweden at Hamburg, May 22, 1762; and with Austria at Hubertsburg, February 15, 1763.

¶ Great Britain concluded peace with France and Spain at Versailles, January 20, 1783, and with the United States and the Netherlands at Paris, 1783.

** War began with an Austrian attack on Belgrade, December 20, 1787, but was not formally declared until February 10, 1788.

†† Turkey concluded peace with Russia at Jassy, 1792, and with Austria at Sistova, 1792.

‡‡ France concluded peace with Spain, Saxony, Hanover, and Prussia at Basel, April 5, 1795; with Savoy at Cherasco, May, 1796; and with Austria at Campo Formio, October 17, 1797.

§§ France concluded peace with Austria and the Empire at Lunéville, February 9, 1801; with Naples at Florence, March 18, 1801; and with Great Britain at Amiens, 1802.

‖‖ The East India Company had fought against Tippu in the first (1780–84) and second (1790–92) Mysore wars.

TABLE 37

LIST OF WARS, 1800–1825

War	Date of Beginning	Date of Ending	Name of Treaty of Peace	Western Europe					Central Europe										Northern Europe			South-Eastern Europe	Asia				Africa	North America									South America										No. of Participants among 43 States	No. of Battles*	Type of War†
				France	Great Britain	Netherlands	Portugal	Spain	Austria	Baden	Bavaria	Hesse	Naples	N. German States	Prussia	Saxony	Venice	Württemberg	Denmark	Russia	Sweden	Greece	India	Burma	Persia	Turkey	Barbary States	Costa Rica	Guatemala	Haiti	Honduras	Mexico	Nicaragua	Salvador	Santo Domingo	United States	Argentina	Bolivia	Brazil	Chile	Columbia	Ecuador	Paraguay	Peru	Uruguay	Venezuela			
Tripoli-U.S.A.‡	5-10-01	6- 4-05	Tripoli																								01									01											2		D
Haytian Revolt‡	2- 3-02	11-19-03	Haut du Cap	02																										02																		2		C
1st Mahratta War‡	2-12-02	1-15-04	Surge Angengaum		03																		03																									2		I
Russo-Persian War‡	-04	12-10-13	Gulistan																	04					04																							2		I
Napoleonic Wars	4-29-03	6- 9-15	Vienna§	03	03	05	07	04	05	05	05	15	05	05	06	05		05	13	05	05																											17	332	B
Third Coalition‖	10- 6-05	12-26-05	Pressburg	X	X	X			X	X	X		X					X		X	X																											..	..	..
Franco-Prussian	10- 9-06	7- 9-07	Tilsit	X	X										X	X				X																												..	..	..
Peninsular War¶	11-30-07	7-20-14	Paris	X	X		X	X																																								..	..	..
Anglo-Danish	7-24-07	1-14-14	Keil		X														X																													..	..	..
Franco-Austrian	4- 6-09	10-15-09	Schönbrun	X					X											X																												..	..	..
Russian Expedition	6-24-12	1-10-13	**	X																X																												..	..	..
War of Liberation	3-27-13	5-30-14	Paris	X	X			X	X	X	X	X	X	X	X	X		X		X	X																											..	..	..
Hundred Days' War	3- 1-15	11-20-15	Paris	X	X	X			X	X					X					X																												..	..	..
Russo-Turkish	12-30-06	8-14-12	Bucharest		06															06						06																						3	20	B
Russo-Swedish	2-22-08	9-17-09	Frederikshavn																08	08	08																											3	2	B
Latin-American Revolt‡	4-19-10	12- 9-24	Capitulation of Ayachuco				20	10																				21	21		21	10	21	21	21		10	10	20	10	12	10	11	20	11	10	19		C
War of 1812‡‡††	6-18-12	12-24-14	Ghent‡‡		12																															12											2	3	B
Austria-Naples	3-30-15	5-20-15	Calvi§§						15				15																																		2	4	B
Algiers-U.S.A.‡	3- 2-15	7- 6-15	U.S.S. "Guerrière"																								15									15											2		D
2d Mahratta War‡	11- 6-17	8- 4-18			17																		17																									2		I
Spanish Civil War	12-12-21	10- 1-23	‖‖‖	21				21																																							2		C
Greek Revolt	3- -21	2- 3-30	London	27	27													22		27		21				21	27																					7		C
Haiti-Santo Domingo‡	3- -23	- -23																												23					23												2		B
1st Central American‡	- -23	- -23																										28	23		23		23	23													5		B
Burmese War‡	3- 5-24	2-20-26	Ava		24																			24																								2		I
La Plata War‡	3-27-25	9-15-28	Rio de Janeiro																																		25		25						25		3		B
Number wars participated in by each state				4	7	1	2	3	2	1	1	1	2	1	1	1	1	1	2	5	2	1	2	1	1	2	3	2	2	2	2	1	2	2	2	3	2	1	2	1	1	1	1	1	2	1	79	361	..

* See Table 31.

† See Table 31.

‡ Wars fought mainly outside Europe.

§ The Final Act of Vienna War signed before the Battle of Waterloo (June 17, 1815).

‖ The first engagement on the Danube between Napoleon and Austria took place on October 6, 1805, though mobilization had begun in August. Great Britain began naval hostilities against France in 1803 and made a naval attack on Spain on October 5, 1804.

¶ On November 30, 1807, the French under Junot entered Lisbon though war had been resolved upon by October 12.

** Murat turned over his command at Posen on January 10, 1813, and returned to Paris. The main body of Napoleon's army had crossed the Niemen at Kaunas in the middle of December, 1812.

†† The Declaration of War on June 18, 1812, had been preceded by the affairs of the "Leopard" and "Chesapeake" (1807) and the "President" and "Little Belt" (1811) and by the Battle of Tippecanoe in which the United States had defeated Indians thought to be supported by the British in Indiana (1811).

‡‡ Hostilities including the Battle of New Orleans continued until February 15, 1815.

§§ Representatives of the Neapolitan army, the Austrian army, and the British admiralty signed a military convention near Calvi on May 20, 1815. Ferdinand IV returned to Naples on June 17.

‖‖‖ The king of Spain issued a decree declaring an end to the constitutional system of the Cortez on October 1, 1823. The capitulations of Cadiz, Badojos, and Carthagena occurred at about the same time.

TABLE 40
LIST OF WARS, 1875–1900

WAR	DATE OF BEGINNING	DATE OF ENDING	NAME OF TREATY OF PEACE	EUROPE										ASIA					AFRICA			NORTH AMERICA							SOUTH AMERICA			NO. OF PARTICIPANTS AMONG 28 STATES	NO. OF BATTLES*	TYPE OF WAR†
				France	Italy	Great Britain	Spain	Russia	Bulgaria	Crete	Greece	Montenegro	Serbia	Afghanistan	China	Japan	Philippines	Turkey	Central Africa	North Africa	South Africa	Costa Rica	Cuba	Guatemala	Honduras	Nicaragua	Salvador	United States	Bolivia	Chile	Peru			
Russo-Turkish	5- 3-77	7-13-78	Berlin§					77				76	76					77														4	38	B
War of the Pacific‡	4- 5-79	3-28-84	Ancon																										78	78	78	3		A
Zulu War†	1-23-79	9- 1-79	Ulundi‖			79															79											2		I
2d Afghan War‡	1- 1-79	10- 3-81	¶			79								79																		2		I
1st Transvaal War†	12-20-80	8- 8-81	Pretoria			80															80											2		B
Tunisian Expedition‡	3-31-81	4- 4-82	Kasr-el-Said	81																81												2		I
Egyptian War‡	7-11-82	9- 7-82	**			82														82												2		I
Tonking War‡	12- -82	8- 9-85	Tientsin††	82											82																	2		I
5th Central American War‡	3-18-84	4-14-85	Acajulta																			84		84	84	84	84					5		B
Serbo-Bulgar War	11-13-85	3- 3-86	Constantinople						85				85																			2		B
Guatemala-Salvador‡	7-23-89	11-15-89	Guatemala																					89			89					2		B
Chino-Japanese‡	8- 1-94	4-17-95	Shimonoseki												94	94																2	5	I
Madagascan Conquest‡	3- 1-95	8- 8-96	‡‡	95															96													2		I
Abyssinian War‡	3- 1-95	10-26-96	Addis Ababa		95														96													2		I
Cretan Revolt	5-24-96	11-26-98	‖‖							96								98														2	1	C
2d Ashanti War‡	-96	1-19-96	§§			96													96													2		B
Costa Rica-Nicaragua‡	3-20-97	4-26-97																				97				97						2		B
Greco-Turkish War	4-17-97	12- 4-97	Constantinople								97							97														2	2	B
Spanish-American War‡	4-21-98	12-10-98	Paris***				98										98						98					98				4	4	B
Boer War‡	12-12-99	5-31-02	Vereeniging†††			99															99											2	8	B
Number wars participated in by each state				3	1	6	1	1	1	1	1	1	2	1	2	1	1	2	3	2	3	2	1	2	1	2	2	1	1	1	1	48	58	

* See Table 31.   † Wars fought mainly outside Europe.   ‡ See Table 31.

§ The Treaty of Berlin was preceded by the Preliminary Peace of San Stefano, March 3, 1878, and followed by the definitive treaty of Constantinople, February 8, 1879.

‖ Hostilities ended with the capture of Cetywayo, the Zulu king, on August 29, 1879, followed by a British proclamation on September 1.

¶ Amir Abdurrahman, who defeated Ayub Khan, conducted his campaign with British backing. The war came to an end with defeat of Ayub on October 3, 1881.

** The war ended with the defeat of the rebel, Arabi, on September 7, 1882. Sporadic hostilities in the Sudan did not end until the fall of Dongola to Kitchener on September 23, 1896.

†† Treaties were signed by France with Annam (June 6, 1884) and Cambodia (June 17, 1884), but hostilities actually continued for a few months more.

‡‡ Queen Ranavale capitulated on September 30, 1895, and on October 1, 1895, accepted the protectorate treaty. Disturbances continued, and France declared the island annexed on August 8, 1896.

§§ War ended without serious hostilities when the tribal king was taken prisoner by the British forces on their entry into Kumansi, January 19, 1896.

‖‖ The Cretan Revolt continued after Greece had settled with Turkey and the Concert of Powers consisting of France, England, Russia, and Italy. Prince George, who had been given the post of high commissioner by the powers on November 26, 1898, landed at Crete on December 21, and hostilities ceased soon after Admiral Noel of the British Navy had hung the ringleaders of the revolt.

*** A preliminary treaty of peace was signed at Paris, April 26, 1897, and the boundary question was settled by arbitration sponsored by the Greater Central American States.

††† A preliminary treaty of peace were signed at Paris, August 12, 1898, but hostilities continued against the Philippine insurgents until 1902.

LIST OF WARS, 1825–50

WAR	DATE OF BEGINNING	DATE OF ENDING	NAME OF TREATY OF PEACE	WESTERN EUROPE						CENTRAL EUROPE					NORTHERN EUROPE			ASIA					AFRICA		NORTH AMERICA								SOUTH AMERICA						NO. OF PARTICIPANTS AMONG 35 STATES	NO. OF BATTLES	TYPE OF WAR
				Belgium	France	Great Britain	Netherlands	Portugal	Spain	Austria	Hungary	N. German States	Prussia	Sardinia	Denmark	Poland	Russia	Afghanistan	Central Asia	China	Persia	Turkey	Morocco	Egypt	Costa Rica	Guatemala	Honduras	Mexico	Nicaragua	Salvador	Texas	United States	Argentina	Bolivia	Brazil	Chile	Peru	Uruguay			
Spanish-Portuguese	11-22-26	-27				26		26	26																														3		B
Russo-Persian†	9-28-26	2-28-28	Iourk-Mantchai														26				26																		2		I
Russo-Turkish	4-26-28	9-14-29	Adrianople														28					28																	2	13	B
Belgian Revolt	8-25-30	-33	London §	30	31	31	30																																4		C
Algerian Conquest‡	6-14-30	12-23-47	Sidi Bralim		30																																			2		I
Polish Insurrection	11-29-30	9-7-31														30	30																						2	7	C
2d Central American‡	-31	-45																							31	31	31		31	31								5		B
Carlist Revolt†	10-4-33	4-2-47	¶		33	33		34	33																													4		C
Egyptian Conquest‡	11- -31	4-5-33	Kutalia																		31		31															2		C
Khivan Conquest‡	-39	-42															39		39																			2		I
Portuguese Revolution	-31	5-24-34	Evora-Monte		31	31		31	31																													4	4	C
Peru-Bolivia‡	7- -35	6-7-42	Acora																													38	34		38	34		4	1	B
Texan Revolt‡	-35	-36																						35			35							2	1	C
Chile-Argentine‡	-36	-36																													36			36			2		B
1st Afghan War‡	10-11-38	9- -42	**			38												38																				2	2	I
2d La Plata War‡	9-2-39	2-3-52	††		49																											38		52			38	3		B
Egyptian War‡	6-8-39	11-27-41	Alexandria		40	40				40												39		39														5		I
1st Opium War‡	6-22-40	8-29-42	Nanking			40														40																		2		I
France-Morocco‡	7-6-44	9-10-44	Tangier		44																		44															2		I
Mexico-U.S.A.‡	5-13-46	2-2-48	Guadalupe Hidalgo																								46				46							2	20	B
Denmark-Germany	3-24-48	1-11-51	‡‡							48		48	48		48																							4	1	B
Austria-Sardinia	3-19-48	3-23-49	§§							48				48																								2	7	B
Hungarian Insurrection	10-3-48	9-13-49	Vilagosh							48	48						48																					3	12	C
Number wars participated in by each state				1	7	7	1	3	3	4	1	1	1	1	1	1	5	1	1	1	1	3	1	2	1	1	1	2	1	1	1	1	3	1	1	2	1	1	65	68	

* See Table 31.   † See Table 31.   ‡ Wars fought mainly outside Europe.

* Wars fought mainly outside Europe.

§ Belgium declared independence October 4, 1830. A preliminary treaty among the great powers recognized this on June 26, 1831, but hostilities continued until 1833, and peace was finally made in the Treaty of London, April 19, 1830.

‖ Warsaw fell September 7, 1831. The Polish insurrectionary forces did not surrender to the Russians but crossed the frontier into Prussia.

¶ An amnesty for all Carlist political offenders was decreed on September 2, 1847.

** The war seems to have come to an end with the British withdrawal from Afghanistan, in September, 1842.

†† Justo Jose de Urquiza, heading a coalition of Uruguayans, Brazilians, and Argentinians, defeated the Argentinian dictator Rosas at Caseros, February 3, 1852.

‡‡ The Stadtholders of the duchies of Schleswig and Holstein issued a proclamation on January 11, 1851, at Kiel.

§§ The Sardinian king, Charles Albert, abdicated in favor of his son, Victor Emmanuel, after the Sardinian defeat by the Austrians at Novara, March 23, 1849.

TABLE 39

LIST OF WARS, 1850–75

WAR	DATE OF BEGINNING	DATE OF ENDING	NAME OF TREATY OF PEACE	WESTERN EUROPE			CENTRAL EUROPE											NORTHERN EUROPE			SOUTH-EASTERN EUROPE		ASIA					AFRICA		NORTH AMERICA										SOUTH AMERICA									NO. OF PARTICIPANTS	NO. OF BATTLES AMONG 45 STATES	TYPE OF WAR
				France	Great Britain	Spain	Austria	Baden	Bavaria	Hanover	Hesse	Naples	N. German States	Prussia	Sardinia (Italy)	Saxony	Württemberg	Denmark	Poland	Russia	Greece	Montenegro	Central Asia	China	India	Japan	Turkey	Central Africa	North Africa	Costa Rica	Cuba	Guatemala	Haiti	Honduras	Mexico	Nicaragua	Santo Domingo	Salvador	United States	Argentina	Bolivia	Brazil	Chile	Columbia	Ecuador	Paraguay	Peru	Uruguay			
3d Central American‡	–49	–58																												54		49		49		59		49											5		B
Taiping Rebellion‡	8– –50	7-19-64	§																					50																								1		C
Conquest of Turkestan‡	7– –52	1-31-64	Askabad‖																	52			52																									2		I
Montenegran War	2-12-53	3-13-53																				53					53																					2		I
Crimean War¶	10-23-53	3-30-56	Paris	54	54										54					53							53																						5	12	B
2d Haiti–Santo Domingo‡	–55	–56																														55				55												2		B
2d Opium War‡	10-22-56	10-24-60	Peking**	56	56																			56																								3		I
Sepoy Rebellion‡	5-10-57	7- 8-59	††		57																				57																							2		I
Moroccan War‡	10-22-59	4-27-60	Fez			59																							59																			2		I
Italian War‡	4-23-59	11-10-59	Zurich	59			59								59																																	3	5	B
Peru-Ecuador‡	–59	–59																																											59		59		2		B
Italian Revolution	5-11-60	2-13-61	‡‡	60								60			60																																	3	5	C
American Civil War‡	4-19-61	4- 2-66	§§																																		61									1	50	C
Japanese Restoration‡	8-13-63	4-17-69	‖‖																						63																						1		C
Mexican Expedition‡¶¶	4- 4-62	6-27-67	***	62	62	62																												62													4	1	B
4th Central American War‡	1-23-63	11-15-63	†††																											63		63		63		63										4		B
Columbia-Ecuador‡	10– –63	12-30-63																																									63	63				2		B
Spain-Peru‡	9-25-65	5- 9-66	Paris‡‡‡			64																																		64		63		63		5		B
Polish Insurrection	1-22-63	8- 1-64	§§§															63	63																												2		C
Lopez War‡‖‖	4-14-65	3- 1-70	¶¶¶																																	64		63		63	64	4		B
Germany-Denmark	2- 1-64	10-30-64	Vienna				64						64	64		64		64																											5		B
Austro-Prussian	6-15-66	8-23-66	Prague****				66	66	66	66	66		66	66	66	66	66																												11	4	B
Spanish Civil War	1- 3-66	9-28-68	††††			66																																							1	19	C
Cretan Revolt	9- 2-66	–69	‡‡‡‡	66	66															66					66																					4		C
Cuban Revolt‡	10-10-68	2-10-78	Lanson		68																								68																		3		C
Franco-Prussian	7-19-70	5-10-71	Frankfort§§§§	70				70	70				70	70		70	70																												7		B
Carlist War	4- 8-72	2-28-76	‖‖‖‖	72		72																																							2	54	C
Ashanti War‡	10-14-73	2-13-74	Kumansi		74																							74																	2		I
Number wars participated in by each state				9	7	6	3	2	2	1	1	1	3	3	4	3	2	1	1	3	1	1	1	2	1	1	3	1	1	1	1	2	1	2	1	2	1	2	1	1	1	1	1	1	3	1	2	1	90	150	

* See Table 31.

† See Table 31.

‡ Wars fought mainly outside Europe.

§ The Taiping Rebellion ended with the killing of its leader in 1864, though desultory fighting occurred after that event.

‖ The conquest of Turkestan ended with an imperial ukase announcing Turkestan as a Russian province in 1864. This was followed by hostilities on the Afghan border involving Russian, British, and native troops.

¶ The Turkish ultimatum to Russia expired October 23, 1853, but hostilities had taken place with the Russian invasion of Turkish territory, January 2, 1853.

** The Treaty of Tientsin, 1858, intended to conclude peace, was not observed but was reaffirmed by the Treaty of Peking, 1860.

†† The Mogul emperor was captured and banished in September, 1858, the Mogul Empire was declared at an end, and the government of India transferred to the Crown, after which, on July 8, 1859, peace was proclaimed.

‡‡ The Italian Revolution ended when King Frances of Naples escaped from the country in a French vessel, February 13, 1861.

§§ According to the Supreme Court in the case of the Protector (12 Wall. 79, 1871) the war began in the Far South by the blockade proclamation of April 19, 1861, and in North Carolina and Virginia by the blockade proclamation of April 27, 1861, and ended by the proclamation of April 2, 1866, except in Texas, where it ended by the proclamation of August 20, 1866. Lee had surrendered at Appomattox on April 9, 1865, and Johnston surrendered the last Confederate army on April 26, 1865.

‖‖ After the defeat of the supporters of the shogunate, restoration of the Emperor's power was marked by grant of the Charter Oath on April 17, 1869.

¶¶ Small French, British, and Spanish forces landed at Vera Cruz in December, 1861, but hostilities did not begin until April 4, 1862, when 30,000 French troops were landed.

*** The emperor Maximilian was shot on June 19, 1867, soon after withdrawal of French troops, and Mexico City was taken by Juarez on June 27, 1867. The Allies had made a treaty with Juarez at Solidad, February 19, 1862, after which Great Britain and Spain had withdrawn from the expedition.

††† The war came to an end when General Carrera of Guatemala defeated General Barrios of Salvador. With Barrios' escape, no legal government existed with which to sign a treaty of peace. Carrera appointed General Duenas acting president of Salvador and retired to Guatemala with his army on November 15, 1863.

‡‡‡ Hostilities ended with departure of the Spanish fleet, May 9, 1866. A truce was arranged through mediation by the United States in 1871 and a formal treaty of peace was signed between Spain and Peru at Paris August 14, 1879, and between Spain and Chile at Lima, June 12, 1883.

§§§ The Polish insurrection ended with the hanging of the insurrectionary leaders at Warsaw in August of 1864.

‖‖‖ Lopez attacked the Argentine on April 14, 1865, though hostilities had occurred on August 26, 1864, between Brazil and Uruguay and on November 13, 1864, between Paraguay and Brazil.

¶¶¶ When Lopez was killed, the war came to an end. The conditions of peace imposed on Paraguay were those decided on by the terms of the treaty of alliance signed May 1, 1865, by Argentina, Brazil, and Uruguay.

**** An armistice was signed at Nikolsburg, July 26, 1866. In addition to the Treaty of Prague with Prussia, Austria made separate treaties with Württemberg (August 13), Baden (August 17), Bavaria (August 28), Hesse (September 3), Saxony (October 21), and Italy (October 3) at Vienna. Venice was ceded to Italy and Prussia annexed Hanover.

†††† The insurgents defeated the royalists on September 28, and the queen fled from Spain. The insurgent army entered Madrid on October 3, and the provisional government of which it was the instrument was recognized by the powers on October 25, 1868.

‡‡‡‡ The Cretan Revolt ended in 1869 when hope for Greek intervention disappeared. Fighting of a sporadic nature continued until the end of that year.

§§§§ The Treaty of Frankfort was preceded by the Preliminary Peace of Versailles, signed February 26, 1871.

‖‖‖‖ The Carlist Rebellion came to an end with the withdrawal of the Carlist forces from Guipuzeon, February 20, 1876. Don Carlos, its leader, left Spain on February 28. On March 4, 1877, a general amnesty was extended to the Carlists who had submitted by March 15.

TABLE 41

LIST OF WARS, 1900–1941

War	Date of Beginning	Date of Ending	Name of Treaty of Peace	Belgium	France	Great Britain	Ireland	Luxemburg	Netherlands	Portugal	Spain	Austria	Czechoslovakia	Germany	Hungary	Italy	San Marino	Denmark	Estonia	Finland	Latvia	Lithuania	Norway	Poland	Russia (U.S.S.R.)	Albania	Bulgaria	Greece	Montenegro	Rumania	Serbia (Yugoslavia)	Afghanistan	Australia	China	Hejaz (Saudi Arabia)	India	Japan	New Zealand	Siam	Turkey	Egypt	Ethiopia	Liberia	Morocco	South Africa	Bolivia	Brazil	Paraguay	Venezuela	Canada	Costa Rica	Cuba	Guatemala	Haiti	Honduras	Mexico	Nicaragua	Panama	Salvador	United States	No. of Participants among 57 States	No. of Battles	Type of War
Boxer Expedition‡	6-17-00	9- 7-01	Peking	00	00	00			00		00	00		00		00									00									00			00																							00	12		I
Venezuelan War‡	12-11-02	2-13-03	Washington			02								02		02																																		02												4		B
Russo-Japanese War‡	2- 6-04	9-15-05	Portsmouth																						04												04																								2	18	B
Central American War‡	7- -06	12-20-07	Washington§																																																	06		06		07		06				4		B
Mexican Revolution‡	11-20-10	12- 1-20	‖																																																					10				2		C
Italo-Turkish War‡	9-29-11	10-18-12	Lausanne													11																								11																				2	10	I
1st Balkan War	10- 1-12	5-30-13	London																								12	12	12		12									12																				5	13	B
2d Balkan War	6-30-13	8-10-13	Bucharest¶																								13	13		13	13									13																				5	6	B
World War I	7-28-14	1-10-20	Versailles**	14	14	14				16		14	18	14	14	15	15							18	14	15	15	16	14	16	14		14	17		14	14	14	17	14			17		14			17				18	17	18	18	18		18	17		17	38	615	B
German War	8- 1-14	7-16-20	Versailles††	X	X	X				X			X			X								X	X			X	X	X	X		X	X		X	X	X	X					X			X		X				X	X	X	X	X		X	X		X			
Austrian War	7-28-14	7-16-21	St.-Germain‡‡	X	X	X				X			X			X								X				X	X	X	X		X	X		X	X	X											X					X	X			X	X		X			
Hungarian War	7-28-14	7-26-21	Trianon‡‡	X	X	X				X			X			X								X				X	X	X	X		X	X		X	X	X											X					X	X			X	X		X			
Turkish War	11- 5-14	8- 6-24	Lausanne§§	X	X	X				X			X			X								X	X			X		X	X		X	X	X	X	X			X									X					X							X			
Bulgarian War	10-15-15	8-19-20	Neuilly‖‖	X	X	X				X			X			X								X	X			X	X	X	X		X	X		X	X	X											X					X	X						X			
Chinese Civil Wars‡	1- 1-16	12-25-36	Sian Agreement¶¶																															16																												1		C
Irish Rebellion	4-24-16	7-20-22	London***			19	19																																																						2		C
Russian Revolution	11-15-17	2- -20	†††		18	18							18												17												18																							18	6	9	B
Russo-Polish War	4-16-19	4-17-21	Riga‡‡‡																					19	19																																			2	21	B
3d Afghan War‡	5- 6-19	8-18-19	Rawal Pindi			19																										19				19																								2		I
Vilna War	4- -20	12-10-27	Geneva§§§																			20		20																																				2		B
Greco-Turkish War	4- -21	8- 6-24	Lausanne‖‖‖																									21												21																				2	5	B
Riffian War‡	7- -21	5-30-25			25						21																																	21																	3		C
Chaco War‡¶¶¶	12- 5-28	6- 2-35	Buenos Aires																																													28		28												2	10	B
Manchurian Hostilities‡	9-18-31	5-31-33	Tangkü Truce****																															31			31																							2	5	B
Ethiopian War‡	10- 3-35	7- 9-36	Geneva††††													35																										35																		2	8	I
Spanish Revolution	7-17-36	4- 1-39	‡‡‡‡								36			36		36																																													3	100	C
Chino-Japanese War‡	7- 7-37				40																						37							37			40																							4	50	B
World War II§§§§	8-30-39			40	39	39		40	40				39	39	40	40		40		41				40	41	40	41	40		41	41		39	41		39	41	39	41			40				40			39		39	41	41	41	41	41		41	41	41	41	42	120	B
Russo-Finnish War	11-30-39	3-12-40	Moscow																	39					39																																				2	2	B
Number wars participated in by each state				3	6	7	1	2	2	1	3	3	3	5	2	7	1	1	1	2	1	2	1	4	7	1	4	5	2	3	4	1	2	6	1	2	7	2	3	5	1	2	1	1	2	1	1	1	1	2	2	3	2	3	1	3	2	2	2	5	151	992	

* See Table 31.   † See Table 31.   ‡ Wars fought mainly outside Europe.

§ A peace treaty between Salvador and Honduras on the one hand and Guatemala on the other was signed on the U.S. warship "Marblehead" on July 20, 1906, but war was renewed by Nicaragua in February, 1907. A treaty of peace between Nicaragua and Salvador was signed at Amapala on April 23, 1907, a peace protocol between all five republics was signed at Washington, September 17, 1907, and a definitive peace treaty was signed at that place December 20, 1907. See D. P. Myers, "The Central American League of Nations," World Peace Foundation Pamphlet Series, VII (February, 1917), 110 ff.

‖ The inauguration of President Obregon, who was generally recognized, is considered to have ended the revolution.

¶ Turkey made peace with Bulgaria in the Treaty of Constantinople, September 29, 1913, and with Greece in the Treaty of Athens, November 14, 1913.

** There were five wars ended by distinct treaties and seventy-nine bilateral wars. Germany, Austria-Hungary, Turkey, and Bulgaria signed a treaty of peace with Russia at Brest-Litovsk on March, 1918, and with Rumania at Bucharest on May 6, 1918.

†† The Treaty of Versailles was signed June 28, 1919, but did not go into effect until January 10, 1920. Russia, Montenegro, Costa Rica, and Luxemburg did not sign it, although they had been at war with Germany. The United States signed a separate peace with Germany at Berlin on August 15, 1921, which antedated peace to July 2, 1921, and China signed a separate peace at Peking on May 20, 1921, which went into effect June 28, 1921. Bolivia, Peru, Ecuador, and Uruguay had broken relations with Germany and signed the Treaty of Versailles, though they had not been at war.

‡‡ Russia, Montenegro, and San Marino, though at war with Austria and Hungary, did not sign the treaties of St.-Germain (signed June 10, 1919, in force July 16, 1920) and Trianon (signed June 4, 1920, in force July 26, 1921).

§§ Of the nine powers at war with Turkey all but Russia and Hejaz signed the Treaty of Lausanne (signed July 24, 1923, in force August 6, 1924). In addition to these seven, Armenia, Belgium, Hejaz, Poland, Portugal, and Czechoslovakia signed the abortive Treaty of Sevres, August 10, 1920.

‖‖ In addition to the six powers at war with Bulgaria which (except for Russia) signed the Treaty of Neuilly (signed November 27, 1919, in force August 19, 1920), ten other allied and associated powers signed this treaty.

¶¶ Civil strife not recognized as a legal state of war was practically continuous in China from the republican opposition to Yuan Shi-kai's effort to re-establish monarchy in 1916, through the Tuchun wars from 1918 to 1925, through the nationalist advance in

1926–27, to the termination of the anticommunist wars by the Sian Agreement following Chiang Kai-shek's capture by Chang Hsueh-liang, in 1936.

*** Articles for a treaty recognizing the Dominion status of the Irish Free State were signed December 6, 1921, and went into force July 20, 1922.

††† The Russian Revolutionary War was not recognized as a war in the legal sense. During its course Great Britain, France, Poland, Japan, and the United States intervened with military forces.

‡‡‡ Signed March 18, 1921, in force April 17, 1921.

§§§ Vilna was assigned to Poland by the Conference of Ambassadors, March 15, 1923, but Lithuania regarded itself in a state of latent war with Poland until the two accepted a resolution of the League Council in December, 1927.

‖‖‖ This treaty also ended World War I, but in fact the latter ended with signature of the abortive Treaty of Sevres. From the diplomatic and military points of view the Greco-Turkish War was therefore an independent incident.

¶¶¶ A truce was signed on January 3, 1929, followed by efforts at conciliation. Diplomatic relations were broken July 5, 1931. Paraguay's declaration of war on May 10, 1933, is said to have been rescinded a few days later (Shepard and Scroggs, The United States in World Affairs, 1934–35, p. 131).

**** There was no legal state of war between China and Japan and diplomatic relations were never broken, but actual hostilities were carried on before and even after the Tangkü Truce.

†††† The resolution of the League Assembly in July, 1936, terminating sanctions may be regarded as terminating this war, although hostilities continued and the major powers did not recognize Italy's conquest until 1938.

‡‡‡‡ No legal state of war was recognized in Spain, but an agreement to prevent assistance to either faction was accepted by most of the European states on August 26, 1936. In spite of this, some assistance continued to be given for a time by Portugal and the Soviet Union, and Italy and Germany intervened with official forces on the side of the rebel government, which they had recognized as the government of Spain.

§§§§ In addition to the forty-two states listed, Danzig, Iceland, Iraq, and Iran had become involved in this war before the end of 1941.

TABLE 42

WORLD WAR I, 1914–18

		GERMANY								AUSTRIA						HUNGARY					BULGARIA				TURKEY					CENTRAL POWERS						DURATION OF WAR IN YEARS				
ALLIED AND ASSOCIATED POWERS		Declaration of War*	Armistice,* Rethondes 11/11/18	Treaty of Versailles Signed 6/28/19	In force 1/10/20	Treaty of Berlin† Signed 8/25/21	In force 11/11/21	Treaty of Peking Signed 5/20/21	In force 6/28/21	Declaration of War	Armistice, Villa Giusti 11/3/18	Treaty of St.-Germain Signed 9/10/19	In for 7/16/20	Treaty of Vienna† Signed 8/24/21	In force 11/8/21	Armistice, Belgrade 11/3/18	Treaty of Trianon Signed 6/4/20	In force 7/26/21	Treaty of Budapest† Signed 8/29/21	In force 12/17/21	Declaration of War	Armistice 9/29/18	Treaty of Neuilly Signed 11/27/19	In force 8/10/20	Declaration of War	Armistice, Mudros 10/30/18	Treaty of Sèvres Signed 8/10/20	Treaty of Lausanne Signed 7/24/23	In force 8/6/24	Armistice 12/16/17	Treaty of Brest-Litovsk Signed 3/3/18	In force 3/16/18	Preliminaries of peace 3/5/18	Treaty of Bucharest Signed 5/6/18	In force 5/6/18	Germany	Austria	Hungary	Bulgaria	Turkey
Principal A. and A. Powers	United States	4/6/17	×	×		×	×			12/7/17	×	×		×	×	×	×		×	×	‡				‡‡‡											4.2	3.6	3.6		
	British Empire	8/4/14	×	×	×					8/12/14	×	×	×			×	×	×			10/15/15	×	×	×	11/5/14	×	×	×	×							5.4	5.9	5.9	4.8	9.8
	France	8/3/14	×	×	×					8/13/14	×	×	×			×	×	×			10/16/15	×	×	×	11/5/14	×	×	×	×							5.4	5.9	5.9	4.8	9.8
	Italy	8/28/16	×	×	×					5/24/15	×	×	×			×	×	×			10/19/15	×	×	×	8/21/15	×	×	×	×							3.3	5.2	5.2	4.8	9.0
	Japan	8/23/14	×	×	×					8/27/14	×	×	×			×	×	×			‡				11/23/14	×	×	×	×							5.3	5.8	5.8		9.8
Allied and Associated Powers	Belgium	8/4/14	×	×	×					8/28/14	×	×	×			×	×	×			‡															5.4	5.8	5.8		
	Bolivia	‖																																						
	Brazil	10/26/17	×	×	×																															2.2				
	China	8/14/17	×	¶				×	×	8/14/17	×	×	×			×	×	×																		3.9	2.9	2.9		
	Cuba	4/7/17	×	×	×					12/16/17	×	×	×			×	×	×			‡															2.7	2.6	2.6		
	Ecuador	**																																						
	Greece	11/24/16	×	×	×					11/24/16	×	×	×			×	×	×			11/28/16	×	×	×	11/24/16	×	×	×	×							3.1	3.6	3.6	3.7	7.7
	Guatemala	4/22/18	×	×																																1.7				
	Haiti	7/15/18	×	×																																1.5				
	The Hejaz	††	×	×	×																‡															2.8				
	Honduras	7/19/18	×	×																																1.4				
	Liberia	8/4/17	×	×	×																															2.4				
	Nicaragua	5/6/18	×	×						5/6/18	×	×	×			×	×	×																		1.6	2.2	2.2		
	Panama	11/10/17	×	×	×					12/10/17	×	×	×			×	×	×																		2.1	2.6	2.6		
	Peru	‡‡																																		1.2				
	Poland	§§	×	×	×					§§	×	×	×			×	×	×																		1.2	2.5	2.5		
	Portugal	3/9/16	×	×	×					3/9/16	×	×	×			×	×	×																		3.9	4.4	4.4		
	Rumania	8/28/16	×	×	×					8/27/16	×	×	×			×	×	×			9/1/16	×	‖‖‖		8/31/16	×	×			×			×	×	×	3.3	3.9	3.9	3.9	9.0
	Serb-Croat-Slovene	8/9/14	×	×	×					7/28/14	×	×	×			×	×	×			10/11/15	×	¶¶		12/2/14	×	×									5.4	6.0	6.0	4.8	9.7
	Siam	7/22/17	×	×	×					7/22/17	×	×	×			×	×	×			‡															2.5	3.0	3.0		
	Czechoslovakia	***	×	×	×					***	×	×	×			×	×	×																		1.5	2.1	2.1		
	Uruguay	†††		×	×																																			
Not at Peace Conference	Costa Rica	5/24/18		§§§																																1.6				
	Luxemburg	8/2/14		§§§																																5.4				
	Montenegro	8/9/14								8/7/14			‖‖‖‖			×					10/20/15				11/3/14											3.6	3.6	3.6	2.4	3.3
	Russia	8/1/14								8/6/14			‖‖‖‖								10/20/15				11/3/14					×	×	×					5.2	5.2		
	San Marino									6/1/15																														
	Average length of wars (4.2)																																			3.2	4.0	4.0	4.2	8.3
	Total number of wars (79)																																			26	19	19	7	8

* The declarations of war are printed in United States Naval War College, *International Law Documents*, 1917, p. 15; *ibid.*, 1918, p. 11. For the Armistices see *ibid.*, 1918; the treaties of peace are conveniently collected in *The Treaties of Peace, 1919–1923*, ed. Lieut.-Col. Lawrence Martin (2 vols.; New York: Carnegie Endowment, 1924), with exception of those by the Central Powers with Russia and Rumania in 1918, which are printed in *International Conciliation*, No. 128, July, 1918.

† Provided for end of war on July 2, 1921, date of passage of peace resolution by United States Congress.

‡ Broke relations.

§ Armenia signed this treaty, but the United States did not.

‖ Broke relations 4/14/17.

¶ Though named in the preamble, China did not sign the treaty.

** Broke relations 12/17/17.

†† Recognized by the Allies 3/19/17.

‡‡ Broke relations 10/6/17.

§§ Recognized by the Allies 11/2/18.

‖‖‖ Though named in the preamble, Rumania did not sign the treaty.

¶¶ Though named in the preamble, the Serb-Croat-Slovene state did not sign the treaty.

*** Recognized by the Allies 6/30/18.

††† Broke relations 10/17/17.

‡‡‡ Broke relations 4/20/17.

§§§ These states were not parties to the Treaty of Versailles, but presumably their wars with Germany ended when that treaty went into force. Montenegro was absorbed by the Serb-Croat-Slovene state.

‖‖‖‖ These states were not parties to the Treaty of St.-Germain, but presumably their wars with Austria ended when that treaty went into force.

TABLE 43

PARTICIPATION OF POWERS IN GENERAL WARS, 1600–1941

1. The Thirty Years' War (1618–48) included Austria, France, Spain, Sweden, the Netherlands, Denmark, and the German states directly. During its course England engaged in the War of the Mantuan Succession (1627–30), which also involved France, Austria, and Spain, and in the Civil War (1642–51). Turkey was engaged in wars with Poland (1621) and with Venice (1644–68).

2. The war between Spain and France continued after the Thirty Years' War until 1659, drawing in England, Lorraine, and Savoy. During its course the Netherlands had wars with England and with Portugal. Russia fought Austria, Sweden, Denmark, Poland, Prussia, and the Netherlands in the First Northern War (1655–60). Turkey was involved in a war with Austria in which France also took part (1657–64), in the long war with Venice (1644–68).

3. The War of the First Coalition against Louis XIV (1672–79) included directly France, Austria, Spain, the Netherlands, Sweden, Denmark, and Prussia. During its course England was engaged in a war with the Netherlands (1672–73) and Turkey in a war with Poland (1673–78).

4. The War of the Second Coalition against Louis XIV (1688–97) involved France, Austria, Spain, the Netherlands, England, Savoy, and Prussia, and during its course Turkey was fighting Austria, Poland, Hungary, and Venice (1682–99). Sweden was not fighting during this period, but the wars of Charles XII began soon after.

5. The War of the Spanish Succession (1701–14) included France, Austria, Spain, Portugal, the Netherlands, England, Prussia, and Sardinia directly, and during its course Sweden, Russia, and Denmark were fighting the Second Northern War (1699–1721), and Russia, Sweden, Turkey, and Poland also had a war (1710–12).

6. The War of the Quadruple Alliance against Spain (1718–20) involved France, Austria, England, the Netherlands, and Sardinia as well as Spain; and during its course Russia, Sweden, and Denmark were still fighting the Second Northern War, in which Prussia had entered in 1715 (1699–1721). Turkey had just concluded a war with Austria and Venice when it began.

7. The War of the Polish Succession (1733–38) included France, Austria, Spain, Prussia, Russia, and Sardinia. During its course Russia and Austria were engaged in a war against Turkey (1736–39). England succeeded in keeping out of war during this period, although she began the War of Jenkins' Ear against Spain the year after it was over.

TABLE 43—*Continued*

8. The War of the Austrian Succession (1740-48) involved Austria, France, England, the Netherlands, Russia, Prussia, Spain, and Sardinia directly, and during its course Russia and Sweden fought a war (1741-42).

9. The Seven Years' War (1756-63) involved France, England, Prussia, Austria, Spain, Portugal, Sardinia, Russia, and Sweden.

10. The American Revolution (1775-83) became a great-power war after France, the Netherlands, and Spain had entered it. Austria and Germany were engaged in the War of the Bavarian Succession (1778-79) at the same time. Russia kept out of war during this period, although she initiated the first armed neutrality (1780) which was participated in by Sweden, Denmark, Prussia, Austria, and Portugal. Immediately after the war, in 1783, Russia seized the Crimea from Turkey.

11. The French Revolutionary Wars (1792-1802) included four overlapping wars. The first coalition (1792-97), which included France, Austria, England, Spain, Prussia, the Netherlands, and Sardinia; the Egyptian expedition (1798-1801), which included France, England, and Turkey; the American naval war with France (1798); the second coalition which included France, Austria, England, Spain, Prussia, Russia, Naples, Portugal, the Netherlands, and Sweden (1799-1802).

12. The Napoleonic Wars (1805-15) included seven wars against Napoleon: the third coalition (1805), which included France, Austria, England, the Netherlands, Sweden, Russia, and Prussia; the war of France against Prussia and Russia (1806-7), the Peninsula War (1807-14), which included France, England, Spain, and Portugal; the French-Austrian War (1809); the Russian expedition (1812), which involved France, Russia, and Prussia; the War of Liberation (1813-14), which included France, Austria, Prussia, the Netherlands, and Sweden; and the Hundred Days' War (1815), which included France, Austria, England, Prussia, the Netherlands, Russia, Sardinia, and Spain. During this period Russia had a war with Turkey (1806-12); England with Denmark (1807); Russia with Sweden (1808-9); and the United States with England (1812-14).

13. The Crimean War (1854-56) included Turkey, France, England, and Sardinia against Russia. Two great powers, Prussia and Austria, were not at war during this period, although Austria became involved in the brief war with Sardinia and France in 1859 and Prussia and Austria joined in the brief war against Denmark in 1864.

14. World War I (1914-19) included Germany, Austria, Bulgaria, and Turkey against Russia, France, British Empire, Japan, Italy, the United States, Serbia, Belgium, Rumania, Greece, Portugal, the Hejaz, China, Siam, Liberia, Brazil, Cuba, Haiti, Panama, Guatemala, Honduras, Nicaragua, and Costa Rica. Czechoslovakia and Poland were recognized as belligerents before the

TABLE 43—*Continued*

war was over, and Bolivia, Ecuador, Peru, and Uruguay, having broken relations with Germany, were recognized as allied and associated powers.

15. World War II (1939——) began with the German invasion of Danzig and Poland, immediately followed by the entry of France and Great Britain with the Dominions except Ireland. Germany invaded Denmark, Norway, Belgium, Luxembourg, and the Netherlands in 1940. Russia occupied a portion of Poland in 1939 and Bessarabia and the Baltic States in 1940. Italy entered the war on the German side and invaded Greece in 1940. The rest of the Balkan states, the Arab states, and Iran were drawn into the war in 1941. Germany induced Hungary, Rumania, and Bulgaria to become allies and in 1941 invaded Jugoslavia and Greece. Czechoslovakia, Egypt, and Ethiopia were recognized as belligerents on the British side, and by legislation in 1941 the United States promised aid to Britain. Austria and Albania had been occupied by Germany and Italy, respectively, before the war began. The short Russian war on Finland and the Chino-Japanese War (begun in 1937) were proceeding at the same time and were merged in the general war through German attack on Russia and Japanese attack on the United States in 1941. The latter attack brought several Latin-American states, as well as the United States, into war with all the Axis powers.

This summary indicates that, with very few exceptions, all the great powers of the time participated in each of these general wars. The list includes all wars with a great power on each side which lasted as long as two years.

Of the countries regarded as great powers during the entire period, France was involved in all fifteen wars and England in all but one (7). Austria, which ceased to be a great power in the twentieth century, and Prussia, which became a great power in the eighteenth century, were involved in all but one (13). Russia, which became a great power in the eighteenth century, and Italy (Savoy, Sardinia), which did not become a great power until the nineteenth century, were involved in all but two (3, 10). Spain, the Netherlands, Sweden, and Turkey ceased to be great powers in the early eighteenth century. Their nonparticipation in these wars was, with one exception, after that date. Omitting World War II, in progress at this writing, Spain did not participate in two (13, 14), the Netherlands in three (9, 13, 14), Sweden in three (4, 13, 14), and Turkey in four (6, 8, 9, 10). Japan and the United States did not become great powers until the twentieth century. Japan was involved in the two twentieth-century general wars (14, 15). The people of United States were involved during ten of these war periods: the Dutch occupation of Swedish Delaware (2), the Dutch reoccupation of New York (3), King William's War (4), Queen Anne's War (5), King George's War (8), French and Indian War (9), Revolutionary War (10), French naval war (11), War of 1812 (12), and World War I (14).

TABLE 43—*Continued*

The summary also indicates a declining length of general wars and, with the exception of the twentieth century, an increasing time between them. The average length of these wars in the four successive centuries was 14, 8, 6, and 4 years, and the average time between them was 6, 8, 33, and 20 years. The following diagram indicates the date and duration of each of the general wars.

DATE AND DURATION OF GENERAL WARS OF MODERN
CIVILIZATION

1618 1650	1700	1750	1800	1850	1900 1941

| 1 | 2 | 3 | 4 | 5 | 6 | 7 8 | 9 | 10 | 11 | 12 | 13 | 14 | 15 |

TABLE 44

SUMMARY OF PARTICIPATION IN WARS OF MODERN CIVILIZATION BY
IMPORTANT STATES, BY FIFTY-YEAR PERIODS, 1480–1941

State	1480–1550	1550–1600	1600–1650	1650–1700	1700–1750	1750–1800	1800–1850	1850–1900	1900–1941	Total
England (Great Britain)	6	6	7	10	8	7	14	13	7	78
France	10	10	6	8	4	4	11	12	6	71
Netherlands	1	1	2	8	5	2	2	0	2	23
Spain	12	7	11	6	7	5	6	7	3	64
Empire (Austria)	13	4	3	8	7	5	6	3	3	52
Prussia (Germany)	0	1	1	3	4	4	2	3	5	23
Savoy (Italy)	0	0	4	1	5	2	1	5	7	25
Denmark	2	1	3	5	1	3	3	1	1	20
Sweden	2	6	4	4	5	3	2	0	0	26
Poland	3	4	7	5	3	2	1	1	4	30
Russia (U.S.S.R.)	2	6	7	8	7	10	10	4	7	61
Turkey	6	5	5	4	3	5	5	5	5	43
United States	0	0	0	0	0	2	4	2	5	13
Japan	0	0	0	0	0	0	0	2	7	9
China	0	0	0	1	0	0	0	4	6	11
World	32	31	34	30	18	20	41	48	24	278

TABLE 45

Summary of Certain Characteristics of Wars of Modern Civilization, by Fifty-Year Periods, 1480–1941

Characteristic	1480–1550	1550–1600	1600–1650	1650–1700	1700–1750	1750–1800	1800–1850	1850–1900	1900–1941	Total
No. of wars fought:										
Mainly in Europe	28	31	31	26	18	13	15	14	11	187
Mainly outside Europe	4	0	3	4	0	7	26	34	13	91
Total	32	31	34	30	18	20	41	48	24	278
No. of important battles:										
Fought in Europe	39	48	116	119	276	496	432	130	744	2,400
Fought outside Europe	9	0	0	0	0	13	11	78	248	359
Total	48	48	116	119	276	509	443	208	992	2,759
No. participating:										
European states	22	18	30	17	19	26	29	27	28	......
Non-European states	6	1	4	5	1	6	24	26	29	......
Total	28	19	34	22	20	32	53	53	57	......
Average no. participating:										
Wars fought mainly in Europe	3.0	2.0	2.6	3.0	3.4	4.4	4.5	4.0	8.5	......
Wars fought mainly outside Europe	2.0	0	2.0	2.0	0	2.4	3.0	2.5	3.2	......
All wars	2.8	2.0	2.6	2.5	3.4	4.0	3.5	2.9	5.7	......
Average no. of important battles:										
Wars fought in Europe	1.4	1.5	3.7	4.6	15.3	39.5	30.9	9.3	62.7	......
Wars fought outside Europe	2.2	0	0	0	0	0.1	0.3	2.0	7.4	......
All wars	1.5	1.5	3.4	4.0	15.3	25.4	11.0	4.3	37.2	......
Average duration of wars:										
Fought mainly in Europe	3.5	4.9	8.2	4.9	4.9	3.6	3.7	1.1	3.7	......
Fought mainly outside Europe	1.0	0	1.0	7.2	0	3.0	4.1	2.8	3.6	......
All wars	3.8	4.9	7.6	5.2	4.9	3.4	4.2	2.7	3.6	......
Types of war participated in by European states:										
Balance of power	18	12	13	14	13	10	8	12	11	111
Civil	4	14	14	8	5	5	8	9	3	70
Defensive	6	5	4	4	0	0	0	0	0	19
Imperial	4	0	3	4	0	5	11	13	4	44
Total	32	31	34	30	18	20	27	34	18	244
Types of war participated in by non-European states:										
Balance of power	0	0	0	0	2	0	10	16	8	36
Civil	0	0	0	0	0	1	4	4	3	12
Defensive	6	5	4	4	0	0	2	0	0	21
Imperial	4	0	3	4	0	5	11	13	4	44
Total	10	5	7	8	2	6	27	33	15	113
Types of war participated in by all states:										
Balance of power	18	12	13	14	13	10	17	23	15	135
Civil	4	14	14	8	5	5	11	12	5	78
Defensive	6	5	4	4	0	0	2	0	0	21
Imperial	4	0	3	4	0	5	11	13	4	44
Total	32	31	34	30	18	20	41	48	24	278

APPENDIX XXI

DURATION AND INTENSITY OF MODERN WAR

The tables in this appendix present materials for judging the variation in the significance of war in different centuries and in different states. There has been a slight tendency for the proportion of time to diminish during which states are formally at war (Table 46). The average duration of war *between pairs of states* was high in the sixteenth and twentieth centuries and low in the thirteenth and nineteenth centuries (Table 47). This corresponds roughly but not exactly with the average duration of wars *treated as historical episodes* presented in Appendix XX, Table 45. Table 48 illustrates the great difference in the amount of time states have devoted to hostilities in the twentieth century. The total campaigning periods of the great powers usually exceeded the 360 months from 1900 to 1930 during that period, thus indicating that they were campaigning somewhere most of the time and in more than one place some of the time. The smaller powers, even those with colonies, spent comparatively few months in campaigns.

Tables 49, 50, and 51 present estimates by Pitirim Sorokin indicating the tendency of war to increase in tensity during the past centuries, with, however, a marked drop in the nineteenth and a lesser drop in the eighteenth centuries. Table 52 suggests that caution is necessary in dealing with estimates of war casualties by exhibiting the wide divergence between two estimates. Tables 53, 54, 55 (Figs. 39, 40, 41) indicate the number and proportion of the population *killed or wounded* in battle in France, Great Britain, and the United States by decades since 1630, and Table 56 gives similar data for the principal participants in World War I. Table 57 contains estimates of the total losses of population through military service in France and England during the last four centuries. This includes death from disease in the military service as well as death in battle and so is not comparable with the figures in Table 56. Since it deals only with deaths, it is not comparable with Tables 50, 53 and 54, which deal with battle casualties (killed or wounded). The proportion of deaths from military service have tended to increase, with the exception of the very small losses by Great Britain in the nineteenth century.

TABLE 46*

Number of Years in Which Eleven Principal European Powers Were at War, by Fifty-Year Periods, 1100–1900

Power	1100–1150	1150–1200	1200–1250	1250–1300	1300–1350	1350–1400	1400–1450	1450–1500	1500–1550	1550–1600	1600–1650	1650–1700	1700–1750	1750–1800	1800–1850	1850–1900	Average 1450–1900
France	26.5	10.0	31.5	17.5	18.0	25.0	35.5	17.0	29.5	31.0	24.0	22.5	25.0	25.5	18.0	17.0	23.5
Austria								37.0	36.0	39.5	40.5	33.0	29.0	19.5	7.5	6.0	27.5
Great Britain	38.0	16.0	19.0	17.0	39.5	25.5	38.0	19.0	16.0	38.5	17.5	26.0	29.0	26.5	26.0	27.5	25.0
Russia								29.5	42.0	36.0	18.0	39.5	29.0	20.5	35.5	17.5	30.0
Prussia											39.0			11.0	30.0	5.5	17.0
Spain								38.0	27.5	45.5	48.0	34.0		19.0	14.5	23.5	33.0
Netherlands											36.0			11.5	6.5	0	22.0
Sweden								21.5	22.5		39.0			7.0		0	17.5
Denmark								15.5	22.5		22.0	10.5	9.0	1.0	10.0	5	11.5
Turkey								42.5	33.0	47.5	47.0	42.0	9.0	14.0	24.0	15.5	30.5
Poland								27.0	26.0	29.0	32.0	36.0	17.0	5.5			24.5
Total	64.5	26.0	50.5	34.5	57.5	50.5	73.5	247.0	254.0	354.5	363.0	298.0	239.0	161.0	178.5	117.5	
Average for states recorded in the period	32.0	13.0	25.0	17.0	28.5	25.0	36.5	27.5	28.0	35.5	33.0	27.0	21.5	14.5	18.0	11.5	
Average percentage of time at war	64	26	50	34	57	50	73	55	56	71	66	54	43	29	36	23	
Average percentage of time at war in century	45.0		42.0		53.5		64.0		63.5		60.0		36.0		29.5		

* Source: Woods and Baltzly, *Is War Diminishing?* (Boston, 1915).

TABLE 47*

TOTAL DURATION OF ALL EUROPEAN WARS, NUMBER OF WARS, AND AVERAGE DURATION OF WARS, BY CENTURIES, 1200–1930

Power	12th	13th	14th	15th	16th	17th	18th	19th	20th (to 1930)	Total 1450–1930
France	36.5/10 = 3.6	49/24 = 2.0	43/20 = 2.1	52.5/25 = 2.1	60.5/34 = 1.8	46.5/28 = 1.7	50.5/21 = 2.4	35/35 = 1.0	26/4 = 6.5	271/147 = 1.8
Austria				37/19 = 2.0	75.5/28.5 = 2.6	73.5/14.5 = 5.1	48.5/15 = 3.2	13.5/22 = 0.6	72/28 = 4.0	320/116 = 2.7
Great Britain	54/16 = 3.4	36/22.5 = 1.5	65/22.5 = 2.1	57/30 = 1.9	54.5/21 = 2.6	43.5/23 = 1.9	55.5/24 = 2.3	53.5/43 = 1.2	28/5 = 5.6	292/146 = 2.0
Russia				29.5/22.5 = 1.3	78.5/32.5 = 2.4	57.5/25 = 2.3	49.5/19 = 2.7	53/32 = 1.7	16/6 = 2.7	284/137 = 2.1
Prussia						58.5/11 = 5.3	31/11 = 2.8	13/13 = 1.0	80/26 = 3.1	182.5/61 = 3.0
Spain				38/7 = 5.4	73/27 = 2.7	82/27 = 3.0	48.5/16 = 3.0	53.5/25 = 2.1		295/102 = 2.9
Netherlands					48.5/3 = 16.2	62.5/12 = 5.5	29.5/10 = 3.0	14.5/4 = 3.8		155/29 = 5.4
Sweden				21.5/4.5 = 4.8	50.5/10.5 = 4.8	50/25 = 2.0	29.5/11 = 2.7	6.5/6 = 1.1		158/57 = 2.8
Denmark				15.5/6 = 2.6	32.5/14 = 2.3	30.5/18 = 1.7	12/4 = 3.0	15/9 = 1.7		105.5/51 = 2.1
Turkey				42.5/20 = 2.1	80.5/18 = 4.5	89/27 = 3.3	23/11 = 2.1	39.5/26 = 1.5	74/14 = 5.0	349.5/117 = 3.0
Poland				27/7 = 3.9	55/23 = 2.4	68/29 = 2.3	22.5/7 = 3.2		4/5 = 1.3	176.5/69 = 2.5
Total duration.. / Total no. wars...	90.5/26 = 3.5	85/46.5 = 1.8	108/42.5 = 2.1	320.5/134 = 2.4	609/211.5 = 2.9	661.5/239.5 = 2.7	400/149 = 2.7	297/215 = 1.4	297/74 = 4.0	2589/1032 = 2.5

* Source: Same as Table 46.

TABLE 48*

NUMBER OF MONTHS' DURATION OF CAMPAIGNS OF FOURTEEN PRINCIPAL
COUNTRIES, BY CLASS OF CAMPAIGN, 1900–1930

Country	Legal War	Inter- vention	Victim of Inter- vention	Civil Disturb- ance	Colonial Hostilities	Border Incident	Total
France..........	66	450	0	7	188	0	711
Austria.........	87	38	0	7	0	3	135
Great Britain....	301	410	0	35	182	13	961
Russia (U.S.S.R.)	101	314	167	85	0	3	670
Germany........	409	54	171	24	95	2	755
Spain...........	0	0	0	14	30	0	44
Netherlands.....	0	0	0	2	2	0	4
Sweden.........	0	0	0	0	0	0	0
Denmark........	0	0	0	0	0	0	0
Turkey.........	205	18	62	85	0	10	380
Poland..........	0	1	0	4	0	8	13
Italy...........	51	226	0	8	155	0	446
United States....	20	605	0	40	19	2	686
Japan..........	24	213	0	1	2	0	240

* Prepared by W. T. R. Fox.

TABLE 49*

SOROKIN'S INDEX OF WAR INTENSITY OF EIGHT PRINCIPAL
COUNTRIES, BY CENTURIES, 1100–1925

Country	12th	13th	14th	15th	16th	17th	18th	19th	20th	Average since 1600
France..........	3	12	35	44	84	1,152	1,262	1,406	24,904	5,761
Austria.........	7	11	7	155	273	2,830	1,946	136	19,825	5,002
Great Britain....	6	8	50	60	61	156	271	132	9,672	2,058
Russia..........	11	19	50	52	155	161	547	731	27,742	5,867
Germany........							1,105	509	47,000	16,204
Spain...........					159	599	341	115	50	253
Netherlands.....						279	152	57	0	122
Italy...........						16	50	103	8,166	2,084
Total........	27	50	142	311	732	5,193	5,674	3,189	137,359	....
Per 1,000,000 pop- ulation........	18	24	60	100	180	500	370	120	3,080	....

* Source: Pitirim Sorokin, *Indices of the Movement of War*, based on duration of wars, size of forces,
number of killed and wounded, number of countries involved, proportion of combatants to total population
involved, presented to American Association for Advancement of Science, December, 1933.

TABLE 50*

SOROKIN'S ESTIMATE OF WAR CASUALTIES IN EUROPE, BY CENTURIES, 1000–1925
(000's omitted)

Country	11th	12th	13th	14th	15th	16th	17th	18th	19th	20th	Average since 1600
France..........	1	4	11	59	61	107	658	1,055	1,769	3,682	1,791
Austria..........	....	8	11	7	100	257	1,560	1,505	226	3,000	1,573
Great Britain....	1	7	17	64	86	91	160	310	141	3,095	901
Russia..........	5	12	29	37	38	118	119	752	777	6,371	2,005
Germany.........	....	....	....	....	....	....	....	360	459	6,060	2,293
Spain...........	....	....	....	....	....	160	559	94	166	44	216
Netherlands	....	....	....	....	....	....	64	290	170	34	......	124
Italy...........	....	....	....	....	....	....	....	17	41	54	1,783	474
Poland and Lithuania..........	....	....	....	....	....	....	66	91	348	219	......	219
Total.......	7	31	68	167	285	863	3,454	4,635	3,845	24,035	......
Per 1,000 population........	....	2	5	8	10	15	37	33	15	54	......

* Source: Pitirim Sorokin, *Social and Cultural Dynamics*, Vol. III, Tables 6–19. See Table 51 below.

TABLE 51*

SOROKIN'S ESTIMATE OF RELATIVE WAR CASUALTIES, BY CENTURIES, 1100–1925
(Per 1,000 Population)

Country	12th	13th	14th	15th	16th	17th	18th	19th	20th
France...........	......	......	......	......	......	37	48	51	92
Great Britain.....	......	......	......	......	......	20	30	5	67
Germany.........	......	......	......	......	......	......	13	95
Austria..........	......	......	......	......	......	130	94	6	48
Russia..........	......	......	......	......	......	8	22	11	41
Italy...........	......	......	......	......	......	......	......	52
Spain...........	......	......	......	......	......	......	12	11	2
Netherlands......	......	......	......	......	......	161	85	6	0
All Europe.......	2	5	8	10	15	37	33	15	54

* The figures in this table resulted from dividing the estimates for war casualties (killed or wounded) for the century by the average population for the century (Sorokin, *Social and Cultural Dynamics*, III, 340, 345, 349).

TABLE 52

COMPARISON OF ESTIMATES BY SOROKIN AND BY KING ON NUMBER ENGAGED AND CASUALTIES IN FRENCH AND BRITISH WARS BY FIFTY-YEAR PERIODS, 1626–1925

DECADE	NUMBER ENGAGED			CASUALTIES		
	King's Estimate*	Sorokin's Estimate†	Ratio S : K	King's Estimate*	Sorokin's Estimate†	Ratio S : K
France						
1626–1675....	826,500	2,929,000	354	123,700	323,350	260
1676–1725....	1,517,350	4,490,000	296	213,770	562,180	263
1726–1775....	1,667,100	2,850,000	111	148,517	376,800	240
1776–1825....	11,716,550	7,597,000	64	1,214,380	1,701,750	140
1826–1875....	2,741,800	3,019,000	110	211,400	484,633	229
1876–1925....	24,000,000	9,337,000	39	2,250,000	3,693,100	166
England						
1626–1675....	420,000	1,059,000	252	71,450	98,140	137
1676–1725....	480,400	1,620,000	337	64,950	280,000	431
1726–1775....	550,850	752,000	137	47,630	53,000	111
1776–1825....	1,125,470	1,166,000	104	99,785	111,170	111
1826–1875....	99,400	611,400	615	22,105	44,148	200
1876–1925....	15,000,000	8,154,400	54	1,113,122	3,112,340	280

* See Tables 53 and 54. The estimates are based upon addition of statistics of the principal battles and so omit losses in minor engagements.

† *Social and Cultural Dynamics*, III, 307, 315. The data on casualties are the same as in Table 50, but the periods of time differ. The estimates result from addition of estimates for each war of the period.

TABLE 53*

NUMBER OF SOLDIERS ENGAGED IN BATTLES, NUMBER OF CASUALTIES, AND POPULATION OF FRANCE, BY DECADES, 1630–1919

(See Fig. 39)

Decade	No. Engaged	No. Killed or Wounded	Percentage of Those Engaged Killed or Wounded	Population	Percentage of Population Killed or Wounded	Average No. Engaged in Five Largest Engagements	Percentage of Population in Largest Engagements
1630–39.....	132,500	15,350	11.58	17,500,000	0.09	23,600	0.13
1640–49.....	266,000	56,900	21.39	18,000,000	0.32	20,800	.11
1650–59.....	78,000	10,000	12.82	18,500,000	0.05	15,600	.08
1660–69.....	15,000	1,000	6.66	19,000,000	0.01	20,000	.10
1670–79.....	335,000	40,450	12.07	19,500,000	0.21	44,800	.23
1680–89.....	8,000	2,200	27.50	20,000,000	0.01	16,200	.08
1690–99.....	512,000	62,650	12.24	20,000,000	0.31	68,200	.34
1700–09.....	678,350	104,270	15.37	18,000,000	0.58	42,600	.24
1710–19.....	319,000	44,650	13.99	17,500,000	0.26	54,600	.31
1720–29.....							
1730–39.....	183,500	20,800	11.33	20,000,000	0.10	43,200	.22
1740–49.....	827,500	77,125	9.32	21,500,000	0.36	86,600	.40
1750–59.....	341,100	31,142	9.13	22,000,000	0.14	55,000	.25
1760–69.....	270,000	17,200	6.37	24,250,000	0.07	39,800	.16
1770–79.....	45,000	2,250	5.00	25,000,000	0.01	15,000	.06
1780–89.....	118,500	9,100	7.68	26,250,000	0.03	15,200	.06
1790–99.....	4,748,000	406,530	8.56	27,500,000	1.48	80,400	.29
1800–09.....	3,065,700	327,600	10.69	29,250,000	1.19	101,400	.35
1810–19.....	3,782,150	470,950	12.45	30,500,000	1.54	159,200	.52
1820–29.....	2,200	200	9.10	32,500,000	0.001	2,200	.01
1830–39.....							
1840–49.....							
1850–59.....	391,800	49,150	12.54	37,000,000	0.13	61,800	.17
1860–69.....							
1870–79.....	2,349,000	162,250	6.91	37,500,000	0.43	189,600	0.51
1880–89.....							
1890–99.....							
1900–09.....							
1910–19.....	8,625,000†	2,250,000‡	8.70	40,000,000	5.63		

* Source: See Appen. XIX, n. *.

† This figure is the total number of men mobilized in the French forces during the entire period of World War I and is not strictly comparable with the foregoing figures in the same column. The other figures were obtained by adding the number of men in all engagements. Hence they are larger than the total number of men in the armed forces for the decade in question, for they count each man as many times as he went into battle. In order to obtain for the decade 1910–19 a figure comparable to the others, the 8,625,000 must be multiplied by a factor equal to the average number of times that the individual soldier took part in an engagement. Such a factor would be very hard to compute accurately. If it were 3—which is surely a very low estimate—the percentage in the fourth column would be 8.70. If the factor were 4, the percentage would be 6.52. Thus, in spite of the very high number killed and wounded during the decade, it is quite certain that the percentage of those engaged who were killed or seriously wounded was not higher than in the wars of the nineteenth century and was lower than in wars of the seventeenth century. Cf. Tables 54 and 55.

‡ Woytinsky (*Die Welt in Zahlen* [Berlin, 1928], pp. 116–18) gives this figure as 3,918,872 and states that 17.4 per cent of those engaged were killed or died of wounds or disease.

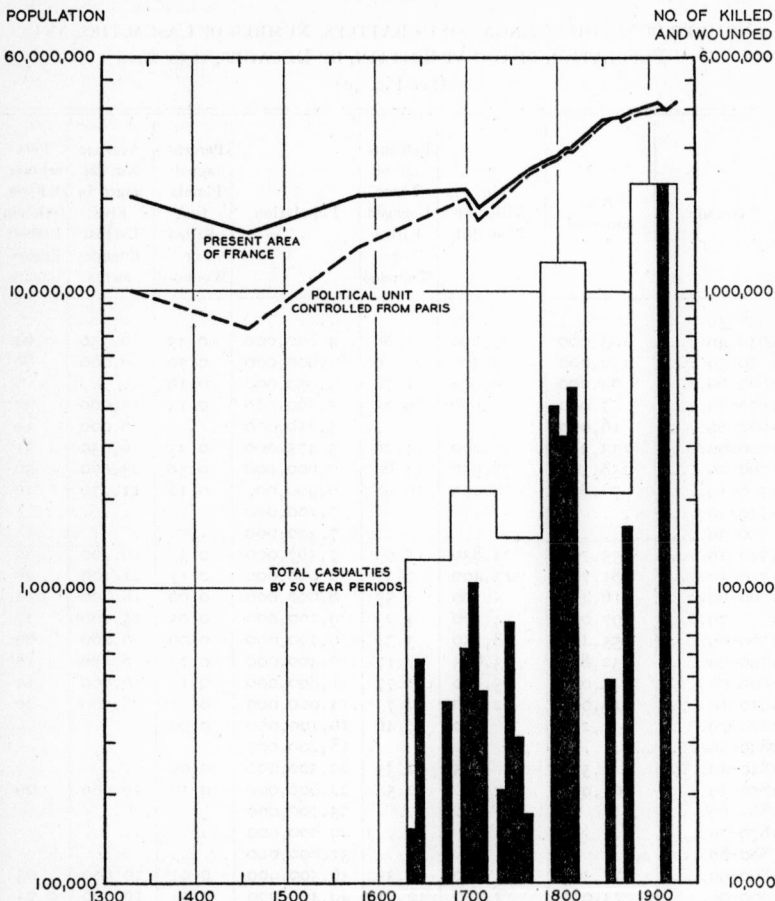

POPULATION

NO. OF KILLED
AND WOUNDED

60,000,000 — 6,000,000

PRESENT AREA
OF FRANCE

POLITICAL UNIT
CONTROLLED FROM PARIS

10,000,000 — 1,000,000

TOTAL CASUALTIES
BY 50 YEAR PERIODS

1,000,000 — 100,000

100,000 — 10,000

1300 1400 1500 1600 1700 1800 1900

Fig. 39.—Population and war casualties in France, 1350–1930, by decades and fifty-year periods (see Table 53).

TABLE 54*

NUMBER OF SOLDIERS ENGAGED IN BATTLES, NUMBER OF CASUALTIES, AND POPULATION OF GREAT BRITAIN, BY DECADES, 1630–1919

(See Fig. 40)

Decade	No. Engaged	No. Killed or Wounded	Percentage of Those Engaged Killed or Wounded	Population	Percentage of Population Killed or Wounded	Average No. Engaged in Five Largest Engagements	Percentage of Population in Largest Engagements
1630–39.....	....	....	....	....	....	....	....
1640–49.....	123,000	22,000	17.89	4,800,000	0.45	30,750	0.64
1650–59.....	152,000	34,500	22.70	4,900,000	0.70	39,000	.80
1660–69.....	68,000	8,000	11.76	5,050,000	0.16	....	....
1670–79....	77,000	6,950	9.03	5,200,000	0.13	17,000	.33
1680–89.....	16,000	....	......	5,250,000	....	10,000	.19
1690–99.....	133,250	19,000	14.26	5,475,000	0.35	16,950	.31
1700–09.....	258,300	37,950	14.69	6,600,000	0.58	23,870	.36
1710–19.....	72,850	8,000	10.98	6,900,000	0.12	11,270	.16
1720–29.....	....	....	......	7,100,000	....	....	....
1730–39.....	....	....	......	7,300,000	....	....	....
1740–49.....	155,700	24,830	15.95	7,567,000	0.33	19,400	.26
1750–59.....	181,700	13,400	7.37	8,000,000	0.17	21,100	.26
1760–69.....	116,450	5,300	4.55	8,600,000	0.06	18,800	.22
1770–79.....	97,000	4,100	4.23	9,100,000	0.05	15,200	.17
1780–89.....	155,400	8,250	5.31	9,700,000	0.09	9,000	.09
1790–99.....	332,870	23,885	7.17	10,400,000	0.23	18,550	.18
1800–09.....	225,000	15,230	6.77	11,800,000	0.13	16,600	.14
1810–19.....	410,000	52,210	12.73	14,000,000	0.37	28,560	.20
1820–29.....	2,200	210	9.46	16,100,000	0.00	....	......
1830–39.....	....	....	......	18,200,000	....	....	......
1840–49.....	1,500	35	2.33	20,500,000	0.00	....	......
1850–59.....	97,900	22,070	22.54	22,900,000	0.10	20,080	.09
1860–69.....	....	....	......	25,700,000	....	....	......
1870–79.....	....	....	......	29,500,000	....	....	......
1880–89.....	....	....	......	32,800,000	....	....	......
1890–99.....	77,300	4,890	6.33	36,500,000	0.01	10,680	.03
1900–09.....	23,000	2,510	10.91	40,400,000	0.01	19,500	0.05
1910–19.....	4,970,902†	1,113,122‡	7.47	42,600,000	2.61	....	......

* Source: Same as Table 53.

† Cf. note †, Table 53. The number in this column is the number mobilized in the British army. In November, 1918, there were 407,000 officers and men in the British navy.

‡ Woytinsky (op. cit., pp. 116–18) gives this figure as 2,436,964 and states that 10 per cent of those engaged were killed or died of wounds or disease.

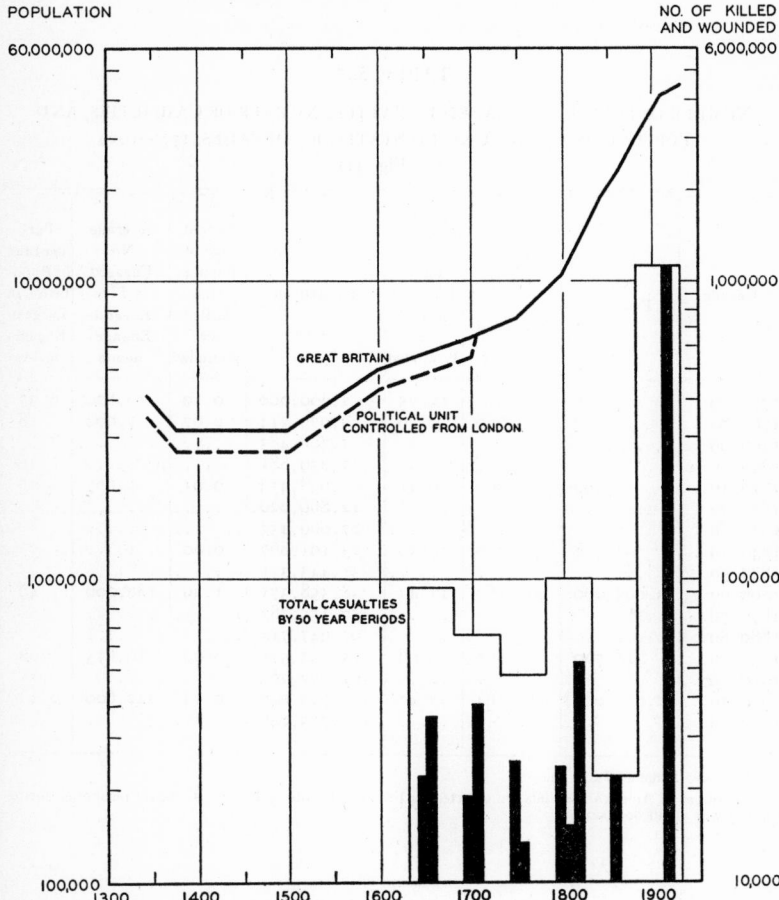

FIG. 40.—Population and war casualties in Great Britain, 1350–1930, by decades and fifty-year periods (see Table 54).

TABLE 55*

NUMBER OF SOLDIERS ENGAGED IN BATTLE, NUMBER OF CASUALTIES, AND
POPULATION OF THE UNITED STATES, BY DECADES, 1770–1929
(See Fig. 41)

Decade	No. Engaged	No. Killed or Wounded	Percentage of Those Engaged Killed or Wounded	Population	Percentage of Population Killed or Wounded	Average No. Engaged in Five Largest Engagements	Percentage of Population in Largest Engagements
1770–79...	44,600	5,910	13.25	2,900,000	0.20	10,800	0.37
1780–89...	28,000	2,600	9.29	3,929,214	0.07	7,000	.18
1790–99...	....	....	......	5,308,483	......	....	......
1800–09...	....	....	......	7,239,881	......	....	......
1810–19...	17,000	1,090	6.41	9,638,453	0.01	5,667	.06
1820–29...	....	....	......	12,866,020	......	....	......
1830–39...	....	....	......	17,069,453	......	....	......
1840–49...	4,400	720	16.36	23,191,867	0.00	....	......
1850–59...	....	....	......	31,443,321	......	....	......
1860–69...	3,995,000	496,380	12.43	38,558,371	1.29	189,000	.49
1870–79...	....	....	......	50,155,783	......	....	......
1880–89...	....	....	......	62,947,714	......	....	......
1890–99...	18,700	1,862	9.96	75,994,575	0.00	16,675	.02
1900–09...	....	....	......	91,972,266	......	....	......
1910–19...	2,086,000†	150,284	2.40	105,710,620	0.14	442,600	0.42
1920–29...	....	....	......	122,775,046	......	....	......

* Source: Same as Table 53.
† Number of American soldiers transported to France (cf. note †, Table 53). Naval personnel during
the war was about 600,000.

662

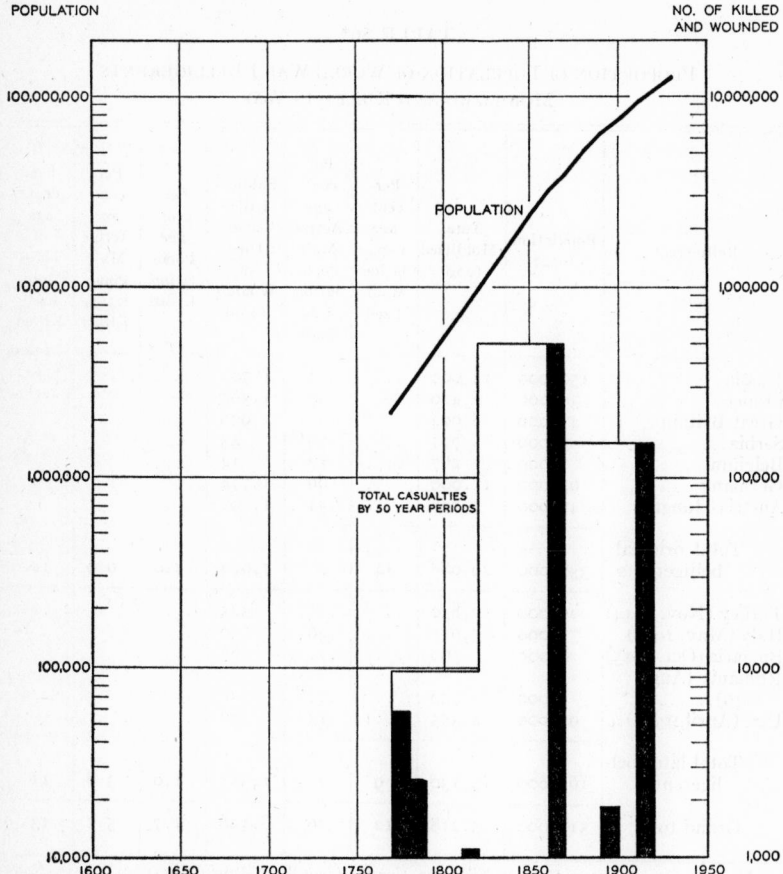

FIG. 41.—Population and war casualties in the United States, 1776–1930, by decades and fifty-year periods (see Table 55).

TABLE 56*

PROPORTION OF POPULATION OF WORLD WAR I BELLIGERENTS
MOBILIZED AND KILLED IN WAR

Belligerent	Population (ooo)	Total Mobilized (ooo)	Percentage Population Mobilized	Percentage Active Male Population Mobilized	Soldiers Killed and Died of Wounds (ooo)	Percentage Population Killed	Percentage Active Male Population Killed	Percentage of Those Mobilized Killed
Russia............	150,000	12,000	......	30	1,700	......	......	......
France............	39,000	8,410	......	59	1,363	......	......	......
Great Britain.....	41,000	8,904	......	39	908	......	......	......
Serbia............	3,000	707	......	70	45	......	......	......
Belgium..........	7,000	267	......	12	14	......	......	......
Germany.........	63,000	11,000	......	66	1,774	......	......	......
Austria-Hungary..	47,000	7,800	......	54	1,200	......	......	......
Total original belligerents.	350,000	49,088	14	42	7,004	2.0	6.0	14
Turkey (Nov. 1914)	26,000	2,850	......	......	325	......	......	......
Italy (May, 1915)..	33,000	5,615	......	46	650	......	......	......
Bulgaria (Oct. 1915)	4,000	560	......	......	87	......	......	......
Rumania (Aug. 1916)............	7,000	750	......	......	336	......	......	......
U.S. (April, 1917)..	92,000	4,355	......	13	126	......	......	......
Total later belligerents....	162,000	14,130	9	27	1,524	1.0	3.0	11
Grand total...	512,000	63,218	12	36	8,528	1.7	5.1	13

* Source: Compiled from Hoffman Nickerson, *Can We Limit War?* (Bristol, 1933), pp. 123–25. Non-European belligerents, except the United States, are omitted (Japan, China, Siam, British Dominions, Latin-American countries, etc.), as are certain of the smaller European belligerents (Portugal, Luxemburg, Greece, etc.). See also Leonard P. Ayres, *The War with Germany: A Statistical Summary* (Washington, 1919), p. 119, and W. Woytinski, *Die Welt in Zahlen* (Berlin, 1928), pp. 116, 118.

TABLE 57*

PROPORTION OF POPULATION OF FRANCE AND GREAT BRITAIN
DIED IN WAR, BY CENTURIES, 1600–1930

Century	Deaths in Military Service	Average Annual Deaths in Military Service	Average Population	Death Rate	Average Annual Deaths	No. Military Deaths per 1,000 Deaths
			France			
17th........	673,000	6,730	18,500,000	0.034	629,000	11
18th........	1,783,000	17,830	22,000,000	.030	660,000	27
19th........	2,522,000	25,220	34,000,000	.025	850,000	30
20th........	1,427,000	42,810	40,000,000	0.017	680,000	63
			Great Britain			
17th........	226,000	2,260	5,000,000	0.030	150,000	15
18th........	314,000	3,140	8,000,000	.028	224,000	14
19th........	273,000	2,730	22,000,000	.022	484,000	6
20th........	807,000	24,210	42,000,000	0.012	504,000	48

* Source: See chap. ix, n. 64.

APPENDIX XXII

MILITARY AND NAVAL DEVELOPMENT
OF THE POWERS, 1850–1937

The accompanying tables (Tables 58–60) indicate the development of armies and navies during the past century and the comparative military standing of the great powers at selected dates during that period so far as that can be judged from the statistics of naval tonnage, army and navy personnel, and military appropriations. They thus throw light both on the changes in the balance of power and in the fluctuations of national anxieties during this period.

Naval tonnage and personnel declined in most of the great powers after 1870 but grew rapidly from 1890 until after World War I, declining in the 1920's and rising again in the 1930's. Over 84 per cent of the world's naval tonnage, and probably a larger proportion of its naval strength, was in 1937 concentrated in the seven great powers (cols. 2 and 3).

The size of standing armies has tended to rise in all countries since 1880 with the exception of declines, especially in Germany and Russia, in the 1920's. In 1937 the great powers maintained twice as many men under arms as in 1880 (col. 4).

The proportion of the total population under arms did not, however, change greatly—about five to the thousand. This ratio has averaged about the same in the great and small states, though in 1937 the American states and the British Commonwealth kept less than half this proportion under arms, while Germany, Italy, and Japan kept twice as large a proportion under arms (col. 7).

The military appropriation figures exhibit more startling changes in time. Among the great powers, with the exception of some decline in the 1920's, military budgets have risen since 1870 with accelerating speed until in 1937 they averaged over twenty-five times what they had been at the earlier date. They multiplied by more than five in the eight years from 1929 to 1937 and have increased greatly since (col. 10).

While the small powers have maintained about as large a proportion of their populations under arms as have the great powers (col. 7), their military budgets have been relatively much less. The extraordinary capitalization of war, manifested by the rapid increase in the expenditure per man in the armed forces, occurred mainly among the great powers. In 1937 each effective in the armed forces involved a cost in maintenance and equipment of over $2,500, compared with a little over $200 in 1870; and in 1937 every man, woman, and child in the great powers was averaging a payment of $25 a year for defense, while in 1870 the cost was only $1.70 per year. The latter figure had not increased among the smaller powers by 1937. The rapid rise in the per capita cost of military

666

preparation among all the great powers, continuous except during the 1920's, is most significant of the rising tensions during the past half-century (col. 16).

In spite of the tremendous growth in military budgets, they have not grown much faster than the total national budgets (col. 12). This proportion has varied greatly in time and among different states because of variations in the scope of governmental activity and in the degree of governmental centralization. In Soviet Russia practically all the national income passed through the national budget in 1937, and in Germany, Italy, and Japan about a third; while in the United States less than 12 per cent did so and in Britain 21 per cent. In 1820, however, less than 1 per cent of the United States' national income went through the federal budget and in 1914 less than 3 per cent. In Great Britain the figure was below 6 per cent in 1870 and below 9 per cent in 1914. Thus has governmentalization and centralization of economic activity progressed (cf. cols. 11 and 13).

The most significant index of militarization is the proportion between military appropriations and national income. This had risen, on the average, among the great powers, from less than 3 per cent before World War I to nearly 10 per cent in 1937. Variations among the powers are, however, very great. While Germany, Soviet Russia, and Japan were spending about a quarter of their national incomes for military preparation in 1937, and Italy nearly 15 per cent, the United States was spending less than 2 per cent, Great Britain less than 6 per cent, and France about 9 per cent (col. 14).

The following notes refer to the figures at the head of the columns of Tables 58–60:

1. At none of the dates selected were any of the great powers at war, with the exception of 1900, when the British Empire was at war in South Africa, and 1937, when Japan was at war in China. The armies of these countries were abnormally large in these years as was the army of the United States in 1870 before the Civil War had been wholly liquidated. The figures for 1870 and 1914 are for the fiscal year preceding the wars which began during these years.

   The smaller countries referred to in Table 60 are as follows: *America*—Mexico, Guatemala, Honduras, Nicaragua, Salvador, Costa Rica, Panama, Cuba, Haiti, Santo Domingo, Columbia, Venezuela, Ecuador, Brazil, Peru, Bolivia, Paraguay, Uruguay, Argentina, Chile; *Europe*—Spain, Portugal, Belgium, Netherlands, Luxembourg, Switzerland, Denmark, Norway, Sweden, Finland, Lithuania, Latvia, Estonia, Poland, Czechoslovakia, Yugoslavia, Rumania, Austria, Hungary, Albania, Greece, Bulgaria; *Asia and Africa*—Turkey, Iraq, Saudi Arabia, Iran, Afghanistan, Siam, Egypt, Liberia. The army and navy personnel and population of dominions, colonies, protectorates, and mandated territories are included in the figures for the governing state, but in the case of appropriations dependencies are listed separately. The appropriations of dependencies are, however, only those of dependencies such as the British Dominions and India, which make independent military and naval appropriations. Where colonial budgets are carried as part of the metropole's budget, they are there included.

2. Naval tonnage includes the total for vessels of all types in use measured by standard displacement. Vessels in process of building during the year in question are omitted. The total tonnage of wooden ships, which constituted the bulk of navies before 1870, was estimated from the number of ships. The navies of British Dominions are included with the British Empire. Figures from different sources often vary materially on naval tonnage because of differences in including over-age vessels (British admiralty reports omitted vessels over twenty years old after 1909 but not before); because of differences in including vessels in process of building (the different times during a year when the data were collected would have an influence); and because of different ways of measuring tonnage (standard and normal displacement, see *League of Nations Armament Year Book, 1937*, p. 5). As the purpose is to indicate general trends, figures of approximate accuracy are considered sufficient. As the *Statesman's Year Book* was the only available source covering most of the period, its data were in general given priority if they showed no great divergence from other sources. Sources: *U.S. Navy Year Book; League of Nations Armament Year Book; Statesman's Year Book;* German, *Taschenbuch der Kriegsflotten;* Austrian, *Almanach für die K. und K. Kriegsmarine.* Cobden ("Three Panics," *Political Writings* [London, 1903], II, 539) gives the figures for Great Britain and France for 1835-59. Helen Fisher ("The Future of Naval Limitation," *Foreign Policy Reports,* October 1, 1936, p. 188) gives figures for 1930 and 1936. Nathan Reich collected materials for this study from the British admiralty reports included in the public accounts submitted annually by the British government.

3. Includes actual number of officers and enlisted men of navy and marines at dates mentioned, not statutory authorizations. Sources same as 2 above.

4. Includes actual number of officers and enlisted men of army and independent air force at dates mentioned. Reservists and militia not in active service are excluded, but colonial troops are included. Thus the figures for France and Italy include considerable numbers of native colonial troops, and the native Indian army constitutes almost half of the British Empire army. Sources: For United States, Heitman, *Historical Register and Dictionary of the United States Army* (Washington, 1903), II, 626, and *United States Statistical Abstract.* For other countries, *Statesman's Year Book; League of Nations Armament Year Book;* Webb, *New Dictionary of Statistics* (1911), p. 48; *Report of British War Office,* February 24, 1908. D. P. Myers lists figures from the *League of Nations Armament Year Book* for 1931 in *World Disarmament* (Boston, 1932), pp. 356 ff.

5. Figures in col. 3 plus those in col. 4.

6. Includes population of colonies, dominions, protectorates, and mandated territories. Sources: *United States Statistical Abstract; Statesman's Year Book; League of Nations Armament Year Book.*

7. Figures in col. 5 divided by those in col. 6.

8. Includes merely national appropriations; thus naval appropriations voted by the British Dominions are not included. Different sources vary considerably because of variations in excluding "nonmilitary" items from the budgets for naval and war departments; because of differences in utilizing estimates and actual expenditures; and because of differences in including supplementary budgets. In the figures here given actual appropriations, whether in normal or supplementary budgets, for the navy and war departments were used without effort to exclude "nonmilitary" items which seldom exceeded 10 per cent, though in the case of the United States

they were sometimes larger. Currencies were converted to dollars at the following rates in American cents, which approximated the current exchange.

Year	Pound	Yen	Franc	Lira	Mark	Ruble	Krone
1870–1914....	500	50	20.0	20	25	50	20
1921.........	400	50	6.6	5	1	....	....
1929.........	500	50	4.0	5	25	....	....
1937.........	500	29	4.0	5	40	20	....

Sources: Exchange rates, League of Nations, *Statistical Year Book, 1937-38*, pp. 13, 231; *United States Statistical Abstract, 1939*, p. 288. Other data same as for 2 above.

9. Includes only appropriations by national governments. Local appropriations such as those by states of the United States for militia and colonial appropriations such as those by the British Dominions and India are excluded. Sources: *United States Statistical Abstract; Statesman's Year Book; League of Nations Armament Year Book; Reich, op. cit.;* W. T. Stone, "Economic Consequences of Rearmament," *Foreign Policy Reports*, October 1, 1938; W. T. Stone and Helen Fisher, "The Rising Trend of Armaments," *Foreign Policy Reports*, February 15, 1937.

10. Figures in col. 8 plus those in col. 9. In some cases the total figure was found and the distribution between army and navy appropriations was estimated. Where the air arm is separate, it is included in the army figure. The 1937 figures for Germany and the Soviet Union follow the estimates by Stone (*op. cit.*), supplemented by the estimates by L. F. Richardson ("Generalized Foreign Politics," *British Journal of Psychology, Monograph Supplements*, XXIII [1939], pp. 17, 79) and Norman Crump ("Economic Conditions in Germany," *Financial Times* [London], December, 1937, p. 22).

11. Includes only appropriations by the national government, thus excluding appropriations by local subdivisions such as states of the United States and Germany, and by colonies and dominions such as Canada, India, Korea. Sources: *United States Statistical Abstract; Statesman's Year Book.*

12. Figures in col. 10 divided by those in col. 11.

13. National income means the total value of the commodities and services produced by the people comprising the nation in a year or the total received by them for engaging in economic activities. See Simon Kuznets ("National Income," *Encyclopaedia of the Social Sciences*, XI, 205), whose tables give several of the figures used and references to numerous other sources. Sources: Kuznets, *op. cit.*, and *National Income and Capital Formation, 1919-1935* (New York: National Bureau of Economic Research, 1937); Robert F. Martin, *National Income of the United States, 1799-1938* (New York: National Industrial Conference Board, 1938); W. I. King, *The National Income and Its Purchasing Power* (New York: National Bureau of Economic Research, 1930); A. C. Bowley, *Statistical Studies Relating to National Progress in Wealth and Trade since 1882* (London, 1904); A. C. Bowley and Sir Josiah Stamp, *The National Income, 1924* (Oxford, 1927); *Japan Year Book, 1938-39*, p. 237; Stone, *op. cit.*

14. Figures in col. 10 divided by those in col. 13.

15. Includes only population of the home country; thus for countries with dependencies it differs from figures in col. 6. As appropriations by the national governments are met mainly by taxes from the people of the home territory, this population figure seemed preferable.

16. Figures in col. 15 divided by those in col. 10.

TABLE 58

MILITARY AND NAVAL DEVELOPMENT OF THE UNITED STATES, THE BRITISH EMPIRE, FRANCE, AND JAPAN, 1820–1937

1 Date	MATERIAL 2 Navy Tonnage (000)	PERSONNEL 3 Navy Personnel (000)	4 Standing Army (000)	5 Total Personnel (000)	6 Total Population (000,000)	7 Per Cent Population	APPROPRIATIONS 8 Navy Appropriations (000,000)	9 Army Appropriations (000,000)	10 Defense Appropriations (000,000)	11 National Appropriations (000,000)	12 Per Cent	13 National Income (000,000)	14 Per Cent	15 Population of Home Territory (000,000)	16 Cost Per Capita
United States:															
1820		2	9	11	10	0.11	$ 4	$ 3	$ 7	$ 18	38	$ 2	0.4	10	$ 0.73
1850	175	8	11	19	23	0.08	8	10	18	40	44	7	0.3	23	0.76
1870	169	10	37	47	39	0.12	22	58	80	203	27	7	1.1	39	1.98
1880	40	9	25	34	50	0.07	14	38	52	264	19	7	0.7	50	1.03
1890		12	27	39	63	0.06	22	45	67	297	23	12	0.6	63	1.06
1900	333	28	68	96	84	0.11	56	135	191	487	39	17	1.1	75	2.53
1910	824	60	67	127	101	0.12	123	156	279	659	42	30	0.9	92	3.03
1914	895	66	98	164	108	0.15	140	174	314	1,045	30	37	0.8	98	3.20
1921	1,225	131	90	221	118	0.27	426	322	748	3,604	31	58	1.3	106	7.05
1929	721	112	137	249	137	0.18	374	453	827	3,994	20	78	1.1	122	6.78
1937	1,099	109	179	288	145	0.20	582	410	992	8,105	12	68	1.5	129	7.69
British Empire:															
1820	500	30	417	456	205	0.20	32		116	345	33			21	
1850	579	39	302	345	228	0.14	49	67	126	365	36	6	2.0	27	3.74
1870	633	43	322	367	240	0.13	51	75	157	438	38	5	2.3	31	3.60
1880	650	45	355	420	282	0.16	69	88	253	668	44	8	2.3	35	4.03
1890	679	65	513	624	366	0.16	146	107	340	761	40	9	3.1	38	6.17
1900	1,065	111	445	576	395	0.13	202	138	384	961	24	11	3.6	41	7.56
1910	2,174	131	381	532	419	0.16	237	147				20	5.8	45	8.53
1914	2,714	151	575	699	440	0.09	330	815	1,144	4,781	13	22	2.5	45	26.00
1921	1,860	124	344	443	441	0.12	275	275	550	4,145	27	22	5.7	44	12.23
1929	1,269	99	533	645	484									45	26.87
1937	1,211	112			554		500	763	1,263	4,690				47	
France:															
1820	200	20			31		17			199				30	
1850	362	25	260	285	39	0.74	35	75	110	318	26			35	3.03
1870	457	74	380	454	42	1.07	43	114	157	411	25			40	4.22
1880	271	40	503	543	44	1.23	44	142	186	616	29			37	4.87
1890	319	40	592	542	56	0.97	73	139	212	658	29			38	5.41
1900	499	42	673	715	60	1.19	74	188	262	699	30			39	6.70
1910	725	56	713	769	82	1.07	90	197	287	877	28			39	7.33
1914	900	64	846	910	89	1.02	57	282	339	1,002	26	6	4.8	39	8.72
1921	461	59	1,018	1,077	91	1.31	98	260	358	1,812	32	6	5.6	41	8.71
1929	406	58	608	666	100	0.66	209	700	909	1,360		8	4.5	42	21.64
1937	552	70	755	825	103	0.80				2,824		10	9.1	42	
Japan:															
1870	15	1	70	71	30	0.20	3	6	9	51	17	0.4	2.2	32	0.25
1880	41	10	74	84	35	0.21	6	18	24	42	58	0.7	3.4	36	0.60
1890	187	24	210	234	40	0.52	30	39	69	123	56	1	6.9	40	1.53
1900	494	46	225	271	45	0.40	37	47	84	274	30	2	4.2	45	1.03
1910	700	56	250	306	51	0.42	48	48	96	283	34	2	4.8	51	1.75
1914	528	82	296	378	55	0.49	258	141	399	770	51	5	8.0	55	6.76
1921	618	85			59	0.31	112	103	215	868	25	5	4.3	59	3.36
1929		85	199	284	64									64	
1937	874	107	850	957	71	0.95	230	900	1,130	1,549	73	4	28.2	71	15.91

MILITARY AND NAVAL DEVELOPMENT OF GERMANY, ITALY, RUSSIA, AND AUSTRIA-HUNGARY, 1870–1937

	MATERIAL	PERSONNEL					APPROPRIATIONS								
1 DATE	**2** Navy Tonnage (000)	**3** Navy Personnel (000)	**4** Standing Army (000)	**5** Total Personnel (000)	**6** Total Population (000,000)	**7** Per Cent Population	**8** Navy Appropriations (000,000)	**9** Army Appropriations (000,000)	**10** Defense Appropriations (000,000)	**11** National Appropriations (000,000)	**12** Per Cent	**13** National Income (000,000)	**14** Per Cent	**15** Population of Home Territory (000,000)	**16** Cost Per Capita
Germany:															
1870	42	7	403	410	40	1.02	$ 6	$ 48	$ 54	$ 58	92	.....	.....	40	$ 1.33
1880	88	7	419	426	43	0.99	11	91	102	135	75	.....	.....	43	2.27
1890	190	17	487	504	63	0.80	23	121	144	283	51	.....	.....	49	2.95
1900	285	29	495	524	70	0.75	37	168	205	404	44	.....	.....	56	3.64
1910	904	58	636	694	79	0.88	103	204	307	710	43	.....	.....	64	4.17
1914	1,305	79	812	891	79	1.13	112	442	554	880	64	$ 12	4.6	65	8.52
1921	117	15	100	115	55	0.21	5	25	30	915	3	12	0.2	55	0.55
1929	157	15	100	115	63	0.18	50	129	179	2,682	7	18	1.0	63	2.97
1937	281	46	720	766	68	1.13	100	3,900	4,000	5,000	80	17	23.5	68	58.82
Italy:															
1870	70	19	334	353	27	1.32	7	32	39	200	19	.....	.....	27	1.44
1880	100	16	200	216	28	0.78	9	41	50	283	17	.....	.....	28	1.80
1890	242	22	262	284	30	0.94	23	56	79	374	21	.....	.....	30	2.63
1900	245	25	230	255	33	0.77	24	54	78	346	22	.....	.....	32	2.44
1910	327	30	292	322	35	0.90	41	81	122	515	23	.....	.....	35	3.50
1914	498	40	305	345	39	0.88	49	92	141	506	28	4	3.5	37	3.81
1921	272	52	250	302	40	0.76	61	190	251	1,249	20	4	6.3	38	6.61
1929	222	48	365	413	43	1.00	57	163	220	1,047	21	5	4.4	40	5.50
1937	444	64	695	759	57	1.33	90	780	870	2,000	43	6	14.5	44	19.77
Russia:															
1870	363	16	700	716	82	0.87	12	98	110	330	33	.....	.....	82	1.34
1880	200	25	766	791	93	0.85	19	130	148	449	33	.....	.....	93	1.59
1890	180	30	647	677	110	0.61	22	123	145	474	30	.....	.....	110	1.32
1900	383	43	1,119	1,162	133	0.87	42	162	204	943	22	.....	.....	133	1.53
1910	401	60	1,225	1,285	163	0.79	47	266	312	1,299	24	.....	.....	163	1.91
1914	679	52	1,300	1,352	171	0.79	118	324	441	1,861	23	7	6.3	171	2.58
1921	254	20	1,500	1,520	132	1.16	46	356	402	1,063	42	3	13.4	132	3.04
1929	130	8	562	570	150	0.38	50	475	525	5,981	9	16	5.3	150	3.60
1937	267	24	1,300	1,324	168	0.80	100	4,926	5,026	19,012	26	19	26.4	168	29.91
Austria-Hungary:															
1870	73	5	247	252	36	0.70	4	37	41	214	19	.....	.....	36	1.16
1880	60	6	240	246	37	0.66	6	60	66	353	18	.....	.....	37	1.78
1890	66	9	337	346	41	0.84	6	58	64	458	14	.....	.....	41	1.56
1900	87	10	375	385	45	0.86	9	59	68	630	11	.....	.....	45	1.51
1910	210	15	410	425	49	0.87	14	73	87	1,040	8	.....	.....	49	1.77
1914	372	20	424	444	52	0.87	38	143	182	1,162	16	3	6.1	52	3.48
Total Great Powers:															
1870	1,813	174	2,473	2,647	535	0.49	135	416	551	1,842	30	.....	.....	323	1.70
1880	1,553	149	2,545	2,694	611	0.44	154	556	710	2,518	28	.....	.....	359	1.98
1890	1,757	205	2,691	2,896	771	0.38	216	653	860	3,025	28	.....	.....	409	2.12
1900	3,084	312	3,683	3,995	867	0.46	417	863	1,280	6,136	30	.....	.....	466	2.75
1910	6,119	456	4,013	4,469	997	0.45	640	1,154	1,794	7,700	29	.....	.....	538	3.33
1914	8,665	628	4,416	5,044	1,039	0.49	832	1,568	2,400	13,507	31	82	2.9	562	4.27
1921	4,717	463	3,924	4,392	956	0.46	1,139	1,775	2,914	20,037	21	108	2.7	473	6.16
1929	3,523	425	2,315	2,740	1,068	0.26	1,016	1,858	2,874	43,176	18	152	1.9	525	5.47
1937	4,728	532	5,032	5,564	1,196	0.47	1,811	12,379	14,190	43,176	33	146	9.7	569	25.00

TABLE 60

MILITARY AND NAVAL DEVELOPMENT OF THE POWERS, 1937

	MATERIAL	PERSONNEL								APPROPRIATIONS					
1 1937	2 Navy Tonnage (000)	3 Navy Personnel (000)	4 Standing Army (000)	5 Total Personnel (000)	6 Total Population (Empires) (000,000)	7 Per Cent Population	8 Navy Appropriations (000,000)	9 Army Appropriations (000,000)	10 Defense Appropriations (000,000)	11 National Appropriations (000,000)	12 Per Cent	13 National Income (000,000)	14 Per Cent	15 Population of Home Territory (000,000)	16 Cost Per Capita
America:															
U.S.A.	1,099	109	170	288	145	0.20	$ 582	$ 410	$ 992	$ 8,105	12	$ 68	1.5	129	$ 7.69
20 others	256	52	271	323	119	0.27	……	……	203	……	……	……	……	119	1.71
Total	1,355	161	450	611	264	0.23	……	……	$ 1,195	……	……	……	……	248	$ 4.82
Europe:															
British Empire	1,211	112	533	645	554	0.12	$ 500	$ 763	$ 1,263	$ 4,690	27	$ 22	5.7	47	$26.87
France	552	70	755	825	103	0.80	209	700	909	2,824	32	10	9.1	42	21.64
Germany	281	46	720	766	68	1.13	100	3,900	4,000	5,000	80	17	23.5	68	58.82
Italy	444	64	695	759	57	0.80	90	780	870	2,000	43	6	14.5	44	19.77
U.S.S.R.	267	24	1,300	1,324	168	0.80	100	4,926	5,026	19,012	26	19	26.4	168	29.91
22 others	432	63	1,484	1,547	273	0.57	……	……	1,000	……	……	……	……	189	5.29
Total	3,187	379	5,487	5,866	1,223	0.48	……	……	$13,068	……	……	……	……	558	$23.42
Asia and Africa:															
Japan	874	107	850	957	101	0.95	$ 230	$ 900	$ 1,130	$ 1,549	73	$ 4	28.2	71	$15.91
China	26	4	1,600	1,604	450	0.33	……	……	95	……	……	……	……	450	0.21
8 others	68	15	527	542	87	0.62	……	……	87	……	……	……	……	87	1.00
Total	968	126	2,977	3,103	638	0.49	……	……	$ 1,312	……	……	……	……	608	$ 2.17
Great powers	4,728	532	5,032	5,564	1,196	0.47	$1,811	$12,379	$14,190	$43,176	33	$146	9.7	569	$25.00
Small powers	782	134	3,882	4,016	929	0.43	……	……	1,385	……	……	……	……	845	1.64
Dependencies	……	……	……	……	……	……	……	……	238	……	……	……	……	711	0.33
World-total	5,510	666	8,914	9,580	2,125	0.45	……	……	$15,813	……	……	……	……	2,125	$ 7.44

APPENDIX XXIII

THE INFLUENCE OF MILITARY MECHANIZATION UPON WAR COSTS

Certain military writers have expressed the opinion that the mechanization of war tends to decrease the size of armed forces and the human costs of war because (1) the machines will be so expensive that they can be provided only for a relatively small force; (2) they require a highly trained personnel which cannot be supplied in large numbers; (3) there will be such reluctance to risk either the expensive machines or the highly trained men that tactics will tend to maneuver rather than mass charge; (4) the professional spirit of such an army will promote reliance upon intelligence rather than fanaticism for achieving military objectives, and this will make for limited war within the rules; and (5) mechanization will benefit the offensive by integrating striking power, mobility, and protection. Thus the great defensive advantage of the invention of long-range arms of precision and speed, like the rifle and machine gun, will be neutralized by the same instrument made mobile and defended in tank or plane. "Today, the obstruction caused by the machine gun and by bloated conscript armies, too unwieldy for maneuver, may be removed by the wise application of armor, the petrol engine, new means of concealment, and a reversion to highly trained professional forces. Thus may the overwhelming evidence of the defensive mastery of the machine gun pave the way, paradoxically, for an era of offensive mobility."[1] It is assumed that this augmentation of the relative power of the offensive will shorten war and decrease its costs.

A comparison of the development of armies and navies perhaps gives some support for this theory. The navy has undergone just this change since the ironclad superseded the wooden ship in the 1860's, and the human cost of naval operations seems to have been considerably diminished. In the Napoleonic Wars the British navy required a third as many men as the army, and the proportion of losses was a little more severe (37 per cent against 29 per cent). The more mechanized navy of World War I required only one-fifteenth as many men as the army, and the proportion of losses was considerably less severe (7 per cent against 10 per cent). In the Napoleonic Wars 30 per cent of the war losses occurred in the navy, while in World War I only 4 per cent were in the navy (see Table 61). In spite of the greater mechanization of the navies, however, as compared with the armies among the great powers, reflected in the greater

---

[1] Capt. B. H. Liddell Hart, *The Remaking of Modern Armies* (London, 1927), p. 17. See also Hoffman Nickerson, *Can We Limit War?* (Bristol, 1933); Col. J. F. C. Fuller, *The Reformation of War* (New York, 1933).

cost per enlisted man for maintaining the former ($1,325 for the navy compared with $355 for the army in 1914),[2] the cost per enlisted man in the peace army did not increase after 1870 as rapidly in the navy as in the army (100 to 166 in the navy compared with 100 to 212 in the army). The armies, however, were prepared for much greater expansion in case of war. Thus in World War I, while the British navy personnel of 1914 was multiplied by only about four during the war, that of the army was multiplied by fifteen (see Table 61).

TABLE 61*

COMPARISON OF BRITISH LOSSES IN THE ARMY AND THE NAVY
IN THE NAPOLEONIC WARS AND WORLD WAR I

SERVICE	MOBILIZED		DIED		PERCENTAGE OF THOSE MOBILIZED WHO DIED
	No.	Per Cent	No.	Per Cent	
Napoleonic Wars					
Army............	748,000	75	219,420	70	29
Navy............	250,000	25	92,000	30	37
Total........	990,000	100	311,420	100	32
World War I					
Army............	8,904,000	94	908,000	96	10
Navy............	600,000	6	42,000	4	7
Total........	9,504,000	100	950,000	100	10

* Source: Dumas and Vedel-Petersen, *Losses of Life Caused by War* (New York, 1923), pp. 29, 138.

The mechanization of the navy, though saving of man-power in war, may not have increased the navy's offensive character. Naval action was less rapidly decisive in World War I than in previous wars. According to J. H. Rose: "It would seem that modern inventions have brought naval warfare to a state resembling deadlock; and at present no way out is apparent. .'. . . Great battle-fleets, like those which did not close at Jutland, are not likely to achieve a decisive result, and naval warfare will probably resolve itself into a prolonged blockade, exerted in reality against the enemy's civil population."[3] Admiral Fiske, however, took a contrary view. "A naval battle is usually much more decisive than a battle on land, and therefore a more important factor in de-

[2] See Appen. XXII, Table 59 ("Total Great Powers, 1914," cols. 8 and 9, respectively, divided by cols. 3 and 4).

[3] J. Holland Rose, *The Indecisiveness of Modern War* (London, 1927), p. 28.

ciding the ultimate defeat or victory of a nation. This has always been the case; and it is becoming increasingly more so, as ships become more and more powerful, more and more complicated, and more and more difficult to repair when injured."[4]

The increased power of the offensive resulting from mechanization shortened particular campaigns in World War II and reduced the casualty rates of the belligerents below those of World War I; but there is little evidence that mechanization has shortened wars.[5]

Thus while the opinion of military men and a comparison of army and navy statistics suggest that mechanization reduces the costs of war, this must be set against the general trend of the last fifty years, in which mechanization has proceeded most rapidly, but the material and human costs of war, whether in preparation or in waging, have also increased with unparalleled rapidity.[6] While it cannot safely be argued that the increasing costs of war have been due to mechanization, it certainly cannot be contended from recent history that mechanization reduces the cost of war.

Perhaps a reconciliation can be found by distinguishing between the costs of war to an armed force and to the nation as a whole. While mechanization may tend to reduce the costs of maintaining an armed force of given power,[7] it may also tend to increase the proportion of national power which can be organized in the armed forces, thus augmenting the absolute and relative costs of war, if political conditions are such as to elevate military power to a rank of major national interest.[8]

[4] *The Art of Fighting* (New York, 1920), p. 356.

[5] See Appen. XXI, Table 47.

[6] Per capita costs of military preparation multiplied by 15 among the great powers from 1870 to 1940 (Appen. XXII, Table 59). Casualties increased with almost equal rapidity (Appen. XXI, Tables 53, 54, 55). Considering longer periods, budgetary costs have increased much more rapidly than human costs. According to Herbert Hoover ("Hope in a Poorer World," *Rotarian*, February, 1941, p. 10): "War has become more terrible every year since the invention of gunpowder. Every half-century has seen more and more men sacrificed on the battlefield. Lowell M. Limpus, in *Twentieth Century Warfare*, says that it cost Caesar about 75 cents to kill a man, that Napoleon almost bankrupted France because it cost a fraction under $3,000 to kill an enemy in his day. The World War ran the cost up to $21,000 per dead soldier, and it is estimated that before the present conflict ends it will have risen to $50,000."

[7] Casualties in proportion to men engaged in battle have declined (Table 61), but the material cost of maintaining a man at the front has increased. The ratio, however, should be in terms of the power organized, not in terms of the number of men engaged. A modern tank with a crew of three men may be more powerful than a thousand men armed only with rifles.

[8] The proportion of the national income spent for military preparation increased among the great powers from less than 3 per cent on the average in 1914 to nearly 10 per cent in 1937.

The influence of mechanization upon the decisiveness of war, that is, upon the probability of war terminating without mutual economic exhaustion, is important to the present discussion on the assumption that wars of attrition are more costly than wars of combat; but this influence seems to be indeterminate. Particular mechanical devices may favor the offensive or they may favor the defensive, though, in the writer's judgment, in the long run mechanization favors the defense, thus tending toward indecisiveness, mutual attrition, and high costs.[9] On the whole it appears that mechanization makes for total war and high costs, if military power is divided. The tendency might be the opposite if military power were united in a world-police.

[9] See above, chap. xii, sec. 3b.

APPENDIX XXIV

THE CHARACTER OF MILITARY UNITS AND MILITARY ACTION IN RELATION TO ORGANIC HISTORY AND THE HISTORY OF CIVILIZATION

The history of life has been divided into four unequal stages successively dominated by animal groups, by primitive cultures, by historic civilizations, and by modern civilization. Table 62 compares the types of fighting units, the forms of stability, and the agencies of change characteristic of each of these stages. Table 63 compares the types of political interest and organization and the characteristics of war in the successive stages of a typical civilization.

TABLE 62

THE UNITS OF POLITICAL AND MILITARY ACTION IN THE STAGES OF ORGANIC HISTORY

Unit	Animal Group	Primitive Culture	Historic Civilization	Modern Civilization
Ultimate units of military action	Individual animal	Clan	Feudal barony or faction	Section or political faction
Normal fighting unit	Animal society	Village	Kingdom or republic	Nation-state or empire
Occasional fighting unit	Animal community or biocoenoses	Tribe, tribal federation, or kingdom	Empire or alliance	Alliance or confederation
Unit constituting a historical whole	Species	People	Civilization	World-community
Dominant form of stability	Static	Dynamic	Oscillating	Adaptive
Dominant agency of change	Natural catastrophe	Military conquest	Social, economic, and political corruption	Ideological conversion

677

TABLE 63

TYPICAL CHARACTERISTICS OF WAR IN THE SUCCESSIVE
STAGES OF A CIVILIZATION*

ASPECTS OF CIVILIZATION AND OF WAR		RISE		DECLINE	
		Heroic Age	Time of Troubles	Time of Stability	Time of Decline
Character of civilization	Dominant interest†	Religion	Politics	Economics	Art
	Typical political organization‡	Warring states	Balance of power	Universal empire or federation	Universal church and political anarchy
Character of war	Destructiveness of war§	Moderate	Severe	Moderate	Severe
	Commonest type of war‖	Imperial (intercivilization)	Balance of power (interstate) '	Civil (intrastate)	Defense (intercivilization)
Technique of war	Typical military strategy¶	Pounce	Charge	Maneuver	Attrition
	Typical military organization**	Chief, retainers, and militia	Citizen army	Professional army	Mercenary army, fortification, and mechanization
Law of war	Internal law of war††	Private internal violence forbidden (king's peace)	Private external violence regulated (letters of Marque)	Public internal violence regulated (constitutional guaranties)	Public external violence regulated (military discipline)
	International law of war‡‡ Resort to war permissible:	to protect natural rights	as an instrument of justice	as an instrument of authority	in self-defense or for police of civilization
Function of war	Typical conception§§ War considered a:	natural solution of conflicts of interest	legitimate procedure to settle controversies (ultima ratio or trial by battle)	status which may properly be created by sovereign authority for reason of state	technique of government and politics to be used when expedient
	Typical objectives‖‖	Expansion of civilization	Achievement of reforms	Preservation of order	Defense of civilization
	Typical effects¶¶	Integration	Change	Stability	Disintegration

* Chap. vii, n. 41. Since the modern period is still in progress, its stages cannot be determined. Modern history may have included thus far only the final stages of the decline of Western and other civilizations and the heroic age of world-civilization. The Renaissance was characterized by the wide disparity between the publicists' exposition of the medieval theory of the just war and the Machiavellian practice of princes, indicative of a period of decline. The situation since has displayed many of the characteristics of heroic ages with indications of a time of troubles more recently. On the other hand, there have been changes which suggest that the modern period may have included a complete but brief civilization, with its time of troubles from the Thirty Years' War to the Napoleonic Wars, its time of stability during the nineteenth-century *pax Britannica*, and its decline begun by World War I, since which there has been a wide disparity between the theoretical justification of war under the Covenant and the Pact of Paris and the Machiavellian practice of the aggressive powers. L. Sturzo (*The International Community and the Right of War* [New York, 1930]) characterized the medieval period as a whole by the theory of "just war." He divided the modern period at the Napoleonic Wars, before which he suggests that "reason of state" was considered sufficient justification for war. In the nineteenth century, according to Sturzo, war has been considered a "bio-sociological necessity" (see above, chap. xiii, secs. 1, 2).

† Chap. vii, n. 42.
‡ Chap. vii, nn. 158, 159.
§ Chaps. vii, sec. 3c; xii, sec. 5.
‖ *Ibid.*
§§ *Ibid.*, and Q. Wright, "Changes in the Conception of War," *American Journal of International Law,* October, 1924; Sturzo, *op. cit.*
‖‖ Chap. vii, sec. 7d.

¶ Chap. vii, nn. 158, 159.
** *Ibid.*
†† Chap. vii, sec. 7c.
‡‡ Chap. vii, sec. 7d.

¶¶ Chaps. vii, sec. 4; x, sec. 1.